The Spanish financial system

Edited by
José Luis Malo de Molina
Pablo Martín-Aceña

The Spanish
financial system

Growth and development since 1900

Published in Spain by Alianza Editorial S.A. in 2011 as
'Un siglo de historiadel sistema financiero español'

First published 2012 by
PALGRAVE MACMILLAN

Palgrave Macmillan in the UK is an imprint of Macmillan Publishers Limited, registered in England, company number 785998, of Houndmills, Basingstoke, Hampshire RG21 6XS.

Palgrave Macmillan in the US is a division of St Martin's Press LLC, 175 Fifth Avenue, New York, NY 10010.

Palgrave Macmillan is the global academic imprint of the above companies and has companies and representatives throughout the world.

Palgrave® and Macmillan® are registered trademarks in the United States, the United Kingdom, Europe and other countries.

ISBN: 978–0–230–35004–5

This book is printed on paper suitable for recycling and made from fully managed and sustained forest sources. Logging, pulping and manufacturing processes are expected to conform to the environmental regulations of the country of origin.

A catalogue record for this book is available from the British Library.

A catalog record for this book is available from the Library of Congress.

10 9 8 7 6 5 4 3 2 1
21 20 19 18 17 16 15 14 13 12

Printed and bound in China

Contents

3.   THE MAIN REFORMS OF THE SPANISH FINANCIAL SYSTEM

M.ᵃ Ángeles Pons

4.   THE SPANISH BANKING SYSTEM FROM 1900 TO 1975

Pablo Martín-Aceña

5.   THE SAVINGS BANKS: 1900-1975

Francisco Comín

6.   THE MACROECONOMIC BASIS OF THE RECENT DEVELOPMENT OF THE SPANISH FINANCIAL SYSTEM

José Luis Malo de Molina

7.   BANKING SUPERVISION AND REGULATION OVER THE PAST 40 YEARS

Raimundo Poveda

8.   SPANISH SECURITIES MARKETS: RECENT DEVELOPMENTS AND KEY CHALLENGES

Fernando Restoy and Rafael Sánchez de la Peña

9.   INTEGRATION, COMPETITION AND STABILITY OF THE FINANCIAL SYSTEM
      Jesús Saurina

10.   THE INTERNATIONALIZATION OF THE SPANISH FINANCIAL SYSTEM
       Ángel Berges, Emilio Ontiveros and Francisco J. Valero

11.   THE SPANISH FINANCIAL INDUSTRY AT THE START OF 21ST CENTURY:
       CURRENT SITUATION AND FUTURE CHALLENGES
       Xavier Vives

List of Figures, Charts, Tables and Boxes

TABLES

Boxes

Prologue

Miguel Fernández Ordóñez
Governor of the Banco de España

This book is the outcome of a project launched by the Bank over two years ago with a view to reflecting on the transformations the Spanish financial system has undergone over the past hundred years of its history. When immersed in a world characterized by frequent and profound changes, from time to time it is worth taking a look back over the past and viewing events from a historical perspective: and better still from a plurality of angles and viewpoints. The book's editors, José Luis Malo de Molina and Pablo Martín-Aceña, decided to take an approach that combined both a historical overview and an applied analysis of the more recent situation. This has taken the form of a collection of essays, enriched by the diversity of the specialists contributing to the analysis.

This timely project elicited reflections and analysis from a group of historians whose in-depth knowledge of the Spanish financial system is a guarantee of the quality and value of the study. On behalf of the Banco de España I would like to thank everyone involved – Ángel Berges, Francisco Comín, José Luis García Ruiz, Santos Juliá, Emilio Ontiveros, María Ángeles Pons, Raimundo Poveda, Fernando Restoy, Rafael Sánchez de la Peña, Jesús Saurina, Gabriel Tortella, Francisco J. Valero and Xavier Vives – for their invaluable contributions.

When we embarked on this project no one could have foreseen the severity of the economic and financial crisis, nor the magnitude of its impact on the Spanish financial system. Indeed, even as we go to print it is still too early to say what its repercussions will ultimately be. Nevertheless, the reflections here offer invaluable insights when attempting to interpret the ramifications of the present juncture. Historical experience shows that the road to our financial system's modernization has been punctuated by recurrent periods of crisis. Overcoming them has always called for an effort from everyone concerned and for changes to be made to remedy latent weaknesses. From the transformations undertaken during periods of crisis the financial sector has emerged strengthened and better able to perform an active role in the development and modernization of our economy.

From this historical perspective we can anticipate that the restructuring currently under way in the Spanish financial system as this book goes to print will culminate in one of the most significant transformations in the system's history, and that this will contribute to the strengthening of the economy as a whole.

Madrid, 2 March 2011.

Introduction

José Luis Malo de Molina and Pablo Martín-Aceña

The financial system plays an essential role in a modern economy. Banking, in the broadest sense of the word, channels savings into investment and provides economic agents with products with which to obtain returns on their surpluses and funds with which to finance their consumption and investment plans. This is an essential task, because savers and investors are not always the same social partners, and because their preferences as regards liquidity, security and returns do not generally coincide. Moreover, as the intermediary in savings and investment flows, the financial system also creates and manages a considerable portion of the means of payment of the economy.

Banking is one of the most ancient economic institutions and can be traced back to the time of the Mesopotamian empires. Many of the credit instruments still in use today, such as bills of exchange, originated at the medieval fairs and in the Renaissance cities. The developments of the 19th and 20th centuries – the industrial revolution, international trade, technological change, rising living standards, etc. – would not have been possible without the support of efficient and sound financial intermediaries. Financial intermediation has been, is and will continue to be fundamental for the working of the economy.

There is a long tradition in the economic literature surrounding the relationship between the financial system and economic growth. More than two centuries ago, Adam Smith, in *The Wealth of Nations,* emphasized the important role played by banking in mobilizing capital:

"It is not by augmenting the capital of the country, but by rendering a greater part of that capital active and productive than would otherwise be so, that the most judicious operation of banking can increase the industry of a country. That part of capital which a dealer is obliged to keep by him unemployed, and in ready money, for answering occasional demands, is so much dead stock, which, so long as it remains in this situation, produces nothing either to him or his country. The judicious operations of banking enable him to convert this dead stock into active and productive stock; into material to work upon, into tools to work with, and into provision and subsistence to work for; into stock which produces something both to himself and to his country".[1]

More recently, in 1911, Schumpeter wrote that the services supplied by financial intermediaries – mobilizing savings, evaluating investment projects, diversifying and managing risk, monitoring corporate activity and promoting initiatives – were essential to promote and facilitate technological innovation and economic development. Gurley and Shaw (1960) investigated the financial aspects of economic development, establishing the theoretical links between growth and finance, and Gerschenkron (1962) advised that in order to know the past and present of an economy, one must first know its financial system, as this will provide a better understanding of why some economies grow and others decline. Goldsmith (1969) followed with an outstanding contribution, the first empirical study to establish the links between finance and growth; he constructed his renowned Financial Intermediation Ratio (FIR) and opened up countless research avenues. McKinnon (1973) continued along this same empirical path, increasing the number of observations and analyzing the post-World War II period in more depth. And Cameron (1967) started a series of specific case studies to determine the role of banking in the industrialization process in European and other nations.

Much progress has been made since these pioneering works were published. Rigorous theoretical studies have illustrated the range of channels through which financial institutions and markets affect, and are affected by, economic growth. A body of increasingly plentiful empirical studies, including works on firms and industrial sectors, and country-specific and comparative country studies, shows that there is a direct and positive connection between the working of the financial system and long-term economic growth. For example, the latest research on emerging Asian markets and on the causes of economic stagnation in Africa insist on the essential role that financial systems play in economic growth [Easterly (1997), Collier and Gunning (1999), Andersen and Tarp (2003) or Ang and McKibbin (2007)].

In 1993, King and Levine published an influential article, formalizing the link between finance and growth. Using data from a broad sample of countries over three decades, and various financial development and economic growth indicators, they found a high and statistically significant correlation between economic growth rates and levels of financial development. A further notable find was that the level of financial development was a

---

[1] A. SMITH, An Inquiry into the Nature and Causes of the Wealth of Nations, Book II, Chapter II, first published in 1776.

good predictor of future long-term growth rates, of physical capital accumulation, and of technological progress and the resultant economic efficiency gains.

At the start of the new century, many researchers have continued along the paths proposed by Goldsmith and Cameron, incorporating not only new evidence but also the analytical progress made in the financial research field. Levine et al (2000) highlighted that institutions and the legal framework are both determinant factors in nations' financial structures and development, which suggests that there is also a close link between these two factors and economic growth, considering its influence on the financial system. On the basis of a huge volume of statistical data, Demirgüc-Kunt and Levine (2001) rigorously established the link between financial development and economic growth, showing that the former accelerates the rate of the latter. Several historical studies [Rousseau and Sylla (2003), and Rousseau (2003)] also analyzed the links between financial development, productivity growth, economic growth and rising income levels, while Bordo and Rousseau (2006) studied the links between finance, growth, legislation and the political framework for a sample of countries between 1880 and 1990. And in 2006, *Explorations in Economic History* dedicated a special edition to research on the historical connections between financial "revolutions" and economic growth.

It should be noted, however, that the very authors and studies that suggest that there is a virtuous link between finance and growth, also note that empirical theory and evidence show that the financial system likewise responds to economic stimuli, i.e. that there could also be causality in the other direction, since the financial system is clearly molded by non-financial factors. Progress in telecommunications and information technology, sectoral policies, monetary and fiscal policies, institutional reforms, the growth of international trade, the increasing flexibility of labor markets and rising industrial competition are all reflected in the financial and capital markets. Accordingly, it is a question of determining, at empirical level, the relative importance of both directions of causality. However, in general, it seems that the studies conducted reflect the strong positive effect that the exogenous component of financial development has on economic growth, maintaining, in fact, that had the less-developed economies enjoyed, between 1960 and 1995, a level of financial intermediation similar to that of the more industrialized countries, their annual GDP per capita growth would have been one percentage point higher than it actually was during that period.

Another issue that is currently high on the agenda and has been analyzed by the literature on financial development and economic growth is the impact of the former on income distribution and wealth. If growth is key to promoting or facilitating prosperity and higher living standards (reducing poverty), and if financial development contributes to economic growth, then an advanced financial system should generate potential benefits and opportunities at all income levels. Insofar as it promotes economic growth, an efficient financial system can, in the long term, help reduce poverty and even inequality. As Greenwood and Jovanovic (1990) showed, this opens up a promising avenue of research, establishing a link between the financial system, economic growth and poverty reduction.

***

The aim of this book is to present an overview of how the Spanish financial system has evolved and transformed over the past century, and how this has affected the development and modernization of the Spanish economy, based on the conviction that to understand the present position of the Spanish financial system, with its strengths and weaknesses, a long-term perspective is essential. The current level of development of banking in Spain is the result of a lengthy transformation. The financial system has progressed from a situation of underdevelopment at the turn of the 20th century, to the present degree of complexity and sophistication; transformed from a system that was lacking in size and diversification, made up of mainly local or at the most regional institutions, into a large, modern, highly diversified, technology-based system whose members operate on the leading international markets. The Spanish financial system is no longer backward, as it was at the turn of the 20th century, but is now on a par with, if not ahead of, the financial systems of the more advanced European Union countries. Moreover, it has evolved in parallel with the vertiginous transformation of the Spanish economy. Indeed the two have been, and remain, interdependent: when strong economic growth has demanded new financial services, banks and savings banks have responded, accelerating the rate of transformation; in addition, and as suggested by much of the literature, financial developments have driven economic growth. Likewise, the structural constraints that have hampered the modernization of the Spanish economy and the economic stagnation and recession episodes witnessed have acted as a drag on the financial system. Progress has not been linear; there have been recurrent imbalances and excesses that have triggered crises and harsh periods of adjustment in which the financial system and the real economy have played an unequal part.

This book is a compilation of articles, the result of a project that aims to present students of the Spanish economy and interested readers with a general overview of the Spanish financial system from a historical standpoint over the past hundred years. The idea was to study both the distant and the more recent keys to the transformation of the financial system and to analyze the most significant facets of this transformation: changes in the regulatory and supervisory framework; technological and financial innovation and its role in economic development; interaction with macroeconomic stability; the internationalization of financial institutions and the markets; and issues connected with stability and efficiency. A further aim was that this historical perspective be used as a basis for analysis of the present challenges and future outlook. The project was launched more than two years ago, when no one knew – or even suspected – the breadth and depth of the present economic and financial crisis and the particular virulence with which it would affect Spain's economy and its financial system. Nevertheless, the uncertainties and doubts raised by the most serious financial crisis since the Second World War, far from hindering the work have spurred it on and have added value to the contributions, giving the authors the chance to reflect on the complex present situation with the intellectual backing of a wealth of knowledge of the near and distant past of the Spanish financial system. A good understanding of the past permits a better interpretation of the present; analysis of the present permits a better understanding of some of the implications of the past.

In keeping with this conviction, the book combines articles by economic historians, who describe the events of yesteryear with a concern for the present and the future, with others by economists, who analyze the problems of today with the advantage of a historical perspective. Lessons can be drawn from all the articles: lessons that can help provide a better understanding of the present crisis, and also lessons for the future, to enable us to be better prepared and to ensure, insofar as is possible, that future crises, which will most certainly arise, are shorter and less destructive in terns of income and employment.

Many lessons may be drawn, but clearly the most important lesson lies in the active role played by the transformation of the financial system in the galvanization of the Spanish economy, and this despite the extremely eventful nature of the trajectory, plagued by crises and recession episodes, which meant that only in the second half of the 20th century did Spain approach the levels of the more advanced European nations. Accordingly, the magnitude of the goals achieved should not obscure the many banking crises experienced in Spain, nor the difficulties involved in the complex correction processes that followed them. The link between financial development and macroeconomic stability has been crucial in the difficulties caused by the twists and turns in the path followed. Periods marked by high spending and debt, with their consequences in terms of inflation, and budget and balance of payments deficits, have generally resulted in financial crises and in a decline in convergence with the industrialized countries, both on the financial plane and in the real economy.

Financial regulation has played a determinant role in this trajectory. Through 1975 it was primarily a constraint on financial development, insufficiently justified by the claim that it provided stability, as the difficulties along the way proved. But it was a decisive and positive driving force when the time came to deregulate the Spanish financial system, establishing at the same time modern prudential supervision and financial stability arrangements. The question of maintaining barriers to protect the solvency of financial institutions, or of opening them up to domestic and foreign competition, was a cause of tension throughout the period, with notable swings and differing outcomes. However, it was finally decided to opt for a competitive model that has seen the system achieve maturity. Moreover, as in so many other areas of the Spanish economy, the harmonization requirements deriving from the decision to join the European Community were also a driving force in this respect, and by the end of the period the Spanish financial system is, in many aspects, one of the most deregulated and most open in the region.

Spanish banking regulation and supervision not only reached an equal footing with those of the more advanced countries, but they were at the vanguard as regards innovative crisis prevention and resolution systems and countercyclical mechanisms. Spain's experience of introduction of the dynamic provisioning system led to universal acclaim of this concept, recognized in the international regulatory reform that is currently ongoing in response to the crisis. Regulatory innovation was gradual and was accompanied by strict banking supervision arrangements, designed in response to successive crisis episodes. The tight control provided by this supervisory model protected Spain's credit institutions from the high-risk practices that triggered and propagated the latest international crisis. The supervisory architecture also evolved in keeping with the demand for greater international coordination, in accordance with the principles established and agreements reached, although only at the end of the period, in light of the failings revealed by the crisis, were the first steps taken to construct an international and European architecture.

All the components of the financial system have been radically transformed, and although the level of banking intermediation remains high, the development of the markets has been fundamental for the dissemination and incorporation of state-of-the-art technologies and financial innovation. This modernization was not incompatible with the continued existence of a traditional business model that has taken advantage of the financing opportunities provided by the wholesale markets, subject to rigorous risk control standards. The main factors of financial instability were all largely connected with overexposure to undercompetitive or oversized domestic sectors, with real estate crises the main sources of vulnerability at the most advanced stages of maturity towards the end of the period. Overall, the level of integration, competition and efficiency of the Spanish banking sector has increased significantly, there has been great progress in innovation and development of new technologies and products, and Spain's large institutions have opened up to the outside world and have embarked on international expansion.

The process of opening up to the outside world was another source of recurrent tension and was settled, just as competition and deregulation finally prevailed, in favor of internationalization of the financial system overall. Spain's participation in the single European financial services market and the position achieved by its two leading banks in the international arena are the best exponents of this approach. As a result, the sources of financing available and the investment destinations have increased, but so have the dependence on external borrowing and exposure to external risks (although with the attendant decline in the exposure to shocks on the domestic market).

At the end of the period analyzed, when the Spanish financial system had reached a high degree of maturity, closely linked to the progress made in macroeconomic stability, the economy has had to face the consequences of a severe international crisis and an unprecedented adjustment process, due to the scale and complexity of the imbalances that had built up during the opening years of the new century. The combination of the two will test the soundness and sustainability of the goals achieved, as exceptional restructuring measures will have to be taken. As we go to press, in early 2011, it is very difficult to foresee the scale of this major shock and it is clearly too early for an in-depth analysis. Some of the key achievements in the area of stability, such as fiscal discipline, have resurfaced as issues outstanding, and some distortions that had remained latent against the backdrop of the economic boom (for example, in the labor market) have emerged with virulence, jeopardizing the capacity to start out on a new high-growth phase with the necessary assurances in terms of stability. All of this has shown that the financial system is oversized and, in some segments, overexposed to real estate risk; these segments are now immersed in large-scale reorganization. The ongoing transformation process will entail a resizing of the Spanish financial system, to correct the excess capacity, higher capital levels, to increase resilience to adverse scenarios, and demutualization at the savings banks, to enhance their efficiency via greater market discipline. This process will most likely be one of the most significant transformations in the recent history of the Spanish financial system, resulting, it is to be hoped, when successfully completed, in a sounder and more efficient system that is more resilient to crisis episodes.

***

The book divides into three parts. The first two chapters present an overall view of Spanish society, politics and economics in the 20th century. The second part comprises three chapters that narrate the history of the financial system between 1900 and 1975, analyzing the trajectory of Spain's banks and savings banks and changes in the legislative framework. The last and most extensive part, comprising six thematic chapters, presents an overview of the development and transformation of the Spanish financial system in the last three decades of the 20th century and of the changes made and ongoing in the first decade of the new century.

In Chapter 1, Santos Juliá begins by asking if the history of Spain in the 20th century has been any different from that of its European neighbors. Is Spain an anomaly among the European nations? Are Spanish institutions and culture so different as to make Spain an exception to the rule? To answer these and other questions, the author analyzes the three periods in the past century when Spanish society debated whether or not it was part of Europe. During the first thirty years of the 20th century there was a clear approximation to the European model. Spanish society underwent a radical transformation: its demographics were modernized, towns and cities began to take over from the countryside, illiteracy levels declined and institutions similar to those existing in other countries began to emerge. Only the two-party political system of the Restoration era remained entrenched, unresponsive to the democratic demands of a country with an increasingly urban population and a growing middle class. After the interlude of the Primo de Rivera dictatorship, the political setting changed under the Second Republic and a series of reforms was introduced (civil liberties, clear separation of powers, separation of Church and State) designed to ensure that Spain was not an exception. But it became an exception after the Civil War and during the long Franco regime that followed. Under Franco, Spain was different (no elections, no political parties, no free trade unions), and while western Europe gradually moved towards democracy, with the help and protection of the United States, Spain remained an exception. And after Franco? The author recalls the deep pessimism with which foreign intellectuals viewed the country's future. But they were mistaken, because although Spain was different politically, in sociological terms Spanish society was not that different from its European neighbors. The political transition, which was just as successful as the democratic transformation of post-war Europe, marked the end of the exception. In this third phase, Spain has returned to normal, most particularly since 1986 when it became a fully-fledged member of the European institutions. The chapter concludes with a phrase that succinctly summarizes the author's core argument: Spain is "simply a normal European country. So normal, in fact, that it has a highly exceptional history. Just like all its neighbors".

Chapter 2, authored by Gabriel Tortella and José Luis García Ruiz, covers the past century of the Spanish economy, which was characterized, in the early 1900s, by archaic demographics, a largely unproductive agricultural sector, industrial backwardness and a limited urban population. This was the legacy of the 19th century, when the Spanish economy had grown at a slow pace, below the average of the more advanced European countries. By the turn of the 21st century, there had been a radical change. Spain was no longer a backward country but rather one of the world's richest nations, with high income per capita and high living standards. The authors describe the factors which, in their view, were key to this change and the periods of most significant growth and transformation. Domestic factors that were crucial for the shift from underdevelopment to development include, for example, higher productivity in agriculture and industry, the adoption of new technology, investment in human capital, and economic policies that tore down obstacles to growth. External factors also played a part; for example, foreign investment and, since 1986, Spain's entry into what was then the European Community. Despite some steps backward, as during the Civil War and the long post-war years, the 20th century was a period of economic progress. As the authors explain, during that time Spain conducted its own industrial revolution and came out of a backwater to achieve economic and social maturity. If it now wishes to make further progress, it will have to face the challenges of the present crisis and implement the reforms necessary, just as it did in the not too distant past and which allowed the backward Spanish economy of the turn of the 20th century to converge with the advanced European economies of the turn of the 21st century.

In the following chapter, "The main reforms in the Spanish financial system", M.ª Ángeles Pons reviews, as the title suggests, the legislative changes seen in the period 1900 to 1975. The author first notes that banking is one of the most regulated sectors of the economy, although the role of regulation has changed over time: initially designed to foster the development of financial institutions, after the depression of the 1930s, stability became the main objective. Banking regulation and stability are both concerned with correcting market failings, for example, to prevent excessive concentration and resolve problems deriving from asymmetric information. The difficulty in all cases is to determine the optimal level of financial legislation. Most of the chapter is devoted to describing how Spanish financial legislation has evolved and the changes that have been made. The author refers in particular to the first Banking Law (LOB) of 1921; this was the starting point for Spanish banking regulations and effectively remained in force until 1936. She also analyzes the savings bank legislation enacted in the period 1926-1929 and in 1933. The Spanish Civil War and the interventionist policies of the post-war regime put an end to the self-regulatory framework established in the 1921 Banking Law, giving rise to a period in which, with the second Banking Law of 1946, the financial sector became tightly controlled, in terms of its operational capacity and its growth potential. The turning point came in 1962 with the third key legislative reform, and from that year through 1975 Spain experienced a slow but continuous process of financial deregulation. The chapter ends with a series of comparisons between Spanish legislation and that of other European countries.

Chapter 4, by Pablo Martín-Aceña, traces the development of banking between 1900 and 1975. At the turn of the century, Spain's financial system was that of an underdeveloped economy with a low level of monetization. The central bank – the Banco de España – had absolute predominance and easily outweighed all other credit institutions. However, between 1900 and 1935, there was a significant transformation, as institutions grew both in number and size and many began to shift towards what would come to be known as the "mixed banking" model, combining commercial activities with the direct promotion of industrial corporations. The Banking Law (LOB) of 1921 introduced the first banking regulations, but the general framework remained quite open. The level of financial intermediation rose, but the level of diversification remained virtually unchanged: there were banks and savings banks, but the Spanish financial system lacked institutions specializing in the different credit segments. Most of the banks that had emerged at the turn of the century failed to resist the passing of time and disappeared, either in one of the crises that marked the first three decades of the century, or as a consequence of the continuous processes of merger and absorption. The end of the Spanish Civil War saw the onset of state interventionism, and both the regulations that introduced the status quo and the 1946 Banking Law (LOB) wrought changes in the existing regulatory framework. Administrative interventionism continued for two decades, up to the enactment of the 1962 Credit and Banking Law (LBOCB) that represented the start of a slow, timid deregulation process. Nevertheless, despite the status quo and the multitude of regulations, the banking system underwent notable growth and transformation and the level of financial intermediation rose, verging on that of other western European countries. There were no open crises during the Franco regime, but there were as many changes in the banking map as in the previous era, as the result of an intense consolidation process. Thus, during the Franco years and despite the status quo, the banking system underwent further significant change; few new banks were created, but many of the existing ones merged or were wound up or absorbed. In 1975 the Spanish financial system was much larger than it was in 1900: it had grown and it had diversified, albeit to a lesser extent than the financial systems of other developed European countries. It had also achieved a level of banking concentration similar to that of the rest of Europe. The legislation introduced since 1962 had relaxed the rigidities of state interventionism and had granted institutions greater freedom in their operations. But the banking sector, like Spain's other economic sectors, had developed under the protection of the State; in general, it lacked the capacity to compete on foreign markets, it suffered efficiency failings, and many credit institutions were too small and were poorly managed. The crisis of the 1970s-80s exposed these and other weaknesses affecting the regulatory framework. However, it also prompted a restructuring of the financial system, placing it in a position to be able to compete on the market that opened up as a result of Spain's entry into the then European Community.

In Chapter 5, Francisco Comín analyzes the development of Spain's savings banks. The story runs from 1900 – when they were immersed in a strong growth phase and were transforming from charitable into financial institutions – to 1975, the last year of the Franco regime and the prelude to deregulation and modernization of the Spanish financial system. The author begins with an analysis of savings banks' financial and community welfare activities between 1900 and 1920. He then examines the troubled inter-war years, from enactment of the 1921 Banking Law (LOB) through to 1935, just before the start of the Spanish Civil War. The growth of the savings banks in the 1920s led to creation of the Spanish Confederation of Savings Banks (CECA), and during the Second Republic the Savings Statute *(Estatuto del Ahorro)* was approved, entailing new political commitments for these institutions. There follows an analysis of how the savings banks fared during the autarky, when the financial pressure exerted by the Ministries of Labor and Finance intensified in an endeavor to control all aspects of their financial and community welfare activities. The savings banks managed to neutralize the most interventionist measures, but the truth is that in the 1940s-50s their operational autonomy declined and they lost control of their community projects. The chapter then moves on to the turnaround in economic policy in 1957, examining the effect this had on savings banks. Their position as financial institutions was consolidated but, in exchange, they had to invest their funds in the sectors determined by the government of the day, against the backdrop of the Development Plans. To control the savings banks' investments, new powers were granted to the Credit Institute for Savings Banks (ICCA), which became a "supervisory" body. To conclude, the author notes that in 1971 the Banco de España assumed control of the savings banks, bringing them in line, in institutional terms, with the banks. This enabled them to prepare for deregulation of the financial system, a process that gained speed as from 1977 and that transformed them into genuine credit institutions, representing the end of an era in which Spain's banks and savings banks had trodden very different paths.

Chapter 6, by José Luis Malo de Molina, studies the relationship between macroeconomic development and the transformation of the financial system from 1975 to date, with particular emphasis on how the efforts made to achieve macroeconomic stability contributed to further development of the financial system, even though this was not a linear process, but was interrupted by steps backward and crisis episodes. Following a brief reference to the relevant analytical literature available, the author presents a general overview of the link between growing macroeconomic stability and the increasing maturity of the Spanish financial system. He analyzes the interaction between the two, offering most detail on each of the three main phases into which the period under study divides: convergence towards stability with full monetary sovereignty; euro area membership; and the economic and financial crisis that emerged in 2007. In the first phase, a distinction is drawn between the role of monetary and fiscal policy. In the case of monetary policy, the author reviews the effects on the financial system of the different stages of instrumentation and strategy of the monetary authorities (from the money supply targets, through participation in the European Monetary System, to inflation targeting), up to the introduction of the euro in 1999.

Regarding fiscal policy, he describes the gradual shift towards rebalancing public finances, from the high deficit levels of the early 1980s that were driven by the oil crises and the social demands that followed the restoration of democracy. Spain's entry into the euro area represented not only consolidation of a framework of macroeconomic stability in keeping with that of the most advanced countries of Europe, but also a series of monetary and financial conditions that were extraordinarily favorable to the Spanish economy. This prompted a long period of economic expansion and development of the Spanish financial system. However, the growth momentum associated with euro area membership was not sufficiently offset by the economic policy instruments that remained in the hands of the national authorities, and as a result a series of imbalances gradually built up (excessive debt of private agents, rising asset prices, foreign trade deficit, etc.). Lastly, the author examines the most recent events, connected with the international financial and economic crisis and the problems it poses for Spain's economy and its financial system. In particular, he notes the differences between the impact of the crisis on Spain and on other developed countries, and the different phases of the crisis, and the main measures taken by the national authorities. By way of conclusion, he highlights the major transformation that is now under way in the Spanish financial system, which will signify a move towards demutualization of the savings banks, significant resizing of the financial system and higher capitalization levels.

In Chapter 7, Raimundo Poveda reviews the main changes in the Spanish financial system since the 1960s in the area of banking regulation and supervision. He begins with the 1962 reform that granted the Banco de España powers of inspection over banks; these powers were extended in 1971 to include savings banks and credit unions and finally, in 1988, to include all other credit institutions. The author then analyzes the events that had the most bearing on the development of the Spanish financial system, starting with the 1977-85 crisis which had a huge impact. The consequences of this crisis were vital for development of the prudential supervision mechanisms, and they were the main driving force for the present supervisory arrangements. The analysis of subsequent crises focuses, in particular, on Banesto due to the scale of the difficulties involved; although in this case special solutions were required, in view of the size of the institution, in general, the supervisory system worked well, with no significant design improvements being needed. The author then examines the process of adaptation to Europe resulting from Spain's entry into the European Community and the euro area. Certain reforms were necessary to adapt the Spanish arrangements to Community regulations and, in some cases, to international regulations (IAS). Another significant reform of the prudential system that is discussed in detail is the introduction, in 1999, of a credit risk provisioning system with a stabilizing (countercyclical) effect on income statements. Under this system, credit institutions would build up provisions during growth phases, to be used at times of crisis when losses started to appear on their banking books. Lastly, the author analyzes the impact of the severe international crisis that emerged in the United States and Europe in 2007, highlighting that the Spanish banking sector was virtually untouched by the wave of major international banking crises seen in 2008. However, it has not been spared the effects of the subsequent economic crisis that has driven up default rates, exacerbated by overexposure to the real estate sector and by refinancing difficulties on the external markets. This has meant that a raft of measures have had to be taken, including, in particular, creation of the FROB (a new mainly public-funded support mechanism that is giving savings banks a second chance to merge and restructure), and reform of the savings banks' regulatory framework.

Chapter 8, authored by Fernando Restoy and Rafael Sánchez de la Peña, is a broad overview of the past development, present situation and future outlook of Spain's securities markets. It begins by placing the Spanish financial system, marked by a high level of banking intermediation, in context. The chapter then examines how the securities markets have evolved since 1988, describing the objectives and the main changes contained in the Securities Market Law (LMV) and its impact on securities issues, issuers, intermediaries and investors, and on transparency rules and rules of conduct. It goes on to describe the present situation of the securities markets, regulation of information on securities and issuers, trading and post-trade infrastructures and the European financial supervision arrangements. The authors analyze the present structure of the regulated markets and multilateral trading systems (MTFs), and the size and activity of trading and post-trade infrastructures and their market participants. To place these developments in context, they examine the importance of the Markets in Financial Instruments Directive (MiFID) and the emergence of competition from the new MTFs. The authors then discuss some of the challenges facing Spain's securities markets, in particular: openness; competition between intermediaries and trading centers; the possible relocation of securities issues; and trading through the new MTFs. They propose greater transparency of information on issuers, products and markets (specifically, more public information on OTC market transactions). Moreover, to combat the crisis of confidence caused by the financial crisis, they indicate the need to improve post-trade regulations and to reconsider certain mechanisms, such as, for example, prevention of market abuse and restrictions on short-selling. They also suggest that the OTC markets be reformed, that central counterparties (CCPs) be created and that the terms and rules of conduct be harmonized. Lastly, after highlighting the foreseeable changes in the future regulatory arrangements as a consequence of the lessons drawn from the financial crisis, the authors conclude with two thoughts. The first focuses on the idea that the new capital accord – Basel III – could reduce banks' capacity to provide companies with financing, which would foreseeably result in a greater demand for the markets to raise their capacity to handle financial flows. The second refers to the need for the Spanish industry to make renewed efforts to adapt to increased competition, both in securities trading (due to the MTFs) and in clearing and settlement systems.

In the following chapter, Jesús Saurina analyzes the relationships between integration, competition and financial stability in the Spanish banking sector since 1975. Over this period there have been enormous changes in Spain, both in regulatory aspects and in the activities pursued by financial institutions. The chapter begins with an overview of how various indicators of integration of the banking system (taken to mean the increase in the number of local or foreign deposit institutions with which firms and households can interact to obtain banking products and services), competition and financial stability have evolved. It then examines the empirical evidence, in Spain, on some of the key questions arising from the theoretical relationships between integration, competition and financial stability. Thus, analyzing the determinants of profitability at Spain's banks, evidence is presented to show that this depends both on their market power and their efficiency. It is also found that extraordinary income (measured by Tobin's Q Ratio) derives, essentially, from winning demand deposits and, to a lesser extent, from extending credit, providing other services and efficiency. The various regulatory changes seen in the period, primarily connected with the deregulation process, have also had a considerable impact on extraordinary income. Finally, evidence is also presented that would point to an inverse relationship between competition and financial stability. The chapter underlines the huge changes seen in the Spanish banking system over the past 35 years: integration, competition and efficiency levels have increased significantly; there have been major advances in innovation and development of new technologies and products; and the large Spanish banks have become more outward-looking and have expanded internationally. At the same time, however, there have also been marked credit cycles, with strong growth periods followed by corrective episodes and even crises. In consequence, the chapter ends advocating strict prudential regulations, considering both micro-prudential and macro-prudential aspects, to temper these credit cycles.

Chapter 10, by Ángel Berges, Emilio Ontiveros and Francisco J. Valero, examines the openness of the two main components of the Spanish financial system (the banking system and the securities markets), from the outside looking in and vice versa. The authors begin by defining the concept of internationalization, which goes beyond merely securing funds from abroad / placing funds abroad, followed by an analysis of the points for and against: on the upside, a broader range of financing sources and investment destinations; on the downside, higher dependence on the foreign sector as regards funding obtained and risks assumed. They then analyze the increasing internationalization of the Spanish economy over the last thirty years, a logical consequence of Spain's entry into the European Community (1986), the single market (1993) and monetary union (1999). This pattern has been even more notable in the case of the financial system. To study how this process of internationalization has evolved, they analyze the entry of foreign banks onto the Spanish market, detailing the successive legal reforms that allowed these institutions to become established in Spain and monitoring a number of ratios to determine the extent of this process. They also examine the international expansion of Spain's credit institutions, by group, by mode of expansion (via subsidiaries, branches, directly or through representative offices) and by target country and activity. To complete this analysis, they then consider the process of internationalization of the securities markets, showing how Spain's gradual integration into the global economy has prompted growing internationalization of its financial activity. This has resulted in heavy dependence on the foreign sector, stemming from the need to fund unbalanced growth accompanied by a domestic savings deficit. In turn, internationalization of the financial system has made it increasingly dependent on the foreign sector, in terms both of funding and of the importance of foreign investor confidence. The presence of foreign banks on the Spanish market, despite their limited market share, has been an important catalyst for development and modernization of the financial system, and Spanish banks have now achieved a highly significant presence abroad, having progressed from the initial focus on Latin America to more recent expansion into the United States and the rest of Europe.

The last chapter of the book, authored by Xavier Vives, focuses on the challenges facing the Spanish banking system in the difficult scenario ahead, in view of the impact of the crisis on Spain's financial institutions and the stricter demands of a reformed regulatory framework. The chapter begins with a brief overview of the main trends in the banking sector worldwide pre-crisis, marked by technological change, market integration and globalization, and increasing deregulation, all of which had prompted a decline in the share of traditional banking activity (loans and deposits) in favor of investment and corporate services, and a move towards consolidation and concentration in the sector. The 2007-08 crisis interrupted these trends, as regards regulatory requirements and also as regards the business model and the role of innovation and internationalization. The author analyzes the development of the Spanish banking sector pre-crisis, marked by: high returns and solvency levels and low levels of default; sharp credit growth, especially on the real estate market; the key role played by the banking system, despite the development of the financial markets; growing branch concentration and a high-density branch network; a decline in institutions' high market power; and the strong pace of internationalization. He then examines the impact of the crisis on the Spanish banking sector, marked by financing difficulties, a sharp deceleration in credit growth, an increase in doubtful assets, and a decline in returns and solvency levels. The main strengths and weaknesses of the banking sector are the next focus of the chapter, with a special section devoted to the savings banks, some of which have borne the brunt of the crisis, owing in part to their singular institutional make-up. The author describes the weaknesses of the savings bank model that were revealed during the crisis and explains the main lines of reform included in the new savings bank regulations approved in July 2010. To conclude, he reviews the key challenges and future outlook for the Spanish banking sector. Among the challenges, he underlines the need to restructure not only the sector's balance sheet but also the sector itself, to eliminate surplus capacity and achieve appropriate capitalization levels. He also indicates that in order for the banking sector to help deleverage and fund the national economy, changes may be needed in the banking business model and balance sheet structure, against a backdrop of stricter capital and liquidity requirements.

***

This book is an initiative of the Banco de España, in the context of its programs of study and discussion of the Spanish economy and the Spanish financial system. The points of view expressed here reflect solely the opinions of the authors and do not necessarily reflect the view of the Banco de España. In our role of editors, we have worked to ensure that the various chapters form a coherent whole, to help the reader gain a comprehensive and coalescent overview of the radical transformation witnessed. We have also aimed to establish certain general editorial criteria, but without in any way intending to achieve a uniform interpretation, but rather to maintain an enriching array of views. We are grateful to the Banco de España for its support for the project, which was initially inspired by the Governor, Miguel Fernández Ordóñez, and to the services of the Banco de España that have collaborated in the coordination and preparation of the book. We are especially grateful to Roberto Blanco and Jesús Esteban, whose help has been essential in order for it to become a reality.

15 February 2011.

References

ANDERSEN, T. B. and F. TARP (2003). "Financial Liberalization, Financial Development and Economic Growth in LDCs", *Journal of International Development,* 15, 2, pp. 189-209.

ANG, J. B. and W. J. MCKIBBIN (2007). "Financial Liberalization, Financial Sector Development and Growth: Evidence from Malaysia", *Journal of Development Economics,* 84, 1, pp. 215-233.

BORDO, M. D. and P. L. ROUSSEAU (2006). "Legal-political factors and the historical evolution of the finance-growth link", *European Review of Economic History,* 10, 3, pp. 421-444.

CAMERON, R. (1967). *Banking in the early stages of industrialization,* Oxford University Press, New York.

COLLIER, P. and J. W. GUNNING (1999). "Explaining African economic performance", *Journal of Economic Literature,* 37, 1, pp. 64-111.

DEMIRGÜÇ-KUNT, A. and R. LEVINE (eds.) (2001). *Financial structure and economic growth: a cross-country comparison of banks, markets and development,* The MIT Press, Cambridge, Mass.

EASTERLY, W. (1997). *The ghost of financing gap: how the Harrod-Domar growth model still haunts development economics,* Policy Research Working Paper Series, 1807, The World Bank.

GERSCHENKRON, A. (1962). *Economic backwardness in historical perspective,* Harvard University Press, Cambridge, Mass.

GOLDSMITH, R. (1969). *Financial structure and development,* Yale University Press, New Haven.

GREENWOOD, J. and B. JOVANOVIC (1990). "Financial development, growth and distribution of income", *The Journal of Political Economy,* 98, 5, pp. 1076-1107.

GURLEY, J. G. and E. S. SHAW (1960). *Money in a theory of finance,* Brooking Institution, Washington DC.

KING, R. G. and R. LEVINE (1993a). "Finance and growth: Schumpeter might be right", *Quarterly Journal of Economics,* 108, pp. 717-738.

— (1993b). "Finance, entrepreneurship and growth: theory and evidence", *Journal of Monetary Economics,* 32, pp. 513-542.

LEVINE, R. (1997). "Financial development and economic growth: views and agenda", *Journal of Economic Literature,* 35, pp. 688-726.

LEVINE, R., N. LOAYZA and T. BECK (2000). "Financial intermediation and growth: causality and causes", *Journal of Monetary Economics,* 46, 1, pp. 31-77.

MCKINNON, R. I. (1973). *Money and capital in economic development,* Brooking Institution, Washington DC.

ROUSSEAU, P. L. (2003). "Historical Perspectives on Financial Development and Economic Growth", *Review of Federal Reserve of Bank of St. Louis,* July, pp. 81-106.

ROUSSEAU, P. L. and R. SYLLA (2003). "Financial Systems, Economic Growth and Globalisation", in M. D. Bordo, A. M. Taylor and J. G. Williamson (eds.), *Globalisation in Historical Perspective. National Bureau of Economic Research,* University of Chicago Press.

1. Spain in the 20th century: The end of the exception?

Santos Juliá

Universidad Nacional de Educación a Distancia

Spain, as usual, is the significant exception.
Charles Tilly, 1969

Observers of Spain, whether Spanish or foreign, have tended to interpret the last two centuries of the country's history in terms of comparisons between what did NOT take place there but supposedly did take place in other European countries or in Europe as a whole. This habit of treating Spain as an exception – which, according to Charles Tilly,[1] as far as violence goes, confirms the rule – aims to explain the ills of the patria, be they the *caciquismo* of the past or the democracy deficit of the present, not so much by means of an analysis of structures, institutions, cultures or internal events, but in terms of the absence or deficit of those factors which transformed our neighbors into democratic states built on flourishing economies, with a public awareness and broad social consensus. This has given rise to accounts of Spain's past that treat it as an anomaly among the group of European nations. This was very much in vogue in the years immediately before, during and after the "Disaster" of 1898, when Spain lost the last vestiges of its colonial empire. And it was also the source of many of the criticisms of the transition to democracy in 1977 which saw it as the cause of the low quality of Spain's democracy.

---

[1] Tilly (1969), pp. 31-32.

Spain as a problem was the heritage of those born in the 1880s, who reached the age of political reason at the time, as Ortega put it, when the last leaves of the legend of the *patria* were falling. Many of them had the opportunity to travel abroad, to further their studies in German, French or British universities, and take part in high-level scientific meetings, allowing them look at their own country's shortcomings and its distorted reflection in the mirror of the countries they visited. A substantial proportion of these young people who studied abroad came to the conclusion that Spain, unlike Germany, lacked science and that this was the root of the country's ills and the reason for its long decline. Another group, more concerned with politics, thought that Spain's decadence, in contrast to France's energy, rather than being due to a lack of science, although it clearly lagged behind, was due to a lack of democracy. A third current, which emerged from the *Institución Libre de Enseñanza* emphasized the idea that unlike Britain, Spain lacked the bedrock of public education on which to build its self-government.

In all three cases, the task this generation of scientifically literate, politically liberal or democratic, and socially and culturally European citizens took upon itself was to return Spain to the mainstream of European civilization so as to make up for lost time and put an end to its being a permanent anomaly. For them, Spain was the problem to the same extent that Europe was the solution. However, the solution was ultimately a fundamental part of the problem: the planned 'Europeanization' devised and carried out by the generation of 1914 and their younger siblings ended with the bombardment of Spanish cities by German and Italian airplanes and the presence of Italian troops and the International Brigades fighting on Spanish soil while France and Great Britain looked on from behind the ramparts of non-intervention.

Towards 1960, twenty years after the defeat of that project of Europeanization and the construction on the authentic Spain of a different State, an exception within the democratic normality of Europe, another generation of Spaniards, born between 1930 and 1945, resumed the same story, convinced that Spain was not just an anomaly but an irrevocable failure from which it could only escape if it became, in the near future, what France, Germany or Italy were in the present. Once again this was a generation which had grown up observing and reflecting on the ills of the *patria,* this time defined by a pointless fratricidal massacre that had split Spain in two and led the nation to ruin. Again, many of them travelled abroad to identify Spain's deficiencies and deformities in the image they saw in the mirror of European countries or the United States. And, again as had happened with previous generations, they had the chance to witness a radical change in living standards, with the resumption of the rural exodus, the chaotic growth of the cities, rapid industrialization and the raising of educational standards: all that remained was to bring the Spanish state up to the level of its European peers.

It was as if history wanted to repeat itself, but whereas the first round had been tragedy, nobody was willing for the second to be farce. They knew about their past – and they made sure their parents did not forget it – and they envied their neighbors: and between what they had learned from their own experience, remembered, and were able to learn from the experience of others, a transition was embarked upon leading from an anachronistic political system, a dictatorship built on a victory in the Civil War, towards a full democracy. This they did always with an eye on Europe, and with the ultimate goal of eliminating a difference, of making Spain at last a State and a nation like others. The pages that follow address these two attempts, and the social transformations on which they were built, which sum up Spanish life in the 20th century.

1 Spain is Europeanized

The desire to Europeanize Spain, which was felt so widely and fervently in the wake of the Disaster of 1898, was the corollary on the cultural and political level of the changes perceptible in Spanish society since the turn of the 20th century. At the start of the century, Spain was an archaic country with an agricultural and pre-industrial economic structure. It was a country rooted in the past, as Antonio Bonet wrote in the introduction to the unique book *Ciudades españolas. Su desarrollo y configuración urbanística,* by Oskar Jürgens, the Prussian Government's chief architect, who came to Spain in 1907 and died here, in El Escorial, in 1923, without having completed his work. Jürgens had not come to Spain to eulogize dead cities, as Pío Baroja and José Martínez Ruiz had done during their journey of initiation through Castile a few years earlier; nor was he driven by the quest for the Spanish soul, even in Toledo, like Maurice Barrès. Jürgens came as an urban architect. He was interested in the morphology of Spanish cities, particularly their old towns, but also the plans for reform and expansion that the majority of them had embarked upon. These were inward reforms to open up wide new avenues to bring fresh air into their streets, and expansions along the lines, of that in Barcelona, which he described as the most prosaic and least artistic imaginable, following a grid pattern of squares or octagons – with the corners of the blocks chamfered to a varying extent – with no special features worthy of note. The time of his journey was the start of what, to use Karl Polanyi's term, could be called the great transformation.

This was because, over the space of just a few years (from the 1890s – with the elegies for the death of Spain now having descended to the sepulcher, as Joaquín Costa saw, while awaiting a savior who would say: "Rise up and walk!" – through the time of the arrival of the Jürgens until the outbreak of the Great War), Spanish cities decided to reform themselves internally and expand outwards: these were signs of a new dynamism that would propel changes on an unprecedented scale over the next fifteen years. In the first third of the century, Spain's population grew at a rate of 0.8% a year. This allowed it to grow without immigration and despite the strong flow of emigration abroad in the first fifteen years, rising from 18.6 million in the 1900 census to 23.56 million in that of 1930. This population growth was moderate, and rested on a simultaneous drop in the birth rate and death rate, highlighting a dramatic reduction in child mortality and substantial rise in the number of women who reached the age of fifteen, which is a good proxy for the general improvement in health-care and hygiene introduced during the period.

This population, which became younger as child mortality dropped, gave up working on the land *en masse* and, no longer able to emigrate to the Americas, migrated to the cities, and to the provincial capitals in particular. Between 1910 and 1930, the agricultural workforce fell from 66.3% to 45.5% of the total active population.[2] Up until 1915 the growing pressure of the population on scarce economic resources had driven large-scale overseas emigration: the net balance of emigration out of Spain over the fifteen-year period was around half a million people. The Great War reversed this trend: not only were emigrants unable to leave, but many were forced to return. The 1920s experienced the fastest demographic expansion ever seen, with natural population growth of 2.28 million inhabitants. The bulk of this new population was entirely in the cities, characterized by burgeoning cohorts in the 15 to 35 year age range. Hence, the metaphor of a young Spain growing on the ruins of the old, which served as the recruiting slogan of the *Partido Reformista* or Reform Party from 1914 onwards, which accurately expressed this abundance of youth that was the defining feature of Spanish cities at the time.

The population grew throughout this period, but not always at the same rate. The urban population, considering towns with over ten thousand inhabitants, doubled in just twenty years, between 1910 and 1930, while the rural and semi-rural population grew fastest in towns with over five thousand inhabitants, to the detriment of those with less than two thousand. The rural scene had ceased to be the dominant note, sharing its position with urban life. Thus, neither entirely rural nor urban, Spanish society was, in this and in many other ways, a society in transition, with a continuous migratory flow to the cities, reaching 1.17 million people in the 1920s. More than natural population growth, it was the influx of migrants that changed the demographics of cities such as Madrid, Barcelona and Bilbao. Seville, Zaragoza and Valencia also received many outsiders, and their pattern of growth was similar: slow during the first half of the 19th century, starting to spill outside the old city walls with the expansion plans of the middle decades, and accelerating their growth as of 1900 and, above all, 1915, as in the case of Granada and Cordoba, which passed the hundred-thousand mark for the first time in this period.

The rapid growth of the cities transformed their urban layout, social structure, demographic pyramid and civic culture. The traditional uniformity around the old town, characterized by the mix of workers, craftsmen and the bourgeoisie, gave way to a clear demarcation between classes. While the middle classes of tradesmen, businessmen, industrialists and professionals occupied the new urban areas or *ensanche* built outside the old city, in buildings equipped with running water and elevators, working class districts sprang up in the outer suburbs and periphery, with few or no amenities, no town planning, and where the dirt and poverty were palpable. The development along the estuary of the river Nervión in Bilbao, the Madrid city plans, city expansions and extensions in Vigo, Badajoz, Gijón, Salamanca, Logroño and Seville: after the end of the Great War there was a sort of frenzy of building which would continued up until the nineteen twenties, when the crisis also began to make itself felt in Spain.

---

[2] Carreras and Tafunell, (eds.) (2005).

The shrinking of the agricultural workforce was accompanied by a rapid and somewhat chaotic process of urbanization, and big strides towards industrialization, induced by the construction boom. This led to the development of the food, paper, textile, chemicals and tobacco industries, and the appearance of large factories. Alongside these changes there was marked growth in school attendance rates at all stages of education. Illiteracy rates fell from an average of 55% at the start of the century to 27% in 1930. However, this was insufficient to close the now perennial gap by which Spain lagged behind countries such as France or Italy. In 1901, in response to the calls for regeneration, a Ministry of Public Instruction was created, taking charge of teachers' pay and extending compulsory schooling from six to twelve years, although rural school buildings and equipment continued to give rise to constant complaints from educationalists that visited them and reported on their needy situation.

In secondary education, the dominant note was the paralysis of the building of new high schools, while the religious orders multiplied the number of their establishments to take in the children of the expanding new middle classes: of the 70,000 pupils enrolled in secondary education in 1930, less than 20,000 attended official establishments. In contrast with this domination by the church were the initiatives to create a higher education sphere beyond its reach with the *Junta para Ampliación de Estudios e Investigaciones Científicas,* which from 1910 onwards sent dozens of Spaniards to study abroad each year with scholarships approved by successive liberal governments. This was the foundation on which a new professional class was built. These professional people shone in fields as varied as architecture, urban planning, engineering, mechanics, geometry, histology, physics, pedagogy, medicine, economics, not to mention literature, music and painting. Cultural associations, clubs, theatres, cinemas, lectures, journals and exhibitions transformed the atmosphere in the cities, which no longer gave cause to lament the decadence and death of Spain, and the conviction took root among the middle class that something new had emerged to replace the old.

The "old" in the parlance of the time, was not society, which was undergoing rapid change, but the political system inherited from the restoration of the monarchy in 1875, and which by 1898 was showing signs of exhaustion. After 1909, with the protests against troops being sent to Morocco, the formation of a left-wing bloc following the Tragic Week in Barcelona, and the "Maura, no" campaign against the Conservative leader, a new phase of factional in-fighting and governmental instability began. Based on the *turno pacífico,* an agreement between the dynastic Conservative and Liberal parties to pass power back and forth peacefully between them, the whole system was built on the foundations of a massive electoral fraud which guaranteed victory to the party calling the elections. Following in the footsteps of his grandmother Isabella II – a bad omen presaging a similar end – the young and inexperienced King Alfonso XIII, who came to the throne in 1902, called upon the leader of first one party then the other to charge them with the task of forming a government. A few weeks later, the chosen party dissolved the Cortes and called elections, which were inevitably won by the ruling party, with the connivance of a network of local election managers or *caciques* who rigged the results at the ballot box. Supported by its new majority, the government would remain in power until the situation was exhausted or problems arose between the different factions formed around the parties' leading figures, the main *caciques*. The time would then come for the situation to change and the king would call the leader of the opposition, and once again the merry-go-round would turn to bring the new government enough members of parliament.

This political system, devised for a rural world and an inward-looking society, was effective because it put an end to a century punctuated by civil wars, *pronunciamientos* or officers' coups, urban revolts and highly unstable government. The *turno pacífico* defused the conflicts arising from the confrontation between absolutism and liberalism and curbed the tendency to turn to the military to settle political arguments. However, the resulting system, in which sovereignty was shared by the king and the Cortes, with its *caciquismo*, electoral fraud, alternation between the parties, and closed political oligarchies, was poorly equipped to tackle the conflicts arising from society's modernization and the transition from an oligarchic liberalism to a mass democracy. It was a system that had been constructed with a view to resolving the disputes of the past, not looking to the future. And when the future came on the scene in the form of the new working class that had emerged in the suburbs of the cities, the professional middle class, and the regionalist movements, the governing political oligarchy, consolidated over decades of pernicious circulation in power, was unable or unwilling to face the looming crisis. Between 1918 and 1923, in a little more than the five-year term the Constitution set as the limit for a legislature, general elections were held five times, the Cortes were suspended on nine occasions, there were twelve changes of government and there were no less than seven different Conservative Presidents of the Council, all well into their sixties.

Meanwhile, with the connivance of the crown, the army had risen to the position of arbiter, and the church had emerged as the staunchest supporter of the crown. When the Congress emerging from the 1923 elections embarked on a search for responsibility for the disasters of the war in Morocco, the army's field marshal in Catalonia, Miguel Primo de Rivera, suspended the 1876 Constitution with a *pronunciamiento* which straight away received royal backing and wound up the whole political system, dynastic political parties included, along with the Constitution. If one had to put a date to the moment when Spanish political life lost its way and was unable to get back on course, it would be this one: 13 September 1923. This was the day the crown demonstrated its incapacity to direct the constitutional reform that would have allowed a peaceful evolution towards a constitutional monarchy based on popular sovereignty. The military coup was the clear demonstration that in Spain liberalism would not lead to democracy. It is true that Primo de Rivera presented himself as the "iron surgeon" ready to extirpate the old politics and restore the Constitution that his *pronunciamiento* had overturned in as short a time as possible. But after just two years, with the problem of Morocco solved, thanks to the decisive intervention of France, the dictator made it clear that he was in power to stay: in September 1926 he addressed a manifesto to the nation announcing the failure of the parliamentary system and proposing that a Supreme National Assembly be called and charged with the task of drafting a corporatist and authoritarian pseudo-constitution for the Spanish monarchy.

When the draft appeared in the press a political debate was sparked off in which a whole spectrum of opinions was voiced: from those, fearing the worst, who called for a return to the Constitution of 1876, to those who felt it to be impossible for things to return to normal, and that the time had come for a new beginning. Spain, which had witnessed a profound social transformation and the emergence of new middle and working classes, had expanded its industrial base and enjoyed a moment of cultural creativity, but lacked a Constitution. The dictator sought to impose a fundamental law that was completely alien to the Spanish constitutional tradition, digging his own grave by persisting in his efforts. Failing to find solid support for his aims, Alfonso XIII dismissed the general he had previously referred to as "my Mussolini" and handed the government over to another ageing general, Dámaso Berenguer, who witnessed in astonishment the sudden transformation of political life in the cities with the outbreak of a new fashion for declaring one's political stance, which so much irritated the director general for security, General Emilio Mola. Everybody wanted to declare their political views, in fact, but from the moment when monarchical politicians such as José Sánchez Guerra began to do so, the dilemma no longer revolved around the question of yes or no to the constituent Cortes, but on who was to convene these Cortes, the King or the president of a provisional government of the Republic.

As people took to the streets to listen, applaud and acclaim those who pronounced themselves in favor of the Republic, those voices that still considered promulgation of a new Constitution with Alfonso XIII remaining on the throne a possibility, fell silent. The socialist Indalecio Prieto made it very clear during a speech he delivered at the Ateneo in Madrid on 25 April 1930: "either you are with the King or against him." And this was what defining one's stance boiled down to: it was necessary to "overturn the monarch" by means of a revolutionary movement. Shortly before, Niceto Alcalá-Zamora, a recent newcomer to the Republican ranks from the monarchist side, had said in Valencia that there was only one legitimate power that could resolve Spain's political problems: a parliament, the Cortes, entirely sovereign and backed by the freely expressed national will. Manuel Azaña, leader of *Acción Republicana,* addressed the crowds gathered at the Madrid bull ring on Sunday 28 September to say that the Cortes arising spontaneously from the popular revolution had delivered the irrevocable verdict of the national will: no more tyrants, no more despotism, which at this juncture, meant: no more monarchy.

Thus, over the course of 1930, a confluence of parties took shape, bringing together republicans old and new, centrists and federalists, and culminating with the meeting on 17 August called by *Alianza Republicana* in San Sebastián. Two months later, in Madrid, the coalition was joined by the two socialist organizations, the party and the labor union, in order to organize a general strike which, accompanied by a military insurrection, would proclaim the Republic and, in the absence of the King, convene the constituent Cortes. "We come," their manifesto said, "to consign the Monarchy to the annals of History and establish the Republic on the foundations of national sovereignty represented by a Constituent Assembly." For the time being, however, they would have to wait: some in jail, others in hiding or on the run: the strike failed to materialize, and the insurrection ended in fiasco. But it was sufficient to convince General Berenguer to call elections for deputies to the Cortes for 1 March and senators two weeks later. By this time the project was so out of place that it lasted just a few days. Shortly after this call, a "Ministerial Declaration" issued by the new government, presided by another military figure, Admiral Juan Bautista Aznar and comprising the old – in all senses of the word – leaders of the dynastic parties, announced a new electoral timetable, with the calling of municipal elections first, followed by elections to the Cortes, which would be "Constituent in nature."[3]

To carry out his plan, Aznar decreed that elections to town halls would take place on Sunday 12 April 1931, leaving the promise of elections to the Cortes up in the air. Of course, in the towns and cities everyone received the announcement of municipal elections as if a plebiscite on the monarchy had been called, and after a lively election campaign in the urban media, this returned an undisputed victory for the Republican-Socialist candidates in the vast majority of provincial capitals, followed by a declaration of the Republic from the balconies of the town halls occupied by their new councilors. On the 13th, seven members of the Revolutionary committee, which was already presenting itself as the Republic's provisional government, signed and published a note treating the votes in the provincial capitals and major towns and cities as a plebiscite "against the Monarchy and in favor of the Republic," and announcing their intention to "act with energy and celerity" to immediately realize the "thirst of the young and eager Spanish majority by creating a Republic."

Such was the advent of the Republic; as a revolutionary popular *fiesta* which merged Republican and Socialist opposition into a single thrust, with a contribution from Catalan and Galician nationalists inspired from the outset by middle-class professionals in coalition with the organized working class. In the midst of this enthusiasm, a provisional government, made up of Republicans, Socialists and representatives of Catalan and Galician nationalisms, undertook the work of political and social reform demanded by the profound transformations Spanish society had experienced since the Great War. Nevertheless, although the Republic arrived, as the poet Antonio Machado said, like a gift of springtime, it was also mature fruit, long-awaited by the new middle class and the working classes that had been emerging in the cities over the preceding fifteen years. Its proponents aspired to create a democratic regime, with parliament as the centre of political life, free and fair elections, and the end of the power of the *caciques*. They sought to free the State from the weight of the two great institutions which had watched over it since time immemorial: the army and the church; establish equality of political and civil rights for men and women; remedy the great social inequalities, exacerbated by the waves of emigration from depressed rural areas to the squalid suburbs of the cities; extend and secularize primary and secondary education, and promote the creation of higher education establishments; and renew the political and administrative autonomy demanded by nationalist parties and movements, particularly in Catalonia.

---

[3]   The documents cited here and in the following paragraph are referenced in Juliá (2009).

This was an ambitious program which touched upon all orders of society and the State, the relationships between social classes, the power of the clergy, the military and landowners. It would affect people's lives from cradle to grave, and the regions' aspirations for political autonomy. In the social imaginary, the Republic was not merely a matter of regime change, and much less a change of government; it was, or promised to be, a change of way of life: the working class was to join the political system and the government of the State, and thereby improve on its miserable condition; women would enter the public sphere and have their full rights of citizenship recognized, starting with suffrage; children and young people would receive a new education, along modern, secular lines, which would end the scourge of illiteracy and the provincialism of a model of education dominated by religious orders – Spanish and foreign – which had flooded in since the end of the 19th century; the regions would fit better into the State; peasants would acquire title to the land they worked; the State would be organized as a democracy, ending the dual sovereignty of the Cortes and King. In short, as befitted the age, life would be more egalitarian, freer, and fairer, thereby fulfilling the demands of the generation that had been in its youth at the time of the Disaster of 1898, had reached middle age by 1914, and was now in power and eager to construct a new State and rebuild society from the bottom up.

It is impossible here to go into all the details of the sequence of events between the Republican fervor of 14 April 1931 and the military uprising against the legitimate government of the Republic on 18 July 1936. However, once again, as had happened several times during the 19th century and had been the case thirteen years earlier, the political process was violently interrupted by the force of arms. This time, however, far from achieving its aim of a rapid seizure of power, it triggered a workers' revolt and an uprising in the countryside, followed by a long drawn-out civil war. There was nothing inevitable about the conspiracy which led to the *coup d'état:* if, rather than conspiring, the army had supported the government of the Republic in its efforts to maintain the peace and social order, as its duty dictated, the Civil War would never have happened; but, given that they had decided to conspire, if they had guaranteed sufficient complicity to strike with a firm hand, with the full backing of the army, they would have seized power: perhaps with more difficulty than in 1923, but with no less success. In July 1936 the rebellion failed to achieve its aims, but the government was unable to quell it, and a situation arose that was as unforeseen by the rebels as it was undesirable to those loyal to the government: a military uprising that had triumphed in its attempt to establish a territorial basis for power, but failed in its goal of taking over the government of the State; and a government that, in order to contain the rebellion and bolster its resistance, handed out weapons to unions and workers' parties, who embarked on a social revolution. It was war, but at the same time, where the military triumphed, it was a counter-revolution, and where those loyal to the government defeated the rebels, a revolution; both accompanied by strategies of political cleansing that resulted in countless murders and massacres.

The Civil War unleashed by the military uprising was first and foremost a Spanish matter, in which various conflicts inherent to a period that the country seemed to have put behind it resurfaced: a military rebellion against the legitimate civil authority, a counter-revolution which was met with a revolution, an armed class struggle, a war of religion, a clash of nationalisms within a single nation, and not only Spanish nationalism against Catalan or Basque nationalisms, but also a clerical and military nationalism among the rebels against the popular and republican nationalism of those loyal to the government. But in just a few weeks the Spanish Civil War went from being an internal struggle over the form of society and State to take on an international dimension. The early and unconcealed intervention of Germany and Italy on the rebels' side, was followed, during the defense of Madrid, by the presence of the International Brigades, who were organized and trained by envoys from the Communist International, and who took up their positions on the battle front. With Germans, Italians, Soviets and the International Brigades on Spanish soil, the war ceased to be simply a domestic matter in which ancient Spanish disagreements were being settled by force of arms, and went from being a civil war to a testing ground for war between European states and between the political and social systems operating in Europe at the time: fascism, democracy and communism.

Thus, the first collective project to Europeanize Spain ended up with Europe playing a major part in the Spanish catastrophe, while it prepared itself to resume its second "Thirty Years' War", which would end in the European catastrophe. Spain's perennial habit of looking at its neighbors to see a reflection of its own deformities and deficiencies left the way open, after the double slaughter of war in Spain and in Europe, to the affirmation of a Spanish difference, which the Archbishop of Toledo, Enrique Pla y Deniel, when about to be elevated to the rank of Cardinal, rushed to proclaim, addressing the allied powers, on the very same day that Germany capitulated, in a pastoral letter setting out the justification of the Spanish Civil War as a crusade against communism. Juan Valera would have termed it an insurrection wrapped in Catholic robes.

2   Spain becomes different

The war in Spain, with the triumph of the Catholic nation supported by the fascist powers over the republican people abandoned by the democratic powers, swept away not only everything that had been gained since the start of the century up until the proclamation of the Republic, but also what had formed the germ of the victors' delirious narrative: the liberal tradition, a foreign graft onto the body of the nation, the origin of the Anti-Spain. To a repression that was methodical and implacable, destined to root out the seeds of the ill, with the result that thousands were sent to their death by firing squad by marcial courts after the war had ended, and hundreds of thousands imprisoned or driven into exile, there was added the re-Catholicization of society, from secondary education up, through to the sanctification of public spaces, with massive ceremonies and trailing processions, and a universal autarky, in social and cultural matters as well as in the economy. From its first steps, the new Spanish State began to build itself on the unique and authentic Spanish nation, rhetorically monarchic and catholic in essence, founded in fascist style under the charismatic leadership of the *caudillo* General Franco, victor on the battlefield, head of the sole party and consecrated by the church as being sent by God to save the *patria*. This was an amalgamation that marked Spain with an eternal difference from any other European country and forced it to project itself backwards to the mythical age of the Catholic Monarchs.

It is not difficult to imagine the immense damage this project to reinvent the Spanish nation on autarkic and Catholic foundations, with a dictatorship governed by soldiers and a fascist "service class", did to Spanish society. By looking for the mythical origins of the State, outside of real historical time, the coalition that emerged victorious from the Civil War broke the continuity of its economic development, paralyzed its population flows, blocked the process of profound social and political transformations that had begun around 1910 and wrecked its political and cultural traditions. The urban and rural working classes were stripped of their union organizations, while their leaders and militants were shot or sent to labor camps; the members of the professional middle class, which had become increasingly reformist and republican over the preceding two decades, were cowed into silence or forced into exile, if they did not want to risk losing their jobs, or even their lives. Relations with the outside world, in European science, thought or art, were completely cut off. From the mid-1940s, this is what Spanish exceptionalism boiled down to.[4]

It was a difference that did not worry the allies on the eve of their triumph over the Axis powers, nor thereafter. Towards 1945 Spain counted for little on the international stage, and its regime, to ward off possible problems, played up its Catholic essence – and the complicities this essence derived from – over and above its fascist components, which it had boasted of at least up until 1943. The democracies, for their part, saw the specter of Communism in the East take physical form with Soviet tanks in the heart of Germany, a fact that, as Raymond Aron commented,[5] would have astounded British or French observers in the 19th century. The irrelevance of Spain as a power, and the Catholic ideological basis of the dictatorship, served to accentuate the myth of its origins as an anti-Communist crusade, while its military component looked, to the eyes of the Western victors, the only possible way of keeping order in a devastated and impoverished society, with Spain's exiles deeply divided by previous confrontations between their main political forces, and unable to put up a common front. The allies declared themselves satisfied with a UN statement condemning the new State as fascist, only to start negotiations two years later that would lead to its becoming a disciplined and subordinate member of the United States' defensive system without its needing to make any changes beyond what Raymond Carr has described as "cosmetic constitutionalism."[6]

Spain was thus excluded from the second wave of democratization, which under the friendly smile of young US marines and the stern gaze of the tribunals ready to initiate

---

[4]   I have written on these topics at greater length in Juliá (2000).
[5]   Aron (1985), p. 297.
[6]   Carr (1982), p. 704.

trials for crimes against humanity, flooded Western Europe. Germany, Italy, France and others consummated their transitions to democracy from fascist or collaborationist regimes, while in Spain, Franco, with something more than the acquiescence of the democratic powers, strengthened his hold without the slightest push towards democracy from Europe or the United States. In 1947, Joseph Schumpeter wrote that the case of Spain was "the least problematic" of any in Europe, because ultimately Franco was doing no more than follow a "pattern well established in the 19th century: he had not done and was not doing anything more than Narváez, O'Donnell, Espartero and Serrano had."[7] The drawback of historical learning is that the present tends to be understood merely as the continuation of the past: Franco and his regime were interpreted as the continuation of a history of Spain whose origins could be traced back to the middle of the 19th century and which was summed up in the conviction that Spain was a country where nothing worked unless there was a general in the presidency, or to express it in the terms the absolutists used, according to Juan Valera's reproach, that this noble, Catholic country, the birthplace of heroes and saints, could only be governed with a stick.[8]

To confirm this, four years after Schumpeter's reflections, in 1951 when the UN had overturned its recommendation to withdraw ambassadors, Gerald Brenan advised the British that they should not hesitate to visit Spain, where they would find the hotels cheap, the rooms clean, and the food plentiful and good. It would be a delusion, he said, to imagine that the alternative to Franco could be a parliamentary democracy. Not a bit of it: if elections were called and the left were to win, there would be a fresh *coup d'état*. Spain, Brenan said, "for some time to come needs to live under an authoritarian régime". And the recently restored European democracies shared his view: for now Spain needed an authoritarian regime. Later, we would see. For the moment, this cauldron in which the cultures of Europe, Asia and Africa had been mixed over the centuries would stop hearing a note that was unlike any other, nostalgic like that of its guitars, such that no one who had heard it could forget it. The people of the North, Brenan concluded, had a lot of reasons to travel to Spain certain that the country would give them "new sensations":[9] Carmen with the guitar in the background, a crucifix on the wall, and a civil guard watching the doorway: this was the Spanish difference, from which British tourists could extract *new,* that is to say oriental, sensations.

Thus excluded from the processes of democratization, but ultimately benefiting from the prosperity that these visitors brought with them, the regime's propaganda retrieved the slogan of Spanish difference to legitimize the persistence of political institutions that originated in the Civil War and in the early post-war years, while society started once again on the process of its grand transformation. That is what Florentino Pérez Embid, an intellectual of the true and unique Spain, called, by way of a warning "Spanishization in

---

[7]   Schumpeter (1979), p. 380.

[8]   Valera (1958), III, p. 736.

[9]   Brenan (1950), XV and XVI.

the ends, Europeanization in the means," a happy synthesis which liquidated the "wounding antinomy of Spanishization or Europeanization."[10] Once again, there was a rural exodus, this time on a vast scale, heading abroad or towards the major cities: from the magnitude, recovered after the Civil War, of 50.5% of the labor force in agriculture in 1940, which was still 47.5% in 1950 – two-tenths of a percentage point higher than twenty years earlier – it dropped to 22.8% in 1970. And together with the end of traditional farming, there was a process of rapid industrialization accelerated by the development plans and a general promotion of education, with universal primary schooling, the building and opening of new high schools and universities. Once again the cities – Madrid, Barcelona and others – doubled in size in under a decade and once again there was a process of secularization, while Spain's bishops, retaining all their privileges, looked on in amazement at the sessions of the Second Vatican Council. And finally, the windows – and indeed wide avenues – were opened up on to the outside world, and travel was no longer limited just to the middle classes but extended to the working classes, who found in emigration a new democratic experience while the beaches filled up with tourists: these were the results of that *Spain is different* which shone like sunlight in the posters distributed to travel agencies by the Ministry of Information and Tourism, headed at the time by Manuel Fraga.

These results explain why, when Santiago Carillo, General Secretary of the Communist Party of Spain (PCE), in exile in Paris, asked the question: *After Franco, what next?* the question echoed across borders and through chancelleries, and among the legion of Hispanicists and political scientists, concerned about the possibility of Spain's falling back into its depraved and somewhat savage political customs. As if Franco was indeed the continuation of Spanish history, his disappearance could lead to the breaking of that continuity and the destruction of what industrialization, urbanization, and the growth of the middle class had achieved, all at the expense of suppressing the occasional bellicose urge for violence that was intrinsic to Spaniards, given their individualistic and rebellious nature, and their demonstrated inability to avoid democracy's ending in chaos. This was at least what a close observer of contemporary Spain, Richard Herr, feared when he wrote in 1971, that the future was shrouded in mystery and would depend on how the question: "After he goes, what?" was answered, typical of countries governed for a long time by a *"he"*, a strong man. Spaniards, he said, were by nature rebellious and politically voluble; fortunately, in recent years they had applied to the economy the energy that they had normally destined to political agitation, a forced sublimation by the prohibition of political activity, Herr wrote, delving into the murky waters of social psychoanalysis. But what would happen when this prohibition was lifted? Herr had heard a lot of people, both friends and enemies of Franco, say – and he did not deny it – that Spaniards would return to their old ways. Had Charles Tilly not written earlier that, as regards violence, Spain always offers a "marvelous array of regressions, mixtures and hesitations"? They may well be "marvelous", but only for the scientific observer of these regressions, who could then

---

[10]   Pérez Embid (1949), p. 160

go on to say that they are "the exception that test[s] the rule". And in 1975, Giovanni Sartori, scarcely more optimistic than Herr or Tilly, expressed the view that Spain could regress to the pattern of the 1930s, "a chaotic, excessively brief and highly polarized experiment with multiparty politics."[11] Simply stated, among foreign scholars nobody held out much hope for what might happen in Spain without Franco: it was to be expected that Spain would return to "normal" by sinking back into its old habits of violence and chaos.

Meanwhile, in Spain, Carrillo's question worried both the politicians in power, in the *Consejo Nacional del Movimiento,* and the leaders of the PCE, in opposition. On a more academic level, it also spurred debate among Spanish social scientists, young sociologists, political scientists and historians who had enjoyed something of a boom in the 1960s and had analyzed the social changes taking place during the decade. With their penchant for crystal-ball gazing, they had explored possible future political avenues, taking a comparative approach, particularly in terms of the levels of industrialization, urbanization, education, and consolidation of a society with new working and middle classes. It was in one of these comparisons that the new social scientists detected the presence of a generation born between 1930 and 1945, dubbed the "new Spaniards," described by Luis González Seara in his presentation of the Foessa report in 1975, who were ready to man a democratic system, being a generation that aspired to a Spain that, in the near future, would come to resemble what other European states were at the time. "We wanted to be like the Swedes, the Dutch, the Belgians. That was our ambition," wrote Félix de Azúa later, recalling the period. And much earlier, José María de la Peña, director of the *Archivo General de Indias* in Seville, wondered, one day in January 1962, in front of an attentive Gabriel Jackson, "if Italy could achieve parliamentary democracy, with Christian democrats and socialists sharing power, why can't we do the same one day in Spain?"[12]

And looking in the mirror at a model with variable similarities to Spain which could serve as a guide to the process that loomed on the horizon, would it not be useful to recall that when Franco died in November 1975, several military dictatorships were in place in Latin America, military juntas were running, or had only recently handed over power, in Turkey and Greece. And in Portugal the army had mounted a *coup d'état* – the so-called Carnation Revolution, to underscore its peaceful nature as a new spring, with carnations in rifle barrels – against the corporativist and authoritarian regime. What prevailed then, in the Mediterranean and in Latin America, was not a model of civilian transitions to democracy, but rather the contrary, with the military playing a major part. A drift in the same direction could not be ruled out in Spain, indeed it formed part of the set of hypotheses circulating about the answers to the question of what would happen after Franco: that of a military authority able to control the transition to an authoritarian monarchy. Neither Latin America nor the Mediterranean countries offered models with which to open up the way to the future; in the best of cases, they were models of what not to do, even for the regime's political

---

[11]   Herr (1971), p. 27. Tilly (1969), l.c. Sartori (1976), pp. 155 and 165.
[12]   González Seara (1976), XIX-XXXII; Azúa (1996), p. 81; Jackson (1993), p. 203.

elite, which answered Carillo's question firmly and concisely: the institutions. They had been working along these lines since the Organic Law of State in 1967: after Franco, the institutions, or what was also termed "organic democracy" or "Spanish democracy".

It is therefore not surprising that both social scientists and the opposition forces – which sought to avoid both intervention by the military and the prolongation in time of the regime's institutions – should look not so much to contemporary examples but to other periods in the past in their search for points of reference to guide the process of change. The period they alighted on was that of the rebuilding of democracies in Western Europe following the Allied victory over the Axis powers in the Second World War. A long way ahead of any third wave of democratization that no one had yet thought to proclaim, Spaniards looking for a point of comparison saw themselves as epigones of the wave that had crossed Europe after the defeat of fascism, led by Germany, Italy and France. The aim was to liquidate the accursed Spanish difference by making up for a centuries-old lag, something that had been achieved in part in the economic field, in social life and in the culture of a new professional middle class and blue-collar working class, but which was blocked in the political domain behind the vain efforts at opening driven from within the regime itself and always ending in fiasco.

And so the social scientists of the sixties, conscious of the weight of the church in the construction of the Spanish Catholic nationalist state, and by no means ignorant of the fascist element visible in institutions such as the *Movimiento Nacional* and the *Organización Nacional de Sindicatos,* began to look to Italy as the most eloquent example from which to draw lessons for the future. Perhaps the first person to hold up Italy as a mirror in which to glimpse the future of Spain was Juan Linz in 1967. An international authority on issues concerning the processes and breakdowns of democracy, Linz wondered what would happen "if Spaniards were to vote like Italians."[13] He hazarded a guess that any multiparty system in Spain would revolve around Christian Democrats and Socialists, with a strong Communist party that would limit the power of the Socialists. Studies and opinion polls conducted in the absence of political parties and constrained to exploring voting trends, enabled predictions based on respondents' answers to the questionnaires – the response rate was barely fifty percent – of strong support for Christian Democrats, Socialists and Communists. This suggested support be split between regime insiders and outsiders. The Communists, who argued for a strategy of transition as a means of reconciliation, and the politically dissident Catholics, who called for dialogue, therefore seemed to be in the best position to occupy the hegemonic positions on the left and right after Franco.

This was the view not only of political scientists, but also that of the Communist party leadership and of Catholics recently converted to Christian democracy with the encouragement of the Vatican, that is to say, the Spanish Communist Party (PCE) controlled without internal opposition by Santiago Carrillo, on the one side, and the various Catholic currents accreting around José María Gil Robles, Manuel Giménez Fernández and Joaquín Ruiz-

---

[13] Linz (1976), pp. 268-271.

Giménez, on the other. That the Catholics looked to the Vatican, and therefore to Italy, as a source of inspiration and no doubt more was clear: Ruiz-Giménez was given suggestions by Pope Paul VI, formerly cardinal Montini, on launching his initiatives for dialogue so as to build bridges with the clandestine opposition and erode the military-ecclesiastical alliance that underpinned the Francoist state. Nor is there any doubt as to the Italian inspiration behind the PCE's policy, to which everyone, starting with the regime, attributed a crucial role in what was to happen after Franco. From the declaration "For national reconciliation, a democratic and peaceful solution to the Spanish problem," agreed in June 1956, a few months after confirming that some of the "sons of the victors" had crossed over to the losers' side, the Spanish Communists adopted a policy inspired by that of their Italian counterparts, which on two occasions had taken the same route towards national reconciliation: in 1936, when the Italian Communist Party (PCI) held out its hand *"ai fascisti nostri fratelli di lavoro i di sofferenze"*;[14] and later, in 1944, when fascism had been defeated and after the bouts of "savage justice" in the final phases of a veritable civil war, with more than ten thousand executions by partisans, Palmiro Togliatti backed a national unity government, and in 1946 presented, as justice minister in the cabinet presided by Alcide de Gasperi, an amnesty law that, in its lax application, not only offered immunity to the partisans who had committed "spontaneous acts of vengeance, but also allowed many condemned fascists to return to their bourgeois lives." In fact, the vast majority of public servants, police prefects and governors who had served the fascist State kept or regained their positions and held them until retirement.[15]

Carrillo was no doubt aware of these precedents. During his first conversation with Suárez in February 1977, a month and a half before his party was legalized, he set out a strategy learned from the "experience of the transition from fascism to democracy in other countries, such as France, after the war. What did the French Communist Party do? It ran a campaign calling on workers to raise production. In Italy, Togliatti did something similar."[16] In reality, Togliatti had gone further: after ordering party militants to hand over their weapons, he argued for a policy identical to that which the PCE had advocated since 1956 and tried to put into practice twenty years later – a government of national unity, an amnesty and maintenance of the monarchy, up until the time when a plebiscite was held in the Italian case, and indefinitely in the Spanish one. He did so with spectacular results, as Carrillo was no doubt also aware: the PCI's membership of 401,960 in 1944 rose to no less than 2,252,716 in 1947.[17] This made it a true mass party, which fought to conquer in society the hegemony that the ballot box denied it. It was a model of success based on the thesis expressed by Togliatti on his return from the Soviet Union, a model that was part Leninist,

---

[14]   Quotes from two publishers of *Lo Stato operaio,* June 1936: "La riconciliazione del popolo italiano è la condicione per salvare il nostro paese della catastrofe" and "La vittoria del Fronte popolare in Francia", are from Spriano (1975), p. 63.

[15]   For an overview see, Woller (1998) I, 526-545, and Focardi and Klinkhammer (2006), pp. 251-290.

[16]   "La transición en España: testimonio de Santiago Carrillo" (1998), p. 161.

[17]   Figures from Gallerano (1981), p. 1070.

part Gramscian, which had enabled the PCI to hold on to a solid position in Italian politics and society for over thirty years. This was the model the PCE aimed to develop, convinced that it would win a third of the total votes in the first elections,[18] which would make it a major mass party able to achieve social hegemony. To do so, the PCE had to avoid the fate of the German Communists after the war, an example Carrillo had "in mind" each time he refused, first to the King's envoys, and then to Suárez, to agree to a delay in the legalization of his party until two or three years after the first elections.[19]

This was the opposition's reference framework after the death of Franco: taking Spain, thirty years late, along the road Europe had taken after the end of the Second World War. Within this framework, it was necessary to improvise a different route to eliminate the difference. First of all, in Spain, unlike France, Germany or Italy, the Allied powers had not lifted a finger – nor would they do so – to cut short the dictatorship by so much as a day: it was certain, everyone accepted, that Franco would not die like Mussolini, which ruled out the possibility of there being a period of fascist hunting. Moreover, in 1975 the break in continuity of the party system had been much more long-lasting and profound and nobody knew how the electorate ought to behave; moreover, the King of Italy had cohabited with the dictator, one as head of state, the other as head of government, whereas in Spain, the King was the successor of the dictator, and as of July 1976, when he dismissed the reformers and *aperturistas* at a stroke, including Arias and Fraga, he put himself at the head of an uncertain process of returning popular sovereignty; in short, although no less important, the generals who had triumphed as lieutenants, captains and majors in the Civil War kept control over the armed forces and national security. To complete the picture, Spain's politicians – both those in power and those in opposition – knew full well that no foreign power would do anything to help them dismantle the regime's institutions. The foreign powers were not concerned by these institutions' anachronism and apparent inability to keep order after the death of Franco, although perhaps they might intervene if the Communists failed to stick to the post-war pact, as they had feared might happen in Portugal. Indeed, Henry Kissinger, the United States Secretary of State, recommended leaving the legalization of the PCE for later, while Willy Brandt, the Chancellor of the Federal Republic of Germany, recommended something similar to Felipe González, namely that he not demand the legalization of the Communists as a precondition for taking part in the elections. Was that not what had happened in Germany after the Nazi defeat?

There was, therefore, a model from which to draw inspiration, namely that established by the allies after the end of the Second World War. However, the variables of time and place were such that the transition would either happen in a totally new way defined by Spain or not happen at all. And it was on this point that a factor arose that nobody had foreseen during the lengthy conversations the opposition had held with dissident groups in the 1940s. The political regime had not been defeated: the public administration and the

---

[18]   As stated by Carrillo during a visit to the president of Algeria, according to Vidal Beneyto (2007), p. 127.

[19]   Interview with Santiago Carrillo, in Prego (1996), p. 54

institutions of the State, with a pseudo-constitution in the form of the Organic Law of State of 10 January 1967, were all still standing. This detail introduced a leading actor that had disappeared from the scene in the fascist systems that had suffered defeat: the fascist political caste, drawn from the bureaucracies of the State and the Movement, which was inwardly not willing to change, nor did it feel itself to be driven to do so from outside. On the contrary, it had shown itself to have sufficient capacity to reproduce itself that some of its younger members, who had not been through the war nor occupied front line positions under the dictatorship, moved up to push the old guard aside and position themselves to occupy, after Franco's death, the space that had been filled in Europe by the Christian Democrats after the end of the Second World War.

Thus, Adolfo Suárez's aim – as the businessman Pere Duran Farell told Carrillo – was to create in Spain a party that would occupy the role played by the Christian Democrats in Italy: giving reassurance to the United States and allowing the Communists to occupy a broad space that divided the left into two parties of similar electoral strength and, therefore, consigned them to perennial opposition. This was how the transition was going to look according to the image seen in the mirror of Italy: Suarez's *Unión de Centro Democrático* (UCD) playing the role of the DCI while the PCE played that of the PCI. Almost from the outset Suárez tried to achieve this by including leading members of the Tácito group – such as Alfonso Osorio, Marcelino Oreja, Landelino Lavilla, who held their get-togethers at the *santa casa* and whose mouthpiece was the catholic newspaper *Ya* – in his first government, and giving them key positions, such that their presence swamped that of those whose background was in the regime, such as Suárez himself and his minister of the interior, Rodolfo Martín Villa. And this effort would culminate a few months later with UCD's devouring the first People's Party, created by Pío Cabanillas and José María de Areilza, to form a party that was destined – with the blessing of the church – to cut the grass from under the feet of the Christian Democrat *Equipo Demócrata Cristiano del Estado Español,* whose impossible name highlighted the historical divisions between the Christian Democrat factions from the confederation of Catholic right-wing parties, CEDA, and the *Movimiento Nacional* (Gil Robles, Ruiz-Giménez), who lacked the support of the Vatican and the Spanish episcopate, which was in no way willing to baptize a new Catholic party in Europe.

The similarities were, therefore, no less significant than the differences. But this did not stop the impression prevailing in political circles that the match would be between a pseudo-Christian Democrat party and an Italian-style Communist party. The Spanish Communists hastened towards their model, right down to the appearances. As Rossana Rossanda suspected, Palmiro Togliatti had felt more at ease playing the part of a leader of the opposition in a capitalist society such as Italy than he would ever have been as the general secretary of the United Workers Party of Poland.[20] And the same, or more so, was true of Enrico Berlinguer, the architect of the *compromesso storico* with the Christian Democrats.

---

[20]   Rossanda (2008), p. 269.

Moreover, his leading Spanish disciple, Santiago Carrillo, convinced that his party was destined to take the lead in the opposition, announced, not accidentally, from Rome, that his was an "agreed break" and hurried to draft and publish a tract on Eurocommunism and managed to arrange things such that George Marchais, general secretary of the French Communist Party, also appeared as a firm supporter of the new way at the meeting the three leaders held in Madrid in early March 1977, one month before the PCE was legalized in bold stroke by the prime minister, swept along by public opinion following the brutal act of terror by the extreme right which cost the lives of four Communist lawyers and their office caretaker.

Ultimately, the most original feature of the Spanish political transition was that the secretary general of the *Movimiento Nacional,* who had blocked the reform of the fundamental laws proposed by the Arias/Fraga government, would behave like an Italian Christian Democrat, without saying so much, and call general elections to the Cortes that, by the sheer force of events rather than any plan by the government, were to be declared constituent Cortes from their very first day. This fact was not a response to the government's intentions, as it had planned the task of the Cortes to be to proceed towards "constitutional reform" on its own initiative, but the result of elections which denied the UCD an absolute majority, while giving second place – to the undisguised disgust of the PCE – to the Spanish Socialist Party, PSOE. The historical memory had worked and the socialists, led by Felipe González, had refashioned the party by breaking away from its ties to its leaders in exile and as Carrillo mentioned, "it was imbued with the idea that its mission was to prevent Spain from following the Italian example",[21] gathering votes from its traditional constituencies and emerging as the main opposition force and leaving the Communists with insufficient resources to repeat in Spain the experience of a *historical compromise,* Spanish style, with the lure of a government of national unity.

The outcome of the elections also represented a rebuff for the legion of prophets of doom who had predicted chaos and a return to violence which would lead to the reproduction of a polarized multiparty system. What happened was the opposite: the number of parties and the seats they obtained were reduced to two main options, left and right, after the fashion of other post-war European democracies. And the political learning curve, together with the need to confront a profound economic crisis, forced them to negotiate over pending issues and plans for the future. Although violence returned as the instrument of terrorist groups, of which ETA was the most significant, the new parliament passed an Amnesty Law on 15 October and the parties went into conversations to tackle the economic crisis through the agreement that came to be known as the Moncloa Pact. At the same time, once the constituent nature of the new Cortes had been confirmed, the committee appointed by the Commission on Constitutional Affairs started work, culminating in the presentation of a draft Constitution agreed from start to finish and in which the most fiercely debated points – and those finally brandished by the Basque Nationalist Party, PNV, to justify its

---

[21]　As mentioned in Prego (1996), l.c.

abstention and thus start a long and profitable career as a free rider – were Article 2, on the recognition of the autonomy of the nationalities and regions, and Title VIII, on the territorial organization of the State.

The climate of accord lasted only as long as it took to promulgate the Constitution. The Spanish Christian Democrats never willingly accepted the leadership of a parvenu with no credentials or track record, and preferred to go down fighting than to consolidate the UCD as a true political party, created as it was out of an agglomeration around personalities unwilling to give up the limelight rather than through the integration of its constituent groups. In 1980, the history of internal rifts and the irresistible decline of the PCE, unable to make headway at the ballot box, ran parallel with the history of the internal divisions and self-destruction of the UCD, torn apart by the rebellion of the Christian Democrats – or whatever they were – against Adolfo Suárez. It was in this situation when it was to be feared, to paraphrase Tilly, that Spain would be, "as usual, the significant exception." But the exception took the face of a lieutenant colonel in the Civil Guard with an old-style moustache, who stood on the rostrum of the Congress of Deputies brandishing a pistol. Fortunately Marx was right: If the first exception, with civil war and dictatorship, was a tragedy, the second, with Tejero and his demand that deputies "sit down, damn it!", was a farce (that said only with the benefit of hindsight).

Thus, the attempted *coup d'état,* with its various demonstrations in Valencia and the armored division in Brunete, followed by the failure and surrender of the insurgents, accelerated the disappearance of the governing party, sunk the PCE a little further and served as a spur to the conquest of an absolute majority by a reformed PSOE, while the right, led by Manuel Fraga, began its long march through the wilderness. The party system would not regain its balance for another ten years, during which the construction of a peculiar system of territorial organization, known as the State of Autonomies, would be completed, and the constitutional predictions were modified with a view to ensuring equal and uniform competencies at the expense of extending seventeen mimetic copies of the central government across the country, with their parliaments, governments, higher courts and their own media channels.

3   Spain becomes normal, but ...

The first outcome of Spain's transition to democracy, which, in its way, followed the path of Italy, Germany and France in the period between the defeat of fascism and the start of the Cold War, was a party system similar to that in those countries, but with the specific differences arising from its timing: after the Second Vatican Council, it was impossible to create a Christian democratic party; the alternative was a State built on a nation and various nationalities with the consequent presence of nationalist parties which immediately sought, as the corollary of their conquest of liberty, to recoup the autonomy they had achieved under the Republic. But, in terms of the State, the fact that two dominant parties emerged, each with its own space, UCD – and in 1982, Alianza Popular (Popular Alliance), later the Partido Popular (People's Party) – occupying the centre right, and PSOE holding the centre left, gave governments a stability that had never previously been seen in Spain's parliamentary system: since 1976 there have been five prime ministers, and since 1982 just three: less than during the last three years of the constitutional monarchy and less than in the two years of the Republic under the Partido Radical (Radical Party) with the CEDA. Therefore, Spain not only had a fully European Constitution and system of parties, but it had completed a political process that brought about a radical change of perceptions among foreign analysts: foreign observers proclaimed Spain to be nothing less than a "very model" of transition by agreement, which, given its success, could be followed by other countries in Europe and the Americas.[22]

It was a success because the transition to democracy, although not without obstacles, violence and hazards, and its consolidation after the Socialist Party's victory in 1982 with an absolute majority, enabled a rapid political transformation. In the final fifteen years of Franco's regime, Spain had been a centralized, highly bureaucratic, authoritarian, Catholic State with organic or corporate representation, an extraordinarily high degree of concentration of power at the apex, and a permanent military presence in government. Its domestic market was highly protected and regulated, and it was excluded from the political institutions of the then European Economic Community. The process of transition turned it into a lay and non-confessional democratic state – although the Catholic Church held on to significant privileges in education and finance – governed by the rule of law, with a welfare state, a division of powers, a government that was accountable to Parliament and with military power fully subordinate to government. Politically and administratively it was devolved into 17 Autonomous Communities, each with its own government and higher courts of justice, and it was fully integrated in Europe. The transition from one form of state to another was not without its vicissitudes, particularly given the persistence of ETA terrorism and the nationalist confusions and tensions which accompanied the creation of the Autonomous Communities. However, given the prevailing view at the start of the process, its consolidation over the course of the socialist party government from 1982 to 1996, and the normality of the second alternation of power, led to its being celebrated as a thoroughgoing success.

The inward transformation of the State was accompanied by a new relationship with the outside world, which although it has had a few ups and downs as a result of the confrontation over the second Iraq war, retained the two main lines of Spain's traditional policy: agreements with the United States since 1953 and a special relationship with the European Economic Community, established by the technocrats in the 1960s. But that politics had impassable boundaries that the consolidation of democracy had just broken through: without losing its trans-Atlantic links, and even strengthening them with its membership of NATO, Spain had turned towards the European Union, of which it became a member on 1 January 1986.

---

[22]   Among others, Przeworski (1991) and Gunther (1992).

This had a considerable impact on all levels, from the possibility of establishing a foreign policy that was less dependent on the alliance with the United States, through to the development of infrastructure that has transformed the landscape with the construction of motorways and high-speed rail lines. The differential with the average of the fifteen-member European Union at the end of the twentieth century had been cut to 80%, while the deep-rooted conviction that Spain was the anomaly in Europe gave way to the feeling that Spain's exceptionality was a thing of the past, reinforced by the evidence that while the structure of a Regional State comprising 17 Autonomous Communities and integration in Europe were being consolidated, substantial shifts were underway in Spanish society that brought it closer to the mainstream of European society.

Indeed, our turn-of-the-century traveler, that urban planner and meticulous observer Oskar Jürgens, would have been struck dumb if he had been able to witness the transformation of the medium-sized cities, provincial capitals and other towns, over the final decades of the century. It was towns with between 100 and 500 thousand inhabitants, followed closely by those with populations between 20 and 100 thousand, that had undergone the most dramatic demographic changes: in 2009, 70% of Spain's population lived in urban centers of over 20,000 inhabitants. These were also those in which urbanization was fastest, accelerating for the first time since 1915, having been interrupted by the Civil War and post-war period, although picking up again in the 1960s. This process was completing the transformation of the predominantly rural Spain that existed at the start of the 20th century, in which 66% of the labor force worked on the land, into an urban society. Urbanization was paralleled by similar growth in the services sector, which now accounts for 71% of all employment.

This process was neither linear nor problem-free. The transition to democracy took place in the midst of an economic crisis with a sharp fall in employment and hence rising unemployment rates. In the early 1980s this reached 24% of the labor force, with a loss of jobs in both agriculture and industry, as loss-making state-owned firms were closed or sold to multinationals, and more women sought to join the workforce. The employed population, which had totaled 12.6 million in 1976, fell significantly over the following ten years and recovered only slowly, returning to around 12.7 million in 1996: it took twenty years to regain the level of employment that had been lost. Not only was this process accompanied by tensions deriving from the new territorial distribution of power: there was also a period of conflicts as workers who found their livelihood and traditional working-class culture being undermined sought to defend jobs in traditional industries.

Over the twenty years of net job destruction, there was a powerful redistribution of the employed population between sectors. The loss of jobs in agriculture and industry could only be offset by an increase in employment in services and construction, with the result that Spain saw an acceleration in the rate at which it turned into a services-based society. Whereas in 1977 the services sector accounted for 40.4% of the labor force, by 2000 the figure was 62.1%, and this share would continue to rise over the first decade of the 21st century. In the fourth quarter of 2009, and in the midst of a new phase of massive job losses, services came to account for 71.7% of employment, industry having fallen by over ten points to just 14.4%, construction accounting for 9.7% (after a peak in the three previous years of 12.7%), and agriculture 4.2%. These figures highlight Spain's progress along the path from an agricultural society to a post-industrial society, which at the same time, substantially increased the amount of work offered to women: the percentage of women in the labor force, which began at values of under 20%, rose over the last 25 years of the 20th century to 37% of the occupied population, and the figure today – in the wake of the loss of two million jobs since the start of the economic crisis in 2007 – is 39%. According to data for the first quarter of 2010, the labor force in Spain comprises 15.94 million people, of whom 9.70 million are men and 6.23 million are women.

Women's demand for a place in the labor force, and the legalization of the contraceptive pill, help explain the third great wave of transformations affecting Spain's demographics in the 20th century. This time, however, the driver of change was not population growth but its rapid contraction. Right from the early stages of the transition, Spain's women decided to bring substantially fewer young Spaniards into the world than had their mothers and grandmothers. In 1900, with a population of 18.5 million, the number of births stood at 650,600, a level at which it remained for the first 62 years of the century. Indeed, so stable was it that it almost appeared as if Spanish women had set themselves this figure as a target, regardless of how many of them there were; although there was a slight but persistent drop during the Civil War and post-war years, only once – in 1939 – did it drop below 500,000. From 1979 on, however, there was a sharp fall, until twenty years later, in 1999, against the backdrop of a population of 39.8 million, there were just over 380,000 births, the lowest figure in the century and only slightly (10,000) more than deaths. In sum, the rate of gross natural population growth in 1964, the year in which the birth rate peaked, reached a record of 13.3‰, but fell to near stagnation, at 0.1‰, at the end of the century.

As noted, the fall in the birth rate is an indicator of the change in the position of women and the impact of this revolution on family relationships. As with almost everything concerning Spanish society in the 20th century, it was not a change that was implemented for the first time in the 1980s: women won the right to vote in the Constitution of the Republic, which recognized the equality of men and women and promoted the presence of women in the public sphere, with significantly improved access to the labor market and higher education. But these conquests were rolled back after the Civil War and the establishment of a dictatorship that encouraged women to return to the private sphere and reduced them to a subordinate role, dependent on their fathers and husbands. As of the nineteen-sixties, women had undoubtedly achieved new public visibility through citizens' movements and feminism. But it would be the transition to democracy that would bring the drop in the birth rate, the relaxing of sexual mores, the emergence of new forms of relationship between men and women, and a widespread increase in the level of middle and higher schooling among girls. Women with higher professional qualifications are those who postpone marriage and childbirth longest, if they decide to marry and have children at all.

Thus, following the pattern set previously by the countries of the North, in the South civil partnerships have also become more common as an alternative to marriage and delaying having children. As a result, the number of children born out of wedlock has also increased. In the 21st century this has reached 30%. Women's average age when they have their first child is close to 30 and barely differs from the mean age at childbirth, which in 2007 was 30.87 years. The age at which both women and men marry has also risen, and the number of annulments, separations and divorces has multiplied, reaching the figure of 118,939 in 2007; just over half of all marriages, which in 2008 totaled 196,613, of which 3,549 were between people of the same sex. While the marriage rate fell for the first time to below five marriages per thousand inhabitants in 2007 (falling to just 4.27 in 2008), the rate of voluntary termination of pregnancy, which is highest in the 20-to-24-year-old age group, rose by 11.5‰ that same year.

Overall, although it remains the buffer or backstop in times of economic crisis, the impression prevails that in Spain the family is not what it was, at least up until the mid-1960s. This is a radical change in public morals which has taken place without major upheavals, although not without street protests defending the family led by the ecclesiastical hierarchy. With the ageing of the population and the rate of marriage separations and break-ups, the number of single-parent households, with a father or mother bringing up children aged under eighteen alone, rose from 169,000 in 2000 to 309,000 in 2007 (of which 268,000 were headed by a single mother). The number of childless couples also increased during this period from 2.53 million to 3.42 million. Living together before marriage has increased, as has the number of stable couples who keep their own homes, and the number of single-person households has risen from 1.86 million to 2.86 million. Moreover, as of July 2005 homosexual partnerships are legally recognized as marriages.

Adding together all these factors, the result is that the traditional family, and the predominance of the two-parent nuclear family with children, has given way in just a few years to a wide range of forms of relationship, in which different models of family coexist, with a clear trend towards replacing traditional values associated with the institution – stability, clear demarcation between the role of men and women, paternal authority over the children, etc. – for new values based on personal fulfillment, autonomy, independence and individualism. The higher educational level attained by women during this period – today outnumbering men at universities – and their joining the labor force *en masse* have been decisive factors in this proliferation of plural forms of family relationship and in the evolution of marriage rates and the number of children born to unmarried mothers.

Against this backdrop of profound social change, one dimension of Spain's political culture gained increasing traction from the start of the transition: the high degree of legitimacy of the democratic political system was bolstered after the attempted coup in February 1981. The mass demonstrations of 25 February put an end to what had been termed the "disenchantment" and again made democracy – after a fall to 49% in 1980 – the political system preferred by 70% of Spaniards, a figure which in 1995 reached 76% and which has consolidated in the first decade of the 21st century at around 80%, leaving the number of people who consider that an authoritarian regime is preferable in some cases at less than 10% and those indifferent to the form of government at 10%.[23]

This high degree of consensus around democracy, with a marked preference for moderation and reformist policies, in which voters identify with the centre ground, has not gone hand in hand with an interest in politics – in 2005 67% of Spaniards declared themselves to have little or no interest in it – nor any feelings of affection towards the political system and its institutions, nor do they rank the people involved in it very highly. What is more, there is a widespread view that the high degree of legitimacy enjoyed by the democratic system is accompanied by a persistent disenchantment with politics and an unfavorable view of politicians, which is reflected in the lack of interest most of society shows in political matters, the low participation rate and widespread cynicism, all of which are deeply rooted in Spanish society since time immemorial. On this point, it may be confirmed that Spain would add the results of a centuries-long history of political cynicism to the pattern of advanced democratic societies, in which democracy is considered an added value, while discontent over its functioning is ever more acute.

Things seem somewhat more complex, as regards both sentiments and conduct. In the case of the former, the following and euphoria that some political leaders have aroused have also marked decisive periods in Spain's history: this happened in 1977 when the new democratic system was set up and occurred again in the early years of the long period of Socialist government, when the new system of Autonomous Communities got off the ground, Spain joined the European Community and a phase of economic growth began in 1986. In both of these two situations, membership was followed by detachment and disaffection, not so much because this constituted a perennial part of the essence of Spaniards' political culture, but in response to the political crises arising, in the first case due to the internal party struggles, and in the second, the death throes of the PSOE government in the early nineties, punctuated by corruption scandals and the dirty war against terrorism. Moreover, supporting political leaders, programs and parties has ceased to form part of the political culture of consolidated democratic systems which, as in the Spanish case, are highly critical of parties, while at the same time, a large majority recognizes that they are necessary for democracy to operate.

Moreover, the still short history of Spaniards' participation in elections does not tally with the reported lack of interest, sense of unease and disaffection towards politics, nor their assumed passivity or demobilization of opinion, but coexists, and indeed prospers, with them, which does not mean that it does not sometimes make its effects felt. In general elections, only those in 1982, which gave the PSOE its first absolute majority, approached a turnout rate of 80%, and only those in 2000, giving the PP its first and only absolute majority, fell below 70%. This suggests that whatever the disaffection and sense of unease towards politics reported by opinion polls, one constant is that turnout at legislative elections is always somewhere between

---

[23]   Percentages taken from the CIS database. Electoral data in the following paragraphs drawn from the *Boletín Oficial del Estado*.

70% and 80%. This is a range that does not differ greatly – above or below– from that seen in democratic systems that have a longer track record than Spain's.

It may be deduced from this electoral behavior that one of the features of Spain's political culture is that the electorate's turnout is greater when people perceive a real possibility of a change of government, that is to say, when the outcome of the elections is in the balance. This is what happened at the end of the period of Socialist government, when in 1993 many of the party's voters returned to the ballot box when they perceived that the right, in the form of the People's Party, had a chance of winning. Similarly, the following elections, which were highly polarized and competitive, saw a turnout rate of 77.4%, one of the highest in the series. Again, the drop in participation in the 2000 elections, which the opinion polls had handed to the PP, did not mark a pattern, as in March 2004, due to the climate of confrontation that followed the attack in Madrid by a fundamentalist terrorist cell linked to Al Qaeda three days before the elections, voter turnout was back up over 75%. In short, something which is attributed to the political culture – low turnout as a result of disaffection – is rather the product of strategic decisions taken by large swathes of voters according to their perceptions of the chance of victory or defeat of the national parties that are potentially able to form a government. In Spain, it is the abstention by PSOE or PP voters, rather than a transfer of votes from left to right, or vice versa, that decides who wins or loses.

This political culture, apart from the much vaunted moderation, has been the bedrock on which, since the elections that ended the long period of socialist domination, the party system has been built, characterized by its stability and tendency to a two-party system, except in the Basque and Catalan systems, where the presence of the nationalist vote can sometimes be decisive for the governability of the State. But these nationalist roots do not show through in the general elections: since 1986 the parties with parliamentary representation have varied from 12 to 10 today. Of these parties, just two, the PSOE and PP, share out an increasing number of seats between them: the 299 of 1986 became 308 in 200 and nine more, 321, in 2008. This is a progression that is due not only to the system by which deputies are assigned, but to an increase in the number of voters concentrating their votes on these two parties, which have gone from 70.5% in 1986 to 82.7% in 2008, while the regional parties that obtained seats received between a maximum of 11.1% of the vote in 2000 and a minimum of 7.6% in 2008. In short, as another feature of the system that has become consolidated over the last twenty-five years, the sum of the votes for the left at national level, PSOE plus United Left (IU), has retained, with the sole exception of 2000, a considerable advantage over the votes for the right, limited to the PP.

Taking into account the changes that have taken place over the last thirty years, and recalling that 20 or 30% of Spain which was not "European" (was it perhaps Asian or African?) in 2000, Howard J. Wiarda put forward a new diagnosis: "Spain is a Southern European country that works. Spain has made it to the ranks of being a 'normal country'".[24] Put that way, it sounds somewhat different from the country Charles Tilly had described

---

[24] Wiarda (2000), p. 61.

some decades earlier as "a significant exception." But does the emphasis on "southern" mean that it is still exceptional that a Southern-European country work? Because if what has happened is that the exceptional has become "normal" why is it necessary to recall that it is *Southern European* and put normality between quotes? Perhaps, when another 25 years have gone by and we have escaped the crisis, some new observer of Spain's exceptionality will discover that it is simply a normal European country. So normal that it has a highly exceptional history. Just like all its neighbors.

References

ARON, RAYMOND (1985), *Memorias,* Madrid, Alianza.

AZÚA, FÉLIX DE (1996), "Tout se complique", in *Salidas de tono. Cincuenta reflexiones de un ciudadano,* Barcelona, Anagrama.

BRENAN, GERALD (1950), *The face of Spain,* London, Turnstile Press.

CARR, RAYMOND (1982), *Spain, 1808-1975,* Oxford, Oxford University Press.

CARRERAS, ALBERT Y TAFUNELL, XAVIER, EDS. (2005), *Estadísticas Históricas de España,* vol. I, Madrid, Fundación BBVA, 2ª ed.

CARRILLO, SANTIAGO (1993), *Memorias,* Barcelona, Planeta,

FOCARDI, FILIPPO, Y KLINKHAMMER, LUTZ (2006), "La rimozione dei crimini di guerra dell'Italia fascista: la nascita di un mito autoassolutorio", in Luigi Goglia, Renato Moro y Leopoldo Nuti, eds., *Guerra e pace nell'Italia del Novecento,* Bologna, Il Mulino.

GALLERANO, NICOLA (1981), *"L'organizzazione nel Mezzogiorno 1943/1947",* in Il Partito Comunista Italiano. Struttura e storia dell'organizzazione 1921/1979, Fondazione Giangiacomo Feltrinelli, Annali.

GONZÁLEZ SEARA, LUIS (1976), "Los nuevos españoles. Introducción a un Informe", *Estudios sociológicos sobre la situación social de España. 1975.* Madrid, Fundación FOESSA.

GUNTHER, RICHARD (1992) "Spain: the very model of the modern elite settlement", in John Higley a Richard Gunther, eds., *Elites and democratic and consolidation in Latin American and southern Europe,* Cambridge: Cambridge University Press.

HERR, RICHARD (1971), *An historical essay on Modern Spain,* Berkeley, University of California Press.

JACKSON, G. (1993). *Historia de un historiador,* Anaya and Mario Muchnik, Madrid.

JULIÁ, SANTOS (2000), "La sociedad", in José L. García Delgado, coord., *Franquismo. El juicio de la historia,* Madrid, Temas de Hoy, 2000.

— (2009), *La Constitución de 1931,* Madrid, Iustel.

"La transición en España: testimonio de Santiago Carrillo" (1998), in Javier Ugarte, ed., La transición en el País Vasco y en España. Historia y memoria, Bilbao, Universidad del País Vasco.

LINZ, JUAN (1967), "The Party system of Spain: past and future", in Seymour M. Lipset y Stein Rokkan, eds., *Party systems and voter alignments: cross-national perspectives,* New York, The Free Press.

PÉREZ EMBID, FLORENTINO (1949), "Ante la nueva actualidad del 'problema de España'", *Arbor,* 45-46, September-October.

PREGO, VICTORIA (1996), "Santiago Carrillo", in Santos Juliá, Javier Pradera and Joaquín Prieto, Eds., *Memoria de la Transición,* Madrid, Taurus.

PRZEWORSKI, ADAM (1991), *Democracy and the market.* New York: Cambridge University Press.

ROSSANDA, ROSSANA (2008), *La muchacha del siglo pasado,* Madrid, Foca.

SARTORI, GIOVANNI (1976), *Parties and party systems. A framework for analysis,* Cambridge, Cambridge University Press.

SCHUMPETER, JOSEPH A. (1979) *Capitalism, socialism and democracy* [1943], London, George Allen & Unwin.

SPRIANO, PAOLO (1975), *Storia del Partito comunista italiano, III. Il fronti popolari,* Stalin, la guerra, Turín, Einaudi.

TILLY, CHARLES (1969), "Collective violence in European perspective", in Hugh D. Graham and

Ted R. Gurr, eds., *The history of violence in America,* New York, Frederick A. Prager.

VALERA, JUAN, (1958), "Sobre el concepto que hoy se forma de España", [1868] in *Obras completas,* Madrid, Aguilar, Tomo III.

VIDAL BENEYTO, JOSÉ (2007), *Memoria democrática,* Madrid, Foca.

WIARDA, HOWARD J. (2000), "Spain 2000: A normal country?", *Mediterranean Quarterly,* summer.

WOLLER, HANS (1998), "The political purge in Italy", in Stein U. Larsen, *Modern Europe after fascism,* New York, Columbia University Press, vol. I.

2. A century of the Spanish economy

Gabriel Tortella and José Luis García Ruiz
Universidad de Alcalá
Universidad Complutense de Madrid

1 The Spanish economy in 1900

1.1 Demographic and agricultural backwardness

At the dawn of the 20th century Spain was a backward country on the periphery of Europe [Tortella (1994)]. Perhaps the clearest evidence of its backwardness lies in its demographic variables [Nadal (1991)]. In 1900 Spain's population retained many archaic demographic features, such as high mortality and birth rates, low rates of urbanization, low female labor-force participation rates, a very large share of the work force dedicated to the primary sector (primarily agriculture), coupled with relatively low mobility. It is around the turn of the century (probably in the last decade of the 19th century) when the rapid changes that marked the start of the so-called "demographic transition" began to appear.

The factors triggering the start of this transition are complex. Economic growth clearly played a major part. There is no doubt that during the 19th century the Spanish economy had fallen behind Europe: the gap between per capita incomes in Spain and its neighbors in northern Europe had widened. This is not to say, however, that the economy contracted or even stagnated; it simply grew more slowly. The most palpable evidence of this was also demographic: the Spanish population grew during the 19th century, but at one of the slowest rates in Europe. Population growth was accompanied by moderate income growth, such that overall, by the end of the century, per capita income was only marginally higher than at the start. Although it was slow, this growth brought a modest dose of structural change.

This sluggish growth in the 19th century was no doubt due to the physical and cultural features of southern Europe, as this slow growth rate was also typical of other countries around the Mediterranean (including Portugal). The geographical features of the Mediterranean basin were not favorable to an agricultural revolution of the type taking place in northern Europe, which was based on a combination of livestock and grain farming, and which did not fit comfortably with the dry and sunny lands of the South. Further more, the mixture of religious, cultural and even geographical factors (within Europe the countries of the South invested less in education, and the southernmost regions of virtually all these countries invested less still) determined the fairly slow progress of education among the population, whether measured using its simplest indicator, the literacy rate, or in terms of other indicators such as school attendance rates or the total budgetary allocation to education. The education deficit could not but have a negative impact on the economy, especially in agriculture, which employed two out of every three workers, and which "lacked skills" [Simpson (2005)], as well as suffering from low productivity and returns. Thus in the late 19th century Spanish agriculture had changed little in structural terms (only a few isolated pockets of market-oriented fruit and vegetable cultivation had developed) and remained primarily reliant on cereal crop dryland farming.

1.2   Dominance of the consumer industry

As is characteristic of an underdeveloped country, Spanish industry in the late 19th century accounted for only a modest fraction of national income, and employed only a small proportion of the workforce. Such industry as there was, was largely devoted to the production of consumer goods such as drinks, food and textiles [Nadal, (ed.), (2003)]. Over the course of the century, industry had become concentrated in just a few urban centers, mainly towns with maritime trade. Mechanization had proceeded at a snail's pace, and there were numerous nuclei of artisan production still scattered all over the country. The main focus of industry was in Catalonia – particularly Barcelona – where there was a long tradition of craftsmanship: this was where the cotton and wool industries were located (and also, although smaller, the silk industry). In Catalonia there was also a milling industry, driven by steam engines and using modern milling methods, in contrast to the traditional windmills or watermills elsewhere in the country. Although of lesser importance, there were also industries such as leather, stationery, glass and ceramics.

The only significant non-consumer industry was mining [Pérez de Perceval et al., (2006)]. Spain's location relatively close to the major industrial centers in Britain, France, Germany and Belgium, and the abundance of mineral resources, often located near the coast, thus facilitating their export, led to the large-scale development of the extractive industry in the last quarter of the 19th century, most of the output from which was sent for export. The skills, capital and even prospection were largely in foreign hands; the local industry barely had its own refining capacity (foundries in the case of metals) or processing capacity, and domestic demand for its output was meager. Most Spanish mineral output was in the form of metallic ores, particularly iron, lead, zinc and mercury, but there was also significant production of pyrites, especially copper pyrites.

The main capital goods industries were metallurgy and chemicals. Metallurgy, especially iron and steel, developed towards the end of the century thanks to the abundance of ore. Located in the Basque Country, the biggest producer and exporter of iron ore, this industry suffered from two serious drawbacks: a shortage of coal and the lack of domestic demand. Spanish coal was expensive and poor quality, and the tariff protection from which its producers benefited pushed up the price of coal imports. The lack of national demand limited the scale of production, which, together with the problem of the coal supply, led to higher unit costs making it difficult to compete internationally: a typical vicious circle of underdevelopment. The chemical industry developed to supply the textile industry (fabric softeners and dyes) and mining (explosives), and was located, logically enough, in Catalonia and the Basque Country.

1.3 Economic policies

At the end of the 19th century Spain's commercial and monetary policy isolated it from its European neighbors [see Sudrià and Tirado (eds.) (2001)]. After a relatively brief period (1869-1890) of hesitant liberalism, the ancestral protectionism (Spain is the birthplace of mercantilism, according to Adam Smith), was reaffirmed by the Cánovas Tariff in 1891. Tariff protection had a delaying effect on both industry and farming. In the case of agriculture it hindered modernization by effectively subsidizing inefficient farms, as Simpson (1995, Chapter 10; 2005) has eloquently and forcefully demonstrated; and in industry it produced the vicious circle just described.

Spain's monetary policy made it an exception in Europe: in an environment where the gold standard prevailed, Spain clung to a silver standard that was in fact a fiat money standard, because silver depreciated in the second half of the century and the face value of coins came to exceed their intrinsic value. Although the Spanish authorities strove to maintain parity of the peseta against major currencies they did not always succeed, and the uncertainty of the exchange rate contributed to Spain's isolation. In the context of a growing international economy, the country's isolation must have been a considerable hindrance; why, and to what extent, things changed in the 20th century is an issue we will address in the following pages.

2   An overview of the 20th century: a glance at the evolution of the main macroeconomic variables

In the 20th century Spain's population grew faster than that of countries such as England, France or Italy. The flu epidemic of 1918 and the Civil War (1936-1939) caused high levels of mortality, but did not alter the trend towards lower mortality rates that had been underway since the late 19th century. This trend was maintained until levels stabilized at the low levels characteristic of the last four decades of the century, mainly as a result of the ageing of the population. Consequently, life expectancy rose from a low of 35 years in 1900 to recent figures which situate Spaniards – and above all Spanish women – among the longest lived in the world. The birth rate adjusted to the fall in mortality, as the model of demographic transition predicts. At the end of the 20th century the number of births was less than that recorded in 1939, in the immediate aftermath of the civil war, and the number of children per woman was one of the lowest in the world. Only immigration in the early years of the 21st century explains the strong growth observed, with the biggest jump at any time in the period (Table 1).

Table 1 also shows the increase in geographical mobility within Spain as the 20th century progressed. Whereas at the beginning of the century, more than 90% of Spaniards said they lived where they had been born, a hundred years later more than a quarter had emigrated in search of new opportunities. Emigration abroad was considerable in the years leading up to the First World War [Sánchez Alonso (1995)] and the preferred destination was Argentina, which took the place of Cuba after 1898. After the Great War, emigration became less important, among other reasons because the conflict had put an end to the first wave of

TABLE 1	VARIATION IN SPAIN'S POPULATION BETWEEN 1900 AND 2010		
	Population	Annual increase (%)	% of population in province of birth
1900	18,616,630	—	91.10
1910	19,990,669	0.71	90.70
1920	21,388,551	0.68	89.20
1930	23,677,095	1.02	87.30
1940	26,014,278	0.95	87.10
1950	28,117,873	0.78	84.40
1960	30,582,936	0.84	80.70
1970	33,956,047	1.05	76.30
1981	37,742,561	0.97	74.80
1991	39,433,942	0.44	75.40
2001	40,847,371	0.35	73.50
2010	45,989,016	1.49	—

SOURCES AND NOTES: For 1900-2001, the population figures are from the Censo de Población, except for 2010 which is the 1 January estimate from the national statistics bureau (www.ine.es). The percentage of the population in the census reported to be living in their province of birth has been taken from Nicolau (2005), p. 154.

TABLE 2	ANNUAL RATES OF VARIATION IN GDPmp PER CAPITA AT CONSTANT PRICES AND INVESTMENT RATE IN THE SPANISH ECONOMY, 1901-2007

Years	Stage	Prados de la Escosura	Maluquer de Motes	Investment rate
1901-1913	Economic "regenerationism"	1.12 (3.41)	1.06 (4.07)	8.71
1914-1918	First World War	-0.57 (2.55)	-0.92 (3.63)	9.76
1919-1923	Post-war recovery	2.78 (2.64)	3.05 (2.95)	10.59
1924-1929	Dictatorship of Primo de Rivera	3.16 (3.39)	3.55 (4.61)	14.00
1930-1935	*Dictablanda* and 2nd Republic	-0.97 (3.19)	-1.24 (3.73)	12.15
1936-1938	Civil War	-11.16 (11.21)	-10.48 (13.34)	10.72
1939-1950	Autarky	1.92 (4.30)	1.76 (5.05)	14.31
1951-1958	"Hinge Decade"	4.85 (3.22)	5.18 (3.17)	20.40
1959-1960	Stabilization Plan	-0.26 (1.50)	-1.07 (3.03)	18.75
1961-1974	"Developmentalism"	6.90 (2.51)	6.64 (2.12)	24.57
1975-1985	Oil Crisis	1.68 (1.54)	0.70 (1.09)	22.81
1986-1991	Membership of the EEC	4.67 (1.44)	3.82 (1.12)	23.79
1992-1993	Readjustment Crisis	0.01 (1.69)	-0.45 (1.37)	22.23
1994-2001	Globalization	3.42* (0.74)	3.35 (1.07)	23.06*
2002-2007	Construction boom	n.a.	1.78 (0.42)	n.a.

SOURCES AND NOTES: (*) 1994-2000.
The standard deviation is given in brackets.
The investment rate is Gross Fixed Capital Formation / GDPmp and has been taken from Prados de la Escosura (2003).

economic globalization. Emigration abroad picked up again after the Civil War, first towards the Americas (particularly Venezuela) and then, from the late 1950s, to Europe (mainly France, Germany and Switzerland). The outbreak of the oil crisis stopped this phenomenon and led millions of Spaniards with low educational levels to cross the border (many as seasonal workers). In 2001, the number of Spaniards living abroad was very similar to the number of foreign residents in Spain. The economic boom in the years that followed shattered this balance by encouraging a strong influx of immigrants.

There is a degree of consensus among historians in defining the major periods of Spanish economic history in the 20th century. Table 2 divides the century up into 14 periods, to which we have added one further period, for the first decade of the 21st century. The key variable defining these periods was the rate of per capita GDP growth (at constant prices), taking data from the two most recent estimates of this variable, Leandro Prados de la Escosura (2003) and Jordi Maluquer de Motes (2009) (the path taken by each of the series is very similar, but the recent series by Maluquer significantly raises the absolute values collected earlier by Prados).

The 20th century began with a spirit of economic regeneration following the loss of the last colonies in 1898. In the years prior to the First World War (1901-1913) per capita income grew at just over 1% a year, and the rate of investment in the economy stayed below the 10% minimum threshold at which (according to W.W. Rostow) one can talk of self-sustaining growth. The balance of the war years was a decline in per capita output in real terms but healthy profits for businesses from exports permitted by Spain's neutrality, which enabled the investment rate to approach 10%.

The end of the First World War was accompanied by a high level of social unrest world-wide, which was not unrelated to the triumph of the Bolshevik Revolution. In the case of Spain, both estimates agree that the years 1919-1923 were a time of significant economic growth, albeit with serious social problems. The period was also one of strong growth in real wages, which partly offset the loss of purchasing power seen during the war years. In order to curb the social unrest, both businessmen and the military supported the establishment of the dictatorship of General Miguel Primo de Rivera in September 1923. The 1920s were a decade of strong economic growth and the investment rate now clearly passed the 10% threshold. Prices remained stable, facilitating a rise in real wages [the behavior of prices can be followed in Maluquer de Motes (2007) and that of nominal salaries in Reher and Ballesteros (1993)].

After the fall of the Dictatorship in the early 1930s, social and political tensions escalated and, in April 1931, the Second Republic was proclaimed. This happened while the world was in the midst of the Great Depression, so it is not surprising that the preceding growth trend should end: the average rate of change in per capita income in 1930-1935 was negative (more so in Maluquer's estimates than in those of Prados, who nevertheless also registered the lowest positive rates in the period 1919-1929). Wage rises, which far outstripped inflation, help explain the difficulties businesses faced during this period.

The combination of economic crisis and the worsening political and social disorder during the Second Republic paved the way for the Civil War, which led to a dramatic fall in per capita income (10-11% a year on average) and a shrinking of the investment rate to negligible levels. The post-war recovery was slow, as Francoism opted for autarky, with disastrous results. The timid liberalization introduced in 1951 encouraged a degree of recovery in the market economy; there was strong growth during the "hinge decade" [to use the expression coined by García Delgado (1987)] and investment rates again rose to over 20%.

Inflation in the second half of the "hinge decade" created the need for the Stabilization Plan in 1959, which, among other things, halted the escalation of prices. After 1961 the Spanish economy returned to growth rates that, up until 1974, were so high as for people to speak of an "economic miracle." The estimates of Prados and Maluquer coincide in registering an average per capita growth rate of close to 7% a year, with investment rates at a record high. However, these two authors diverge over the years 1975-1985 (and the years of the "oil crisis"), as the average annual rate reported by Prados is more than twice Maluquer's. It is difficult to reconcile Prados's figure with the very high level of unemployment registered during the period. Moreover, this unemployment was accompanied by rising wages in real terms, which the authorities sought to control by means of restrictive monetary policies.

Spain returned to vigorous growth when the oil crisis ended, which coincided with the country's joining the European Economic Community (EEC) in 1986. These were years in which a downward trend in inflation began and Spain committed itself to globalization. The process was halted temporarily in 1992-1993, but continued rapidly between 1994 and

2001. The tensions on the international scene in the early years of the current century, due to the scourge of terrorism, and the emergence of highly competitive countries in Asia, partly explains why the Spanish economy grew more slowly from 2002-2007 and began to look for an alternative in the domestic market in the form of the construction sector. This choice lead to severe imbalances, and the global economic crisis in 2007-2008 is having an unexpectedly powerful impact on Spain's economy and society.

The external sector of the Spanish economy was relatively insignificant prior to Spain's joining the EEC; moreover statistics on it have had to be reconstructed by historians and economists due to the lack of reliable official data until recently. Table 3 gives a summary of the balance of payments figures, including the recent reconstruction by Leandro Prados de la Escosura (2010) for the period 1901-1913. According to these estimates, there was an accumulation of surpluses on the goods account of the balance of payments (due to substantial mineral ore exports, for example) and on the transfers account (remittances from emigrants), while there was an export of capital (which does not fit well with reports from the time and the strong deficit in the income balance, which would be made up primarily of dividends on foreign investments). The trade surplus disappeared in the 1930s and 40s, when, according to the statistics the Banco de España began to prepare at this time, the trade balance came close to equilibrium. As the table shows, in these years the Spanish economy's export balance was relatively unimportant. This was largely due to the trade and monetary policies in place and the impact first of the Great Depression and then of the Second World War.

During the years of the "hinge decade," the process of opening up to the outside world led to a sizeable deficit in the trade balance, which could not be offset by other items and exhausted the country's reserves. The Stabilization and Liberalization Plan restored the balance and opened the door to foreign capital inflows. In the years of "developmentism" the

TABLE 3	BALANCE OF PAYMENTS, 1901-2008 (% OF GDP)					
	Goods	Services	Income	Transfers	Current Account	Long-term Capital
1901-1913	1.83	-0.17	-2.68	1.93	0.91	-0.73
1931-1934	-0.74	-0.05	-0.06	0.74	-0.10	0.11
1940-1950	0.01	0.11	0.02	0.08	0.21	0.16
1951-1958	-2.08	0.35	0.11	0.34	-1.28	0.18
1959-1960	-0.80	1.71	-0.02	0.72	1.61	0.99
1961-1974	-5.24	3.61	-0.31	1.53	-0.41	1.49
1975-1985	-3.85	3.25	-1.08	0.75	-0.93	1.49
1986-1991	-4.86	3.74	-1.23	0.92	-1.42	2.16
1992-1993	-3.96	2.10	-0.91	0.94	-1.83	0.60
1994-2001	-3.76	3.45	-1.26	0.45	-1.12	0.92
2002-2008	-7.03	2.57	-2.06	-0.33	-6.85	0.80

SOURCES AND NOTES: For 1901-1913, balance of payments from Prados de la Escosura (2010) and GDP from Prados de la Escosura (2003); for the remainder, balance of payments from Tena (2005), except in 2002-2008 where figures from the Banco de España have been used (www.bde.es), and the GDP figure given in Maluquer de Motes (2009). No comparable information is available for 1914-1930 and 1935-1939.

balance on the long-term capital account rose to 1.5% of GDP. This was a figure only surpassed in the years after Spain joined the EEC. The strong trade deficit was offset by surpluses in services (e.g. tourism) and transfers (e.g. remittances from emigrants), which almost made it possible to balance the current account. In the 1970s and 80s there was a clear positive balance on the capital account, but from the 1990s on, the conversion of large Spanish corporations into multinationals and the slowing of investments caused it to fall sharply. Spain's joining the euro at the start of the 21st century meant the loss of the competitiveness that came with a weak currency such as the peseta, and the trade deficit soared to new historic highs. To make matters worse, the balance on the current transfers account turned negative (due to remittances by immigrants living in Spain) and the balance on the services account shrank (due to the fact that Spaniards were travelling abroad more often). The result was that the current account deficit rose to levels that had never been seen before.

3   The original features of the Spanish economy in the 20th century

Although undoubtedly falling within the European pattern, certain features distinguish the Spanish economy from those of northern European countries, whose economic development since the 18th century may be regarded as canonical. Within the European context, the Spanish economy undoubtedly shares features typical of a Mediterranean country, as several works attest [O'Brien and Prados de la Escosura, (1992), Tortella (1994), Dobado (2004a and 2004b)]. The "Mediterranean" or "Latin" pattern is characterized by growth getting off to a late start in the 19th century and then partially catching up in the 20th century. Spain fits this pattern perfectly. However, when looking more closely at the details, certain characteristics, such as rates of growth and regression, are exclusively Spanish.

3.1   Geographical factors

The three big European-Mediterranean peninsulas (Iberian, Italian and Greek) have notable geographical similarities. They are all mountainous, with a sunny climate and relatively dry soil, and have lower rainfall and higher temperatures than northern Europe. All these factors have contributed to the development of land-use patterns that are sufficiently distinctive for them to have given their name to an agricultural model: "Mediterranean agriculture."

Of these three peninsulas, the Iberian Peninsula is the largest and most extreme. Its solid landmass and high central plateau mean that, despite being a Peninsula, a large share of its land surface is remote from the sea, which, coupled with its high and scattered mountain ranges, makes transport difficult and its markets remote from one another. This explains both their historic isolation and a tendency towards economic and political fragmentation.

Mediterranean agriculture had serious difficulty adapting to the so-called "agricultural revolution" that took place in northern Europe and which served as the launch pad for industrial and commercial development in the countries where it took place during the 18th and 19th centuries. This agricultural revolution consisted of integrating arable farming with livestock, and combining various crops with cereals (wheat in temperate regions of Europe, rye in colder countries). The shortage of pasture in the South made livestock farming difficult, and the arid soils produced low yields from cereals. Mediterranean soils are well suited to woody crops (vines, olives, fruit trees) and to horticulture. The difficulties of transport hindered trade in fruits, vegetables and even oil; only wine has traditionally been widely traded. Overall, this backward pattern of agriculture in the South meant farming did not play the role of a source of capital and labor, or as a market for industrial products. Moreover, the fact that this backward sector employed a large share of the population is an additional factor in the explanation for the economic backwardness of the Mediterranean, and of the Iberian Peninsula in particular.

3.2   Growth rates

On this point too the Spanish economy fits in with the "Latin pattern." Although in the early modern age the economies of the countries of southern Europe performed brilliantly, thanks in large part to the development of navigation and trade, the drag of agriculture caused them to lose their shine. Thus, when the economies of the countries of the North began to take off in the 18th and 19th centuries, those of the South remained stagnant. In the second half of the 19th century, however, this relative decline bottomed out and the southern economies began to grow at rates comparable to those of the North. Northern Europe had begun to pull the Mediterranean economy along with it. Northern Europe's demand for products from the South, combined with advances in transport and preservation methods, enabled exports that were previously impossible, such as canned fruit and vegetables. Moreover, capital from the North headed south in search of these products and stimulated local business.

The Spanish case clearly reflects this pattern. Exports of fruit, wine, canned foods, and ores, together with imports of capital (both from Europe and America, after the demise of the vestiges of the colonial empire in 1898), boosted the modernization of Spanish industry and society in the early years of the 20th century. Neutrality during the First World War enabled a notable export boom, which led to the country's first broad wave of industrial expansion in the 1920s. Spain was among the European countries achieving the highest growth rates during the decade. The "Roaring Twenties" were livelier in Spain than in its European neighbors, partly no doubt because of a combination of having avoided the war and built up significant gold reserves. However, as if to compensate for this prosperity, the next two decades were the great blot on the Spanish economy in the 20th century.

The extent and depth of the impact of the Great Depression (1929-1939) on the Spanish economy is still being debated, and this issue will be discussed below. In view of the figures just given, there is no doubt that Spain was seriously affected by the crisis, even excluding the catastrophic civil war years. However, more serious was the exasperating slowness with which the economy recovered in the decade after the war. The prewar peaks were not reached again until the mid-1950s, whereas after the Second World War, Germany and France needed just three years to recover; Belgium four; and Italy and Austria, five [Catalan (1995) p. 27].

The astonishing delay in the post-war recovery is sadly the Spanish economy's genuinely original accomplishment in the 20th century. While it is true that in this period the Second World War led to serious difficulties obtaining supplies, the surprising thing is that during those years the rate of recovery, while not brilliant, was continuous. Not dazzling perhaps, but acceptable. The worst thing was that once world peace was restored, incomes again fell. The failure of economic policy in the post-war years could not be more glaring. As an internal Banco de España report put it in 1946, "Spain has not yet reached the levels of production of the years 1930-1935 [...] The excesses of the drive for self-sufficiency have made some people believe that Spain's economic reconstruction could be achieved by the work of Spaniards alone. While this might be possible, it of course has made it slower, more difficult and more costly" (cited in Tortella and García Ruiz, 2004, p. 108).

3.3   Economic policy: levels of intervention

It is broadly true that Spain's economic history could not but follow the ups and downs of the international situation. Something similar is true of economic policy. As we saw at the start of this chapter, in terms of its trade policy, in the 19th century Spain followed the same swings back and forth as its European neighbors. As regards monetary policy, here Spain was totally original, being the only European country never to have adopted the gold standard. However, in the 20th century this unique feature of Spain's monetary policy was no longer so striking, particularly after the Great War, when currency convertibility was suspended; and when, during the 1920s, Europe returned to the gold standard, its return was so bumpy and short lived (seven years in England, the creator of the system), that the Spanish silver standard did not stand out so much.

Spain's trade policy in the 20th century also loosely matched the general outline, but was locked up in protectionism, with strict quantitative restrictions and persistent international trade barriers, setting it apart as one of the most extreme cases of protectionism. The Cánovas Tariff in 1891, which was already very protective, was followed by others in 1906 and 1921 (the Salvador and Cambó Tariffs) which raised tariffs yet further and closed the few gaps that remained. When, in the interwar period, and in particular the Great Depression, monetary and quantitative controls were imposed on trade, Spain eagerly welcomed them. After the Civil War Franco's regime reinforced and heightened the international trade barriers to strangle trade almost completely. In the wake of the Second World War there was a concerted international effort to lower trade barriers, an effort that Spain ignored, clinging to a doctrine of isolationism in a world that was moving in precisely the opposite direction. The result was the collapse of trade in the late 1950s and the need to resort to external aid and to improvise the 1959 Stabilization Plan. But a long time was to pass, and it was not until after the death of the dictator, the establishment of a democratic system and accession to what is today the European Union, that Spain's commercial and monetary policies achieved full normality.

3.4   Isolation

One characteristic, therefore, which partly derives from this economic policy is the isolation of the Spanish economy which has been mentioned by numerous authors, including a Banco de España report from 1934 which spoke of the Spanish "economy's total closure" (p. 354). However, not everything can be attributed to economic policy. As we have seen, geography is also a factor, given that Spain is characterized by its compact and solid plateau and the height and abundance of its mountains.

The consequences of this isolation, both imposed and voluntary, have almost always been negative. The inevitable limitations of the country's resources have always made it desirable to increase exchanges so as to obtain the positive effects that economic theory has been demonstrating since the time of Adam Smith and David Ricardo, if not before. Empirical studies corroborate the theoretical recommendations: broadly speaking, the periods of economic openness have brought greater prosperity to the Spanish population. Spaniards have paid a high price for their economic isolation.

3.5   Education and human capital

In this field too, Spain has a long tradition of isolation, while also having many parallels with its southern neighbors. The tendency to isolate itself from the main currents of modern thought goes back at least to the Counter-Reformation, while the opposing trend towards openness and cosmopolitanism has been weaker and less constant. The long dictatorship of General Franco represented a return to the obscurantist spirit in the middle of the 20th century.

Spain lags considerably on the main education indicators. The simplest, literacy and school attendance rates, in unison with most of its economic and social variables, lagged behind those of the rest of Europe in the 19th century, such that the country entered the 20th century with educational indicators that were low (a literacy rate of well below 50%). The founding of the Ministry of Education at the turn of the century was a positive development, which certainly produced results. However, throughout the century Spanish education always fell short of expectations, and of average European levels. The indicators of "social commitment to education" [Núñez (2005, p. 172)] situate Spain badly relative to its European neighbors.

Moreover, the way education has been organized has suffered from a surprising degree of irrationality in an area that one would expect to be characterized by precisely the opposite. It is difficult to understand, for example, how it is that private enterprise (with a predominance of religious orders) was allowed in primary and secondary education, while the State kept an almost total monopoly of university education. It is also hard to understand why vocational education was almost completely sidelined, with the imposition of an almost exclusively academic route through education. The effects of this single educational route have been harmful in many ways, particularly to the economy. One of its consequences has been that Spanish employers are almost totally polarized between graduates and those who have only primary schooling or even less. Secondary-level education is rarely found on Spanish businessmen's curriculums. The few comparative empirical studies that have been conducted on this issue show that education has contributed little to the success of Spanish entrepreneurs, for example in comparison to their English counterparts [Tortella et al., (2008)]. Institutional arrangements to promote technical progress were also slow and inadequate. There was certainly no lack of individual talent in Spain: "some significant inventions [were made], but their industrial exploitation frequently took place abroad" [José María Ortiz-Villajos in Tortella et al., (2008) p. 162].

4   The main periods

4.1   1900-1930: gestation of the protectionist, nationalist and interventionist model

The loss of the American (Cuba, Puerto Rico) and Asian colonies (the Philippines) to the United States in 1898 was a severe blow to the Spanish collective consciousness. But, as Jordi Maluquer de Motes has shown (1999), there was a reaction to the "Disaster" and Spain went from complaining about the "ills of the *patria*" to taking effective measures to remedy them. The first reaction was liberal. The Conservative Raimundo Fernández Villaverde pushed through tax reforms, while curbing spending and reorganizing the public debt. This had the result that the first eight years of the 20th century produced a surplus [Comín (2002)]. The health of the Treasury strengthened the peseta and encouraged the repatriation of capital from the colonies, which was mainly invested in the creation of a genuine banking system. As many as 15 new banks opened their doors for business between 1898 and 1914, particularly in the Basque Country and Madrid [García Ruiz (1998)].

However, Fernández Villaverde's liberal orientation would soon be replaced by that of Antonio Maura, whose economic program combined protectionism with new elements of nationalism and interventionism. Spain remained neutral during the First World War, which benefited its economy. There are various differing estimates of the trade balance, but all agree that there was a strong trade surplus between 1915 and 1919. Analysis of output suggests that, together with an acceleration of traditional exports, items that under normal circumstances would never have been sold abroad also made their way across Spain's borders. The accumulated surpluses were, in all likelihood, the most important factor in explaining the jump in the Banco de España's gold reserves from 710.9 million in June 1914 to 2,506.3 million in December 1919. The benefits of neutrality also encouraged the nationalization of assets held by foreigners [Roldán and García Delgado (1973), Sudrià (1990)].

Spanish output in the 1920s continued on an upward path, driven by a policy of public works and the strength of the world economy [Velarde (1973)]. However, the model of development implemented by José Calvo Sotelo, the Ministry of Finance under the dictatorship of General Primo de Rivera, who was inspired by Maura, was characterized by three heterodox notes from an economist's point of view: interventionism, protectionism and nationalism. Calvo Sotelo's main concern was obtaining the resources needed to launch a huge plan of public works. In view of the failure of his tax reform, in 1927 he instead created a large monopoly in the oil business: the Compañía Arrendataria del Monopolio de Petróleos, S.A. (CAMPSA) [Tortella et al., (2003)]. At the same time public-sector banks were given a boost, with some institutions being reorganized (Banco Hipotecario de España, Banco de Crédito Industrial) and others created (Servicio Nacional de Crédito Agrario, Banco de Crédito Local, Banco Exterior de España).

The imbalances in the economic model (government and trade balance deficits), the enmity of the oil multinationals earned by Spain's creating the state monopoly CAMPSA, and mistrust of all things foreign even before the nationalist dictatorship, explain the decline of the peseta after 1927. In many people's eyes, this proved that the dictatorial economic system did not work. Calvo Sotelo made the mistake of attaching highly symbolic value to the peseta, even beyond the economic sphere, by talking in terms of its representing "moral realities" and "racial capabilities." This bet on the peseta cost him dearly, as the currency continued its downward slide, even with intervention. When Calvo Sotelo resigned in early 1930, he could still not understand why all these efforts to strengthen the economy and back Spanish companies had not been accompanied by an appreciation of the peseta.

The fall of Calvo Sotelo was followed by that of the dictator himself. General Dámaso Berenguer, who formed a government with Manuel Argüelles as finance minister, tried to keep the dictatorial regime in place (although somewhat watered down in the form of the *"dictablanda"* or soft dictatorship). However, this merely tilted public opinion towards Republican and revolutionary ideas. For his part, Manuel Argüelles was determined to pursue fiscal orthodoxy, settling the 1930s budget with barely a deficit. This caused a steep fall in public investment at precisely the moment the Great Depression was extending across the globe. If there was a "Berenguer mistake" (as the philosopher José Ortega y Gasset put it) which prevented progress towards democracy in 1930, there was also an "Argüelles mistake" [García Delgado (1979)] which left Spanish industry in serious difficulties. The combination of these two errors helps explain the proclamation of the Second Republic on 14 April 1931.

4.2   1931-1959: depression, war, the first Francoism

With the exception of the War of Independence, the 1930s are perhaps the most dramatic period in contemporary Spanish history, and the political drama had its economic counterpart. This decade and that which followed it were characterized by a deep and prolonged decline in the main macroeconomic indicators. There has been much debate about the duration and intensity of the Great Depression's impact on the Spanish economy. Evidence and reports from the time suggest that the contraction was not as deep as in the United States or Germany [see, for example, Banco de España (1934)], but it is nevertheless clear that the crisis had an impact in Spain, and that it aggravated a number of endogenous factors, both political (in particular the fall of the monarchy) and economic (political tensions inherent in the growth that undoubtedly took place in the early decades of the century) [Hernández Andreu (1980), and Palafox, (1991)]. One demographic sign of the depth of the recession in Spain which has received little attention – except by Amando de Miguel (1987, p. 169) – is the very abrupt decline in the marriage rate that began in 1931.

The Republic's active social policy offset the negative impacts of the crisis in some sectors. An expansionary fiscal policy aimed particularly at redistribution and social spending undoubtedly produced a rise in real wages, which led to an increase in consumption among the lower classes. This at least partially offset the contractionary effects of the depression. At the same time, Spain's not having adopted the gold standard turned out to be an unexpected blessing in the circumstances of 1931, as it allowed the country to pursue an expansionary monetary policy that staved off the banking and currency crises that afflicted Austria, Germany, Italy, Britain and the United States [see the Banco de España's *Memoria* from 1932, pp. 8, 15 and 16, and Martín Aceña (1984), and Tortella (1999), pp. 174-175].

But, once the crisis of 1931 had passed, the Republican authorities got their monetary and exchange rate policy badly wrong. The fall in the peseta exchange rate at the end of the Dictatorship persuaded the Republicans that they had to halt its depreciation. They therefore continued the policy pursued by the governments of both the Dictatorship and the *"Dictablanda"*, namely building up gold and foreign currency reserves to buy pesetas on the international market when the price dropped. The consequences were harmful: gold reserves were diminished and the high value of the peseta exacerbated the trade deficit. After Britain left the gold standard in 1931 and the United States in 1933, Spain remained obsessed with propping up the value of its currency, aiming for parity with the French franc, which had become the central currency of the "gold bloc." To this end, interest rates were kept relatively high, which together with rising wages, further damaged the competitiveness of exports and widened the trade gap. This policy no doubt also contributed to rising unemployment. Very probably, the period saw the emergence of a two-tier labor market, characteristic of advanced economies, with rising wages and rising unemployment [García Ruiz, (2006)].

In other matters too the Republic's government was unfortunate. The most urgent economic problem it faced was agrarian reform, which even in those difficult circumstances could be neither postponed nor avoided. The public expected the new government to resolve what it considered to be the most serious economic and social problem to have been weighing on Spain for centuries: the inequitable and inefficient distribution of land ownership. The question, however, was more complex than it seemed at first sight, as the structure of ownership and cultivation systems varied dramatically from region to region, making it difficult to offer a universally applicable solution. Furthermore, any land reform involves readjustments on such a scale that the short-term economic effects are almost inevitably negative, something that in the 1930s was extremely dangerous. The measure therefore required careful study and full parliamentary debate. The law's gestation consequently proved lengthy: it was finally passed in September 1932 and proved to be of considerable legal complexity. As Jackson (1965, p. 84) remarks, it seemed to have been designed more to combat unemployment among lawyers than agricultural laborers. As a consequence, the pace of land being settled by new owners was very slow. What is more, the law was only in force for just over a year, as its application was suspended after the elections of 1933. In short, land reform satisfied very few, alarmed conservative groups, and contributed to the polarization which paved the way for the Civil War.

The outbreak of the war divided Spain physically, splitting its territory and society, and with them its institutions and economy. In the first few weeks of hostilities, the Republic appeared to have the best economic assets in its hands: it controlled all the major cities except Seville, and thus the industrial and commercial centers, and the headquarters of large corporations. The Republican side also held the country's capital, Madrid, and with it, important economic assets such as central government and the Banco de España, with its gold reserves, which were among the largest in the world. It also controlled the most important ports and the crafts and export agriculture areas of the Levante on the east coast. It was, moreover, the legitimate government: an important diplomatic asset.

However, the divisions which opened up within the Republican ranks had powerful negative impacts on the economy, because they led to a lack of discipline in factories and farms, demoralization and abandonment by numerous businessmen and officials, and the serious damage to output and productivity caused by the famous spontaneous collectivizations that took place both in industry and in agriculture. Eloquent testimony has come down to us of how businessmen, and particularly bankers, were treated in Republican Spain [Sánchez Asiaín (1999), Tortella (2004)]. These reports reveal how businesses ceased to function effectively as managers, disappointed and terrified, seized the first opportunity that offered itself to go over to Franco's Spain, even if that had not been their intention in the early months of the war. The inflation that soon took hold in the Republican zone is eloquent proof of the prevailing economic chaos, produced by shortages and administrative disorder as well as political fragmentation. Inflation, as is almost inevitable in war, occurred in both Spains; but was far higher on the Republican side. All this helps explain why the Soviet Union under Stalin was the only European country willing to fight to maintain Republican legality in Spain [Viñas (1979), Martín Aceña (2001), Martín Aceña and Martínez Ruiz, (eds.) (2006)].

As is well known, the economic consequences of the Civil War were disastrous. Destruction, death and exile were terrible in themselves, but they also had serious repercussions for the economy, given the substantial loss of human capital. The fact that the victors barely changed their economic policy when peace came was also highly detrimental, because what had been effective during the conflict then became a shackle on the economy, leading to a post-war decade as arduous, or more so, than that under the infamous tyranny of Ferdinand VII. For a decade after the war, incomes and investment suffered unprecedented stagnation. The hardships of the war and its aftermath also showed up in the height of soldiers, which dropped significantly [Quiroga (2002) esp., Chap. 6]. Education indicators also took an alarming step backwards. The economic wounds caused by the conflict took many decades to heal.

The victors of the Civil War sought to play up the number of victims and destruction that occurred during the conflict when looking for a culprit for the Spanish economy's poor performance during the first 15 years of Francoism [Catalan (1995), Tortella and García Ruiz (2004)]. The transport crisis goes some way towards explaining the collapse of the economy – the most severe in contemporary Spanish history – but it seems clear that, since there had been relatively little destruction of productive assets, a rapid post-war recovery should have been possible. The fundamental problem was that General Franco's new State opted for a self-sufficient and interventionist economic model. Although the macroeconomic figures remain somewhat confusing, there is little doubt that this policy was a total failure [Barciela (ed.), (2003)].

The creation of the government holding company, the *Instituto Nacional de Industria* (INI), in 1941 would confirm the autarkic direction taken by the new State [Schwartz and González (1978), Martín Aceña and Comín (1991), San Román (1999), Gómez Mendoza, (ed.), (2000)]. This orientation would last until 1951, when at the height of the Cold War the United States decided to consider Francoist Spain an ally on whose soil to build military bases of great strategic importance. The 1950s were characterized by a gradualist approach to the transition to a market economy, but serious economic and social conflicts could not be avoided. The result was that the economy grew rapidly, but suffered strong inflationary pressures, making the approval of a Stabilization and Liberalization Plan necessary in 1959.

4.3   1959-1975: the economic policy of "Developmentalism"

The policy of autarky so much widened the gap between the path taken by Spain and the more developed European countries, that even with the undeniable growth in the 1960s it is impossible to argue that overall Francoism promoted convergence [Carreras and Tafunell (2010)]. Moreover, the "developmentalism" of these years was externally induced. US support allowed Franco's Spain to accede to international organizations (the United Nations in 1955; the OECD, IMF, and World Bank, in 1958), but called for changes in the socio-economic structure. Thus, the main measures introduced by Decree-Law 10/1959 of 21 July 1959 – commonly known as the Stabilization and Liberalization Plan, as it proposed "economic organization" along both axes – included: 1) stabilization by means of tax increases and credit controls; 2) gradual liberalization of imports and control of monopolistic practices in the domestic market; 3) support for inflows of foreign investment; and, 4) convertibility of the peseta, accompanied by strong devaluation and regulation of the foreign exchange market. All in all, the government hoped to obtain "internal and external stability of the economy, equilibrium in the balance of payments, strengthened confidence in the currency and, overall, the normalization of Spain's economic life."

The plan was submitted to the Cortes by Alberto Ullastres, who had been appointed Minister of Commerce in February 1957. At that time a change of government had allowed in a group of well-qualified men who had in common their membership of Opus Dei. Together with Ullastres, the group included the new finance minister, Mariano Navarro Rubio, and Laureano López Rodó, who had been technical general secretary of the office of prime-minister since the previous year. All of them were well connected to the world of banking and business, an environment which considered this "normalization of our economic life" of which the 1959 Decree-Law spoke, to be absolutely essential. The recommendations of the first OECD report on Spain (March 1959) were not lost on the group of prestigious economists such as Joan Sardà, Manuel Varela and Enrique Fuentes Quintana who contributed to the drafting of the Plan. Nevertheless, the Plan met with resistance among those closest to the Falange and raised doubts even in Franco's mind [Fuentes Quintana (1984 and 2003), and interviews compiled in Perdices de Blas and Baumert, (eds.), (2010)].

In May 1960 a new tariff schedule was adopted, known as the Ullastres Tariff. This was very high, as it took the place of the preceding autarkic legislation. On 9 February 1962 the Spanish government applied to the European community for negotiations to be opened with a view to Spain's "association." On 17 May 1962 the Council of Europe issued a statement spelling out that, without democracy, Spain could not aspire to be a full member of the EEC, but that there was the possibility of "some type of economic arrangement" [Sánchez-Gijón (1974)]. Finally, on 29 June 1970 a preferential trade agreement between Spain and the EEC was signed in Luxembourg, entailing further tariff dismantling by Spain.

The Spanish economy showed considerable capacity to assimilate the conditions offered by the international market. The rate of growth over the decade 1960-1970 was the highest in Spain's history and one of the highest in the world. It was a period of rapid industrialization, large-scale modernization of farming, growth of the services sector and increasing trade with the outside world [Barciela et al. (1999)]. The authorities guiding economic policy sought to channel growth through three four-year Social and Economic Development Plans which they launched in 1964, along the lines of the French indicative planning model. Above all, the plans sought to promote industrialization in poorer areas, for which they designated "industrial development zones" (where there was little existing industrialization) and "industrial promotion zones" (where industrialization was non-existent), which were backed with incentives to attract private initiative [De la Torre and García-Zúñiga (eds.), (2009)]. A Plan Commission was set up, headed by López Rodó, and in 1973, this was turned into the Ministry of Development Planning, which was abolished shortly after the end of the dictatorship. Spanish indicative planning, as pointed out by

Ramos and Pires (2009), was judged harshly during the transition to democracy following the Franco's death. Scandals such as the "Matesa case" contributed to its loss of prestige [Tortella and Jiménez (1986), Chapter VI]. Enrique Fuentes Quintana (1990a) noted the "paradox" that growth on the basis of the foundations laid by the Stabilization Plan in the 1960s was strong and yet the Development Plans impeded it.

4.4   1975-1985: from the economic crisis to membership of the EEC

The 1970s were a watershed for many countries' economies and policies and for the international economy as a whole. For Spain, this decade was particularly crucial because it signaled the end of the dictatorship and the transition to a democratic political system and market economy. After the turbulence of the preceding decade, the 1980s were a decade of recovery for the Spanish economy and the world economy as a whole. There are many similarities and parallels between the international crisis in the 1970s and crisis in Spain, but there are also many differences and divergences. These were sufficiently important to constitute what Fuentes Quintana (1990a, p.36) has called "the differential character of the Spanish crisis."

As is well known, the international crisis began with the abandonment of the Bretton Woods monetary system in 1971, as a result of the US's economic problems. It was exacerbated by sharp increases in oil prices in 1973 and 1979, and led to "stagflation" (i.e. stagnation combined with inflation). In Spain, the crisis produced oscillations similar to those in international economies, but they were made more pronounced by the rigidities inherited from Francoism. The weakness of Franco's final governments had induced them not to pass on soaring oil prices to the domestic market, delaying the inevitable adjustment. However, as a result of labor market rigidities, unemployment soared. The labor market was segmented between those who enjoyed stable employment and were pressing for higher wages, and a growing number of unemployed, who barely had union representation. Stable workers (with permanent contracts) supported the union's militancy, and the unions made full use of the right to strike granted by the Industrial Relations Law of 1976. As a consequence, during the crisis many companies were forced to pay wages above productivity, while taxpayers bore the cost of unemployment insurance. This gave rise to the paradox that wage levels increased even while the unemployment rate was rising: this was the other side of the "stagflation" coin. The rigidity of the labor market thus fuelled inflation and contributed to the widening budget deficit.

The Francoist economy was also plagued with monopolistic and oligarchic elements that contributed to low productivity and the technological backwardness of the productive system. During the crisis of the 1970s, the banks, which had been the main source of finance for businesses, were trapped in an situation from which there was no obvious way out: inflation and rising interest rates (now deregulated) gave the advantage to debtors (customers) against creditors (bankers). The latter, accustomed to the peaceful life they had enjoyed under the previous regime, and mired in imprudent investments made during times of optimism, found themselves unable to resolve the problems posed by this state of affairs. This led to one of the biggest banking crises in Spanish history, and undoubtedly the biggest of the 20th century [Cuervo (1988), Tortella (1996), pp. 569-571].

Another serious rigidity was fiscal. At the end of the dictatorship Spain's tax structure was archaic. The only substantive reform that had been undertaken dated from 1845 (the famous Mon-Santillán reform), and the changes made to the system since that time were mere tinkering (including the 1889-1900 Fernández Villaverde reform, which had been the most ambitious). In 1975, indirect taxes still predominated, and direct taxes were based on a crude traditional system of "quota and product" [Fuentes Quintana (1990a), in particular pp. 370-415; Comín (1996), for a broader long-term view]. As a result, as well as being iniquitous, taxation was inflexible and inadequate. In the crisis of the 1970s, this rigidity produced a deficit and stoked up inflation.

The weak governments of the early stages of the transition did not dare to take the radical measures necessary for fear of provoking rejection from all sides. It was not until the government produced by the first democratic elections (15 June 1977) was formed that the much cited Fuentes Quintana, newly appointed second Deputy Prime Minister and Minister of the Economy, achieved a consensus between groups and parties representing a broad majority in the country, with a view to adopting an economic plan to address the dire state of affairs in which the country found itself, in which the annual inflation rate was above 25%, the balance of payments and the budget were in deficit, external debt was growing and per capita incomes had virtually stagnated. The so-called "Moncloa Pacts", published in October, comprised a stabilization plan which sought to curb money supply growth, place limits on government spending, and impose wage restraint on labor unions, which had obtained big increases in previous years. To achieve equilibrium in the balance of payments, it had first been necessary to devaluate the peseta by 20%. Wage restraint and restrictive monetary and fiscal measures brought with them difficulties for large segments of the population. In order to share out the burden of sacrifice more fairly and be able to offer more social spending without widening the deficit, a tax reform was envisaged that aimed to promote fairness, flexibility and budgetary efficiency.

This tax reform was implemented through a series of laws and decrees inspired by the reports drafted or backed by Fuentes Quintana in previous years while he was president of the *Instituto de Estudios Fiscales* [Fuentes Quintana (1990b)]. Some of these provisions were adopted after Fuentes had resigned in 1978, while Fernández Ordóñez was Finance Minister, such that this complex reform must, in all fairness, be attributed jointly to Fuentes Quintana and Fernández Ordóñez, in that order. The increased revenues enabled public services and social security benefits to be improved. As noted by González-Páramo (1990, pp. 249-257), over the five-year period from 1977 to 1982, the foundations of the welfare state were laid, largely with a view to European integration. Inevitably, the government's public spending as a share of Spain's GDP grew much more rapidly than in neighboring countries, including Sweden and Italy, which were famous at the time for their high levels of public spending [Tortella (1994), Table XVI-1].

On 28 October 1982 the Spanish Socialist Party (PSOE) won the general elections. Felipe González's new government adopted plainly restrictive measures in order to get quick results in three areas: controlling inflation, narrowing the trade gap, and reducing the government deficit. One of the first measures taken to achieve these goals was the devaluation of the peseta in December 1982. Monetary and budgetary policies, meanwhile, tried to keep the growth of domestic demand within certain limits, as the only efficient and realistic way of eliminating the imbalances. But what the government was unable to achieve was to alleviate rising unemployment.

The result of these measures could be described as encouraging. GDP grew moderately up until 1986. The inflation rate was also brought down, although it was still close to 9% in 1985. However, the adjustment also had its negative side. This included high levels of unemployment (21.4% in 1985) and a persistent budget deficit, which in 1985 was 5.3% of GDP. The main reasons for the deficit were the high cost of industrial restructuring, higher social security spending caused by the rise in unemployment, corporate and financial crises such as that affecting the Rumasa group (expropriated in 1983, in one of the new government's most controversial measures) and the rising cost of servicing the public debt.

Two more reforms deserve mentioning in this brief review of the accomplishments of the first socialist governments after the transition: the reform of the securities exchanges and reform of the education system, particularly the universities. In 1988 a Stock Market Law was passed, which drew its inspiration from the radical reforms undertaken in the London and Paris stock exchanges. The key reforms under this Law were the elimination of the former stock market agents, whose role had barely changed since Pedro Sainz de Andino first promoted the Madrid stock exchange in 1831, and the creation of a National Securities Market Commission, the CNMV. But, whereas stock-market reform was a success, the same cannot be said of educational reform. Both the University Reform Law of 1983 and the General Organic Law on the education system in 1990 raised enrolment rates at the expense of standards and confirming temporary teachers in their posts, despite many of them having inadequate qualifications.

4.5   1986-2000: membership of the European Union and the euro

Although Spain joined the European Community in 1986, as we have seen, the initial talks had begun a quarter of a century earlier. In fact, membership was the ultimate goal towards which the economic policies put in place since the establishment of democracy were aimed. Malo de Molina (1994, p. 83) describes the climate of those years: "Spain's joining the European Union was viewed with considerable trepidation and uncertainty. It was accompanied by significant economic expansion and a certain climate of euphoria, even overconfidence, which would later have serious repercussions."

It was not only the lack of democracy which held back Spain's entry in the 1960s, as from 1977 Spain had a government elected by universal suffrage; it was also the country's economic structure that hindered the process. If the negotiations lasted eight long years, this was mainly due to the difficulties that Spanish agriculture, a sector of considerable size and low productivity, could cause for the EEC. Aware of the difficulties, negotiators from both sides closed the industrial chapter first, establishing a transitional period of seven years. The Spanish negotiators avoided the sharp initial reduction their EEC counterparts sought. A general transitional period of seven years was also applied, but Spain agreed to a special timetable for exports of its competitive "Mediterranean" products (e.g. fruit and vegetables) in exchange for not being flooded by "continental" goods (e.g. dairy products, beef, breadmaking common wheat) [Badosa Pagés (2005)].

Spain's membership of the EEC led to a sharp increase in foreign trade and foreign investment. In addition, the balance of income and payments was clearly in Spain's favor, which benefited from the Common Agricultural Policy (CAP) and the structural and cohesion funds (which replaced migrants' remittances on the transfer balance). Taken together, these factors explain why, with the exception of the crisis of 1992-1993, Spain's economic growth was very satisfactory in the final years of the 20th century [Betrán et al. (2010)].

The crisis of 1992-93 had to do with the peseta's entering the European Monetary System (EMS) in 1989, which it was believed would help control inflationary pressures. However, the overvaluation of the peseta undermined the international competitiveness of Spain's companies, leading to country's position becoming untenable as soon as difficulties arose within the EMS. In the summer of 1992, the Bundesbank raised interest rates to curb the inflation triggered in the wake of German reunification. Shortly after, the pound, the Italian lira, and the Spanish peseta were attacked by speculators, who bet that none of these three currencies would be left unscathed by the new state of affairs. The result was that in mid-September the pound and the lira left the Exchange Rate Mechanism (ERM) and the peseta was devaluated by 5%. One month later, the peseta was to devaluate again, taking the Portuguese escudo down with it. In May 1993, the peseta and the escudo were again devalued. In August 1993, the decision was made to widen the exchange rate fluctuation band to 15%, which in practice meant that the ERM was no longer operational. The path of monetary union was abandoned until May 1998, when it would be taken up again, leading rapidly and successfully to the euro.

The Spanish crisis of 1992-1993 has been explained by José Luis Malo de Molina (2005, pp. 11-13) in the following terms: "When the financial markets, in the international context described [the Maastricht Treaty of 1991], became aware of the unsustainability the accumulated loss of competitiveness [for Spain], it was inevitable that a series of successive devaluations would begin, and that they would trigger a sharp contraction in output, which would be amplified and transmitted to employment. As a result of the prevailing dualism of the labor market, as much net employment was destroyed in just a few quarters as had been generated over the past few years of expansion." At the root of the loss of competitiveness was a series of "highly imbalanced policies" where the whole stabilization effort fell on monetary policy. The independence of the Banco de España, granted by the government in 1994 as part of the implementation of the Maastricht Treaty, would help "establish medium-term targets for inflation, which gradually gained credibility [and] facilitated the containment of those public spending items most closely tied to inflationary behavior, while the progressive reduction in interest rates was cutting the heavy burden of interest on the public finances." The orthodox policies pursued by the Socialist minister Pedro Solbes (July 1993-May 1996) were continued and stepped up by the Conservative minister Rodrigo Rato (May 1996-April 2004), allowing Spain to join the euro, in a climate of euphoria among economic agents, who spurned the opportunity to discuss the pros and cons of this event in depth.

At the same time as the government was making efforts to complete the internationalization of the Spanish economy, the private sector set in motion a parallel process. Whereas up until the 1980s, the international activity of Spain's businesses was confined to the importing capital and technology for the domestic market, the crisis of the 1970s had made it necessary to look for markets abroad. The internationalization of Spain's business took place in two phases, first exporting goods and services, and then capital and technology. The crisis in the 1980s, especially in Latin America, encouraged Spanish companies to look for ways of gaining a foothold in these countries, where opportunities were plentiful. This process, led by large public corporations (such as Telefónica and Repsol), the banks, but also including construction companies, utilities and communications companies, etc. began in this decade and gathered pace in the decades that followed *[Información Comercial Española* (2009)].

5   Conclusions: looking to the future

There is no doubt that, despite its uneven progress, the Spanish economy's performance in the 20th century was its most brilliant ever. During the century the country underwent its industrial revolution and made the leap from backwardness to social and economic maturity. However, as we have seen, although it has certain distinctive features, the Spanish economy clearly falls into the pattern of Mediterranean Europe – albeit with differences in timing – and it has followed a similar path to the region as a whole.

That said, we must add one further trait to these distinctive characteristics, which being political, we have not mentioned in the corresponding section. In an extraordinarily turbulent and belligerent century for the world as a whole, Spain followed a path of its own in terms of tragedy and violence: it avoided taking part in two world wars and yet had its own civil war when the rest of the world was nominally at peace. This divergence speaks volumes about the degree of isolation of Spanish society in the 20th century and helps explain the eccentricities of its pace of economic development.

The second half of the 20th century, however, was characterized by convergence among European countries, largely as a result of a deliberate policy, the most obvious sign of which was the creation of what is now the European Union. Spain, like all other southern European countries, was among those with most to gain from integration, a fact which did not escape the attention of its governments, whether under dictatorship or democracy, which pursued membership through all the diplomatic means at their disposal. The democrats achieved it, and justly so. Having reached a per capita income that ranks Spain among the 20 most developed countries of the world, and as one of the biggest members of the European Union, Spain can look forward with confidence to a future of stability and development.

But not everything should be congratulations. First, the current crisis has shown serious cracks in the grandiose European edifice, and one of those cracks runs west to east, separating the north and the south along a dividing line that until recently we thought had been overcome, such that the unity and stability of Europe today do not seem as safe as they did a few years ago. Secondly, the crisis has also highlighted the Spanish economy's own problems, which had been forgotten in the boom years following the introduction of the euro: the Spanish economy is excessively prone to unemployment, inflation, stagnating productivity, and a trade deficit. These are all interrelated phenomena that require rigorous structural policy measures to solve them, because otherwise they risk becoming a heavy drag on the development we all wish for. Related to these problems are also the structural weaknesses of the educational and research system, and other legal, administrative and political scourges that have profound economic consequences. If Spaniards want the 21st century to be as brilliant as the 20th – but without the severe turbulence and discontinuities of the past – they need to apply themselves to remedying these serious problems.

References

BADOSA PAGÉS, J. (2005). "La adhesión de España a la CEE", *Información Comercial Española*, 826, pp. 99-106.

BANCO DE ESPAÑA (1932). *Memoria*.

— (1934). *Ritmo de la crisis económica española en relación con la mundial*, Madrid.

BARCIELA, C. (Ed.) (2003). *Autarquía y mercado negro. El fracaso económico del primer franquismo, 1939-1959*, Crítica, Barcelona.

BARCIELA, C., M. I. LÓPEZ, J. MELGAREJO and J. A. MIRANDA (1999). *La España de Franco (1939-1975). Economía*, Síntesis, Madrid.

BETRÁN, C., A. CUBEL, M. Á. PONS and T. SANCHÍS (2010). *La España democrática (1975-2000). Economía*, Síntesis, Madrid.

CARRERAS, A., and X. TAFUNELL (2010). *Historia económica de la España contemporánea (1789-2009)*, Crítica, Barcelona.

CARRERAS, A., and X. TAFUNELL (Coord.) (2005). *Estadísticas históricas de España, siglos XIX-XX*, 3 Vols., Fundación BBVA, Bilbao.

CATALÁN, J. (1995). *La economía española y la segunda guerra mundial*, Ariel, Barcelona.

COMÍN, F. (1996). *Historia de la Hacienda Pública*, 2 Vols., Crítica, Barcelona.

— (2002). "El Plan de Estabilización de Raimundo Fernández Villaverde", *Cuadernos de Información Económica*, 168, pp. 189-196.

CUERVO, Á. (1988). *La crisis bancaria en España, 1977-1985*, Ariel, Barcelona.

DE LA TORRE, J., and M. GARCÍA-ZÚÑIGA (Eds.) (2009). *Entre el mercado y el Estado: los planes de desarrollo durante el franquismo*, Universidad Pública de Navarra, Pamplona.

DE MIGUEL, A. (1987). *España cíclica. Ciclos económicos y generaciones demográficas en la sociedad española contemporánea*, Fundación Banco Exterior, Madrid.

DOBADO, R. (2004a). "Un legado peculiar: la geografía", in Enrique Llopis (Ed.) (2004), *El legado económico del Antiguo Régimen en España*, Crítica, Barcelona, pp. 97-119.

— (2004b). *Geografía y desigualdad económica y demográfica de las provincias españolas, siglos XIX y XX,* Working Paper 2004-20, de la Facultad de Ciencias Económicas y Empresariales de la Universidad Complutense de Madrid.

FUENTES QUINTANA, E. (1984). "El Plan de Estabilización Económica de 1959: veinticinco años después", *Información Comercial Española,* 612-613, pp. 25-40.

— (1990a). "Tres decenios de la economía española en perspectiva", in J. L. García Delgado (Coord.), *España. Economía,* 2nd edition, Espasa Calpe, Madrid, pp. 1-78.

— (1990b). *Las reformas tributarias en España: teoría, historia y propuestas,* Crítica, Barcelona.

— (2003). "Joan Sardà y el Plan de Estabilización y Liberalización de la economía española", *Papeles y memorias de la Real Academia de Ciencias Morales y Políticas,* 11, pp. 156-185.

GARCÍA DELGADO, J. L. (1979). "La política económica española de 1930: el "error Argüelles", *Papeles de Economía Española,* 1, pp. 43-47.

— (1987). "La industrialización y el desarrollo económico de España durante el franquismo", in Jordi Nadal, Albert Carreras and Carles Sudrià (Eds.), *La economía española en el siglo XX. Una perspectiva histórica,* Ariel, Barcelona, pp. 164-189.

GARCÍA RUIZ, J. L. (1998). "La nueva banca mixta en el Madrid de comienzos de siglo", in Pedro Tedde (Ed.), *Economía y colonias en la España del 98,* Síntesis-Fundación Duques de Soria, Madrid, pp. 261-297.

— (2006). "Política y Hacienda en el período de entreguerras", in Agustín González Enciso and Juan Manuel Matés Barco (Coord.), *Historia económica de España,* Ariel, Barcelona, pp. 619-648.

GÓMEZ MENDOZA, A. (Ed.) (2000). *De mitos y milagros. El Instituto Nacional de Autarquía, 1941-1963,* Universitat de Barcelona, Barcelona.

GONZÁLEZ-PÁRAMO, J. M. (1990). *El papel del sector público en España: de la crisis económica al mercado único europeo,* FUNCAS, Madrid.

HERNÁNDEZ ANDREU, J. (1980). *Depresión económica en España, 1925-1934. Crisis mundial antes de la Guerra Civil española,* Instituto de Estudios Fiscales, Madrid.

INFORMACIÓN COMERCIAL ESPAÑOLA (2009). "La internacionalización de la empresa española en perspectiva histórica", 849 (July-August).

JACKSON, G. (1965). *The Spanish Republic and the Civil War, 1931-1939,* Princeton University Press, Princeton.

MALO DE MOLINA, J. L. (1994). "Diez años de la economía española", in *Historias de una década. Sistema financiero y economía española, 1984-1994,* AB Asesores, Madrid, pp. 81-108.

— (2005). *Una larga fase de expansión de la economía española,* Documentos Ocasionales, no. 0505, Banco de España, Madrid.

MALUQUER DE MOTES, J. (1999). *España en la crisis de 1898. De la Gran Depresión a la modernización económica del siglo XX,* Península, Barcelona.

— (2007). *La paradisíaca estabilidad de la anteguerra. Elaboración de un índice de precios de consumo de España, 1830-1936,* Documento de Trabajo 2007-07, de la Unitat d'Història Econòmica de la Universitat Autònoma de Barcelona.

— (2009). "Viajar a través del Cosmos: la medida de la creación de riqueza y la serie histórica del Producto Interior Bruto de España, 1850-2008", *Revista de Economía Aplicada,* XVII (51), pp. 25-54.

MARTÍN-ACEÑA, P. (1984). *La política monetaria en España, 1919-1935,* Instituto de Estudios Fiscales (Ministerio de Hacienda), Madrid.

— (2001). *El oro de Moscú y el oro de Berlín,* Taurus, Madrid.

MARTÍN-ACEÑA, P., and F. COMÍN (1991). *INI. 50 años de industrialización de España,* Espasa Calpe, Madrid.

MARTÍN-ACEÑA, P., and M. Á. PONS (2005). "Sistema monetario y financiero", in Albert Carreras and Xavier Tafunell (Coord.), *Estadísticas históricas de España: Siglos XIX-XX,* Vol. II, pp. 645-706, Fundación BBVA, Bilbao.

MARTÍN-ACEÑA, P., and E. MARTÍNEZ RUIZ (Eds.) (2006). *La economía de la Guerra Civil,* Marcial Pons, Madrid.

MINISTERIO DE ECONOMÍA Y HACIENDA (2009). *Recaudación y estadísticas del sistema tributario español, 1997-2007,* Madrid.

NADAL, J. (1991). *La población española, siglos XVI a XX,* 4th edition, Ariel, Barcelona.

NADAL, J. (Supervisor) (2003). *Atlas de la industrialización de España, 1700-2000,* Crítica, Barcelona.

NICOLAU, R. (2005). "Población, salud y actividad", in Albert Carreras and Xavier Tafunell (Coords.), *Estadísticas históricas de España: Siglos XIX-XX,* Vol. I, pp. 77-154, Fundación BBVA, Bilbao.

NÚÑEZ, C. E. (2005). "Educación", in Albert Carreras and Xavier Tafunell (Coord.), *Estadísticas históricas de España: Siglos XIX-XX,* Vol. I, pp. 155-244, Fundación BBVA, Bilbao.

O'BRIEN, P. K., and L. PRADOS DE LA ESCOSURA (1992). "Agricultural Productivity and European

Industrialization, 1890-1980", *Economic History Review,* XLV (3), pp. 514-536.

PALAFOX, J. (1991). *Atraso económico y democracia. La Segunda República y la economía española, 1892-1936,* Crítica, Barcelona.

PERDICES DE BLAS, L., and T. BAUMERT (Coord.) (2010). *La hora de los economistas. Entrevistas a cuarenta economistas que han contribuido a la modernización de la economía española,* Ecobook, Madrid.

PÉREZ DE PERCEVAL, M. Á., M. Á. LÓPEZ-MORELL and A. SÁNCHEZ RODRÍGUEZ (Eds.) (2006). *Minería y desarrollo económico en España,* Síntesis, Madrid.

PRADOS DE LA ESCOSURA, L. (2003). *El progreso económico de España, 1850-2000,* Fundación BBVA, Bilbao.

— (2010). "Spain's International Position, 1850-1913", *Revista de Historia Económica,* 28 (1), pp. 173-215.

QUIROGA, M.ª G. (2002). *Medidas Antropométricas y Condiciones de vida en la España del siglo XX,* Tesis Doctoral, Universidad de Alcalá.

RAMOS, J. L., and L. PIRES (2009). "Spanish Economists Facing Indicative Planning in the 1960s", *Storia del Pensiero Economico,* 1, pp. 79-110.

REHER, D. S., and E. BALLESTEROS (1993). "Precios y salarios en Castilla la Nueva: la construcción de un índice de salarios reales, 1501-1991", *Revista de Historia Económica,* 1, pp. 101-151.

ROLDÁN, S., and J. L. GARCÍA DELGADO (with the collaboration of Juan Muñoz) (1973). *La formación de la sociedad capitalista en España, 1914-1920,* 2 Vols., Confederación Española de Cajas de Ahorros, Madrid.

SAN ROMÁN, E. (1999). *Ejército e industria. El nacimiento del INI,* Crítica, Barcelona.

SÁNCHEZ ALONSO, B. (1995). *Las causas de la emigración española, 1880-1930,* Alianza, Madrid.

SÁNCHEZ ASIAÍN, J. Á. (1999). *Economía y finanzas en la Guerra Civil española, 1936-1939,* Real Academia de la Historia, Madrid.

SÁNCHEZ-GIJÓN, A. (1974). "Cronología básica del Acuerdo España-CEE", *Revista de Instituciones Europeas,* 2, pp. 627-638.

SCHWARTZ, P., and M. J. GONZÁLEZ (1978). *Una historia del Instituto Nacional de Industria (1941-1976),* Tecnos, Madrid.

SIMPSON, J. (1995). *Spanish Agriculture. The Long Siesta, 1765-1965,* Cambridge University Press, Cambridge.

— (2005). "Spanish Agriculture in the Long Run, 1760-1960", in Magnus Jerneck, Magnus Mörner, Gabriel Tortella and Sune Akerman (Eds.), *Different Paths to Modernity. A Nordic and Spanish Perspective,* Nordic Academic Press, Lund, pp. 74-105.

SUDRIÀ, C. (1990). "Los beneficios de España durante la Gran Guerra. Una aproximación a la balanza de pagos española, 1914-1920", *Revista de Historia Económica,* 2, pp. 363-396.

SUDRIÀ, C., and D. A. TIRADO (Eds.) (2001). *Peseta y protección. Comercio exterior, moneda y crecimiento económico en la España de la Restauración,* Universitat de Barcelona, Barcelona.

TENA, A. (2005). "Sector exterior", in Albert Carreras and Xavier Tafunell (Coord.), *Estadísticas históricas de España: siglos XIX-XX,* Vol II, pp. 573-644, Fundación BBVA, Bilbao.

TORTELLA, G. (1994). *El desarrollo de la España contemporánea. Historia económica de los siglos XIX y XX,* Alianza, Madrid.

— (1996). "La transición bancaria", in Santos Juliá, Javier Pradera and Joaquín Prieto (Eds.), *Memoria de la transición,* Taurus, Madrid, pp. 569-574.

— (1999). "The Role of Banks and Government in Spanish Economic Development, 1850-1935", in Richard Sylla, Richard Tilly and Gabriel Tortella (Eds.), *The State, the Financial System and Economic Modernization,* Cambridge University Press, Cambridge, pp. 158-181.

— (2004). "Guerra en la guerra: el Banco Central en años difíciles, 1930-1942", in José Pérez Fernández, Carlos Sebastián Gascón and Pedro Tedde de Lorca (Eds.), *Estudios en homenaje a Luis Ángel Rojo* (Vol. II). *Economía y cambio histórico,* Editorial Complutense, Madrid, pp. 125-147.

TORTELLA, G., and J. L. GARCÍA RUIZ (2004). "Spanish Banking after the Civil War: a Halting Reconstruction under Fascism", in Edwin Green, John Lampe and Franjo Stiblar (Eds.), *Crisis and Renewal in Twentieth Century Banking,* Ashgate, Aldershot, pp. 104-128.

TORTELLA, G., and J. C. JIMÉNEZ, (1986). *Historia del Banco de Crédito Industrial,* Alianza, Madrid.

TORTELLA, G., A. BALLESTERO and J. L. DÍAZ FERNÁNDEZ (2003). *Del monopolio al libre mercado. La historia de la industria petrolera española,* LID, Madrid.

TORTELLA, G., J. L. GARCÍA RUIZ, J. M. ORTIZ-VILLAJOS and G. QUIROGA (with the collaboration of Ignacio Moral) (2008). *Educación, instituciones y empresa. Los determinantes del espíritu empresarial,* Academia Europea de Ciencias y Artes, Madrid.

VELARDE, J. (1973). *Política económica de la Dictadura,* Guadiana, Madrid.

VIÑAS, Á. (1979). *El oro de Moscú. Alfa y omega de un mito franquista,* Grijalbo, Barcelona.

3. The main reforms of the Spanish financial system

M.ª Ángeles Pons
Universidad de Valencia

This chapter aims to explore how the main legislation affecting the Spanish financial system evolved over the course of the 20th century. In terms of legislative developments, four main periods can be distinguished: the period from the early legislation in 1856 up until 1920; from 1920 through to the Civil War in 1936; Francoism from 1939 to 1975; and, finally, the phase of deregulation between 1975 and 2000. After a short introduction, we will examine below the first three of these four phases in chronological order.

1 Introduction: The influence and importance of the legislative framework

The financial system has historically been a highly regulated sector compared to other industries. However, the role of regulation has changed over time. In the formative stages of the financial system, the goal of regulation was to encourage financial institutions to emerge and grow. However, as financial business developed, the purpose of the regulatory framework changed, and stability became the priority objective, particularly after the crisis of 1929-1933. The changes in the financial sector since the early 1980s and the crisis which broke in 2007 have reawakened interest in the sector's regulation. Rapid financial innovation and the process of globalization have not only heightened the risk of a financial crisis emerging, but have increased the likelihood of its spreading around the world. This raises a series of questions, such as: Why is the financial sector regulated? What forms of regulation could make it more efficient, and are therefore economically justified? What is the optimal level of regulation?

The financial sector is crucial for economic activity as it provides the means of payment the economy needs, and handles the process of financial intermediation. According to certain hypotheses, the resource allocation resulting from a free-market situation is optimal; however, when these conditions are not met, market failures occur, creating the need for economic policy makers to intervene. What are the main market failures? Some authors consider the sector's tendency to organize itself monopolistically due to economies of scale and scope to be a significant market failure. Regulation might allow the sector to exploit the benefits of size without monopolistic behaviors emerging (Gowland 1990, Baltensperger and Dermine 1990 or Baltensperger 1990). The empirical evidence on which to assess the existence of economies of scale and scope is inconclusive, however[1]. Moreover, this argument presupposes that the State's intervention limits monopolistic behaviors, when, in fact, in many cases the legislation itself has reinforced financial systems' monopolistic structure by limiting competition [Pons (2002)].

The second market failure concerns imperfect information. The banking system suffers from an information asymmetry between the banks and their customers. Depositors cannot judge precisely the quality, and thus the solvency, of the assets the bank offers them. Likewise the bank cannot be entirely sure of the "quality" of its customers and the likelihood of their repaying its loans, although it will, as far as it is able, try to estimate the risk associated with each customer. These information asymmetries between depositors and banks, and between banks and borrowers, increase the likelihood of a banking crisis. Here, regulation would aim to introduce the mechanisms necessary to improve information flows and insure the various agents against a possible crisis. However, other sectors also have information asymmetry problems, thus it is a matter of assessing whether this problem is more serious in the financial sector, and consequently whether or not special regulation is warranted.

Another market failure associated with information issues is the emergence of externalities. These arise when a crisis at a "bad" bank is propagated to banks that are operating correctly or, in other words, when there is "contagion" from one institution to another. In markets with imperfect information, if the public begins to doubt the solvency of a particular bank, the perceived likelihood of an insolvency occurring at any other financial institution will be augmented. However, some authors do not share the idea of the greater vulnerability of the banking industry as they consider the likelihood of bank runs to be small and that the "contagion effect" also occurs in other branches of the economy[2]. Nevertheless, the 1997 financial crisis, and to a greater extent the crisis which broke in 2007, exposed the financial sector's vulnerability, and above all, the fact that the sector has much greater potential for its

---

[1]   Lawrence (1989), pp.368-379; Vives (1988), pp.62-76.
[2]   Gowland (1990), p.13

crises to spill over into the rest of the economy than other industries have. The crisis in 1997 revealed the problems global financial integration can cause in emerging countries. After the crisis erupted in Thailand in July it rapidly spread to Indonesia, South Korea and Malaysia, until it finally developed into a full-blown global financial crisis. These emerging economies had opened up rapidly to the outside world and received copious amounts of foreign investment, expanding their domestic financial sectors in lightly regulated markets. Serious economic imbalances had built up during this process of rapid deregulation, resulting in a loss of confidence in the countries concerned and a sharp devaluation of their currencies. This in turn led to a financial panic which then spread to other parts of the world. The crisis of 2007, however, has mainly affected the developed countries, emerging in the United States and then subsequently spreading to Europe. In this case, the crisis initially appeared to be local and concentrated in the real-estate sector. However, it soon took on global dimensions as a result of the international integration of the banking business. These two crises have therefore revealed that, in both developing countries and in the industrialized world, the risk of suffering a financial shock has increased and that in both cases the problems of lack of regulation or inadequate regulation have been the key to explaining the crisis.

These arguments, among others, attest to the need to regulate the sector[3], although they tell us nothing about what the optimal level of financial legislation might be. The legislative framework is not independent of the country's political and economic circumstances and needs to be defined accordingly. The financial sector needs prudential standards of behavior to ensure stability. Mechanisms need to be in place ensuring adequate capitalization, funding and reserves of liquidity. And a deposit guarantee system needs to exist that is able to evaluate risks, and adjusts premiums to avoid moral hazard. Moreover, a system of supervision over the activities of the financial industry is required, along with a lender of last resort which will only intervene under very specific circumstances in order to avoid banks taking excessive risks, safe in the knowledge that they will be rescued by the authorities as soon as they get into difficulties. Finally, as the IMF recommends, international cooperation in the current context is essential. The increase in cross-border business prevents governments from acting unilaterally and calls for the adoption of international cooperation measures in finance, which will no doubt shape the international agenda over the years to come.

2 The stage prior to 1920: the formation of the Spanish financial system and its legal framework

The origins of the current legislation governing the Spanish financial system reach back over a century and a half. Up until the mid-19th century the number of financial institutions in Spain

---

[3] As well as the reasons linked to stability and efficiency, regulation has had other justifications, such as the desire of the authorities to use bank funds to support government policy goals, for example. In this latter case regulation is not justified on the grounds of the intrinsic characteristics of the banking industry [Pueyo (2003), p.63].

was small and the legislation was permissive. The first legislation regulating the conditions under which banks could be created was the 1848 Corporations Law, passed in the wake of the stock-market crash and financial crisis of 1847. This ended a period of relative freedom to enter the sector by laying down that issuing banks could only be created with authorization from the Cortes (parliament) and prohibiting the creation of non-issuing banks unless they demonstrated their "public utility." A new law in 1851 gave the Cortes the authority to grant new bank licenses. However, it was in 1856 that the laws configuring the legal framework on which the banking system developed were passed, namely the Issuing Banks Law and the Credit Companies Law. These two laws defined a relatively liberal legislative framework in which there was barely any supervision. This situation was to remain until the 1921 *Ley de Ordenación Bancaria* or Banking Law (LOB) was passed [Tortella (1970) and Martin Aceña (1985)].

The Issuing Banks Law of 28 January 1856 allowed for a plurality of issuers, but limited them to one per locality. As Pérez de Armiñán (1980) has pointed out, these new banks were to take the form of joint-stock companies, with their capital fully paid-up before starting business, their shares were to have a minimum nominal value, and they were to be approved by decree. Their loans to the Treasury were regulated and they were not allowed to use their own shares as collateral. Dividends were limited so as to ensure adequate growth of their reserves. Moreover, they were obliged to publish their balance sheets in the *Gaceta* every month. In order to ensure convertibility, banknote issuance was limited to three times paid-up capital and reserves of precious metals. The government gave the governor of the Banco de España the task of monitoring compliance with these issuance rules, with the appointment of a royal commissioner to oversee each of the banks [Tortella (1970)]. For its part, the Credit Companies Law, passed at the same time as the Issuing Banks Law, allowed these institutions to undertake a wide range of activities, including lending to the government and public bodies, collecting taxes, promoting, merging and transforming companies, lending, buying and selling shares, taking deposits, and making collections and payments for third parties. Under the aegis of these two laws there was a significant expansion of the financial system, which went from just five banks in 1855 (three of which were issuing banks) to 19 in 1857 (with 10 issuing banks) and on to 58 institutions in 1858.

In 1866 a financial crisis was triggered in the wake of the railway boom, and as a consequence, the number of credit institutions shrank drastically. This crisis left some of the surviving banks in a precarious state, making it difficult for them to provide loans to the Treasury at a time when the government urgently needed funds. Nevertheless, the authorities did not introduce any significant legislative changes and the burden of adjustment was left to the market. Indeed, subsequent measures further liberalized the sector. On 19 October 1869 a law was passed giving the freedom to create land banks, agricultural banks, issuing banks, discount banks and credit companies, and mortgage lending firms in industry or trade. However, this law was only in effect for five years, as in 1874 the Banco de España was given the sole privilege of issuing currency.

It was the government's difficulties that prompted the legislative change passed in 1874 and which gave the Banco de España its privileged status as the sole issuing bank for a period of thirty years. The aim was to "create, based on the Banco de España, and with the aid of the provincial banks, a National Bank, as a new financial powerhouse that would come to the aid of the Treasury, without neglecting the functions intrinsic to any issuing bank." Therefore, in the early stages, the fundamental goal of the Banco de España was to raise funds with which to meet the government's needs. Thus, in 1890 almost all the money in circulation was absorbed by direct or indirect loans to the state. By the end of the century the Banco de España had handed over to the state all its capital and almost all the bank-notes in circulation. By granting the privilege of issuance to the Banco de España the other banks had the option to wind themselves up, be absorbed by the Banco de España – and thus become into branches of it – or to continue as independent banks, but without the issue privilege. Most banks took the second option. Only four choose to carry on as independent banks, those of Barcelona, Reus, Bilbao and Santander.

In the case of the unlisted savings banks *(Cajas de Ahorros),* the legislation in force in the mid-19th century was highly interventionist. Thus, in 1853 a Royal Decree was passed which regulated the organization and operation of the savings banks, turning them into municipal charitable institutions [Titos (1999)]. However, the popular opposition to the decree meant its application was left in suspense. The 1880 Savings Banks Law defined the legislative framework within which the savings banks operated for over 40 years. This legislation gave the savings banks more freedom, going back to the 1835 regulations and the abortive 1853 Royal Decree. Legal recognition was given to the specific nature of the statutes and the independence of each of the savings banks, which undoubtedly reduced the uncertainties in the sector. However, in the 1880 Law the government reserved the right to approve the statutes freely adopted by the savings banks. It also committed the State to promoting their creation in those provinces in which none yet existed. The savings banks and *Montes de Piedad* (a form of charitable pawnbrokers) formally regained their freedom to lead a separate existence provided the cajas were able to invest their capital in assets other than loans through the *Monte de Piedad,* and that the latter had a source of funding independent from the savings banks. This meant that from this time on, new savings banks no longer needed to have a *Monte de Piedad* associated with them, as happened in the case of the Guipúzcoa, Álava, Vizcaína, Manlleu, and Carlet savings banks and the Caja de Pensiones de Barcelona [Comin (2008)]. Finally, the 1880 Law continued to consider the cajas as charities, thus enabling them to benefit from tax exemptions under charity law, without this necessitating their being brought under municipal control.

In 1885 a new Commercial Code was passed. This set out a very vague legal framework for banking institutions with the result that the existing framework was not substantially altered. The legislative measures around the turn of the century were marked by problems of the depreciation of the peseta linked to the inflation caused by the Banco de España as a result of measures taken by the State. Thus, without altering the prevailing legal framework, steps were taken to shore up the national accounts and reduce the Treasury's pressure on the central bank, as well as to modify the Banco de España's portfolio in order for it to supply credit to the private sector as well as to the government.

In the case of the stock market, the first officially recognized exchange was opened in Madrid in 1831. Although its regulations were initially rudimentary, it envisaged both spot and forward transactions. However, stock-market stability problems led to the passing of a Royal Decree in 1846 which prohibited forward transactions. Despite this provision, this type of transaction carried on outside the stock exchange, leading to its being authorized again in 1847 and then prohibited again in 1848, which is an indication of the swings back and forth typical of the economy and politics of the period.

In 1869 freedom was granted to create commercial exchanges, their operations being subject to the Commercial Code and the Civil Code, but the regulations of the existing stock exchanges remained in place. Subsequently this rule was abrogated in 1874 and a Decree-Law passed regulating the stock market. This recognized the *Bolsa de Madrid,* as an official stock exchange, guaranteeing it a monopoly on all transactions with intermediaries and licensed agents in those cities in which there was no official stock exchange. The 1885 Commercial Code established the functions of stockbrokers and commercial brokers, and constituted the legislation regulating the sector up until 1936. This allowed the public authorities, quasi-public corporations such as chambers of commerce, and even private companies, to apply to create a stock exchange in any city of Spain. Following an application, the government reserved the right to grant authorization and turn it into an official exchange. In any event, the real changes with respect to the preceding situation were minor [Rojo Cagigal (2008)]. Although the 1885 code appeared to establish more liberal legislation, this greater openness was a response to the pressure from other regions against the centralized model of a single stock exchange in Madrid.

The *Bolsa de Barcelona* became an official exchange in 1915. However, as there was a self-regulating "old exchange," the legislation caused a conflict between the interests of the existing exchange and the official one. This was only resolved in 1916 when an agreement between the two institutions was reached [García Ruiz (1999)]. Along with the Madrid and Barcelona exchanges, the *Bolsa de Bilbao* had been in operation since 1890, together with a few smaller provincial exchanges. However, the stock exchanges played a minor role in the Spanish financial system as a whole, and although they did carry out some "sophisticated" financial transactions, such as holding current accounts for securities and valuables, the volume of trading was small. Given the country's limited level of industrialization, the stock market was basically a market for public debt, created on official initiative rather than as a result of demand from the private sector. Private securities were limited to shares in a few railways, banks and insurance companies. These accounted for less than one percent of total trading and were highly illiquid.

Spain's neutrality during the First World War brought it substantial economic benefits and Spanish banks experienced rapid growth during the period,[4] consolidating their character as mixed banks[5]. However, the end of the war led to a wave of insolvencies among

---

[4] Muñoz (1978, p.159), Roldán, García Delgado and Muñoz (1973, pp.183-253) or Tortella and Palafox (1984, pp.33-45).

[5] The creation of mixed banks was a fairly widespread phenomenon over the period of consolidation of the banking systems in many European countries such as France and Germany.

the banks, with many of them being wound up. The subsequent increase in government intervention in the financial sector taking place between 1919 and 1923 in various countries (Denmark, Norway, etc.), together with Spain's financial crisis registered during the post-war years, were two factors clearly influencing in the legislative changes that took place in 1921.

3 From the 1921 Banking Law to the Civil War

3.1 The 1921 Banking Law

In 1921 the issue privilege which had been granted to the Banco de España in 1874, and subsequently extended in 1891, ended. In 1918 a commission was set up, including members of the Treasury, the Banco de España, and representatives of various branches of the economy, to gather information and draw up proposals for the creation of a new legislative framework. The most significant ideas included the need to turn the Banco de España into a true central bank and give the commercial banks a definitive organizational structure. These two points therefore formed the basic guiding principles of this reform.

The Banking Law of 1921 (LOB) took its inspiration from the bill establishing the United States Federal Reserve and created the new legislative framework regulating the functioning of the Spanish financial system up until the Civil War [Tortella (1970) and Pons (1999)]. As noted, the 1921 Law had two objectives. Primarily, the reform sought to consolidate the Banco de España's position as a central bank. The Law also introduced a number of new features. One was that it allowed the banks registered with the *Consejo Superior Bancario,* or Banking Council, to discount bills with the Banco de España at a subsidized interest rate. A second feature of the Law was that it set a limit on the loans that the Banco de España could supply to the treasury and limited its portfolio of public debt. The Law also regulated the volume of banknotes in circulation[6]. Ultimately, however, the changes were modest. The Law limited itself to extending the Banco de España's issue monopoly for a further 25 years, without taking the definitive step of making it a true central bank and guaranteeing its greater independence. Although the Law regulated the relationships between the government and the Bank, limiting the loans the treasury could obtain from it and setting the maximum volume of banknotes in circulation, these limits were ultimately subject to the government's approval. This meant an opportunity to normalize the central bank's activity and shape it according to the pattern being followed by other central banks in the developed world was wasted [Olariaga (1933)]. Another example of the Bank's lack of independence was in the provisions linked to exchange rate control. The Banco de España was prohibited from exporting gold without the prior

---

[6] Martín Aceña (1984), pp.25-27

authorization of the Council of Ministers, and the government was authorized to intervene in the foreign-exchange market.

The second objective of the Law was to create a new legal framework for the commercial banks. The authorities established various control and supervision measures applicable to the banks, thus breaking with the *laissez-faire* model that had formerly prevailed. The Law therefore defined the concept of a bank, and the conditions institutions had to satisfy in order to obtain a banking license. Its other provisions included minimum capital requirements, the possibility of defining proportionality between equity and debt, the setting of tariffs or limits on interest rates, and the setting of maximum interest rates for current accounts and deposits. A Register of banks and bankers was set up, on which those entities complying with the Law's requirements were to be registered. The Law also assigned significant powers to the *Consejo Superior Bancario* (CSB), as the body regulating and representing commercial banks, replacing the former *Comité Central de la Banca española* (Central Committee of Spanish Banks). The CSB was a consultative body and was responsible for compiling banking statistics and publishing some of the information sent to it each month by banks in the form of a standardized balance sheet. It was also empowered to investigate and monitor banking operations and impose penalties, thus effectively playing the role of an official channel of communication between the private-sector banks and the authorities. This corporate body was given a broad range of functions: not only was it entrusted with the task of overseeing the proper functioning of the banking institutions, but it also monitored certain essential features such as each institution's minimum capital requirements, the minimum interest rates on deposits, and the ratio of paid-in capital to total reserves plus deposits. Consequently, the period from 1921 through to 1936 was effectively one of self-regulation by the sector under the supervision of a Royal Commissioner appointed by the Finance Minister.[7]

It was in this regulatory framework that the financial crisis of 1929 took place, although the crisis did not affect the Spanish economy particularly severely [Palafox (1991)]. Nevertheless, between 1930 and 1931 a number of institutions found themselves in difficulties. There were two main factors limiting the scope of the international financial crisis. The first was that, for the first time, the Banco de España acted as a lender of last resort and together with the Treasury undertook a series of operations guaranteeing liquidity to those banks that needed it.[8] Secondly, the banks had considerable reserves of liquid assets, which they were able to turn into cash when necessary.

Despite the limited impact of the crisis of 1929-1933, the sector's problems at the start of the 1930s led to reform of the Banking Law by the Finance Ministry in 1931. This reform focused on the role and responsibilities of the Banco de España and did not directly affect the banking sector or its supervisory mechanisms. Broadly speaking, the reform sought to increase the government's control over the Banco de España. It therefore ensured repre-

---

[7]   Faus (2001), pp.69-118.
[8]   Martín Aceña (2001), p.134.

sentation of the government on the Banco de España's board, to which it appointed three representatives. An inspectorate was also set up, comprising civil servants from the Treasury, and finally, government intervention in monetary policy was bolstered by its setting the discount rate and managing intervention in exchange rates. The government was also authorized to draw upon the Bank's gold reserves in the form of advances to the Treasury [Sardá (1970), p.288]. To some extent, what this led to was a discharging of monetary policy onto the issuing bank and a reduction of the bank's business with private customers to a minimum, so as to turn it into the "bankers' bank" [Olariaga (1933)]. At the same time, a process began whereby the Banco de España was drawn ever further into the apparatus of the state, culminating in its nationalization in 1962.

The fierce competition for deposits between banks and savings banks led to the savings banks' also calling for a specific legislative framework enabling them to compete in the new scenario brought about by the 1921 LOB.[9] The first legislation to be passed this direction was a Royal Decree on 9 April 1926 which aimed to update that which existed previously. One of this Law's most important innovations was a change in the ministry responsible for the savings banks, with their being passed from the Directorate-General for Charities, under the Interior Ministry, to the Ministry of Labor, Trade and Industry. The Law obliged the savings banks to be listed on a specific register and imposed severe restrictions on their investment portfolios. Finally, it envisaged the transformation of all the savings banks into joint-stock companies. The new regulation did not satisfy the savings banks, which worked on forming an association which finally gave rise to the creation in 1928 of the Spanish Confederation of Charitable Savings Banks *(Confederación Española de Cajas de Ahorro Benéficas* or CECA). This body became the visible head of the Spanish savings banks.

In 1929 the Savings Statute was passed. This new legislative instrument sought to improve on the 1926 legislation by clearly differentiating between the savings banks' social goals and the activities of other savings bodies aimed at the public. Among other things, the Statute defined the legal personality of the savings banks, guaranteeing official inspection, formally transferring authority over them to the Ministry of Labor and Welfare, and establishing the characteristics of the operations the savings banks were allowed to conduct. The Statute's regulations were extremely detailed and the savings banks undoubtedly benefited from the fact that their business and activities were governed by general rules that applied equally to all of them. The Statute differentiated between general savings banks aimed at the public and specific savings institutions. The general savings banks included the institutions of the official boards and protectorates, collaborating institutions of the *Instituto Nacional de Previsión* (National Welfare Institute) and the nonprofit provisional and municipal savings banks whose purpose was to encourage savings. The remainder were considered specific savings institutions. The name "Monte de Piedad", referring to the charitable pawn-broker's associated with the savings banks, was reserved for institutions under public tutelage which had been recognized as such.

---

[9] Maixé (2003), p.126

In 1933 the *Estatuto de las Cajas Generales de Ahorro Popular* or Statute of the General People's Savings Banks was passed. This clearly defined the savings banks and differentiated them from other credit and savings institutions. It also confirmed their charitable status and delimited the social purpose of their investments (public debt, provincial and municipal bonds, shares in industrial corporations expressly classified as eligible by the government, purchase of real estate, granting of loans and mortgages, corporate lending against security or personal guarantees, and lending against stock as collateral, such that obligatory investments could not exceed 30 percent of savings deposits). This legislation delimited the types of investments these institutions could make and obliged them to set aside reserve funds that were to be equivalent to at least 10 percent of deposits.[10] Their loan portfolio was also regulated, with the setting of limits on the maximum terms and percentages of the guarantees given. Membership of the regional federations and of the Spanish Confederation of Savings Banks (CECA) was also made obligatory. The Statute therefore clearly defined the social nature of the savings banks, but gave them broad functions, which undoubtedly enabled their subsequent development [Titos (1999)]. In 1933 the Savings Banks Credit Institute *(Instituto de Crédito de las Cajas de Ahorro)* was also created, with a view to its being an intermediary between the savings banks and those public – and particularly government – bodies that wished to obtain finance from them. In late 1933 the conflicts between the banks and savings banks resurfaced, with pressure from the CSB, which wanted the savings banks' legislative framework of 1929 to be restored. In the end, a Decree on 3 May 1935 laid down that the savings banks would come under the purview of the Ministry of Finance insofar as their economic and banking functions were concerned, and under the Ministry of Labor as regards their social and charitable roles. This duality remained until 1957. The Decree also established that the financial activities of the savings banks would be subject to governmental delegation from the CSB.[11] The tensions between the banks and the savings banks led to this agreement's being overturned, although the rest of the legislation remained and went on to become the legal basis regulating the sector almost up until 1977.

As regards the stock market, the economic dynamism of the years of the First World War was reflected in the value of shares in industries such as water, gas, electricity, mining, iron and steel and chemicals. However, the end of the war led to a sharp drop in share prices, putting the market back to where it was in the 1920s. In any case, whereas private stocks barely represented three percent of all shares at the turn of the century, in 1930 they accounted for almost 68 percent.[12] In the 1930s a series of measures were approved that curbed the scope of the Spanish stock markets and the already somewhat rigid Spanish stock market was further weakened in this period [García Ruiz (1999)].

---

[10]   Maixe (2003), p.129
[11]   Maixé (2003), p.130
[12]   Hoyo (2007), p.145

3.2   The Civil War

The Civil War disrupted the functioning of the Spanish economy on all levels. The country's physical and economic division also affected the legal framework. The existing legislation was suspended and each side in the conflict passed its own legislation. One of the most immediate consequences of the war was the appearance of two pesetas: one in Nationalist territory and the other in the Republican-held areas. The Banco de España was also split in two.

After the outbreak of the conflict a number of urgent measures were passed, such as the freezing of accounts to prevent massive withdrawals of cash from the banking system, and measures to avoid monetary flight (controls on exports of gold, silver, currencies and Banco de España banknotes).[13] Despite this, the authorities on the Republican side suffered severe difficulties in monetary matters, particularly as regards monetary control.[14] In the Nationalist zone, the administrative apparatus was created along highly interventionist lines and the monetary disorder was more limited. The first issue of Banco de España banknotes in Nationalist-held Burgos took place on 21 November 1936 and there were no local issues (except in isolated cases). Moreover, the Nationalists deemed all banknotes put into circulation in the Republican zone after 18 July 1936 null and void, with an operation invalidating all Banco de España banknotes that had not been stamped.[15]

The financial institutions in the Republican zone were not nationalized, although they did suffer from government intervention and harassment from labor unions and political organizations. Moreover, their boards of directors were replaced by committees including worker representatives. In the Francoist zone, however, shareholder representatives remained on the boards of directors, although the Finance Ministry kept a close eye on the financial institutions [Martín Aceña (2006)]. The war also forced a hiatus in stock market activity, and trading was not restored until 1940.

4   The Francoist period: interventionism during the first phase of Francoism (1939-1962) and the changes begun in the 1960s (1962-1975)

4.1   The legislative reforms of the 1940s and 1950s

The legislative measures adopted after the end of the Civil War had two goals: normalizing the financial situation and laying the foundations for the use of the financial system as

---

[13]   Sánchez Asiaín (1999), p.109.

[14]   Martorell (2006), pp.343-344.

[15]   Sánchez Asiaín (1999, p.152) goes so far as to talk of "monetary warfare" between the Nationalist and Republican pesetas, given that as well as cancelling the Republican currency, the Francoists stockpiled large quantities of banknotes as they captured Republican areas and used them to generate mistrust in the Republican peseta.

an extra tool to support Francoist economic policy. In order to make progress towards monetary reconstruction, on 7 December 1939 the *Ley de Desbloqueo* ("Unfreezing" Law) was passed, with a view to unfreezing accounts and unifying the national currency, while seeking to avoid the emergence of inflationary pressures. Given that the Republican zone had suffered faster inflation, an "equivalence" table was used to convert old Republican pesetas into Nationalist ones.[16] As Sardá (1970) has pointed out, the *Ley de Desbloqueo* restored the monetary community and avoided runaway inflation taking hold, although the conversion process penalized holders of deposits in Republican pesetas excessively harshly.

The Law of 9 November 1939 declared banknotes to be full legal tender, suspending the system of precious-metal guarantees established by the 1921 Banking Law, and it authorized the Banco de España to buy public and treasury debt as the balancing item for the cash in circulation. In part, this was a response to the asset and liability position of the Banco de España, although it also reflected trends in most other countries. It should not be overlooked that the account item representing the gold and silver owned by the Banco de España was fictitious, as the Bank's precious-metal reserves had been used by the Republican government to pay for its war effort.[17] It was also necessary to include the borrowings of Franco's side during the conflict. For this reason, the Law passed on 13 March 1942 tried to clarify the state of the Banco de España's accounts at the end of the war, with the merger of the accounts of the two banks, and an assessment of the real asset and liability position of the Bank.

Other measures approved after the war included the dissolution of the *Comité de Moneda Extranjera* (Foreign Currency Committee) by a Law passed on 25 August 1939, and the creation of an independent body called the *Instituto Español de Moneda Extranjera* (Spanish Foreign Currency Institute), which was given responsibility over all exchange-rate policy matters. This Law was extremely important as it represented a separation of interior and exterior policy, with the difficulties that this entailed when formulating a consistent overall program of action at the macroeconomic level.

The banking regulations adopted in the 1940s were highly restrictive in terms of barriers to entry, limits on opening new branches and interest rate controls. Many of these measures were introduced provisionally in 1942 and made permanent in the Banking Law of 1946. This Law replaced that passed in 1921, ratified the legislation in force up until that time, and established the Spanish economy's guiding principles in terms of finance and banking for almost twenty years.[18] As regards the Banco de España and rules on issuance, although the preamble to the Law stated that it introduced no new features in this regard, two measures

---

[16]   Paris Eguilaz (1945), p.31 and Ridruejo (1954), p.45.

[17]   Viñas (1976) and Martín-Aceña (1991, 2001).

[18]   For example, the Ministerial Order of 15 January 1936 on interest rates set the minimum charges applicable to both lending and borrowing; the Law of 27 August 1936 on governmental powers relating to banking matters gave the Treasury Ministry the authority to determine credit policy and make inspections of banks or bankers; the Decree-Law of 17 May 1940 prohibited the creation of new banks or branches; and the Decree of 31 December 1941 limited the distribution of dividends by banks, a measure which was also included in the Banking Law of 1946.

contradict this claim. Firstly, by ratifying the interim measures enacted at the end of the war, the Law broke with the requirement for new money issues to be backed by reserves of precious metals; thus, banknotes became full legal tender in their own right, as had been established by the Law of 9 November 1939. Secondly, the Law granted the government full authority to dictate general rules for credit policy and to set discount rates and open market operations, ratifying the Law of 27 August 1938.

The Banking Law of 1946 renewed the Banco de España's issue privilege, a right it had enjoyed since 19 March 1874 and which was due to expire in December of that year. Although it retained its legal status as a private institution and its shareholders retained their majority on the Board of Directors, the government strengthened its control over the institution, although it did give the shareholders the option of selling their shares to the government at the official rate. The body mediating between the government and the privately owned banks was the *Consejo Superior Bancario* (Banking Council). From the legal point of view this was merely a consultative body. Although it was chaired by the Director General for Banking and the Stock Market, and its deputy chairman was the Deputy Governor for Banking and the Stock Market, it was a body representing the private-sector banks. Despite the increase in government control and intervention in banking issues, no form of incompatibility rules were imposed on members of the Board to ensure that the decisions they took were in the national interest rather than in the interests of the representatives. In any event, the government always had the right to veto any decisions taken by the Board.

As regards the private-sector banks, the first control measure established by the new Law was the introduction of barriers to entry to the sector, ratifying a preceding provision from 1939, which would remain in force until 1962. Although there is nothing in the measure itself about its being temporary, the literature of the time spoke of it in terms of its being a "transitional" measure.[19] However, these barriers remained unaltered until 1962. This control over entry to the sector not only allowed the existing entities to consolidate their position, but also prevented foreign banks from establishing themselves in Spain.

Banking regulations, as well as preventing firms from freely entering the sector, established an additional series of measures directly affecting the conduct of their business. First of all, interest-rate controls were established, setting an upper limit on borrowing rates and a minimum for lending rates. Some of the interest rates on credit were also set.[20] It is worth noting that these levels were barely altered over the course of the period. This regulation had significant impacts, limiting the scope for competition and, above all, the incentives to compete, by making lending and credit an unattractive business for banks. This could be one of the factors explaining Spanish banks' high level of direct investment in industry. Bearing in mind that interest rates were regulated and that the government offered incentives for the financing of corporations it considered to be of "national interest",

---

[19]   Sáez de Ibarra 1954, pp.23-24.
[20]   For more on interest rates during this period, see Pons (2001a).

the rate of return on investments in the various sectors of the Spanish economy was totally distorted by regulation, a fact which undoubtedly affected Spanish banks' investment decisions.

Secondly, the LOB of 1946 established rules for the distribution of dividends. The legislation laid down that if the net profits obtained by an institution exceeded four percent of its capital plus reserves, at least 10 percent should be deducted and set aside for special reserves. These measures tried to make up for the lack of a series of ratios or standards to ensure a given level of reserves.

Thirdly, controls were established on the terms of assets and liabilities. Banks could not grant loans for terms of longer than 90 days. Although in practice these loans were continually rolled over, the absence of a long-term credit policy meant an increase in risk and made it difficult for Spanish to obtain finance. This problem was particularly acute among small and medium-sized businesses, which had less access to capital markets than large corporations.

Fourthly, the LOB of 1946 regulated the number of banks both by raising barriers to entry and controlling mergers. Although a considerable number of mergers took place in the 1940s and 1950s (there were over a hundred mergers between 1941 and 1970), there were none between large banks. Thus, the wave of mergers in Germany between the wars, Scotland in the fifties, or the UK as a whole in the 1960s, did not take place in Spain during Francoism. Likewise, there were controls on any expansion in the number of bank branches and offices.[21] The result was a structure of offices that was geographically highly concentrated, with most branches belonging to the national banks, and in particular to the big five, and the rate of growth of branches relative to the population was slower than in other developed countries such as Italy or the UK.

In the case of the saving banks, the regime sought to promote the expansion of these institutions that it considered essential in promoting savings. For this reason, the Confederation (CECA) was charged with undertaking a study of their extension across the country, establishing branches and agencies in all towns of more than 4,000 inhabitants, and setting up a service providing loans to farmers without physical deposit of collateral. However, the freedom to open branches, agencies and offices ended in 1946 with an Order by the Ministry of Labor that required the ministry's prior authorization to create branches, together with other rules regulating the savings banks' operations. Control over the savings banks' expansion therefore tightened, to the point that in 1949 the Ministry of Labor prohibited the savings banks from opening branches with a savings balance of less than ten million pesetas, only allowing them to open agencies. A Decree passed on 6 June 1947 established complex regulations that nevertheless gave them greater flexibility, in exchange for their ceding a large part of their control over their *Obra Social,* or charitable and welfare activities [Titos (1999)]. Between 25 and 50 percent of net profits had to be

---

[21]   The Decree of 17 May 1940 had prohibited the creation of new banks and bank offices. However, the Decree of 12 December 1942, amended by that of April 1945, established certain conditions under which offices could be opened.

devoted to reserves and the rest invested in social and charitable activities (85 percent in activities of their own choosing and the remainder through the common social welfare fund run by the Ministry of Labor which it invested in welfare work it considered to be of national interest).

This increase in regulation and the introduction of limits on the type of operations conducted also affected the stock market, which from 1940 onwards found any transactions other than those in cash to be excluded. This prohibition remained in force until 1988, again relegating the stock market to a marginal role. Levels of trading during the 1940s remained stable, thanks to the increase in public debt, as variable income, which in the twenties and thirties had accounted for more than 50 percent of total trading, dropped to levels below 30 percent and, in two years during the period, even to as little as 13 percent [Bolsa de Madrid (1994)]. As García Ruiz points out (1999), more than fifty years were to pass before the Spanish stock market was to develop "modern" operations. Only from the 1960s was the level of real effective business to recover its levels of the start of the century [Hoyo (2007)].

Although the Spanish economy began to make tentative steps towards opening up to the outside world in the 1950s, there were no significant changes in banking and finance. A few Decrees were published aimed at expanding on the provisions of the LOB of 1946. Thus, the Decree of 16 October 1950 approved the regulations on the functioning of the *Consejo Superior Bancario* (CSB). Changes in the rules governing the opening of banks and offices were also minimal. The Ministerial Order of 3 July 1952 on dividend payments perhaps stands out. This defined the effective reserves to be used in the calculation of dividend payments.

Realizing the funding possibilities the savings banks represented, the regime's authorities began to control them through investment coefficients. A Decree in 1951 laid down that 60 percent of savings banks' total deposited funds was to be invested in public debt, and that no less than three-quarters of these funds would be Spanish national floating or consolidated debt, or debt backed a government guarantee. The savings banks therefore became an important source of funding for the public investment projects the government decided to undertake.

From 1957 on, new reforms were passed (raising the discount rate, freezing the limits on banking rediscount, and a minor tax reform) intended to solve the most pressing economic problems the Spanish economy faced, such as inflation and the government's budget deficit. This same year, as already mentioned, the savings banks, which had been under the supervision of the Ministry of Labor, and previously under the Interior Ministry, came under the authority of the Finance Ministry. In 1958 the legal and tax framework for *Sociedades de Inversión Mobiliaria* (Non-Real Estate Investment Firms) and the Law of 26 December regulating the functioning of *Entidades de Crédito a Medio y Largo Plazo* (Medium- and Long-term Credit Institutions) were passed, with the aim of fostering long-term borrowing. However, there were no significant changes in the legal framework governing the financial system.

4.2   The 1962 Basic Law and subsequent implementing norms

In 1961 the authorities put forward a bill to reform the financial system, on which they solicited views from various bodies (the Banco de España, the *Confederación Nacional de Cajas de Ahorro* (CECA), the *Consejo Superior Bancario* (CSB), the *Consejo Superior de Cámaras de Comercio* or Higher Council of Chambers of Commerce, the *Organización Sindical* or Labor Union Organization, the *Instituto de Estudios Políticos* or Institute for Policy Studies, and the *Consejo de Economía Nacional* or National Economic Council). The *Ley de Bases de Ordenación del Crédito y la Banca,* or Basic Law on Credit and Banking Organization, drew upon the initial draft bill presented by the government and the reports submitted by the institutions consulted.

The Basic Law of 1962 highlighted the main problems faced by the Spanish banking system and defined the general lines along which change in the industry was to develop. The financial system suffered from four main defects. Firstly, although a number of attempts had been made, the Banco de España lacked sufficient power to be able to act as the regulatory authority for the credit system. Firstly, the problem of the mechanism for implementing monetary policy had yet to be resolved. Secondly, despite the laws passed since 1957, there was a severe shortage of medium- and long-term credit. This situation had encouraged an idiosyncratic funding system based on the continuous rolling over of loans with terms of not more than 90 days, but which 'de facto' constituted the usual form of longer-term finance.[22] Thirdly, the authorities took an unfavorable view of the relative weight of mixed banking in Spain and considered that this feature was crucial to explaining Spanish businesses' funding problems. Finally, the economic authorities expressed their concern about potential mismatch between the volume of accrued savings and the placement of these funds. The law opted for official intervention to guide these funds towards productive activities.

The authorities did not, therefore, back a market-based approach to the banking sector. Although the 1962 financial reform sought to re-establish market mechanisms in some fields, in others it stepped up the interventionist mechanisms. Thus, controls on interest rates remained in place, and the structure of interest rates remained unchanged between 1959 and 1969. The privileged funding channels were reinforced, thereby increasing the relative weight of the official banks and tightening controls over private-sector banks and savings banks [Poveda (1980)]. The Spanish banking system remained a closed system, under rigid protection and controlled by the country's big five banks.

The Basic Law of 1962 led to the nationalization of the Banco de España, with the multiple objectives of controlling money creation and facilitating the implementation of

---

[22]   The Treasury Ministry's memorandum on the banking and credit system [Ministerio de Hacienda (1961), pp.9-10] emphasizes the problems Spanish firms faced in obtaining funding and the responsibility of the legislation and government intervention in this state of affairs. In any event, the report pointed out that the lack of funding was not a result of discriminatory practices by the banking industry but of a lack of demand.

monetary policy. Financial activity was therefore regulated by three entities: the Banco de España, which was basically responsible for supervising private-sector banks; the *Instituto de Crédito a Medio y Largo plazo,* which controlled official credit; and the *Instituto de Crédito de las Cajas de Ahorros,* which supervised the savings banks.

The authorities' intention to revitalize the role of monetary policy was clear, and a number of measures to facilitate monetary control were introduced. A Decree-Law on 6 December 1962 established cash, liquidity and guarantee ratios, and stipulated mandatory deposits, in order both to enhance security and facilitate the design of monetary policy. In 1963 the liquidity ratio was officially set at 10 percent and the authorities increased it to 12 percent later that same year. It was subsequently raised again, to remain at 13 percent between 1965 and 1970. Moreover, in 1965 a complementary public debt ratio was set which began at 15 percent, although the authorities increased it annually, until it reached 22 percent in 1969. Finally, in 1960 the Finance Ministry was empowered, with advice from the Banco de España, to order private-sector banks to set aside special reserves in the form of cash or public debt, which would be set at around 10 percent of the value of their deposits. These reserves were to be held at the Banco de España. A Ministerial Order of 9 August 1974 established a minimum guarantee ratio for commercial banks, set at 8 percent of their paid-in capital and reserves, although the Banco de España was empowered to modify this ratio and set it to between 7 and 10 percent.

As regards the private-sector banks, the Basic Law of 1962 sought to encourage specialization among the banks by creating industrial and commercial banks. Thus, the Decree of 29 November 1962 laid down the rules for the process of specialization, and this was expanded upon by the Ministerial Orders of 21 and 31 May 1963 on the interim system applicable to banks intending to convert into industrial and commercial banks, and the Order of 13 December 1966, on the types of activities these banks were authorized to conduct. However, this attempt was not a great success and in 1974 the distinction between the different types of bank was abolished.

The Law also revealed the concern with limiting the influence of the large banks on other credit institutions and on business activity in general. However, the measures taken were not sufficiently effective and were unable restore competition to the sector, which was essential if the excessive power the authorities considered the largest banks to wield was to be limited. Moreover, the defense of the creation of industrial banks was contradictory, if the aim was to promote a type of financial institution that did not have a strong hold over the industrial sector.

One of the most significant aspects of the Basic Law was undoubtedly the greater control it imposed on the allocation of resources. Specifically, two types of measure were passed: those aimed at encouraging long-term finance and those intended to alter the market-based allocation of resources. The measures intended to lengthen the term for which finance could be granted allowed the banks to extend terms to 18 months, but required specific authorization to be obtained for longer-term transactions. Programs were designed for the privileged funding channels that were, by their nature, medium-to-long term. In relation to the allocation of financial resources, the necessary mechanisms were put in place for funds to be directed towards those activities considered to be priorities. In this area, the legislation expanding on the 1962 Basic Law was somewhat ambiguous. On the one hand, the preamble to the Law highlighted the poor operation of the Spanish capital market and the difficulties small and medium sized businesses had in obtaining funding, but on the other, the sectors identified as priorities were those in which large corporations predominated.

Up until the 1960s the privileges granted to firms considered to be priorities for the national interest were regulated by the Law of October 1939. Law 152/1963 replaced this concept with that of "industries of national interest." The purpose of this change was to replace support for specific firms with support for sectors so as to avoid the discriminatory effect the former type of incentive created. However, the government reserved the right to give preferential treatment to firms in a sector it considered to be of national interest, which meant that discretionary measures did not entirely end. In any event, what is clear is that the legislation did not restore market mechanisms, but was merely a reform of the National Interest Law.[23] Additionally, the Order of 13 December 1966 on the transactions industrial and commercial banks were authorized to perform defined the priority sectors to be capital goods (which continued to receive support under the orders of 16 September 1967 and 18 December 1969), the export sector, and shipbuilding. These sectors basically comprised large corporations, which meant that the problem of financing small and medium-sized businesses, which had been one of the Law's rationales, remained unresolved.

Thus, during the 1970s the measures aimed at encouraging the financing of certain sectors showed the orientation of the legal framework to be less deregulatory than the 1962 Basic Law had suggested. As Poveda (1980) points out, while in the early 1970s privileged funding accounted for 35 percent of total resources in the credit system, in the late 1960s this had been 45 percent. Only between 1969 and 1973 did the Francoist authorities reduce the weight of privileged funding channels. Even so, in 1979 sector-specific intervention affected 37.7 percent of the resources channeled through the credit system [Poveda (1980), p.117]. To sum up, interventionism and the role of official credit hindered the increasing competition in the financial sector that was necessary to put an end to the advantages that the Law acknowledged the banks had obtained from the *status quo*.

These interventionist measures continued to be highly significant through the early 1960s. Thus, for example, the Order of 24 March 1972 established a regime for a consortium between the Official Credit Institute and private-sector banks to finance shipbuilding for the domestic market, and Decree 670 of 7 March 1974 and the Order of 21 March of the same year headed in the same direction. Similarly, the Order of 31 January 1973 updated Decree 715 of 1964, according to which these institutions were to devote a percentage of their depos-

---

[23]   The incorporation of "concerted actions" reinforced this process. When a firm bound itself to a concerted plan of action, it undertook to achieve a given level of production and productivity, and in exchange received aid in the form of tax exemptions and financial support. In short, this was simply another means of reinforcing the interventionism typical of Franco's regime.

its, set by the Treasury Ministry, to certain specific purposes. Although this order recognized the need to adapt the ratios to the prevailing economic conditions, it nevertheless imposed strict limits on financial institutions.

The Basic Law of 1962 did not introduce any significant changes in terms of interest rate controls, although from this point onwards the caps on interest rates set by the Law were minimal. To give an idea of the lack of modulation of interest rates as a function of the changing economic climate, suffice it to say that the interest rate on deposits with a term of more than a year remained unchanged at 3 percent from 1938 to 1964. At the end of this year it rose by one point and then rose again to 4.5 percent in 1969.

Changes in the Banco de España's basic interest rate were more frequent in the 1960s. However, the Basic Law of 1962 and later provisions left one of the fundamental elements of the banking system out of the deregulation process. Despite this fact, it is worth highlighting that in the 1970s an effort was made to bring interest rates closer to the market. For instance, in 1969 there was liberalization of the interest rates on lending for terms of over three years and on deposits with terms of over two years, and of the interest rates applied by various types of credit institution.

One of the most significant measures in the 1962 Banking Law was the easing of the sector's barriers to entry. The Law therefore promised the use of simpler criteria when deciding whether to authorize the creation of new institutions or allowing banks to expand their network of offices. Nevertheless, there were no substantial changes. The results of this moderate relaxation of the barriers to entry were also limited. The number of banks rose from 109 in 1962 to 125 in 1965, and then fell back to 111 in 1969 and 105 in 1972. This initial increase in the number of banks was the result of the creation of 15 industrial banks. However, 10 of them were tied to existing commercial banks which were trying to comply with the provisions of the legislation as regards specialization. In any event, the percentage of loans and deposits held by these banks was not significant, which highlights the limited impact this piece of legislation had in real terms.

The Basic Law of 1962 had a big impact on the number of bank offices. The total number of offices rose considerably, particularly after 1963. Decree 2245 of 9 August 1974 gave banks the freedom to open new branches, the only restriction being a requirement for each new branch to have a certain minimum level of resources. The outcome was a spectacular rise in the number of branches, particularly in the case of regional and local banks. The Basic Law of 1962 therefore changed the trend that had persisted throughout the 1950s, whereby national banks had increased their numbers of branches to a much greater extent than regional and local ones.

The 1962 Basic Law was also applicable to the savings banks, which remained under the supervision of the *Instituto de Crédito de las Cajas de Ahorro*. The Basic Law of 1962 and subsequent legislative instruments had a major influence on banking diversity, particularly as a result of the changes introduced in the legislation affecting savings banks. As noted above, one of the hallmarks of the Spanish financial system under Francoism was its scant diversification, with the result that the banks very much overshadowed all the other types of financial institution. The only non-bank financial intermediaries that had acquired any scale were the savings banks, which were institutions strongly rooted in the business of attracting savings from the working classes. However, the legislation clearly discriminated against the savings banks as the government controlled a large share of their resources. The 1962 Basic Law narrowed the gap in the legislation on the banks and savings banks but did not close it altogether. Thus, for example, the savings banks were obliged to maintain a large proportion of their deposits in government bonds and bonds issued by corporations considered to be of "national interest."[24] Commercial and business banks also had to keep a share of their deposits in the form of public debt and were obliged to invest part of these resources in certain forms of medium- and long-term credit. However, the measure clearly harmed the savings banks, which again shows that the 1962 Basic Law's intention to liberalize the market was somewhat half-hearted.

The 1962 Basic Law allowed the savings banks to expand their range of activities, and in particular, their lending, which meant an increase in their share of the total financial market. Even so, as just mentioned, the savings banks' lending activities were closely tied to the government's programs. This rigid regulation prevented the banks and savings banks from developing in a competitive market. The savings banks focused on small savers, and the main tool they used to attract deposits was to open more branches. This led to a situation in the 1960s where the savings banks had more branches than the banks, although their volume of deposits was smaller. Although the differences between the banks and savings banks in terms of banking ratios and other requirements narrowed considerably in the 1970s, they were not entirely eliminated, and remained particularly restrictive in the case of lending. The outcome was that the Spanish financial system diversified less than that in more developed European countries.

Finally, the failure of the securities market regulations, such that stock markets failed to establish themselves an essential funding mechanism for Spanish businesses [López Roa (1981)], also stands out. In 1956 almost 60 percent of issues were public debt and only from 1959 onwards did the share of private issues increase, such that public issues represented 38 percent in 1959.[25] In fact, the 1962 Basic Law hardly devoted any attention to the securities markets at all. In 1964 a Decree-Law was passed in which the government continued to reserve the right to create official stock exchanges, and that the Finance Ministry could authorize small exchanges to be set up in those localities where the volume of trading justified their existence. This Decree created the *Consejo Superior de Bolsas* (Stock Market

---

[24]   In 1962 the savings banks' portfolio of public debt accounted for almost half of their borrowings. An order passed in August 1962 set the share of the increase in deposits that was to be devoted to public debt at 60 percent. However, as this proportion exceeded the available public debt issues, securities issued by industrial corporations classed as eligible by the Finance Ministry were also allowed. In 1964 a Decree on 26 March and a Ministerial Order on 20 August set the investment ratios applicable to the savings banks. In the end, the savings banks obligatory finance, which in 1962 came to 60.8 percent of borrowings –50 percent public debt and 11 percent industrial securities and special loans– reached 75.8 percent in 1969 [Poveda (1980), p.124].

[25]   Sardá (1964), p.358.

Council) as the body representing the exchanges, being responsible for coordinating stock exchanges and acting as a consultative body on those issues over which it had authority. The Decree regulated the differentiation between simple price quotations and qualified price quotations and allowed forward transactions for securities with qualified quotations, maintaining the prohibition on this type of transaction imposed by the 1940 regulation for other securities. Finally, the Decree delegated to the government the setting a quota for the number of active stockbrokers and entrusted the Finance Ministry with preparing the general securities market regulations, which were approved in 1967. These regulations were both broad and detailed, dealing with transactions, intermediaries, etc. The entry of foreign capital, which took place in the 1960s partly focused on the purchasing of stock, explains the stock market's expansion during the decade, although it remained insufficient [Sardá (1964)]. The main inference is, therefore, that the legislation under Francoism impoverished stock market activity and led to the configuration of a capital market that remained narrow until the 1970s [García Ruiz (1999), p. 200]. The Ministerial Order of 4 August 1977 proposed the creation of a Stock Market Study Commission. The report this produced proposed far-reaching changes in order to enable this institution to perform its role in the economy [Moreno Castaño (2006)]. Nevertheless, the 1967 regulation was kept in place until the 1980s and it was in 1988 that the Stock Market Law was passed [Moral (1997)].

5 Concluding remarks

The legislative framework governing the Spanish financial system changed substantially over the course of the 20th century. The first changes took place in the 19th century, with the 1848 Corporations Law, followed by the Issuing Banks Law and the Credit Companies Law in 1856. In the case of the savings banks, the main legislation was passed in 1880, in which the government showed its clear intention to promote the growth of savings institutions of this kind.

This set of laws sought to organize the expansion of a financial system that up until very late in the 19th century was somewhat underdeveloped.

The economic and financial problems arising in Spain in the wake of the First World War led to the Banking Law's being passed in 1921. This aimed to put in place a definitive set of regulations for the banking sector and gradually turn the Banco de España into a genuine central bank. Some of the characteristic features of the Spanish financial system began to emerge in this period: a lack of diversification; a preponderance of the banks, basically in the form of mixed banks; a relatively high degree of concentration in the sector; and a weak stock market.

After the Civil War Spain's financial legislation became more interventionist. The Banking Law of 1946 set up barriers to entry to the sector, controlled expansion by limiting the opening of new branches, setting interest rates, and defining the terms of and lending and borrowing. Thus the existing features of the system became even more pronounced. Thanks to the maintenance of the *status quo,* the banks became the leading financial intermediaries, with an increase in the concentration of the banking business up until the early 1950s. The Francoist authorities used the banking system as a tool with which to finance their industrialization policy and increased their level of control over the resources available in the financial system, drawing upon both the banks and the savings banks, but on the latter in particular. In exchange, the legislation limited the level of competition in the sector, particularly favoring the private-sector banks.

In 1962, the legislation changed course with the passing of the Basic Banking Law. In theory, this Law was intended to initiate a process of gradual liberalization of the financial sector. However, the reality was more complex. The government had no intention of giving up its *dirigisme,* but the economic and social system obliged it to introduce certain reforms. For this reason, the process of liberalization was beset with numerous contradictions. Thus, alongside a number of measures to open up the system, other provisions were applied that maintained or reinforced state interventionism (interest-rate control, establishing "privileged financing circuits," etc.). This slow liberalization held back the modernization of the financial system. In any event, over the course of the 1960s and in the early 1970s, legislative modifications were introduced which opened the way for the subsequent modernization of the financial system, which began to arrive in the 1980s. These were to gradually reduce the discrimination against the savings banks, allow the expansion of the branch network, and deregulate interest rates.

The legislative changes taking place in the Spanish financial system between 1900 and 1975 need to be viewed in the international – and particular European – context. Was Spain's financial legislation during much of the 20th century more interventionist than in other countries? This question is difficult to answer as there is no single European "legislative model." However, it can safely be said that Spanish legislation was not particularly unique. In broad terms, the legal framework governing the Spanish financial system was not substantially different from that in Italy, were a Banking Law extensively regulating the sector was passed in 1926. As with the 1921 Banking Law in Spain, this Law ended a period of freedom to enter the sector and, subsequently, setting up a new bank or branch required alicense. The same was true of mergers and acquisitions. The Law also established minimum capital and reserve requirements and controls on lending activities, limiting the volume of credit an individual customer could receive [Gigliobianco, Giordano and Toniolo (2009)]. The fundamental differences between the Spanish and Italian financial systems at the time lay in the fact that, whereas in Spain the system was relatively concentrated, in Italy there was a large number of financial institutions and one of the aims of the 1926 legislation was precisely to encourage consolidation (Alhadeff 1968). The *Convenzioni* in 1934 and the 1936 Banking Law reformed this legislation by introducing mechanisms intended to ensure the stability of the financial system. As Gigliobianco, Giordano and Toniolo (2009) have pointed out, the Law favored stability at the expense of competition by establishing controls on interest rates and regulating any instruments that might facilitate free competition. The Law also had clear objectives regarding the assignment of resources. Credit control became an important tool with which the government could reassign resources to those sectors it considered priorities. It was not until the 1970s that Italy embarked on a process of deregulating its financial system. Thus, aspects such as the existence of barriers to entry, limits to the expansion of banking offices, or interest-rate controls, are common traits to both the Spanish [Pons (2001a)] and Italian [Alhadeff (1968)] banking systems.

In Spain and Italy regulation was reinforced by agreements between institutions governing the terms under which they conducted asset and liability transactions. The 1936 Italian Banking Law, conscious of the limitations imposed by the barriers to entry, put the power of the State behind the banking cartel. This cartel had emerged voluntarily in 1929, strengthening the ties between institutions with the signing in 1954 of an interbank agreement between the banks that held 98 percent of all deposits. This agreement, as Alhadeff points out (1968), although not given official status by the Italian monetary authorities, nevertheless received their tacit acceptance. In Spain, although there is no evidence of there having been a formal cartel, there were ad hoc agreements to set some of the terms on which banks would compete [Pons (2001a)]. Formal agreements were rare or non-existent, and links were established informally through cooperation agreements or through directors who sat on the boards of several banks.

A number of common features with the French case are also evident. In France, the most important legislative instrument was the 1941 Banking Law. This legislation had a number of similarities with the Spanish LOB of 1921. In both cases the legislation increased the power of the banks controlling the sector, resulting in a situation which could be described as self regulation. The 1945 Banking Law altered this by increasing the French government's influence over the banking sector. Thus, the *Conseil National du Crédit* established the general outlines of lending policy, regulated entry to the sector, approve mergers, interest rates – setting a maximum interest rate for savings deposits, and a minimum for loans – etc. In France, the process of reform began in 1964 and the aim was basically for banks to become more effective tools for the government's planning policy. However, at the same time, free competition was restored in some areas (minimum interest rates on loans, and restrictions on the term of deposits, etc. were lifted). In any event, generally speaking, although the degree of legislative intervention in the French financial system was relatively high, banking activities were less constrained by legislation in France than in Spain.

The legislative framework with which the biggest differences existed was Britain's. By contrast to the wide-ranging and detailed legislation governing the French and Italian financial systems, Britain maintained a non-interventionist approach. Like the French banking system, that in Britain was highly concentrated, and the eleven London clearing banks controlled almost 90 percent of deposits. These institutions basically formed a cartel which laid down the basic lines of action in the sector. However, formal agreements were rare, basically dealing only with interest rates on deposits. Agreements of this type also arose in other European countries, although in some cases, such as Italy or Finland [Tarkka (2009)], the agreements took place under the supervision of the State.

To sum up, the increase in interventionism seen in the Spanish financial system from the turn of the century onwards, and which was stepped up after the Civil War, was not an isolated phenomenon. Financial legislation – particularly concerning the banks – in other European countries, such as Italy and France, also intensified the controls over the sector. This does not mean that there were no significant differences. One of the biggest was the more limited diversification of the Spanish financial system, accentuated by legislation which clearly discriminated against non-bank financial intermediaries, giving the banks a degree of market power that was greater even than that which these institutions enjoyed in countries with a more concentrated banking system. Although in Spain the only non-bank financial intermediaries of note were the savings banks, which the legislation limited to certain types of operations, in Great Britain, for example, the options for deposits were much wider, including building societies (thrifts), trade unions, friendly societies, etc. As well as giving the Spanish banks greater market power, this lack of diversification also had important long-term consequences, as in some cases the modernizing drive in the financial sector came precisely from the non-bank entities [Collins (1990)].

Another difference was the influence of legislation on Spanish banks' balance-sheet structure and the implications this had for corporate finance. The legal restrictions imposed after the Civil War basically favored short-term lending. Although in practice the banks tried to sidestep the legal limits, and short-term loans were rolled over to become longer-term transactions [Prados Arrarte (1958)], financial conditions of this type led to a high degree of instability in Spanish business in comparison with other countries, such as Italy or Germany, where the percentage of longer-term lending to fund business ventures was higher [Martín Aceña and Pons (1994)]. This was all the more important given that the ability of Spanish firms to access the capital markets was more limited than in most industrialized countries. This form of borrowing made businesses highly dependent on the banks, not only for their investment projects, but their day-to-day operations could depend on whether the loans granted were rolled over or not [Pons (2001b)].

Finally, two particularly complex topics are the level of intervention of the State in the lending mediated by the financial system, with the aim of allocating resources, and the role of financial legislation in the activities of central banks and the implementation of monetary policy. There was clearly more State intervention to manipulate the allocation of resources in Spain than in other countries. In Italy and in Britain the government might offer suggestions or guidelines on credit policy, but stopped short of laying down specific rules modifying how lending was allocated. Even in France, where as well as indirect interventions (via recommendations) direct interventions also took place, the priorities were only ever set at the sector level and never, for example, at that of individual companies.

As regards legislation's influence on the configuration of the Banco de España as a true central bank and on the implementation of monetary policy, the Banco de España was probably more beholden to government's interests than were its counterparts in other countries. Indeed, many authors have noted that from the end of the Civil War through to

1959 there was no monetary policy of any kind in Spain.[26] Nevertheless, this situation was not so different from that encountered in other European countries. After the Second World War, and during the post-war reconstruction, most European governments adopted measures to ward off a possible depression, giving it priority over the fight against inflation. For example, as Collins (1990) observes, the way in which the British government sought to achieve economic recovery, through controls and increased public-sector intervention in the economy, meant that monetary policy did not play a significant role during this period. Moreover, the predominance of Keynesian ideas during this period should not be ignored, as they made fiscal policy the main instrument used by various governments, taking precedence over controlling the money supply.

Nevertheless, there were also clear differences between Spain and other European countries in the strictly monetary field. The first was the indiscriminate use of inflationary State financing instruments (issues of money or debt which could automatically be used as collateral), which led to a faster rate of money-supply growth than in most other countries. For comparison, in the United Kingdom, between 1940 and 1958 the money supply grew by 5.8 percent, whereas in Spain it grew by 11.3 percent, despite the fact that this period includes five years of world war.[27] In Italy the 1940s were also characterized by a period of runaway inflation, forcing the government to adopt measures to moderate price rises in 1947. However, in this case the inflationary process ran in parallel with strong economic expansion and the government was able to control prices without driving the economy into recession [Catalán (1992)].

The second difference was the length of time that monetary policy remained in the background. In the British case, the election of a Conservative government in 1951 meant a significant change in how monetary policy was used, although the role given to monetary instruments was still not a very active one. By contrast, throughout the fifties Spain remained without clear inflation-control mechanisms, although the 1957 reform and the 1959 Stabilization Plan sought to move in that direction.

To conclude, the increase in interventionism that began to be apparent in Spain's financial legislation from 1921 and which was accentuated after the Civil War, responded in part to the trend seen in other countries such as France or Italy. However, the use the Francoist regime made of the legal framework to promote its industrialization program gave the financial system certain peculiar features which undoubtedly influenced the ability of Spanish firms to obtain funding and caused serious financial imbalances, such as high rates of inflation, in particular.

---

[26]   Poveda (1981, p.43), Fanjul, Fernández and Rodríguez (1987, p.21), or Rojo (1963, p.48).

[27]   After 1945 the growth in money supply in the United Kingdom was more moderate. Thus between 1945 and 1950 the growth rate was 3.97 percent, dropping to 1.93 percent between 1950 and 1955 and 1.66 percent between 1955 and 1958.

References

ALHADEFF, D. A. (1968). *Competition and controls in banking, a study of the regulation of bank competition in Italy, France and England,* University of California, Los Angeles.

BALTENSPERGER, E. (1990). "The Economic Theory of Banking Regulation", in E. G. Furubotn and R. Richer, *The economics and law of banking regulation,* Center for the study of the New Institutional Economics, Universität des Saarlands, pp. 1-21.

BALTERNSPERGEN, E., and J. DERMINE (1990). "European Banking: Prudential and Regulatory Issues", in J. Dermine (Ed.),*European Banking in the 1990s,* Blackwell Publishers, Oxford, pp. 17-41.

BANCO DE ESPAÑA (1941). *Informe sobre el balance de diciembre de 1941 y régimen de desbloqueos,* Informe D-6824.

— (1960). *Informe del comité director del acuerdo monetario europeo sobre la ejecución del programa de estabilización,* Informe D-1191.

BOLSA DE MADRID (1994). "Una visión cifrada de la historia de la Bolsa", *Revista Bolsa de Madrid,* no. 25, pp. 4-22.

CASARES, A. (1962). "Consideraciones sobre el sistema bancario español y la nacionalización del Banco de España", *Seminario central de política económica,* Madrid.

CATALÁN, J. (1992). "Reconstrucción, política económica y desarrollo industrial: tres economías del sur de Europa, 1944-1953", in L. Prados de la Escosura and V. Zamagni (Eds.), *El desarrollo económico en la europa del sur: España e Italia en perspectiva histórica,* Alianza Editorial, Madrid.

COLLINS, M. (1990). *Money and banking in the uk: a history,* Routledge, London.

COMIN, F. (2008). *Historia de la cooperación entre las cajas de ahorros. La confederación española de cajas de ahorros,* 1928-2003, CECA, Madrid.

FANJUL MARTÍN, E., D. FERNÁNDEZ NAVARRETE and G. RODRÍGUEZ PRADA (1987). "La política monetaria española (1940-1978)", *Monografías del instituto de estudios fiscales,* no. 7.

FAUS, E. M. (2001). *Regulación y desregulación. Notas para la historia de la banca española,* Ed. Península, Barcelona.

FERNÁNDEZ, V. (1975). "La deuda pública", in *Datos básicos para la historia financiera de españa,* IEF, Madrid.

GARCÍA RUIZ, J. L. (1999). "Otras instituciones de crédito", in P. Martín-Aceña and M. Titos Martínez (Eds.), *El sistema financiero en españa,* Universidad de Granada, Granada, pp. 183-202.

GIGLIOBIANCO, A., C. GIORDANO and G. TONIOLO (2009). "Innovation and Regulation in the Wake of Financial Crises in Italy (1880s-1930s)", in A. Gigliobianco and G. Toniolo (Eds.), *Financial market regulation in the wake of financial crises: the historical experience,* no. 1, Seminari, Convegni, Workshops and Conferences, Banca de Italia. November, pp. 45-74.

GOWLAND, D. (1990). *The regulation of financial markets in the 1990s,* Edward Elgard, Worcester.

HOYO, A. (2007). *Economía y mercado de valores en la españa contemporánea: la evolución de la bolsa antes del big bang español,* 1831-1988, Servicio de Publicaciones de la Universidad de Cantabria, Santander.

LAWRENCE, C. (1989). "Banking Costs generalized functional forms and estimations of economies of scale and scope", *Journal of money, credit and banking,* pp. 368-379.

LÓPEZ ROA, A. (1981). *Sistema financiero español,* Nueva Generación de Editores, Alicante.

MAIXÉ, J. C. (2003). *El ahorro de los gallegos. Orígenes e historia de Caixa Galicia* (1876-2002), Fundación Caixa Galicia, La Coruña.

MARTÍN-ACEÑA, P. (1984). *La política monetaria en España, 1919-1935,* Instituto de Estudios Fiscales, Ministerio de Economía y Hacienda, Madrid.

— (1985). "Desarrollo y modernización del sistema financiero, 1844-1935", in N. Sánchez Albornoz (Compiler), *La modernización económica de España 1830-1930,* Alianza Editorial, Madrid, pp. 121-146.

— (1991). *Los problemas monetarios al término de la guerra civil,* Papeles de trabajo de Historia contemporánea, Instituto Universitario Ortega y Gasset, Madrid.

— (2001). "El Banco de España entre dos siglos: de banquero del Estado a prestamista en última instancia", *Las claves de la españa del siglo XX. Las transformaciones económicas,* Sociedad Estatal España Nuevo Milenio, Madrid.

— (2006). "El sistema financiero", in P. Martín-Aceña and E. Martínez Ruiz, *La economía de la guerra civil,* Marcial Pons, Madrid.

MARTÍN-ACEÑA, P., and M. A. PONS (1994). "Spanish banking after the Civil War, 1940-1962", *Financial History Review,* Vol. 1, Issue 2, pp. 121-138.

MARTORELL, M. (2006). "Una guerra, dos pesetas", in P. Martín-Aceña and E. Martínez Ruiz, *La economía de la guerra civil,* Marcial Pons, Madrid.

MINISTERIO DE HACIENDA (1961). *Informe del banco de españa, consejo superior de cámaras de comercio, industria y navegación, consejo superior bancario, organización sindical, instituto de estudios políticos, ceca, consejo de economía nacional, sobre el memorándum del ministerio de hacienda sobre el sistema bancario y crediticio,* Ministerio de Hacienda, Madrid.

MORAL, C. (1997). "La segunda reforma bursátil en España. Hacia un mercado único de valores", *Cuadernos de estudios empresariales,* no. 7, pp. 255-272.

MORENO CASTAÑO, B. (2006). *La bolsa de Madrid. Historia de un mercado de valores europeo,* Universidad de Cantabria, Santander.

MUÑOZ, J. (1978). "La expansión bancaria entre 1916 y 1926: La formación de una banca nacional", *Cuadernos de información comercial Española,* no. 6, pp. 98-162.

OLARIAGA, L. (1933). *La política monetaria en españa en 1977,* reprinted by Servicio de Estudios de la Banca Mas Sardá.

PALAFOX, J. (1991). *Atraso económico y democracia. La segunda república y la economía española, 1892-1936,* Ed. Crítica, Barcelona.

PARIS EGUILAZ, H. (1945). "Sobre algunos problemas de la Ley de Desbloqueos", *Moneda y crédito,* p. 31.

PÉREZ DE ARMIÑÁN, G. (1980). *Legislación bancaria española,* Banco de España, Madrid.

PONS, M. A. (1999). "La legislación bancaria española, 1850-1960", in P. Martín-Aceña and M. Titos Martínez (Eds.), *El sistema financiero en España,* Universidad de Granada, Granada, pp. 35-51.

— (2001a). "Oligopolio y tipos de interés en la banca española, 1942-1975", *REVISTA DE HISTORIA ECONÓMICA,* no. 3, pp. 679- 703.

— (2001b). "La evolución del sistema bancario español en el siglo XX. Una perspectiva comparada", *Estudis d'historia económica,* no. 17-18, pp. 177-212.

— (2002). *Regulating Spanish Banking, 1939-1975,* Aldershot, Ashgate.

POVEDA, R. (1980). "Circuitos privilegiados de financiación del sistema crediticio", *Papeles de economía española,* no. 3, pp. 114-135.

— (1981). "Funcionamiento del mercado financiero español", *PAPELES DE ECONOMÍA,* no. 9, pp. 42-67.

PRADOS ARRARTE, J. (1958). *El sistema bancario español,* Aguilar, Madrid.

PUEYO, J. (2003). *Las condiciones de la competencia en la banca española, 1921-1974: colusión, regulación y rivalidad,* Tesis doctoral, Universidad de Barcelona.

RIDRUEJO, E. (1954). "El sistema bancario español", *Moneda y crédito,* no. 51, pp. 149-216.

ROJO CAGIGAL, J. C. (2008). *Choosing a legal framework for spanish stock markets, 1800-1936,* Working Papers in Economic History, WP 08-03, Universidad Carlos III de Madrid.

ROJO, L. A. (1963). "La política monetaria", in E. Fuentes Quintana (Ed.), "El desarrollo económico de España", *Revista de occidente,* Madrid.

ROLDÁN, S., J. L. GARCÍA DELGADO and J. MUÑOZ (1973). *La formación de la sociedad capitalista en españa,* Confederación de Cajas de Ahorros, Madrid.

SÁEZ DE IBARRA, L. (1954). "La regulación de la banca en España", *Moneda y crédito,* no. 51.

SÁNCHEZ ASIAÍN, R. (1999). *La banca española en la guerra civil,* 1936-1939, Real Academia de la Historia, Madrid.

SARDÀ, J. (1959). "Aspectos monetarios de la estabilización", reedited in R. Ortega (Ed.), *Escritos (1948-1980), Juan Sardà Dexeus,* Banco de España, Madrid, pp. 375-388.

— (1964). "El sistema financiero español", *Boletín de estudios económicos,* Vol. 19, no. 62, May-August, pp. 349-362.

— (1970). *El Banco de España, una historia económica,* Banco de España, Madrid.

TARKKA, J. (2009). "Financial regulation in finland from the 1950s until the 1980s: stability at what price?", in A. Gigliobianco and G. Toniolo (Eds.), *Financial market regulation in the wake of financial crises: the historical experience,* Seminari, Convegni, Workshops and Conferences, no. 1, November, Banca de Italia, pp. 75-94.

TITOS, M. (1999). "Las Cajas de Ahorros, 1853-1962", in P. Martín-Aceña and M. Titos Martínez (Eds.), *El sistema financiero en España,* Universidad de Granada, Granada.

TORTELLA, G. (1970). "La evolución del sistema financiero español de 1856-1868", in P. Schwartz (Coord.), *Ensayos sobre la economía Española a mediados del siglo XIX,* Servicio de Estudios, Banco de España, Madrid.

— (1999). *El desarrollo de la españa contemporánea. Historia económica de los siglo XIX y XX,* Alianza Editorial, Madrid.

TORTELLA, G., and J. PALAFOX (1984). "Banking and industry in Spain, 1918-1936", *The journal of european economic history,* Vol. 13, no. 2, pp. 81-111.

VIÑAS, A. (1976). *El oro español en la guerra civil,* Instituto de Estudios Fiscales, Madrid.

VIVES, X. (1988). "Concentración bancaria y competitividad", *Papeles de economía española,* pp. 62-76.

4. The Spanish banking system from 1900 to 1975

Pablo Martín-Aceña
Universidad de Alcalá

1 The Spanish banking system prior to 1900[1]

The history of the modern Spanish banking system began in 1856 when the Cortes (parliament) passed the Issuing Banks Law and the Credit Companies Law. The first of these Laws enshrined the principle of plurality of issuance and, at the same time, renamed the Banco Español de San Fernando the Banco de España, the name it has retained to the present day. A significant number of establishments were founded under the aegis of the Issuing Banks Law. By 1866 the number of banks had thus risen from three (the Banco Español de San Fernando, the Banco de Barcelona and the Banco de Cádiz) to 21. The second of the two Laws, the Credit Companies Law, led to the creation of a series of institutions authorized to conduct a wide range of activities, from bill discounting and trade credit, through to long-term lending and investments in company shares and bonds. In Madrid, the Sociedad de Crédito Mobiliario Español, the Sociedad Española Mercantil e Industrial and the Compañía General de Crédito, were founded, each with a portion of French capital. These were not the only banks to be created, as investment banks also sprang up in all of

---

[1]   The origins and early stages of the Spanish banking system are described in Canosa (1945), Martín-Aceña (1985 and 2005), and the articles included in Martín-Aceña and Titos (1999), Tedde (1974, 2001) and Tortella (1970).

Spain's regions. Businessmen were particularly active in Catalonia and Valencia, and it was there that three of the most significant establishments emerged: the Sociedad Catalana General de Crédito, the Crédito Barcelonés and the Sociedad Valenciana de Fomento.

The list of the 35 banks existing in 1899 is shown in Table 1. The cities with the most were Madrid, Barcelona, and lagging somewhat behind, Bilbao. The list reveals clearly how few of these institutions have survived to the present day. Some of them were wound up as a result of one or other of the successive crises that occurred and vanished without trace; others merged or were taken over by larger institutions. Thus, of the 34 (excluding the Banco de España), only three remain in existence today: those of Bilbao (today BBVA), Santander and Sabadell.

In addition to the banks established as corporations, and the savings banks, studied in another chapter of this book, at the end of the 19th century there was also a class of banker-tradesmen who had provided exchange, current account and security deposit functions since the 18th century.[2] The size and composition of this group is difficult to determine precisely. The figure could have reached 150 towards 1874 and 239 in 1900, when their number peaked. Most operated in Madrid and Barcelona. The presence of foreign banks was minimal, with just three foreign-owned institutions operating in Spain: The Banco Hispano-Alemán, Crédit Lyonnais and the Union Bank of Spain and England. These were small and their business was at the mercy of the volatility of the Spanish currency, particularly in the later years, which prevented them growing and carving out a niche for themselves in what was at the time a competitive financial system.[3]

Although at the end of the 19th century the business of the banks, savings banks, credit unions and private bankers had clearly taken off, their level of development and modernization still lagged a long way behind that of Europe's leaders. With little regulation, as the legislation did not impose restrictions on the activities of credit institutions, they had nevertheless been unable to go beyond being relatively simple non-specialist deposit-takers. According to Raymond Goldsmith's "Financial Intermediation Ratio," which is defined as the ratio between total assets issued by financial institutions and the market value of national wealth, the degree of development of the structure of the Spanish banking system in 1900 was well below the European average, with a figure of 39 compared to the average of 104. If we agree with Goldsmith that an intermediation coefficient of 100 is indicative of a country with an advanced financial sector which has reached a satisfactory – although not optimal – level of intermediation, Spain was clearly a long way short of this threshold at the end of the 19th century.[4]

---

[2]   For more on this segment of the financial system, see García López (1985 and 1989); and also Titos (1999).

[3]   Tedde (1974), pp. 332 and 333

[4]   For the calculation of the financial intermediation ratio for Spain and a comparison with other countries, see Martín-Aceña (1985), pp. 134-139.

TABLE 1	CENSUS OF BANKS IN 1899

Institution	Year Founded
Banco de España	1782
Banco Hipotecario	1873
Banco de Crédito Zaragozano	
Banco de Barcelona	1844
Crédito Navarro (Pamplona)	1864
Crédito Mercantil de Barcelona	1864
Banco de Reus	1863
Banco de Bilbao	1857
Banco de Santander	1857
Sociedad Catalana General de Crédito (Barcelona)	1856
Crédito Mobiliario Español (Madrid)	1856
Banco de Castilla (Madrid)	
Crédito Balear	1864
Crédito Gallego	
Banco Hispano Colonial (Barcelona)	1877
Banco de Préstamos y Descuentos (Barcelona)	1881
Banco de Villanueva (Villanueva y Geltrú)	1881
Banco de Tortosa	1881
Banco de Manresa	1881
Banco de Valls	1882
Banco de Tarrasa	1882
Banco de Sabadell	1882
Banco de Felanitx	1883
Crédito y Docks de Barcelona	1883
Crédito de Fomento de Gracia (Barcelona)	1883
Banco de Ciudadela	1887
Crédito Felaginense	1888
Banco de Sóller	1889
Crédito Industrial y Mercantil (Ciudadela)	1890
Banco del Comercio (Bilbao)	1891
Fomento Agrícola, Industrial y Comercial (Lluchmayor)	1893
Sociedad Anónima de Crédito y Ahorro (Barcelona)	1894
Fomento Agrícola de Mallorca (Palma)	1895
Banco Agrícola de San Isidro (Madrid)	1899
Banco Asturiano	1899

SOURCES : Tedde (1974), vol. II, pp. 221-223 and Faus (2001), pp. 383-387.

2   Expansion and consolidation, 1900-1919

2.1   The blossoming of the financial system at the turn of the century[5]

The most important phenomenon in the banking sector during the early years of the 20th century was the opening of numerous entities across the country, some of them with sub-

---

[5]   Tedde (1974), Chap. IV, pp. 374-455); BBVA (2003 and 2004); Canosa (1944), remains a valuable source.

stantial equity capital. Between 1900 and 1914 around fifty banks were created, although many of them were the outcome of the transformation of old commercial houses and the conversion of some well-known banking firms into corporations.

One of the larger institutions, the Banco Español de Crédito (1902), was the product of the reorganization of Crédito Mobiliario. Another emblematic institution was Banco Hispano Americano (1901), which was created as an investment venture by a group of Spanish businessmen based in the Americas who had brought their capital back to Spain. In the Basque Country, which had the peninsula's most dynamic regional economy, the banking system was transformed dramatically: alongside the venerable Banco de Bilbao firms as significant as Banco de Vizcaya (1901), Crédito de la Unión Minera (1901) and Banco Guipuzcoano (1900) emerged; other banks created in the Basque Country during this period included the Banco de Vitoria (1900), the Banco de San Sebastián (1909), the Banco de Tolosa (1911) and the Banco de Comercio (1900). Mighty new institutions also sprang up in various cities on the Cantabrian coast: in Santander, the Banco Mercantil (1899) and the Crédito Industrial y Comercial (1899), which merged in 1900; in Asturias, the Banco Asturiano de Comercio (1899), the Banco de Gijón (1899), the Crédito Industrial Gijonés (1900) and the Banco Herrero (1911); and in Galicia, which had less of a banking tradition, the Banco de Vigo was founded in 1900. Fewer new institutions opened in Catalonia, which already had a dense bank network extending across the region and was home to a flagship institution: the Banco de Barcelona. Nevertheless, there were some noteworthy changes, such as the transformation of the venerable Manuel Arnús y Compañía, the Crédito y Fomento de Ahorros and the Sindicato de Banqueros de Barcelona into corporations, the *statu* of the latter being changed in 1910.

Some new banks were also created in the centre of the peninsula (Castile and Aragón), including the Banco Castellano (1900) in Valladolid, Banco de Burgos (1900), and a little later Banco Aragonés de Seguros y Crédito (1906), Banco Zaragozano (1910), the Banco de Aragón (1910), and Banco de Albacete (1910) and Banco Riojano (1911). The wave of new banks also reached the Mediterranean coast and the Balearic islands: the Banco de Valencia was founded in 1900 and the Banco Español Comercial in 1908; the blossoming on the islands was spectacular, with the appearance of various institutions in Majorca and Minorca, such as the Banco de Comercio de Mahón in 1906, Crédito Mercantil de Menorca in 1911 and the Banco Agrario de Baleares in 1912, among others. And in Andalusia, which lacked a home-grown financial system, there were also numerous initiatives, the most significant of which being the Banco de Andalucía (1900), in Seville. The progress registered in the first decade and a half of the 20th century is confirmed by the figures in Table 2. Aggregate bank deposits increased from 374 million pesetas in 1900 to 707 million in 1913. The two main items on the asset side also grew significantly: Loans and credit from 161 to 464 million pesetas and the investment portfolio from 201 to 443 million pesetas. Thus, the private-sector banks, excluding the Banco de España, doubled in size. This was partly as a result of the increase in the number of institutions, but also because the new institutions were themselves larger.

TABLE 2	PRIVATE-SECTOR BANKS: MAIN ASSET AND LIABILITY ACCOUNTS. BALANCE AT END OF EACH YEAR, IN MILLIONS OF PESETAS		

Years	Loans and Credit	Investment Portfolio	Deposits
1900	160.6	201.2	374.3
1905	277.1	341.0	447.2
1910	443.4	432.5	685.5
1913	464.1	443.1	707.4

SOURCES: *Anuarios Financieros y de Sociedades Anónimas,* 1900 and 1913 and Martín-Aceña (1985), Table I-1.

However, most of the banks continued to be small, and their sphere of activity was circumscribed to the town or city in which they were based, or at most extended to the surrounding province. Only a handful of institutions reached a level of paid-up capital of over ten million pesetas, a long way short of the Banco de España's 150 million, and only a few of them started to project their business nationally by creating a network of branches outside their home city. Those that did so aimed to attract more resources and bolster their capacity to supply credit and build up an investment portfolio.[6]

The majority of the banks that emerged in these first two decades of the century took the form of typical credit and discount firms, undoubtedly their primary activity, but they also showed an early vocation for efforts to promote the economy of the region in which they were based, whether through industry, mining or export-led agriculture. Thus, alongside traditional investments, short-term bills and trade lending, the value of shares in manufacturing and services companies soon came to represent a significant proportion of their investment portfolios.[7]

The expansion of the banks during this first decade and a half of the 20th century was not, however, free of difficulties and even the occasional serious setback. Together with the wave of newly founded banks, the period was also marked by some significant closures, as well as complications for some institutions. Between 1900 and 1914 twenty institutions were wound up, some of them old ones and others created recently. Indeed, no less than eleven of those founded in 1900 and 1901, often with limited capital and managed by people from outside the banking business, folded shortly after opening their doors to the public. One of the most serious crises, although it did not end in bankruptcy, was that which affected the Banco Hispano Americano.[8]

---

[6]   This was the situation of the small group of banks that had been the 'big-four' since the turn of the century: Banco de Bilbao, Banco de Vizcaya, the Banco Hispano Americano and the Banco Español de Crédito. This quartet, as well as demonstrating greater financial strength and technical expertise, had come to account for around 40% deposits and lending by 1914. If the weight of the three biggest Catalan banks (Banco de Barcelona, Banco Hispano Colonial and Crédito Mercantil de Barcelona) is added to this quartet, the proportion rises to 70%.

[7]   The mixed nature of Spanish institutions as retail and investment banks should not, however, be overstated, as the "investment portfolio" account included both public and private securities, without it being possible to know for sure what proportion of each type they held.

[8]   For more on the Banco Hispano Americano's crisis, see Tedde (1974), pp. 426-430 and Martín-Aceña (2001).

2.2   The banking system during the First World War, 1914-1919

The First World War gave a fresh boost to the financial system. Spain's neutrality placed its economy in an advantageous position to meet demand from abroad arising as a result of the conflict: exports of goods and services boomed, leading to a balance of payments surplus and an influx of gold and foreign currency into credit institution's accounts; firms made extraordinary profits and the peseta rose. The exceptional conditions produced by the war spurred a rapid process of import substitution, with new companies being formed in all sectors of the economy and existing companies expanding capacity. The banking sector was not unaffected by these changes: between 1915 and 1920 the number of institutions grew, paid-up capital tripled and deposits rose five-fold. The Banco de Bilbao, Banco de Vizcaya, Banco HispanoAmericano and Banco Español de Crédito were joined by the institutions that subsequently became the big six of the epoch.

In 1918, Banco Urquijo was founded through the transformation of a firm of the same name; and in 1919 Banco Central was created out of the firm of Aldama y Cía; and in Barcelona the firm of Fábregas y Recaséns became the Banco de Cataluña in 1920.[9]

Before the start of this expansion phase, the outbreak of war in August 1914 ushered in a brief period of uncertainties both in Europe and in Spain.[10] Francisco Bernis has given a vivid description of the impact of war's breaking out in Europe: "ruinous bankruptcies, bottlenecks in the stock market, closed exchanges, selling of assets at rock-bottom prices. Contraction of bank lending, unprecedented demand for cash, withdrawals of deposits from banks and savings banks, bank runs in Bilbao, brought under control by the Banco de España and the government; difficulties obtaining supplies of raw materials, particularly imports (cotton) or in collecting payment for exports, particularly from Catalonia; bottlenecks in the circulation of various industries, for example in cork manufacturing, and a severe blow to the mining industry."[11] The Madrid Stock Exchange remained open, but trading was minimal. The Barcelona Stock Exchange was hit by panic and had to close until June 1915. The Bilbao Stock Exchange also suffered serious difficulties, to the extent that it was not possible to summarize the year's trading as most shares had no quoted price.

The situation of the banks was also serious, with widespread panic in many financial centers.[12] There were severe strains on liquidity in almost all the country's provinces and all institutions in all the financial centers requested that the Banco de España, as the issuing bank, make extraordinary credit lines available. The city in which the difficulties were most dramatic was Bilbao: shares in the main banks (Banco de Bilbao and Banco de Vizcaya)

---

[9]   The establishment of these institutions can be followed year by year in the financial yearbooks of corporations published since 1900.

[10]   For more on the impact of the outbreak of the World War on Spanish business, see Roldán and García Delgado (1973).

[11]   Bernis (1923), p. 95

[12]   What follows is taken from Martín-Aceña (2001).

fell sharply and trading was suspended. A particularly significant event was Crédito de la Unión Minera's going into receivership, as it had been affected by the halt in the exports of iron ore and slump in freight, two businesses to which the institution was heavily exposed, although it cannot be ruled out that there was an excessive concentration of industrial risks, or that its managers, who were relatively inexperienced, reacted slowly to the situation created by the conflict.[13] In this instance the Banco de España supplied the liquidity the system needed and most institutions were able to weather the storm. Nevertheless, the crisis left its mark on banks' balance sheets, and in 1914 most banks suffered a drop in profits. After the early stressful months were over, in early 1915 the Spanish banks began a phase of strong growth in line with, or even outpacing, that in other sectors of the economy. This expansion showed up in the creation of new establishments and in the growth of the main items on credit institutions' balance sheets.[14]

The most complete list of the banks existing in 1920 is given in the renowned Ministry of Finance Memorandum published at the time of the Banking Law in 1921. This exceptional list gives the details of 120 institutions, including not only the institutions' names and head offices, but also their corporate purpose, nominal and paid-up capital, their deposits and main asset items. A number of other institutions existed which were not included on the Memorandum's list: seven small banks and 22 credit firms that were not recorded in the Ministry of Finance's statistics but nevertheless appear in the yearbooks of the time. Moreover, the banking houses or banker-tradesmen also need to be included, of which there may have been more than fifty, although they did not take long in being transformed into corporations, as in the case of Banco Pastor and Soler y Torra.[15]

The war also encouraged the larger banks to embark on a policy of expansion by opening branches at a wide range of locations across country as a means of expanding their deposits base and growing their business. In this way they sought not only to establish themselves beyond their original area of operations and reinforce their foundations, but also to chip away at the financial hegemony still enjoyed by the Banco de España. Opening branches across the whole of mainland Spain was the only way of growing and facing the competition of the issuing bank.

The number of banks multiplied, their business increased and their capital and reserves grew, along with their deposits and borrowings. Loans and credit also expanded rapidly, and credit institutions became involved in funding industry, thereby broadening their investment portfolio. Paid-up capital (Table 3) grew three-fold, from 258 million pesetas in 1915 to 730 million in 1920. This trajectory was the combined outcome of the swelling ranks of institutions and the succession of capital increases they underwent, particularly towards the end of the period. In parallel, there was an increase in reserves, which jumped

---

[13]   Anes (1974), pp. 204 and 205; Tedde (1974), pp. 387 and 388.

[14]   Canosa (1945), pp. 67-71 gives an excellent description of the events of those years.

[15]   Ministerio de Hacienda, Ordenación Bancaria Española (1921); also Roldán and García Delgado (1973), table 16, p. 213

TABLE 3	EXPANSION OF PRIVATE-SECTOR BANKS DURING THE FIRST WORLD WAR. 1914-1920. IN MILLIONS OF PESETAS

Years	Number of Banks	Paid-up Capital	Reserves	Total Deposits
1914				628.3
1915	52	258.2	52.0	837.4
1916	47	259.9	58.3	1,050.2
1917	56	274.4	70.1	1,393.6
1918	72	397.4	107.4	2,184.8
1919	73	467.1	186.5	2,704.7
1920	91	730.0	256.1	3,223.2

Years	Loans and Credit	Investment Portfolio	Total Assets
1914	382.0	428.0	
1915	289.0	564.8	2,012.2
1916	364.0	699.9	2,417.0
1917	501.2	830.4	3,177.9
1918	945.2	1,071.2	5,491.3
1919	1,226.1	1.484,2	6,434.1
1920	1,580.9	1,880.1	7,944.3

SOURCES: *Anuarios Financieros y de Sociedades Anónimas de España,* 1915-1919 and 1923; and Martín-Aceña (1985), Table I-2.

from 52 million pesetas to 256 million. Deposits, including the sum of both current and savings account balances together with term deposits, increased five-fold, from 628 million pesetas in the year war broke out, to 2,705 million pesetas in the year it ended. The following year the increase was particularly strong, taking credit balances to over three billion pesetas.

The banks' two main types of earning asset, namely their lending and their investment portfolios, continued on an upward path until 1920. The increase was marked in both cases: the first rose sharply from 382 million pesetas in 1914 to almost one billion pesetas in 1918, and on to over 1.5 billion in 1920. The investment portfolio behaved similarly: private securities, shares, bonds and debentures in commercial and industrial firms, and public bonds, primarily national debt, grew rapidly between 1914 and 1917, and from this year on their growth accelerated as a result of the ease with which the securities issued could be used as collateral, such that in 1920 the banks' portfolio had risen to a value of 1.88 billion pesetas. In percentage terms, credit and loans accounted for 15% of assets in 1915 and 20% in 1920, whereas investments went from 28% in 1915 to 24% in the final year of the period.

Table 4 shows the ranking of Spain's banks in 1920. Banco Hispano Americano stands out, having made a strong recovery from the crisis, along with Banco Español de Crédito, one of the institutions that would take on an increasingly prominent role in subsequent decades. Overall, deposits in these ten institutions totaled 1,653 million pesetas, almost 40% of the banks' total deposits and borrowings. The Table also shows the number of branches this group of institutions had: 156, almost 50% of the total.

TABLE 4   BANKS: SIZE AND RANKING IN 1920

Banks	Deposits (Millions of Pesetas)	Number of Branches (more than five)
Hispano Americano	437.5	49
Español de Crédito	335.5	32
Urquijo	255.4	
Bilbao	138.1	8
Barcelona	116.4	
Crédito Unión Minera	106.7	
Vizcaya	86.1	24
Mercantil	66.1	17
Herrero	55.7	13
Guipuzcoano	55.7	18
TOTAL	**1,653.2**	**156**

SOURCES: *Anuarios Financieros y de Sociedades Anónimas de España*, 1915-1919.

The banks also enjoyed excellent health in other respects, with growing profits and a steady rise in their stock-market valuation. The banking system's level of development in the war years can also be measured using the intermediation coefficient, which is the ratio of bank deposits to gross domestic product (GDP). In 1913 the coefficient was 3.6 whereas at the end of 1919 it had risen to over 10 per cent. In parallel with the increase in the level of banking intermediation a change in the composition of the money supply or amount of money in the hands of the public can also be observed. In 1900 private-sector bank money (excluding current accounts at the Banco de España) represented just 12% of the total, whereas in 1920 the share had risen to almost 40%.

One significant feature of these years was the consolidation of mixed banks. During the war years we know that banks stepped up their role in the promotion and financing of industry. The influx of banks into business promotion was considerable and took two forms: a) underwriting third-party debt issues, and b) owning a fixed stake in companies with a view to controlling them. For a perceptive observer like Olariaga the need for Spanish deposit-taking banks to be mixed was beyond doubt: "for the three fundamental reasons that Spanish capitalism is very limited and that it will not be easy to promote large-scale industrial firms without the financial support of the large banks; that the country has not built up sufficient savings to make it feasible to develop the country's industry without the application of a share of the national income that is deposited in these institutions; and that there is insufficient business for the majority of Spain's banking firms to be profitable if they devote themselves solely to commercial transactions."[16]

---

[16]   Olariaga (1961), p. 160

3   Crisis, reforms, progress and set-backs, 1920-1935

3.1   The post-war crisis[17]

The end of the First World War in November 1918 brought radical changes to the business world. The preceding upward trend gave way to a downward phase in the cycle, leading to widespread paralysis of industry and trade. The post-war crisis was long and deep, fomenting a level of social unrest that had not previously been witnessed.

In the financial sector, the post-war difficulties put a stop to the creation of new banks, and exposed the fragility of many institutions that had emerged during an unusually favorable period which proved unsustainable beyond the armistice of November 1918. A year after the hostilities had ended a number of institutions began to face liquidity and solvency difficulties, followed by a number of resounding crises. The banks had embarked on new types of transactions during the war. The expansion of their activities, however, was not accompanied by specialization or any differentiation in their roles; all the banks aspired to undertake the whole range of banking transactions, and in conjunction with often inadequate paid-up capital, this led to situations of excessive risk with hazardous fixed-asset positions, bearing in mind the equity capital they had available to them. The banks had gained capacity and become more complex, but their management structure was weak; there were too many people on the boards of directors, many of whom lacked a detailed understanding of the banking business, but were almost solely concerned about dividends. Also, many of the banks' managers had little experience in the business world and insufficient technical training to manage risks.

The banking crisis was particularly acute in Catalonia, the region where the most resounding bankruptcy occurred, namely that of the venerable Banco de Barcelona. The bank failed for two reasons: excessive speculation in the foreign-exchange market, in particular in German marks, and an ill-judged lending and investment policy. The deflation that began in mid-1920 and the plummeting of the mark seriously compromised the institution's solvency, which it was unable to resolve by itself. Nor did it receive any help from the Banco de España, which was reluctant to provide its support without the necessary guarantees. A short time earlier, for similar reasons, and again without the Banco de España coming to the rescue, another flagship Catalan institution, the Banco de Tarrasa, had gone into temporary receivership.

Although the banking crisis was basically confined to Catalonia, its impact was felt throughout the country. And while it is unlikely that all the institutions concerned had made the same mistakes as the Banco de Barcelona, it seems plausible that many of them suffered from a degree of asset impairment as a result of falling prices. It also seems likely

---

[17]   What follows draws upon Martín-Aceña (2001). Together with Roldán and García Delgado (1973). On the crisis at Banco de Barcelona, Cabana (1965 and 1978). For a contemporary account, see Tallada (1926).

that the first unequivocal signs of the changes in the economic cycle were emerging. Consequently, the risk on many loans granted before the changing circumstances had risen, as debtors were now finding it much more difficult to meet their commitments. This was compounded by the fact that the banks were registering losses on their public debt portfolio due to the slow, but continuous, decline in the market value of debt securities. A significant number of private securities also fell in value, which again increased the losses registered on the securities portfolio as a whole.

Fear of bankruptcies spreading, and the conviction that in view of their special nature credit firms ought to be under some form of control, made it look advisable to bring some sort of order to the financial system. This took shape with the famous Banking Law *(Ley de Ordenación Bancaria or LOB)*, which was passed by the Cortes Generales in 1921. This Law, which would remain in force, with amendments introduced in 1931, until the Civil War, affected both the Banco de España and the private-sector banks, but the savings banks were excluded from its purview. [18]

3.2 The banking census

Determining exactly how many banks, bankers and credit firms there were at the start and end of this period is extremely difficult. The diverse range of sources provides non-uniform and inconsistent data, and the statistical shortcomings, combined with the turbulence of the times, characterized by bankruptcies, liquidations, defaults and receiverships – both temporary and definitive – mergers and acquisitions, which meant that new institutions were created and others changed name or legal status, in most cases by being transformed into corporations, making them hard to track over the period. The most thorough treatment of the composition of the banking system over period from 1921, after the passing of the Banking Law, up until 1935, just before the Spanish Civil War, is that by Faus Mompart. However, as he acknowledges, the situation in this period is complicated by the short lifespan of many firms and the fact that the majority of sources limit themselves to institutions registered as corporations.

In 1922 the *Gaceta de Madrid* published an Annex[19] listing 164 institutions registered with three banking associations: those of the Centre, North and Barcelona. Once the LOB had been passed, a register of banks and bankers was created, and the registrations can be followed in the books kept by the Commissioner for Banking Organization. In the first year (1922), 105 institutions were registered and in the subsequent years up to 1929, a further 39. Another 22 companies were added to the register between 1930 and 1935. This made a total of 166 banks, credit firms and private bankers: a number close to that published in the *Gaceta*. However, this similarity in the numbers does not necessarily

---

[18]   The LOB is discussed in more detail in Chapter 3 of this book.

[19]   Reproduced in Faus (2001), pp. 390-395.

TABLE 5   NUMBER OF BANKS, 1922-1935 (a)

Years	Registered	Unregistered	Total
1923	106	44	150
1924	107	40	147
1925	104	32	163
1926	112	31	151
1927	116	74	190
1928	122	77	199
1929	123	80	203
1930	126	85	211
1931	123	85	208
1932	122	94	216
1933	124	103	227
1934	122	95	217
1935	120	90	210

SOURCE: *Boletines del Consejo Superior Bancario.*

a. Number of banks submitting their balance sheet to the Banking Council (CSB).

mean that the institutions listed in the *Gaceta* in 1922 are the same ones as those registered over the following decade and a half. Many of those existing in 1922 disappeared for various reasons, such as winding up, liquidation, merger, receivership and bankruptcy, and there were also some changes of name. Moreover, over this same period a number of new banks were created and added to the register.

The Banking Council's bulletins gave statistics on the number of banks on the register and those not included on it, but which submitted their balance sheets. As Table 5 shows, in 1923 there were 150 (106 registered and 44 unregistered banks); in 1929 the number rose to 203 (123 registered and 80 unregistered banks) and by the end of 1935 the figure came to 210 (120 registered and 90 unregistered banks). There were also a number of small entities that were neither registered nor sent their balance sheets to the Banking Council (CSB). These were not even listed on the register of authorizations created in 1926, but operated outside the official books. In fact, according to the "Libro de estadísticas de la banca privada", published by the Banking Council (Consejo Superior Bancario, CSB), in June 1936 there were 229 entities in operation, including banks, credit firms and private bankers.

3.3 Progress and set-backs in the private-sector banking system between the wars[20]

When the post-war crisis subsided, a mood of optimism returned. During the 1920s the Spanish economy benefited from the favorable climate of international expansion, boosted by strong public and private investment. The result was notable growth in national income and a no less remarkable structural transformation, with a shrinking of farming and mining's share of GDP and an increase in that of industry and services. By contrast, during the thirties, the disaster of the Great Depression led to the Spanish economy's stagnating: industrial production and foreign trade declined, the stock markets fell, the business outlook worsened and investment slumped.

In the twenties the financial system grew and underwent significant structural changes. The most relevant indicator with which to measure this expansion – more so than the number of institutions – is the development of the banks' aggregate balance sheet. As Table 6 shows, banks' assets grew rapidly between 1923 and 1930, from 7,657 million pesetas to 12,425 million, with a slight inflection in 1925, as a result of the financial crisis discussed below. The difference between the two figures represents an increase of over 60%. Indeed,

TABLE 6   PRIVATE-SECTOR BANKS. MAIN FINANCIAL ASSETS AND LIABILITIES, 1922-1935. BALANCE AT THE END OF EACH PERIOD, IN MILLIONS OF PESETAS

Years	Loans and Credit	Portfolio: Bills of Exchange	Portfolio: Public Debt	Portfolio: Other	Total Portfolio	Deposits	Paid-up Capital	Assets
1922	1,929	1,090	1,000	647	2,737	4,350		
1923	1,822	1,106	1,291	724	3,121	4,488	1,466	7,657
1924	1,770	1,309	1,028	727	3,244	4,169	1,380	7,773
1925	1,654	1,269	1,250	731	3,250	3,927	1,357	7,656
1926	1,639	1,292	1,348	735	3,376	4,135	1,400	8,451
1927	1,788	1,455	1,539	938	3,933	4,874	1,446	9,244
1928	1,867	1,547	1,914	1,312	4,773	5,531	1,486	10,090
1929	2,314	1,709	2,142	1,475	5,325	6,208	1,611	11,702
1930	2,433	1,757	2,433	1,574	5,765	6,749	1,803	12,425
1931	1,861	1,460	2,363	1,475	5,297	5,587	1,770	11,232
1932	1,875	1,558	2,475	1,455	5,488	5,942	1,717	12,205
1933	2,028	1,524	2,617	1,473	5,614	6,217	1,743	12,693
1934	2,028	1,617	3,007	1,576	6,200	6,217	1,708	12,611
1935	1,802	1,702	3,307	1,460	6,469	7,262	1,681	13,296

SOURCES: *Boletines del Consejo Superior Bancario* and Martín-Aceña (1985), Table I-7.

NOTE: Includes the accounts of banks registered with the Banking Council (CSB) and those that were not.

---

[20] This period has been studied by, among others, Cuesta (1944); a broad overview is given in Muñoz (1978), Tortella and Palafox (1988), Martín-Aceña (1995) and BBVA (2003).

the rate of growth of assets was around 6%, above the rate of growth of national income during these same years. As a consequence the intermediation coefficient rose to 75%, which was high, but still a long way short of 100%, which is the minimum level at which a financial system can be classed as advanced. This noteworthy expansion was above all the fruit of the exceptional growth of the banks' deposits, which rose from 4,350 million pesetas in 1922 to 6,749 million pesetas in 1930. As a result, the ratio of deposits to national income more than doubled from 10% to 21%.

The banks' two main items on the assets side also increased. Loans and credit went from 1,822 million pesetas in 1923 to 2,433 million pesetas in 1930 (33%) and the total portfolio, including commercial bills and securities, rose from 3,121 million pesetas to 5,765 million (85%). As the banks' portfolios grew faster than their lending, their share of total assets rose from 26% to 31%. Trade credit, including bill discounting, went in the opposite direction with its share dropping from 39% to 34%. This difference in behavior between these two items was basically the result of the massive purchase by credit institutions of public debt issued by the State in large quantities to cover the budget deficit and finance its major infrastructure projects. State debt paid a good return and was highly liquid, as it was automatically valid as collateral at the Banco de España, making it an attractive investment, particularly for large institutions. It is also true that at the same time the banks increased their portfolio of private securities, the value of which rose from 724 to 1,574 million pesetas, that is to say, from 9.5% to 13.0% of total assets.

Over the same period a process of consolidation also took place, such that in 1929 a group of five institutions (Banco Hispano Americano, Banco Español de Crédito, Banco Central, Banco de Bilbao and Banco de Vizcaya) came to control 50% of paid-up capital and 70% of total deposits in the system. These same institutions embarked on a process of geographical expansion, opening up branches right across the country, breaking out of their narrow regional frame to become genuinely national banks. They also intensified their character as mixed institutions, combining commercial discount and short-term credit activities, with others to promote industry (buying company shares and bonds). At the end of the decade the investment portfolio was distributed almost equally between the two types of operation.

Although the decade was clearly one of expansion, it was not entirely free of difficulties and the occasional serious financial crisis. The most significant episode was the crisis between June 1924 and May 1926. In the interim, six major institutions folded and a considerable number verged on insolvency, although they ultimately managed to survive. Particularly serious were the difficulties experienced by the Banco Central, the fall of which would have amplified the crisis, with unpredictable consequences for the national economy.

As on previous occasions, the Banco de España, still reluctant to take on the role of lender of last resort, generally took a neutral and passive line. When the calls for help arrived, essentially in the form of requests for liquidity by extending exceptional lines of credit, it examined them more from the point of view of the collateral the stricken institutions could offer than the danger in which they found themselves. If the collateral was not sufficient, the Banco de España usually turned down the request. Thus it allowed most troubled institutions to fail. There was only one exception: that of the Banco Central, which found itself suffering from serious liquidity problems in the spring of 1925. In this instance the Banco de España's apparent change of heart was brought about by pressure from the authorities, who felt that it was essential to keep the bank afloat.

The expansion of the twenties ended in 1930. In the thirties the system suffered the impact of the economic depression, which although less virulent in Spain than elsewhere, nevertheless made its mark on various sectors, including banking, and slowed growth rates. Asset and liability accounts, shown in Table 6, scarcely grew between 1930 and 1934. The volume of loans, credit and the portfolio of bills stagnated or contracted, clear evidence of the dual impact of the crisis on both credit supply and demand. The same was true of the portfolio of private securities and only the public debt investment portfolio, a safer and more stable investment, grew during this five year period. Deposits also suffered from the financial stagnation over this period, which no doubt contributed to a second episode of banking difficulties at the start of the decade and which followed a course parallel to the difficulties affecting other countries in Europe.

The crisis broke in 1931, with the collapse of the central European banking system and the advent of the Second Republic in Spain, which caused jitters that manifested themselves in the capital markets. The movement began with a massive withdrawal of deposits, which shrank by 20% in just two months. However, unlike what had happened in the twenties, the sharp fall in current accounts and savings deposits did not bring a series of bankruptcies of credit firms in its wake. The only noteworthy cessations of payments were those of Banco de Cataluña and its associated institutions, Banco de Reus and Banco de Tortosa. Most institutions managed to obtain the funds they needed to meet their short-term commitments and obligations, and to re-establish their normal levels of liquidity. This was made possible by the attitude of the authorities at the Ministry of Finance and the credit policy adopted by the Banco de España, which enabled a rapid and "orthodox" solution to the crisis. Another important factor explaining the absence of bankruptcies among the banks was the nature of the structure of the Spanish banking system's assets. In particular, the fact that public debt securities could be used as collateral, enabling their holders to automatically monetize them and immediately draw upon cash reserves. In situations of crisis, this monetizable debt was a genuine stabilizing mechanism for the system, as it provided considerable flexibility and, to a certain extent, made the money market independent from possible irresponsibility by the authorities (the Banco de España and the Ministry of Finance). Indeed, the ample portfolio of public funds in the banking system at the beginning of 1931 provided one of the means by which the financial institutions restored their levels of liquidity and responded to the public's unexpected demand for cash.

3.4   The origins of the official banking system[21]

One significant new feature in this period was the emergence of official credit institutions, which aimed to meet the financing needs of special sectors. These institutions were created with private capital, but under public supervision and granted a privileged *statu*. The first, the Banco de Crédito Industrial, was founded in 1920 with the purpose of supporting business projects linked to industry. It was followed in 1925 by the Banco de Crédito Local, which aimed to meet the needs of municipal authorities and finance public works and services. At almost the same time, the Servicio Nacional de Crédito Agrícola (National Farming Credit Service) was created, which was the embryo of the future Banco de Crédito Agrícola (1926). Finally, in 1929 the Banco Exterior de España was set up to meet the needs of the import and export trade.[22]

Up until their nationalization in 1962, all these banks had private capital, despite their being regulated and controlled, directly or indirectly, by the State. Thus, although the government backed their creation and determined their corporate purpose, the private sector was given the task of establishing and managing them. The authorities reserved the right to appoint the governor, who became their official representative. In some cases, they also appointed other members of the boards of directors. Apart from their public nature, another feature which characterized these official entities was their high degree of specialization. These institutions had been created to meet the credit needs of a specific sector, namely particular industries or economic activities that it was felt were not being adequately served by the commercial deposit-taking banks. Moreover, their operations followed special, and in general more complex, administrative procedures. The third distinctive feature of the official banking system was its source of funds. Indeed, although these institutions were called banks, this was not strictly speaking true, as they did not take deposits from private individuals, or did so only in a limited fashion. Instead they used alternative mechanisms to obtain the resources they needed. Firstly, they could receive funding directly from the Treasury and, secondly, the State granted them certain privileges regarding their taking on debt, the most important of which was the right to issue special securities, which were generally treated as public or government-backed debt.

In terms of the resources the public-sector banks had at their disposal at the end of this period, they were large institutions, comparable to the largest of the deposit-taking institutions. In 1929 they were already on the list of the country's twelve largest credit institutions (Table 7), with the Banco Hipotecario de España (BHE) in first place (behind only the Banco de España). The Banco de Crédito Local (BCL) was in fourth position, the Banco de Crédito Industrial (BCI) in ninth and the Banco Exterior de España (BEE) in twelfth place. In 1935, as a proportion of the banking system as a whole, public-sector banks accounted

---

[21]   What follows is a summary of Martín-Aceña (1991) and of the bibliography included with this chapter.

[22]   In 1935 there were five official or semi-official credit institutions and a further two sui generis firms that could be classed as such.

TABLE 7	RANKING OF THE TWELVE LARGEST BANKS BY VOLUME OF BORROWINGS IN 1929. FIGURES IN MILLIONS OF PESETAS
Banco Hipotecario de España	1,235
Banco Español de Crédito	946
Banco Hispano Americano	923
Banco de Crédito Local	568
Banco de Bilbao	476
Banco de Vizcaya	391
Banco Central	267
Banco Mercantil	127
Banco de Crédito Industrial	112
Banco Guipuzcoano	110
Banco Pastor	110
Banco Exterior de España	76

for 20% of total resources. This was by no means a trivial percentage, although it was true that this was largely due to the weight of the BHE, as the BCI, BCK and BEE accounted for just 7%.

3.5 The presence of foreign banks in Spain[23]

Foreign institutions have operated in the Spanish financial sector ever since the origins of the banking system. The leading role was undoubtedly played by the Banco de París y de los Países Bajos, the main backer of the Banco de Castilla (1871), the Banco Hipotecario de España (1872) and of the transformation of Crédito Mobiliario into the Banco Español de Crédito (1902). It was followed by Crédit Lyonnais, which was founded in 1862, and which opened an office in Spain 1876. Next came the German banks linked to the mighty Deutsche Bank: the Banco Hispano-Alemán in 1889 and the Banco Alemán Transatlántico, in 1907. Other foreign-owned banks included the Union Bank of Spain and England, founded in 1881, and the Argentinean Banco Español del Río de la Plata, created in 1903. Before 1914, in addition to those just mentioned, the Banco di Roma, the French banks Comptoir National d'Escompte (as of 1901) and Société Générale (as of 1905, through the Société Générale de Banque pour l Étranger et les Colonies) also had branches in Spain.

The apparent prosperity of the First World War attracted numerous financial institutions. The first were two English banks, the Anglo-South American Bank, in 1916, and the London County Westminster&Parr's Bank, in 1917. In 1918 the arrivals of the Royal Bank of Canada and the Mercantile Bank of America were also registered. Two more banks set up in Spain in 1919: the International Banking Corporation (IBC), founded in 1901, and the Banco Español de Chile. These were followed by the Banco Germánico de la América del Sur, which was established in 1906 by Dresdner Bank, the Bank of British West Africa, a

---

[23] García Ruiz (2001) and BBVA (1999).

London-based institution founded in 1894 which from 1902 had business in the Canary Islands and on the island of Fernando Po (Bioko).

The reason why some authors talk of an "invasion of foreign banks" is bound up with the war economy, which created lucrative business opportunities financing the burgeoning export trade. It was also a result of the absence of barriers to entry and the fact that banks could set up in Spain with relatively little capital. A number of authors have pointed out that the weakness of Spain's banking system at the start of the war offered an attractive opening for foreign banks; Spanish trade needed to turn to the branches of established foreign banks for finance, which attracted in other institutions to meet the needs of the Spanish economy. Other reasons for their expansion included the possibility of channeling investments into foreign securities and the fact that these foreign banks offered a wider variety of banking services and lower interest rates.

Foreign banks primarily focused on retail banking, offering the whole range of banking services, although with particular emphasis on those dedicated to financing foreign trade. These banks were mainly linked to head offices operating in countries with more sophisticated financial systems and they introduced a degree of modernity into the Spanish system, stimulating the diversification of business and encouraging the opening of new branches.

The influx of foreign banks ceased at the end of the war. According to the information provided by the Banking Council's bulletins, of the 13 banks on the Register in 1922, with total assets of 1,276 million pesetas, by the end of 1926 the number had dropped to nine, and assets to 1,025 million pesetas. A brief recovery followed, such that in 1929 there were 12 foreign banks, with assets of 1,774 million pesetas, although the number fell back to 9 again in 1934, with assets down to 1,023 million pesetas. Part of the reason for this was more restrictive legislation. The first deterrent measure was the agreement signed on 1 July 1918 between the Banco de España and the Central Committee of Spanish Banks (Comité Central de la Banca Española) under which only Spanish banks could benefit from a 1% rebate on the rediscount of bills and the automatic acceptance of public debt up to 80% of its value. The Banking Law (LOB) in 1921 and its regulations in 1927 maintained these benefits for registered national banks, but excluded foreign banks. Moreover, foreign banks were barred from direct access to the clearing houses created in 1923, obliging them to submit their documents to the clearing houses through a national institution. Then, the Great Depression buffeted foreign banks, given their exposure to international trade and foreign-currency transactions; the depreciation of the peseta and government restrictions on foreign-exchange business cost them market share, with the result that between 1930 and 1934 the percentage of total private bank deposits in the hands of foreign-owned banks fell from 12.3% to 6.0%. In the face of declining business and growing problems in Spain and abroad, many of them shut up shop and left the country.

Foreign banks virtually disappeared after the Civil War. The regime's nationalism and policy of autarky sounded the death knell for those institutions still operating in Spain: some closed and others were taken over by Spanish banks. The only foreign banks listed in the 1947 CSB bulletins were the Bank of London and South America (which had taken over the Banco Anglo-Sud Americano), Société Générale, Crédit Lyonnais, the Banco Alemán Transatlántico and the Banco Germánico de América del Sur. These all had their offices in Madrid, except Société Générale, which was based in Barcelona.[24]

4 The interlude of the Civil War, 1936-1939[25]

4.1. The division of the financial system

The military uprising in July 1936 divided the country into two opposing sides from which two antagonistic States emerged, splitting the financial system in two. The currency was also split and for three years two different currencies called the peseta were in circulation: the Republican peseta and the Nationalist peseta. The war brought massive state intervention in the economy and the conflict's financial needs consumed the Banco de España's gold reserves, drove up public debt, and swelled the supply of cash in circulation, leading to rampant inflation, and a decline in the internal and external value of both currencies. The conflict dislocated Spanish commercial life. In both zones measures were taken to limit cash withdrawals and interest payments and public debt repayments were suspended. At almost the same time the maturities of trade bills and mortgages were extended to avoid a cascade of defaults that would have led to the general insolvency of the system.

The country's being divided in two affected the majority of its banking institutions. Given that their head offices were mainly located in the republican sector, a plethora of branches scattered across the territory under Franco's control lost their links to their respective parent banks. As the Civil War meant the suspension of legal provisions and company bylaws regarding the formulation of balance sheets and calling of general shareholders' meetings, it led to a loss of communication for almost six years between credit institutions' governing bodies and shareholders and to relationships between the banks and their customers no longer being governed by the normal contractual conditions.

The Republican government modified the Banking Council (CSB), which came under the Finance Ministry, and ordered the replacement of financial institutions' boards of directors by executive committees comprising representatives of the Finance Ministry, shareholders, current-account holders, and the National Banking Federation (Federación Nacional de la Banca). This change was a response not only to pressure from labor unions

---

[24] To these must be added Banca Nazionale del Lavoro, which was founded in 1919 and set up in Nationalist Spain in 1937, with offices in Burgos, Seville and Salamanca, with the ostensible purpose of managing the savings and remittances of Italian soldiers.

[25] The content of this section draws upon two recent publications by Martín-Aceña (2006) and Sánchez Asiaín (2008) These give a detailed account of developments affecting the financial system during the war and ad hoc references to events affecting the main banking institutions.

and workers' parties, but also the exodus of directors and executives to the zone controlled by Franco's forces.

The latter adopted measures in the opposite direction. Drawing upon a few regional entities and the branches of the major banks, with the help of directors resident in the Nationalist zone, they rebuilt a highly government-controlled financial system, designed to serve the war effort, but respecting private property. The Nationalist government established the National Spanish Banking Committee (Comité Nacional de la Banca Española), a body conceived as an instrument of coordination and monitoring of credit institutions' activities. Later on they abolished the CSB and the National Spanish Banking Committee was turned into the National Credit Board (Consejo Nacional de Crédito), a consultative body on credit policy and organization under the Finance Ministry. They also created a Commissioner for Official Banks (Comisaría de la Banca Oficial), who was assigned the functions of the governors of the Banco de España and the official banks. The banks themselves established boards of directors and management bodies from among the directors already in the Nationalist zone at the start of the war and those gradually emigrating from the Republican cities.

4.2   Financial activity during the war

The war prevented banks from conducting their business normally. Institutional factors, the progress of the war, the consequences of monetary measures and customers' spirits all contributed to the design of a type of business that was difficult and atypical. Moreover, by shattering the unity of the market, the traditional flows of savings and investment were interrupted, as on the one side there were zones with sizeable credit investments (basically the industrial regions situated in Republican territory) and on the other, zones with a volume of deposits or savings that exceeded their credit demand (the agricultural regions of Nationalist Spain). However, there were differences between banks on each side of the divide. On the Republican side, business gradually declined as the business base shrank in parallel with the progressive loss of territory and the decomposition of the currency. Conversely, on the Nationalist side, as institutions were reconstructed they managed to move with a degree of ease within a less hostile political environment. They fulfilled the tasks entrusted to them by the new state as regards internal and external funding and the implementation of monetary policy. They also maintained more normal operations, despite the imbalance caused by the sharp increase in customer liabilities, which was not matched by a similar growth in the volume of lending.

At the start of the war, the credit institutions operating in both zones had to pledge securities with the Banco de España to meet the strong demand for cash from the public. Although the government limited immediate cash withdrawals, the current accounts of the Banco de España reveal the rapid increase in repaid balances. Banks on the Nationalists' side also faced liquidity problems and only by resorting to the Banco de España's branch in Burgos were they able to avoid insolvency. These same liquidity problems also made it prudent to limit asset operations during the first six months of the conflict.

Subsequently, the financing of military operations led to the opposite situation. The common trait in both sectors was the creation of money and the swelling of bank deposits, a phenomenon that was more marked in the Republican than the Nationalist zone. In the former, the higher level of issuance and a certain fear that the banknotes would not be recognized in the other zone led to their being deposited in current accounts, where their owners felt they would be more secure. And in the latter, the measures dictated for the stamping of banknotes led to substantial inflows into the creditor accounts, thereby overcoming the liquidity problems of the first few months.

As regards asset operations, the paralysis of trade resulting from the conflict rapidly affected the banks' investment activities. The fall in demand for credit from companies and individuals, the closure of the stock markets, and the brake on the contracting of new issues, all had an impact on the number and size of bank transactions. Moreover, whether out of prudence or fear, financial institutions themselves also scaled back their investments in new companies' capital, at least during the early months of the war. This contraction affected both sides, although it was more pronounced in the sector controlled by the Republicans, given the greater complications traders and businessmen faced. Banks on both sides of the conflict also had to respond to the demands of their respective governments, and repeated requests for aid from a multitude of official bodies, such as provincial and local governments, and quasi-official organizations, such as labor unions and workers' committees. This institutional demand compensated in part for the lack of ordinary investment activity, although it subsequently resulted in losses for the banks as a significant proportion of the loans granted were never repaid. In the Republican zone the banks operated under the socio-political pressures of the time, such that on occasions loans were granted against inadequate collateral. Many official bodies created new forms of account with names such as "for war losses," "for damage caused by the fascist uprising," or "for the General Repairs account." In the Nationalist zone banking operations had a peculiarity in the form of the demands from the national services (wheat, cotton, almonds) created by the state, which the banks were obliged to meet. Similarly, from mid-1938 the banks contributed to the placement of the debt issues by Franco's government, by this time well-established militarily and with a recently constructed administrative structure built around a series of new ministerial departments.

The four official credit institutions in operation, Banco Hipotecario de España, the Banco de Crédito Industrial, the Banco de Crédito Local and the Banco Exterior de España suffered the effects of the conflict as much or more than private institutions; none of them was able to function normally, and as the months passed, they fell into a profound lethargy from which they were not to emerge until many years after the end of the war.

In short, the financial system did not collapse during the war, but its functioning reflected the abnormalities of the social and economic life of the time. On both sides, the banks and savings banks bore the burden of state intervention and harassment from political organizations and labor unions. On the Republican side, the common feature was the replacement of boards of directors by executive committees including employee representatives. The banks were not nationalized, but they operated as if private property had ceased to exist. On the Nationalist side, directors representing the shareholders remained present, but the Finance Ministry took on a central role and placed financial institutions under strict vigilance. There were numerous anomalies. These included the non-publication of balance sheets and income statements, through to the suspension of shareholders' meetings, which could not be held during the three years of the war or for a further two years during the post-war period. The rarefaction of the life of the financial system was also aggravated by the seizure of accounts, the forceful opening of safety-deposit boxes and the requests for assistance, in the form of loans and donations, which the banks and savings banks also had to respond to.

Deposit taking, extending credit, buying and selling shares, all nonetheless continued despite the multitude of difficulties both lenders and borrowers faced. However, in terms of the number and volume of transactions, this activity was a pale reflection of pre-war business.

5   The banking system between 1939 and 1962[26]

5.1   The status quo and interventionism

After the civil war it was necessary to rebuild the fabric of the financial system. The first measure taken by the economy's new authorities was to modify the precepts of the former Banking Law of 1921 that had become inapplicable, such as those referring to the ratio of precious metal reserves to fiduciary circulation and the links between the Banco de España and the Treasury.[27] This was followed by preparation of the "Unfreezing" Law *(Ley de Desbloqueo)* of 7 December 1939, which aimed to restore normality after the situation created by the wartime legislation, which had effectively rendered all financial transactions registered in the zones controlled by the Republican government *sub-judice*.

One extremely significant piece of legislation, in view of its long-term consequences, was the adoption of the so-called banking status quo introduced by the Ministerial Order of 19 October 1939, establishing a *numerus clausus* for both the banks operating in Spain and their branch networks. The status quo not only prevented the creation of new credit institutions but also prohibited the opening of new agencies and branches without the relevant government per-

---

[26]   The banking system in the forties and fifties has been covered in various works by Olariaga (1951), Ridruejo (1954), Prados (1958), Sánchez Pedreño (1961), Sardà (1964) and Clayton (1973) and Martín-Aceña and Pons (1994); and more recently by Lukauskas (1997) and Pons (2002 and 2007), who provide an extensive bibliography.

[27]   Sardá (1970) and Martín-Aceña (1994)

mission. A few months later, a decree on 17 May 1940 prohibited the creation of new banking institutions; the setting up of new agencies and branches; the change of premises of existing branches, any modification to the nature and legal *status* of banks and bankers; agreements for transfer and merger; the purchase of shares in other banking businesses and capital increases or circulation of banking institutions throughout 1940. This policy reflected a profound mistrust of private initiative and the functioning of the market. The aim was also to introduce a mechanism that would prevent the financial crises of the past from being repeated. It also revealed a clear intention to bar the way to competitors and possible consolidation in the financial industry through uncontrolled mergers and takeovers.[28]

The post-war legislative framework was completed with the Banking Law *(Ley de Ordenación Bancaria, LOB)* of 31 December 1946, passed when ending the Banco de España's privilege of issuing banknotes, and intended to regulate the ensemble of credit institutions, commercial and official banks, although excluding the savings banks.[29] One interesting feature of the Banking Law of 1946 was how it divided the financial system into three types of institution: official banks, private-sector banks (national, regional, local and foreign) and savings banks.

5.2 The progress of the banking census

In 1936 there were 116 banking institutions on the Register of banks and bankers, a further 48 were noted down in the Register of licenses and 65 more submitted their balance sheets to the Banking Council (CSB), making a total of 229 credit firms of one sort or another. As a consequence of the measures taken after the war, the licenses to use the name of bank or banker obliged firms and individuals wishing to continue in the sector to apply for a new authorization from the still acting Central Committee for Spanish Banks (Comité Central de la Banca Española), the body which had replaced the Banking Council (Consejo Superior Bancario). Between 1939 and 1946 the Committee agreed to the addition of over 60 entities, most of which been in operation before the war.[30]

Following the restoration of the Register of Banks and Bankers in 1947, a total of 119 Spanish entities were registered in the various categories that existed (national, regional and local), plus Banco de Londres y América del Sur in the foreign banks category: bringing the total to 120.[31] In subsequent years there were new additions to the register, many of which were institutions which had previously had some form of license to operate. Table 8 shows the progress of registrations between 1947 and 1962: 160 entities accessed the Register, 153 of them Spanish – 10 national, 17 regional and 126 local – and 7 foreign

---

[28] Although the *status quo* formally remained in place until 1962, it is nevertheless true that its application was gradually relaxed over time [García Ruiz (2002) and Pons (2001a)].

[29] The 1946 LOB and its developments are covered in Chapter 3 of this book.

[30] Over the same period 92 entities were removed from the register, 55 as a result of mergers and acquisitions.

[31] The full list of national, regional and local banks is published in Faus (1991), pp. 423-425.

| TABLE 8 | ENTRIES ON THE REGISTER OF BANKS AND BANKERS BETWEEN 1947 AND 1962 |

Years	Number
1947	120
1948	22
1949	6
1950	6
1951	2
1952	1
1953	1
1954	2
1955-1962	–
TOTAL	160

SOURCE: Consejo Superior Bancario (1973).

institutions.[32] Relatively few (just 11) new banks were added to the census: ten Spanish and one foreign bank, all of which were small. One noteworthy event, in view of the institution's subsequent importance, was the establishment of the Banca Catalana in 1948, out of the venerable and respected Banca Dorca. This period also saw the creation of Comercial Trasatlántico in 1950, which was the heir to and continuation of the Banco Alemán Transatlántico.

The mergers and acquisitions during the period were more significant. Between 1940 and 1946 a total of 52 such operations took place, of which 34 involved the six largest banks.[33] Subsequently, between 1946 and 1962 a total of 55 were registered, which, as Table 9 shows, resulted in a total of 14 banks, although four of them – Banco Español de Crédito, Banco de Bilbao, Banco Central and Banco Popular – accounted for 39 operations, i.e. more than half. This process of absorptions was precisely one of the mechanisms whereby the large banks were able to increase their scale and capture a growing share of the market.

The information in the Register of banks and bankers offers a snapshot of the annual census of private banking institutions, drawing upon the information on registrations, discontinuations and mergers. As Table 10 shows, in 1950 there were 306 institutions on the register, of which 202 were subsequently removed. In 1960 the number was 261. In 1950 the Spanish banking system comprised 35 national institutions, 12 regional ones and 54 local ones. Ten years later: the system comprised 21 national institutions, 12 regional ones and 46 local ones. The number of foreign banks went from three in 1950 to four in 1960.[34]

---

[32] The list of entities refused authorization to operate, being excluded from the register, comprised 45 bankers and banking houses, and again were small credit firms with a local, or at most regional, scope. The list of 45 credit firms is given in Faus Mompart (1991), p. 433

[33] The numbers of institutions absorbed by each of the six biggest banks before the LOB was passed in 1946 were: Español de Crédito: 13; Hispano-Americano: 9; Bilbao: 5; Central: 3; Santander: 3; Vizcaya: 1.

[34] The full census of banking institutions is given in Consejo Superior Bancario (1973)

TABLE 9   ACQUISITIONS AMONG REGISTERED BANKS BETWEEN 1947 AND 1962

Acquiring Bank	Number
Central	12
Bilbao	10
Español de Crédito	9
Popular Español	8
Zaragozano	4
Vizcaya	3
Santander	2
Hispano Americano	1
Aragón	1
Comercial Transatlántico	1
Rural y Mediterráneo	1
Coca	1
Guipuzcoano	1
Crédito Balear	1
TOTAL	55

SOURCE: Consejo Superior Bancario (1973).

TABLE 10   BANKING INSTITUTIONS ON THE REGISTER OF BANKS AND BANKERS BETWEEN 1950 AND 1960

Category	1950	1960
National banks	35	21
Regional banks	12	12
Local banks	54	46
Foreign banks	3	4
Total (of above)	104	83
Other institutions (a)	202	178
TOTAL	306	261

SOURCE: Consejo Superior Bancario (1973).

a. Institutions existing on each date but subsequently removed from the Register.

5.3   Growth during the status quo years

As we have seen, the extreme interventionism of these years did not prevent significant changes in the bank census, nor was it an obstacle to the strong growth of the financial system. This can be seen in both the banks' aggregate balance sheet, and the growth in the number of offices (including branches and agencies).

Table 11 shows the private-sector banks' consolidated balance sheet, which gives a view of the developments taking place between 1947 and 1962. The expansion registered over these 15 years can be readily confirmed by examining the asset figures, which

TABLE 11   AGGREGATE BALANCE SHEET OF PRIVATE-SECTOR BANKS. IN BILLIONS OF PESETAS

ASSETS	1947	1952	1957	1962
Cash and banks	6,998	12,698	27,501	59,223
Bills portfolio	12,782	32,209	75,423	170,819
Bills with maturities of up to 90 days	12,677	31,760	74,349	159,127
Longer-term bills	105	182	447	10,657
Other bills	–	267	627	1,035
Securities portfolio	19,038	34,181	72,717	81,716
Public debt	14,661	26,413	57,371	58,934
Misc.	4,377	7,768	15,346	22,782
Credit	13,409	25,267	51,342	104,430
Secured loans	2,337	4,078	8,001	12,274
On demand	963	2,352	5,826	12,189
Term	9,783	17,662	35,957	77,643
Foreign currency	326	1,175	1,558	2,324
Other Assets	13,007	43,159	115,471	232,283
TOTAL ASSETS	**65,234**	**147,514**	**342,454**	**648,471**
LIABILITIES				
Equity capital	2,774	3,719	5,386	7,526
Reserves	1,587	3,294	7,735	15,836
Borrowings	38,793	77,633	165,262	341,541
Sight deposits	25,656	47,732	99,989	173,005
Maturities over one month	9,927	22,885	44,647	97,483
Longer maturities	2,956	5,868	18,424	67,548
Foreign currency	254	1,148	2,202	3,505
Other Liabilities	22,080	62,868	164,071	283,568
TOTAL LIABILITIES	**65,234**	**147,514**	**342,454**	**648,471**

SOURCE: Consejo Superior Bancario (1973).

rose from 65,234 million pesetas to 648,471 million pesetas, i.e. growing approximately ten-fold. The most significant increases took place at the end of the period, from 1957 to 1962, as a result of the inflation that struck the Spanish economy in the late fifties. However, there was also a significant increase when the effects of the 1959 Stabilization Plan were assimilated.

All the banks' balance sheet items made a contribution to this increase in activity, but particularly their bills portfolio. Indeed, whereas in 1947 they represented 20% of the total, at the end of the period this proportion had reached 26%. Discounting, basically of trade bills with maturities of up to 90 days, was the basic instrument through which the Spanish economy obtained short-term credit. This also included so-called *"letras financieras"* or financial bills of exchange, which were often not based on an underlying commercial transaction, but issued in order to obtain credit in the form of an advance with which to refinance operations, or alternatively were used to obtain a larger amount of funds than involved in the underlying commercial transaction. The bill of exchange portfolio had the advantage that the bills could be rediscounted at the Banco de España, with a rebate for registered banks, although in practice most institutions made little use of this facility. One possible explanation was that it was not obligatory for the Banco de España to grant this facility, such that it was at the Bank's discretion rather then being subject to objective criteria.

Credit and loans to business made up the second most important item on the balance sheet. This rose from 13,409 million pesetas to 51,342 million 10 years later, and up to 104,430 million in 1962. Maturities were up to 90 days, although they were frequently renewed, such that in practice so-called business credit was extended over longer periods and could even exceed 12 months; this was in a fact a form of lending to companies with close links to the institution. There were four categories of debtors:

- Firstly, those posting collateral, either in the form of goods or real estate;
- The second category, "sight," included all short-term or temporary overdrafts;
- The third included term debtors, corresponding to loans granted with no other guarantees than the solvency of the company in the eyes of the bank, and was usually formalized as a credit policy;
- The fourth group comprised debtors proper, consisting of short-term transitory credit, given the prohibition on the banks' holding permanent foreign-currency balances.

As may be observed, all these items grew, although long-term debtors increased most. In this case, as in that of discounting discussed above, although these were in theory short-term operations, in practice many of these loans were renewed until they became much longer-term transactions and an essential source of finance for businesses and individuals. There was a practical limit on this process in the case of corporations, which were able to obtain finance from other sources. Thus, as Spanish private-sector banks were authorized to hold shares and bonds issued by private firms on their portfolio, a sizeable share of funding was obtained by issuing securities which the bank covered with its own resources and included in its securities portfolio.

Thus, if we look at the securities portfolio, we find that as well as public debt, the banks held a significant private securities portfolio. The public-debt securities held by the banks increased significantly in the first ten years as a result of the volume of debt issued to fund the national budget, in conjunction with the fact that it was automatically accepted by the Banco de España as collateral, giving banks a high level of second-degree liquidity. In the later years of the period the trend was reversed and the fastest growing category was that of private securities. In 1947 the portfolio represented 30% of the total, although it later dropped, falling to 21% in 1957 and 13% in 1962.

The lack of a distinction between retail and investment banking meant that private-sector banks lacked any true specialization. They carried out both discounting and lending, as well as taking shareholdings in companies, and thereby building up a portfolio of securities that included private securities such as shares and bonds, as well as public debt. The proportion of total assets the portfolio of private securities represented was always small, tending even to decline over the period. However, as a share of the total portfolio, the proportion was slightly over 20%, reaching 28% in 1962, after the interruption in public debt issues. This is by no means a trivial percentage and is sufficiently large for the Spanish banks of this period to be considered mixed. The data also reveal that national banks had an investment portfolio that was larger than that of regional and local banks, and that banks had stable and close relations with the manufacturing firms that appeared in their debtors' accounts.

On the liabilities side one can observe that the expansion in asset operations was matched by a similar progression in their borrowings, namely bank deposits with various maturities. Demand deposits also lost ground, but less rapidly: 66% in 1947, 61% in 1952 and 1957, and 51% in 1962. The volume of term deposits was smaller, although it followed an opposite path, such that at the end of the period it accounted for half of the total. Despite the growth in accounts receivable, it was nevertheless true that check use was not widespread and transfers were also fairly uncommon, despite the fact that there were four official clearing houses (Madrid, Barcelona, Bilbao and Zaragoza) and three private ones (Valencia, Seville and San Sebastián).

In 1947, the banks' equity, that is to say, their paid-up capital plus reserves, was equal to 6.7% of their total liabilities. Ten years later, both items can be seen to have increased, although their weight in the balance sheet had dropped to 3.8%. In 1962, the end of the period discussed here, the share was around 3.6%. One noteworthy feature was the rapid increase in reserves, which ended up exceeding the banks' capital and becoming the main source of equity. This was a result of the 1946 Banking Law which placed legal restrictions on dividend payments. Thus, banking corporations that obtained net profits of more than four per cent of their paid-up capital plus reserves had to deduct from these profits at least 10% to set aside reserves of up to half of the banks' capital. This provision was added to another which had been in force since 1942, under which Spanish banks could not distribute a dividend worth more than six percent of the sum of their paid-up capital and reserves. The effect of these rules was that banks built up reserves rapidly, making capital increases, which were, moreover, subject to strict administrative regulations, largely unnecessary. This explains why, whereas in 1947 the figure for paid-up capital exceeded that of reserves, by 1962 the latter was twice the figure for shareholder's equity.

There are methodological difficulties in measuring the overall liquidity and solvency of the banking system as it is necessary to properly define the concepts and then include the appropriate items in each of them. A traditional approach to liquidity is to calculate the ratio of reserve requirements (the cash in hand and banks account) to aggregate deposits (on the liabilities side). The figures shown in Table 12 suggest that during this period Spanish banks enjoyed high levels of liquidity, never dropping below 15%. If we also take their public debt portfolio into account, which could automatically be used as collateral at the Banco de España, we must conclude that the system was essentially liquid. Up until the

TABLE 12   LIQUIDITY AND SOLVENCY OF SPANISH BANKS

A) Liquidity

Years	Cash / Current accounts	Cash / total deposits	Cash + government debt / Deposits
1947	27.3	18.0	55.8
1952	26.6	16.4	50.4
1957	27.5	16.6	51.4
1962	34.2	17.3	34.6

B) Solvency

Years	Capital + reserves / Deposits	Capital + reserves / Loans + private-debt securities
1947	11.2	24.5
1952	9.0	21.2
1957	7.9	19.7
1962	6.8	18.4

SOURCE: Consejo Superior Bancario (1973).

1959 Stabilization Plan, second line liquidity was extremely high, at levels of over 50%. It dropped to 35% when the issuance of readily monetizable public debt was interrupted. This did not prevent some institutions from suffering liquidity problems, which they were able to resolve, if the authorities saw fit to allow them to do so, by accessing some of the Banco de España's rediscount lines.

Solvency is even more difficult to calculate, however, as an adjusted measure would require that the level of risk on each of the assets in the calculation be determined. It is therefore necessary to make do with the apparent solvency estimated using two coefficients: firstly, the ratio of equity (paid-in capital and reserves) to borrowings (total deposits); and secondly, the ratio of equity to the profitable portion of assets (lending and the portfolio of private securities). The estimated solvency according to the first criterion was fairly high at the start of this stage, but declined over the years until it reached around 7% in 1962, a level that was still reasonable, but somewhat tight. If equity is measured against the potential exposure – the second possible estimate – the solvency levels seem reasonable, even in 1962 when the percentage was at its lowest. Moreover, bearing in mind that the lending and borrowing interest rates were controlled by the authorities, solvency was virtually ensured by decree, although it could happen that an institution might find itself in difficulties, in which case before its reaching bankruptcy, it would be saved by being taken over by a larger institution in better shape.

The banks' aggregate balance sheet offers a way of tracking their quantitative growth over these two decades of the status quo. Another way of confirming this growth is by observing the number of offices, taking the sum of their branches and urban agencies. The evidence is shown in Table 15. The number offices open for business just before the Civil War, in July 1936, was 1,903. By 1948 this number had risen to 2,157. That is to say, 254 offices had been opened; not a large number if one considers that 10 years had passed. The number then continued to rise, albeit slowly: reaching 2,298 in 1950; 2,449 in 1955;

and 2,610 in 1958. By 1961 the total had risen to 2,728. Thus, over the decade-and-a-half as a whole, 571 branches and agencies were opened: equivalent to a rate of 44 a year. The number of bank offices undoubtedly rose, but the growth was by no means as rapid as it would become in the following decades. In this case the status quo clearly exerted a restraining effect.

What the status quo could not avoid was the trend towards increasing levels of concentration in the banking industry already observed. In 1960 the fourteen national banks accounted for almost 80% of offices and the remainder were shared out between the regional banks (15%) and local banks (6%). To refine this a little further, the "big five", at that time comprising the Banco Español de Crédito, the Banco Central, the Banco Hispano Americano, the Banco de Vizcaya and the Banco de Bilbao, together had 1,673 branches and agencies: 62% of the total. If we add in Banco Santander and Banco Popular, to make a group of seven, the proportion rises to 71%.[35]

5.4   Official credit

As already mentioned, alongside the private-sector banks there were also five official banks and two ministerial departments able to provide credit, all of which had been created prior to or immediately following the Civil War. Three of these institutions obtained their resources from issuing fixed-income securities: the Banco Hipotecario de España, Banco de Crédito Local and the Banco de Crédito a la Construcción (created in 1939 as the Instituto de Crédito para la Reconstrucción). A further two, the Banco de Crédito Agrícola (created in 1925 as the Servicio Nacional de Crédito Agrícola) and Crédito Social Pesquero (created in 1919 as Caja Central de Crédito Marítimo y Pesquero) were funded with loans from the private-sector banks or the savings banks in the form of instruments that could be monetized by using them as collateral with the Banco de España. And one, the Banco de Crédito Industrial, received cash advances directly from the Treasury. The Banco Exterior de España, on the other hand, was more like a commercial credit institution in that it raised its funds in the market.

The 1946 Banking Law established that the official banks would be governed by their own specific provisions, although the Finance Ministry had the authority to set interest rates and fees, approve or reduce dividends, and decide on the opening and closure of branches. The following ten years were, in any event, fairly sluggish for the official banks.[36]

Subsequently, the Law of 20 December 1958 on Medium- and Long-Term Credit Institutions tried to reinvigorate official credit such that it complement the activities of private-sector banks. The Law also sought to establish the necessary coordination between the official institutions by setting up a mechanism viewing them as a whole and directing their lending

---

[35]   This trend towards concentration among the banks may also be detected by looking at bank deposits: in 1946 around ten institutions held 60% of total resources, while in 1960 the five biggest, plus Santander, controlled almost 70% of all the sector's assets and liabilities.

[36]   A full study of the official banks in this period can be found in Arias (1986).

and borrowing according to the investment plans approved or authorized by the government. The overall aim was to ensure that all the resources available could be combined effectively to meet the needs of the national economy. This resulted in two innovations. Firstly, the institutions were to be financed through the Treasury, with the creation of investment certificates, and a maximum volume of operations was defined for each institution; and secondly, management bodies were set up (the consultative committee and medium and long-term credit committee) to make it possible to modify how these entities operated and were organized. Although the rule was not applied to all the banks (the Banco Exterior de España and the Banco de Crédito Local were excluded), some institutions were included that were not strictly speaking banks, although they could perform lending activities (for example, the National Housing Institute: Instituto Nacional de la Vivienda). This Law was also important on account of its defining the starting point from which the subsequent restructuring of official credit began in 1962.

6 Reorganization and growth, 1962-1975[37]

6.1 Nature and significance of the Basic Law on Credit and Banking Organization of 1962

This final period covered by this chapter was marked by the passing and implementation of the Basic Law on Credit and Banking Organization *(Ley de Bases de Ordenación del Crédito y la Banca)* of 14 April 1962, which put an end to the long period of the status quo and opened the way for a phase of reforms and changes in the Spanish financial industry. With this new provision the government was authorized to reorganize the whole system, including the Banco de España (which was nationalized), private-sector banks, savings banks, official credit institutions, collective investment entities, long-term sales finance institutions and the stock exchanges. The financial sector underwent significant changes in its structure, with the creation of new institutions and a series of mergers, takeovers and liquidations. The level of intermediation rose as a result of the gradual deregulation and expansion of banking business, the diversification of operations and the creation of an extensive network of branches. The map of the banking system changed, and new types of institution appeared, such as the Institute of Medium- and Long-Term Credit (Instituto de Crédito a Medio y Largo Plazo), which was transformed into the Official Credit Institute (Instituto de Crédito Oficial) in 1971, and the Savings Bank Credit Institute (Instituto de Crédito de las Cajas de Ahorros, ICCA). The period ended just before the start of one of the most severe financial crises to affect the Spanish economy, sweeping away almost half

---

[37] Good studies of this period include Fanjul and Maravall (1985), Gil (1986), López (1981), Lukauskas (1997), Poveda (1980) and Pons (2002 and 2007)

of the banks that had been in business around the middle of the decade. As a result of the crisis the map of the Spanish financial system was again radically altered.

The preamble to the Law of 1962 set out the rationale for reforming the financial system as a whole. The first reason was the inadequacy of the mechanisms at the Banco de España's disposal to implement monetary policy. The second was that the shortage of medium and long-term credit was holding back the growth of the Spanish economy. Thirdly, the lack of specialization among the credit institutions that were expected to meet all the market's demands meant that there was an absence of banks able to meet industry's borrowing needs. And finally, the lack of coordination between saving and investment processes, which called for the adaptation and improvement of the financial mechanisms enabling economic flows to be channeled adequately.[38]

One of the Law's most significant features from the point of view of this chapter was its intention to establish a clear distinction between commercial and investment banking, investing in industry and business. To achieve this, regulations were laid down concerning the creation of investment banks. These banks were required to have equity of at least a million pesetas, fully paid-up in cash at the time of their incorporation, such that no non-cash contributions to their capital were permitted. By way of a guarantee these new institutions were guaranteed their independence and there was a prohibition on other banks, on aggregate, holding more than fifty percent of their capital. Despite this quest for specialization, mixed banks survived, although their long-term investments were more limited and their purchasing of new industrial stock was subject to express authorization from the Finance Ministry. The existing mixed banks had the option to apply to be licensed as investment banks.[39] The creation of new institutions was also regulated, with prior authorization being required from the Finance Ministry, following a proposal by the Banco de España and a report from the Banking Council (Consejo Superior Bancario). New banks' minimum capital requirements varied according to their location, but had to be entirely paid-up.

Despite the 1962 Law's reforming and renewing intent, the degree of State intervention was barely reduced and was only relaxed in later years, and then very gradually: asset and liability operations remained subject to controls and regulations, and interest rates were still set by the authorities.[40] Privileged credit circuits remained, with obligatory coefficients for the banks and savings banks. The official banks also took on a more central role in the financing of public investments and activities the State considered strategic. In 1969 timid steps began to be taken to deregulate interest rates. A basic rediscount rate was set by the Banco de España and the rates applicable to lending and borrowing by other credit institutions were

---

[38]   A detailed study of this law is given in Chapter 3.

[39]   This was the option chosen by Banco Urquijo, Banco Forestal (which was renamed Banco Industrial del Sur), the Banco Hispano Suizo (renamed as Banco de Financiación Industrial) and the Banco de Progreso Agrícola (renamed as Banco de Progreso).

[40]   A Decree-Law of 6 December 1962 authorized the Finance Ministry to impose reserve, liquidity and collateral requirements on the banks.

linked to it by positive or negative marginal differences. In 1970 and 1971 reserve ratios for banks and savings banks were put in place, replacing the existing liquidity coefficient.

A more important step towards the deregulation of the financial system came with the regulations approved in 1974, when a series of measures were enacted introducing an increasing degree of deregulation into the system and tending towards greater uniformity in the legislation relating to different institutions while eliminating compartmentalization. These new features included greater flexibility over the creation of savings banks, new possibilities for attracting borrowings by means of deposit certificates, deregulating long-term bank interest and making cash ratios, and collateral and investment coefficients more generally applicable. The aim was to promote free competition between banks by authorizing new institutions and deregulating the opening of offices, promoting greater operational uniformity between institutions by treating banks and savings banks in a more unified way, and enabling more flexibility over interest rates on term transactions.

As regards the official banks, the 1962 Law created the Institute of Medium- and Long-Term Credit (Instituto de Crédito a Medio y Largo Plazo, ICMLP) and nationalized the Banco Hipotecario, Banco de Crédito Industrial and Banco de Crédito Local; it also reorganized the Instituto de Crédito para la Reconstrucción Nacional, the Servicio Nacional de Crédito Agrícola and the Caja Central de Crédito Marítimo y Pesquero.[41] These six institutions were given the collective title of Official Credit Institutions (Entidades Oficiales de Crédito, EOC). The Banco Exterior was excluded from this nationalization and subject to the same regulation as the private-sector banks, although it remained an official bank. The next step in the restructuring of the EOCs was taken in June 1971, with a new regulation on the Organization and Framework for Official Credit. The intention was that asset operations by the Official Credit Institutions be oriented according to the targets set in the economic and social development plans. Institutions were required to maintain the financial equilibrium of their activity; official credit was to be complementary to private credit and channeled through the capital market, and official credit was to be coordinated with private credit to achieve an efficient allocation of financial resources. One key feature of the 1971 reform was the creation of the Official Credit Institute (Instituto de Crédito Oficial, ICO), which replaced the ICMLP. At the same time the ICCA was dissolved and the two institutions' supervision and inspection functions passed to the Banco de España. The Official Credit Institute (ICO) became the backbone of the management of official credit.

As regards foreign banks, the Law of 1962 delegated their regulation to the government, setting the requisite limitations based on the so-called "reciprocity principle." The mandate was not fulfilled until 23 June 1978, the date on which a Royal Decree was passed in which three modes were envisaged in which foreign establishments could operate:

---

[41]   The Instituto de Crédito para la Reconstrucción Nacional was created by Decree-Law of 7 June 1962, and the other institutions were reorganized and nationalized in successive decrees.

  − Representative offices.
  − Branches.
  − Subsidiaries.

And thus, between 1979 and 1981 the branches of 24 foreign banks joined those of the four banks that had operated in Spain since the end of the Second World War.

6.2   A decade-and-a-half of growth

The end of the status quo paved the way for the creation of new credit institutions. The 1962 Law indicated that "more freedom and greater ease of access to, and exercise of, the banking profession" would be given. As a result, between 1963 and 1969 22 new entities were added to the Register and between 1970 and 1975 a further nine, making a total of 31 banks, including investment banks (financing industry and business) and retail banks. The full list is given in Table 13. None of the institutions founded at this time went on to become a major player or alter the existing financial ranking, however. The majority suffered from serious management shortcomings, leading to disproportionate growth which as the years went by, made them vulnerable to insurmountable difficulties. These new institutions were the main players in the crisis of the mid-seventies and were placed under the control of the authorities and subsequently wound up or taken over by other banks.

The total number of banks at this time comes to 132, if the 31 newly created banks are added to the 101 that existed in 1963 (including the Banco Exterior de España, which was classed as both official and national). However, the figure that is given in the CSB's statistics for the number of banks in 1975 is 111, which is 21 less. This was a result of the continual process of mergers and takeovers, which, as Table 14 shows, were led by the major banks, which continued the progress towards consolidation of the financial industry begun in the preceding period. Banco Central and Banco de Bilbao took over the largest number of smaller institutions. As regards the other banks, of the 111 entities on the Register of banks and bankers in 1975, we know 40 to have been national; 12 belonged to the regional bank group, 55 were classed as local banks; and there were a further four foreign institutions.[42]

One way of understanding the progress of the banking sector in these years is to look at how their networks of branches expanded. In effect, the development of the financial sector was framed by the so-called "expansion plans" prepared for each financial year by the Banco de España, which determined the growth capacity of each institution by means of a complex formula, which set the number of new branches which each bank could open.[43]

---

[42]   The full list of banks can be consulted in the Consejo Superior Bancario's statistical yearbook published in 1976. It is also reproduced in Patxot (1999).

[43]   Faus (2001), pp. 182-192

TABLE 13 NEW BANKS CREATED BETWEEN 1963 AND 1975

1963
Banco del Desarrollo Económico Español
Banco de Fomento
Unión Industrial de León
Unión Industrial Bancaria

1964
Banco Industrial de Bilbao
Banco del Noroeste
Banco de Soto (later renamed Banco de Lugo)
Banco de San Adrián (later renamed Banco de Navarra)
Banco de Granada (later renamed Banco Granada-Jerez)
Banco de Langreo (later renamed Banco de Asturias)
Banco Europeo de Negocios (later renamed Banco Popular Industrial)
Banco Catalán de Desarrollo (later renamed Banc Català de Crèdit)
Banco Occidental

1965
Banco de Levante
Banco de Huelva
Banco de la Exportación
Banco Comercial de Talavera (later renamed Banco de Toledo)
Banco de Burgos
Banco de Alicante
Banco Intercontinental Español
Banco Industrial de Cataluña

1969
Banco Industrial Fierro (later renamed Banco Luso Español and Banco de Finanzas)

1972
Banco Industrial del Mediterráneo

1973
Banco de Promoción de Negocios
Banco de Europa
Nuevo Banco
Banco de Descuento

1975
Banco Árabe Español
Banco de la Industria Exportadora (later renamed Banco de Expansión Industrial)
Banco Industrial de Guipúzcoa
Banco de Coordinación Industrial (later renamed Banco de los Pirineos)

SOURCE: Consejo Superior Bancario.

Nine plans were drawn up in all (the last in 1974), permitting a total of 2,549 new offices to be opened, almost as many as the 2,758 that existed at the end of the period shaped by the *status quo*.

One essential feature of the plans cited was a quantity termed the "banks' capacity for expansion." This was calculated as the sum of their equity and borrowings on 31 December of each year, minus the value calculated for the bank's offices as a whole, a value which

TABLE 14   TAKEOVERS AMONG REGISTERED BANKS, 1962-1975

Acquiring banks	Acquired bank
Hispano Americano	Banco de San Sebastián (1975)
Vizcaya	Banca de Vilella (1969)
Bilbao	Banco de Irún (1970)
	Banco Asturiano de Industria y Comercio (1970)
	Banco Castellano (1970)
	Banco de La Coruña (1970)
Central	Crédito y Docks de Barcelona (1970)
	Banco de Aragón (1970)
	Banca Nogueira (1971)
	Banco de Canarias (1971)
	Crédito Navarro (1972)
Santander	Banco Industrial de Barcelona (1970)
	Banco Continental (1971)
Mercantil e Industrial	Banco Aragonés de Crédito (1969)
	Banco de Burgos (1971)
Guipuzcuano	Barcaiztegui y Maestre (1962)
Atlántico	Banco de Málaga (1972)
Catalana	Expansión Comercial (1971)
Crédito e Inversiones	Crédito y Fomento (1964)
Galicia (before, Banco de Vigo)	Banco de Lugo (1973)
DISCONTINUED	Banco Comercial de Menorca (1967)

SOURCE: Consejo Superior Bancario.

varied according to the size of the financial centre. Rules of preference were established for the awarding of offices, and to this end the banks were classed into five groups:

- Local banks operating in a single province;
- Local banks operating in a banking district;
- Local banks operating in several banking districts;
- Regional banks.
- National banks.[44]

Allocations were made in groups and within each group according to the ratio between the total capacity and the consumed capacity, as well as by the order in which the places had been applied for. For their part, the locations to be awarded were classed into four groups according to their features:

- Shortage of banking services.
- Inadequacy of the service provided.

---

[44]   Spain was divided into 9 banking districts: Center; Basque Country-Navarre; Catalonia-Balearic Islands; Aragón; Asturias-Galicia; Castile-León; Levante (east coast); Andalusia-Extremadura; and the Canary Islands and the cities on the African mainland.

- Inadequacy of the service bearing in mind the economic development plans for the financial center and its surrounding area.
- The advisability of greater competition at the location in question.[45]

The expansion plans were in effect over the 10 year period from 1963 to 1973. Although they were produced annually, in most cases new openings were phased over a period of two to three years. The plans were implemented as follows:

- The first plan was approved in October 1964 and included 210 branches and 68 urban agencies, of which 179 and 68 were allocated and opened, respectively.
- The second plan, dated October 1965 authorized 399 branches and 57 agencies, of which 307 and 40 were awarded, respectively.
- The third plan, approved on 17 January 1967, envisaged 218 branches and 74 agencies, and the numbers allocated were 197 and 74, respectively.
- The fourth plan, in December 1967, envisaged 221 offices, of which 190 were awarded.
- The fifth plan, approved on 30 October 1968, envisaged 220 offices, of which 210 were awarded.
- The sixth plan, in the last quarter of 1969, 224 offices, of which 202 were awarded.
- The seventh plan was approved in 1970, with 151 offices of which 144 were awarded.
- In 1971, rather than a new expansion plan, the Ministry published an Order amending the regulations (establishing 'open access' for 80% of the usable capacity) and under this new Order the eighth plan was approved in March 1972, with 172 offices, of which 17 were allocated, whereas 326 were granted by 'open access'.
- The ninth and final plan was approved on 6 February 1973 and included 154 offices of which 116 were awarded, while 387 were opened under 'open access'.

Table 15 shows the annual growth of the number of offices.

True deregulation of the opening of offices came with the Decree of 9 August 1974. From that point on the opening of new branches was solely dependent on the capacity ratios defined in relation to equity capital. The result of this liberalization was an extremely rapid expansion of the network of branches: in the following four years 5,658 offices were opened, until the crisis slowed the pace of this excessive proliferation of branches. At the end of the period, before the onset of the banking crisis, Spanish banks had grown from 2,775 offices in 1963 to 11,095 offices in December 1978. This route was one of the few mechanisms of competition used by Spanish banks at the time.

---

[45] The regulations changed with the expansion plans, affecting in particular the rules on capacity for expansion and other points such as minimum distances between branches.

TABLE 15   ANNUAL CHANGE IN THE NUMBER OF BANK OFFICES

Year	Total	Annual change	Accumulated change
1948	2,157	–	–
1949	2,197	40	40
1950	2,226	29	69
1951	2,260	34	103
1952	2,298	38	141
1953	2,336	38	179
1954	2,391	55	234
1955	2,449	58	292
1956	2,519	70	362
1957	2,562	43	405
1958	2,610	48	453
1959	2,637	27	480
1960	2,697	60	540
1961	2,728	31	571
1962	–	–	–
1963	2,775	47	618
1964	3,037	262	880
1965	3,421	384	1,264
1966	3,689	268	1,532
1967	3,875	186	1,718
1968	3,881	6	1,724
1969	4,092	211	1,935
1970	4,291	199	2,134
1971	4,437	146	2,280
1972	4,911	474	2,754
1973	5,437	526	3,280
1974	5,625	188	3,468
1975	7,569	1,944	5,412

SOURCE: Consejo Superior Bancario.

The growth of the banking sector can also be followed by examining the variation in the aggregate balance sheet items in Table 16. The figure for total assets grew more than 15 fold between 1960 and 1975, from 466,418 million to 8,308,555 billion pesetas. If the miscellaneous and memorandum accounts are subtracted from these sums, as they may distort the comparison (especially in 1975, when they were particularly large), the increase is somewhat more moderate, but nevertheless considerable. The whole set of account items on the balance sheet was involved in this rapid growth of assets, in particular the bills portfolio (discounting and commercial lending) and credit (under the debtors heading); the securities portfolio, by contrast, behaved more moderately.

The structure of the balance sheet largely reflected the account given above. Commercial paper accounted for a constant proportion, at around 22% of assets investments and credits for around 15%; i.e., overall, the banks channeled approximately 40% of their investments through their lending and credit. By contrast, the weight of the securities portfolio fell by 10 points: from 17% to 7%. This was due to the smaller issues of national debt, which led to

TABLE 16   AGGREGATE BALANCE SHEET OF THE PRIVATE-SECTOR BANKS. IN BILLIONS OF PESETAS

Assets	1960	1965	1970	1975
Cash and banks	42,002	98,971	278,926	856,795
Bills portfolio	103,876	322,789	644,019	1,866,699
Bills with maturities of up to 90 days	101,116	275,246	542,986	1,309,716
Longer-term bills	1,952	45,714	97,717	527,357
Other bills	808	1,829	3,316	29,626
Securities portfolio	81,714	112,233	295,084	624,745
Public debt	61,001	84,067	233,082	413,019
Misc.	20,713	28,166	62,002	211,726
Credit	71,526	145,543	301,065	1,161,727
Secured loans	9	19,179	37,346	119,708
On demand	8,029	20,213	45,839	145,073
Term	52,329	104,729	209,104	757,927
Foreign currency	-	-	-	-
Other Assets	46,416	108,116	207,895	628,156
Memorandum and miscellaneous accounts	120,884	309,013	969,266	3,170,433
TOTAL ASSETS	466,418	1,096,665	2,696,255	8,308,555
Liabilities				
Capital	6,096	19,200	50,614	180,989
Reserves	11,946	24,498	50,057	170,207
Borrowings	233,621	570,341	1,163,057	3,173,239
On demand	122,371	278,605	482,215	1,284,296
Maturity greater than one month	72,519	186,264	323,742	733,732
Longer maturities	38,731	105,472	357,100	1,155,211
Foreign currency	-	-	-	-
Other Liabilities	214,755	482,626	1,432,527	4,784,120
TOTAL LIABILITIES	466,418	1,096,665	2,696,255	8,308,555

SOURCE: Consejo Superior Bancario.

these securities playing a smaller role on the banks' balance sheets. In fact, the participation of public funds receded, giving way to investments in private securities; whereas public securities represented 75% of the portfolio in 1960, 15 years later their share had fallen to 66%; investments in company shares and bonds had clearly gone in the opposite direction.

Capital and reserves also grew rapidly during this period, which was characterized by a succession of capital increases, once the barriers existing prior to the Law of 1962 were eliminated. This led to paid-up capital being multiplied by a factor of 30, such that in 1975 the figure shown on the aggregate balance sheet exceeded that of reserves. Reserves had also increased considerably, but somewhat less than capital. Overall, capital and reserves went from 18,042 million pesetas in 1960 to 351,196 million in the final year of the period. Liability items also continued their ascent, as can be seen in the lower part of the aggregate balance sheet. One noteworthy change was the greater weight acquired by term deposits relative to current accounts. While the proportion of the latter descended from 52 to 41%, deposits rose from 48 to 59% between the start and end of the comparison.

The liquidity ratios also suggest that this was a phase in which banks had a comfortable and expanding position (Table 17). Banks as a whole enjoyed liquidity levels of over 20%, a percentage that could be classed as high. Second-line liquidity, although lower than in the previous period, was also high, at around 40%. From these figures one can only conclude that the Spanish banking system as a whole did not suffer from liquidity problems at any time during the period and that the problems that arose were confined to smaller, badly managed, institutions. The solvency ratios are higher than those estimated in the preceding period; thus, we can observe that the ratio of equity to borrowings and deposits rose from 7.7% in 1960 to 11.1% in 1975.

The banking crisis that struck two years later brought the banking industry's expansion described here to a halt and overturned the map of the Spanish financial system. With the crisis, which endured until the mid-eighties, no new institutions were created and numerous institutions disappeared, including almost all of those created during this first phase of financial deregulation. Of the 110 banks in operation in Spain on 31 December 1977, the crisis affected, to a greater or lesser extent, 56 banks and 23 banking firms. That is to say, it had an impact on 52% of Spanish banking institutions and more than 27% of savings, with an associated cost that reached 15% of GDP of the time. Of all the banks affected, around twenty were entities created between 1963 and 1979. At the start of the crisis it affected small and medium-sized banks, but as of 1981 it began to make its mark on bigger entities such as Banca Catalana, the Rumasa Group and Banco Urquijo.[46]

TABLE 17   LIQUIDITY AND SOLVENCY OF SPANISH BANKS

a) Liquidity

Year	Cash / total deposits	Cash + government debt / Deposits
1960	18.0	55.8
1970	24.0	50.4
1975	27.0	51.4

b) Solvency

Year	Capital + reserves / Deposits	Capital + reserves / Loans + private debt securities portfolio
1960	7.7	19.6
1970	9.2	27.8
1975	11.1	25.6

SOURCE: *Anuarios Financieros y de Sociedades Anónimas de España,* 1915-1919 and 1923; and Martín-Aceña (1985), Table I-2.

---

[46]   The banking crisis is covered in Chapter 7.

7   The transformation of the Spanish banking system: a long-term view [47]

This chapter has discussed the evolution of the Spanish banking system between 1900 and 1975. Over these seven decades-and-a-half the banking industry has grown and modernized. At the start of the century the country's financial structure was that of an underdeveloped economy with a low degree of monetization. The Banco de España had absolute pre-eminence, and it was far bigger than any of the other credit institutions. Only the other official institution, the Banco Hipotecario, and three private-sector banks, the Banco Hispano Colonial, the Banco Español de Crédito and the Banco Hispano Americano came anywhere close to it. Between 1900 and 1935 there was a remarkable transformation: the number of institutions multiplied, they gained in size, and many of them started to develop into what were termed "mixed banks," combining retail business and investment activities aimed at industry. The 1921 Banking Law led to the first regulations being applied to the system, but the general framework remained fairly open. The degree of financial intermediation rose, but the level of diversification barely changed: although it included banks and savings banks, the Spanish system lacked institutions that specialized in different credit segments. One noteworthy change, however, was the loss of weight of the Banco de España and the emergence of national banks in the form of five large institutions, the Banco de Bilbao, the Banco Central, the Banco Español de Crédito, the Banco Hispano Americano and the Banco de Vizcaya, with an extensive network of branches. The financial map underwent considerable modifications, with numerous entities being added and others disappearing. This reflected both economic events, and political ones, such as the world war.

Most of the banks created in the early years of the century did not stand the test of time and disappeared either during one or other of the crises that punctuated the first three decades of the century, or as a result of the continuous process of mergers and takeovers.

After the end of the Civil War, state interventionism made itself felt. The rules ushered in by the status quo and the Banking Law of 1946 altered the regulatory framework that had previously existed. This interventionism by the authorities remained in effect for two decades, until the Basic Law in 1962, when a half-hearted process of deregulation began. Nevertheless, despite the status quo and the multiplicity of regulations in force, the banking system grew and was transformed considerably, with an increase in the level of financial intermediation, which came closer to that in other Western European countries. There were no overt crises during Francoism, but the banking map was transformed as much as it had been in the preceding period, this time through a process of consolidation. Comparing the list of banks in 1900, or indeed that of 1930, with the list in 1975 is the best evidence of the fluidity characterizing the system. At the same time, a central core of banks formed, comprising half-a-dozen institutions that dominated the Spanish financial landscape until recent times.

---

[47]   For an overview of the financial system during this period, see Villalonga (1962), Tedde de Lorca (1988 and 2001), Pons (2001c), Cuevas and Hoyo (2003), Martín-Aceña (2005) and Pueyo (2006).

These included two of the oldest banks, Banco de Bilbao and Banco de Santander, which were joined in the early 20th century by Banco Hispano Americano, and the Banco Español de Crédito, Banco de Vizcaya, and Banco Urquijo, and somewhat later by Banco Central and Banco Popular Español. Thus, during Francoism, despite the "status quo" the structure of the banking system again underwent considerable changes. Few new institutions were founded, but many of the existing ones were wound up, merged or taken over.

As regards the level of banking concentration, the trend was downwards. The absolute index shows that while in 1874 the five, ten or fifteen biggest banks accounted for more than 90% of the paid-up capital, by 1915 the percentage had dropped to 63%, 77% and 84%, respectively. The reduction, measured using Herfindhal's index, is – if possible – more significant, dropping from 0.2908 to 0.0695. Over the following two decades the degree of banking concentration barely changed, which implied that the oligopolistic power of the financial institutions during this period was maintained and with it their market power. It seems that the forces in favor of competition, which had been so strong up until 1915, had been neutralized. However, after the civil war the level of banking concentration continued its initial trend, with a drop of 10 points. The decline was very sharp between 1952 and 1975, two decades in which the major banks appeared to lose positions of market control. The more technical Herfindhal index corroborates these findings as it offers a decrease of 0.1163 to 0.0650, implying a reduction of more than 40%.[48]

Among the factors that explain Spain's historical experience of progress towards greater competition in the banking sector over the last third of the 19th century and first decade-and-a-half of the 20th century, are the lack of significant legal barriers to entry, such as requirements regarding initial capital, scant regulation of the system, and a rapid development of the deposit market. Other factors include the increase in the number of institutions, which could have been an essential driving force towards greater competition, and also the fact that small and medium-sized firms greatly outnumbered the larger ones. In the following decades (between the wars and after the Civil War), with consolidation and modernization of the Spanish banking system, the forces in favor of concentration prevailed. The main reason could be the introduction, after the Banking Law (LOB) of 1921, of the first administrative measures, laying down the rules for the conditions of entry and regulating a variety of credit activities. Economies of scale also emerged, with the consequent reduction in unit costs as size increased, thus possibly contributing to the increase in the level of financial concentration. The banks embarked on processes of mergers and acquisitions in order to achieve these economies of scale and they implemented policies aimed at maximizing internal growth in order to bring down their unit costs faster and thus gain market share.

In 1975 the Spanish financial system was much bigger than in 1900: it had grown and diversified, although less so than in other developed countries in Europe. The level of concentration in the banking system was similar to the European average. The regulations

---

48   The calculations are given in Martín-Aceña and Pons (1996).

approved since 1962 had made state interventionism less rigid and introduced a measure of freedom into institutions' operations. However, Spanish banks, like other sectors of the country's economy, had developed under the protection of the state and, in general, lacked the ability to compete abroad. They also suffered from an efficiency deficit. Many credit institutions were too small and their internal management inadequate. The crisis of the seventies and eighties highlighted these weaknesses and revealed others in the regulatory framework. This same crisis also served to restructure the system and place it on a footing on which it could compete in the open environment that Spain's membership of what was then the European Community would entail.

References

ANES ÁLVAREZ, R. (1974). "El Banco de España (1874-1914). Un banco nacional", in G. Tortella (Supervisor), *La banca española en la Restauración,* Banco de España, Madrid.

ARIAS, X. (1986). *La banca oficial en España,* Instituto de Estudios Fiscales, Madrid.

BBVA (1999). Actividad de la banca extranjera en España entre 1920 y 1935, Cuadernos del Archivo Histórico, Bilbao.

— (2003). *La banca en España en el período de entreguerras,* 1920-1935, Cuadernos del Archivo Histórico, Bilbao.

— (2004). *La banca como motor de desarrollo en España.* 150 años de historia bancaria, Cuadernos del Archivo Histórico, Bilbao.

BERNIS, F. de (1923). *Consecuencias económicas de la guerra,* Junta para la Ampliación de Estudios e Investigaciones Científicas, Madrid.

CABANA, F. (1965). *La banca a Catalunya,* Edicions 62, Barcelona.

— (1978). *Història del Banc de Barcelona,* 1844-1920, Edicions 62, Barcelona.

CANOSA, R. (1945). *Un siglo de banca privada en España, 1845-1945,* Nuevas Gráficas, SA.

CLAYTON, G. (1973). "España", in R. S. Sayers, *La banca en Europa occidental,* Labor, Barcelona, pp. 317-349.

CONSEJO SUPERIOR BANCARIO (1973). *Un cuarto de siglo de banca privada,* 1947-1972.

CUESTA GARRIGÓS, I. (1944). "Los grandes bancos españoles. Su evolución, 1922-1943", *Moneda y Crédito,* 11, pp. 36-65.

CUEVAS CASAÑA, J., and A. HOYO APARICIO (2003). "Los flujos de financiación de la actividad económica y empresarial en la España contemporánea, siglos XIX y XX", *Cuadernos de Economía y Dirección de Empresa,* 17, pp. 67-95.

FANJUL, O., and F. MARAVALL (1985). *La eficiencia del sistema bancario español,* Alianza, Madrid.

FAUS MOMPART, E. M. (2001). *Regulación y desregulación. Notas para la historia de la banca española,* Ediciones Península.

GARCÍA LÓPEZ, J. R. (1985). "Banqueros y comerciantes banqueros, clave oculta del funcionamiento del sistema bancario español del siglo XIX", *Moneda y Crédito,* 175, pp. 59-85.

— (1989). "El sistema bancario español en el siglo XIX: ¿Una estructura dual? Nuevos planteamientos y nuevas propuestas", *Revista de Historia Económica,* VII, 1, pp. 111-132.

GARCÍA RUIZ, J. L. (2001). "La banca extranjera en España tras la Restauración, 1874-1936", in C. Sudrià and D. A. Tirado (Eds.), *Peseta y protección,* Edicions Universitat de Barcelona.

— (2002). "Los arreglos interbancarios durante el franquismo", *Revista de Historia Económica,* 2, pp. 365-386.

GIL, G. (1986). *El sistema financiero español,* Estudios Económicos, no. 29, Banco de España.

LÓPEZ ROA, R. (1981). *Sistema financiero español,* Alicante.

LUKAUSKAS, A. J. (1997). *Regulating finance. The Political Economy of Spanish financial Policy from Franco to Democracy,* Ann Arbor University Press, Michigan.

MARTÍN-ACEÑA, P. (1985). "Desarrollo y modernización del sistema financiero, 1844-1935", in N. Sánchez Albornoz (Ed.), *La modernización económica de España,* Alianza Editorial.

— (1991), "Los orígenes de la banca pública", in F. Comín and P. Martín-Aceña, *Historia de la empresa pública en España,* Espasa Calpe, Madrid.

— (1994). "Los problemas monetarios al término de la Guerra Civil", *Hacienda Pública Española,* monografía 2, pp. 63-88.

— (1995). "Spanish Banking in the Interwar Period", in C. H. Feinstein (Ed.), *Banking, Currency and Finance in Europe between the Wars,* Clarendon Press, Oxford, pp. 502-527.

— (2001). "El Banco de España entre dos siglos: de banquero del Estado a prestamista en última instancia", in A. Morales (Ed.), Las claves del siglo XX. *Las transformaciones económicas, Sociedad Estatal Nuevo Milenio,* Madrid, pp. 95-139.

— (2005). "La conformación histórica de la industria bancaria española", *Mediterráneo Económico,* 8, pp. 21-44.

— (2006), "El sistema financiero", in P. Martín-Aceña and E. Martínez Ruiz (Eds.), *La economía de la Guerra Civil,* Marcial Pons Editores, Madrid.

MARTÍN-ACEÑA, P., and M. A. PONS BRIAS (1994). "Spanish Banking after the Civil War, 1940-1962", *Financial History Review,* 1, 2, pp. 121-138.

— (1996). "Estructura y rentabilidad de las empresas financieras en España, 1874-1975", in F. Comín and P. Martín-Aceña (Eds.), *La empresa en la historia de España,* Editorial Civitas.

MARTÍN-ACEÑA, P., and M. TITOS MARTÍNEZ (1999). *El sistema financiero en España, Una síntesis histórica,* Universidad de Granada.

MINISTERIO DE HACIENDA (1921). Ordenación Bancaria de España, Gráficas Reunidas, SA, Madrid.

MINISTERIO DE HACIENDA. DIRECCIÓN GENERAL DE BANCA, BOLSA E INVERSIONES (1961). *Memorándum del Ministerio de Hacienda sobre el sistema bancario y crediticio,* Madrid.

MUÑOZ, J. (1978). "La expansión bancaria entre 1919 y 1926. La formación de una banca nacional", *Cuadernos Económicos de ICE,* 6, pp. 98-162.

OLARIAGA, L. (1951). "La liquidabilidad de los bancos de depósito españoles", *Moneda y Crédito,* 38, pp. 12-20.

— (1961). *El dinero. II: Organización monetaria y bancaria* (2nd edition), Madrid.

PATXOT, V. (1999). *Medio siglo del Registro de Bancos y Banqueros,* 1947-1997, Banco de España.

PONS BRÍAS, M. A. (2001a). "Oligopolio y tipos de interés en la banca española, 1942-1975", *Revista de Historia Económica,* 19, 3, pp. 679-706.

— (2001b). "Banca e industria en España, 1939-1985: la influencia de la banca universal en el crecimiento económico", *Revista de Historia Industrial,* 19-20, pp. 249-274.

— (2001c). "La evolución del sistema bancario español en el siglo XX: una perspectiva comparada", *Estudis d'Història Econòmica,* 17-18, pp. 177-212.

— (2002). *Regulating Spanish Banking,* 1939-1975, Ashgate Publishing Ltd.

— (2007). "Banca e industria en España durante la etapa franquista", in R. Dobado, A. Gómez Gal-varriato and G. Márquez (Eds.), *México y España. ¿Historias paralelas?,* Fondo de Cultura Económica, Mexico, pp. 621-648.

POVEDA, R. (1980). "Circuitos privilegiados de financiación del sistema crediticio", *Papeles de Economía Española,* 3, pp. 114-135.

PRADOS ARRATE, J. (1958). *El sistema bancario español,* Editorial Aguilar.

PUEYO SÁNCHEZ, J. R. (2006). *El comportamiento de la gran banca en España, 1921-1974,* Estudios de Historia Económica, no. 48, Banco de España, Madrid.

RIDRUEJO, E. (1954). "El sistema bancario español", *Moneda y Crédito,* 51.

ROLDÁN, S., and J. L. GARCÍA DELGADO (1973). *La formación de la sociedad capitalista en España,* Confederación Española de Cajas de Ahorros, Madrid.

SÁNCHEZ ASIAÍN, J. Á. (2008). "La banca en la Guerra Civil", *Economía y economistas españoles en la Guerra Civil,* Vol. II, Real Academia de Ciencias Morales y Políticas/Galaxia Gutenberg, Barcelona.

SÁNCHEZ PEDREÑO, A. J. (1961). "Tres casos de banca comparada", *Banca y Seguros,* trimestre II, pp. 3-21.

SARDÀ DEXEUS, J. (1964). "El sistema financiero español", *Boletín de Estudios Económicos,* XIX, 62, pp. 349-362.

— (1970). "El Banco de España, 1931-1962", *El Banco de España. Una historia económica,* Banco de España, Madrid.

TALLADA, J. M. (1926). *Economía de la posguerra. Moneda y Crédito,* Editorial Minerva, SA, Barcelona.

TEDDE DE LORCA, P. (1974). "La banca privada española durante la Restauración, 1874-1914", in G. Tortella (Supervisor), *La banca española en la Restauración,* Banco de España.

— (1988). "El sector financiero", *Enciclopedia de Historia de España,* I, Economía, Sociedad, Alianza Editorial.

— (2001). "El sistema financiero en la España del siglo XX", in A. Morales Moya (Ed.), Las claves de la España del siglo XX. *Las transformaciones Económicas, Sociedad Estatal España Nuevo Milenio,* Madrid.

TITOS MARTÍNEZ, M. (1999). "Banca y banqueros privados", in P. Martín-Aceña and M. Titos Martínez (Eds.), *El sistema financiero en España. Una síntesis histórica,* Universidad de Granada.

TORTELLA CASARES, G. (1970). "La evolución del sistema financiero español de 1856 a 1868", in *Ensayos de la economía española a mediados del siglo XIX,* Editorial Ariel.

TORTELLA CASARES, G., and J. PALAFOX (1988). "Banca e industria en España, 1918-1936", *Investigaciones Económicas,* 20, pp. 33-64.

VILLALONGA, I. (1962). "La banca española en lo que va de siglo", *Arbor,* pp. 189-190.

5. The savings banks: 1900-1975

Francisco Comín
Universidad de Alcalá

1 Introduction

This chapter studies the historical evolution of Spain's unlisted savings banks, or *cajas de ahorros,* from 1900 when their business entered a stage of rapid growth and they began mutating from charitable organizations into financial institutions, up until 1975, the final year of Francoism and the prelude to the liberalization and modernization of the Spanish financial system. Along with this introduction, this chapter comprises six further sections, devoted to the successive stages of the history of Spanish savings banks; a history shaped by political circumstances, given powerful impact of legislation on the *cajas.*

The second section focuses on the new financial and social activities of the *cajas de ahorros* from 1900 to 1920, taking the sector's structure at the turn of the century as its starting point. The third section examines the turbulent inter-war period, beginning with Cambó's Banking Law in 1921 and ending in 1935, on the eve of the Spanish Civil War. The sector's growth in the 1920s led to the creation of the Spanish Confederation of Saving Banks (Confederación Española de Cajas de Ahorros or CECA), followed, during the Second Republic, by the promulgation of the Statute of Savings *(Estatuto del Ahorro).* This section also looks at the savings banks' new political commitments and other features of their development in this period. The fourth section examines the savings banks' vicissitudes during Spain's period of economic autarky, and the financial constraints imposed by the Ministry of Labor and the Ministry of Finance in their effort to bring the *cajas'* financial and social welfare activities entirely under their control. The savings banks managed to neutralize the most interventionist of these measures, but in the 1940s and 1950s they lost their operational independence in both the financial and social spheres.

The fifth section of this chapter looks at how the new course taken by government economic policy after 1957 influenced the savings banks, enabling them to consolidate their status as financial institutions in exchange for their making their resources available to provide preferential finance to support the government's policy goals. This required a reorganization and change of command at the Spanish Confederation of Savings Banks (CECA) to orient the savings banks' investment policy; a change which met with resistance from some quarters. The sixth section examines the intensification of the financial constraints on the *cajas,* which were placed at the service of the Development Plans from 1964 onwards. To control their investments, new powers were given to the Savings Bank Credit Institute (Instituto de Crédito de Cajas de Ahorro, ICCA), which went on to become the supervisory body for the savings banks, its financial and service functions being devolved to the CECA. From that time on, the government intervened in all the savings banks' operations, both on the deposit-taking side (by setting interest rates and controlling the authorization of "new savings accounts") and on the investment side, by channeling their investments through increased mandatory investment coefficients. Finally, the seventh section covers the savings banks during the twilight years of Francoism, from 1971 to 1975. The most noteworthy legal change during this period, and that which shaped their future course, was that the *cajas* came under the supervision of the Banco de España (putting them on an equal footing, in institutional terms, with the commercial banks). The final years of Francoism also saw some important operational changes at the CECA and in the savings banks themselves, paving the way for growth once the financial sector was liberalized in 1977. The chapter ends with some concluding remarks in section eight.

2   Financial and social activities (1900-1920)

The *cajas de ahorros* or savings banks first emerged as charitable organizations under legislation passed in 1835. The role assigned to them was that of promoting savings among the lower classes and providing charitable lending to the neediest segments of the population through their *montes de piedad,* a form of charitable pawnbrokers. Initially, the law obliged all savings banks to be linked to a *monte de piedad.* Together with the charitable aims of the *cajas de ahorros,* liberal governments also granted them financial functions: thus as well as mobilizing the working class's savings, the *cajas* were intended to compete with pawnbrokers and bring down the exorbitant interest charged on pledge loans. Initially the State's involvement in the savings banks was indirect, being limited to regulating their operations and laying down guidelines for the action of their governing bodies. The State merely encouraged the creation of savings banks by private philanthropists. The Savings

Banks Law *(Ley de Cajas de Ahorros)* in 1880 established the savings banks as charitable organizations with independence from the State. In 1880 the role of the savings banks as intermediaries between savers depositing their money and the *montes de piedad*'s borrowers remained unaltered. Importantly, the savings banks were eligible for the tax exemptions granted to charitable institutions. The 1880 Law also clearly defined the operations of the *cajas de ahorros* and their associated *montes de piedad.* The main novelty was that, henceforth, savings banks could be founded without a *monte de piedad.* This was an option certain savings banks in the more developed regions, such as the Basque Country and Catalonia, were quick to take advantage of. By contrast, in the country's southern provinces, the savings banks continued to be tied to their *montes de piedad,* because their social role remained paramount in view of the greater poverty in these regions. The greater organizational freedom stimulated the creation of numerous savings banks. The Law of 29 June 1880 represented a boost to the founding of new *cajas de ahorros,* the creation of which had slowed since the Royal Decree of 1853, which was never really implemented. Thus, between 1880 and 1900 a total of 34 new institutions were created, whereas between 1835 and 1880 just 36 had been.

2.1 The starting point: the savings banks in 1901

Table 1 shows the situation in the savings sector at the start of this period with the basic details of the savings banks existing in 1901. At that time there were 47 *cajas* of widely differing sizes, both in terms of deposits and numbers of depositors. The marked increase in the number of savings banks is a clear sign of the sector's growth. This was confirmed by the reduction in the level of concentration in the sector, although in 1901 this remained substantial. In particular, the two largest savings banks (those of Madrid and Barcelona), accounted for 46.2% of total deposits; the five largest savings banks accounted for 76.3% and the top ten, accounted for 84.5%. In terms of depositor numbers, the top two savings banks (in this case the order being reversed, with Barcelona's savings bank having the largest number of depositors) also accounted for a large share of the total (48.4%). But as new savings banks were added, the percentage of depositors declined in relation to deposits, as the five biggest savings banks in terms of customer numbers accounted for 67.3% of all customers and the top ten accounted for 78.6%. This meant that although they had fewer customers, the top five and top ten savings banks had a larger share of total deposits. This implies that, in general, the balance per depositor was bigger among the larger savings banks, although with notable exceptions, such as the case of the Caja de Barcelona.

It is necessary to qualify this statement, however, in view of the final column of Table 1, which shows high degree of dispersion of average deposits. What is more, the average balance did not depend so much on savings banks' size as on the socio-economic environment in which they operated. This explains why the average balance of the Caja de Barcelona was half that of the Caja de Madrid, as there was a predominance of wage earners and professionals

TABLE 1	SPANISH SAVINGS BANKS IN 1901
	(Ranked by deposits)

	Savings Banks	Number of depositors	Percentage of depositors	Ranked by depositors	Deposits (thousands of pesetas)	Percentage of deposits	Deposits/ depositors (Pesetas)
1	Monte de Piedad y Caja de Ahorros de Madrid	52,088	22.3	2	42,780	29.3	821
2	Caja de Ahorros y Monte de Piedad de Barcelona	60,969	26.1	1	24,730	16.9	406
3	Monte de Piedad y Caja de Ahorros de Valencia	22,371	9.6	3	14,964	10.3	669
4	Monte de Piedad y Caja de Ahorros de Sevilla	12,587	5.4	4	9,913	7.8	788
5	Caja de Ahorros Provincial de Guipúzcoa (a)	9,264	4.0	6	9,780	6.7	1,056
6	Caja de Ahorros y Monte de Piedad Municipal de San Sebastián	10,112	4.3	5	7,911	5.4	782
7	Caja de Ahorros y Monte de Piedad de Zaragoza	4,788	2.0	8	3,540	2.4	739
8	Caja de Ahorros y Monte de Piedad Ciudad Vitoria	3,469	1.5	10	3,178	2.2	916
9	Caja de Ahorros y Monte de Piedad de Jerez de la Frontera (a) (b)	2,402	1.0	15	2,666	1.8	1,110
10	Caja de Ahorros y Monte de Piedad de Las Baleares	5,590	2.4	7	2,600	1.8	465
11	Caja de Ahorros y Monte de Piedad de Córdoba (a)	3,993	1.7	9	2,416	1.7	605
12	Monte de Piedad y Caja de Ahorros de Valladolid (a)	2,598	1.1	13	2,388	1.6	919
13	Caja de Ahorros y Monte de Piedad de Santiago	2,888	1.2	12	2,067	1.4	716
14	Caja de Ahorros y Monte de Piedad de La Coruña	2,396	1.0	16	1,992	1.4	831
15	Caja de Ahorros de Sabadell	3,340	1.4	11	1,559	1.1	467
16	Caja de Ahorros y Monte de Piedad Municipal. Pamplona		0.0		1,377	0.9	
17	Caja de Ahorros y Montepío de Lérida	1,427	0.6	22	1,360	0.9	953
18	Caja de Ahorros y Monte de Piedad de Alicante	1,745	0.7	18	994	0.7	570
19	Caja de Ahorros de Manresa (b)	1,644	0.7	20	977	0.7	594
20	Monte de Piedad y Caja de Ahorros de Alcoy	2,338	1.0	17	954	0.7	408
21	Monte de Piedad y Caja de Ahorros de Oviedo	2,470	1.1	14	822	0.6	333
22	Caja de Ahorros de Mataró (a) (b)	1,635	0.7	21	804	0.6	492
23	Caja de Ahorros y Monte de Piedad de Salamanca (a)	1,102	0.5	27	791	0.5	718
24	Caja de Ahorros de Tarrasa	1,714	0.7	19	743	0.5	433
25	Caja de Ahorros y Monte de Piedad de Ávila (a)	1,411	0.6	23	582	0.4	412
26	Monte de Piedad y Caja de Ahorros de Pontevedra (a) (b)	454	0.2	31	582	0.4	1,282
27	Caja de Ahorros y Montepío de Manacor (a) (b)	1,353	0.6	24	489	0.3	361
28	Caja de Ahorros de Elche (a) (b)	1,046	0.4	28	367	0.3	351
29	Caja de Ahorros de Logroño (b)		0.0		355	0.2	
30	Caja de Ahorros de Palafrugell (b)	721	0.3	29	335	0.2	465

SOURCE: *Historia cuantitativa de las Cajas de Ahorro españolas en 1901-1927* (II), Madrid; CECA, 1969, pp. 6 and 7.

a. The number of depositors has been estimated.
b. Deposits have been estimated.

TABLE 1	SPANISH SAVINGS BANKS IN 1901 (cont'd) (Ranked by deposits)

	Savings Banks	Number of depositors	Percentage of depositors	Ranked by depositors	Deposits (thousands of pesetas)	Percentage of deposits	Deposits/ depositors (Pesetas)
31	Caja de Ahorros y Monte de Piedad de Segorbe	651	0.3	30	330	0.2	507
32	Caja de Ahorros de Cádiz (b)	426	0.2	33	313	0.2	735
33	Monte de Piedad y Caja de Ahorros de Granada		0.0		184	0.1	
34	Caja de Ahorros y Socorros de Orihuela	1,188	0.5	25	152	0.1	128
35	Monte de Piedad y Caja de Ahorros de León	207	0.1	38	150	0.1	725
36	Monte de Piedad de Alfonso XIII y Caja de Ahorros de Santander	448	0.2	32	150	0.1	335
37	Caja de Ahorros y Monte de Piedad de la Cámara Agrícola de Jumilla		0.0		126	0.1	
38	Caja de Ahorros y Monte de Piedad de Almería		0.0		120	0.1	
39	Monte de Piedad y Caja de Ahorros de Segovia	1,134	0.5	26	102	0.1	90
40	Caja de Ahorros de Manlleu		0.0		101	0.1	
41	Monte de Piedad y Caja de Ahorros de Teruel	357	0.2	34	91	0.1	255
42	Monte de Piedad y Caja de Ahorros de Palencia	331	0.1	36	87	0.1	263
43	Caja de Ahorros de Játiva	216	0.1	37	79	0.1	366
44	Caja de Ahorros y Monte de Piedad del Sindicato Agrícola de Pollensa	168	0.1	39	55	0.0	327
45	Caja de Ahorros de Béjar	142	0.1	40	53	0.0	373
46	Caja de Ahorros y Monte de Piedad de Onteniente	38	0.0	41	40	0.0	1,053
47	Caja de Ahorros y Monte de Piedad de Mahón	341	0.1	35	39	0.0	114
	TOTAL FOR ALL SAVINGS BANKS INCLUDED	233,566	100.0		146,188	100.0	626

SOURCE: *Historia cuantitativa de las Cajas de Ahorro españolas en 1901-1927* (II), Madrid; CECA, 1969, pp. 6 and 7.

a. The number of depositors has been estimated.
b. Deposits have been estimated.

in the latter's customer base. Among the savings banks with the largest average deposits, the Caja Provincial de Guipúzcoa, and the Jerez de la Frontera, Pontevedra and Onteniente savings banks, stand out as having an average deposit of over a thousand pesetas, compared with a sector average of 625.8 pesetas. The average balance in the accounts of savings banks in the industrial cities (Barcelona, Alcoy, Mataró and Tarrasa) stood at around 400 pesetas; smaller deposits (less than 300 pesetas) tended to be seen in savings banks in rural towns, and smaller provincial capitals, such as Segovia, Teruel and Palencia. That is to say, as Martínez Soto and Cuevas (2004) have pointed out, the savings banks' average balance depended on the economic environment in which they operated, because this determined the type of customers they had. The increase in the average balance in all the savings banks corroborates the moderate progress of the sector, rising from 578 pesetas in 1875 to 626 pesetas in 1901. Between 1854 and 1913 the average value of deposits held in savings banks was low, indeed average deposits stagnated after 1890 and declined from 1900 onwards. The small deposit size reveals both the social background of depositors and the limits certain savings banks imposed on the size of deposits. The decline in the value of average deposits from the end of the 19th century may be indicative of a shift in the clientele towards lower-income wage earners. A similar process seems to have taken place in the case of average deposits in the cities: the Madrid, Seville, Jerez and Valladolid savings banks had larger average deposits than those of Barcelona, Valencia, Zaragoza and Sabadell, indicating that the former included more members of the bourgeoisie in their customer base, whereas the customers of the latter were mainly drawn from the working class.[1]

2.2   Spanish savings banks in the international context

The world of the *cajas de ahorros* has traditionally been a complex one. Although they were institutions created with similar goals and forms of operation, the way in which they were organized in the period examined here depended on their statutes, with the result that there was considerable variety among them. International comparisons are, of course, made even more difficult by the fact that each country had its own model of savings bank, as they are highly regulated entities governed by legislation that varies from one country to another. Nevertheless, the history of the Spanish *cajas* can be viewed from within the perspective of Europe's experience of savings banks if one focuses on the economic aspects of their operations, at the highest level of abstraction. Historians of savings banks in Europe distinguish five traits characterizing these institutions, which are applicable, with some variations, to the Spanish savings banks, prior to Decree 2290 (in 1977) and the Law on Savings Bank Governance (LORCA) in 1985, as we shall see below.[2]

First of all, the ideological roots of the legislators and founders of Spanish savings banks lay with the thinkers of the Enlightenment and they were inspired by a philanthropic spirit and a desire to help those in need. Ideas and practices that had spread in other European countries were known in Spain and attempts were made to emulate them. Secondly, there was a mixture of ways in which institutions were established, given that their founders were inspired by the experience of various different countries. Up until the late 19th century the British example was the most widely followed, and Spanish savings banks were predominately founded by private individuals. In the 20th century, however, local and provincial authorities came to fore among the founders of the *cajas,* a pattern more typical of Germany. Thirdly, as regards the legal forms they took, in Spain the model followed

---

[1]   This chapter is based on the bibliography listed at the end, however to avoid an excessive number of references, only the main references are cited in the text. The chapter draws mainly on the works of Comín (2001, 2004, 2005, 2007a, b and c and 2008). All the charts are taken from Comín (1988). The sources of the charts are given in the commentary on them. The book Comín (2008) was written in collaboration with Eugenio Torres Villanueva. The author would like to express his thanks for the comments by the book's publishers, who have contributed to substantially improving this chapter.

[2]   For more on the complex issues involved in international comparisons of savings banks and the historical evidence of the features Spanish savings banks shared with their European counterparts, see: Américi (2002), Bonin (2005), Comín (2008), Hertner (1996), Llamby (2006), Moss and Slaven (1992), Mura (1996), O' Gráda (2001), Ross (2001) and Wysocki (1996).

was mainly that of Italy, with some features of the French model, as although the savings banks had different sponsors in each case, the State established relatively flexible common legislation for all of them. As in other countries, the activity of the Spanish savings banks responded – with broad autonomy, in practice, up until the advent of Francoism – to a single set of economic policy rules as a result of the country's political centralization. Except for a few savings banks that took the form of joint-stock companies, as was the case with certain Andalusian savings banks, those in the American colonies, and the many local savings banks created under Francoism, most of them had a somewhat ill-defined legal structure. Those considered to be "*cajas ordinarias*" (ordinary savings banks) were private institutions under public protection, similar to the status of foundations in Britain.

Fourthly, as regards the operations they were able to undertake, what emerges is that over and above the considerable diversity in the size of savings banks in Spain and in Europe, the different specialization in various asset and operations, and the differing nature of their customers – resulting from differences in the socio-economic context in which they operated – there was nevertheless a series of general features they all shared. Like their European counterparts, up until the 1960s the Spanish savings banks operated along retail banking lines. Up until the 1960s they demonstrated a clear specialization in low- and middle-income customers and low-value transactions. In terms of borrowing, European savings banks targeted low income social groups with a low or zero propensity to save. The fundamental goal was precisely to promote and attract the "potential savings" of poor individuals, families and workers. To do so, they had to instill the virtues of thrift among small property owners and wage earners through advertising and by offering rewards. As happened elsewhere in Europe, to attract these savings from lower-income groups, up until 1964 Spanish savings banks concentrated on deposits as their sole liability product. They therefore used the savings-book account as the basic vehicle for deposits. The savings banks paid interest on these deposits and sought to demonstrate to potential savers that they were a safe place for them to put their money, in view of the people managing them and the low risk of their investments. Over time, the Spanish savings banks started to follow widespread practices in Europe, dropping the limitations on deposits and accepting deposits of any size. They also began to diversify their investments. Initially, however, Spanish savings banks had followed the German and Italian patterns, and the government imposed on them the obligation to finance the *montes de piedad.* However, this special feature of the Spanish case disappeared after 1880 when savings banks were allowed to be created without an associated *monte de piedad.*

The fifth characteristic was that, as in most European countries, the *cajas* had more legal limitations on the scope of their activities than did the banks; they were prohibited from undertaking risky or speculative investments, and the transactions they could and could not undertake were more strictly defined. This was one of the reasons for their higher survival rate during financial crises.

Additionally, in Spain as elsewhere in Europe, the savings banks initially operated at local level, and their geographical focus sharpened over the period, such that their activities were limited exclusively to a relatively small geographical area. This contributed to enhancing the security offered to depositors. The proximity of depositors made it easier to make new deposits, as customers' knowledge of the institution and its backers and boosted their confidence. This local presence also made the charitable activities of the savings bank more visible, thus further reinforcing customer loyalty. This trust, in conjunction with the high profile of their charitable work, whether directly or through their *montes de piedad,* was crucial in these institutions' development. Their specialization in a limited geographical area also made it easier for them to break into new business lines, such as granting personal, commercial, industrial or farming loans. This territorial specialization is also behind the origins of the operational diversity of the savings banks. Their ability to adapt to changing legislation was combined with their remarkable flexibility to adapt to a diverse range of economic and social environments. However, on top of these basic commonalities, the *cajas* had individual features in terms of their personality, nature, size and specialization.

In some respects the Spanish savings banks lagged behind their counterparts elsewhere in Europe. Up until 1928, the main difference was that savings banks in Spain continued to act individually without coordination with their peers. In Europe the first savings banks associations were created in the 1880s, whereas in Spain the regional associations would not appear until the 1920s, followed later by the Spanish Savings Banks Confederation (Confederación Española de Cajas de Ahorros). The development of an association of Spanish savings banks in the 1920s was a late, but faithful reflection, of the experience of these institutions in many other countries since the end of the 19th century, and the First World Thrift Congress (held in Milan in 1924) was the launch pad from which it finally took shape. Most of the world's savings banks, like those in Spain, had been created with a primarily local focus. However, the strengthening of nation states in the second half of the 19th century, economic growth and rapid improvements in communications brought savings banks' activities into closer contact, and convinced them of the need for joint action, so as to put up a common front against public authorities to defend their freedom of action and ensure their specific features were recognized when legislation on savings was being drawn up. Another important goal was to effectively foster a spirit of thrift among the population. And finally, there was the savings banks' desire to improve their technical and administrative organization by utilizing each others' experience and to establish a single system of supervision and control over their activity so as to enhance public trust. Spanish savings banks followed suit, creating the Spanish Confederation of Confederated Savings Banks (Confederación Española de Cajas de Ahorros Confederadas) in 1928. The *cajas* also went on to join the World Savings Banks Institute and followed the strategies and procedures this body recommended to all its members.

2.3 The expansion of the savings banks: 1901-1920

The savings banks' phase of development between 1890 and 1920 has been described by Forniés (1991) as "fragmented growth." According to Forniés, 119 savings banks were founded between 1890 and 1920. All of them were small, and most were set up by labor unions, which were becoming increasingly powerful at the time. These savings banks were trammeled by the progress of the unions and their small size led to their being absorbed by larger institutions. The bourgeoisie, land owners and local authorities scaled back their sponsorship of new savings banks, although they continued backing well-managed, larger, city-based savings banks. These included the savings banks in Granada (1893), Guipúzcoa (1896), Santander (1898), Almería (1900), León (1900), the Caja de Pensiones de Barcelona (1905), the Caja de Cáceres (1905), the Caja Municipal de Bilbao (1907) and the Caja de Ronda (1909). The expanding number of savings banks brought with it an increase in the volume of savings channeled through them.

According to other estimates, the number of savings banks grew significantly in the first decade of the 20th century (a total of 41), but more slowly in the second decade. The total rose from 50 savings banks in 1899 to 91 in 1909 and 101 in 1919. The period seeing the greatest expansion in the number of savings banks was 1905 to 1909 (with an increase of 31). This increase was basically explained by the support given by new legislation passed in 1905. The development of farming organizations in the first three decades of the 20th century, rising incomes, and the modernization of the Spanish financial system, also played a part in this expansion. Moreover, these figures for the number of savings banks do not include all the credit unions, of which there were around 50 at this time, according to estimates by Martínez Soto (2000). According to Martínez Soto the savings banks were very diverse. Most of them were founded by private patrons and came under the legislation that classified them as charitable institutions, although some of them (such as the Caja de Ahorros y Monte de Piedad de Orihuela, which distributed dividends to its shareholders) did not manage to get themselves recognized as charities, despite repeated attempts. There was also growth in deposits and the number of depositors (Martínez Soto and Cuevas, 2004). Deposit growth, which since 1880 had outpaced growth both in GDP and in savings deposits with commercial banks, remained high between the turn of the century and 1920. Average deposits with savings banks grew more slowly, however, indicating that the increase in savings was a result of there being more savings institutions, with savings banks spreading right across the country, and above all, an increase in the number of depositors. On the asset side, savings banks' loans also grew during this period. Lending remained more or less stable throughout the First World War. Thus, in 1895 the difference between savings banks' deposits and loans widened, as they began to diversify their investments, acquiring other assets such as public debt and private securities.

The success of the savings banks during the first few decades of the 20th century is comparable to that experienced in other Western European countries, in that various different forms of saving institution and cooperative became widespread in the last three decades of the 19th century. This was the experience in the benchmark countries, such as Germany, France, Italy and Great Britain, although the institutional aspects of the process were different in each case. The consequence of this delay was that the figures for popular saving in Spain did not catch up with those of more developed European countries until the inter-war period, particularly the 1930s.

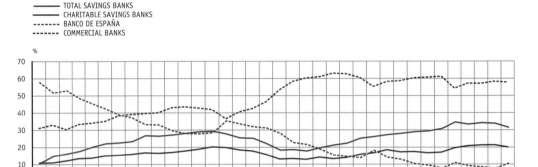

SOURCE: Comín (2008).

Charitable savings banks' deposits as a share of the total grew to 20.3% in 1913 (Chart 1), a much smaller percentage than those of the Banco de España and the commercial banks (which developed in entirely the opposite direction: a fall in the first case and rise in the second), but greater than the share held by the commercial savings banks, which at that time, accounted for half of the total. From the start of the First World War the share of deposits held by charitable savings banks declined, falling to below 13% in 1920. Commercial savings banks followed a similar – indeed more marked – trend as their share of deposits in 1920 was lower than at the start of the century. Conversely, the share of deposits held by commercial banks grew over the period, slowing slightly in 1914-15, possibly as a result of the difficulties suffered by a number of major banks, such as Banco Hispano Americano and Crédito de la Unión Minera, caused by the outbreak of the Great War. This growth in both bank and in savings bank deposits was at the expense of deposits held with the Banco de España, whose share of deposits in the system as a whole fell dramatically, such that by 1920 it held less than half the share of twenty years earlier. Over this period, therefore, the Banco de España's predominance in terms of deposits was taken over by commercial banks, whose weight was even greater if the deposits of the banking cajas, or commercial savings banks, are also considered. The charitable savings banks increased their share of deposits, but did so modestly: between 1900 and 1920 their share increased by two percentage points, as part of the gains made prior to 1913 were lost during the war and post-war years.

From the regional perspective, significant changes can be observed which point to a tendency for the savings banks, and savings in general, to develop more in those regions undergoing rapid economic modernization. Thus, from the first decade of the 20th century, the Basque savings banks expanded in parallel with their local banks. The same was not true in Madrid, however, where the Caja de Ahorros de Madrid, which had been the biggest institution by deposits at the end of the 19th century, found itself overshadowed by large new commercial banks. However, it was in Catalonia that the savings banks developed most in this period, subsequently consolidating – prior to the Civil War – a trend that had lasted throughout the 20th century and which placed these savings banks (Caja de Pensiones and Caja de Barcelona) at the summit of the Spanish financial system. In Andalusia, among other factors, the regional economic decline and scant development of agricultural cooperatives, led to the savings banks in the region starting to lose importance among the major national savings institutions as of the end of the 19th century. In the *Levante,* on Spain's east coast, where the network of popular savings institutions was fairly dense, in parallel with a commercial banking network that was thinner on the ground – the Banco de Valencia was the biggest institution – the Caja de Ahorros de Valencia held its own against the leading players in the first few decades of the century. Thus, over this period the popular savings market reflected ever more clearly the pre-eminence of the urban wage-earning and middle classes, together with smallholders and small farmers.

At the turn of the 20th century there was also a change in the founding patrons of the savings banks. Rather than being founded by individuals, the new savings banks were being set up by agricultural associations, labor unions, local government and councils, workers' centers, and to a lesser extent, the rural oligarchy. While the State had kept out of creating savings banks, local bodies began to found them during this period. Some time later, the State would create the post-office savings bank, the Caja Postal de Ahorros. Many of these new savings banks did not have an associated *monte de piedad,* but had other features better reflecting their new role as "insurers of savings" rather than their traditional charitable work. The clearest example of this was the Caja de Pensiones de Barcelona. The activities of the *montes de piedad* in fact declined, although the name was kept in some cases so as to be able to take advantage of the tax advantages savings banks were able to derive from their status as charitable institutions.

It was at this time that the savings banks also began to reorient their investments. In the early days of their existence, the savings banks had difficulty meeting their commitment to finance the loans granted by the *montes de piedad.* But after the Restoration in 1874, the problem was precisely the opposite. Demand for finance from the *montes de piedad* was insufficient to ensure a return on the deposits held in the savings bank. They therefore had to look for alternative investments, the nature of which depended on the decisions of each individual savings bank. Some opted for personal loans, backed with personal guarantees or public-debt securities, whereas others lent to town councils. Personal loans (particularly those by the Caja de Madrid) caused a reaction from the banks, which managed to get the senate to debate the possibility of prohibiting the *cajas* from operating in this segment of the banking intermediation business. Although parliament did not eventually pass any laws to this effect, the Caja de Madrid began to withdraw from this market. In order to balance its books, the Caja de Madrid opted for a strategy of restricting interest-bearing deposits on the one side, and creating a securities portfolio on the other. At the end of the 19th century, therefore, the savings banks not only continued to perform their charitable role in attracting popular savings and financing the *montes de piedad,* but had also expanded their financial role, despite the legal restrictions. Nevertheless, the expansion of commercial banks since the start of the 20th century created serious difficulties for the *cajas*. Competition with the banks took the form of their pursuing popular savings, creating "banking" *cajas* within their own organizations, but without giving them a separate legal identity. This meant that the savings deposited with these bank *cajas* were tied to the fate of the parent bank, and their depositors did not enjoy any special protection.

The new situation forced the savings banks to change strategy, such that pledge loans began to decline in importance, while other activities, such as mortgage lending, became more significant. These changes were originated by the shift in demand for credit. The economic and social change had shrunk the numbers of the needy, and at the same time, there had been an increase in the number of wage earners, members of the middle classes and farmers, whose credit needs were different. The needs of these economic agents called for loans focusing on productive or commercial activities, to meet the needs of merchants, industrialists and farmers. The increase in the number of depositors, especially from certain segments of the urban middle class, and savings deposited in these institutions, was another sign of these underlying economic and social changes. But the financial success of the savings banks alerted the banks to the potential of this market segment, formerly the preserve of the savings banks, and they began to target it.

3 The inter-war period (1921-1935)

A new stage in the history of Spain's savings banks began after the end of the First World War. Cambó's Banking Law of 1921 was a milestone that has been somewhat underappreciated in the past. This Law favored the banks but somewhat ignored the interests of the savings banks. Also, the Ministry of Labor was created in 1920, taking over responsibility for social security and welfare issues from the Ministry of the Interior, and thus taking a new approach to them. Social insurance became compulsory in 1919, accompanied by a package of social measures, such as the eight-hour day, passed that same year. At the end of the Great War the state was more interventionist, but less so than in the European countries directly involved in the conflict. Aid for industry and transport was stepped up and became more systematic in the post-war period, and the corporate element of society and the State increased. This interventionist and corporatist tendency was further reinforced during the Dictatorship of Primo de Rivera and the Second Republic.

3.1 The expansion of the savings banks in the 1920s

During the 1920s the number of savings banks rose by 115 (from the 101 that existed in 1919 the total went up to 155 in 124 and to 216 in 1929), returning to the number that existed before the First World War. The 1920s saw the biggest increase in the number of charitable savings banks, and the same thing happened in the case of the *montes de piedad,* which increased in number by 67. During the decade the *cajas* also expanded geographically, but somewhat unevenly. Deposits in charitable savings banks as a share of total deposits in the financial system grew moderately during the 1920's, but did not return to the peak seen in 1913. This growth was concentrated in the first half of the decade, as between 1927 and 1930 half of the previous years' gains were lost (Chart 1). This moderate growth contrasted with the stagnation in the share of deposits held by commercial banks, at around 61%, and the *Caja Postal* at around 2.5%. There was also a sharp decline in the share held by the Banco de España. This moderate growth also contrasted with the spectacular recovery in the share of deposits held by the bank *cajas,* which grew threefold over the period to exceed the previous high-water mark of 1908-1912. Thus, if we add this share to that of the commercial banks, not only do they emerge as having a clear predominance in terms of total deposits in the financial system, but there was also considerable growth in their total share, and this was basically at the expense of the Banco de España. Therefore, as Chart 1 shows, it is true to say that the expansion of the commercial banks in the twenties translated into an increase in their already considerable predominance on the deposits side of the financial system, and that this was not at the expense of the share held by the savings banks, as this also grew, albeit modestly.

Similarly, over this period the savings banks increased their volume of investments of types other than welfare lending through their *montes de piedad,* with the continuing gradual decline of the latter and the *cajas'* consolidation and diversification. However, the process of regulation of the savings banks, which began in 1926, slowed this trend by establishing the first mandatory investment coefficients for the sector. Although each savings bank's investment strategy was different, the granting of loans and purchasing of a portfolio of public and private securities were the most important investment types. In the case of loans, mortgage loans secured with either rural or urban property increased, in particular, and came to account for almost two-thirds of the total funds devoted to this type of investment. Loans with listed shares as collateral also increased, but their relative importance was smaller, and that of personal loans was much smaller still. The increase in the new type of loan, especially mortgages, was consistent with the urban development of the cities and urban public services, on the one side, and the financing of innovations in agriculture and the purchase of agricultural land, on the other. The expansion of the savings banks' mortgage lending for investments was an extremely important factor.

As regards securities portfolios, from the turn of the century many savings banks, particularly those that were not linked to a *monte de piedad,* increasingly invested a share of their funds in public and private securities, both domestic and foreign, according to the guidelines laid down by their governing bodies. In the early 1920's the *cajas,* particularly larger urban ones, held highly diversified portfolios and, although the setting of mandatory investment coefficients in 1926 reduced their degree of diversification somewhat, this type of voluntary investment continued, at least among the larger institutions. The savings banks' portfolios were largely made up of government bonds.

	Savings Banks	Deposits (thousands of pesetas)	% total confederated savings banks	% charitable savings banks
1	Caja de Pensiones de Barcelona	276,162	17.65	17.26
2	Caja de Ahorros y Monte de Piedad de Barcelona*	188,717	12.06	11.80
3	Caja de Ahorros Municipal de Bilbao*	163,695	10.46	10.22
4	Caja de Ahorros Provincial de Guipúzcoa*	111,316	7.11	6.95
5	Caja de Ahorros y Monte de Piedad de Valencia*	88,549	5.66	5.53
6	Caja de Ahorros y Monte de Piedad de Madrid*	82,409	5.27	5.15
7	Caja de Ahorros Vizcaína	70,638	4.51	4.42
8	Monte de Piedad y Caja de Ahorros de León*	57,459	3.67	3.59
9	Caja de Ahorros y Monte de Piedad de Zaragoza*	45,771	2.93	2.85
10	Caja de Ahorros Municipal de San Sebastián	41,404	2.65	2.58
11	Caja de Ahorros de Navarra	35,763	2.29	2.23
12	Caja de Ahorros y Monte de Piedad de Vitoria	34,952	2.23	2.18
13	Caja de Ahorros y Monte de Piedad de Castellón	28,898	1.85	1.80
14	Caja de Ahorros y Monte de Piedad de Las Baleares	25,753	1.65	1.61
15	Caja de Ahorros y Monte de Piedad de Salamanca*	24,576	1.57	1.53
16	Monte de Piedad y Caja de Ahorros de Santander*	19,696	1.26	1.23
17	Caja de Ahorros y Monte de Piedad de La Coruña*	15,099	0.96	0.94
18	Caja de Ahorros y Monte de Piedad de Alicante*	14,080	0.90	0.88
19	Caja de Ahorros de Tarrasa	13,222	0.85	0.82
20	Caja de Ahorros Municipal de Vigo*	11,828	0.76	0.74

TABLE 2   MAIN CONFEDERATED SAVINGS BANKS, 1928

SOURCE: *Historia cuantitativa de las Cajas de Ahorro españolas en 1928-1935,* pp. 16-18.

NOTE: (*) Not included in the Confederación Española de Cajas de Ahorros.

The larger confederated savings banks played a much less significant role, however. Table 2 shows the wide disparities existing between the twenty largest *cajas* in terms of their deposits. The difference between the first three – two of which were Catalan – and the rest was considerable, and confirmed the concentration of deposits, which was one of the characteristics of these institutions in the 19th century, although it was gradually diluted over time. Indeed, the degree of concentration in the three largest institutions in 1928 was approximately half of what it had been in 1885, when the Caja de Madrid had absolute supremacy in the charitable savings sector.

The importance of the confederated savings banks from the regional point of view and in terms of the geographical distribution of savings deposits is of interest here because the Confederation was a union of Regional Federations rather than of individual savings banks. The Catalan and Basque savings banks dominated the national scene, accounting for no less than two-thirds of all the savings held by the confederated savings banks. Moreover, the four biggest *cajas* were located in these regions. The number of savings banks in 1928 totaled 134, although some of them (marked with an asterisk in the table) did not belong to the CECA at this stage, because it had been created that same year. Most of them went on to join it the following year.

3.2   The savings banks during the Second Republic

The creation of savings banks during the Second Republic was slowed by the economic depression and climate of political instability. Between 1930 and 1935 only ten new savings banks were created; many fewer than in the previous five year period. In 1935 the number of savings banks registered in the CECA totaled 222. The increase in the number of depositors also slowed: whereas between 1925 and 1930 depositor numbers had grown from 2.1 to 3.5 million, between 1930 and 1935 they rose more slowly, reaching just 3.7 million.

The slower growth in total deposits in the financial system during the Second Republic accentuated competition between institutions as they sought to attract depositors. Chart 1 shows how the general savings banks gained ground against "non-charitable" savings banks, because commercial banks increased their share more than general savings banks between 1931 and 1935. The bulk of the growth in savings banks' deposits during the first half of the 1930s was among institutions that were members of the CECA. Nevertheless, the loss of ground by the commercial savings banks reduced the predominance of commercial banks as a whole. Among the charitable savings banks, between 1928 and 1935 the growth of the Caja de Pensiones para la Vejez de Barcelona and the other Catalan *cajas* was particularly strong. By taking over a series of smaller savings banks in Catalonia and the Balearic islands, the Caja de Pensiones' share of deposits came to account for a quarter of all the deposits held by the confederated savings banks. The dynamism of the Catalan savings banks was favored by the absence of a strong commercial banking sector, and the more limited impact of the crisis in the thirties on the consumer goods industry. This contrasted with the relative loss of importance of the Basque savings banks, in particular the Caja de Ahorros Municipal de Bilbao, the president of which was the chairman of the CECA.

Between 1926 and 1939 the confederated savings banks continued to invest in securities portfolios (58%), loans (33%) and real estate (9%). Welfare funds allocated to the *montes de piedad* continued to decline in importance. Mortgages still dominated lending activity, including loans backed by personal guarantees or with securities as collateral. However, lending to local authorities, sometimes against inadequate collateral, also increased. According to Forniés (1991), between 1926 and 1939, mortgage lending accounted for 65% of the total loans granted by the savings banks, in most cases being secured by urban property. Personal loans (18%), corporate loans (9%) and pledge loans (8%) were less important. Loans to build low-cost housing declined in significance, being interrupted in mid-1933 due to the suspension of government subsidies, despite the fact that from July 1931 the Patronato de Política Social Inmobiliaria del Estado, a body endowed with somewhat limited resources for the goals for which it had been created, was operating under the aegis of the Ministry of Labor. From 1933 on, the savings banks worked with the republican government to provide agricultural loans, with or without collateral, in an attempt to solve the problem of the wheat shortage. These operations were possible because the reform of the 1933 Savings Statute allowed the savings banks to discount bills of exchange issued in relation to loans backed by the wheat crop. The biggest and most profitable investments by the savings banks were their securities portfolios, which were, however, badly affected by the economic crisis. From 1931 onwards the savings banks were affected by the problem of the falling value of the securities they held on their portfolios, and the declining dividend revenues, or interruption in the payment of coupons on corporate bonds. The savings banks' portfolio was oriented towards public debt even before the mandatory investment coefficients imposed in 1926. The 1933 Statute obliged savings banks to invest 30% of their total deposits in public debt. This was an unnecessary imposition as the *cajas* already held more than 60% of their investments in public debt prior to 1933.

4   The savings banks during the period of autarky: financial repression (1940-1957)

The 1940s were a difficult period for the Confederation and the saving banks, as they were for the Spanish economy as a whole, not just because of the profound crisis, but also as a result of wide-ranging and arbitrary state interventionism.

4.1   The savings banks' loss of operational independence

During the period in which the Francoist government pursued economic autarky, the savings banks found their freedom of operation encroached upon by increased government intervention in both their investments and social welfare activities. First of all, during the immediate post-war years, the government obliged the savings banks to increase their mandatory investments. Over this period the savings banks' investments in public securities exceeded their mandatory investment coefficient as the economic crisis had led to a drying up of demand for credit from the private sector. The government did not therefore find it necessary to raise the existing coefficient for mandatory investments in public securities. Nevertheless, the savings banks found themselves obliged to enter into certain loan operations under favorable conditions for their beneficiaries, such as loans to farmers and to the Ministry of Labor. By negotiating as a body, the savings banks were able to minimize the negative impact, enabling them to improve the conditions under which loans were granted in terms of interest rates and minimizing credit risk. Even so, these were transactions the commercial banks were not willing to engage in as they did not conform to market terms. Secondly, the savings banks also lost a large part of their independence in relation to their social and welfare activities. The activities to which they devoted funding ceased to be freely chosen by the *cajas,* as the government strictly defined how funds were to be allocated, in line with its own priorities. Indeed, in the post-war period, the savings banks were obliged to devote the lion's share of their resources (no less than 85%) to charitable social activities in the areas and sectors laid down by the government. All they managed to achieve was the freedom to assign a small part of this 85% at their own discretion. However, this social spending continued to be undertaken by the savings banks, which meant that in appearances at least they continued to fulfill their specific statutes regarding social activities, except that they were no longer "free" but mandatory, which is to say, imposed by the state. Nevertheless, although mandated by government, this social work continued to be perceived by the population as an activity performed by the *cajas*. What was more serious was that the remaining 15% of the *cajas'* allocation to social work had to be transferred directly to the Ministry of Labor for "national social work." The savings banks thus lost control over the benefits of this spending in terms of promoting savings or targeting it on their customer base or areas of operation, as they were no longer associated with the spending, given that it was carried out directly by the Ministry of Labor as it saw fit. This was against the savings banks' statutes, but obviously successive Francoist governments did not let that get in their way.

However, it was not all bad news; governments in the post-war period also passed some measures that benefited the savings banks. The most noteworthy was the freedom the savings banks obtained to expand nationwide by setting up new branches and institutions (this was complete freedom until 1946 and regulated freedom after that time). Nevertheless, this concession by the State did not come without a price, as this geographical expansion by the savings banks and their setting up new branches went hand in hand with their collaborating with government by granting loans to farmers on favorable terms, which were therefore not very profitable for them. Farm credit had traditionally been neglected by the commercial banks and the state wanted the savings banks to take it on. This policy of expansion enabled them to create a national charitable savings network, which in time would become one of the pillars on which the expansion and strength of the *cajas* would be based. This territorial and institutional expansion by the savings banks was in contrast to the *status quo* maintained by the private banks, whose association did not allow a single new bank to be created during the period of autarky. Moreover, the most profitable financial businesses during this period were the preserve of the commercial banks, which kept the savings banks out of them, despite their repeatedly expressing their interest. In the 1950s the savings banks continued the territorial expansion they had begun in the preceding decade, by setting up agencies and branches under the Order of 26 May 1955, which repealed the previous Order of 13 February 1946. The Ministry of Finance's financial control over the savings banks was also stepped up in the 1950s, as is shown by the 1951 decree doubling the mandatory investment coefficient to set it at "at least" 60% of their borrowings.

4.2   The savings banks' accounts during autarky

The Civil War had a serious impact on the savings banks' share of deposits. Although the data series are not homogeneous, the savings banks' market share (by deposits) in 1935 was approximately 27%, whereas by 1942 it had fallen below 18%, nine percentage points lower, a measure of the substantial cost to the savings banks of the Civil War. The

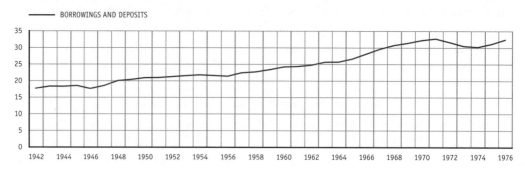

CHART 2   MARKET SHARE OF THE SAVINGS BANKS (1942-1976)

—— BORROWINGS AND DEPOSITS

SOURCE: Comín (2008).

savings banks' market share began to recover gradually after 1942, reaching a maximum in the 1950s, and then stagnating somewhat (Chart 2). Therefore, although the *cajas* did not recover the share of deposits they had held in 1935, the volume of savings deposited with them nevertheless rose between 1940 and 1957, insufficiently to regain the ground lost during the Civil War.

From the regional perspective there were also significant changes in the way in which savings were distributed, as shown in the ranking of the main confederated savings banks (Table 3). As in the thirties, during the post-war period there was a concentration of savings in Catalonia, which strengthened its dominance between 1940 and 1955, coming to account for almost half of the savings sector. Catalonia was home to the country's two largest savings banks, and they both increased their share of deposits over the period, which contributed to strengthening their position of leadership. Andalusia and Aragon also saw an expansion in regional savings. In Andalusia, this growth was spread across various medium-sized *cajas* (those of Seville, Córdoba, Jerez de la Frontera, Ronda, Antequera and Granada), none of which achieved sufficient scale to take a place among the top twenty. In Aragón, growth centered on the Caja de Ahorros de Zaragoza, which had become the third-largest in Spain in deposit terms by 1955. The trend begun in the 1930s towards the declining importance of the regional savings banks in areas such as the Basque Country and Navarre, León and the Balearic Islands also continued.

In the 1940's the savings banks stepped up their social welfare work. This was because in 1947 the Ministry of Labor obliged them to devote 15% of the resources they allocated to social welfare activities to 'National Social Work', as defined by the government. To compensate, the savings banks thus devoted a larger share of their income to social activities, rising from 20% to 33% between 1947 and 1957 (Chart 3). However, the main application of the savings banks' profits continued to be the reserve fund, which was a reflection of their prudential management, thus giving their depositors the guarantees they needed.

TABLE 3	MAIN SAVINGS BANKS, 1940-1955 (Deposits as percentage of total held with confederated savings banks)		

	Savings Banks	1940	1955	Variation
1	Caja de Pensiones de Barcelona	25.71	28.13	2.42
2	Caja de Ahorros y Monte de Piedad de Barcelona	9.45	10.06	0.61
3	Caja de Ahorros Municipal de Bilbao	5.95	3.73	-2.22
4	Caja de Ahorros Provincial de Guipúzcoa	5.61	3.99	-1.62
5	Caja de Ahorros y Monte de Piedad de Valencia	4.92	4.04	-0.88
6	Caja de Ahorros y Monte de Piedad de Zaragoza	4.61	6.01	1.40
7	Caja de Ahorros Vizcaína	3.99	3.82	-0.17
8	Caja de Ahorros y Monte de Piedad de Madrid	3.60	3.15	-0.45
9	Caja de Ahorros de Navarra	3.05	1.92	-1.13
10	Monte de Piedad y Caja de Ahorros de León	3.04	1.41	-1.63
11	Caja de Ahorros Provincial de Barcelona	2.30	2.85	0.55
12	Caja de Ahorros y Monte de Piedad de Las Baleares	2.26	1.02	-1.24
13	Caja de Ahorros y Monte de Piedad de Salamanca	2.14	1.53	-0.61
14	Caja de Ahorros y Monte de Piedad de Vitoria	1.93	0.92	-1.01
15	Caja de Ahorros y Monte de Piedad de San Sebastián	1.90	1.46	-0.44
16	Caja de Ahorros Municipal de Vigo	1.56	1.48	-0.08
17	Caja de Ahorros y Monte de Piedad de La Coruña	1.51	1.22	-0.29
18	Caja de Ahorros Municipal de Burgos	1.20	1.32	0.12
19	Caja de Ahorros de Sabadell	1.13	1.16	0.03
20	Monte de Piedad y Caja de Ahorros de Santander	0.76	0.62	-0.14

SOURCE: *Historia cuantitativa de las Cajas de Ahorros españolas en 1940-1955*, IV, 21-22 and 30-31.

CHART 3	DISTRIBUTION OF PROFITS BY SAVINGS BANKS (1947-1976)

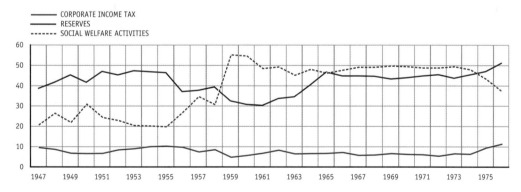

SOURCE: Comín (2008).

During the period of autarky, the savings banks' two main investments were their securities portfolios and loans. The larger investment of the two was, of course, securities, primarily in the form of public debt. This was not just because these investments gave the *cajas* more security, but because from 1951 onwards the savings banks were subject to a mandatory investment coefficient whereby they were obliged to devote 60% of their total resources to public debt. Despite this, in relative terms loans and credit increased from the end of the 1940s, when the severe post-war economic crisis began to subside and demand for credit from the private sector began to pick up.

5   The savings banks as financial institutions (1957-1963)

A new stage began for the *cajas* in 1957 when they came under the supervision of the Ministry of Finance, leaving their social activities under the tutelage of the Ministry of Labor. The Ministry of Finance began to treat the savings banks as financial institutions.

5.1   The refocusing of the savings banks

Changes at the Ministry of Finance in 1957 had a big impact on the savings banks. The government urgently needed new channels of finance to lighten the national budget's expenditure – all those included under the letter C, among which was the government holding company, the INI (Instituto Nacional de Industria) – and reduce the deficit. Thus, in 1957 the government began to weigh up the possibilities offered by the savings banks. Although at the time the savings banks' mandatory investment coefficient had already been doubled, they were still under the supervision of the Ministry of Labor, which prevented the Treasury from exploiting the full potential of the savings sector as a source of finance, given that the ministry continued to view the savings banks more as charitable organizations than financial institutions. For this reason, in 1957 it was decided that responsibility for the savings banks should be transferred to the Ministry of Finance. This was one of the most important milestones in the history of the sector, as it gave it more scope for growth, as we shall see in this section and the next.

Indeed, as of 1957 the new government realized that it was necessary to take a new approach to the savings banks, in order to ensure their closer cooperation with economic policy. As well as occasionally applying the stick, the Ministry of Finance frequently also offered the savings banks carrots to encourage them to collaborate more or less voluntarily. Despite the power some of Franco's ministers achieved between 1940 and 1957 (and which they exercised crudely with the savings banks) it was plain to see that the *cajas* were not willing to cede their financial independence lightly. Although they lost their autonomy over social activities, it remained the *cajas* that disbursed the funds, apart from the 15% they were obliged to devote to "national social work" through the Employment Ministry. However, the savings banks defended their financial independence as best they could, as it was on this, and their negotiating at least a basic return on their mandatory investments, that their survival as savings banks depended.

From the early fifties the government's intervention in the savings banks had been firmly focused on their integration in the financial system as institutions at the service of economic policy, in general, and to finance public investment, or privileged private investment, in particular. The purpose of the 1951 Decree on investments in public funds was basically for the savings banks to be obliged to devote at least 60% of their borrowings to the purchase of public funds: twice the amount established in the 1933 Savings Statute. As the initiative for this provision came from the Ministry of Finance, this Decree therefore marked the start of the one-way street down which the *cajas* would proceed until they ultimately came fully under the tutelage of this ministry. This meant recognition of the important lending role the savings banks already played in the economy, particularly in terms of lending to government.

However, the savings banks did not formally come under the supervision of the Ministry of Finance until the change of government in February 1957. One of the measures taken in 1957 and 1958 to pave the way for the Stabilization Plan, oriented fundamentally towards controlling the deficit and domestic prices, was put in place by the new Finance Minister, and was the transfer of the supervision of the savings banks from the Ministry of Labor to the Ministry of Finance, such that they would be subject to the economic policy directives – particularly as regards credit – dictated by this latter ministry. This entailed their explicit recognition as credit institutions, which came to take the upper hand over their charitable nature, which had been their dominant feature up until this time. 1957 therefore marked the start of a new phase in the history of the savings banks. Subsequently, the savings banks would be required to collaborate more closely with the public authorities; initially by subscribing to the INI's bond issues and by financing vocational training. As a result of this, given the Ministry of Finance's desire to make greater use of the savings banks as a source of finance, they were granted broader borrowing capacity. Over the longer term this new situation would prove profitable for the savings banks, as they gradually expanded their financial operations within the new scope allowed to them.

5.2   The institutional reorganization of the savings banks

In order to be able to supervise the savings banks, a reorganization took place at the Ministry of Finance (Decree of 10 May 1957) whereby the former Directorate-General for Banks and the Stock Exchange became the Directorate-General for Banks, the Stock Exchange and Investments, and took on a new role in the organization and supervision of savings banks of all types, including "charitable" savings banks, which were those under the umbrella of the Confederation of Spanish Charitable Savings Banks (Confederación Españolas de Cajas de Ahorros Benéficas), which at this time began to drop the adjective "charitable." This represented a decisive step in the Ministry of Finance's taking control over these institutions. The savings banks reacted by informing the Ministry of Finance that if they had to come under its supervision, they would do so "conserving their autonomy and independence" from other institutions under the new Directorate-General for Banks, the Stock Exchange and Investments, and that they should be under the supervision of a single body. The government conceded both points, as the tutelage of the Ministry of Labor was replaced by that of the Ministry of Finance by a Decree on 26 July 1957. However, the transfer of supervisory functions affected only the savings banks' financial activities, as their welfare activities continued to be overseen by the Ministry of Labor, and in particular, by the National Social Fund (Fondo Social Nacional). Moreover, another similar provision on 30 July created the Subdirectorate-General for Savings and Investments, which took direct responsibility for overseeing the savings banks. With this, the Ministry of Finance aimed to utilize the savings banks' capacity to "mobilize resources" to finance state-owned companies, particularly those under the Instituto Nacional de Industria (National Industry Institute, INI), which, as Martín Aceña and Comín (1991), have pointed out, from 1958 had to finance itself by issuing bonds either in its own name or in those of its subsidiary companies. In order to overcome the savings banks' reluctance to buy these bonds issued by the INI or its companies, however, the chairman of the CECA had to apply all powers of persuasion and exploit the good institutional relations that existed. As compensation, it was also necessary to meet some of the demands from the *cajas,* such as a State "guarantee" for these INI and INI-owned-company bonds; for the savings banks the security of the investment remained fundamental.

In 1959 the government imposed the obligation on the savings banks to devote a larger percentage of their annual increase in resources to buying debt issued by the INI. Without clear legislation, this new obligation was superimposed on the requirement that had existed since 1951 whereby the savings banks were to devote 60% of new deposits to buying public securities, and the obligation imposed in 1957 to provide loans to finance the construction and purchase of protected housing. The savings banks fought against this superimposition of mandatory investment coefficients, but were unsuccessful. The legal situation was somewhat confusing, as the Ministry gave out contradictory signals, and the savings banks exploited the confusion to resist compliance with the "three coefficients" for obligatory investments that had been layered one on top of another. In any event, the INI securities were not a bad thing for the savings banks, as 1960 heralded a period in which investment was sluggish, affecting both public and private investments in Spain, as a result of the paralysis of activity following the Stabilization Plan. When even INI issues started to become scarce, the savings banks found themselves with excess liquidity, as their "savings funds" or customer deposits continued to grow while credit to the private sector fell. This gave rise to a "sterilization of funds" in the savings banks' treasuries, which was not viewed favorably by the government. The Ministry of Finance resolved the issue rapidly in 1962 by obliging the *cajas* to cover the full investment coefficient by buying "qualified private company bonds," selected in advance by the Ministry's Investments Board, when there were insufficient INI bonds available. This opened up a new line of business for the savings banks, which began to provide "mandatory" finance to large private firms which had previously given government access to this "privileged credit" as the interest paid was below the market rate.

6 The savings banks at the service of the Development Plans (1962-1970)

This section will look at how the 1962 Banking Organization Law and the first Development Plan, launched in 1964, gave the Savings Banks new "investment obligations." These were superimposed on those already described, and were intended to finance small and medium-sized businesses in farming, industry and commerce, the building and purchase of homes, and even to allow wage earners at the large state-owned companies to buy shares.

6.1 Attracting deposits: interest rates, monetary policy and the "new savings accounts"

Following the Banking Organization Law of 1962 there were three types of banking transactions savings banks were prohibited from undertaking: discounting bills, foreign exchange arbitrage, swaps and any other form of speculation. From that time, however, they progressed significantly in terms of bringing their range of transactions into line with that of the commercial banks, particularly in terms of liability products. As can be seen in another chapter of this book, the regulations on the savings banks were strongly biased towards asset transactions, through the mandatory coefficients, which obliged them to finance large corporations and grant so-called social credit as suited the government's interests. Nevertheless, in order for the *cajas* to be able to finance these "obligatory investments" the government tried to make it easier for them to attract deposits by giving them greater freedom, as the more deposits they obtained, the greater the volume of the obligatory investments.

As Titos and Piñar (1993) have noted, in addition to traditional savings deposits (ordinary, children's and home savings) and term deposits, the savings banks were able to develop new "linked savings deposits" which were a form of goal-oriented saving, intended for a specific investment, complemented by credit from the savings bank. Thus, as of 1966, they were able to open home-savings deposits, share-savings deposits from 1967 and emigrant savings deposits from 1970. In the 1960s the savings banks also began to provide current accounts, enabling them to offer customers a range of new services (checkbooks, direct debits and funds transfers) in return for lower interest rates. These new instruments bolstered the growth of the *cajas'* deposits between 1965 and 1971. This increase, however, was driven by Spaniards' rising per capita income, in particular among the middle classes, a sector of the population that was drawn to the savings banks by the new services on offer that had previously only been available from the banks. This led to the *cajas* changing their strategy, particularly as regards how they marketed their products and competed to attract deposits. The expansion of the network of branches also contributed to their growth, as did their policy of lending to sectors that were underserved by the commercial banks, although this was through "social loans" and the small portion of "free" lending the savings banks were permitted.

In short, the savings banks had two strategies with which to attract deposits: modifying interest rates and offering new types of savings accounts. However, interest rates offered little scope for their use as the basis of competition as they were set by the government. In 1964 the interest rates and minimum charges both the commercial and savings banks were allowed to apply were set by the government. Later, the government continued setting interest rates and resorted to quantitative lending restrictions to curb inflation. Between 1964 and 1970 the government also put a cap on the interest the savings banks could receive on their deposits with banks. The *cajas'* other possible way of attracting new customers was to create new products. In 1966 they were allowed to offer home-savings accounts and share-savings accounts to stimulate saving and attract deposits. An insurance-saving account was also created with the same aim. The provisions regulating the implementation and operation of home-savings and share-savings accounts were published in the State Official Gazette (BOE) in November 1966. The home-savings account offered 4 percent interest, which entailed limitations being imposed on this formula to avoid the majority of current accounts (which paid interest at 2%) switching to home-savings accounts. Share-savings accounts, implemented in March 1967, were intended to attract a segment which until that time had only had contact with "other credit institutions." In April 1968 the *cajas* continued offering new products so as to provide fresh incentives for people to deposit their savings with them. The most advanced was the "insurance-saving" scheme, but they also came up with ideas such as "deferred salary savings," "emigrant savings," and "progressive saving" schemes.

6.2   Mandatory investment coefficients

The savings banks were manipulated by the government as a means of financing the policy implemented through the Development Plans. As of 1964 further obligatory investment requirements were imposed on them, increasing their mandatory investments to 80% of deposits. This left savings banks with little leeway to provide loans to their traditional customers, and jeopardized their returns (the savings banks' discretionary or "free" lending was more profitable) while increasing the risk on their investments. The Development Plans were obligatory for the public sector and indicative for the private sector. Nevertheless, the Plans increased the financial repression, in the form of mandatory investment coefficients. This affected the commercial banks, and of course, the savings banks. The latter were obliged to finance the State and also certain sectors and companies, both public and private, on preferential terms (for beneficiary companies) at below-market interest rates. The state took this approach because the paucity resources in its budget prevented it from funding all the projects envisaged in the 1st and 2nd Development Plans through subsidies and tax rebates. The indicative plans needed preferential finance in order to redirect business investment towards those sectors considered strategic. Of the various instruments available in Spain, that which was cheapest for the State was chosen, although it was the

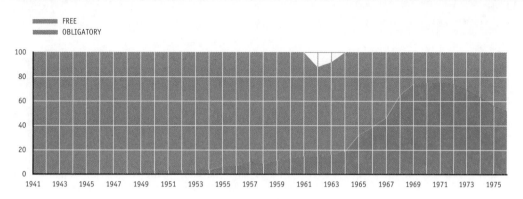

CHART 4   CREDIT STRUCTURE OF THE SAVINGS BANKS (1941-1976)

SOURCE: Comín (2008).

most expensive for the economy as a whole, given how the mandatory investment coefficients imposed on the banks and savings banks distorted the financial markets. Allocation
of financial resources in the Spanish economy was inefficient, as sectors privileged by this
captive finance had access to cheap capital, while sectors which did not have access to
these privileged credit channels had to pay higher interest than they would have done if
this financial repression had not existed. Moreover, financial repression also harmed the
interests of depositors in both the banks and savings banks, who received lower returns on
their savings, as a result of the lower returns the *cajas* earned on their investments.

The *cajas*' investment coefficients were legislated by various legislative instruments
over the period 1964 to 1967, the year in which their investments in public funds were reduced and they were given greater liberty to find other, more appropriate investments. Although this legislation increased the percentage of obligatory investments (Chart 4), these
modifications responded to some of the demands made by savings banks, as they reduced
the percentage investment in public and other eligible securities. This gave them more
room to maneuver when granting loans, as these transactions allowed them more options
to provide loans to customers in their environment. Moreover, some of these loans had a
contribution from official banks and even government subsidies.

When issues of public-debt securities and those by INI companies were insufficient to
absorb the *cajas*' investment coefficients, the Ministry of Finance obliged them to buy
debt issued by "eligible" private companies. It was the ministry's Investment Board that
was authorized to declare private-debt issues eligible. This opened up the way for large
private corporations able to influence the Francoist government to place their bond issues
with the *cajas* at preferential interest rates. It also broadened the latter's range of possible
investments, as these private securities offered better returns than public ones. Thus, the
savings banks opted for private securities (Chart 5), and tried to avoid subscribing to INI
securities. This brought with it the problem of the increased risk of these investments in pri-

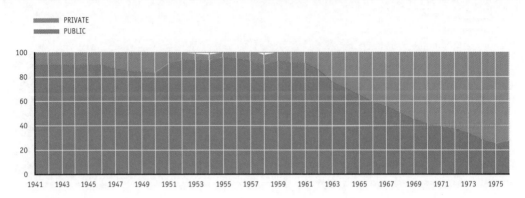

SOURCE: Comín (2008).

vate securities, which although recommended by the State, lacked its guarantee or backing. As the intermediary in this nascent fixed-income market, the Confederation, with the *cajas'* support, played an essential role in three ways: by, a) negotiating with the INI, Telefónica and other private corporations the conditions under which the securities the *cajas* were due to buy would be issued; b) by analysing the risk on private issues and offering studies on the issuing companies and the fixed-income market for the *cajas* and their customers; and, c) by representing the *cajas* on the bondholders' committees of the various issuers. This new line of financial activity began in the second half of the sixties and developed considerably over the subsequent decades.

The savings banks' lending to farmers took longer to get off the ground, primarily because collaboration with the official bodies was more difficult. This was despite the fact that the business of many *cajas* was predominantly in rural areas. Some savings banks supported farming in interesting ways, such as by promoting agricultural companies, providing business, economic and technical advice, with a view to ensuring the lending they provided was used efficiently. The relationships between the savings banks and the Banco de Crédito Agrícola and other Ministry of Agriculture bodies were far from smooth, however. Meanwhile, home loans began to gain in importance for savings banks, although the confused legal situation hindered progress in this direction. Finally, the *cajas* began to work with the Banco de Crédito Local to finance the Provincial Works and Services Plans. In the end, the government decided to expand lending to foster home ownership among the "middle class", given that its previous attempts, limited to the "working class", had met with little success. This fresh attempt to expand popular capitalism with money from the savings banks also failed to take root at this stage, but not for want of cooperation from the *cajas*.

7 The savings banks during the twilight years of Francoism (1971-1975)

During this final period examined here, a series of important changes took place affecting the savings banks, which have tended to go unnoticed, but which prepared them for the competition that would prevail in the financial sector after the return to democracy.

7.1 The savings banks under the supervision of the Banco de España

In 1971 the savings banks were put on an equal footing with the banks by placing them under the control and supervision of the Banco de España. In parallel the Savings Banks' Confederation (CECA) bolstered the financial functions inherited from the ICCA, which had formally been transferred to it in 1967, and began to offer the *cajas* new operational services. This led the CECA to become more than merely an association representing the savings banks, launching it on a new stage in which it reinforced and expanded its financial role, in a manner more characteristic of a credit institution. Following the *cajas* being put on same institutional footing as the banks, as of 1971 a swathe of new legislation was passed that changed the face of the savings banks. The new financial measures pursued a degree of liberalization of certain banking operations, a "de-specialization" of institutions and a reduction in their mandatory investments. Despite the timid attempts at deregulation in 1971 and 1975, as the sun set on Francoism, the banking system still suffered from serious rigidities and wide-ranging state intervention. With the exception of operations with a horizon of more than two years, interest rates continued to be set by the authorities, the mandatory investment coefficients remained too high; banking institutions were overly specialized, as a result of their obligations under the legislation; the commercial and investment banks, savings banks and credit unions all received different treatment, and operated under unequal conditions, to the detriment of the savings banks. Nevertheless, the specialization of the banking institutions only concerned their investments; on the deposit-taking side they all fought over the same customers and offered the same banking products, with the exception of the privileges enjoyed by the investment banks regarding long-term liabilities.

At the same time, the persistence of out-of-date regulations hampered the emergence of non-bank financial intermediaries. Thanks to the mandatory investment coefficients, the savings banks during this period (1971-76) continued to act as a palliative for the central government's deficient fiscal and social policy. Privileged access to credit offloaded from the public budget the financing of certain public investments and social functions which the State was insufficiently solvent to meet. It would be necessary to wait for the tax reform under the democracy in 1977 for the State to be able to do without the privileged financing of the savings banks to sustain its economic and social policy. At the end of this period, therefore, the *cajas* still had severe institutional restrictions on their activity, and their freedom to make financial decisions was very limited, but it had increased since 1971.

7.2 Statistics on the savings banks between 1957 and 1977

7.2.1 The savings banks' financial accounts

The savings banks gained market share in virtually every year between 1957 and 1977, except during the slight stagnation from 1972 to 1974 mentioned above (Chart 2). In terms of attracting deposits, the *cajas* went from holding 28.8% to 49.4% of the banking sector's borrowings between 1957 and 1977. In the case of private sector deposits the pattern is similar, although the percentage is slightly higher. Thus, at the end of the period the *cajas'* market share in terms of deposits was half that of the banks. This increase in deposits was achieved despite the reduction in the number of savings bank branches relative to those of the banks over this twenty-year period, resulting from the official policy of promoting the expansion of the banks more strongly after 1964 (Table 4). Between 1957 and 1963 the savings banks increased the number of their branches more rapidly than did the banks, rising from 97.6% to 119% of their number. However, the new government policy regarding the regulation of the expansion plans tipped the balance in favor of the banks; between 1964 and 1971 the *cajas* maintained their rate of new branch opening and even accelerated it, but from 1972 onwards they lost ground rapidly, falling from 120% to 70.6% between 1971 and 1977. From 1963, on the other hand, branch sizes, measured in terms of deposit volumes, increased relative to those of the banks; particularly up until 1967, and between 1975 and 1977, mainly due to the greater expansion in the number of banking branches. In 1971 the savings banks achieved institutional parity with the banks, but they clearly lost the battle for branches. This may explain why in 1972 and 1973 the rate at which savings banks were able to attract deposits slowed, leading them to change strategy, as we have seen. Indeed, between 1971 and 1973 the *cajas* focused on expanding the granting of credit, after losing market share to the banks. And in 1974 they began to balance their relative position, which was no mean feat given the ground lost in terms of number of branches. In 1977, the position of the savings banks in the credit market was even weaker, as their credit portfolio only came to 22.6% of that of the banks. Conversely, the *cajas* gained ground against the banks in terms of securities portfolios, as their portfolios grew in size from 87.1% to 110.3% of those of the banks between 1971 and 1977. Thus, in particular, from 1973 on, the *cajas'* securities portfolio exceeded that of the banks (Chart 4).

Home loans had been the *cajas'* biggest single form of lending, accounting for 53.8% of loans in 1964, but shrinking to 39.7% in 1968 (Table 5). Lending for home purchases subsequently recovered, reaching 57.4% in 1976. Industry was the second sector in importance for the savings banks' loans, accounting for 10.4% of loans in 1964 and 24.3% in 1970, when it stagnated, and in 1973 the share of loans going to industry had fallen to 14.9%, although it remained second in importance. Farming credit remained at around 20% of total lending until 1970 when it collapsed, falling to just 4.3%. In 1972 lending to farmers recovered to 14.7%, but then fell back again to 6.9% in 1976. Savings banks' lending to retailers was

TABLE 4   COMPARISON OF SAVINGS BANKS AND BANKS (1957-1977)
(percentages savings banks/banks)

Year	Borrowings and deposits	Private sector deposits	Offices	Lending portfolio	Securities portfolio	Deposits/office
1957	28.8		97.6			
1958	29.3		103.4			
1959	30.6		105.2			
1960	31.9		106.3			
1961	32.2		105.1			
1962	32.9	34.6	105.1			33.0
1963	34.5	35.3	119.1			29.7
1964	34.6	35.3	108.8			32.4
1965	36.2	37.5	96.6			38.8
1966	39.1	40.6	102.6			39.6
1967	42.0	43.4	107.5			40.4
1968	44.3	44.8	115.9			38.6
1969	45.8	45.8	118.6			38.7
1970	47.5	48.8	119.9			40.7
1971	48.6	48.8	120.3	23.5	87.1	40.6
1972	46.3	46.8	113.2	22.3	97.0	41.3
1973	43.9	45.1	112.2	21.8	108.1	40.2
1974	43.2	45.0	109.7	22.1	104.4	41.0
1975	45.2	47.4	84.1	22.1	103.5	56.3
1976	48.4	49.3	73.6	22.6	110.4	67.0
1977	49.4	50.9	70.6	22.6	110.3	72.1

SOURCE: Hernangómez (2003).

TABLE 5   SAVINGS BANK LENDING BY SECTORS (1964-1976)
(percentages)

Year	Industry	Housing	Agriculture	Trade	Misc.	Corporate
1964	10.4	53.8	19.7	4.2	10.1	1.9
1965	13.0	53.1	19.0	4.5	8.8	1.6
1966	18.2	47.4	17.7	6.3	8.9	1.5
1967	20.6	43.8	18.8	7.0	8.5	1.3
1968	23.7	39.7	16.4	5.8	6.9	0.9
1969	23.5	44.5	20.9	4.5	5.8	0.7
1970	24.3	44.9	4.3	18.6	7.4	0.6
1971	22.9	48.0	4.1	16.9	7.6	0.5
1972	22.7	50.8	14.7	4.2	7.1	0.5
1973	20.3	50.0	12.6	4.8	11.9	0.5
1974	18.3	51.9	10.5	5.0	13.8	0.5
1975	16.5	54.6	8.2	5.2	15.1	0.5
1976	14.9	57.4	6.9	5.5	14.9	0.4

SOURCE: Titos and Piñar (1993).

limited, except in 1970 and 1971, although this sharp increase, with a simultaneous drop in farm lending, suggests that there may actually be a problem with the way the figures have been recorded. Finally, corporate lending was meager throughout the whole period.

7.2.2 The savings banks' social activities and obligatory reserves

Chart 3 shows the distribution of the savings banks' profits. Obviously, the columns do not add up to a hundred as, just as in the other tables, certain other items are not shown. Except in 1976, the percentage of earnings the savings banks paid as corporate income tax was limited to between 5% and 10%. What is most striking is the increase in the percentage of earnings set aside for reserves. Although this fell between 1957 and 1961, it later rose from 30.3% to 55.2% between 1961 and 1977. The 45% limit would not be broken until 1972, and the 50% barrier in 1976. Little by little, the *cajas* managed to devote a larger share of their resources to reserves, thus building their equity. The share of earnings devoted to social and charitable activities was always more than a third, and in 1959 and 1969 it was over half. The allocations to social and charitable activities fell slightly below 50% up until 1975 when the Decree passed that year changed the applicable legislation. Thus, the contribution of funds to social activities by the *cajas* would not be affected by the new distribution of the surplus ordered by the Decree passed on 3 July 1975, which sought to increase the reserves held by all the savings banks.

Between 1957 and 1975, the savings banks' social and charitable activities were spread fairly widely across the various categories (Chart 6). The most important category was the contribution to the National Social Welfare Fund which the *cajas* were obliged to transfer to the Ministry of Labor. Despite the repeated complaints from the ministry that the savings banks were in breach of their obligations, it may be observed that as of 1963 the opposite was the case, that is, that their contributions exceeded the theoretical 15% imposed by the

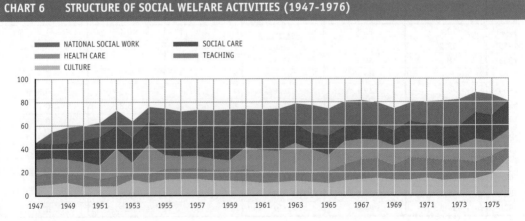

CHART 6   STRUCTURE OF SOCIAL WELFARE ACTIVITIES (1947-1976)

NATIONAL SOCIAL WORK   SOCIAL CARE
HEALTH CARE   TEACHING
CULTURE

SOURCE: Comín (2008).

1951 Law. Next in importance were healthcare, cultural activities, schooling, child protection and vocational training. Overall, education received a substantial portion of the *cajas'* social funding, if the "workers' universities" (included in the 15% paid to the National Fund), vocational training and schooling are all included. The protection of the elderly also became significant recipient of funding from 1973 onwards.

7.2.3   The end-point: the savings banks in 1975

Table 6 lists the *cajas* that existed in 1975, the final year covered by this study. Their number had practically doubled since 1901, rising from 47 to 88. In 1975 their size, in terms of deposits, remained highly uneven. The sector's concentration had fallen substantially since the start of the century, although it remained considerable. The two biggest savings banks (the Caja de Pensiones and the Caja de Madrid) alone accounted for 21.6% of total deposits (half of their share in 1901); or for their part, in 1975 the five biggest savings banks (the above two, plus the Caja de Zaragoza, Caja de Barcelona and Caja de Valencia) held 36.82% (somewhat less than half their share in 1901); finally, the ten biggest (adding to the above the Caja de la Diputación de Barcelona, Caja de Bilbao, Caja de Guipuzcoa, Caja Vizcaína and Caja del Sureste de España) together held 51.27% (60% of their share at the start of the century). The concentration therefore remained significant, but was down on that at the start of the 20th century. The reason for this was the emergence of numerous new savings banks, although many of them were tiny. The sector continued to be dominated by the Catalan, Madrid and Basque cajas. There is no record of any savings banks going bankrupt during the period covered by the study because the strict regulations (Savings Statute of 1929, which remains in force) and supervision by the relevant ministries (Interior, Labor and Finance, successively) prevented these institutions from making high risk investments. Nevertheless it is true that some *cajas* disappeared. The reason being that they were absorbed or merged with others.

Up until the transition to democracy and, more specifically, Decree 2290/1977 which granted the savings banks operational equality with the banks, the institutional and operational characteristics of the Spanish savings banks were fairly similar to those in other European countries, barring the obvious national differences. These include, in the case of Spain, the existence of forty years of dictatorship which implemented indicative planning in the 1960s, bringing with it greater financial repression of the savings banks, as has been discussed. By way of compensation, the *cajas* were permitted to start conducting new types of financial transaction that were prohibited to most of their European counterparts. And it also allowed the CECA to take on two roles as an association: as well as representing the savings banks, which it had done since 1928, it also began to provide them with finance, a role ceded to it by the ICCA. Elsewhere in Europe these two functions were performed by separate bodies. Combining these two roles in the CECA gave the *cajas* greater leverage when it came to lobbying the government. This explains why Decree 2290

TABLE 6   CONFEDERATED SAVINGS BANKS IN 1975 RANKED BY VOLUME OF DEPOSITS AND BORROWINGS
(millions of pesetas and percentages of total)

	Savings Banks	Total deposits and borrowings	% of total
1	Caja de Pensiones para la Vejez y de Ahorros	224,279.35	14.81
2	Caja de Ahorros y Monte de Piedad de Madrid	102,368.69	6.76
3	Caja de Ahorros y Monte de Piedad de Zaragoza, Aragón y Rioja	81,905.33	5.41
4	Caja de Ahorros y Monte de Piedad de Barcelona	81,331.19	5.37
5	Caja de Ahorros y Monte de Piedad de Valencia	67,699.71	4.47
6	Caja de Ahorros de la Diputación de Barcelona	57,700.06	3.81
7	Caja de Ahorros y Monte de Piedad Mpal. De Bilbao	43,012.70	2.84
8	Caja de Ahorros Prov. de Guipuzcoa	42,779.79	2.82
9	Caja de Ahorros Vizcaina	39,581.50	2.61
10	Caja de Ahorros del Sureste de España	32,794.87	0.10
11	Caja de Ahorros y Monte de Piedad de La Coruña y Lugo	30,887.93	2.04
12	Monte de Piedad y Caja de Ahorros de Ronda	28,500.77	1.88
13	Caja de Ahorros de Asturias	27,787.60	1.83
14	Caja de Ahorros y Monte de Piedad Mpal. de Vigo	27,394.97	1.81
15	Caja de Ahorros Prov. de Orense	24,493.77	1.62
16	Caja de Ahorros y Monte de Piedad de Granada	22,857.13	1.51
17	Caja de Ahorros de Navarra	22,385.49	1.48
18	Caja de Ahorros y Monte de Piedad Mpal. de San Sebastián	21,307.60	1.41
19	Caja de Ahorros de Sabadell	18,519.74	1.22
20	Caja de Ahorros y Monte de Piedad de León	17,608.57	1.16
21	Caja de Ahorros de Santander	16,968.69	1.12
22	Caja de Ahorros del Penedés	16,915.76	1.12
23	Monte de Piedad y Caja de Ahorros de Córdoba	16,662.57	1.10
24	Caja Insular de Ahorros y Monte de Piedad de Gran Canaria.	16,622.99	1.10
25	Caja de Ahorros y Monte de Piedad de Salamanca	16,307.55	1.08
26	Caja de Ahorros y Monte de Piedad de Las Baleares	14,907.02	0.98
27	Caja de Ahorros Mpal. de Burgos	14,732.68	0.97
28	Caja de Ahorros Prov. de San Fernando de Sevilla	13,845.50	0.91
29	Caja General de Ahorros y Monte de Piedad de Santa Cruz de Tenerife	12,700.92	0.84
30	Caja de Ahorros Prov. de Toledo	12,301.11	0.81
31	Caja de Ahorros de la Inmaculada de Zaragoza	12,077.58	0.80
32	Caja de Ahorros Prov. de Tarragona	11,710.65	0.77
33	Caja de Ahorros de Manresa	11,204.72	0.74
34	Caja de Ahorros y Monte de Piedad de Santiago de Compostela	11,049.26	0.73
35	Caja de Ahorros y Monte de Piedad CCO de Burgos	10,724.20	0.71
36	Caja de Ahorros y Monte de Piedad de Segovia	10,225.88	0.68
37	Caja de Ahorros y Monte de Piedad de Cádiz	9,972.90	0.66
38	Caja Prov. de Ahorros de Álava	9,837.64	0.65
39	Caja de Ahorros "Sagrada Familia" de Barcelona	9,814.57	0.65
40	Caja de Ahorros Prov. de la Diputación de Gerona	9,748.68	0.64
41	Caja Prov. de Ahorro de Cuenca	9,669.43	0.64
42	Caja de Ahorros de Tarrasa	9,628.57	0.64
43	Monte de Piedad y Caja de Ahorros de Almería	9,628.34	0.64
44	Caja de Ahorros Layetana	9,383.10	0.62
45	Caja de Ahorros y Monte de Piedad de la Ciudad de Vitoria	8,718.56	0.58

TABLE 6 CONFEDERATED SAVINGS BANKS IN 1975 RANKED BY VOLUME OF DEPOSITS AND BORROWINGS (cont'd) (millions of pesetas and percentages of total)

	Savings Banks	Total deposits and borrowings	% of total
46	Caja de Ahorros y Monte de Piedad de Castellón	8,549.64	0.56
47	Caja de Ahorros Prov. de Pontevedra	8,295.15	0.55
48	Caja Prov. de Ahorros y Monte de Piedad de Huelva	8,224.05	0.54
49	Caja Gral. de Ahorros y Monte de Piedad de Avila	8,140.77	0.54
50	Monte de Piedad y Caja Gral. de Ahorros de Badajoz	7,858.38	0.52
51	Caja de Ahorros de Jerez de la Frontera	7,814.00	0.52
52	Caja de Ahorros y Monte de Piedad de Plasencia	7,758.10	0.51
53	Caja de Ahorros Prov. de Alicante	7,648.63	0.03
54	Caja de Ahorros y Monte de Piedad Mpal. De Pamplona	7,464.07	0.49
55	Caja de Ahorros Prov. de Albacete	7,358.24	0.49
56	Monte de Piedad y Caja de Ahorros de Sevilla	6,922.23	0.46
57	Caja Gral. de Ahorros y Préstamos de Soria	6,751.80	0.45
58	Caja de Ahorros y Monte de Piedad de Cáceres	6,673.08	0.44
59	Caja Prov. de Ahorros de Córdoba	6,432.96	0.42
60	Caja Prov. de Ahorros de Logroño	6,245.02	0.41
61	Caja de Ahorros y Monte de Piedad de El Ferrol	5,123.62	0.34
62	Caja de Ahorros Prov. de Valladolid	5,117.78	0.34
63	Caja de Ahorros Prov. de Málaga	4,944.33	0.33
64	Caja de Ahorros de Torrente	4,895.13	0.32
65	Caja de Ahorros de Ntra. Sra. de Monserrate	4,883.24	0.32
66	Caja de Ahorros y Préstamos de Antequera	4,645.03	0.31
67	Caja de Ahorros Comarcal de Manlleu	4,373.96	0.02
68	Caja de Ahorros Prov. de Zamora	4,184.06	0.28
69	Caja de Ahorros de Novelda	3,935.85	0.26
70	Caja de Ahorros y Monte de Piedad de Palencia	3,828.42	0.25
71	Monte de Piedad y Caja de Ahorros de Alcoy	3,700.83	0.02
72	Caja de Ahorros Popular de Valladolid	3,692.90	0.24
73	Caja de Ahorros Prov. de Murcia	3,620.54	0.24
74	Caja de Ahorros y Socorros de Sagunto	3,372.23	0.22
75	Caja Central de Ahorros y Préstamos de Avila	3,277.13	0.22
76	Caja de Ahorros Prov. de Guadalajara	2,685.65	0.18
77	Caja de Ahorros y Monte de Piedad de Lérida	2,502.63	0.17
78	Caja de Ahorros Prov. de Lugo	2,389.75	0.16
79	Caja de Ahorros y Monte de Piedad de Onteniente	1,820.41	0.12
80	Caja de Ahorros Ntra. Sra. de los Dolores de Crevillente	1,631.93	0.11
81	Caja de Ahorros de Alhama de Murcia	1,539.01	0.10
82	Caja de Ahorros y Monte de Piedad de Ceuta	1,521.79	0.10
83	Caja de Ahorros Insular de La Palma	1,408.76	0.09
84	Caja de Ahorros y Préstamos de Palencia	824.98	0.05
85	Caja de Ahorros y Monte de Piedad de Segorbe	655.96	0.04
86	Caja de Ahorros y Préstamos de Carlet	611.78	0.04
87	Caja de Ahorros de Pollensa	370.65	0.02
88	Caja Prov. de Ahorros de Granada	334.55	0.02
	TOTAL	1,514,585.27	100.00

SOURCE: *Historia cuantitativa de las Cajas de Ahorro Españolas en 1970-1985,* (VI), CECA, Madrid, 1989, pp. 18 and 19.

was passed, which greatly benefited the savings banks as it allowed them to operate under equal conditions to the banks and started to free them from the political and regulatory ties on their activities. Unlike what happened elsewhere in Europe (with the possible exception of Norwegian savings banks), since then the Spanish savings banks have found themselves in a strong competitive position compared to that of their counterparts in other European countries. But that part of their history lies outside the scope of this chapter.[3]

8 Concluding remarks

Between 1900 and 1975 the *cajas* underwent a series of transformations driven by changing government regulations at the hands of the ministries responsible for them: first the Interior Ministry, then the Ministry of Labor and finally the Ministry of Finance. Obviously, the savings banks influenced these developments, particularly as of 1928 when they organized themselves under the umbrella of the Spanish Confederation of Savings Banks or CECA (the sector's employers' association), and when in 1933 the Savings Bank Credit Institute or ICCA (the savings banks' financial body) was set up. When the ICCA ceased to exist in 1971, the CECA took over both roles, representing the savings banks and providing them with financial services. This helped boost the development of the savings banks as financial institutions. In the first three quarters of the 20th century Spain's savings banks went from being charitable organizations to financial institutions. As of 1926, and particularly after the Savings Statute in 1933, the *cajas* were obliged to invest a percentage of their deposits in public securities, and this percentage was doubled in 1951. Under Francoism the "financial repression" suffered by the savings banks increased, but to offset this, the government conceded them progressively more freedom to act as banks, with a view to increasing the resources they could raise and subsequently invest in public securities.

This transition towards their playing a financial role was further accelerated in 1957, when the Ministry of Finance stimulated the savings banks' activity as financial intermediaries in order for them to make a bigger contribution to the "privileged financing" of public investments, and in particular by providing finance to the companies belonging to the government holding company, the INI, and other state-owned companies such as Telefónica. When these public issues were insufficient to absorb the investments the savings banks were required to make in public securities, they were obliged to subscribe to bond issues by private companies selected in advance by the Ministry of Finance. With the Development Plans the savings banks acquired new obligations to grant "privileged credit" to certain sectors and companies, until around 85% of their deposits were committed to investments of this kind, leaving them little margin for "free" or discretionary investments. As the Ministry of Finance was keen to increase the *cajas'* lending power, it gradually authorized them to undertake new types of financial transactions and attract savings through new instruments,

---

[3] See Comín (2008) and Pampillón (2003) for more on this topic.

including new types of savings books and current accounts. Finally, in 1971 the savings banks came under the supervisory authority of the Banco de España, which meant their being placed on an equal institutional footing with the banks. This allowed the *cajas* to start preparing themselves for the liberalization of the financial system in 1977, which turned the savings banks into fully-fledged financial institutions, giving them operational equality with the banks and obliging them to change their statutes following the Law on Savings Bank Governance (LORCA) in 1985.

This chapter has studied the profound transformations the savings banks have undergone since 1900, which enabled them to compete against other financial institutions in the market. The period also saw a transformation in the way the savings banks' profits were distributed, going from being simply charitable to their being a "social welfare" activity. Under Franco, the Ministry of Labor also obliged the savings banks to devote a share of their social funding to specific welfare, healthcare, cultural and educational activities. Moreover, when they were turned into financial institutions, the profits the *cajas* set aside to fund social and welfare activities became subordinate to their capacity to produce "reserves", which took priority in order to bolster the savings banks' equity, as this acts as a guarantee of solvency for depositors. Without these transformations taking place during the period from 1900 to 1975 it would be impossible to understand the developments affecting the savings banks during the democracy, which have been very different from those in other European countries.

References

AMÉRICI, L. (2002). "Preparing the People for Capitalism: Relations with Depositors in a French Savings Bank during the 1820s", *Financial History Review,* 9, pp. 5-19.

BONIN, H. (2005). "Las estrategias de expansión de las cajas de ahorros francesas durante los siglos XIX y XX", *Papeles de Economía Española,* no. 105-106, pp. 93-108.

COMÍN, F. (2001). "Las cajas de ahorros en la España contemporánea (1835-2000)", in *Ibercaja, una aportación al desarrollo económico y social, 1876-2001. 125 aniversario,* Caja de Ahorros y Monte de Piedad de Zaragoza, Aragón y Rioja, Zaragoza.

— (2004). "La Confederación Española de cajas de ahorros entre 1971 y 1976", in *Estudios en homenaje a Luis Ángel Rojo,* II, Editorial Complutense, Madrid, pp. 339-357.

— (2005). "El nuevo papel de la CECA y las Cajas ante las mayores exigencias de financiación del Estado (1957-1963)", *Papeles de Economía Española,* no. 105-106, pp. 27-47.

— (2007a). "Los Planes de Desarrollo, la CECA y las Cajas de Ahorro (1964-1970)", in *Miscel·lània Ernest Lluch i Martín,* Vol. II, Fundación Ernest Lluch, Vilassar de Mar, pp. 163-188.

— (2007b). "Las cajas de ahorros tras la liberalización del sistema financiero en España (1977-1985)", in S. de Dios, J. Infante, R. Robledo and E. Torijano (Coord.), *Historia de la propiedad, crédito y garantía,* Servicio de Estudios del Colegio de Registradores, Salamanca, pp. 425-457.

— (2007c). "The Spanish Savings Banks and the Competitive Cooperation Model (1928-2002)", *Revista de Historia Económica. Journal of Iberian and Latin American Economic History,* año XXV, autumn, no. 2, pp. 199-230.

— (in collaboration with E. Torres Villanueva) (2008). *Historia de la cooperación entre las cajas de ahorros. La Confederación Española de Cajas de Ahorros, 1928-2003,* CECA, Madrid.

COMÍN, F., and E. TORRES (2003). "Una historia urgente de la Confederación Española de cajas de ahorros", *Papeles de Economía Española*, no. 97, pp. 246-284.

— (2005). "La Confederación Española de cajas de ahorros y el desarrollo de la red de servicios financieros de las cajas de ahorros durante el siglo XX (1900-1976)", *Papeles de Economía Española*, no. 105-106, pp. 48-64.

COMÍN, F., and P. MARTÍN-ACEÑA (1996). "Rasgos históricos de las empresas en España", *Revista de Economía Aplicada*, 12, pp. 75-123.

— (eds.) (1996). *La empresa en la historia de España*, Civitas, Madrid.

COMÍN, F., and R. VALLEJO (2009). "Los Programas de Inversiones Públicas (1964-1976): ¿El instrumento presupuestario al servicio de los Planes de Desarrollo?", in J. de la Torre and M. García-Zúñiga (Eds.), *Entre el Mercado y el Estado. Los planes de desarrollo durante el franquismo*, Universidad Pública de Navarra, Pamplona, pp. 89-145.

CONFEDERACIÓN ESPAÑOLA DE CAJAS DE AHORROS (1964). *La Obra Social de las cajas de ahorros*, Madrid.

— (1986). "La red de oficinas de cajas de ahorros en España, 1950-1985", *Temas Económicos*, 39, Departamento de Estudios y Programación.

— (1987). *Historia cuantitativa de las Cajas de Ahorro españolas en 1940-1955*, IV, CECA, Madrid.

— (1988). *Historia cuantitativa de las Cajas de Ahorro españolas en 1955-1970*, V, CECA, Madrid.

— (1989a). *Historia cuantitativa de las Cajas de Ahorro españolas, 1901-1927*, II, CECA, Madrid.

— (1989b). *Historia cuantitativa de las Cajas de Ahorro españolas en 1970-1985*, VI, CECA, Madrid.

— (1990). *Historia cuantitativa de las Cajas de Ahorro españolas en 1928-1935*, III, CECA, Madrid.

— (1928-2002). *Libros de Actas del Consejo de Administración de la Confederación Española de cajas de ahorros*, Archivo de la Secretaría General de la CECA, Madrid.

FERNÁNDEZ RAMOS, J. C. (2006). *Historia del Instituto de Crédito de las cajas de ahorros en el período 1933-1962*, Universidad Complutense de Madrid, Madrid.

FORNIÉS, J. F (1978). "El nacimiento de la Confederación Española de Cajas de Ahorro y su vinculación con la política financiera nacional", *Cuadernos Económicos de ICE*, 6, pp. 163-177.

— (1989a). "Las cajas de ahorros españolas en una etapa crucial de su historia: 1926-1939", *Fuentes para la historia de las cajas de ahorros y Montes de Piedad españolas*, 5, November.

— (1989b). "Los períodos de la historia de las cajas de ahorros españolas y los grupos sociales fundadores", in *I Simposio de Historia de cajas de ahorros y Montes de Piedad*, Madrid.

— FORNIÉS, J. F. (1991). "Interpretación básica de la historia de las cajas de ahorros españolas", *Papeles de Economía Española*, no. 46, pp. 39-51.

FORNIÉS, J. F., M. M. TORRES and A. RUBIO (1976). *Historia de la Caja de Ahorros y Monte de Piedad de Zaragoza, Aragón y Rioja, 1876-1976*, Zaragoza.

GONZÁLEZ ENCISO, A. (Supervisor) (1998). *Caja de Ahorros y Monte de Piedad Municipal de Pamplona. 125 años de Historia. 1872-1997*, Caja de Ahorros Municipal, Pamplona.

HERNANGÓMEZ, F. (2003). *Estadísticas de las cajas de ahorros y de la Confederación Española de cajas de ahorros*, CECA, Madrid.

HERTNER, P. (1996). "Italy", in J. Mura (Ed.), *History of European Savings Banks*, Bon, Deutscher Sparkassenverlag GmbH, pp. 193-227.

LLAMBY, L. de (2006). *60 ans de construction du Groupe Caisse d'Épargne. Une histoire pour demain*, Caisse Nationale de Caisses d'Épargne, París.

LÓPEZ YEPES, J. (Supervisor) (1979). *La Caja de Ahorros y Monte de Piedad de Valencia. Su historia y su obra, 1878-1978*, Caja de Ahorros de Valencia, Valencia.

LÓPEZ YEPES, J., and M. TITOS MARTÍNEZ (1993). *Historia de la Caja de Ahorros de Badajoz, 1889-1992*, Badajoz.

— (1995). *Historia de la Caja de Ahorros y Monte de Piedad de Madrid (1702-1970)*, Caja de Ahorros de Madrid, Madrid.

— LÓPEZ YEPES, J., and M. TITOS MARTÍNEZ, et ál. (1999). *Cien años de Caja Cantabria*, Santander.

MAIXÉ, J. C. (2003). *El ahorro de los gallegos. Orígenes e historia de Caixa Galicia*, Fundación Caixa Galicia, La Coruña.

MARTÍN-ACEÑA, P. (1984). *La política monetaria en España, 1919-1935*, Instituto de Estudios Fiscales, Madrid.

— (2003a). "La España de la Restauración. Expansión y consolidación institucional de las cajas de ahorros (1880-1923)", *in Siglo y medio de ahorro en España*, CECA, Madrid, pp. 93-119.

— (2003b). "Las cajas de ahorros en la historia económica española", *Economistas*, no. 98, pp. 26-34.

MARTÍN-ACEÑA, P., and F. COMÍN (1991). *INI. 50 años de industrialización en España*, Espasa Calpe, Madrid.

MARTÍN-ACEÑA, P. and M. A. PONS (2006). "Sistema financiero", in A. Carreras and X. Tafunell (Coord.), *Estadísticas Históricas de España,* Fundación BBVA.

MARTÍNEZ SOTO, A. P. (2000). "Las cajas de ahorros españolas en el siglo XIX: entre la beneficencia y la integración en el sistema financiero", *Revista de Historia Económica,* XVIII, no. 3, pp. 585-628.

MARTÍNEZ SOTO, A. P., and J. CUEVAS (2004). *Estadísticas de las cajas de ahorros españolas (1840-1935),* Universidad de Murcia, Murcia.

— (2004). "La expansión y consolidación de las cajas de ahorros en el sistema financiero español, 1880-1936", *Revista de Historia Económica,* XXII, no. 1, pp. 65-110.

MARTÍNEZ SOTO, A. P., J. CUEVAS and A. HOYO (2005). "La historia económica de las cajas de ahorros españolas. Una perspectiva institucional y regional (1830-2004)", *Papeles de Economía Española,* no. 105-106, pp. 6-15.

MOSS, M., and A. SLAVEN (1992). *A History of the TSB in Scotland from 1810 to 1990,* Glasgow.

MURA, J. (1996). "Germany", in J. Mura (Ed.), *History of European Savings Banks,* Bon, Deutscher Sparkassenverlag GmbH, pp. 105-131.

NADAL, J., and C. SUDRIÀ (1983). *Historia de la Caja de Pensiones. La Caixa dentro del sistema financiero catalán,* Barcelona.

O' GRÁDA, C. (2001). *An Institutional Import: Irish Savings Banks c. 1820-1860,* Working Paper 01/17, Centre for Economic Research, Department of Economics, University College, Dublin.

ORIBE, A. (1979). *100 años al servicio de Guipúzcoa. La Caja de Ahorros Municipal de San Sebastián (1879-1979),* Caja de Ahorros Municipal de San Sebastián, San Sebastián.

PAMPILLÓN, F. (2003). "Los modelos históricos europeos de cajas de ahorros", *Papeles de Economía Española,* no. 97, pp. 62-78.

PÉREZ MENÉNDEZ, M. A. (1987). *Caja de Ahorros de Asturias. Historia de cien años, 1881-1980,* Caja de Ahorros de Asturias, Oviedo.

QUINTÁS, J. R. (2003). "Las cajas de ahorros Españolas en el siglo XXI: Modernización y Capital Social", *Perspectivas del Sistema Financiero,* no. 77, pp.1-26.

ROSS, D. (2001). "Penny Banks and Working Class Saving in Glasgow, 1850-1914", in *Savings Banks Conference 19th-20th,* Centre for Business History in Scotland, University of Glasgow.

TITOS MARTÍNEZ, M. (1987). *Historia de la Caja General de Ahorros y Monte de Piedad de Granada (1891-1986),* Granada.

— (1990). "El papel de la Obra Social en el contexto económico de las cajas de ahorros", in *La Obra Social de las cajas de ahorros españolas,* CECA, pp. 61-135, Madrid.

TITOS MARTÍNEZ, M. (1991). "La respuesta histórica de las cajas de ahorros a las demandas de la sociedad española", *Papeles de Economía Española,* no. 46, pp. 12-37.

— (1998). "La fundación de las cajas de ahorros. Motivaciones, protagonistas y evolución numérica", *Papeles de Economía Española,* pp. 74-75.

— (1999). "Las cajas de ahorros (1853-1962)", in P. Martín-Aceña and M. Titos Martínez (Eds.), *El sistema financiero en España. Una síntesis histórica,* Universidad de Granada.

— (2003). "Economía y finanzas en la España liberal. La época fundacional de las cajas de ahorros (1835-1874)", in *Siglo y medio de ahorro en España,* CECA, Madrid, pp. 55-91.

— (2005). "Las cajas de ahorros en Andalucía y su papel en el desarrollo regional", *Papeles de Economía Española,* no. 105-106.

TITOS MARTÍNEZ, M., and J. PIÑAR (1993). *Ahorro popular e inversión privilegiada. Las cajas de ahorros en España, 1939-1975,* Caja de Madrid, Madrid.

TORRES, E. (2005). "Intervencionismo estatal y cambios en el marco regulador de las cajas de ahorros durante el primer franquismo (1939-1957)", *Papeles de Economía Española,* no. 105-106, pp. 16-25.

VALDALISO, J. M. (2007), BBK (1907-2007). *Cien años de compromiso con el desarrollo económico y el bienestar de Bizcaia,* BBK, Bilbao.

WYSOCKI, J. (1996). "Introduction", in J. Mura (Ed.), *History of European Savings Banks,* Bon, Deutscher Sparkassenverlag GmbH, pp. 9-25.

6. The macroeconomic basis of the recent development of the Spanish financial system

José Luis Malo de Molina [1]
Banco de España

1 Introduction

The development and modernization of the Spanish financial system in the final quarter of the 20th century and the early years of the 21st has been closely linked to profound changes in the Spanish economy and particularly to how it has operated on the macroeconomic level. From the macroeconomic point of view, the history of this period has been characterized by the difficulties encountered in establishing a stable framework, something that was only successfully achieved with Spain's joining Economic and Monetary Union (EMU). The last few years have been shaped by the severe international financial crisis, which caught the Spanish economy by surprise at a time when it had already embarked on a process of adjustment to correct imbalances which had built up over the years since membership of Monetary Union. This would represent the biggest perturbation in the country's post-war economic history, test the solidity of the progress achieved by the financial system, and trigger a radical reorganization of the sector. The aim of this chapter is to elucidate the significant influence that macroeconomic developments have had on the transformation of the financial system over the period and look in detail at the most

[1] I am grateful to Roberto Blanco Escolar, Ignacio Hernando Castellet and Jorge Martínez Pagés for their assistance in the preparation of this chapter.

decisive factors. The first section therefore gives a short introductory overview of the role of macroeconomic stability on the development of financial systems, drawing upon the existing analytic literature. The second section sketches out the close relationship that has existed in Spain between progress on macroeconomic stability and the modernization of the financial system, which is the main theme of the chapter. The remaining sections are organized around the three main stages into which the period can be divided: convergence towards stability in a context of full monetary sovereignty; membership of economic and monetary union; and, finally, the economic and financial crisis.

2   Macroeconomic stability and the development of the financial system

The importance of the development of the financial system for economic growth has motivated numerous authors to identify those factors which have contributed most to the development of markets and financial intermediaries in various countries. In particular, these factors include institutional aspects (property law, the degree of transparency and supervision of the financial system, the level of financial deregulation and internationalization, etc.) and macroeconomic conditions (see, for example, Levine [2005]). The literature on the subject has focused on those restrictions arising from the way economic policy and the public sector, through a series of constraints, such as limits on interest rates, mandatory investment coefficients, high reserve requirements or capital controls, which prevented financial intermediaries from offering attractive returns to their investors, and thus limited the volume of assets they have available to lend. McKinnon (1973) and Shaw (1973) were the first to highlight the importance of this phenomenon, which they termed "financial repression."

From this viewpoint, the main source of financial repression comes from attempts to meet substantial public sector borrowing needs by raising funds cheaply, thus disrupting the possibility of the efficient functioning of financial markets (Bencivenga and Smith [1992] and Roubini and Sala-i-Martin [1995]). These mechanisms include, in particular, monetary financing of the public deficit, which, by causing high inflation rates, allows taxation by stealth through seigniorage, with the consequent distortion of funding flows. Thus, the duo of public deficit and inflation appear in the literature as important factors in inhibiting and distorting the financial system and various empirical studies have identified a negative relationship between these two variables, which are indicative of macroeconomic instability, and financial development (see, for example, Huybens and Smith [1999], Boyd et al. [2001], Cotarelli et al [2004] and Hauner [2006]). As a result, reducing the public deficit – and financing it by orthodox means – makes an important contribution to the development of the financial system by releasing resources for the private sector. This enables greater development of financial intermediation, and produces a low-risk asset market for investors (in the form of public debt) which can provide reference prices for alternative investments and instruments for the implementation of monetary policy. It should come as no surprise, therefore, that in many countries the establishment of a framework of healthy public finances and monetary stability has been fundamental in the early stages of financial modernization, as Rousseau and Sylla (2003) have shown.

One should not lose sight, however, of the fact that macroeconomic stability's contribution to the maturation of the financial system also flows through more subtle – but no less decisive – channels such as the reduction in uncertainty as to the future progress of economic agents' real wealth and income. This greater certainty allows investors to increase their portfolios' risk exposures (through investments in equities, private fixed income, venture capital, etc.), allows intermediaries to reduce the cost of intermediation, and borrowers to take on a larger volume of debt. Equally important is the relationship between the degree of macroeconomic stability and the level of financial fragility. The clearest case is when macroeconomic imbalances end up causing crises among financial institutions which may be of systemic importance. A number of studies have shown (see, for example, Demirguc-Kunt and Detragiache [1998 and 2005]) how banking crises tend to be more likely in situations characterized by economic weakness, high real interest rates and high inflation.

One final important issue for the analytical literature on the topic is the evidence of the role of financial deregulation and internationalization in the broad revitalization of the system (see, for example, Chinn and Ito [2006], Henry [2000] and Tressel and Detragiache [2008]). This role is manifest both in the increase in alternative sources of funding and greater competition within the resident financial sector (Rajan and Zingales [2003], Braun and Raddatz [2008]). There is little doubt, however, that successful financial deregulation requires a context of macroeconomic stability and there are numerous examples of cases where the process of internationalization has not been accompanied by a sufficient degree of macroeconomic stability, ending in financial and currency crises as a result (see IMF [2001] and Loayza and Ranciere [2006]). In particular, Claessens et al. (2006) conclude that a high public deficit and inflation tend to hold back not just financial development but also financial internationalization.

3   Progress towards the stability and maturity of the Spanish financial system in recent economic history

When the period from the transition to democracy to the present day is looked at as a whole, the parallel between progress towards macroeconomic stability and greater economic dynamism, which enabled the prosperity gap between Spain and other industrialized economies to be narrowed, is readily apparent [Rojo (2002) and Malo de Molina (2003 and 2005)]. The conditions of stability that enabled faster growth rates to be sustained were also those that supported the profound transformation the financial system experienced during the period. Stability gains, the clearest manifestations of which was a reduction in

CHART 1   MACROECONOMIC AND FINANCIAL INDICATORS

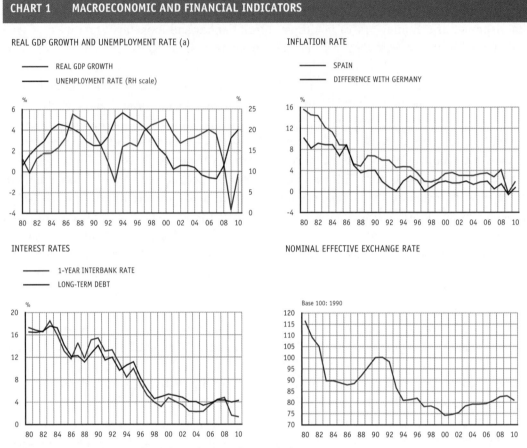

REAL GDP GROWTH AND UNEMPLOYMENT RATE (a)

——— REAL GDP GROWTH
——— UNEMPLOYMENT RATE (RH scale)

INFLATION RATE

——— SPAIN
——— DIFFERENCE WITH GERMANY

INTEREST RATES

——— 1-YEAR INTERBANK RATE
——— LONG-TERM DEBT

NOMINAL EFFECTIVE EXCHANGE RATE

SOURCES: Eurostat, Instituto Nacional de Estadística and Banco de España.

a. Data up to third quarter of 2010.

inflation and interest rates, together with exchange rate stabilization (Chart 1), gave a structural boost to the development of the financial system by fostering the emergence of new instruments and markets and inducing significant changes in the composition of agents' portfolios. To this was added the influence of macroeconomic fluctuations on the expansion of markets and financial intermediaries.

From the beginning of the democratic period until well into the 1980s, the Spanish economy experienced persistent high inflation rates as a result of both external (oil shocks) and internal (wages) upward pressures and a clearly expansionary fiscal policy, which put the burden of the difficult task of stabilization exclusively on monetary policy. Under these conditions, the strong increase in lending to the public sector put pressure on the conditions under which funds were available for the non-financial private sector; a clear example of crowding out. The high interest rates resulting from this combination of circumstances led to scant demand for borrowing by private agents, thus limiting the incentives for the development of the financial system. As a result, the ratio of financial assets to GDP grew only slightly in the

CHART 2   FINANCIAL ASSETS AND STOCK-MARKET CAPITALIZATION (a)

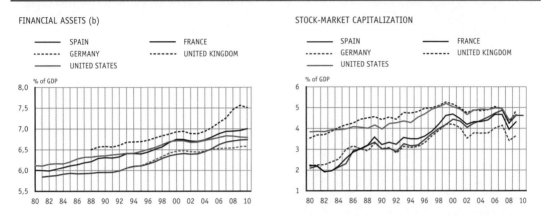

SOURCES: Instituto Nacional de Estadística, Banco de España, Federal Reserve, Banque de France, Deutsche Bundesbank, UK National Statistics.

a. Series in logarithms.
b. 2010 data are for last quarter of 2010, except in the case of Germany, where they are for the second quarter.

1980s, remaining below the levels in other developed economies (Chart 2). During this period, bank lending to the private sector was sluggish, and neither the stock market nor the corporate bond market progressed significantly.

The switch to the use of more orthodox financial instruments in the mid-1980s, while maintaining an expansionary fiscal stance, reduced the public sector's recourse to credit institutions and encouraged the development of the public-debt market. Stimulating this market was fundamental to both avoiding the monetary financing of the government deficit and to ensuring that it was possible to implement an independent monetary policy. The measures introduced to pursue this goal included the introduction of public-debt investment coefficients in 1984 and the creation of a book-entry public-debt market in 1987.

The introduction of the tools of a monetary and financial policy capable of pursuing stability goals paved the way for the financial system to begin a phase of major transformations underpinned by financial innovations and legislative reforms. The main legislative reforms implemented included sweeping liberalization of the operations of institutions and markets and international capital flows, as is discussed in other chapters of this book. Here, however, it is worth stressing how progress towards an environment of greater macroeconomic stability, linked to an incipient process of nominal convergence with neighboring economies, laid the foundations for financial decisions by economic agents that would foster development of the financial system.

The steps made toward controlling price rises allowed inflation expectations to be moderated and interest rates brought down, thus establishing the conditions that enabled more sophisticated financial investments. This expanded the possibilities for disintermediation such that the share of cash and deposits in agents' portfolios shrank while other financial instruments with higher expected returns and higher risk gained in

CHART 3   FINANCIAL ASSETS AND LIABILITIES (a)

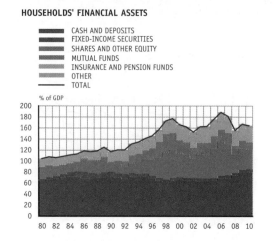

HOUSEHOLDS' FINANCIAL ASSETS

- CASH AND DEPOSITS
- FIXED-INCOME SECURITIES
- SHARES AND OTHER EQUITY
- MUTUAL FUNDS
- INSURANCE AND PENSION FUNDS
- OTHER
- TOTAL

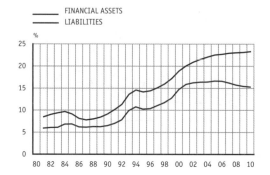

FINANCIAL ASSETS AND LIABILITIES VIS-À-VIS THE REST OF THE WORLD (b)

- FINANCIAL ASSETS
- LIABILITIES

SOURCES: Instituto Nacional de Estadística and Banco de España.

a. 2010 data are for the third quarter.
b. Assets as percentage of total assets. Liabilities as percentage of total liabilities.

significance, facilitating the expansion of corporate bond markets and the development of institutional investors (Chart 3, left panel).[2]

Improved macroeconomic stability also created favorable conditions for the legislative reforms introduced and technological developments to lead to growing internationalization of financial flows and domestic economic agents' portfolios. This manifested itself in significant growth in the share of foreign assets in Spanish economic agents' portfolios and the volume of Spanish financial assets held by non-residents (Chart 3, right panel). Similarly, this progress created incentives for longer-term decision-making, as the narrower fluctuation of interest rates and financing terms reduced the need for frequent review of investment and financing strategies. In this vein, the strong increase in the average maturity of public debt in circulation since the early 1990s stands out.

However, the process of moderating the serious imbalances which marked the start of the democratic period – the most serious manifestation of which being inflation – was neither linear nor free from its vicissitudes. As will be made clear over the course of this chapter, the period included a number of episodes of macroeconomic and financial instability, which had a powerful impact on the development of the financial system. The clearest example was the crisis of the early 1990s, when the application of an imbalanced combination of policies to tackle an overheating economy caused efforts at nominal convergence with the more stable countries of the European Union (EU) to come off the rails. This led to a resurgence of the government deficit and inflation, with the consequent increase in interest and exchange rate volatility. The exchange rate stability gains that had

---

[2]   For more details about these markets and intermediaries, see Chapter 8 of this book.

been achieved through progress towards macroeconomic stability – and the credibility they brought – were not utilized to strengthen internal economic discipline, but to alleviate demand for increased social spending that had emerged as the economy modernized and expectations were raised of greater distribution of the prosperity gains achieved. The result was a severe bout of instability, which led to a serious currency crisis, in which the peseta was devalued five times, accompanied by a rapid rise in unemployment that in turn led to financial strains resurfacing and a partial reversal of the progress made.

This cycle was also reflected in the stability of the financial system. The severe macroeconomic tensions that accompanied the economy in the early days of the democracy had led to one of the most serious banking crises in the developed world since the Second World War and required a group of institutions accounting for almost 50% of the liabilities in the credit system to be rescued at various times.[3] Macroeconomic progress and strengthening of the macroprudential system had managed to reinforce and stabilize the system. Nevertheless, the crisis in the early 1990s increased the risks in broad segments of the system and episodes of banking crisis reappeared, requiring one of the big Spanish banks to be taken under the control of the authorities and bailed out, which again highlighted the close links between macroeconomic stability and financial stability.

It was not until Spain's membership of EMU in 1999 – after meeting the convergence objectives in 1997 – that it was possible to consolidate the often frustrated desire to achieve sufficiently entrenched macroeconomic stability, under common rules of fiscal discipline, and sharing monetary policy with other EMU member countries. It was under these conditions, which also made possible the longest expansionary cycle in Spain's recent economic history, that the Spanish financial system can be considered to have finally reached maturity and fully assimilated the standards prevailing in comparable developed countries. This was true to such an extent that for the first time the Spanish financial system found itself on a par with those of the most solid and developed countries, even beyond the country's position in terms of economic size, with some Spanish institutions ranking among the leaders in the European banking system. This strong progress was made possible by the fortuitous combination of internal consolidation of systemic stability, external conditions that were unusually favorable to financial expansion – conditions that would subsequently reveal themselves to be unsustainable, with dramatic consequences – and a regulatory and prudential framework which combined a large dose of liberalization with enhanced safety mechanisms drawing on lessons learned from previous episodes of macroeconomic and financial instability, whose high costs were still fresh in the memory of economic agents and policymakers.

The reduction in inflation and financial costs that came with the implementation of the single monetary policy represented a powerful expansionary stimulus for the economy and the financial system. This was supported by a context of sustainable low interest rates and increased confidence in future income generation, which drove significant changes in

---

[3] This and other banking crises are covered in more detail in Chapters 7 and 9 of this book.

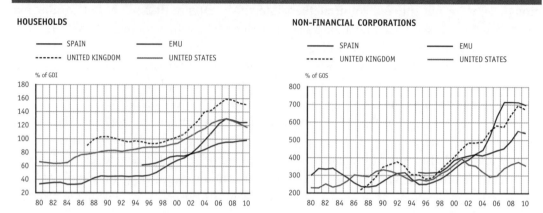

CHART 4   COMPARISON OF HOUSEHOLD AND CORPORATE DEBT RATIOS (a)

SOURCES: Instituto Nacional de Estadística, Banco de España, Federal Reserve, European Central Bank and UK National Statistics.

a. 2010 data are for the third quarter.

agents' asset positions and financial institutions' balance sheets. Households and businesses rapidly increased their debt such that the relevant ratios, which started out very low as a result of the country's tradition of instability and high financial costs, rose rapidly to reach – and surpass – those in other developed economies in just a few years (Chart 4). In turn, the significant fiscal consolidation that took place as part of the process of nominal convergence and membership of EMU caused a significant drop in public debt as a share of overall lending to non-financial sectors, and a change in the trend in the balance of public debt, with its being lower than that in other developed economies (Chart 5). These forces laid the foundations for rapid expansion by financial intermediaries and a significant transformation in the composition of their balance sheets. Private-sector agents' increased borrowing requirements also represented a strong stimulus to corporate bonds, encouraged by reduced competition from public debt, privatizations and the fact that they were accepted as collateral for monetary policy operations. Under these conditions, as happened in other developed economies, the Spanish securitization market also boomed.

Membership of a stable system such as monetary union does not, of itself, eliminate the risk of imbalances building up. It simply means a change in the nature of the risks and the way in which they manifest themselves. If the economic policy instruments that remain under national sovereignty are not managed in a way that sufficiently matches the need to control domestic demand in order to keep costs and price formation in line with the standards of the area, even if there are no marked divergences in inflation rates and it is not possible to suffer a currency crisis, latent competitiveness losses and unsustainable debt excesses may build up. If this happens, the accumulated imbalances will end up triggering an adjustment through various mechanisms tending to re-establish a favorable cost relationship and reduction in debt levels.

The conditions which would have allowed the demand pressures produced by reduced financial costs and improved expectations induced by monetary integration to be mitigated

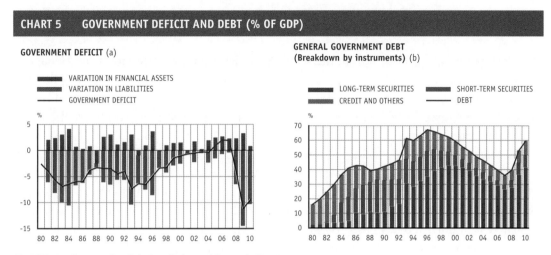

CHART 5   GOVERNMENT DEFICIT AND DEBT (% OF GDP)

GOVERNMENT DEFICIT (a)

- VARIATION IN FINANCIAL ASSETS
- VARIATION IN LIABILITIES
- GOVERNMENT DEFICIT

GENERAL GOVERNMENT DEBT
(Breakdown by instruments) (b)

- LONG-TERM SECURITIES
- SHORT-TERM SECURITIES
- CREDIT AND OTHERS
- DEBT

SOURCES: Instituto Nacional de Estadistica and Banco de España.

a. 2010 figures accumulated over four quarters up to third quarter
b. 2010 figures are for November.

did not entirely arise in Spain, with the result that imbalances built up in the form of cost and price differentials, excess investment in the property sector, and household and corporate debt. The adjustment of these imbalances began gradually in late 2006, even before the onset of the worst international financial crisis since World War II. However, the intensity and scope of the crisis had a particularly powerful impact on the Spanish economy, with the result that, ultimately, the necessary readjustment had to take place under extraordinarily adverse circumstances. This proved to be a dramatic test of the solidity of the progress made by the Spanish financial system, setting in motion a process of profound restructuring, the final scope of which will still take some time to be known.

The following sections discuss in more detail how macroeconomic developments over this period have shaped the progress of the financial system, with a view to establishing a reference framework for the more specialist topics covered in later chapters. Particular attention will be paid to the contribution of monetary and fiscal policies, while distinguishing between the period in which Spain maintained monetary sovereignty, its membership of EMU, and the international financial crisis.

4   The period of convergence in the context of full monetary sovereignty

When discussing the period of convergence, during which economic policy still had full use of monetary sovereignty, it is worth covering the role played by monetary and fiscal policy separately, despite the multiple interconnections and interfaces between them, in order to take a closer look at the specific implications of each of these factors for developments in the financial system.

4.1   The role of Spanish monetary policy in the development of the financial system

Monetary policy is a central link in the relationship between macroeconomic and financial development, as it has a direct impact on the behavior of financial markets both through the instruments chosen and itheir influence on the main macroeconomic variables, in particular, the aggregate behavior of prices and inflation expectations, which are monetary policy's principal targets.

The selection and design of the instruments used, and in general the operational framework of monetary policy, has a strong impact on price fluctuations in the various financial products and how they develop. Thus, for example, a monetary-policy instrumentation based on a strict control of the monetary base or reserves may lead to highly volatile short-term interest rates compared with other models based on managing central-bank intervention rates. In turn, the activity of certain markets, such as inter-bank or public-debt markets, is highly dependent on how monetary policy is implemented. Operations to inject or drain liquidity in order to control bank reserves or influence interest rate formation are crucial to the functioning of these markets, while they also play a fundamental role in transmitting monetary policy decisions. Moreover, the definition of the list of assets acceptable as collateral for monetary policy operations can influence the development of certain instruments and markets by influencing their liquidity and relative attractiveness for banks.

However, ultimately, the extent to which monetary policy is successful at achieving its overall stability goals is the crucial determinant of how the financial system develops. Financial activity will obviously benefit greatly from a regime of low and stable inflation which allows interest rates to be kept at levels that reduce uncertainty, encourages the expansion of credit and the development of longer-term instruments.

As Spanish monetary policy has undergone substantial changes during the country's recent economic history, both in terms of its strategic design and operational model, and in the extent to which it has achieved its price stability objectives, it is useful to differentiate the most significant stages, in this period. These may be identified as: (1) establishing an active monetary policy; (2) membership of the European monetary system; and, (3) renewal after the 1993 recession, culminating in membership of EMU [Rojo (2001) and Ayuso and Escrivá (1997)].

4.1.1   From the construction of an active monetary policy to integration in the European Monetary System (1973-1989).

At the start of the democratic period efforts to implement an active monetary policy able to exercise independent influence over the monetary determinants of price formation had still not reached fruition in Spain. These efforts had been based on the establishment of a two-level target system, in which the aim of achieving the final objectives of inflation control and economic growth were pursued by setting intermediate quantitative targets for a broad monetary aggregate, which was initially M3. To achieve these objectives, in line with the quantitative model used by most central banks at the time, strict control of bank reserves, was applied. This control was only possible if significant fluctuations in interest rates were allowed. The resulting high volatility, in a context in which interest rate risk hedging instruments did not exist, hindered the development of financial markets. The protection against potential exchange-rate volatility promoted by the scheme was based on by controls on capital movements, which also acted as a limitation on financial development. However, these first steps established the basis for a monetary policy that enhanced stability, and the development of inter-bank and debt markets, on which transformation of the financial system would depend.

This model had to face the difficult challenge of combating the extreme inflationary pressures unleashed in the late 1970s and early 1980s when rising oil prices were combined with upward pressures from wages, lack of budgetary control and the political instability of the transition to democracy. Learning monetary policy under such testing conditions led to efforts at adaptation, leading to the use of a broader concept of liquidity (liquid assets held by the public or ALP) as an intermediate target and greater flexibility in implementation, which came to rest on intervention rates, thus enabling greater stability to be achieved in interest rates and monetary markets. This would yield better conditions for financial intermediaries to operate and provide a stronger stimulus for the introduction of innovations. The increased emphasis on controlling short-term interest rates gave a more central role to liquidity control by means of open-market operations. The creation of a Government Debt Book-Entry System at the Banco de España in 1987, which improved the efficiency of clearing and settlement for public debt securities, was an additional stimulus for the use of this type of operations using government debt and conducted with a group of specialist entities that played the role of market-makers.

The boost given to Spain's economic and financial integration by its joining the then European Community in 1986 made controlling exchange-rate fluctuations more important, thus relegating the monitoring of ALP to a secondary role. The setting of implicit exchange-rate targets limited the leeway for monetary policy to act as a stabilizer, given that it also had to address the complications originating from the predominantly expansionary stance of fiscal policy. The effort to control inflation made it necessary to keep interest rates relatively high, which created upward pressure on the value of the peseta. Financial development was encouraged by increasing integration and the entry of foreign banks, which brought innovations in terms of products and distribution channels, for both assets and liabilities, but faced obstacles resulting from a combination of imbalanced policies. To curb the upward pressures on the peseta that these produced, exchange-rate controls were put in place, which together with the increased volatility of interest rates, put a drag on financial development. However, during this period inflation followed a downward trend, approaching the average levels in countries characterized by greater price stability (Chart 1) and laying the groundwork for more solid progress towards financial modernization. Nevertheless, in the final years of the period, in the context of a vibrant economy, the inflation rate again rose.

4.1.2   From membership of the European Monetary System to the 1993 recession (1989-1993).

In order to tackle the tensions produced by the stabilization efforts to mitigate the procyclical nature of budgetary policy and the upward wage pressures emanating from labor-market rigidity more decisively, the decision was ultimately taken to incorporate the peseta in the EMS exchange-rate mechanism. It was hoped that the adoption of a limited band of exchange-rate fluctuations would provide a stabilizing effect thanks to the enhanced credibility and discipline the system provided, in a context in which financial innovation and the free movement of capital limited the effectiveness of monetary policy and inflation was tending to rise [Malo de Molina and Pérez (1990), and Pérez Jurado (1997)].

However, life in the EMS was not easy or free of obstacles to the development of the financial system. Exchange-rate stability promoted international financial integration and innovation in domestic markets and among resident institutions, but the sustained inflows of capital, often of a speculative nature, constrained monetary policy's room for maneuver. In a step which represented a reversal of the process of liberalization and opening up to the outside world, capital controls were resorted to in order to alleviate these pressures, but their effectiveness was limited and transitory. Efforts were also made to reconcile price and cost-control measures with maintaining exchange-rate discipline by imposing administrative controls on credit growth. This was another backward step in the articulation of monetary policy based on market mechanisms. This slowed the expansion of bank balance sheets, but encouraged the commercial paper market, which represented an innovation with a somewhat spurious component. The difficulties faced in articulating a policy of stability in this period led to considerable tensions in the development of the financial system. However, nothing prevented the high interest rates applied to curb inflationary pressures and offset the influence of budgetary imbalances from driving the peseta up to the highest value allowed within its range of fluctuation, exacerbating the loss of competitiveness and widening the trade gap. When the exchange-rate turbulence spread through the EMS in late 1992 the financial markets realized that Spain's situation was inherently unsustainable and the direction of capital flows reversed. This ended up dragging the peseta through a series of successive devaluations that led to a period of harsh adjustment and recession, together with a crisis in the macroeconomic policy framework that had previously been in force (Chart 1).

From the point of view of macroeconomic stability, membership of the EMS failed to meet the expectations raised, arguably because rather than taking advantage of its benefits in terms of reputational gains to make the necessary changes to adapt to the new system, these reforms were postponed or even abandoned. Macroeconomic policy failed to prevent overheating of the economy, which was being driven by excessive credit growth, and made it inevitable that the adjustment would take place through a recession that was particularly costly in terms of unemployment. The credibility gained was squandered, and the devaluation of the peseta was the penalty the markets imposed for having followed policies that diverged from stability objectives.

From the point of view of its influence on the financial system, the inability to articulate a sufficiently stabilizing policy resulted in numerous tensions that at times distorted the functioning of the markets. In particular, excessive credit expansion represented a high risk that necessarily materialized when the economy went into recession, with the reappearance of episodes of crisis among financial institutions, to the point that one of the major banks would require intervention by the authorities for the first time. The prudential and supervisory mechanisms that had been established in response to the banking crisis of the previous decade worked effectively to contain the spread of systemic risk and prevent the way the financial system worked itself becoming a factor in worsening the recession. However, events have made the importance of macroeconomic stability for financial stability patently obvious, and revealed that when imbalances accumulate, in the long run they pose a risk to the financial system itself.

4.1.3   From the 1993 recession to euro entry (1994-1998).

The severity of the recession and, above all, the derailment of the process of convergence towards patterns of stability, forced a thorough rethink of the orientation and implementation of economic policy. In general, this meant a better definition of the ultimate goals, within the timetables and criteria established as a condition for access to monetary integration, and a more harmonious and balanced conception of the contributions of monetary and budgetary policy, respectively.

The contribution of monetary policy to restoring stability – once the adjustments induced by the recession and the sharp realignment of the exchange-rate had enabled competitiveness to be restored and the financial position of businesses and households to be stabilized – rested on an in-depth review of the whole institutional and strategic framework of monetary policy, which would have far reaching implications in the macroeconomic and financial spheres [Gutiérrez (1997)]. On the institutional level, the cornerstone of the new approach was the Law of the Autonomy of the Banco de España in 1994, which formally granted the Banco de España independence to define how it implemented monetary policy, although subject to, and conditional upon, a specific mandate to pursue price stability and with an obligation to comply with explicit transparency commitments. The new framework freed the bank from the interference that might arise from its subordination to goals incompatible with price stability, meeting the public sector's funding needs, or being influenced by electoral cycles. It was a framework that enhanced the potential effectiveness of monetary policy and equipped it with the instruments necessary to bolster its credibility. Enshrining a prohibition on all monetary financing formulas for the public sector in the Bank's statutes was a key development as it meant removing what had traditionally been the main obstacle limiting the capacity to exercise effective monetary control and efficiently channel the economy's financial flows. However, the issuing bank's independence was not a panacea and would not be sufficient on its own to solve all the tendencies towards imbalance rooted in the habits of the economy's agents and the inherited structural weaknesses.

On the strategic level a new monetary policy framework was adopted based on the direct pursuit of inflation targets, relegating monetary aggregates to the role of complementary indicators and maintaining wide bands of fluctuation for the exchange-rate that avoided the emergence of dilemmas such as those encountered during the previous period. Meeting direct inflation targets was facilitated by the credibility that the overall orientation of economic policy was gaining and by the change in expectations that came with the prospect of EMU membership. During this period substantial progress was made towards achieving price stability, laying the groundwork for greater financial development. Thus, the inflation rate went from just over 4% at the start of the period to below 2% after 1997, comfortably complying with the Maastricht convergence criteria (Chart 1). This decisive progress towards convergence made it possible to articulate a gradual process of intervention rate reduction, until full alignment was achieved with the central banks that would form the initial core of monetary union. These reductions were passed on through the monetary markets to the final rates paid by borrowers, who benefited from a significant reduction in the cost of the available financial resources. A period of strong financial expansion therefore began, based on the initial stabilization of business and household balance sheets, which started out from relatively low levels of debt. This was encouraged by the dual prospect of maintaining financial costs at moderate levels – well below those that had been common in the past – and the improved expectations of future income, resulting from the anticipated benefits of EMU membership.

4.2 The contribution of the behavior of the public finances to the development of the financial system

In the early 1980s, Spanish fiscal policy faced a series of serious challenges resulting from the public spending pressures created by the economic crisis and the powerful social demands spurred by the advent of democracy. Fiscal reform in 1979, with the consequent increase in tax collection, was insufficient to offset these pressures, such that growing public deficits emerged (Chart 5). Government borrowing requirements rose sharply, and the State, in view of the underdevelopment of Spain's financial markets and the absence of an orthodox deficit financing tradition, sought to bring down the high financial cost of its borrowing by resorting to loans from the Banco de España, thereby hindering the active control of monetary policy. The only instrument that was available to prevent this monetary financing of budget deficits from feeding through into excessive money supply growth was the use of successive increases in reserve requirements. In this way, credit institutions were forced to hold resources paying returns below market interest rates, thus paying an implicit tax that increased seigniorage revenues and intermediation costs. In 1984, a mandatory investment coefficient, for investments in *pagarés del Tesoro* (short-term government bonds) was introduced. Initially this was potentially profitable for the banks, although it became less so after the passing of Law 14/1985 on the tax treatment of financial assets and the subsequent reduction in the interest paid on these assets, due to the tax premium associated with their opacity.

From the mid-1980s, it became increasingly clear that there was a need to moderate the excessive growth of the public deficit – and consequently spending – and to assume the financial cost of the deficit under market conditions. This was necessary to avoid the multiple inefficiencies and distortions that the previous pattern had been causing in the activity of financial intermediaries and the Banco de España. Budgetary restraint was facilitated at this time by the economic recovery. The government deficit therefore fell in percentage terms of GDP from 6% in 1985 to around 3% in 1988, although subsequently there was a fresh reversal. In parallel, a series of measures were introduced that were oriented towards orthodox deficit funding, beginning in 1987 with the creation of the Banco de España's book-entry system and the first *letra del Tesoro* (Treasury bill) issues.

In 1989 the gradual elimination of the mandatory public-debt investment coefficient began, ending with its complete abolition in 1992. In 1990 reserve ratios were reformed bringing them down from 17% to 5%, although the resources freed up by this reform would temporarily be immobilized in a mandatory investment in Banco de España certificates, which had a progressive repayment schedule ending in 2000. That same year, the General Budget Law prohibited the State from increasing the balance of the Treasury's borrowing from the Central Bank and the Law of the Autonomy of the Banco de España in 1994 consolidated this prohibition, making it apply throughout the year and covering both credit facilities and public-debt purchases. Thus, the State's borrowing needs had to be met primarily through issues of tradable securities under market conditions. This put an end to one of the main obstacles holding back the development of the financial system.

These changes had to be supported by the establishment of a number of mechanisms to make the purchase of these securities attractive to investors, and these mechanisms would ultimately be crucial to the modernization of the financial system. The creation of the Banco de España book-entry system in 1987 was the first decisive step. The elimination of physical securities and their replacement by mere book entries, together with the new market's institutional framework, brought about a considerable improvement in the efficiency, rapidity and simplicity with which securities issued by the State could be traded. Also important was the establishment of so-called "market-makers", the definitive standardization of issue instruments (bills, bonds) and the establishment of regular schedules of auctions for debt issues.

Nevertheless, high official interest rates in the late 1980s and early 1990s, together with considerable uncertainty about their future direction, led to an excessive concentration of issues in the short-term (Chart 5). In fact, even bond issues ended up being bought by the public only as short-term investments, through temporary transfer arrangements with the banks (repos). The creation of direct accounts at the Banco de España (1990) and the promotion of *Fondtesoros* (mutual funds with a portfolio comprising solely public debt) were not sufficient to avoid repos being the common route by which public debt was marketed to the public during this period.

A major milestone on this path was the tax exemption in 1991 on public debt yields for non-residents. This measure, together with the prospect of gains associated with the expected drop in interest rates, led to a sharp increase in demand for bonds by the foreign sector. The entry of these foreign investors spurred further improvements and greater sophistication of the trading and clearing mechanisms. A more efficient and liquid market for public debt assets thus began to develop, which would become a fundamental part of the national financial system. This market offered an attractive investment alternative for savers, provided reference prices for the valuation of other assets, was a means of implementing a non-distorting monetary policy, and represented a source of discipline in the public sector.

However, as of 1988 fiscal policy took an expansionary turn which, in the first instance, halted the process of deficit correction and, subsequently, with the onset of the crisis in the early 1990s, again gave rise to strong public borrowing requirements. Against this backdrop, despite the orthodox financing of the public sector, there was little space for the development of alternative private-sector financing markets, with the bulk of issues and trading being in public-debt securities.

When the process of fiscal consolidation was resumed in the mid-1990s with the goal of meeting the requirements of EMU membership, the reduced absorption of resources by government allowed domestic investors to diversify their portfolios with a greater share going to private fixed-income instruments and equities (Chart 3). Thus, convergence towards fiscal stability was combined with stimulation of credit and the internationalization of financial flows, both encouraged by increasing macroeconomic stability, and propitious conditions were created for what would become the financial system's phase of most significant advances. With membership of EMU, the budgetary stability and economic growth binomial would provide a solid foundation for the most significant period of development of the Spanish financial system, such that it could reach levels of efficiency, profitability and creditworthiness comparable to those of the soundest in the developed world.

5 Monetary integration within the EMU

Spain's participation in EMU from its inception represented the culmination of its entry into the EU's structures and its definitive incorporation in the growing process of global economic integration. From the macroeconomic and financial viewpoint, this important milestone represented the country's renunciation of its having a currency and economic policy of its own, in favor of participation in the common currency and monetary policy of an area with an established tradition of macroeconomic stability. All the previous attempts to bind the Spanish economy to areas of monetary stability, whether loosely or tightly structured, had been unsuccessful. This historic achievement was the result of the macroeconomic and financial policy efforts described in the preceding sections and led to a radical transformation in the financial factors shaping the Spanish economy. The implications would necessarily be far-reaching [Peñalosa and Restoy (2005), Malo de Molina (2007) and Estrada et al. (2009)].

From an operational standpoint, the implementation of common monetary policy brought significant changes. These manifested themselves in reduced market intervention compared with the preceding framework (weekly auctions of liquidity, but not daily open market operations) and contributed significantly to the modernization and improved efficiency of the markets underpinning the financial system's activity. These topics are covered in Chapter 8 of this book, so it is sufficient here to note the importance of the implementation of TARGET for the integration of inter-bank markets (which became a single market free of national barriers) and the acceptance of private securities as collateral for Central Bank loans, which stimulated the development of markets such as the securitization and covered bond markets.

However, the fundamental root of the major transformation undergone as a result of monetary integration lay in the setting of interest rates according to the price-stability needs of the area as a whole and depending on the objectives and strategy of the single monetary policy, and not the specific requirements of the Spanish economy. This change not only affected the interest rates set by monetary policy, but also longer-term rates, given that membership of a system of macroeconomic stability was perceived as overcoming many of the sources of disruption and uncertainties that had traditionally given rise to significant risk premiums. There was, therefore, a substantial reduction in the cost of financing the economy, which was perceived, moreover, as being largely permanent, despite being influenced by conditions of weak growth in Central Europe, which led to abnormally low interest rates, and global financial expansion encouraged by a tendency to underestimate risks.

The expansionary stimulus that slack financial conditions would entail was reinforced by the boosted income expectations deriving from the new macroeconomic regime, which ensured patterns of stability and eliminated the obstacles that had traditionally stifled opportunities for growth and eroded the economy's profitability. The result was a strong upsurge in demand which – in conjunction with other concurrent supply-side factors – translated into a period of unprecedented economic expansion fuelled by unusually favorable financial conditions. However, although this was a response to the improvement in macroeconomic fundamentals, it also contained the seeds of potential imbalances. The possibility of cyclical excesses cannot be ruled out even in solidly grounded stability regimes, leading to adjustments that may at times be abrupt. Both factors, namely rapid expansion and the gradual build-up of imbalances, would shape the transformation of agents' decision-making and drive the notable acceleration of financial development witnessed during the first ten years of EMU membership.

The opportunities for stable growth, and the stimulus to the financial system which came with monetary integration, were threatened by the possibilities that an excessive expansion of credit would led to painful adjustments under the strict conditions of monetary union. To avoid these risks, economic policy was obliged to act on two fronts: budgetary consolidation, with the use of the budget as a stabilizer to compensate for excessively slack monetary policy on the one hand; and structural reforms to give the economy sufficient flexibility to adapt, without inflation and without devaluations, to the demands of competitiveness, on the other. Spanish fiscal policy after the start of EMU maintained the approach taken during convergence and allowed further progress to be made towards fiscal consolidation. This enabled moderate budget surpluses to be achieved and the public debt, which had reached almost 70% of GDP in 1996, to be brought to below 40% in 2007 (Chart 5). Increased public saving, however, was not sufficient to counteract the sharp increase in borrowing by domestic private-sector agents, making the stabilizing effect of fiscal policy insufficient. Meanwhile, although liberalization measures were introduced in various sectors of the economy, the progress of structural reforms was limited and half-hearted, possibly because the climate of rapidly growing prosperity created the illusion that it was less important for the economy to persevere along the path towards stability. In any event, some of the distortions that had plagued the functioning of markets for factors of production and goods and services remained unresolved, limiting the capacity for a flexible response on the supply side to strong pull from demand.

The renunciation of monetary sovereignty meant not only the loss of interest rates and exchange rates as instruments of stabilization and adjustment, but also having to accept the inability to control the development of domestic liquidity and credit. This meant that the Banco de España ceased to have effective leeway to contain or modulate the growth of lending in the economy and to address possible excesses that might arise under the excessively slack conditions that were to prevail. However, as both banking regulator and supervisor, the Banco de España could take prudential measures to contain and, where possible, prevent the effects of excessive credit expansion on the stability of the financial system. This was the concern that prompted the regulatory innovation of establishing a system of countercyclical or dynamic provisions which obliged credit institutions to make provisions in good times to increase their resilience during periods of adjustment, based on the philosophy that risks must be faced when they are taken rather than wait until they materialize. This regulatory innovation, which is explained in Chapter 7 of this book, was not of itself able to curb credit excesses, but did at least enable the resistance of the financial system to perturbations or reversals of the cycle to be enhanced, as would become apparent in the subsequent crisis. This experience is of considerable interest not only because of the influence it subsequently had on the debate about financial regulation, but because it shows how the analysis of macroeconomic and financial stability conditions can have significant implications in the macroprudential field. What happened at that time shows that it is possible to diagnose in advance the emergence of dangerous imbalances for stability and growth and that this diagnosis can be translated into operationally effective regulatory formulas. It could also be argued that it is easier to draw macroprudential inferences from the analysis of macrofinancial equilibriums when the financial supervision architecture ensures the greatest possible proximity between the authorities responsible for monetary and financial stability, on the one hand, and banking regulation and supervision, on the other. It is hard to imagine that Spain would have innovated with the creation of dynamic provisioning if the Banco de España had not also been the banking regulator and supervisory authority. Over the years subsequent to the crisis the Spanish model would earn much praise from around the world, not only for the results achieved in protecting the financial system, but for being practically the sole innovation in the conventional framework of policies that ventured into the use of instruments of financial regulation as a policy tool for macrofinancial stabilization, in line with what would be the generally accepted new orientation that emerged as one of the key lessons of the crisis (Blanchard et al. [2010]).

In any event, the consolidation of a new stability scenario brought by EMU membership, which was perceived as irreversible, contributed, as noted, to a profound transformation in financial decision-making among agents and a notable expansion of the financial system. In particular, the new conditions contributed to a substantial increase in the optimal level of business and household debt [Malo de Molina and Restoy (2004)]. As the starting point was a situation in which the debt ratios in both sectors, but particularly households, were low – as a logical consequence of the financial tensions that had accompanied the redressing of financial instability – the cut in the cost of borrowing, curbing of its volatility and development of financial innovations, all added significant dynamism to credit demand (Chart 6). This led to credit growth that was much faster than in comparable countries. The new instruments

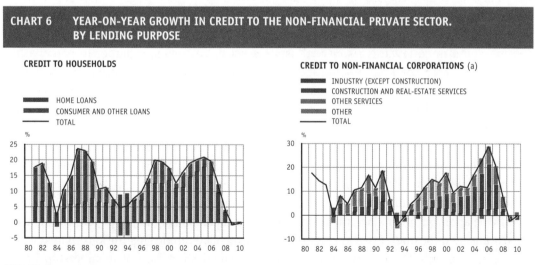

CHART 6   YEAR-ON-YEAR GROWTH IN CREDIT TO THE NON-FINANCIAL PRIVATE SECTOR.
           BY LENDING PURPOSE

CREDIT TO HOUSEHOLDS

- HOME LOANS
- CONSUMER AND OTHER LOANS
- TOTAL

CREDIT TO NON-FINANCIAL CORPORATIONS (a)

- INDUSTRY (EXCEPT CONSTRUCTION)
- CONSTRUCTION AND REAL-ESTATE SERVICES
- OTHER SERVICES
- OTHER
- TOTAL

SOURCES: Banco de España.

a. 2010 data are for the third quarter.

included, in particular, variable interest loans facilitating credit for home purchases. These spread rapidly, coming to account for more than 95% of home loans.

This started a long and powerful cycle of credit expansion which encouraged spending and financed growth, but systematically outpaced income growth by a wide margin. Although it was logical that credit should grow faster than output, the fact that its rate doubled or tripled that of output over an extended period was an unquestionable sign that unsustainable trends were being incubated. The household debt ratio, which had already been on an upward trend during the convergence phase, doubled over the course of the first decade of monetary union, rising from a level below the EMU average to one that comfortably exceeded it (Chart 4). In the case corporate debt, although the process was initially less intense, it accelerated rapidly after 2005, also greatly surpassing the euro-area average. The ratio of private-sector debt to income (gross operating surplus) came to reach levels similar to those in other countries with high debt levels, such as the United Kingdom.

Credit expansion was particularly intense in the real-estate sector, being a business that is highly sensitive to financing conditions. This sector received a strong stimulus from the transition to a context of low interest rates and the innovations that facilitated their being passed on rapidly to the financial charges effectively borne by households. These purely financial factors, which fuelled a property boom of unprecedented proportions, were reinforced by other changes in fundamentals that stimulated demand for homes, including, in particular, high immigration flows, an increased rate of household formation, and the favorable performance of household incomes as a result of the rapid pace of job creation. Demand for housing by non-residents, whether for vacation use or for retirement, was further stimulated by the fact that adoption of the euro had eliminated the risk of a loss of value being caused by a depreciation of the exchange rate. The conjunction of these real and financial factors resulted in unprecedented vibrancy in the mortgage market and in the market for loans to property developers and construction companies (Chart 6). The presence of these fundamental factors, which could explain high long-term demand for housing and a trend towards rising real-estate asset prices, made it harder to perceive the excesses that were potentially being incurred in terms of prices and investment (Chart 7) as well as debt, and sharpened the natural tendency for real-estate business to overreact, deriving from the length of the process of urban growth and the lack of transparency in the various markets involved.

At the same time, the new framework established with membership of monetary union helped to create the right conditions for the development of the financial system in a way that would meet these high borrowing requirements from the rest of the economy. Financial institutions adopted new strategies, developed innovative products and promoted specific market segments to meet the strong expansion in demand for credit from households and businesses. This demand far exceeded credit institutions' capacity to finance it from traditional deposit-taking mechanisms (Chart 8), but membership of the euro area increasingly allowed them to draw on funds from abroad relatively cheaply, as foreign investors no longer demanded an exchange rate risk premium [Fuentes (2008)].

CHART 7 REAL-ESTATE MARKET

RESIDENTIAL INVESTMENT AS A SHARE OF GDP (a)

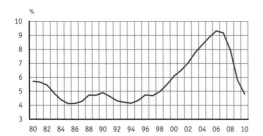

HOUSE PRICES (YEAR-ON-YEAR GROWTH RATE) (b)

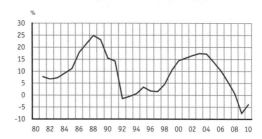

SOURCES: Instituto Nacional de Estadística, Ministerio de la vivienda and Banco de España.

a. 2010 data are accumulated over four quarters, up to the third quarter.
b. Average annual growth. 2001-base series until December 2004, and 2005-base series thereafter.

CHART 8 CREDIT-DEPOSIT GAP AND NET BORROWING (a)

CREDIT - DEPOSIT GAP (b)

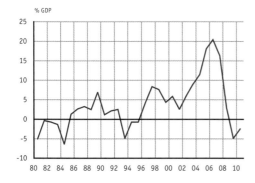

SPAIN'S NET BORROWING VIS-À-VIS THE REST OF THE WORLD

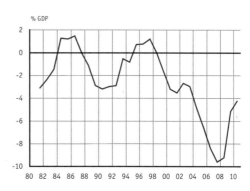

SOURCES: Instituto Nacional de Estadística and Banco de España.

a. 2010 data are accumulated flows over four quarters, up to the third quarter.
b. Difference between annual credit flow and annual deposit flow.

This new opportunity for Spanish banks was encouraged in particular by the abundance of liquidity that then existed in international markets and the widespread search for yield that led to minimal discrimination between the risks different demanders of funds represented.

The banks took advantage of this opportunity to bridge the gap between credit and deposits by issuing tradable securities, including securitizations and covered bonds in particular, which investors worldwide embraced with open arms. Thus, between December 2000 and June 2007, 77% of fixed-income securities issued by Spanish financial intermediaries were purchased by non-residents – mainly financial institutions. It is important to note, however, that unlike securitizations in other countries, which mainly sought to transfer risks institutions had incurred, in the Spanish case the use of these instruments was aimed at raising funds with which to expand credit, with the originator retaining the management and much of the underlying risk associated with the asset [Fuentes (2007)].

From a broader perspective, this behavior was a reflection of the fact that the introduction of the euro, by eliminating exchange-rate risk and currency conversion costs on financial transactions between countries in the euro area, led to an acceleration in the internationalization of financial flows and the portfolios of domestic economic agents, a process which had begun to manifest itself in the early 1990s [Blanco and García-Vaquero (2005)]. Thus, the degree of openness of the financial system – measured as the sum of assets and liabilities vis-à-vis the rest of the world as a share of total financial assets and liabilities— increased from 15.1% in 1998 to 19.5% in 2008. This process took place on both the asset and liability sides (Chart 3), although its intensity differed from one agent to another. On the asset side, the sector in which the process of geographical diversification was most intense was that of institutional investors, whereas on the liability side, as noted, it was monetary financial institutions which substantially increased their demand for foreign funding, although general government also did so, in relative terms if not in absolute ones. Thus although the amount of debt relative to GDP fell, the share of that balance in the hands of non-residents doubled to reach levels of around 45%.

In this context, the Spanish banks stepped up their process of internationalization considerably.[4] Back in the 1980s and the first half of the 1990s Spanish banks had made some isolated acquisitions of Latin American and European institutions. It was, however, in the last five years of the century that this phenomenon began to take off on a large scale, driven by the narrowing margins and increasing competition in the domestic market and the opportunities created by deregulation and privatization programs in certain countries. Spanish credit institutions, especially the two largest, bought banks in Europe, the United States and, especially in Latin America, exploiting their comparative advantages in terms of technology platforms, management capability and business models. In general, their international expansion was aimed at diversifying risk and, in some cases, at exploiting the growth potential in economies with relatively low levels of bank penetration. As a result of this process, the two largest Spanish banks have become major multinational groups.

A key feature of the increasing openness and integration of the Spanish financial system under membership of EMU was the development of new markets and instruments enabling them to attract foreign resources and promote their expansion, expanding the range of financing sources available and enabling risk diversification for investors and the deepening of market liquidity. This resulted in a better allocation of resources and reduction in the cost of capital in the Spanish economy, although it also increased sensitivity to developments in international financial markets.

---

[4]   For more details of this process, see Chapter 10 of this book.

The transformations in the financial system during the period played a significant role in sustaining the long phase of expansion and job creation enjoyed by the Spanish economy starting at the time of joining the euro and lasting up until 2007. Financial institutions were able to mobilize the resources the Spanish economy needed by raising them abroad so that households and businesses could maintain high levels of spending – well above their levels of income generation – by taking on more debt, thanks to easy access to credit at interest rates below those matching conditions of demand in Spain. The strong stimulus to demand that the ready channeling of external resources allowed was not sufficiently tempered by the stabilizing efforts of budgetary policy, which, as noted, were insufficient. Nor was the supply-side stimulus that came with population growth or the timid structural reforms, which fell short of meeting the challenges the economy faced, capable of curbing the widening gap that was opening up between domestic spending and output. This led to an excessive build-up of private-sector debt alongside a growing trade deficit. The Spanish economy, which at the inception of EMU did not require external financing (the net balance of financial transactions with the rest of the world was zero at the end of 1998), had a net borrowing that came to exceed 9% of GDP in 2000 (Chart 8).

The economic policy instruments that remained under the control of the national authorities proved inadequate to curb the potential imbalances that accompanied a financial and monetary policy that was excessively slack for the conditions prevailing in the Spanish economy. These, therefore, continued to build up, becoming ever harder to sustain and increasing the vulnerability of the various economic sectors (both financial and non-financial) to external shocks. The level of debt reached by companies and households made maintaining the previous patterns of expenditure difficult. The excesses of the real-estate sector led to an inevitable adjustment and the financial system found itself in a situation of excess capacity, disproportionate exposure to developments in the property market and vulnerability to events in the wholesale financial markets on which it relied to cover the gap between credit and deposits. It was also sensitive to macroeconomic developments, given that the quality of its loan portfolio was extremely dependent on the economic cycle. Fortunately, it had the protective buffers provided by its accumulated provisions and high levels of profitability and creditworthiness deriving from the business model that had been developed, together with management and efficiency improvements introduced during its expansion, as well as the close supervision of the Banco de España. All of this was put to the test when the necessary correction of these imbalances was unfortunately triggered at the same time as the severe international financial and economic crisis that began in 2007 and worsened seriously in 2008 and 2009. The change in the monetary policy cycle in late 2005 led to a gradual correction of these imbalances starting in 2006, beginning with a slight slowdown in credit growth, but the outbreak of a financial crisis on a scale unprecedented in the recent past, followed by a global recession, precipitated the process and caused an abrupt adjustment on a huge scale.

6 The impact of the financial crisis and the Great Recession on the financial system [5]

The outbreak of the international financial crisis seriously disrupted the complex but gradual process of correcting the accumulated imbalances. This process was already subject to considerable uncertainty as a result of its having to take place under the unknown conditions created by EMU membership, which made it necessary to do without some of the instruments that had played a decisive role in resolving similar situations in the past. Even under normal circumstances, compensating for the necessary slowdown in domestic spending with genuine competitiveness gains that would allow alternative support to be found in a substantial improvement in net external demand would have tested the degree of flexibility of the economy's functioning given the restrictions of EMU membership. There was a risk that if these flexibility conditions were not met the economy would be trapped on a path of low growth and scant job creation. The exceptional virulence of the international financial crisis, and its rapid transformation into a major global recession, led to the dramatic scenario of having to deal with these adjustments under the most adverse of conditions and to the sudden materialization of latent vulnerabilities. The drastic deterioration in financial conditions and the sharp reversal in expectations put a brake on household and business consumption and investment decisions in both productive and residential assets, which particularly affected the overheated real-estate sector. Only the rapid drop in imports allowed the huge contractionary impact of the decline in spending to be mitigated. The magnitude of the shock was exacerbated by institutional weaknesses in the labor market which had not been corrected because of the mirage of intense job creation during the expansion. These weaknesses meant that in the event of swings at macroeconomic level the burden of adjustments was placed on employment, amplifying the severity of oscillations in spending.

In the exceptional circumstances of the global crisis, economic policy in all countries had to face unprecedented challenges in order to stave off a possible collapse of the financial system and a self-reinforcing contractionary spiral in spending. At international level, the G20 and the EU took emergency measures to bail out bankrupt and near-bankrupt institutions, to provide the funding the markets had stopped supplying, such as by offering guarantees or public capital injections (Chart 9), and to activate demand stimuli through the aggressive use of monetary and fiscal drivers. These measures were put in place on a temporary basis with a view to returning to equilibrium in the medium term. In Spain, this led to a drastic relaxation of the conditions set by the ECB's monetary policy (both in terms of low interest rates, which were close to zero, and the exceptional procedures to inject unlimited amounts of liquidity), the articulation of measures to

---

[5] A more detailed analysis of the global financial crisis can be found in Bean (2009), Claessens et al. (2010) and Reinhart and Rogoff (2008). The effects of the crisis on the Spanish economy are described in more detail in Banco de España (2009 and 2010).

CHART 9　RECENT BEHAVIOR OF PROFITABILITY, PUBLIC AID FOR THE BANKING SYSTEM AND FINANCIAL MARKETS

BANKS' ROE (a)

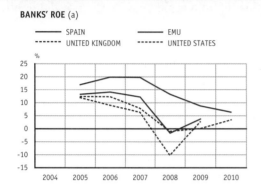

PUBLIC CAPITAL INJECTIONS (b)

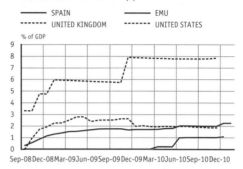

GUARANTEES (c)

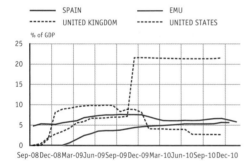

CREDIT SPREADS BY GEOGRAPHICAL REGIONS

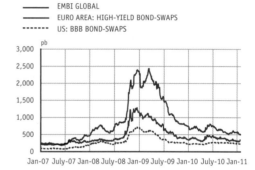

STOCK-MARKET INDICES

IMPLICIT VOLATILITIES (d)

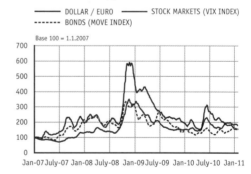

SOURCES: FDIC Quarterly Income Profile Spreadsheets, Merrill Lynch, Datastream, Bloomberg, European Central Bank and Banco de España.

a. 2010 data cover the last four quarters up to the third quarter of 2010.
b. United States: Includes capital injections under the various TARP programs and recapitalization of mortgage securitization agencies. United Kingdom: Includes recapitalization of Royal Bank of Scotland and Lloyds-HBOS together with measures to finance rescued institutions through the deposit guarantee fund.
c. US: Includes the Temporary Liquidity Guarantee Program and the Asset Guarantee Program. United Kingdom: Includes the Credit Guarantee Scheme and the Asset Protection Scheme.
In the EMU the guarantees include those for debt issued by financial institutions and collateral for assets on the balance sheets of banks and their subsidiaries.
d. 20-day moving averages.

support the financial system designed specifically for its unique situation, and the adoption of expansionary fiscal policy. In conjunction with the sharp fall in tax revenues and the effect of automatic stabilizers, this fiscal stimulus led to a rapid deterioration of the public accounts (Chart 5), which in just two years went from a surplus of around 2% of GDP in 2007 to a deficit of over 11% in 2009. This was accompanied by an even more pronounced increase in the debt ratio, although it remained below the European average, thanks to the legacy of the preceding fiscal stabilization policy. The perception that room for maneuver in terms of fiscal policy was running out alerted the markets to the possibility of an emerging fiscal crisis in certain countries, such that the existence of large public deficits became an additional vulnerability factor complicating the management of economic policy and the task of addressing the crisis. Within the euro area, the Greek fiscal crisis, which led to the Greek government's needing to turn to financial support from other euro area members and the IMF, took on a systemic dimension and spread to other countries with big imbalances, despite the considerable differences between them. Fiscal consolidation thus became a priority for all countries, although it was more pressing in those cases in which the deterioration had been faster. The Spanish authorities adopted a stringent stability program which set as its target a return to a deficit of 3% of GDP in 2013, according to the timetable set by the European Council under the Stability and Growth Pact. Achieving this target called for efforts on a scale previously unseen in Spanish fiscal policy, but was nevertheless essential to avoid suffering a serious loss of reputation that could trigger another focus of tension. Under these circumstances, the main economic policy instruments with which to address the complicated challenges of overcoming the crisis, together with fiscal consolidation, lay in supply-side policy and structural reform to increase the economy's flexibility, productivity and growth potential.

However, with the Greek fiscal crisis and the triggering of a serious sovereign debt crisis in the most vulnerable countries of the euro area, the difficulties facing the Spanish economy and its financial system were seriously worsened, adding a new degree of urgency to the economic policy response. The possibility that a Member State might be unable to meet its payment obligations and need to be rescued by its partners in the euro area and the IMF triggered a process of contagion that seriously affected the risk premiums on public debt in various countries, including Spain (Chart 10). This came to threaten the functioning of bond markets in the euro area and became the epicenter of a new phase of international financial instability, this time focusing on Europe. The seriousness of the situation made it necessary for the European authorities at the level of the Council and the ECB, along with the governments most directly affected, to adopt emergency measures. The heads of government of the Eurogroup and Ecofin established a European stability mechanism backed with €750 billion with which to rescue those countries whose ability to meet their debt repayments was at risk of being undermined, subject, in return, to conditionality, requiring them to step up and accelerate their programs of fiscal consolidation and structural reform. The ECB, for its part, re-established some of the unconventional measures to supply unlimited long-term liquidity which had been

CHART 10   INDICATORS OF TENSIONS IN FINANCING MARKETS

**TEN-YEAR GOVERNMENT DEBT
YIELD SPREAD VS. GERMANY**

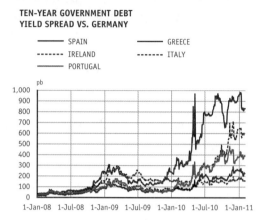

**FIVE-TO-SEVEN YEAR COVERED BONDS.
ASSET SWAP SPREAD** (a)

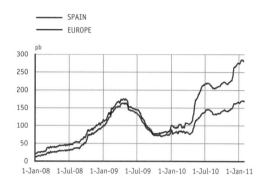

SOURCES: Reuters, Bloomberg, Datastream and Banco de España.

a. Five-day moving averages.

withdrawn, and announced a bond purchase program, which was unique in terms of its operational and institutional framework, in order to ensure the normalization of markets and the correct transmission of monetary policy.

The severity of the sovereign debt crisis, which reached a new peak when it became necessary to put in place a rescue plan for Ireland, forced a review of some of the aspects of the institutional design of the euro area which had been compromised by the extent of the destabilizing tensions unleashed. To avoid a future recurrence of fiscal indiscipline, the European Council launched a reform of economic governance in which, alongside the strengthening of the Stability and Growth Pact, it introduced new mechanisms of monitoring and control over macroeconomic and competitiveness imbalances, and established a permanent financial assistance facility for member countries in difficulties, subject to strong conditionality.

A crisis of this magnitude caught the Spanish economy at a moment of considerable weakness. The adjustment process that had begun had not yet completed, meaning that the country was perceived by international organizations and the markets as a major risk, given the high-level of private-sector debt, the rapid growth of the government deficit, high unemployment, and the need to bring about competitive disinflation, all while restructuring of the banking system was still underway. The spreads on Spanish sovereign debt rose to levels not seen since beginning of the process of convergence (Chart 10). Economic policy faced an emergency that required an immediate and vigorous response, as a loss of confidence could lead to a drying up of the sources of funding in the foreign markets on which the economy depended. The funding mechanisms that mere membership of the EMU had provided had broken down and the continuity of necessary flows depended on the external perception of the Spanish authorities' commitment to the stability of the public finances, and a willingness and ability to advance rapidly towards structural reform, particularly in the case of the labor market, and restructuring of the banking sector. The government decided to accelerate and strengthen the fiscal consolidation plans with drastic measures to cut public spending, which included salary cuts for all public employees for the first time, designed to rapidly reduce the structural component of the public deficit, in line with the requirements of Europe's decision-making bodies, in order to ensure the support of the other partners. The government also decided to embark on a thorough reform of the labor market and pension system, and bring forward the deadlines for completing the ongoing restructuring of the banking system.

This would all have a powerful impact on the Spanish financial system. However, it is important to note that in Spain the situation differed from that in other countries, where the unfolding of the crisis was immediately reflected in the deterioration of the financial system, which was directly contaminated by chains of bankruptcy or finding itself with inadequate resources or provisions to cope with the deterioration. In the Spanish case the difficulties did not manifest themselves until a later stage, more as a consequence of the worsening macroeconomic situation than a direct result of the initial origins of the international financial crisis. Nevertheless, it would subsequently become more complicated as a consequence of phenomena triggered by the spread of the sovereign debt crisis and the rescue of Greece and Ireland.[6] It is therefore worth analyzing the impact of the crisis on the Spanish financial system in a way that distinguishes the successive phases or waves of this process.

The trigger for the first wave was the rise in defaults on sub-prime mortgages in the United States, although the underlying cause of this was a series of factors which had been present as a result of developments in the financial system taking place during previous years: undervaluation of risks; excessive exposure by certain investors and institutions; the concealment of risks in unregulated institutions closely linked to regulated ones; development of complex products that were difficult to value; delegation by investors of the task of assessing risk to the rating agencies; inadequate management control at certain institutions; poor management of liquidity risk; and a lack of transparency regarding institutions' exposures and certain financial products. This was an important set of failings which put in doubt the trust that had been placed in the functioning of financial markets and revealed substantial gaps in regulatory frameworks and the architecture and conduct of supervision. The loose management of macroeconomic and financial policies at global level, based on an overestimate of efficiency and productivity gains in conjunction with an underestimate of the risks that were being incubated by the overvaluation of assets and excessive liquidity, contributed to these shortcomings to an extent that is difficult to precisely determine. Rising defaults on sub-prime mortgages were transmitted through the rapid depreciation of the products linked to them, mainly securitizations. The lack of transparency regarding financial institutions' exposures to the most seriously affected assets produced a climate of widespread mistrust that caused significant tensions in some

---

[6]   A more detailed analysis of the implications of the crisis in Spain's financial system can be found in Chapter 11 of this book.

of the key markets such as the interbank market and the securitization market in general, and falls in the stock market valuation of financial institutions began to occur in the summer of 2007 (Chart 9). This first wave, which was purely financial in nature, directly affected those institutions with the greatest exposures to the most seriously affected products (which came to be known as toxic assets) either directly or through off-balance-sheet vehicles (such as SIVs). However, it also had an impact on institutions which had significant refinancing needs and did not have sufficient liquid assets to meet maturity renewals. In many industrialized countries this all seriously affected banks' earnings and made it necessary to bail out large portions of the financial system to avoid panic and global collapse (Chart 9). The countries most seriously affected included the United States, the United Kingdom, Germany, the Netherlands, Ireland and Iceland.

Spanish banks were left relatively unscathed by this first wave, as they had no direct or indirect exposure to toxic assets. This was a result both of the retail orientation of their business model and stricter banking supervision, which had not allowed investment in these products through off-balance-sheet vehicles. Moreover, although Spanish institutions had drawn extensively on wholesale markets to bridge the gap between credit and deposit growth, the bulk of their liabilities were long-term, which made their short-term refinancing needs manageable. Institutions were able to temporarily accommodate part of their financing needs by issuing short-term securities, the markets for which had been comparatively less affected. Subsequently, emergency measures such as guarantee programs for securities issues, introduced by the Spanish government, in line with the measures agreed at global and European level, helped facilitate the issue of securities (Chart 9), while the policy of massive injection of liquidity by the euro system eased short-term tensions.

The spread and deepening of the financial crisis beginning in the autumn of 2008 with the bankruptcy of Lehman Brothers, ended up triggering a major global recession, which was closely linked to the deterioration in confidence, the impact of declining asset values, and tighter credit supply. This was the worst shock to be suffered by the market economy since the Second World War, categorically refuting the expectations of a prolonged phase of growth which had been encouraged by the opportunities offered by a combination of the new technology revolution and market globalization. In Spain, the powerful external contractionary forces generated by this severe economic crisis were superimposed on the adjustment that had begun to take place in order to absorb the imbalances that had accumulated during the long period of economic growth, in terms of excess investment in real estate and overvaluation of the property market, increasing household and corporate debt, with an excess dependence on foreign savings, and imbalances in relative prices and costs. Thus, what had begun as a gentle process, ended, as we have seen, by turning into an abrupt adjustment in domestic spending and a sharp rise in unemployment, which would have a strong impact on the financial system (Chart 1).

This second wave of the economic and financial crisis affected Spanish institutions more powerfully due to the deterioration of their loan portfolios in the wake of plummeting economic growth and employment and the sharp correction in domestic spending resulting in more pessimistic expectations of future income generation in the private sector and higher risk premiums. The greater impact of the recession on Spanish institutions' asset-portfolio quality was a consequence of their retail orientation, which placed greater relative importance on the loan portfolio. But above all, it was a result of their overexposure to a real-estate sector undergoing a severe process of adjustment. Spanish banks were able to confront the effects of this second wave from an initially solid position, as they had barely been affected by the first wave and because, as well as their strong earnings, they had built up significant safety buffers during the years of expansion, thanks to the regulatory innovations that were introduced with the establishment of dynamic provisioning, as discussed earlier. Nevertheless, these buffers were progressively exhausted as the recession dragged on and assets were increasingly eroded, while at the same time profitability levels declined (Chart 11). Viewed as a whole, the Spanish financial system remained strong overall, but with a time lag and with certain specific characteristics, the fragilities began to emerge that had accumulated in a segment of the financial system that had exposed itself to bigger risks during the period of rapid credit growth and made excessive investments in real estate, particularly in the property development sector, which suffered from high rates of doubtful loans and bankruptcy (Chart 11). This crisis was not on the same scale as in other countries, as it was limited to a specific set of institutions (Charts 9 and 11), but it had a systemic facet due to its influence on the reputation of the system as a whole and the danger that the prolongation of the effects of the crisis and possible entry into a phase of sluggish growth with high unemployment might broaden its scope.

The Spanish financial system, therefore, faced the need to embark on a restructuring that would lead to its resizing after the excessive growth it had undergone during the expansionary phase and the cleaning up of the balance sheets of the most severely affected institutions. It was inevitable that Spanish institutions would join, with their own specific characteristics, the general process of deleveraging taking place in economies and financial systems worldwide, after the reassessment of the risks triggered by the crisis led to levels of debt that had previously been considered optimal now coming to be perceived as excessive.

An adjustment of the financial system along these lines gave rise to additional risks for the development of the economy, already immersed in a severe recession and undergoing a harsh correction. This adjustment could interfere with financial flows if it led to a widespread credit crunch or, in the worst case, if it became a general financial crisis jeopardizing the solvency of the financial system as a whole. This demanded the adoption of exceptional financial policies as part of a strategy for an orderly restructuring of the banking system in a way that combined mechanisms for the recapitalization or bailout of institutions with the adoption of stringent and credible viability plans, which would be the precondition for receiving support from public funds. It was with this purpose in mind that the Fund for Orderly Restructuring of the Banking Sector (Fondo de Reestructuración Ordenada Bancaria, FROB) was created, as a facility specifically designed to meet the needs of the Spanish financial system based on the accrued experience within the supervisory model from

CHART 11 CREDIT QUALITY AND PROFITABILITY INDICATORS

DOUBTFUL RATIO. OTHER RESIDENT SECTORS (a)

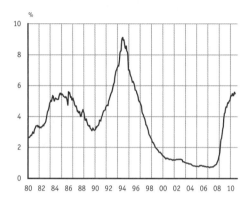

PROVISION COVERAGE RATIO. CREDIT INSTITUTIONS (a)

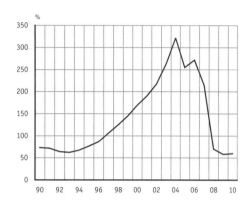

DOUBTFUL RATIO. SECTOR BREAKDOWN (a)

——— HOME LOANS
——— CONSUMER CREDIT, ETC.
------ CONSTRUCTION AND REAL-ESTATE
------ OTHER PRODUCTIVE ACTIVITIES

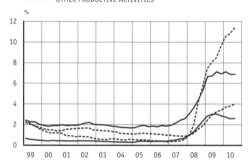

**PRE-TAX PROFITS.
DEPOSIT-TAKING INSTITUTIONS** (a)

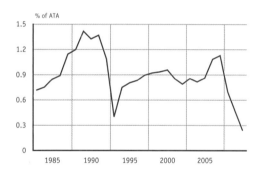

**DISTRIBUTION OF CREDIT INSTITUTIONS' TOTAL CREDIT BY
DOUBTFUL RATIO INTERVALS. DECEMBER 2009.**

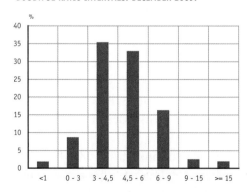

**DISTRIBUTION OF TOTAL CREDIT INSTITUTION ASSETS BY
ROE INTERVALS. DECEMBER 2009**

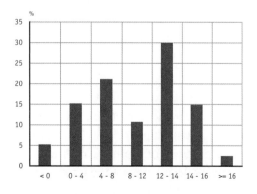

SOURCES: Instituto Nacional de Estadística and Banco de España.

a. 2010 data is for third quarter.

previous episodes of banking crisis and restructuring. Under this scheme, vulnerable institutions can receive financial support in the form of capital injections, provided they are able to present a viable restructuring plan approved by the Banco de España. Vulnerable institutions that are not able to draw up a viable solution suitable for approval by the supervisory authorities will be taken over by the Banco de España and be restructured by new directors appointed by the FROB. In fact, even before this new strategy had been launched one institution had to be taken over by the Banco de España in view of its risk of insolvency. This institution underwent restructuring by means of the conventional procedure with support from the corresponding deposit guarantee fund.

This model of action has some significant differences from that applied in other countries that have had to undertake massive bank rescues or large-scale restructuring. These divergences are a result of differences in timing and the distinctive features of how the financial crisis emerged in Spain, as well as the Spanish supervisory tradition. Given the starting point and the negligible incidence of the first wave of international shocks, the most important symptoms of the financial crisis manifest themselves in Spain with an additional delay, in the wake of the second wave. This was not just because the trigger was more macroeconomic than financial in origin, being linked to the deepening of the process of economic contraction, but also because the shocks generated were transmitted more gradually, being more closely linked to the occurrence of defaults than swings in asset valuations, which tend to be more abrupt as they depend on the formation of expectations. Furthermore, these effects tend to be transmitted in a more localized way, which means their systemic implications have been less obvious in Spain than in many countries where the dense interconnections between institutions were revealed by the sudden loss of value of many assets during the first wave of the crisis.

Although the plight of Spain's financial institutions was not as severe or deep as in other countries, the financial restructuring strategy was a cornerstone of the economic policy designed to tackle the profound economic crisis and to lay the groundwork for economic recovery. This recovery will depend, among other things, on the existence of a healthy financial system able to channel the necessary funds, once the process of deleveraging and consolidation of balance sheets in the non-financial private sector has been completed. In any event, the potential effectiveness of a strategy of this type is closely linked to the progress of fiscal consolidation and reforms to remedy the latent structural weaknesses that have emerged during the crisis as a serious obstacle to the resumption of growth. If the economy is unable to achieve fiscal discipline and economic dynamism, financial restructuring will be more difficult and costly, despite the potency of the instruments applied.

The progress of the bank restructuring strategy articulated through the FROB faced the difficulties deriving from the idiosyncratic institutional configuration of the savings banks; a segment in which the most significant downsizing, recapitalization and cost reduction needs are concentrated. Their vague ownership structure, idiosyncratic corporate governance and the regulatory powers assigned to the Autonomous Communities, stretched out the process of mergers in which both the triggering of public capital injections and the definition of viability plans had to be framed. This process proved slower than initially expected and extended until the very end of the set deadline of 30 June 2010. In the final stage of the process serious new difficulties would arise as a result of what could be considered the third wave of the crisis. This wave was the result of contagion effects and mistrust in Europe triggered by the fiscal plight of Greece and other European Union Member States. The doubts about the scope of the Spanish savings banks' problems and the effectiveness of the restructuring process the authorities had designed added a further factor undermining confidence in the Spanish economy to those deriving from the weakness of the macroeconomic situation and the deteriorating fiscal situation. In this new bout of financial instability, focused on Europe and with its attention on the most vulnerable peripheral economies, the situation of the Spanish financial system, which as a whole continued to depend on external finance and wholesale markets, faced the threat of being unable to attract the financial flows necessary and thus find itself facing a serious liquidity crisis, which would constitute the most serious setback in the recent history of the Spanish financial system. The Treasury's difficulties in meeting its considerable financing needs from the markets and the spiraling cost differentials on Spanish public debt (compared to the debt of more stable countries) would trigger a loss of confidence in the economy and a drying up of its sources of financing, threatening the stability of the financial system. In response to these tensions, the Spanish economic authorities promoted greater transparency among financial institutions concerning their risk exposures in order to allay market concerns about the situation of the financial system. This culminated in the carrying out of stress tests to measure institutions' resilience to extreme shocks, an initiative which was joined by other European countries in a joint exercise coordinated at European level, and whose results were published, with detail at the level of individual institutions, in July 2010.[7] In parallel, a major reform of the regulation of the savings banks was passed, the main objectives of which were to expand their routes for recapitalization, raise the professional standards of their management, and extend their business models, envisaging the possibility that the savings banks might transfer their financial business to a bank.[8] These measures, together with other actions taken at both European and national level (structural reforms and consolidation of the public finances), contributed significantly to easing the tensions in financial markets, but tensions resurfaced after the Irish debt crisis, in November 2010 which led to Ireland's rescue by its European partners and the IMF. Once again, the market's doubts about the solvency of the Spanish financial system, and in particular, the savings banks, played a role in this episode as it was a key factor in international investors' loss of confidence. This translated into new challenges for the financing of the Spanish economy, which had to refinance outstanding debt that had been issued in previous years as well facing the continuing need to finance the external deficit, although this was progressively

---

[7]   For more details, see Chapter 11 of this book.
[8]   For more details, see Chapters 7 and 11 of this book.

shrinking. This situation necessitated new measures aimed, firstly, at increasing the transparency of institutions' liquidity risks and credit exposures, and secondly, at bolstering their solvency by setting more stringent capital requirements. This requirement applied especially to unlisted institutions such as the savings banks, in which private investors do not have a significant presence and which are more reliant on wholesale funding. Moreover, the FROB was empowered to participate in the recapitalization of institutions which so requested, or which found themselves unable to achieve the new capital requirements by the stipulated deadline. Recapitalization with support from the FROB requires that the savings banks first be converted into commercial banks, along the lines of one of the models envisaged in the new savings bank regulations.

7   Concluding remarks

The period covered in this chapter, in which the Spanish financial system finally reached maturity hand in hand with the economy's progress towards macroeconomic stability, ends at a delicate juncture in which, as this book goes to press, the economy is facing a process of adjustment which is unprecedented in terms of the magnitude and complexity of the imbalances which need to be corrected. This is a process made even more complex by the fact that it is taking place within the constraints of EMU membership. Some of the biggest achievements in terms of stability, such as fiscal discipline, have resurfaced as pending challenges, and some of the distortions that remained latent during the boom period – such as the distortions of the labor market – have re-emerged forcefully, jeopardizing the economy's ability to start out again on a new phase of high growth while ensuring the required macroeconomic stability. The valuable experience gained during this period indicates that when economic agents and economic policy managers address these situations – which are not unknown in recent history – with sufficient reforming drive to bring Spain closer to the patterns of stability and efficiency of the most advanced countries in the euro area, the economy has sufficient reserves to enable it to react vigorously. On this occasion the reaction will also be crucial for the capacity for growth in the medium term and the final impact of the crisis on the Spanish financial system and therefore on the sustainability of progress made during this phase.

Recent changes in the financial system suggest that the process of transformation begun will involve a resizing of the industry to correct excess capacity, raise levels of capital, and enhance institutions' ability to withstand adverse shocks, together with a tendency towards the savings banks to transform themselves into banks, which will contribute to raising their efficiency through increased market discipline. This process will probably be one of the most significant transformations in the history of Spain's financial system. It is to be hoped that the successful completion of this process will lead to a stronger, more efficient and more crisis-resistant financial system.

References

AYUSO, J. and ESCRIVÁ, J. L., (1997). "La evolución de la estrategia de control monetario", in *La política monetaria y la inflación en España*, Alianza Economía.

BANCO DE ESPAÑA (2009). *Informe Anual 2008.*
— (2010). *Informe Anual 2009.*

BEAN, C. (2009). *The Great Moderation, the Great Panic, and the Great Contraction*, Schumpeter Lecture, Annual Congress of the European Economic Association, Barcelona, 25 August.

BENIVENGA, V. R. and SMITH, B. D. (1992). *Deficits, Inflation and the Banking System in Developing Countries: the Optimal Degree of Financial Repression*, Oxford Economic Papers, 44, pp. 767-790.

BLANCHARD, O, DELL'ARICCIA, G. and MAURO, P. (2010). *Rethinking macroeconomic policy*, Staff Position Note no. 2010/3

BLANCO, R. and GARCÍA-VAQUERO, V. (2005). "El sistema financiero", in *El Análisis de la Economía Española, Servicio de Estudios del Banco de España*, Alianza Editorial.

BOYD, J. H., LEVINE, R. and SMITH, B. D. (2001). *The impact of Inflation on Financial Sector Performance*, Journal of Monetary Economics, vol. 47, pp. 221-248.

BRAUN, M. and RADDATZ, C. (2008). *The Politics of Financial Development: Evidence from Trade Liberalization*, The Journal of Finance, vol. 63(3), pp. 1469-1508.

CHIN, M.D. and ITO, H. (2006). *What Matters for Financial Development? Capital Controls, Institutions and Interactions*, Journal of Development Economics, 81, pp. 163-192.

CLAESSENS, S., DELL'ARICCIA, G., IGAN, D. and LAEVEN, L. (2010). *Cross-country experiences and policy implications from the global financial crisis*, Economic Policy, vol. 25, n.º 62, pp. 267 - 293

CLAESSENS, S., KLINGEBIEL, D. and SCHMUKLER, S. L. (2006). *Stock Market Development and Internationalization: Do Economic Fundamentals Spur Both Similarly?*, Journal of Empirical Finance, vol. 13, pp. 316-350.

COTTARELLI, C., DELL'ARICCIA, G. and VLADKOVA-HOLLAR, I. (2005). *Early Birds, Late Risers and Sleeping Beauties: Bank Credit Growth to the Private Sector in Central and Eastern Europe and in the Balkans*, Journal of Banking and Finance, vol. 29, pp. 83-104.

DEMIRGUC-KUNT, A. and DETRAGIACHE, E. (1998). *The Determinants of Banking Crises in Developing and Developed Countries*, IMF Staff Papers, vol. 45(1), Marzo, pp. 81-109.

DEMIRGUC-KUNT, A. and DETRAGIACHE, E. (2005). *Cross-Country Empirical Studies of Systemic Bank Distress: A Survey*, National Institute Economic Review, vol. 192(1), Abril, pp. 68-83.

ESTRADA, Á., JIMENO J. F. and MALO DE MOLINA, J. L. (2009). "La economía española en la UEM: los diez primeros años", *Documentos Ocasionales*, n.º 0901, Banco de España.

IMF (2001). *World Economic Outlook*, Octubre, capítulo 4.

FUENTES, I. (2007). "La titulización en España: principales características", *Boletín Económico del Banco de España*, December.

FUENTES, I. (2008). "Evolución de la brecha crédito-depósitos y de su financiación durante la década actual", *Boletín Económico del Banco de España*, December.

GUTIÉRREZ, F. (1997). "La política monetaria tras la ley de autonomía del Banco de España", in *La política monetaria y la inflación en España*, Alianza Economía, pp. 253-298.

HAUNER, D. (2006). Fiscal Policy and Financial Development, IMF Working Paper 06/26.

HENRY, P. B. (2000). *Stock Market Liberalization, Economic Reform and Emerging Market Equity Prices*, The Journal of Finance, vol. 55(2), pp. 529-564.

HUYBENS, E. and SMITH, B.D. (1999). *Inflation, Financial Markets and Long-Run Real Activity*, Journal of Monetary Economics, 43, pp. 283-315.

LEVINE, R. (2005). *Finance and Growth: Theory and Evidence*, in Aghion, P. y Durlauf, S. (eds.) Handbook of Economic Growth, vol. 1A, Chapter 12.

LOAYZA, N. V. and RANCIERE, R. (2006). *Financial Development, Financial Fragility and Growth*, Journal of Money, Credit and Banking, vol. 38(4), pp. 1051-1076.

MALO DE MOLINA, J. L. (2003). "Una visión macroeconómica de los veinticinco años de vigencia de la Constitución Española", *Economía Industrial*, no. 349/350, pp. 29-50.

— (2005). "Una larga fase de expansión de la economía española", *Documentos Ocasionales,* no. 0505, Banco de España.

— (2007). "Los principales rasgos y experiencias de la integración de la economía española en la UEM", *Papeles de Economía Española,* no.111.

MALO DE MOLINA, J. L.and PÉREZ, J. (1990). "La política monetaria española en la transición hacia la unión monetaria europea", *Papeles de Economía Española,* 43.

MALO DE MOLINA, J. L. and RESTOY, F. (2004). "Evolución reciente del patrimonio de empresas y familias en España: Implicaciones macroeconómicas", *Documentos Ocasionales,* no. 0402, Banco de España.

MCKINNON, R. I. (1973). *Money and Capital in Economic Development,* Washington DC: Brookings institution.

PEÑALOSA, J. and RESTOY, F. (2005). "Implicaciones de la integración en la UEM y en el nuevo contexto internacional", in *El Análisis de la Economía Española, Servicio de Estudios del Banco de España,* Alianza Editorial.

PÉREZ JURADO, M. (1997). "El SME y la convergencia en inflación: el papel de la credibilidad cambiaria", in *La política monetaria y la inflación en España,* Alianza Economía, pp. 139-180.

REINHART, C. and ROGOFF K.S. (2008). *Is the 2007 U.S. Subprime Crisis So Different? An International Historical Comparison,* American Economic Review, vol. 98 n.º 2, pp. 339–344.

RAJAN, R. and ZINGALES, L. (2003). *The Great Reversals: The Politics of Financial Development in the Twentieth Century,* Journal of Financial Economics, vol. 69, pp. 5-50.

ROJO, L. A. (2001). "El largo camino de la política monetaria española hacia el euro", in Banco de España, El camino hacia el euro. *El real, el escudo y la peseta,* pp. 117-132.

— (2002). "La economía española en la democracia (1976-2000)", in Historia Económica de España, Crítica, pp. 397-436.

ROUBINI, N. and SALA-I-MARTIN, X. (1995). *A Growth Model of Inflation, Tax Evasion and Financial Repression,* Journal of Monetary Economics, vol. 35, pp. 275-301.

ROUSSEAU, P. and SYLLA, R. (2003). *Financial Systems, Economic Growth, and Globalization,* in Bordo M., Taylor, A. and Williamson, J. (eds.), *Globalization in Historical Perspective,* University of Chicago Press, pp. 373-416.

SHAW, E.S. (1973). Financial Deepening in Economic Development, New York: Oxford University Press.

TRESSEL, T. and DETRAGIACHE, E. (2008). *Do Financial Sector Reforms Lead to Financial Development? Evidence from a New Dataset,* IMF Working Paper 08/265.

7. Banking supervision and regulation over the past 40 years

Raimundo Poveda [1]

1 Introduction

At the start of the 1960s, the solvency of Spain's credit institutions was primarily based, not on prudential regulation, which was still rudimentary, or supervision, which was still underdeveloped, but on an institutional framework that offered little room for competition. The key components of this framework were:

- The banking status quo of the 1940s and 1950s, which obstructed the emergence of new banks and severely limited branch openings.
- A strict interest rate schedule (with capped deposit rates and minimum lending rates) that protected banks' margins.
- A highly compartmentalized financial system that the authorities reinforced by splitting the mixed banking model into commercial banks and industrial and investment banks.

[1] I would like to thank Miguel Angel Almazán, José Manuel Gómez de Miguel, Joaquín Latorre, Rafael Prado, Luis Javier Rodríguez and Fernando Vargas for their comments and suggestions, and Mariano Amor and Valentín Pérez for the data supplied. My memory is based on two works that are not expressly cited here: *Regulación de las entidades de crédito españolas,* by Joaquín Latorre; and, for the early years of the period covered, *Legislación bancaria española,* by Gonzalo Pérez de Armiñán. Lastly, I would also like to thank the editors, and especially José Luis Malo de Molina, for their guidelines and suggestions.

There were no banking crises, or if any did arise they were settled discreetly, thanks to the leading banks' eagerness to acquire banking licenses and branch networks at any price, an appetite that was clearly whetted by the status quo.

This framework was unsustainable in the market economy system dominant in the OECD area, and it was gradually replaced by modern regulation and supervisory arrangements, in a long – sometimes event-driven and not always faultless – process that is described below. The first step was the centralization of the supervisory function at the Banco de España.

2   The Banco de España: supervisory authority

Under the 1962 reform of the financial system, banking inspection was transferred from a State body (since 1946, the Directorate of Banking, Stock Markets and Investment at the Ministry of Finance) to the Banco de España, the recently nationalized central bank. This important and controversial decision generated no debate. The Credit and Banking Law was backed by a consultative memorandum of the Ministry of Finance, based on opinions submitted by all the public and corporate bodies concerned. Other parts of the reform project did attract discussion, with dissenting opinions, but all the parties consulted agreed that the inspection function be transferred to the Banco de España. It was viewed as a means of monitoring compliance with all the legal regulations and technical management rules applicable to private sector banks,[2] possibly because, at that time, this limited inspection role (there was still no mention of *supervision)* was considered an issue of secondary importance.

With the enactment of the Credit and Banking Law, the Banco de España immediately became responsible for inspection and administrative control of the private sector banks,[3] but supervision of all other credit institutions remained in different hands. Savings banks were supervised by the Credit Institute for Savings Banks (ICCA) and public-sector banks by the Institute for Medium and Long-Term Credit (ICMLP), while credit unions remained under the stewardship of the Ministry of Labor and Trade Union Organization until 1967, when the supervisory function was assumed by the Ministry of Finance. The smaller credit institutions remained in a legal limbo, except those engaged in financing capital goods which were so closely controlled by the ICMLP that the latter even had a representative on their boards, with the power to suspend board resolutions.[4]

Under the Credit and Banking Law, the financial authority retained its complex architecture, with the Governor of the Banco de España also acting as chairman of the ICCA and the ICMLP. In theory, this should have permitted top-level coordination of the different supervisory activities, but this was not the concern that determined the arrangement. Rather, the aim was to coordinate lending policies: selective intervention in funding channels was the

---

2   Ministry of Economy and Finance (1961), p. 6.
3   Law 2/1962, Base 2, and Decree Law 18/1962 on nationalization of the Banco de España, Art. 17.
4   Decree Law 57/1962, Art. 6.

great technical instrument of the Development Plans of the time. But the structure collapsed in 1969 in the wake of the Matesa scandal; Matesa was a company that received plentiful funding for fictitious exports that neither the Banco de Crédito Industrial, which granted the funding, nor the ICMLP, which was responsible for its control, was able to detect in time.

In the subsequent reorganization of public sector finance, the Governor of the Banco de España lost his central role, among other reasons, owing to the gradual exclusion of the central bank's privileged access (the traditional automatic pledge of public debt, the new special rediscount facilities) from the selective-intervention process, since it interfered with the needs of incipient monetary control. The Banco de España thus focused on its two basic functions: monetary control and supervision of credit and savings institutions. In 1971 it assumed the supervision both of savings banks (together with the staff of the defunct ICCA) and credit unions.[5] Much later, in 1988, this process was completed when it became responsible for supervision of the official credit institutions (including their parent entity, the Official Credit Institute, a financial body that succeeded the administrative body that was the ICMLP), the specialized lending institutions (ECAOLs) and the mutual guarantee companies.[6]

Securities market institutions (securities dealers and brokers, investment firms, mutual funds, securitization funds, etc.) and insurance institutions have their own supervisory bodies, but there is contact with the Banco de España. With the development of the concept of consolidated supervision, the Bank may obtain, from the respective parent institutions and competent supervisory bodies, information on securities market and insurance institutions that belong to groups under its supervision. Moreover, given the confluence of many financial activities conducted by institutions of different kinds, it has become necessary to coordinate the regulations and policies applicable. In the European Union, this has resulted in common prudential legislation for credit institutions and investment services. In Spain, this coordination is also seen in the exchange of Directors between the Banco de España and the National Securities Market Commission (CNMV) which is responsible for supervising the securities markets and their participants.

3   The 1977-85 crisis and its consequences

The severe crisis that ran from 1977 to 1985 had a huge impact on the private banking sector and a not inconsiderable impact on the other two main families of deposit institutions. It also

---

[5]   Law 13/1971, Additional Provisions Two and Three. In 1973, the Banco de España became responsible for exchange rate policy, absorbing the Spanish Foreign Currency Institute, but the Ministry of Economy and Trade retained the attendant supervisory functions (exchange rate fraud, monetary offences). Under Law 40/1979 on exchange control, these functions were assigned to an interministerial control committee, with a supporting body located at the Banco de España. However, the liberalization of foreign payments and capital movements removed a hitherto significant source of supervisory concern.

[6]   Law 26/1988. Under Law 3/1994, the Banco de España assumed the supervision of appraisal companies.

had far-reaching effects on supervisory policy: new resolution mechanisms had to be created; the supervisory function was strengthened[7] and supervisory targets redesigned. The crisis also demanded in-depth and immediate reconsideration of bank accounting standards, and subsequently of prudential regulations; in fact, it proved to be a turning point for supervision of Spanish credit institutions.

3.1   Extent of the crisis

Between December 1977 and January 1985, the Spanish Bank Deposit Guarantee Fund (FGDEB) assumed control of 29 banks and the State expropriated 20 banks belonging to the Rumasa group, for reasons of "public utility and social interest". A few others also experienced serious difficulties and received special credit support from the Banco de España, or had to be quietly absorbed by their parent institutions or other banks. According to one expert on the crisis, a total of 56 banks were affected, representing 27% of the deposits held at private sector banks. The crisis cost the public sector an estimated 1,216 billion pesetas and the banking sector 365 billion, between contributions to the FGDEB and special operations (Rumasa, Urquijo-Unión), plus a possible further 200 billion in intra-group restructurings (amounts estimated in 1985 pesetas).[8]

The financial crisis had a similarly severe impact – proportionate to their size – on credit unions. A handful of small institutions were wound up and their assets and liabilities (but not their banking licenses, due to the barrier between species) taken over, in most cases by savings banks; there was just one case of one credit union being absorbed by another. And in 1984, nineteen rural savings banks (including Caja Rural Nacional), representing 20% of overall sector deposits, had to be restructured by means of a public program run by Banco de Crédito Agrícola. This program included, inter alia, support from the Credit Union Deposit Guarantee Fund (FGDCC) amounting to 42.3 billion pesetas in the form of loans and purchases of impaired assets.[9]

The crisis also affected a number of savings banks. The impact was less severe and more gradual and this, together with the solidarity of these institutions, meant that the problems were borne and resolved discretely. There were no threats of collapse, but by 1986 the Savings Bank Deposit Guarantee Fund (FGDCA) had granted a total of 11.6 billion pesetas to four institutions.[10] Throughout the rest of the decade, some continued to record difficulties, and even to need further assistance. They would subsequently be absorbed in the wave of savings bank mergers that took place between 1990 and 1992, with support

---

[7]   See Annex and Table 6.

[8]   Cuervo (1988), Chapters 2 and 5; these figures have been criticized, but they remain the best estimates available.

[9]   FGDCC (1984).

[10]   FGDCA (1986).

from the DGF that included, as a new feature, acquisition of subordinated bonds of the merged institutions.

3.2 Causes of the crisis

Such a deep and far-reaching crisis was clearly due to a range of factors. There were general economic factors: the first and second oil crises, which sharply halted growth; and the most severe inflationary episode ever experienced in Spain, with price dislocation, failed revaluation expectations and, in due time, the inevitable corrective measures. There were also political factors, as the political situation throughout most of the period did not encourage the introduction of strong financial policies. And there were factors intrinsic to the banking sector and its regulatory framework. With no disregard to the importance of the economic and political factors, here we are more concerned with the latter.

Moreover, the economic and institutional explanations are not incompatible. The Bank Deposit Guarantee Fund discussed the causes of the crisis in several of its annual reports. In 1981 it argued that the difficulties faced by the banks were not a specifically Spanish phenomenon, but rather a reflection of the general economic climate following the 1974 oil crisis. However, it also added:

> *"Furthermore ... some of Spain's difficulties derive from the way in which the banking status quo was broken up in the wake of the 1962 Credit and Banking Law. In some cases, the Law produced artificial splits, and institutions were created that lacked sufficient own funds and experienced human resources. These institutions were, therefore, particularly vulnerable to an industrial crisis such as that seen in the non-oil producing countries since 1974. Between 1962 and 1974, in light of the Spanish economic boom, new banks were created and existing banks changed hands; some of these institutions launched expansion policies of a more or less speculative nature, with high risk concentration at the controlling groups, all funded with high-cost borrowing. Some industrial banks that created or became involved in companies that were unable to make sufficient profit to meet their interest payments materialized losses in overvalued assets and thus became trapped in a vicious circle, having to continue to meet unsustainable financing needs, at an increasingly high cost, thus making the companies' survival ever more precarious. While economic growth remained strong, poorly-managed banks were able to handle these difficulties, but as the general economic crisis began to bite, the situation became untenable ...".*[11]

---

[11] FGDEB (1980), pp. 6 and 7.

As an inevitable corollary to these vicious circles, the DGF detected the emergence of irregular or unlawful practices, in particular relating to concentration, with third parties being used to bypass the existing limits.

In 1984, when the crisis was virtually at an end, the Bank DGF returned to the subject, summarizing the causes as follows:[12]

-   The general increase in interest rates, which since 1977 had raised the cost of funding unproductive or speculative assets.
-   Keen competition for deposits, forcing many new banks to offer extraordinarily high interest rates.
-   High overheads, with oversized fixed asset and organizational structures in proportion to real business volume.
-   High-risk investments: less solvent customers accepting higher rates, property investments or investments in financial corporations; when the economic situation changed, these marginal customers became loss-making, resulting in capital losses on the investments.
-   Risk concentration: almost all the banks in difficulties had close ties to corporate groups that were funded by them, resulting in high risk concentration.
-   Accounting practices that masked losses.
-   Market support for own shares, which resulted, in practice, in depleted capital levels.

These problems were concentrated in particular among new banks or "new bankers" (businessmen or non-financial groups that had acquired existing banking licenses), to the extent that of the 51 banks affected by the crisis, 47 were new banks or bankers (according to the DGF's 1983 reckoning).[13] Thus, the distant cause of the crisis among the banks (but not among other types of credit institutions) was the policy to dismantle the domestic status quo, marked not only by significant design defects, but also by inadequate regulatory and supervisory measures. By contrast, the much-feared entry of foreign banks into the Spanish market had no harmful effects, and the other key aspect of the opening-up process – the deregulation of interest rates and banking fees – was characterized by great regulatory prudence, with the process extending over an extraordinarily long period to prevent tension building up in income statements.

---

[12]   FGDEB (1983), pp. 13 and 14.

[13]   Of the 34 banks created between 1962 and 1979, 24 were restructured by the DGF, deregistered or absorbed by other banks. The other 10 survived the crisis: the five industrial banks created by the large banks, two foreign banks and three small institutions.

3.3　An ill-prepared break-up of the banking status quo

Since 1940 there had been a ban on the creation of new banks.[14] The first move to dismantle the status quo came in 1962, when regulations were introduced for the creation of industrial and investment banks, with the clear intention of new banking licenses being granted.[15] The aim of the legislator in this respect was to encourage business development and long-term financing, to separate it from strictly commercial and payment activities. For this reason, the industrial and investment banks were allowed to accept long-term deposits, including certificates of deposit, earning interest above the general schedule, and to issue short-term bonds with maturity of more than two years, with significant financial advantages, although their commercial lending activities were restricted. The advantages granted may have attracted certain groups of promoters to an inappropriate type of banking license that, in their hands, represented significant risk.

In 1963, new regulations opened up the licensing of commercial banks, which were not allowed to hold shares or shareholdings.[16] The scope of long-term business at the non-industrial banks' was reduced[17] and a series of incompatibilities was established, limiting the number of management posts (chair, directors, senior executives) that bank executives could hold in other companies.[18] But the aim to do away with the old mixed banking model was condemned to failure from the start. The ban on shareholdings did not extend to existing banks, owing to vested interests, and eventually all the large banks created industrial and investment banking subsidiaries to exploit the advantages granted to these institutions.

The minimum capital requirements imposed on the new banks were totally insufficient (between 10 and 100 million pesetas, depending on the population of the town or city in which they were based). The new banks were also subject to strict limitations on branching, a political obsession of the time. Banking licenses were granted by the Ministry of Finance, at the proposal of the Banco de España, but the criteria for granting them included no assessment of either the viability of the projects or the suitability of their promoters. Instead it depended rather on the "interest for the national economy of the founding program", the kind of intrinsically arbitrary criterion that would subsequently be eliminated by the European Community directives. Between 1963 and 1965 some twenty licenses were granted, but it seems the initial results of this opening-up process did not please the authorities, as these were followed, over the next eight years, by just two new licenses, both for industrial and investment banks. When new licenses were granted again, as from 1973, the capital requirements were much higher (1.5 billion pesetas),[19] but the restrictions on

---

14　Decree of 17 January 1940, ratified by the 1946 Banking Law (LOB).
15　Decree Law 53/1962 and Ministerial Order of 21 May 1963. There were also regulations for existing banks to convert into industrial and investment banks (Ministerial Order of 31 May 1963).
16　Decree 1312/1963.
17　Ministerial Order of 30 November 1963.
18　Law 31/1968.
19　Decree 63/1972, I.

branching remained and the new banks were subject to annual inspections during their first years of operation. A dozen licenses were granted under this new regime before the process came to a halt once more. The problem lay not in the legal conditions, following adjustment of the capital requirement, but rather in an unfortunate combination of:

- Promoters' business expectations, based on memories of the banking market *before* the break-up of the status quo and of the economic situation *before* the oil crisis.
- The lack of supervisory criteria in the granting of licenses, which in many cases depended more on connections than on the suitability or viability of the projects.

The banking regulations of the time were not short of limits on risk concentration and insider and connected risk, the key threat posed by the new banks. In 1968 banks were barred from granting loans to their own senior executives, save with the express authorization of the Banco de España,[20] and in 1969 a limit of 2.5% of own and borrowed funds was placed on loans extended by commercial and mixed banks to single customers, or to groups of banks' subsidiary companies, again save with the express authorization of the Banco de España.[21] However, many banks (both new and old) founds ways – whether or not lawful – to elude these limits, until risk concentrations and group risk were gradually unearthed by inspections, and the Banco de España was forced to issue a circular, obliging banks to keep accounting records of guarantees and restricting the crossed loans used to elude these limits.[22]

There were also controls on purchases of one bank by another, which were subject to administrative authorization, but not on purchases of banks by individuals or by other companies, including financial corporations. This led to widespread and uncontrolled transfers of banking licenses and, in particular, to the creation of the Rumasa banking group.[23] For a considerable time the Banco de España seemed unworried by Rumasa, even granting it credit lines connected with the purchase of a number of banks in difficulties (Banco de Siero and Banco de Murcia in 1967, Banco del Noroeste in 1974), despite the fact that the last acquisitions were made at absurd prices, higher than the value of the deposits of the banks acquired.

Geographical expansion was the next stage of the break-up of the status quo. The Expansion Plans, drawn up by the Administrative Services for Credit and Savings Institutions and characterized by their elaborate nature and their lack of economic sense,[24]

---

[20]   Law 31/1968, Art. 5.1.

[21]   Decree 702/1969. A lower limit was applicable in the case of secured loans.

[22]   Banco de España Circular 172 of 13 July 1979.

[23]   Not all the group's banks had the same parent institution: for some it was the central holding company of the industrial financial conglomerate, for others financial subsidiaries of the holding company (the "Rumasinas") and for yet others trustee companies.

[24]   At that time, the question of whether or not a local banking correspondent collecting bills of exchange was actually a branch in disguise was considered an important issue that could lead to penalty proceedings.

authorized some two hundred branch openings per year, applying obsolete deconcentration criteria that penalized the development of branch networks in the big cities. In 1972-73 the rate of authorizations accelerated and in 1974 the Plans were eliminated. They were replaced by a limit on branch numbers, based on each bank's own funds and on "consumption" of own funds per branch, according to a scale based on the population of the town or city in which they were located.[25] But these were not severe restrictions and over the next three years private sector banks' branch networks grew dramatically, by 35% in 1975, 20% in 1976 and 12% in 1977. In this three-year period, and counter to a generally poor economic situation, some 4,600 new bank branches were opened, and over the next five years, up to 1982, the rate of growth held steady at around 1,000 new branches per year. In comparison, the savings bank branch network, which was still subject to severe restrictions on geographical expansion, grew at a rate of less than 6% per annum in the period 1975-77.

This growth in the competitive capacity of the established banks made life a little harder, not only for the new banks but also for the established banks themselves: operating expenses rose from around 2.4% of total assets in the five years previous to the elimination of the Plans to 3.5% in 1979-80. In the following decade they adjusted downwards, but they never returned to their former levels. And this despite the fact that the new branches were cheaper to run in terms of staff: the number of employees per branch in the Spanish banking sector fell from around 25 in 1974 to fewer than 10 in 1985.[26]

The break-up of the status quo was a decisive factor in the crisis; the entry of foreign banks onto the Spanish market, an inevitable development since the 1962-63 opening-up process, was not. Competition from abroad arrived in 1978,[27] but with two severe restrictions that confined its role to the wholesale markets and to certain special products: the new foreign banks could not open more than three branches in Spanish territory (in fact many opened just one), and their non-interbank debt could not exceed 40% of their investment in loans and securities of Spanish companies, plus their liquidity coverage ratio assets. Nor could they hold shares or shareholdings, another prohibition typical of the time. Many foreign banks did enter the Spanish market (35 over the next decade), but their deposit market share never rose above 2%. Many of these banks never really took root in Spain, the most notorious example being the ten or so Japanese bank branches that closed, virtually unnoticed, in the 1990s. As a result of their dependence on interbank funding, they had to operate with floating-rate instruments, a technical revolution that would soon be copied, for good and bad, by the Spanish institutions, just as they copied all other financial innovations from abroad.

---

[25]   Decree 2245/1974.
[26]   Martínez Méndez (1991), Tables I.47 and I.38.
[27]   Royal Decree 1388/1978.

3.4   Deregulation of banking transaction terms

The deregulation of interest rates and banking transaction fees was a slow and cautious process that took the authorities 18 years to complete and was not without the occasional step backwards (see Box 1). It did not play an important role in the crisis. A different matter altogether is that troubled institutions, in their desperate search for funding, were particularly prone to disregarding the interest-rate ceilings, paying higher rates or formalizing as long-term deposits (already deregulated) products that promised liquidity on demand. These practices were widespread, and prompted more than one Ministerial Order or Banco de España Circular reminding the industry that the deposit-rate ceilings were still in force. For many years, an obligatory part of any inspection was to hunt out unlawfully high interest rates and unrecorded transactions.

Interbank terms were deregulated quite quickly: in 1964 a notified Ministerial Order freed rates in cross-transactions between institutions of the same kind, although the 4% ceiling on cross-transactions between institutions of different kinds (for example, between banks and savings banks) remained until 1969. The Banco de España was not granted the right to freely set interest rates on its liquidity-regulating transactions until much later, in 1977.

In the case of transactions with customers, deregulation began in 1969 with the creation of a mechanism that linked almost all lending and deposit rates to the Banco de España's bank or discount rate that was set by Orders of the Ministry of Finance.[28] An experiment in rationalization perhaps, but most certainly not a market mechanism. Nevertheless, the same regulatory package was the start of the approximation to the market, as it deregulated industrial and investment banks' two-year deposits, deposits in convertible pesetas at more than three months, deposits in foreign currency, and loans with maturity of more than three years. The aim was to extend the options open to industrial and investment banks and encourage long-term lending, while also acknowledging that foreign markets could not be run by administrative fiat.

The next step, four years later, was an ambiguous one. In 1973 two-year deposits were moved back into the regulated fold, but they were opened up to all banks and savings banks. As their official interest rate (6%) was one percentage point higher than that which these institutions could offer on one-year deposits, the readjustment represented, if not deregulation, then at least greater flexibility. In 1974 interest rates on two-year deposits were deregulated once more, and the regulator, by then disenchanted with the industrial and investment banks, opened up the right to issue certificates of deposit to all other institutions.

In 1977 the artificial bank-rate mechanism was done away with, one-year deposits were deregulated and rates on transactions eligible for inclusion in investment ratios moved

---

[28]   There were seven changes in the bank rate over the next nine years. In many cases, they interrupted the original margin schedule on the short side, as rate changes in demand deposits and savings accounts were more moderate than changes in the bank rate.

closer to market levels, although they continued to be set administratively. Financial policy broadened its scope to include the promotion of transparency, an area that would grow in importance and that led to the need to provide customers with accurate and detailed information on their transaction costs. TAE, the Spanish acronym for standardized annual rate, would soon become an everyday term.

Another four years passed before the next steps were taken. In 1981, lending rates were deregulated, save on loan transactions eligible for inclusion in investment ratios, as were six-month deposits of one million pesetas or more and deposit institutions' transactions with other financial institutions and local government. Fees and commissions not linked to loan transactions were also freed (fee schedules had to be published), and the Banco de España was authorized to regulate and supervise the transparency of transaction terms and to establish valuation and settlement standards.

The process culminated in 1987 when the last restrictions on interest rates and fees were removed, after a long interval that may have been due to the banking crisis. The complete deregulation of interest rates and transaction terms extended the responsibilities of the Banco de España as regards the overseeing of fee schedules and preparation of transparency rules. It was also entrusted with creating and managing a Claims Service, with pre-arbitral functions.

During this lengthy deregulation process, Spain witnessed a severe inflationary episode. As a result, lending and deposit rates soared, reaching their peak in 1980-81. Some interest rates reacted sharply to deregulation: for example, one-year bank deposit rates, which leapt from around 6% before 1977 to 10% in 1978. But in general, lending and deposit rates rose in parallel, so that, overall, interest rate spreads remained quite stable. Between 1970 and 1974, the difference between the average return on loan portfolios at private sector banks and the average cost of their deposits was around 3.3%.[29] Between 1975 and 1980, this difference widened to 4.5%, and then narrowed again, but in 1988, the first year following the completion of the deregulation process, it was still 4.2%. Thus, interest rate spreads were *wider* at the end of the process than they were before it started. Clearly, there are many other factors that affect spread movements apart from interest rate ceilings, but this trend suggests that lending and deposit wars were not widespread in the 1977-85 crisis, even though non-compliance with the limits still in force had an adverse impact on the accounts of the "problem banks", especially those of the industrial and investment banks.

---

[29] Martínez Méndez (1991), Table I.28.

BOX 1 INTEREST RATES AND FEES: THE LENGTHY DEREGULATION PROCESS

(Notified) Ministerial Order of 4 December 1964 (not published in the Official State Gazette)
- Interest rates on transactions between deposit institutions of the same class were deregulated. Those on transactions between institutions of different classes (e.g. banks and savings banks) were capped at 4%.

Ministerial Order of 21 July 1969
- The interest rate schedule was rationalized, linking rates to the Banco de España's bank (discount) rate via fixed margins. Under subsequent Ministerial Orders, the bank rate underwent the following changes: 21 March 1970: +1 (except for demand and savings deposits: +0.5); 21 January 1971: -0.25; 3 April 1971: -0.25; 21 October 1971: -1 (except for savings deposits: -0.5; and demand deposits which were left unchanged); 26 July 1973: +1 (except for demand deposits: +0.25; and savings deposits: +0.5); 9 August 1974: +1 (except for demand and savings deposits: +0.25); and 23 July 1977: +1.
- Deposits and certificates of deposit at more than two years were deregulated for industrial and investment banks, together with loans with maturity of more than three years, deposits in convertible pesetas at more than three months and deposits in foreign currency.
- In loan transactions, maximum rather than minimum limits were placed on interest rates and fees and commissions, but fee schedules remained unchanged.
- Competition was encouraged, with institutions required to publish prime rates below the maximum limits.

(Notified) Ministerial Order of 28 October 1969 (not published in the Official State Gazette)
- Interest rates between deposit institutions were deregulated (extended a year later to include securities funds).

Ministerial Order of 19 October 1971
- Interest payments were barred on any increases in convertible peseta accounts up to three months; this conjunctural measure was strengthened in 1973 (Ministerial Orders of 6 February and 16 March 1973).

Ministerial Order of 29 February 1972
- Fees for (non-credit) services became minimum levels. Interbank fees were deregulated.

Ministerial Order of 26 July 1973
- Interest rates on deposits at more than two years were set at 6% (no longer deregulated for industrial and investment banks) and these deposits were opened up to commercial and savings banks (whose deposits were previously capped – at one year – at 5%).

Ministerial Order of 9 August 1974
- Interest rates on deposits at more than two years were deregulated and commercial and savings banks were allowed to issue certificates of deposit (previously confined to industrial and investment banks).

- Institutions had to publish their maximum interest rates on deregulated transactions.

Ministerial Orders of 20 and 30 April 1977
- The link between short-term rates regulating liquidity at the Banco de España and the bank rate was eliminated. These short-term rates will be freely established by the Banco de España.

Ministerial Order of 23 July 1977
- All Banco de España rates, except for the discount rate, were deregulated.
- The link between bank interest rates and the bank rate was eliminated.
- Interest rates on deposits at one year or more were deregulated.
- The 1971 prohibitions on foreign accounts in pesetas were eliminated.
- The obligation to publish prime rates was eliminated.
- Institutions were required to provide customers with detailed information on transaction costs (Banco de España Circular 142 for banks and 24 for savings banks).
- Interest rates on transactions eligible for inclusion in investment ratios were moved closer to market levels, although they continued to be set administratively.

Decree 1851 of 10 July 1978
- Fees and commissions for placement and underwriting of fixed-income issues were deregulated.

Ministerial Order of 17 January 1981
- Interest rates on 6-month deposits of 1 million pesetas or more were deregulated (rates on smaller deposits were raised by 1 pp), but 4 pp penalties were set on early withdrawal of deposits and loans secured by deposits.
- Transactions between deposit institutions, other financial institutions and local government were deregulated.
- Interest rates on loans were deregulated, except for those included in investment ratios, but their fees and commissions were set as ceilings.
- Fees and commissions on services not linked to loan transactions were deregulated; publication of these fee schedules was made compulsory.
- Floating rate transactions became generally acceptable (these were initially tolerated for foreign banks).
- Powers over the transparency of transaction terms and valuation and settlement standards were granted to the Banco de España (materialized in its Circular 13/1981).

Banco de España Circular 2/1982
- The ceilings on the rate of discount of bills were brought into line with those on fixed-term deposit rates.

Ministerial Order of 3 March 1987
- The remaining deposit rate ceilings were eliminated.
- The caps on fees and commissions on loans were eliminated.
- Transparency was strengthened (also, Ministerial Order of 16 June 1988, Banco de España Circulars 15/1987 and 15/1988, Ministerial Order of 12 December 1988 and Banco de España Circular 8/1990).
- The Banco de España Claims Service was established.

3.5   Consequences of the crisis

3.5.1   Supervisory aims

In the early years and up to the mid-1970s, the supervisory authority's aims were largely in keeping with the role envisaged in the memorandum of the Credit and Banking Law: detection of breaches of the rules, and little else. Over time, this penalty-based approach evolved into a more financial approach, essentially focused on matters of financial health and solvency, as problem banks began to emerge. The changes made in the upper echelons of the Banco de España in 1977 were not unrelated to this change in focus, aims and even attitudes towards banking groups with high-risk profiles. Finally, despite its limited means, it was the supervisory authority that brought to light the cases deserving of intervention.

3.5.2   Resolution regime

In 1977 the Spanish supervisor suspected that a banking crisis was imminent, although naturally it could not foresee the eventual scale of the crisis. What are now known as resolution regimes had to be created, since commercial law provisions on bankruptcy and insolvency proceedings were insufficient or inappropriate to provide an orderly solution to the problems of deposit institutions. Neither the 1946 Banking Law (LOB) nor the Decree Law nationalizing the Banco de España envisaged precautionary measures for assumption of control of a problem institution. However, at that time not everyone shared the Banco de España's concern. The large banks, at least while the crisis was centered on small banks that they viewed as upstarts, were able to continue to uphold the "orthodox" view that bad banks and their imprudent customers should be allowed to fail.[30] Caught between these two points of view, for the government of the day problems had to be seen to be believed. Accordingly, resolution regimes and mechanisms were developed on a tentative and experimental basis, and they would only be completed when the crisis spread to larger banks, some with a long-standing tradition, revealing the extent of the distress to which the system was exposed.

The first step was the creation, in 1977, of the deposit guarantee funds (DGFs).[31] Originally constituted at the Banco de España, they had no legal personality. They were funded by their member institutions, with a one-off contribution of 1 per mil of their deposits, and by the Banco de España, which matched this amount, and guaranteed deposits up to 500,000 pesetas in the event of bankruptcy or insolvency. The contributions

---

[30]   Years later, the chairman of the Spanish Banking Association (AEB) continued to maintain that it would have been best to let the bad banks (including Rumasa and Banesto) fail, to obtain a healthy and efficient financial system; see Termes (1995), p. 193.

[31]   Royal Decrees 3047/1977 and 3048/1977, creating the Savings Bank and Bank DGFs. The Credit Union DGF appeared five years later (Royal Decree Law 18/1982).

were in the form of deposits at the Banco de España: deposits that were even eligible for inclusion in the depositing institutions' cash ratio, and that would not be classed as an accounting charge until they were used by the DGF to enforce the corresponding guarantees. The circumstances in which the DGFs could come into play were very limited. The authorities' aim was to prevent such extreme situations from arising; this was the main difference in approach between the Spanish Bank DGF and the US Federal Deposit Insurance Corporation (FDIC) on which it was modeled. However, after just two months in operation (but already facing crises at Banco de Navarra and Banco Cantábrico), these circumstances were extended to include situations representing the *threat* of insolvency, enabling the DGF to grant advances to banks in distress. In this first review, the supervisor was also authorized to order banks to take the necessary measures to re-establish their solvency levels, and to expel from the DGF any banks that refused to do so, a radical measure that was more a threat than a solution, as it would be their death knell.[32]

The lack of legal personality prevented the deposit guarantee funds from pursuing not only financial activities other than those envisaged in their regulations but also management activities. During the first phase of the crisis, a private law solution was employed to take control and assume the management of problem banks. In March 1978, Corporación Bancaria was created, a corporation jointly owned (50/50) by the banks and the Banco de España, which was to purchase the shares of problem banks, restore them to health and sell them on to other institutions as promptly as possible. It was allocated capital of 500 million pesetas, which would not permit many purchases, save at a symbolic price. However, at the same time, the Banco de España was authorized to suspend the management bodies of banks that were under threat and temporarily replace them with persons appointed by it, or alternatively, to appoint controllers to validate the acts of management of the institutions' own managers.[33] Thus, with the supervisory powers significantly strengthened, acquisitions were made at a symbolic price and Corporación Bancaria took control and assumed management of a handful of institutions. But in its first three years it was less successful in the second part of its mission, selling on institutions that it had restored to financial health: the large banks, which were the only potential buyers on the domestic market, showed no interest whatsoever.

The reticence of the private co-owners of Corporación Bancaria, and its limited financial resources in view of all the banking problems that were emerging, prompted the financial authority to take the next and decisive step in the design of the resolution regime. In 1980 the Bank DGF (FGDEB) was granted legal personality,[34] taking the form of a management

---

[32] Royal Decree 54/1978.

[33] Royal Decree Law 5/1978.

[34] Royal Decree Law 4/1980 and Royal Decree 567/1980. The Savings Bank DGF, with no immediate urgency, and the Credit Union DGF were both granted legal personality in 1982 (Royal Decree Law 18/1982). The reform of the Bank DGF had to be via Decree Law, as various provisions of the Spanish Corporations Law – on notice of call and quorum requirements at Shareholders' Meetings – were amended to facilitate operations involving reductions and subsequent increases in capital. The 1980 reform was preceded by a report from the Banco de España (sometimes known as the Boyer Report) to the Government, dated December 1979, on the causes of the crisis and the shortcomings of the existing solutions; for the conclusions of this report, see FGDEB (1980), p. 10.

company governed by a board on which the Banco de España and the private sector banks had equal representation but which was chaired by the Bank's Deputy Governor, with a casting vote. The Bank DGF was authorized to hold shares of problem banks and to participate in their capital increases; it was also authorized to purchase assets (for their nominal value, implying that the DGF would absorb their losses).[35] As a result, there was no longer any need for Corporación Bancaria. Initially, the management company used its services, but it soon preferred to act on its own behalf, absorbing the teams that had been trained by Corporación Bancaria, which eventually disappeared, several years later, when the lawsuits that inevitably accompany supervisory interventions concluded.

This reform also transformed the *one-off* contribution of 1 per mil into an *annual* contribution of the same amount. The deposit guarantee was raised to 750,000 pesetas, and to 1.5 million pesetas a year later. These moves assuaged public opinion, but were of little real significance when the policy was to save the institutions that had been intervened. In fact, throughout the crisis only two banks (the pioneer, Banco de Navarra, and Banco de los Pirineos) went bankrupt or saw insolvency proceedings filed, with the deposits guaranteed being paid by the Bank DGF.

Over the following three years, the regime resulting from this latest reform would resolve the banking sector's problems by means of reductions and subsequent increases in capital, as follows:

-   The supervisor would order the bank in question to take measures to re-establish its financial position within one month, something the institution could not do.
-   The bank would "voluntarily" sell its capital to the DGF for a symbolic price (one peseta), or for a price which, if not symbolic, was very low, in cases in which it was understood that there were "innocent" shareholders deserving of some level of protection.[36]
-   The institution, with a new management team, supplied initially by Corporación Bancaria and subsequently by the DGF, would be granted an aid program to restore its financial health. This could include a temporary exemption from meeting compulsory liquidity, cash and investment ratios.
-   A capital issue would be subscribed by the DGF.
-   Within one year, the institution, restored to financial health, would be sold, by restricted tender, to a suitable bank.

The Spanish banking sector's reluctance to buy banks resulting from this process faded when the DGF sold two banking licenses to foreign banks.

---

[35]   Royal Decree 1620/1981.

[36]   Capital was reduced by 99% or 100% in fifteen cases, by between 35% and 67% in eight cases and in three cases (subsidiary banks controlled through their parent institutions) there was no capital reduction; see FGDEB (1983).

Over the next few years the regime changed very little. The annual contribution to the Bank DGF was adjusted several times: it was first raised, to pay off the losses that had built up during the crisis, and in 1990 reached 2.5 per mil for the banks, although only half that figure for the Banco de España (which nevertheless retained its casting vote on the board); it was then reduced, when this objective had been met. The contributions to the Savings Bank and Credit Union DGFs were adjusted separately, according to their respective needs.

In 1996, Spain's entry into the EEC prompted a significant change in these contributions, to free the DGFs from the stigma of receiving State aid. All the DGFs' annual contributions were set at 2 per mil of the deposits covered, but the Banco de España's contribution was terminated; henceforth, it could only make contributions in exceptional circumstances and following approval by law. Moreover, it was established that contributions would be reduced when a DGF's net worth was sufficient to meet its objectives, and that they would be stopped completely when such net worth, minus the support programs to which it was committed, amounted to 1% of the deposits of its member institutions. The cover was raised to ECU 20,000 per account-holder, to comply with Community legislation.[37]

The regime described was not used to resolve the Rumasa case. DGFs do not generally have sufficient funds to absorb the problems of a large institution or group. This was the case in 1983, and again, ten years later, in the Banesto crisis. The solutions for the difficulties of so many leading US and European banks in the global crisis of 2007-08 also had to be sought beyond the confines of the established resolution channels.

The financial problems of the Rumasa group's banks were first detected in the mid-1970s. It was no secret that their lending was concentrated on group companies, that the banks, which had been acquired via crossed loans, lacked real capital and that, in a desperate search for funds, unlawfully high interest rates were being paid. Capitalization of interest was rife at companies that were in no position to pay. But Rumasa obstructed the ordinary inspection procedures, and consolidation of accounts, which would have revealed the stark reality of the problems and would have provided the legal grounds for immediate intervention, was not compulsory under the legislation in force at the time. Attempts were made via the audit procedure: in January 1982, the Bank DGF filed (Notarial) requests for audits of 18 of the group's banks and of group companies whose solvency could affect that of the banks. In February 1983 no audits had been received. The requests were repeated, this time to be received within one month, but before this period had elapsed the Government expropriated all the shares of the group companies, "considering of public utility and in the social interest the defense of the stability of the financial system and the legitimate interests of deposit-holders, employees and third parties".[38] The operation was financed by the State by means of an extraordinary debt issue subscribed by the banking sector. The DGF made no asset purchases and extended no credit lines, although its services were used to manage the expropriated banks.

---

[37] Royal Decree 2606/1996, which transposed Directive 1994/19/EC.
[38] Royal Decree 2/1983.

The solution to the problem also lay beyond the confines of the normal channels. The expropriation of Rumasa had created widespread fear that Spain's new socialist government could be intent on nationalization, but this fear was dissipated when the group was rapidly reprivatized.[39] Two of the expropriated banks, which were only marginally contaminated by the group's problems, were sold off, one to a medium-sized bank with which it had traditional ties, and the other to a small consortium including several foreign banks. The rest were sold, in 1984, en bloc to a consortium of 14 banks comprising all Spain's large and medium-sized banks plus a few smaller ones. By means of subsequent, strictly commercial, transactions, these banks were ultimately incorporated into the "big seven" banking groups.

A belated consequence of the financial crisis was the review of the procedures for sanctions and intervention of credit institutions, contained in the 1988 Banking Discipline and Intervention Law (LDI).[40] The supervisors had criticized the defects and shortcomings of the sanctions regime throughout the crisis.[41] On occasions, as was acknowledged in the preamble to the Law, the principle of legality could fail (in the allocation of sanctioning powers to the authorities and the supervisor, in the precise typification of infringements). In any case, the pertinent legislation extended across an array of sectoral rules that were uncoordinated and had legal loopholes. The new Law, which covered all credit institutions, provided a detailed definition of infringements, the corresponding sanctions and procedural rules, and indicated which authority was competent to apply such sanctions and rules, in all cases under proposals by the Banco de España. The Law also envisaged two circumstances in which the Banco de España could take control of an institution or provisionally replace its management bodies: in exceptionally serious situations as regards the stability, liquidity or solvency of an institution; and in cases in which it is impossible to deduce an institution's situation from its accounts and there is sound evidence of an exceptionally serious situation.

3.5.3 Conservative accounting rules

Initially, the Banco de España could request specific information from the private sector banks for its inspection purposes, but both the public and confidential financial reporting formats (the latter for the eyes of the supervisor only) were established by Ministerial Order; a balance sheet breakdown of something as innocuous as, for example, short-term bonds, needed Ministerial approval.

In 1968, when new monthly balance sheet and annual financial statement reporting formats were introduced, the Ministry of Finance authorized the Bank to define the content and significance of the different headings, and to create subheadings in the confidential formats.[42] This

---

[39] Banco Exterior and the official credit institutions were also privatized by socialist governments in the 1990s.
[40] Law 26/1988.
[41] See, for example, De Juan (1983).
[42] Ministerial Order of 1 July 1968.

authorization, which was extended some twenty years later,[43] prompted extensive regulatory activity, both in statistical aims (monitoring the development and generation of monetary and credit variables) and supervisory aims (monitoring the financial position of institutions, controlling their regulatory obligations and legal limits). Highly prudent valuation standards were applied; indeed, they are a distinctive feature of Spanish accounting rules, even after their adjustment to current international accounting standards which do not accept the old prudential valuation criteria. When they were first introduced, and in each subsequent review, these standards were accepted with reluctance by the institutions and their management bodies, which argued that it would make them less competitive than their foreign peers. This has proved otherwise, and the prudent approach established in the Banco de España circulars has given compliant institutions added strength in times of crisis.

The prudential approach pervades the credit risk provisioning rules. When the 1977-85 crisis first began to unfold, supervisory activity revealed that banks were reluctant to recognize doubtful debts and to set aside provisions to meet potential losses. Apart from the most obvious cases of non-performing loans, these situations were not sufficiently well defined in the accounting rules of the day, with the institutions themselves left to assess probable losses.[44] All institutions erred on the side of optimism regarding their risk quality and the adjustments needed; however, at the troubled institutions, these accounting failings were becoming more severe.

In response, in 1978 the Banco de España published what came to be known as the "pastoral circular" (in fact it was actually two circulars, as the banks and savings banks still had different accounting regimes).[45] The accrual accounting principle was introduced, together with the suspension of this principle for doubtful assets, to prevent the attendant interest from being included in results until it was actually collected, and the circumstances in which assets were to be defined as doubtful were established. The general criterion whereby losses were to be valued individually on a case-by-case basis was maintained, but another, more objective rule, depending not on a subjective and questionable valuation but rather on a verifiable fact, was added to this orthodox criterion, namely the time elapsed since the obligation became past due.[46] Default would automatically require provisions to be

---

[43] Article 48.1 of the 1988 Banking Discipline and Intervention Law (LDI), empowering the Ministry of Economy and Finance to establish accounting standards for credit institutions, authorized it to delegate this power to the Banco de España. The Ministerial Order of 31 March 1989 did so, with a broad criterion, establishing that the central bank's accounting regulations would replace any other such regulations (for example, those contained in the General Charts of Accounts) for the institutions under its control, requiring no more than a non-binding prior consultation to the Spanish Institute of Accounting and Auditing (ICAC). For more details on the Banco de España's accounting rules, and especially its provisioning rules, by someone who was closely involved with them for many years, see Prado (2002), pp. 45-93.

[44] This situation was not remedied by the Banco de España's first major accounting circular (35/1968), which included very little information on non-performing loans. In fact it did not even stipulate that provisions be charged to the income statement; instead, they figured as an application of earnings.

[45] Banco de España Circular 157 on banks and Banco de España Circular 39 on savings banks, both of 15 December 1978.

[46] Default is a legal concept, arising when a credit obligation, whether principal or interest, is past due more than 90 days; this grace period is designed to rule out any trivial or easily remedied situations.

set aside: minimum percentages according to the time elapsed, based not on statistical calculations, which were still impossible at the time, but on a conventional scale designed by the regulator. This mechanical and effective rule would settle previously unsolvable disputes between bank examiners and accounting managers on the opportuneness of the provisions made (disputes in which the latter pleaded their greater understanding of the real situation of their portfolios). But it would not be the end of the matter. Credit institutions would soon discover how to rearrange their past-due transactions so as to record them as current. In 1980, admissibility criteria for rearrangements had to be introduced to put an end to these schemes.

The initial impact of this regulation, and of many other subsequent measures introduced to strengthen it or to meet other contingencies, was tempered by the lengthy adaptation periods. This refutes the accusation that these accounting rules were designed to camouflage results for political reasons in years in which they were too high.

The essential principle of the specific provisioning regime established in the 1978 "pastoral circulars" remains today, following subsequent adjustments and refinements (see Box 2). In 1982, in light of the economic crisis, the schedule was tightened, the system was strengthened (introducing a minimum provision of 1.5% of the banking book and unsecured off-balance-sheet risks) and the "drag criterion" (whereby default on a certain number of loan repayments would drag the entire balance outstanding into default) was added. But the calculation basis of the provisions was refined, excluding, for example, transactions with State guarantees.[47]

---

[47] Implicitly in 1982 (and then explicitly in 1983), the Ministry of Finance admitted as tax deductible expenses, loan-loss provisions made in accordance with the criteria established in the Banco de España's accounting circulars, thus abating credit institutions' criticisms of the specific provisioning regime.

BOX 2   HISTORY OF COMPULSORY LOAN PROVISIONING.
MINIMUM LEVELS

BE Circular of 1 October 1978 (adaptation period: up to 1981)

Months in default	6 to 12	>12 to 18	>18 to 24	>24
General	25	50	75	80

Mortgage loans are exempt.

BE Circular 1/1982 of 26 January 1982 (adaptation period: up to 1986)

Months in default	3 to 9	>9 to 15	>12 to 18	>18
General	25	50	75	100

A minimum of 1.5% is set for all lending and unsecured off-balance-sheet transactions. A minimum of 25% is set for all other doubtful loans.

BE Circular 25/1987 of 20 October 1987 (adaptation period: initially up to 1989, later shortened to 1988)

Months in default	6 to 12	>12 to 18	>18 to 21	>21
General	25	50	75	100

Years in default	3 to 4	>4 to 5	>5 to 6	>6
Mortgage loans	25	50	75	100

The 1.5% minimum is replaced by a general provision of 1% (0.5% for mortgage loans).

BE Circular 9/1999 of 17 December 1999

Months in default	3 to 6	>6 to 12	>12 to 18	>18 to 21	>21
General	10	25	50	75	100

No changes in the mortgage scale, but the general scale is applied if the LTV ratio is over 80%. Incorrectly documented loans: 10%.

BE Circular 4/2004 of 22 December 2004

Months in default	Up to 6	>6 to 12	>12 to 18	>18 to 24	>24
Corporate loans	5.3	27.8	65.1	95.8	100
Secured corporate loans	4.5	23.6	55.3	81.4	100
Other customer loans	4.5	27.4	60.5	93.3	100
Secured other customer loans	3.8	23.3	47.2	79.3	100

Years in default	Up to 3	>3 to 4	>4 to 5	>5 to 6	>6
Mortgage loans	2	25	50	75	100

Foreclosed real estate assets are exempt from provisions, but a cost of sale of 30% is assumed.
The general provision is eliminated. The subprime risk category is introduced: 10% provision for non-documented risks and at least the generic rate (see section 6 below) for all others.
A minimum of 25% is set for other doubtful loans.

BE Circular 3/2010 of 29 June 2010

Months in default	Up to 6	>6 to 9	>9 to 12	>12
All exposures	25	50	75	100

Provisions apply to the part of loans not covered by collateral, which is taken not at its full value but at the following percentages:
- Completed housing that is the main residence of the borrower: 80%.
- Rural non-development land and completed offices, commercial and multipurpose industrial premises: 70%.
- Other completed housing: 60%.
- Other real estate assets: 50%.
- Pledges: 90% of the fair value of the asset pledged.
Foreclosed real estate assets, whose carrying amount cannot exceed that of the assets applied (at amortized cost, taking into account loan loss impairment), require provisions of 10% during their first year on the balance sheet, 20% during the second year and 30% thereafter.

In 1987 the general schedule was relaxed and a new schedule was introduced for residential mortgage loans or similar (previously exempt). This second schedule was more lenient, coming into effect only after three years of default; the fact that it obliged institutions to provision 100% after six years, even though total loss on residential mortgages seems unlikely, should be viewed as a way of penalizing institutions for the lack of interest shown in recovering non-performing loans, or as a cautionary measure in light of any potential hidden difficulties that might impede realization of the collateral. The drag effect was also extended: borrowers defaulting on any of their loans by more than 25% of their aggregate total would find all their positions classed as doubtful. Insufficient documentation too became cause for provisioning. Several conventional minimum provisioning criteria for doubtful debts for reasons other than default were added and, lastly, the minimum provision of 1.5% was replaced by a supplementary provision of 1% (0.5% for mortgage loans).

The statistical provision (analysed below) was introduced in 1999, when the regime was tightened further, establishing provisions for amounts that were three months past due. In addition, residential mortgages with loan-to-value (LTV) ratios over 80% became subject to the general schedule rather than the more lenient mortgage schedule, in what proved to be a rather unsuccessful attempt to put a stop to overly leveraged transactions.[48]

In 2004, the adaptation of Spanish accounting rules to international accounting standards, which were still based on the "orthodox" approach to valuation adjustments in impaired assets, signified conceptual difficulties for the Banco de España's provisioning criteria. But the Bank resolved to maintain the prudent accounting policy that had served it so well, and kept the regulatory provisions based on time past due, but with further refinements.[49] First, it drew more distinctions in the provisioning levels, which were slightly higher for firms (especially in the case of amounts that had been past due longer) than for other customers, and slightly higher for unsecured transactions than for transactions secured other than with residential mortgages. Second, the percentages applied were no longer round numbers (multiples of 25), but were taken from statistical estimates based on Central Credit Register (CCR) data. The traditional scale was maintained for residential mortgages, plus a small 2% provision for mortgage default up to three years, and the general 1% provision disappeared, to be included in a revised statistical provision.

The treatment of country risk followed a similar pattern. It was first introduced by the supervisory authority in 1984,[50] also in response to a crisis, but in this case an

---

[48]   At end-2009, mortgages with LTV ratios over 80% represented 19.1% of all residential mortgages held with Spanish credit institutions, according to the Banco de España (2010), Table 2.3.D.

[49]   This conceptual polemic is reflected in Banco de España Circular 4/2004. The main body of the text states that the present value of a financial asset (and thus its impairment in respect of its contractual value) is obtained from the future cash flows estimated by the institution, an orthodox approach described in great detail (Rule 29). But there follows a short paragraph which adds that in the case of credit exposures, the methods and criteria set out in Annex IX shall apply, and it is this Annex, which in practice annuls the provisions of Rule 29, that contains all the singularities of the Spanish system on credit risk provisioning (specific and general) and country risk provisioning.

[50]   Banco de España Circular 34 of 16 October 1984.

international one: the first payments crisis in emerging economies, which was affecting the growing activities of Spanish banks in Latin America. Other supervisors chose to compile lists of doubtful countries and demand conventional country-risk provisioning, but the Spanish regulator adopted a more diplomatic approach, preferring to draw up a series of highly-detailed criteria and circumstances that enabled the banks to group the different countries into six categories. The last such category (non-performing loans) required total immediate coverage. The preceding three categories, in ascending order of doubt, required provisions of 5%, 10% and 20%; in this last case, the highly doubtful category, with a schedule that raised coverage to 100% in year 5, with suspension of the accrual criterion. Naturally, bank examiners had their own informed criteria on country risk and could discuss with the banks any classifications deemed inappropriate.

Over the next three years, as the debt crisis unfolded, provisioning levels were tightened, rising to 15%, 20% and 50% from the outset, plus a schedule that raised provisions in the doubtful and highly doubtful categories to 35% and 90%, respectively, after two years. In addition, suspension of the accrual criterion became applicable to all three categories subject to provisioning.[51] Moreover, a minimum provision of 35% was added to the total risk of these three categories, a simple formula that for some time enjoyed considerable prestige among international supervisors. But this minimum provision did not fit well into the overall design of the country risk provisions and in 1997 it was eliminated.

The criteria and circumstances for classifying countries were fine tuned on many occasions, but the country risk coverage schedule was finally simplified in the 2004 accounting reform. Problem countries were classified using broad economic criteria[52] and the provisioning schedule was tempered (these were boom years virtually across the globe), with provisions set at 10.1% (countries with temporary difficulties), 22.8% (doubtful countries) and 83.5% (highly doubtful countries) and no upward scales.

The calls for prudent accounting during and after the banking crisis of 1977-85 were not confined to credit risk. Since 1980 the circulars had been advising of the need, where appropriate, for credit institutions to set aside the actuarial provisions required to meet pension supplements. In 1986 the recommendations became compulsory for pension commitments to retired employees, and a year later for commitments to current employees,[53] in both cases with very generous adaptation periods.

---

[51] Banco de España Circulars 22/1985 of 3 December 1985, 8/1986 of 28 April 1986 and 26/1987 of 20 October 1987.

[52] With one exception. Previously, the two categories of countries with sound economies included, respectively, those classified as such for the purposes of export credit insurance, and all others regarding which there were no grounds for doubt (Banco de España Circular 4/1991). Circular 4/2004 replaced the export credit insurance criterion with a list that includes Norway, Switzerland, Iceland, the US, Canada, Japan, Australia, New Zealand and the EU Member States; this list has not been amended.

[53] Banco de España Circulars 15/1986 of 23 September 1986 and 11/1987 of 13 March 1987.

Regarding banks' annual results and dividends, the Banco de España has always favored a policy of discussion with the banks, employing moral suasion, with recommendations also based on prudential criteria.[54]

3.5.4   A novel capital requirements policy

Although since 1921 Spanish banking legislation had permitted the creation of a guarantee ratio, it was not actually established until 1963 for industrial and investment banks, followed by all other banks (1974), savings banks (1975) and credit unions (1979).[55] This first ratio was a minimum of 8% (10% for industrial and investment banks) for the quotient between own funds (paid-up capital and recorded reserves) and non-interbank deposits and short-term bonds, calculated on a solo basis; it was not a leverage ratio (nor its reciprocal), as significant elements of funding, such as interbank funding, were excluded from the denominator. When the crisis erupted the guarantee ratio was a relative novelty: for banks the adaptation period ran through 1978, while for credit unions the ratio was still a thing of the future.

In 1985 the equivalent of a risk-weighted ratio was introduced as the centerpiece of the solvency rules,[56] based on the assumed risk level of the various asset and off-balance-sheet exposures. For the next seven years this was complemented by a simple ratio (redefined as the minimum proportion between own funds and non-weighted real and financial investments), of minor significance. The new system was inspired by the formulas used by the more advanced supervisory regimes, and by the preparatory work for what would become Basel I and the 1989 European Solvency Directive. The influence from abroad meant that subordinated debt, which was nonexistent in Spain at that time, was added to own funds. In turn, the Spanish rules included some stricter and some interesting new features all of their own, many of which had to go when they were adapted to Community rules.

Risk categories were established, not dissimilar to the subsequent Basel and European rules (see Table 1). The solvency requirements were also similar, especially after the ratios were reviewed by the Banco de España in 1989. As in the case of the provisioning

---

[54]   Another application of the prudent approach: before being adapted to international accounting standards, goodwill amortization periods were less generous (but not unjustifiably so) under Spanish accounting rules than in other countries.

[55]   Ministerial Orders of 21 May 1963 and 9 August 1974, Decree 1838/1975 and Ministerial Order of 26 February 1979. Since 1971, the branching regulations penalized banks with ratios of own to borrowed funds below 8%. The so-called "guarantee ratio" at the savings banks was, strictly speaking, no such thing, but rather a mechanism to establish the part of the surplus to be carried to reserves. The Banco de España was authorized to adjust the ratio for the banks between 7% and 10%, but it did not do so.

[56]   Law 13/1985, Royal Decrees 1370/1985 and 1371/1985 and Banco de España Circular 28/85 of 29 October 1985. This new regime was first applied only to deposit institutions. Four years later, by means of Royal Decree 1044/1989, it was extended to public sector banks and specialized lending institutions. Note the paradox that public sector banks' debt with other banks was classed as sovereign risk, while at the same time they were required to meet the solvency ratio.

TABLE 1	SOLVENCY REQUIREMENTS. 1985-1992 (as % of risk)

Type of risk	Range	1985	1989
Cash, Banco de España, Spanish public sector and official credit institutions, *RENFE (Spanish national railways)*, assets guaranteed by these entities, monetary collateral loans, *forward foreign currency purchases, undrawn credit lines*	0 to 0.75	0.25	0.25
Credit institutions (excluding shareholdings), OECD member country central banks and governments, international financial organizations, assets insured by CESCE (Spanish export credit insurance corporation), documentary credit, *50% of forward purchases and sales of financial assets*	0.5 to 1.5	1	1.25
Mortgages (excluding those on operating assets), loans secured by pledge or listed securities, loans guaranteed by Spanish or OECD member credit institutions, *or by mutual guarantee companies,* companies with majority State capital, technical guarantees, *undrawn commercial paper credit lines, leasing of housing and multipurpose commercial premises*	2 to 4	3	3.75
All other lending (including rediscounted or doubtful) and fixed-income securities (except for subordinated bonds), all other *leasing,* guarantees, transactions in progress, foreclosed real estate assets (for five years), *the part of guaranteed or secured risks that exceeds the value of the guarantee or collateral, open foreign currency positions, sale of unhedged options,* miscellaneous items	5 to 8	6	7.5
Shares or shareholdings and subordinated debt (except for that issued by credit institutions)	5 to 16	8	16
Real assets, bank shares, *savings banks' equity units (cuotas participativas),* contributions to credit unions, subordinated debt issued by credit institutions, *leasing to non-consolidable group companies, loans to employees for purchase of bank or group shares*	10 to 35	25	35
Fictitious assets not deducted from own funds, *loans to third parties for purchase of bank or group shares*	100	100	100
MEMORANDUM ITEM: General (simple) ratio	4 to 6	4	5

Classification according to Banco de España Circular 19/1989; the items in italics were not included in Royal Decree 1370/1985.

legislation, the system was introduced with a set of relatively unexacting requirements and long adaptation periods (three years), to take into account possible differences between the starting positions of different institutions, and was subsequently tightened.[57] In 1989 the ratio applicable to standard risk-weighted positions, initially set at 6%, was raised to 7.5%, nearing the Basel I ratio of 8%.

The requirements were stricter than international standards in the case of: shares and shareholdings, with a ratio of 16% in 1989; subordinated debt and holdings in other banks, together with certain intra-group transactions, with a ratio of 35%, also applicable to real assets; and funding extended to third parties for acquisition of the bank's own shares, with a ratio of 100% (in this case, to prevent disguised treasury stock holdings: at international

---

[57]   Banco de España Circular 19/89 of 13 December 1989. This circular recast several specific amendments, as a result of the growing importance of certain transactions not included in the initial breakdown, specific concerns arising from supervisory experience and pressure from the relevant sectors.

TABLE 2	SOLVENCY RATIO MULTIPLIERS DUE TO RISK CONCENTRATION. 1985-1992

A) 1985-1987

Exposures as percentage of total assets	General	Non-consolidable group companies
Up to 1.25	—	2
From 1.25 to 2.5	2	3
From 2.5 to 5	3	4
From 5 to 7.5	4	6
Over 7.5	4	10

B) 1987-1992

Exposures as percentage of own funds	General	Non-consolidable group companies
Up to 15	—	2
Over 15	2	3
Over 30	3	5

supervisory fora this is known as the "Spanish rule"). Under Basel I all these were subject to the standard 8% ratio, although in the case of capital instruments of other banks, countries could choose to deduct them from own funds if they exceeded certain limits; this was the choice made by the EEC.

Another new feature was the introduction of surcharges on high exposures. In the 1985 version, ratios could increase by up to four times if exposure to a person, company or economic group exceeded certain percentages of a credit institution's total assets. In the case of a non-consolidable company in the credit institution's group, the multipliers were calculated from the first peseta of risk and rose to a maximum of 10 (see Table 2); the memory of Rumasa was still very fresh. In 1987, these surcharges were redefined on the basis of own funds and became less progressive, with maximum multipliers of three (general exposures) and five (exposures to non-consolidable group companies).[58]

Both the risk-weighted and simple ratios were calculated on banking groups' consolidated accounts, with no solo obligations for group members. In the 1985 regulations, the consolidation framework referred to a "banking group" comprising at least one deposit institution and "financial institutions"; these included holding companies, the various kinds of finance companies and instrumental companies for real estate and other tangible asset holdings, expressly excluding insurance companies. There was no mention of investment services firms, since they were only created three years later with the securities market reform.[59] The requisite for consolidation was the existence of decision-making unity, i.e.

---

[58]   Royal Decree 1549/1987. The change in definition was suggested by the technique employed in a Commission Recommendation of 1987 on large exposures.

[59]   Law 24/1988.

when a deposit institution controls all the other institutions or is controlled by them, and also when deposit institutions and finance companies are controlled by persons or entities that do not belong to the consolidation framework and should not therefore be consolidated. This was, at the time, another singularity of Spanish legislation. Naturally, control exists when there is a majority stake in capital or a majority of voting rights, by virtue of express agreements with other shareholders. But decision-making unity may also exist, thus making consolidation compulsory, in the case of non-majority stakes that exceed a minimum threshold (set in the regulations at 20%).

The 1985 prudential regulations had their own, not especially severe, remedy against solvency deficits; deficits over 20% required that all profit be transferred to reserves; in the case of deficits below that limit, any distribution of profit (and branch openings) required the prior authorization of the supervisor.

4 Adapting to Europe

When Spain joined the European Economic Community (EEC), European banking legislation was still embryonic. The acquis communautaire consisted solely of:

-   A number of general principles on freedom of establishment and non-discrimination between nationals of the Member States.
-   Condemnation of discretionary powers (euphemistically called the "economic needs of the market" criterion) in the granting of banking licenses, in exchange for a series of rather vague demands for sufficient own funds and suitable senior management.[60]
-   Mandatory supervision of credit institutions on a consolidated basis, as a result of which, subject to guarantees of professional secrecy, supervisory authorities were required to share the information needed to monitor cross-border groups.

Spain's entry into the EEC prompted changes in Spanish banking legislation,[61] but the Spanish negotiators were unwilling to suddenly surrender what was left of the status quo. Hence the long seven-year transition period, during which time the "economic needs of the market" criterion could still be applied, and subsidiaries and branches of other Member States' banks remained subject to restrictions on branch openings and domestic market funding. These restrictions were gradually lifted in accordance with a complex schedule. Spain's demands had a good precedent in the First Council Directive, which was full of options for deferral and exceptions favoring local whims (the Spanish exception was the Official Credit Institute, minus subsidiaries). In practice, however, the schedule negotiated

---

[60]   First Council Directive 77/780/EEC.
[61]   Royal Decree Law 1298/1986.

was unnecessary, as most foreign banks that entered the Spanish market showed little interest in the retail segment and made little use of the growth avenues that gradually opened up to them, both during and following the transition period.

In all other respects, the adjustment caused no major difficulties. Likewise, the new Community directives and recommendations on financial statements, large exposures and deposit-guarantee systems issued in subsequent years. One immediate consequence of the incorporation of Community law was that it intensified the incipient trend in favor of applying the same treatment and one set of rules to all credit institutions alike.[62]

The main legislative impetus for the creation of a common banking market came in the form of the Second Directive and the Solvency Directive, both of which appeared during the Spanish presidency in 1989.[63] The Second Directive created the "single passport", which allows an institution holding a banking license in one Member State to provide banking services, with or without a physical establishment, in any other Member State, subject only to administrative formalities. In exchange, minimum prudential standards were introduced, supervisory powers over cross-border institutions were established and cooperation between supervisory authorities was envisaged, although over the next decade it would prove to be quite ineffective.[64] In order to obtain and keep their banking licenses, institutions had to meet an undemanding capital requirement (ECU 5 million, which could be reduced to ECU 1 million at the discretion of each Member State) and have suitable principal shareholders. The suitability defined in the Second Directive for senior managers (capacity to ensure sound and prudent management) is, unfortunately, difficult to assess *ex ante*. In the Spanish transposition, the initial capital required both of banks and savings banks was significantly higher (3 billion pesetas),[65] and suitability was translated as good repute (respect for commercial and financial law and for good commercial, financial and banking practice, along with no criminal record for a series of related offences), knowledge, and experience (minimum of five years' senior management experience).[66]

Since the single banking market came into being, the number of foreign banks operating in Spain has risen almost continuously and now totals more than 100. Most of the first arrivals were subsidiaries (acquired in the resolution processes of the 1977-85 crisis or created from scratch), and then later branches (see Table 3), a more flexible arrangement. However, their penetration level remains low: after 30 years in Spain, foreign banks have a deposit market share of some 4.5% and a loan market share of around 8%. The strong

---

[62]   For example, Banco de España Circular 4/1991, which transposed the Financial Statements Directive, was a single text applicable to all credit institutions.

[63]   Second Council Directive 89/646/EEC and Council Directive 89/647/EEC.

[64]   The supervisory authorities were linked through a network of memorandums of understanding that had no legal value and little practical relevance. Only once, in the case of the Bank of Credit and Commerce International (BCCI), was a precedent set for the future colleges of supervisors, but even this did not prevent a widely-heralded failure.

[65]   Royal Decree 1245/1995.

[66]   Royal Decree 1144/1988.

TABLE 3   INSTITUTIONS SUPERVISED BY THE BANCO DE ESPAÑA

	1982	1993	1998	2005	2009
Spanish banks (a)	104	90	76	53	48
Foreign banks	32	78	77	87	106
Of which: subsidiaries	*4*	*22*	*24*	*22*	*17*
Savings banks	83	51	51	47	46
Credit unions	154	100	97	85	83
Money market companies	7	2	—	—	—
Specialized credit institutions	476	221	103	78	69
Electronic money institutions	—	—	—	—	1
Subtotal: CREDIT INSTITUTIONS	**856**	**542**	**404**	**350**	**353**
Credit institutions, excluding branches of foreign banks	*828*	*486*	*351*	*285*	*264*
Mutual guarantee companies	23	28	24	23	24
Reguarantee companies	—	—	1	1	1
Currency-exchange bureaux	na	na	(10)	57	63
Appraisal companies	na	na	106	58	54
TOTAL			**(545)**	**489**	**494**

SOURCES: 1982 and 1993, Termes (1995); 1998 to 2008, Banco de España, Banking Supervision (various dates).

a. Includes the public sector banks (official credit institutions, Caja Postal and Banco Exterior).

competitive pressure exerted by Spanish institutions prevents them from making gains in the retail segment; rather, their interest seems to lie in cornering specific niche markets.

It is also market saturation, rather than the severity of the regulations on market entrants, that explains the limited number of applications for authorization for new Spanish banks (none at all for savings banks) and for other credit institutions in the last three decades. Together with the concentration processes analysed in the next section, this has prompted a sharp drop in the number of Spanish credit institutions.

The most important European prudential standard was the Solvency Directive, a minimum standard that allowed Member States to adopt stricter rules. In the Spanish transposition,[67] the regulator took advantage of this option in the definition of own funds,

---

[67]   Law 13/1992, Royal Decree 1343/1992, Ministerial Order of 30 December 1992 and Banco de España Circular 5/93 of 26 March 1993. It should be noted, incidentally, that the regulatory powers of the Banco de España in prudential matters are in practice quite limited (despite being recognized in Law 13/1994, the Law of Autonomy of the Banco de España); in other countries, most implementation of this (highly technical) legislation is left to the supervisory authorities. The exception is the accounting legislation where, as has been seen, the Bank has full regulatory powers. In the case of important issues, this results in a long series of regulations (laws passed by parliament, decrees passed by the government, possibly ministerial orders and Banco de España circulars) that have meant that Spain has frequently failed to comply with the deadlines for transposing banking directives. The Solvency Directive is a perfect example, as the deadline for transposition into national law was 1 January 1991. However there was an upside to this delay, as when it was finally transposed it also included the new directive on supervision on a consolidated basis (Council Directive 92/30/EEC) and, in advance, a new directive that was soon to be approved on large exposures (Council Directive 92/121/EEC of 21 December 1992), and even one which, several months later, would cover market risk.

excluding certain minor items of negligible value and, most importantly, adding in, or conserving from previous legislation, certain significant deductions.[68] Conversely, it did not take advantage of the possibility to tighten either the weightings table or general capital requirements, signifying that the high weightings applied in 1985 to shares and shareholdings, intra-group transactions, tangible fixed assets and concentrations were eliminated. Accordingly, when the Spanish solvency ratio was adapted to Community law, capital requirements were weakened somewhat, but only in theory, as in practice Spanish credit institutions continued to post solvency levels well in excess of the minimum requirements. Long term, however, capital quality did deteriorate, due to the proliferation of subordinated and hybrid debt.

Spain adopted a novel approach to consolidation. Groups of credit institutions were defined in broad but orthodox terms in accordance with Community law, and groups of securities dealers and brokers and of insurers were regulated, each with their respective solvency requirements on a consolidated basis. But mixed groups, comprising institutions of different kinds, including insurers, were also regulated and made subject to solvency requirements, with original formulas combining the different prudential regimes. Thus, a bank owning an insurance company would be subject to a dual capital requirement, as a banking group and as a mixed group. These regulations, introduced in 1992, were designed to deal with the problem of complex financial conglomerates, ten years ahead of the corresponding Community legislation.[69] For its part, Basel has still not addressed this problem.

Credit risk was the main focus of the Spanish solvency regulations of 1985 and the Community regulations of 1989. Market risk was included in the Community regulations in two stages: in 1993, when standardized risk-management methods were introduced; and in 1998, when internal models, developed by the institutions themselves, were added.[70] This risk had to be covered, but the traditional value-at-risk (VAR) methods, even with the supposedly rigorous safety margins added by the regulators, would prove insufficient. It was revised by Basel II in 2005, seeking to enhance the management of credit risk embedded in trading book instruments, and again, across the board, in 2009, following the onset of the severe international crisis.

The Spanish transposition of the market risk regulation was faithful to the Directives, with one exception. A selective reading was made in the case of counterparty and position

---

[68] Treasury stock held through front men or disguised as sales with a buyback option, loans to third parties for purchase of an institution's own capital instruments, instruments held by non-consolidable subsidiaries up to the extent of their stakes, loans or guarantees to these subsidiaries, shortfalls in provisions or allocation funds. On transposition of the Solvency Directive, see Poveda (2010), Ch. 2, VI.

[69] Directive 2002/87/EC.

[70] Council Directive 93/6/EEC and Directive 98/31/EC. The 1993 Directive copied a draft recommendation of the Basel Committee that did not envisage internal methods, which were a source of serious concern for the supervisors. The Directive was issued because the EEC, which was regulating investment services, urgently needed some form of regulation of the trading book, which was their predominant financial activity. It was three more years before the Basel text appeared, time enough for the large US and UK banks to convince their authorities of the value of their models. The Directives were amended, with no haste, to adapt to the new Basel criteria.

risks, initially opting for the standardized methods; the internal models were not admitted until 2003.[71] It was more conservative on positions in stocks, where the Banco de España decided not to apply some optional reductions permitted by Brussels (and that were eliminated following the onset of the crisis), but it was more lenient in the specific case of covered bonds, which already received favorable credit risk management treatment.

Banking policy in the EU in the past decade has gradually evolved from a set of minimum prudential standards that the Member States could tighten if they deemed appropriate, to a set of single standards with no margin for stricter options. Spanish regulations were both the pioneers and the most conservative in matters such as consolidation or dynamic provisioning; in the future, this will be more difficult.

5   From the remodeling of the banking system to the Banesto crisis

To a certain extent, the other main problem faced by the Spanish banking sector – the Banesto crisis – was a distant consequence of the policy of concentration of the large banks that had been backed by the Spanish financial authorities since the mid-1980s. There are numerous possible reasons for this backing, ranging from a purely defensive stance, seeking to protect the Spanish institutions from colonization by foreign banks (an approach adopted, for example, by the Italian authorities), to the most ambitious approach, aiming to create Spanish banking champions capable of securing a presence in banking markets worldwide. And including, between these two extremes, the desire to see changes at certain traditional banking houses that were considered incapable of meeting the challenges of the modern financial world, or that were making too many mistakes. In earlier decades, the absorption of banking licenses by large banks had led to a model based on seven big banks; seven now seemed too many.

This policy was backed, in the academic world, by Jack Revell, an internationally-renowned banking expert whose study in 1987 of the Spanish banking system was widely read.[72] Revell offered a number of reasons – some more valid than others – for merger among Spain's large banks: to take advantage of economies of scale and automation; to meet large customers' borrowing requirements; to rationalize the branch network; to achieve international status; and to stand up to competition from foreign banks. He admitted there would be efficiency losses during the merger processes, but that did not prevent him from proposing some specific pairings of more dynamic banks with others that were larger in size but less adaptable.[73] His views were prophetic, as the big six Spanish banking groups and the public sector banks did in effect merge, into not four but just two groups. But none of

---

[71]   Banco de España Circulars 12/1993, 5/1998 and 3/2003. See Poveda (2010), Ch. 3, III.5.3.

[72]   Revell (1987).

[73]   Revell paired Banco Central with Banco Vizcaya, Banesto with Banco Santander, and Banco Hispanoamericano with Banco Popular, leaving Banco de Bilbao unpartnered.

his pairings proved correct, and twelve years would elapse before the concentration process among the large banks was complete, when the market players of the 1980s were long gone.

The background to the Banesto crisis is connected with this concentration process. Banesto, in its last bid to become Spain's leading bank, having lost its first place when Banco Central absorbed Banco Ibérico, made two unfortunate acquisitions: Banco Coca (in 1977) and Banco Madrid (in 1978). Both resulted in significant losses, later compounded by those of another subsidiary, Banco Garriga Nogués. Banesto also presented high risk concentration and a real capital shortfall, both disguised through a network of holding companies (the ISAs) that were created by Banesto's main shareholding groups and were used to park treasury stock and shareholdings. This type of group structure explains some of the singularities of Spain's consolidation rules of 1985. Banesto overcame this first crisis, but it was left with weaknesses, both in its financial position and its senior management. And perhaps this was why, in 1987, Banco de Bilbao first proposed a friendly merger with Banesto. The offer was rejected and Banco de Bilbao then launched a hostile takeover bid which failed.

Banco de Bilbao overcame that failure by merging in 1988 with Banco de Vizcaya to form BBV, a combination of two efficient banks that Revell would not have advised. Likewise the merger, three years later, between Banco Central and Banco Hispanoamericano to form BCH, as in his view these were two inefficient banks. Although he would have approved of the subsequent merger, in 1999, between Santander and BCH. The concentration process was completed that same year when BBV and Argentaria – the former public sector bank that had by then been privatized – merged to form BBVA. All these mergers, which enjoyed significant accounting incentives (recognition of revaluation reserves in headings previously recorded at historical cost) were organized as mergers between equals. This was a must in the circumstances, but it meant that the formation of senior management teams, network rationalization and systems integration at the resultant institutions were all longer and more complex processes.

The concentration process was not confined to banks; between 1989 and 1993 a wave of mergers and absorptions affected 45 savings banks, reducing their total number by around 30. There were various reasons for these moves: a few were the final solution for institutions that had presented weaknesses since the 1977-85 crisis and were made with support from their Deposit Guarantee Fund; others granted viability to local institutions that were too small (some only created in the 1970s) and that were absorbed by larger savings banks. The main reason, however, was the change in the geographical model associated with the emergence of Spain's regional governments, which assumed powers over the types of deposit institutions that at the time, in practice or by law, had limited geographical reach, that is, savings banks and credit unions. Accordingly, part spontaneous, part driven, the savings-bank map evolved, albeit incompletely, from a predominantly provincial to a regional model. But there were also mergers at a provincial level, in provinces where there was more than one savings bank. And there were a few cases of large institutions that were not prepared to operate solely within regional confines (in fact some had been employing imaginative formulas to sidestep the old restrictions on geographical expansion for some years.)

Conversely, the large-scale disappearance between 1991 and 1995 of specialized lending institutions was due not to mergers, but rather to the non-viability of a multitude of institutions that had been established in years in which it was impossible to obtain a banking license, and to their unwillingness to meet the minimum capital requirements established in 1989.[74] Over this period, 256 institutions were deregistered (especially companies financing installment sales and financial leasing companies). Their numbers, which had reached some 500, would continue to fall, to stabilize at around 70 in the first decade of the new century (see Table 3).

Returning to Banesto, one immediate consequence of the failed bid launched by Banco de Bilbao was a change at the top, as the Banesto chairman had been in favor of the bid, against the opinion of his board. The new chairman launched Banesto on a high-risk lending and investment spree that soon began to concern the supervisor. The circumstances of the moment did not help, as unlike the situation in the 1977-85 crisis, in this case there was fierce competition for deposits, triggered not by marginal players but by market leaders. In fact, Banco Santander started the deposit war in 1989 when it launched its high-interest-bearing deposits *("supercuentas")*. No one, save the depositors, gained from this war, which was eventually won not by the institutions that paid the highest interest rates, but by those that opened most branches. As in the 1977-85 crisis, the recession, which peaked in 1993, dashed the hopes of capital gains being obtained on speculative portfolios and drove loan defaults up to what are still record levels to date.

Determining the extent of the deterioration at Banesto was neither an easy nor a quick task, with the auditors taking refuge in a silence that was scarcely broken by cryptic indications. In light of the delaying tactics and obstacles placed in the path of the Banco de España's examiners, their work was divided into two stages. The first, completed in early 1993, revealed significant shortfalls in the portfolio segments analyzed, and prompted a demand for a plan to strengthen the institution's own funds. Disconcertingly, this plan, which included issuance of a series of capital instruments in several phases, received the surprise backing of a leading US investment bank. However, the second inspection stage revealed even greater shortfalls in the new portfolio segments examined, and further deterioration in those analyzed previously. It also revealed what were euphemistically described as creative accounting methods, which would lead to a forgery conviction in the courts. The US investment bank withdrew its support for the issues pending and in December 1993 the Banco de España resolved to assume control of Banesto and replace its directors.

The Banesto crisis was settled by means of a somewhat atypical reduction and subsequent increase in capital. The restructuring needs (latent portfolio losses) were estimated at 605 billion pesetas, confirmed by an audit post-mortem. Under the recapitalization plan approved by the Banco de España and the Deposit Guarantee Fund (DGF) in February

---

[74]   500 million pesetas for mortgage lending and financial leasing companies, and 300 million for finance companies (Royal Decree 771/1989). In 1996 the figure was raised to 850 million for all these institutions (Royal Decree 692/1996).

1994, and by the Shareholders' Meeting in March 1994, Banesto contributed 320 billion pesetas to help plug this gap (via application of reserves, a partial capital reduction and a tolerated deferment in appropriation of necessary provisions); the remaining 285 billion was assumed by the DGF, which in a single transaction purchased assets from Banesto for 460.19 billion and sold them back to Banesto for 175.19 billion. In other restructurings, the DGF had assumed assets that took decades to clear, but it would have been unable to handle a portfolio of this size. However, just filling the gap was not sufficient; a capital increase was made for 180 billion pesetas, subscribed by the DGF, and a four-year loan of 315 billion was granted on highly favorable terms (entailing net aid of 41 billion). All the above was financed by means of a debt issue made by the DGF (445 billion pesetas, also at four years) which was subscribed by the large banks. This restructuring plan was the first that had to be approved by the Community authorities, which did so with no objections. In April 1994 Banesto was acquired by Banco Santander, via a tender bid restricted to the large banks, and was incorporated into, but not absorbed by, the Santander group. The good price obtained reduced the DGF's losses to 192.5 billion pesetas.[75] The financial problem had been resolved in less than five months; the legal consequences would last for five years and would result in sentences for fraud and misappropriation.

The 1977-85 crisis had a considerable impact on prudential and accounting regulations and on resolution mechanisms and procedures for deposit institutions. The Banesto crisis had no such consequences, but it was a harsh reminder that no supervisory system, however efficient, is infallible, that well-meaning rules on the suitability of top management are not sufficient to prevent crises and, clearly, that problems at large institutions require special solutions.

Aside of Banesto, over a period of 17 years there were crises at five small or medium-sized banks (three in the recession of the early 1990s, one in 1996[76] and another in 2003). This is in keeping with the normal course of events in the financial world, and all these crises were settled via the ordinary resolution procedures. But, in a change of approach from that seen in the 1980s, possibly due to a change in attitude on the part of the authorities, or to the fact that none of the institutions concerned had systemic repercussions, there were no reductions and subsequent increases in capital. Instead, the institutions were declared insolvent and were wound up in an orderly manner, with the Bank DGF meeting the deposits guaranteed.

6   The last accounting innovation: dynamic provisioning

The last significant addition to the system designed to underpin the health of Spain's financial institutions – dynamic provisioning – was introduced by the Banco de España in 1999 and

---

[75]   FGDEB (1993) and (1994).

[76]   BCCI, a subsidiary of the global bank of the same name that was acquired in the resolution of the 1977-85 crisis, which was bailed out after being rendered non-viable by the collapse of its parent entity.

redesigned five years later.[77] This approach, which reflects the idea that credit-risk provisions should cover not only losses on transactions with clear signs of impairment, but also potential losses on apparently healthy transactions, was not new to banking doctrine and is highly consistent with Basel II's advanced approaches, although it has few precedents in practice. The provisions were criticized by the accounting establishment, as they were not backed by the international accounting standards which are based on the *incurred loss* approach. They were also fiercely opposed by the banking sector, with the usual argument that they would make Spanish institutions less competitive in comparison with their foreign rivals, subject to less exacting criteria.

In addition to strengthening credit institutions for future contingencies, dynamic provisions are funded in a manner that is very comfortable for institutions. Provisions are built up in good years, when default rates are low and results are expected to be good, to be used in bad years. In effect, the regulations require that a gross allocation be calculated in each fiscal year, applying a vector of conventional coefficients to credit *exposures* classified into six groups according to their risk potential (see Box 3). Since the 2004 reform, a second vector of coefficients is applied to *increases* in these exposures (see Table 4). This addition speeds up the rate of provisioning in years of high economic growth, or at banks that record most growth, on the premise that strong credit growth eventually leads to credit quality impairment. To determine the net allocation, the net credit impairments revealed during the accounting period (that is, the specific provisions for incurred losses, minus recoveries) are then subtracted from the gross allocation. In years of good economic growth and, normally, low default rates, the minuend is small and most of the gross allocation is effectively provisioned; in years of high default rates the opposite is true, meaning that the gross allocation is insufficient to meet the impairments observed and the funds are depleted. The system thus has a stabilizing (countercyclical) impact on income statements.

Provisioning does not continue indefinitely: the 1999 Circular established a ceiling of three times the gross allocation; the 2004 Circular sets a limit of 125% of the amount resulting from applying the vector to the increases in exposures.[78] Once this ceiling is reached, as in a prolonged period of economic boom, dynamic provisions cease to play a stabilizing or countercyclical role.

The introduction of these provisions was timely: the economic situation augured a period of several years over which funds could be built up for future cyclical turnarounds, as proved to be the case. But this economic boom was also a political disadvantage when it came to calibrating the system.

---

[77] Banco de España Circulars 9/99 of 17 December 1999 and 4/04 of 22 December 2004, Appendix IX. Introduced as "statistical provisions", they were renamed "generic provisions" when revised in 2004. For the origin and basis of these provisions, see Poveda (2000) and Fernández de Lis et al (2000).

[78] Despite the conceptual difference, in practice, in a typical bank, the two limits should be quite similar, because in the principal categories the coefficients applicable to increases are two to three times higher than those applicable to exposures.

BOX 3   DYNAMIC PROVISIONING RISK CATEGORIES

No appreciable risk: Mainly securities issued or guaranteed by EU Member States and other countries with no appreciable country risk; securities issued or guaranteed by credit institutions; and securities guaranteed by public funds or debts of credit institutions, provided their market value exceeds the amount guaranteed, or with collateral guarantee in the form of holdings in money market funds, provided 90% of their redeemable value exceeds the amount guaranteed.

Low risk: Assets accepted as collateral by the ECB not included in the former category; residential mortgage loans with LTV ratios below 80%; mortgage-backed securities; exposure to firms with credit ratings "A" or higher; and local currency central government securities of countries not included in the former category.

Medium-low risk: Financial leases; exposures secured by other forms of collateral that meet the amount outstanding.

Medium risk: A catch-all category for exposures not included elsewhere.

Medium-high risk: Consumer loans, not for business purposes nor recorded in the Registry of Installment Sales of Personal Property; exposure to residents of countries other than those mentioned in the first category (but with no country-risk coverage).

High risk: Credit card balances, overdrawn current and loan accounts.

NB: The general coverage applies to credit exposures (on-balance-sheet loans and debts, contingent exposures) whose status is normal, i.e. not subject to specific (credit or country-risk) provisions. Debts stated at fair value are excluded, because decreases in fair value are reflected in results and thus any impairment is already implicitly included in fair value (an issue that has been discussed in depth at international level and that has led to solvency charges being applied due to "incremental risk").

TABLE 4   DYNAMIC PROVISIONING: COEFFICIENTS BY RISK CATEGORY

Coefficient	Risk categories					
	None	Low	Medium-low	Medium	Medium-high	High
On increases in exposure (2004)	0.00	0.60	1.50	1.80	2.00	2.50
On credit exposures (2004)	0.00	0.11	0.44	0.65	1.10	1.64
On credit exposures (1999)	0.00	0.10	0.40	0.60	1.00	1.50

The factors applicable to exposures in the initial provisioning model were based on an estimate of the average annual burden represented by impairment losses in the banking book over a complete economic cycle. The burden was not estimated by individual risk category, but for the aggregate portfolio of the banking system and of the main types of credit institutions. A vector of coefficients compatible with the aggregate burden was then sought for the six risk categories (the vector was reasonable and intuitive, but it had no statistical grounding). Over the period analyzed (1986-98), this burden had been 0.79% of the banking book at the savings banks and 0.88% at the banks. Nevertheless, the final calibration was between 0.4% and 0.5%, little more than half the historical burden. Three reasons were given for this underestimation:

- The period considered included several upward revisions of the provisioning rules, together with the effect of a banking crisis that was deemed exceptional and unrepeatable.
- Credit management and recovery procedures had improved in recent years.
- The improvements in macroeconomic management would assuredly lead to longer and less abrupt economic cycles.[79]

These seemed plausible arguments in 1999, but they were optimistic, and in many cases the funds thus established have proved insufficient to absorb the losses associated with a crisis of the present dimensions.

The calibration of the revised system in 2004 faced similar or even greater pressure than the first calibration in 1999, since the economic boom appeared to be lasting indefinitely. Also by that time there were Central Credit Register statistics available on probabilities of default, allowing more well-founded coefficients to replace the conventional ones. The vector applied to exposures was increased, and that applied to increases in exposures was set considerably higher (see Table 4). At the same time, however, other changes were made in the general provisioning table (the former general provision was eliminated, the subprime category was introduced, country-risk provisions were tempered), making comparisons more difficult. In fact, all the above, together with the changes in ceilings, which were already halting the build-up of dynamic provisions, prompted a decline in 2005 not only in net allocations but also in the absolute volume of these provisions, which had been rising at a strong pace through 2004.[80] These levels then recovered, up to the onset of the international financial crisis.

Initially, dynamic provisions were not included in own funds, consistent with the idea implicit in Basel II's advanced approaches that capital is there to cover unexpected losses and provisions to cover expected losses. However, within certain limits, both the Basel and

---

[79] Poveda (2000), pp. 8 and 9.

[80] Under IAS, tax on non-tax-deductible general provisions may be recorded as a fiscal asset; this prompted further moderation in the impact of the general provisions.

Community rules allow general banking risk provisions, which would include dynamic provisions, to be included in the calculation. Their exclusion meant that the Spanish coefficient was considerably stricter (by up to two percentage points) than the Community one. Following the 2004 reform, Spanish regulations were brought into line with EU regulations.

7 The international financial crisis[81]

The long succession of financial crises that beset the international markets in the 1980s and 1990s had virtually no repercussions on Spanish banking regulation save for the creation of country-risk provisions. By contrast, the crisis that erupted in the United States and Europe in mid-2007 has already prompted a raft of significant measures, in addition to those being adopted by the international bodies and the European Union. Moreover, the creation of a European supervisory architecture may have consequences for banking supervision in Spain, although its true significance is still difficult to assess at this stage.

The crisis initially centered on a very specific family of financial instruments, some new to the market and with a little-understood risk potential (securitizations, resecuritizations, CDSs), and had a particularly harsh impact on the banks and other intermediaries that created these instruments, and the trading books of those that invested in them. The first stage of the crisis (summer 2007 to autumn 2008) rapidly caused deep distress (when not complete shutdown) on the interbank and capital markets, forcing central banks to take categorical action, followed by a wave of huge losses at the western world's leading banks. Startled by the lethal consequences of the US decision to let the investment bank Lehman Brothers fail, governments were forced to shore up banks on the verge of collapse, with urgent and improvised bail-outs on an unprecedented scale (involving some €300 billion in capital instruments). At the time, the impending threat of a widespread domino effect silenced any criticism of this use of public funds that could distort competition.

Inevitably, the financial crisis triggered extensive risk aversion on the part of financial intermediaries, forcing them to restructure their balance sheets, deleveraging sharply and with zero credit growth. This, together with the end of an extraordinary boom in real estate activity in the United States and in certain European countries led, in a second phase, to a severe macroeconomic crisis. In the banking sector, all banking books (not just those affected in 2007) began to record impairment losses, with the consequent need for provisions and erosion of income statements. Moreover, after 2008 this impairment was not confined to the leading banks. These problems were not new in an economic downturn, but the scale of the difficulties revived the debate on the procyclicality of banking, possibly heightened by the latest solvency regulatory models that were highly sensitive to risk perception.

---

[81] On the international financial crisis and the measures adopted or under discussion, see Poveda (2010), Ch. 15 and 16.

It was soon recognized that calibration of the solvency rules of the instruments responsible, and of market risk in general, was insufficient, and it was corrected in a rapid response from the Basel Committee. It was also decided to do away with the fair-value accounting method – considered too uncertain and too volatile – in certain market circumstances and for certain books (incidentally, an approach upheld in the past in the Banco de España's accounting regulations). It became clear that, despite the numerous supervisory recommendations on good governance, the risk-management procedures – both new and old – were weak and inadequate; this was a more difficult problem, which has been addressed with more recommendations and a number of rules aiming to establish a link between compensation for executives and the risks generated by them. It was generally agreed that an in-depth review of the whole system of prudential and accounting regulations was required. In the case of banking solvency regulations, this review includes:

- Refining the concept of own funds.
- Stricter common equity requirements (shares or share equivalents, unrestricted reserves), setting a minimum common equity requirement of 4.5%.
- Creation of an additional capital buffer of 2.5% of common equity, which while not covered would place restrictions, inter alia, on profit distribution.
- Another countercyclical buffer, which the national supervisory authorities could impose in high-growth years, to be used in periods of crisis.
- A complementary non-weighted leverage ratio, extending to off-balance-sheet transactions.
- Further tightening of capital charges on certain transactions (derivatives or others with counterparty risk, positions with leading banks).

Discussions are ongoing on the creation of additional charges on systemic banks, that is, those which, owing to their size or other characteristics, can generate systemic risk. The introduction of a liquidity coverage ratio (LCR) and a net stable funding ratio (NSFR) is also being considered. These are areas in which there is little international regulatory experience, meaning that the Basel proposals, which are complex in design and could present difficulties for the supervisory authorities, are still at a provisional or experimental stage. More interventionist measures in the fields of activity open to banks, or in their tax treatment, have not been ruled out, while in the accounting terrain a review has begun of the international standards on credit risk provisions, to bring them more in line with the expected loss approach.

Stricter solvency and liquidity regulations will have an unequal impact on the banking systems of the world's leading economies and institutions, as their starting points vary enormously. Moreover, this tightening of regulations poses a conflict with another immediate political objective, that is, the restoration of credit growth, to stimulate economic activity and employment. Both problems may affect the design of the measures and will, in any case, delay their implementation. In fact it is likely to be at least two years before they come into force, and then with lengthy adaptation periods, through 2013 up to 2019. In some cases (leverage ratio, LCR, NSFR), the information obtained in coming years could lead to adjustments in the final regulatory proposals.

The crisis has also had repercussions on the political organization of the supervisory function, since the problems spread fast and wide, advising coordination of efforts at the highest level. This materialized in the creation of the G20, whose first meetings set the basic outline for the prudential reform, and in the creation of an international body – the Financial Stability Board (FSB) – to lead regulatory efforts. It was decided to complement the regulation and supervision of financial institutions (the micro-prudential approach) with institutionalized monitoring of the problems affecting the financial system overall and the consequent recommendations (the macro-prudential approach). National authorities will continue to be responsible for the control and supervision of banks and for crisis resolution, but the exchange of information on financial groups with an important presence outside their home country will be enhanced, creating, to this end, supervisory colleges for the leading banking groups. In addition, some countries, notably the United States, have reviewed the structure of their supervisory arrangements.

In the European Union these ideas took shape in the Larosière report,[82] which proposed a weighty review of the EU supervisory architecture. The three existing committees of financial supervisors (banking, securities and insurance) have been redesigned; their advisory powers in the adoption and implementation of regulations and the harmonization of supervisory procedures have been amplified, and they may now also act as mediators between national supervisory authorities in matters involving cross-border groups. The banking committee, renamed the European Banking Authority (EBA), has been upgraded, becoming an independent EU body.[83] The EBA will not be responsible for supervising institutions or for crisis resolution – these functions remain in the hands of the national authorities – but in certain emergency situations (failure by the national authorities to apply regulations or to resolve problems that may affect the integrity of the financial markets or the stability of all or part of the EU financial system), and in respect of systemic institutions, the EBA would be able to take decisions affecting individual institutions. The financing of crisis solutions will also remain in the hands of the national authorities, to the extent that these authorities may block decisions of the EBA if they interfere with their own taxing powers. But a directive is in process that will harmonize the funding of the national DGFs, a matter that was not included, at the time, in the directive on deposit-guarantee systems. And studies are ongoing on other

---

[82]   Larosière (2009).

[83]   The EBA succeeds the Committee of European Banking Supervisors (CEBS), which in turn in 2004 succeeded the Basel Committee on Banking Supervision (BCBS). Both were initially purely committees, with hardly any activity other than their regular meetings. However, in 2009 the CEBS was assigned a headquarters (in London) and its own staff, with a secretariat and a steering committee, preparing it for functions that are no longer simply advisory. In the preparatory discussions for creation of the EBA, there were Eurocentric positions (the European Parliament's proposal) in favor of centralizing the supervision of systemic banks at the EBA.

tax burdens that could be imposed on credit institutions to offset any systemic problems generated by them.

The creation of the European Systemic Risk Board, another body with a complex structure, close to the European Central Bank, completes the new financial architecture. The ESRB will be responsible for macro-prudential oversight within the European Union, to prevent or mitigate risks that pose a threat to financial and macroeconomic stability, and it may issue recommendations, in some cases public recommendations, monitoring their application.[84]

8   The impact of the crisis on Spanish banking regulation[85]

The Spanish banking system came out of the first phase of the international crisis relatively unharmed, but it has been affected by the long period of macroeconomic weakness that followed, and by the characteristics of its own credit growth in the preceding boom. Spain's growth profile had three features in common with that of the United States, where the problems originated:

- Strong growth in real estate financing, and a deterioration in the quality of the transactions when the cycle matured.
- Widespread use of securitizations and covered bonds to refinance mortgage portfolios, although Spain was spared the worst excesses of the originate-to-distribute model[86] and recourse to commercial paper was limited.
- High dependence on external refinancing, a reflection to some extent of an imbalance on the balance of payments, largely covered by the external borrowing of banks and savings banks.

The general financial position of the Spanish banking system meant that it was not tempted to invest in the foreign toxic assets that devastated the trading books of so many banks in the western world. But clearly, like the rest of the world, Spain's credit institutions suffered the immediate impact when the interbank markets seized up and the normal markets for new asset-backed securities and covered bond issues evaporated. All countries addressed these problems with ad hoc solutions: credit lines and state guarantees, and acceptance as collateral by the central banks – the ECB – of securities rejected by the markets.

---

[84]   For more details on the new financial architecture in Europe, see Chapter 8.

[85]   This section covers events up to September 2010.

[86]   Spanish legislation made a twofold contribution in this respect: the quality standards required of covered bonds and mortgage securitizations; and the fact that most securitized assets remained on the books of the originating groups, and therefore in the denominators of their solvency ratios, as a result of the strict criteria placed on their separation from originators.

The initial turmoil has been followed by a long period of penitence. The real-estate boom left in its wake a huge stock of unsold housing and unfinished developments, and a mountain of virtually unrecoverable loans. The lending readjustment long overdue in the property sector spread to others when the financial crisis became a severe economic crisis. Credit institutions were forced to review their general credit standards and, as in the rest of the euro area, credit growth in Spain fell to zero.

Overall, Spain's credit institutions enjoyed a comfortable position pre-crisis: high solvency ratios, a good specific provisions framework, with the additional cushion provided by the dynamic provisions, and profit levels that continued to generate reserves, albeit at a slower pace. Default rates rose sharply but, save in the real-estate construction and development sector, they remained well below the levels of the worst years of the last recession in the early 1990s. The Europe-wide official stress tests evidenced the resilience of Spain's credit institutions. Indeed the Spanish banking system was not hit by the global chaos that followed the collapse of Lehman Brothers; there were no crises at any large institutions and, in the circumstances, the collapse of a couple of medium-sized ones was no more than could be expected.

And yet, the Spanish regulator has not been inactive.

In the accounting field, the Banco de España has revised its rules on specific credit-risk provisions (see Box 2). The complex table of provisioning schedules established in 2004 has been replaced by just one, a radical simplification. The threshold set for this single schedule is in principle stricter: immediately following default, 25% must be provisioned, rather than the almost symbolic levels of the previous version, and once a year has elapsed, rather than two or more years, credit risk must be fully provisioned. These percentages reflect a return to conventional provisioning. However, in the case of mortgage or secured loans, the provisions are established not on the outstanding amount of the loan, but on the part not covered by collateral, adjusted, for reasons of prudence, according to the nature of the mortgaged asset or the collateral.[87] In addition, in anticipation of difficulties in disposing of institutions' swollen real estate portfolios, an initial impairment of 10% is applied to foreclosed real estate assets, rising to 20% once they have been in portfolio for a year, and to 30% after two years.[88] The rules also include a series of conditions on credit institutions' lending and risk-management policies, methods and procedures.[89]

A review of the existing resolution mechanisms was also deemed advisable, considering that weak institutions could need further support if the crisis continued. The contributions

---

[87]   It is noteworthy that although the general tone is stricter, some loans receive more favorable treatment: in particular, residential mortgages that meet the 80% LTV limit are now exempt from provisioning.

[88]   The receipt of these assets cannot give rise to accounting gains or to the reversal of any provisions in the case of doubtful loans. This means that impairments will be calculated on their book value, or on the present appraised value of the property, whichever is lower.

[89]   The new rules will signify a 2% rise in provisions and a 10% decline in results in 2010, with a "more significant" impact in 2011, according to Banco de España estimates; this impact will differ greatly between banks.

to the Deposit Guarantee Funds provide them with relatively modest resources, sufficient to solve problems at only a very limited number of small or medium-sized institutions.[90] Save for a readjustment in savings banks' contributions, these criteria were not modified. However, to complement their potential and avoid improvisation, a new support mechanism, the Fund for the Orderly Restructuring of the Banking Sector (FROB), was created.[91] The FROB, which covers the various arms of the banking sector, has a similar legal regime to the DGFs (which have a minority presence on its governing body, where the Banco de España also has the final say). But it has a different funding mechanism, having been allocated funds of €9 billion, 75% of which charged to the State Budget and 25% to the three DGFs in proportion to the deposits held by their members. It may raise extra funds via fixed-income issues or market loans.

The FROB's modus operandi is also different, with two scenarios envisaged, in principle providing institutions with more initiative:

-   Institutions facing difficulties that threaten their viability can approach the FROB and submit a restructuring plan. If the plan is accepted by the Banco de España, the FROB can offer them support, channeled through the corresponding DGF. If the plan is rejected, the institution will be intervened and the FROB will take control, authorizing the necessary support measures: capital contributions, equity units *(cuotas participativas),* loans, acquisition of assets, or transfer of business to other institutions.

-   Institutions which, while not presenting the weaknesses described above, are keen to strengthen their position via integration processes (which must include structural rationalization plans), or are advised to do so by the Banco de España, can also approach the FROB. In this case, the FROB will subscribe preference shares, eligible as capital for the purposes of the solvency ratio and convertible after five years into shares or equity units if not previously redeemed.[92] In the case of savings banks, and as an exception, while held by the FROB the equity units will have voting rights (granting the right to take part in Assemblies, in proportion to the share in equity).

---

[90] In 2009, in one single operation, the Savings Bank DGF used 30% of its funds (€1.3 billion) to acquire preference shares of Caja Castilla La-Mancha. As a result, contributions had to be increased, from 0.4 per mil to 1 per mil (Ministerial Order of 29 December 2009); banks' contributions stand at 0.6 per mil and credit unions' at 0.8 per mil. No DGF applies the 2 per mil limit established by law.

[91] Royal Decree Law 9/2009.

[92] The EU antitrust authorities generally tolerate competitive distortions caused by public aid when it is used to prevent bank failures, considering the greater problem that would be created if the credit institution were allowed to collapse, as was clearly the case during the key months of the global crisis. The second scenario does not fit well here, but the FROB was granted a transitional window of opportunity in 2010; once this is closed, its operations will be subject to the standard authorization procedure.

However, the situation has opened up – or reopened – two specific areas of concern.

The first is connected with certain management weaknesses inherent to the different kinds of institutions. All institutional formats have their typical problems relating to good governance and risk management. The problems of credit unions (where lenders are controlled by their borrowers) are well known, as are those of large corporations (where shareholders are ineffective to control senior management and long internal reporting lines make management difficult); in fact these problems have prompted the international bodies to issue a raft of recommendations, which have proved more extensive than effective. But the focus has now shifted to savings banks, since although all credit institutions were affected to some extent by the crisis, the most serious weaknesses emerged at savings banks with particularly serious management failings.

In general, the savings banks' problems may be attributed to the singular nature of their governing bodies. With the impetus of their founding fathers long gone, the process of appointment of senior executives had degenerated into a co-option process prone to nepotism and inefficiency. Attempts were made to remedy this situation three decades ago, with well-meaning formulas that, in practice, gave representatives of regional and local authorities a significant presence on their governing bodies,[93] a situation which, apart from creating occasional tensions when it came to renewing these appointments, could affect their investment policies. Overall, the model has worked better than may have been expected. For three decades the savings banks have, on the whole, performed successfully, adding diversity to the Spanish banking system and becoming larger by volume than the banks themselves, while at the same time fulfilling their founding role in the area of community-welfare projects. Serious problems of the kind described above have been few and far between, but they have arisen, and the Spanish regulator has recognized the need to correct or at least mitigate these problems. Clearly this issue is not specifically linked to the present moment in time, but as is always the case, it is at times of crisis that latent difficulties emerge.

The second concern is connected with credit institutions' future capitalization. As their profit margins decline, so does their accumulation of unrestricted reserves, an important – if not the most important – source of core capital. These flows will remain weak while default rates continue to rise and lending remains depressed. Moreover, the ongoing reform of the Basel rules will set higher capital requirements, specifically for core capital. Both may create potential difficulties for credit institutions of any kind, but in this case also the savings banks stand out, because the institutions hardest hit by the crisis have all been savings banks and, especially, because the Spanish savings banks, which are basically foundations, cannot issue shares.

---

[93] Royal Decree 2290/1977, Law 31/1985 and abundant regional legislation. When Spain's regional governments were created, it was imprudent to grant them powers both of supervision and control of savings banks. The regional governments are key potential (direct or indirect) customers for the savings banks and they also provide them with a large number of senior executives, thus creating a conflict of interest that should rule them out as supervisors. In practice, the overlapping of supervisory powers has given rise to friction, but it has not prevented the Banco de España from exercising its functions in matters relating to the financial health and solvency of savings banks and credit unions.

These concerns resulted, in July 2010, in a pivotal Royal Decree Law on savings banks' capital instruments, governing bodies and legal regime. This reform includes an optional mechanism, allowing savings banks to transfer their financial activity to instrumental banks.[94]

This is the second review of the legal regime of the savings banks' capital instruments, the *cuotas participativas* or equity units. These units were designed in 1990, not by the market but by the regulator, as a core capital component (with indefinite duration, variable remuneration and the ability to absorb losses on a going concern basis). Under both previous regimes, there were virtually no issues of units.[95] Under the new regime, the limit on holdings per investor (5% of the amount issued) has been lifted and voting rights granted, meaning that unitholders may form part of savings banks' governing bodies (Assembly, Board, Control Committee, although not the Community Welfare Project Committee) in proportion to their share in equity.[96] Both changes, although irrelevant to retail investors, have made these units attractive to those interested in playing an active part in the management of savings banks.

The legislator has approached the problem of the governing bodies via enhanced professionalism. Specifically, the following changes have been made:

- General government senior executives, and elected officers, can no longer belong to savings banks' assemblies or boards.
- The representation of general government and of public law entities and public corporations on the governing bodies has been reduced from 50% to 40%.[97]
- Regional government appointees (designated through the regional parliaments) must now have acknowledged professional standing, and in general the demands of suitability and professionalism have been heightened, especially for board members.
- There will no longer be a regional government representative on the Control Committee.

As part of the good-governance rules, the savings banks' internal committee framework has been revised and they must now produce an annual corporate governance report with extensive information on the institutions and their activities.

---

[94]   Royal Decree Law 11/2010.

[95]   Royal Decrees 664/1990 and 3024/2004. In fact there were no issues under the 1990 regime and just one under the 2004 regime.

[96]   As in the case of any market instrument, the regulations on equity units control and limit treasury stock holdings, for which the 5% threshold is maintained. But units held by the central entity of an IPS are not classed as treasury stock and could, therefore, become the vehicle through which an IPS can participate in the senior management of the savings banks in its group.

[97]   The reduction will be sharper at savings banks that have issued equity units, since this percentage, like those assigned to the other groups represented on the governing bodies, is calculated on voting rights after subtracting those corresponding to unitholders.

Lastly, the savings banks have been given the option to pursue their activities through instrumental banks to which they would transfer all their financial business. In principle, the instrumental banks will operate under the same name as the savings banks and will belong to the Savings Bank DGF, but they will be able to make their own equity issues, thus opening up a new path of access to the capital markets. However, if savings banks' holdings fall below 50% of the voting rights in the instrumental bank, they will lose their credit institution status and will become "special foundations", dedicated to community welfare activities. Savings banks may also voluntarily choose to become special foundations, or may be obliged to do so if they are intervened.

A point to note is that all the operations involved in the transfer of business to an instrumental bank (creation or purchase of the bank, transfer of the business, transformation of the corporate purpose) were possible under the previous legislation, if the governing bodies had so wished and with the necessary permission from the competent authorities, but they would have entailed a significant fiscal cost. The real new development, apart from demonstrating the supervisor's willingness to favor these transformations, is the broad package of tax exemptions granted.

Real or potential weaknesses at the savings banks have triggered a second major wave of mergers which, if completed as projected, will transform the existing 46 savings banks into some 17 groups or institutions. In several cases, the mergers, projected before July 2010, do not follow the classic format, but instead use institutional protection schemes (IPSs), an atypical EU banking regulation figure unknown to date in Spain. Savings banks that join an IPS will maintain their legal personality, their community welfare projects and their retail business, but they will sign a long-term agreement[98] (a minimum of ten years), signifying the creation of a central unit and strong mutual solvency guarantees between the member institutions. These guarantees take the form of a solvency and liquidity commitment that must extend to at least 40% of each institution's eligible capital, accompanied by pooling of at least 40% of their profits, to be redistributed according to each institution's share in the scheme. The central unit, which in practice will be a bank in which the IPS members have stakes (and which could take the form of an instrumental bank) will assume functions such as treasury activities, IT or risk management for the group, and may make its own issues of capital instruments. Legal solvency requirements will be met at a consolidated level. These groups will be entitled to FROB support, in the second of the two scenarios envisaged, provided they commit to rationalization and restructuring plans.

The fact that the original savings banks survive in the IPS model, and the pressures exerted in some cases by financial straits for which the regional governments had no solution, have removed the formal obstacle that stopped the savings banks from forming inter-regional groups.

---

[98]   The commitment to a long-term presence, one potential weakness of the IPSs, is strengthened by a two-year advance notice period, penalizations on exit and a Banco de España report on the viability of both the institutions and the group post-separation (Royal Decree Law 11/2010, Art. 4). The tax exemptions envisaged in the Royal Decree Law also extend to the operations of the IPSs.

9   Conclusions

Over the last 40 years the Spanish banking sector has experienced three crises. During the first, in the period 1977-85, several banks and other credit institutions collapsed, but none were large institutions and the banks specifically were mostly new market entrants. Apart from reasons connected with the economic cycle, this crisis was the direct consequence of an ill-prepared break-up of the banking status quo that was insufficiently backed by appropriate prudential regulation and supervision. As a result of the second crisis ten years later, the Spanish banking map was redrawn, with mergers between the leading banks, expansion (both in theory and practice) of the areas of activity of the savings banks, many of which also merged, and rationalization and restructuring at the smaller institutions. In this case there were no widespread bank failures, but one large institution did collapse. This second crisis was triggered by the higher competition resulting from deregulation, and the saturation of the banking market; the opening up of the market to foreign competition may have spurred on the merger processes, but it did not disrupt the core retail segment. The third and ongoing crisis is an imported one, in terms of its origin and its financial dimension, but it has revealed certain problems specific to the Spanish banking system. As a result, global prudential regulations are being tightened, and all credit institutions will have to adapt to these new regulations.

The first crisis had a crucial impact on prudential regulation and supervision in Spain. Both the size and quality of the inspection corps was strengthened. There was a huge improvement in the information on credit institutions. The Banco de España's supervisory powers relating to intervention and disciplinary procedures were clarified and expanded. A powerful resolution mechanism for crisis situations was created. Conservative accounting standards were developed, dominated by prudential criteria and including new credit-risk provisioning proposals that would be completed, in later years, with the introduction of dynamic provisioning. And modern solvency regulations were introduced that were particularly strict with the banking problems that had triggered the crisis (risk concentration, treasury stock, tangible fixed assets and atypical banking groups).

The new resolution mechanism – the deposit guarantee funds – proved to have insufficient resources when first Rumasa and then Banesto had to be bailed out, and recourse had to be had to special solutions, including public aid. But this is as it should be. These funds' resources are calculated to cover statistically foreseeable events; it would be unreasonable to raise funding levels to the amounts required for potential bail-out of a leading institution that may never be needed.

Throughout the 1980s and 1990s, the inspection corps continued to expand, in keeping with the new demands posed by market developments and inspection techniques, as did supervisory information. But autonomy was lost in terms of prudential, and then accounting, regulation when Spain joined the European Economic Community. The EEC developed its own body of prudential regulations, before assuming, rather precipitately, the IASB's international accounting standards. Spanish legislation had to adapt to all these changes:

in some aspects it was ahead of European legislation, which eventually adopted similar proposals; in others, transposition of European regulations entailed some degree of relaxation of Spanish prudential standards.

The circumstances, and several timely and relatively modest support measures, saved the Spanish banking system from the international wave of severe banking crises in 2008. It is now facing higher default rates as a consequence of the economic crisis, exacerbated by some excesses in the real estate sector and by refinancing difficulties in the external markets. But the regulatory and supervisory framework has provided the banking system with a sound financial base. The present crisis is doing less widespread harm than the 1977-85 crisis, and there is no sign of a specific banking collapse comparable to that seen in the second crisis of the early 1990s, despite the far greater decline in the economic situation.

Nevertheless, conjunctural weaknesses have arisen at a number of savings banks, adding to the weaknesses deriving from their atypical institutional nature. In consequence, the support mechanism has been strengthened, with the creation of the FROB, a new fund endowed with mainly public monies and which, while not confined to the savings banks, is providing them with a second opportunity for concentration and restructuring. Extensive changes have also been made to their regulatory framework: savings banks have been granted the option to change their institutional nature, to make it easier for them to access top-quality capital, and their management teams have become more professional, reducing the presence of public authorities on their governing bodies.

ANNEX

Banking supervision: organization and resources

In the Banco de España's organization chart, banking supervision and regulation have always been separate: the supervisory area as such, responsible for oversight of credit institutions, including inspection visits and continuous off-site monitoring based on the data obtained from inspections; and a second area, responsible for a series of administrative and ancillary tasks, partly related to other Banco de España functions, and for preparation of most legislative proposals on supervisory matters (preparation of draft circulars on accounting and prudential matters, collaboration with other bodies in the preparation of draft legislative proposals on prudential and disciplinary matters).

The structure of the supervisory area has gradually become more complex: the Banco de España now supervises a wide range of institutions; it employs many more bank examiners, demanding a more complex organizational framework and the creation of an intermediate management level;[99] banking activities and techniques, and their regulatory framework, have become more complex, requiring the creation of specialist supervisory niche areas (debt markets, Latin America, money laundering, advanced solvency approaches, etc.); and, in the past decade, there has been a proliferation of coordination work on international supervisory policies.

The second area initially comprised two sections: the Administrative Services for Credit and Savings Institutions, and the Central Credit Register (CCR). The first of these issued the administrative authorizations corresponding to the central bank, it kept the various official registers of private sector banks and it processed their accounting and statistical data that was used for inspection purposes and for preparation of monetary and financial information. Initially it also prepared disciplinary files, until this task was assumed by the Legal Services. The second section, the CCR, ran this system, a direct product of the Credit and Banking Law, receiving individual data on the risk positions of credit institutions' customers and supplying these data to credit institutions and to the inspection corps. In 1981 the two sections were merged to form what would become Banking Regulation, as in addition to the two functions described, and others relating to transparency (authorizations regarding fee schedules and advertising), it also assumed the legislative work described above.

Banking supervision and regulation have gradually gained importance within the Banco de España; a first indication of this is evident in the organization chart. Initially, they came under one single Director General, who was also responsible for other areas. However, the

---

[99]   Initially, all bank examiners were part of a pool, available for inspection visits at any institution. Subsequently, teams of examiners have been permanently assigned to specific institutions, groups of institutions or special functions, resulting in greater specialist knowledge at the expense of flexibility.

TABLE 5	BANKING SUPERVISION AND REGULATION STAFF

Date	Total	Banking supervision	Banking regulation	Administrative banking services	CCR
1971	122	70	—	16	36
1972	169	101	—	31	37
1976	210	114	—	42	54
1982	249	170	79	—	—
1988	283	205	78	—	—
2001	473	336	137	—	—
2009	588	434	154	—	—

SOURCE: Banco de España. 1971 to 1988, *Escalafones por Dependencias;* 2001 and 2009, Banking Supervision Reports.

post of Associate Director General for Banking Supervision was created in 1982, followed in 1985 by that of Director General for Banking Supervision. The post of Associate Director General for Banking Regulation was created in 1987, and that of Director General for Banking Regulation in 1995.

A second indication of this relative importance is the number of banking supervision and regulation staff (see Table 5), which has risen steadily from 122 in 1971 (including division heads down to auxiliary personnel) to 588 at end-2009. Over the same period, the number of staff engaged in banking supervision and regulation and related work has also risen as a percentage of total Banco de España headcount, from 3% to 22%.

The number of serving bank examiners may be a more immediate indicator of the Bank's supervisory capacity (see Table 6). In 1971 there were 30 bank examiners. Over the following two years, as the Bank assumed responsibility for savings banks and credit unions, this figure doubled, and then stabilized and even fell slightly through 1976.[100] In light of the prolonged crisis at credit institutions that followed the collapse, that year, of Banco de Navarra, the inspection corps was strengthened again. The staff shortage at the start of the crisis possibly explains why, for several years, the Banco de España urged that audits be performed, when they were still neither a legal requirement nor common practice. But these audits, which lacked depth and provided little more than a snapshot of the current position, were never a good substitute for the Bank's own inspection procedures. There are notorious cases of credit institutions that received favorable audit reports, or reports containing only cryptic qualifications, just months before decisive losses emerged.

The increase in the number of bank examiners intensified in the mid-1980s, with the introduction in 1985 of the new prudential framework and assumption by the Bank in 1988

---

[100] Initially, bank examiners were appointed from Banco de España staff, but by 1977 a fresh source of talent was needed and the competitive examinations were opened up to external candidates. Table 5 does not include, for 1976, the appointment of nine junior bank examiners who in subsequent years became fully-fledged bank examiners.

TABLE 6	CREDIT INSTITUTION SUPERVISION STAFF

Date	Bank examiners*	IT auditors**	Background
1971	30 (April)		
1972	45 (January)		BE assumes competence over savings banks and credit unions
1973	63 (April)		
1974	63 (January)		
1975	58 (January)		
1976	54 (January)		
1977	59 (January)		Start of the 1977-85 crisis
1978	67 (January)		
1979	68 (January)		
1980	78 (January)		
1981	78 (January)		
1982	92 (January)		
1983	90 (January)		Rumasa crisis
1984	93 (July)		
1985	120		
1986	130	1	
1987	144	2	
1988	152	2	BE assumes competence over official credit and specialized lending institutions
1989	na	2	
1990	152	6	
1991	163	6	
1992	174	11	
1993	173	11	Banesto crisis
1994	175	11	
1995	172	21	
1996	189	21	
1997	191	21	
1998	199	20	
1999	201	20	
2000	200	28	
2001	214	36	
2002	196	34	
2003	210	35	
2004	204	32	Basel II
2005	222	39	
2006	235	42	
2007	237	42	
2008	238	42	
2009	242	42	

SOURCES: (*) Banco de España, *Escalafones de personal*. The 2009 figure is taken from the Banking Supervision report. The chronological differences between 1971 and 1984 are due to the headcount publication dates (in brackets); since 1985, all figures refer to December. (**) Banco de España. Includes Division heads.

of additional supervisory powers; thus, by 1988, there were more than 150 serving bank examiners. Also in the mid-1980s, an auxiliary corps of IT auditors was created. The number of bank examiners leveled off again in the first half of the 1990s, as the number of deposit institutions declined in the wake of the concentrations seen in the late 1980s and early 1990s, before rising again (through 2006) as the number of special tasks increased.[101] The total number of institutions supervised has fallen in recent years, from 545 in 1998 to 494 in 2009; the number of credit institutions (excluding foreign bank branches, which are largely supervised by the parent institutions' supervisor) has fallen somewhat more, from 351 to 264 (see Table 3).[102]

Clearly the supervisory authorities also have other resources apart from staff at their disposal. Over the last four decades there have been a continuous increase and improvement, not only in the data available but also in the manner in which these data are processed, all of which has strengthened oversight capacity. This process is difficult to quantify, but the case of the Central Credit Register (CCR) may serve as a good example. In 1971, a primitive CCR based on punch cards handled 109,500 declarations and issued some 60,000 reports, with a staff of 36. Five years on the staff had risen to 54 (not including the staff at the Bank's own branch offices, who processed the data received on paper until the electronic receipt of these data made this task redundant). At that time the inspection corps hardly used the CCR's services; in fact the CCR hindered rather than helped, as bank examiners had to verify that the declarations made by institutions were correct. By contrast, in 2008, a fully automated CCR was processing exposures of 17.6 million borrowers and issuing 309 million reports. The CCR is now used on a day-to-day basis by bank examiners and is highly valuable for statistical and analytical purposes, and all with a staff of less than 30.[103] It is possibly an extreme example, but the breadth of the accounting, statistical and prudential data of the institutions and consolidated groups of institutions supervised by the Banco de España has also increased significantly, and the handling of these data has improved enormously.

However, it has not all been productivity gains in banking supervision and regulation. Mergers and concentration processes in the domestic market reduced the supervisory burden, but globalization has had the opposite effect. Participation in international standard-setting and in the international bodies that generate prudential standards and coordinate supervisory

---

[101]   Similarly to supervisory bodies in other countries, the Banco de España sees its inspection corps depleted from both sides: internally, due to promotions; and externally, due to market demand for good financial analysts. Approximately 10% of non-retired bank examiners are on permanent leave of absence.

[102]   Table 3 depicts only institutions operating through establishments. Accordingly, it excludes any representative offices and foreign institutions that provide banking services without a permanent establishment (included, by order of EU directives, in a register that has no useful purpose). It also excludes foreign-exchange bureaux that are not authorized to make transfers; these are very small entities whose number (which reached several thousand) fell dramatically with the introduction of the euro. The categories excluded generate virtually no supervisory burden.

[103]   Data taken from Prado (1983), Banco de España, CCR (2009) and Table 4.

activities has become essential, and absorbs a considerable volume of top-quality human resources with no immediate benefit. Work in this area expanded sharply in the first decade of the new century, initially with the need to prepare and implement Basel II and then with the onset of the international financial crisis,[104] without forgetting the demands of oversight of cross-border banking groups.

---

[104] In 2009 the Banco de España participated in 93 committees or working groups of international bodies on supervisory matters (attending a total of 278 meetings). See Banco de España, Banking Supervision (2010), p. 62.

References

BANCO DE ESPAÑA, CIR (2009). *Memoria de la Central de Información de Riesgos,* 2008.

BANCO DE ESPAÑA, BANKING SUPERVISION (2002). *Report on Banking Supervision in Spain,* 2001.

— (2010). *Report on Banking Supervision in Spain,* 2009.

BANCO DE ESPAÑA (2010). *Financial Stability Report,* March.

CUERVO, Á. (1988). *La crisis bancaria en España, 1977-1985.*

DE JUAN, A. (1983) "La supervisión de las entidades de crédito y ahorro en España", in AEB, *Crisis bancarias, soluciones comparadas,* July.

FERNÁNDEZ DE LIS, S., J. MARTÍNEZ PAGÉS and J. SAURINA (2000). *Credit Growth, Problem Loans and Credit Risk Provisioning in Spain,* Working Paper, no. 0018, Research Department of the Banco de España.

FONDO DE GARANTÍA DE DEPÓSITOS EN CAJAS DE AHORRO (FGDCA) (1986). *Memoria correspondiente al ejercicio.*

FONDO DE GARANTÍA DE DEPÓSITOS EN COOPERATIVAS DE CRÉDITO (FGDCC) (1984). *Memoria correspondiente al ejercicio.*

FONDO DE GARANTÍA DE DEPÓSITOS EN ESTABLECIMIENTOS BANCARIOS (FGDEB) (1980). *Memoria correspondiente al ejercicio.*

— (1983). *Memoria correspondiente al ejercicio.*

— (1993). *Memoria correspondiente al ejercicio.*

— (1994). *Memoria correspondiente al ejercicio.*

HIGH-LEVEL GROUP ON FINANCIAL SUPERVISION IN THE EU (2009). *Report,* Brussels, February.

LATORRE, J. (1997). *Regulación de las entidades de crédito en España,* FUNCAS.

MARTÍNEZ MÉNDEZ, P. (1991). *Los beneficios de la banca, 1979-1989,* Banco de España.

MINISTERIO DE ECONOMÍA Y HACIENDA (1961). *Memorándum sobre el sistema bancario y crediticio e informes sobre el mismo. Resumen elaborado por el Consejo de Economía Nacional,* p. 6, Madrid, mimeo.

PÉREZ DE ARMIÑÁN, G. (1983). *Legislación bancaria española,* Banco de España, 6th edition.

POVEDA, R. (2000). "La reforma del sistema de provisiones de insolvencia", Banco de España, *Boletín Económico,* January.

— (2010). *Basilea II,* second edition, FUNCAS.

PRADO, R. (1983). *La Central de Información de Riesgos,* Fundación FIES.

— (2002). "La provisión para insolvencias de las entidades de crédito. Presente, futuro y pasado", *Notas de Estabilidad Financiera,* no. 1, Banco de España, March.

REVELL, J. (1987). *Mergers and the role of large banks,* Institute of European Finance, Research monograph in banking and finance, No. 2, Bangor University.

TERMES, R. (1995). "Los últimos doce años del sistema bancario español", in AB Asesores, *Historias de una década. Sistema financiero y economía española (1984-1994).*

8. Spanish securities markets: recent developments and key challenges

Fernando Restoy and Rafael Sánchez de la Peña [1]

National Securities Market Commission (CNMV)

1 Introduction

When reviewing the development or characteristics of the Spanish financial system, as in various chapters of this volume, one essential point to note is the high level of penetration of banking services in Spain. In fact, credit institutions play a fundamental role in channeling financial flows in the Spanish economy: traditional banking products, such as deposits, are still the main savings vehicle for households, and commercial loans are still the main source of borrowing for companies and households.

This high level of commercial activity on the part of credit institutions has conditioned the development of the securities markets. Nevertheless, the products traded on these markets represent a considerable proportion of corporate debt and private sector savings. Thus, in 2009, the outstanding balance of shares and shareholdings, fixed-income securities and derivatives represented around 70% of the outstanding balance of loans and deposits.[2]

---

[1] We would like to thank Óscar Arce, Nikolay Arnaudov, Roberto Blanco, Maribel Cambón, Nieves Gómez, Montserrat Martínez Parera, Antonio Mas and the editors for their suggestions.

[2] See Banco de España (2010): *Financial Accounts of the Spanish Economy.* Table 2.5.a. Total economy. Financial balance sheet.

Moreover, activity on the securities markets cannot be viewed as a substitute for traditional banking activity. In fact, the sharp rise in bank credit against a backdrop of more limited growth in traditional deposits can only be explained by the increase in securities issued by credit institutions, and especially by the development of the securitization markets.

In Spain, there is a particularly close connection between market development and banking activity. As will be seen later in this chapter, credit institutions are responsible for a substantial part of issuance, they manage most institutional investment vehicles and they dominate the financial intermediary industry whether directly or through their investee investment services firms.

At the time of writing, securities market operations, similarly to other areas of financial activity, are under close scrutiny by the public authorities and other interest groups. The crisis that first unfolded in the summer of 2007 revealed substantial shortcomings in market regulations that facilitated the spread of the shocks and exacerbated their effects. In particular, the appearance and uncontrolled development of new products and markets emerging from the intense process of financial innovation had a severely destabilizing influence. More recently, the public debt crisis, which has caused severe turmoil in the euro area since the spring of 2010, calls for reflection on the rules governing the public-debt markets.

Looking forward, however, following the corresponding regulatory review, the role of the markets as a channel for financial flows will foreseeably increase. Thus, the changes envisaged in prudential regulations will entail a significant tightening of the restrictions already in place on the composition and size of banks' balance sheets (in terms of volume and quality of capital, liquidity and leverage). This could reduce, to some extent, the banks' capacity to finance productive activity via conventional credit instruments and could, therefore, encourage non-financial companies to seek funding directly on the markets. In this setting, the markets should increase their capacity to broker the flow of funds between savers and borrowers, to contain the possible restrictive effects of the new prudential regulations and thus maximize their positive impact on financial stability and economic growth.

In this context, the markets' governing bodies and regulators should review the relevant regulations so as to make the securities markets more attractive to potential issuers and investors. This is particularly important in countries such as Spain where, despite the progress made in recent years, banking products still represent a higher proportion of companies' debt than in most other developed economies.

The important role played by the securities markets in the Spanish financial sector, the foreseeable growth in this role and the intense ongoing regulatory debate provide the perfect setting for an assessment of the situation of the Spanish markets and the challenges they face. For this purpose, it is useful to look back over the recent trajectory of the industry and, in particular, to see how it has adapted to regulatory change and to the transformation of the competitive environment. This is the aim of this chapter, which is structured chronologically: section 2 reviews the most recent regulatory and organizational developments; section 3 describes the present regulatory framework and analyzes the activity of markets and market participants; section 4 examines the regulatory and operational challenges facing the Spanish markets and the market outlook; and section 5 presents a series of final comments.

This analysis of market activity distinguishes between three essential processes:

- *Issuance,* the process of creating and placing marketable securities with subscribers or purchasers.
- *Trading,* the process of matching the interests of buyers and sellers, to reach an agreement (via a public or private document) on the price and volume of a trade.
- *Post-trade (clearing, settlement and registration),* which is essential for completion of trades.[3]

2   Development of the securities markets since 1988

In the mid-1980s, the Spanish securities markets comprised the country's four traditional stock exchanges (Barcelona, Bilbao, Madrid and Valencia) and, as from 1987, the public debt market. All these markets dealt exclusively in *cash* securities; at that time there were no organized *derivatives* markets.

Shares were the main instruments traded on the four stock exchanges, although there was also trading in debt instruments issued by private-sector companies. The whole system revolved around individual stockbrokers, who were the only parties authorized to process orders.

The different stages of post-trading (clearing, settlement and registration) of cash securities was an auxiliary service managed internally by each of the stock exchanges (through the *"Juntas Sindicales"*).

2.1   The Securities Market Law

The Securities Market Law (LMV)[4] of 1988 prompted numerous changes in the structure of the Spanish securities market.

First, it significantly enhanced the flexibility of the requirements for issue and transfer of securities: it unified the conditions for admission to listing on all four stock exchanges; it removed all kind of formal administrative authorizations for securities issues; and it

---

[3]   *Post-trade* processing comprises, in turn, three separate phases: i) *clearing,* when the number and price of the securities traded is determined for each security and party (whether trading on their own account or on behalf of a client); ii) *settlement,* which consists in moves in securities accounts and cash between buyers and sellers; and iii) *registration,* which entails book entries and thus formal recognition of the change in ownership resulting from the trade.

[4]   Law 24/1988, of 28 July 1988.

established the principle of free transferability, in accordance with the provisions of the corresponding European Directives.[5]

Second, it introduced transparency regulations for issues, in particular with the transposition into Spanish law of the obligations contained in two Directives,[6] one on the periodic information to be published by companies listed on official secondary markets in Europe, and the other on the information to be published in the event of acquisition or sale of qualifying holdings in listed companies.

Third, it raised the professional profile of brokerage on the securities markets. Specifically, the provision of services relating to the purchase and sale of shares was assigned to securities dealer firms *(Sociedades de Valores)* and securities brokerage firms *(Agencias de Valores)*[7] which were subject to administrative authorization and specific regulations.

Fourth, it drew up the basic market-infrastructure map. The stock exchanges and the public debt market became *official markets,* a status they would share with any new secondary markets, and the Stock Exchange Interconnection System (SIBE) was created to integrate the secondary share markets. This system, which is still in operation, provides an electronic trading platform to receive, cross and match orders. The Law also introduced a book-entry system, to replace physical share certificates for securities listed on secondary equity and corporate bond markets, and it created a specialist company separate from the stock exchanges to perform the post-trade process. The Securities Clearing and Settlement Service (SCLV) was established in 1992 and was the precursor of the present service, *Sociedad de Gestión de los Sistemas de Registro, Compensación y Liquidación de Valores,* which operates under the commercial name of Iberclear.

Lastly, the Securities Market Law established a supervisory framework, creating the National Securities Market Commission (CNMV) to oversee market transparency, correct price formation and investor protection. The supervisory powers of the CNMV relate to four specific areas of activity:

- Verifying securities issues.
- Monitoring the information available on cash securities and derivatives traded on the Spanish markets.

---

[5] Council Directive 79/279/EEC coordinating the conditions for the admission of securities to official stock exchange listing, and Council Directive 80/390/EEC coordinating the requirements for the drawing up, scrutiny and distribution of the listing particulars to be published for the admission of securities to official stock exchange listing.

[6] Council Directive 82/121/EEC on information to be published on a regular basis by companies whose shares have been admitted to official stock exchange listing, and Council Directive 88/627/EEC on the information to be published when a major holding in a listed company is acquired or disposed of.

[7] These were the first investment services firms (ISFs), a term that was incorporated into the first reform of the Securities Market Law in 1998. In the 1988 Law they were granted exclusive authorization to receive and convey client orders, to execute these orders on the markets, to manage client investment portfolios at their discretion, and to place financial instruments. Securities dealers, unlike securities brokers, were also able to trade on their own behalf and to underwrite issues.

- Overseeing the conduct and activities of participants on the markets and in their relations with investors.
- Supervising compliance by intermediaries of organizational, solvency and capital requirements.

2.2 Key subsequent developments

The 1988 Securities Market Law was the first step in a continuous process of modernization and expansion of the Spanish markets. The following subsections describe the key features of this process.

2.2.1 Role of the markets in the Spanish economy

The regulatory reforms of the late 1980s enabled the Spanish markets to adjust to new investment and financing patterns consistent with the development of the Spanish economy and its convergence with the economies of the EU Member States.

Thus, from 1990 up to the onset of the recent crisis, in Spain the rate of growth of financial assets held by households – between 8% and 12% of GDP per annum up to 2007 – was higher than that seen in the United States or in the euro area.

This higher rate of growth of financial assets was accompanied by a gradual increase in the proportion of securities in the portfolios of Spanish households, which rose from 23% in 1990 to 37% in 2009, after verging on 50% in the years previous to the present crisis (see Chart 1). At the same time, the proportion of cash and deposits gradually declined, although it rebounded somewhat in the last two years of the period. As a result, the value of the investment portfolios of Spanish households has converged, as a proportion of total financial wealth, to average euro-area levels. Nevertheless, it is still a long way behind the levels seen in the United States, where transferable securities account for some 55% of total financial wealth and banking products for some 15%.

Turning to the corporate sector, corporate borrowing rose significantly in the two decades analyzed, as a logical consequence of the intensity of the investment process against the backdrop of continued economic growth. Most of this borrowing took the form of bank loans; only a quarter of these funds were channeled through securities issues.

As Chart 2 shows, the proportion of corporate debt held in the form of securities rose markedly in the 1990s, before falling back in the past decade in favor of bank loans, a development that was closely linked to the real-estate boom. This pattern continued up to the onset of the financial crisis, when the relative weight of securities issued began to rise again. As a source of funding, securities issues play a smaller part in Spain than in the euro area and the United States; conversely, bank loans in Spain account for more than 40% of corporate debt, while in the US and the euro area they account for some 30%.

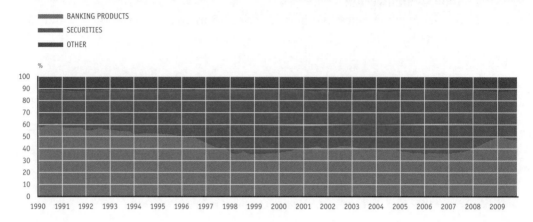

CHART 1   BREAKDOWN OF PORTFOLIOS OF SPANISH HOUSEHOLDS

SOURCE: Banco de España.
NB: Banking products include cash, demand and term deposits. Securities include fixed income, listed and unlisted shares, mutual funds and pension funds.

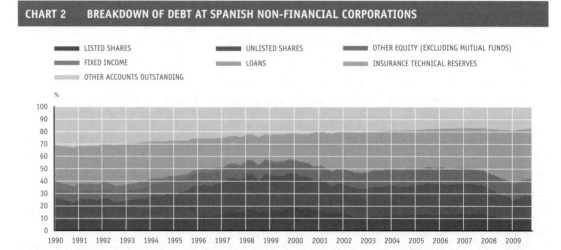

CHART 2   BREAKDOWN OF DEBT AT SPANISH NON-FINANCIAL CORPORATIONS

SOURCE: Banco de España.

Moreover, some two-thirds of funding obtained through securities comes from unlisted instruments. In fact, as a corporate funding vehicle, fixed-income issues play an almost residual role in Spain; they play a slightly larger role in the euro area and a much larger role in the United States, where fixed-income issues represent approximately 20% of the total.

2.2.2 Development of the infrastructures

A range of markets and trading infrastructures gradually emerged in the wake of the Securities Market Law. In 1991 the AIAF *(Asociación de Intermediarios de Activos Financieros)* was authorized as an unofficial secondary market specializing in admission and trading of private fixed-income securities or corporate bonds. The same year also saw the creation, as official secondary markets, of the futures and options markets for equities (MEFF RV) and fixed income (MEFF RF).

The AIAF market recorded continuous growth from the very beginning. In the early years, this expansion was favored by restrictions on bank lending which encouraged firms to issue market securities. However, the definitive boost came in 1999 with the introduction of the euro, as the single currency prompted a marked increase in issues, especially by financial institutions.

Specifically, the sharp growth in demand for credit that accompanied Spain's entry into the euro area prompted an increase in corporate-borrowing needs that was met by issuance of securities – mainly commercial paper and covered and other bonds – and asset securitization.[8] In fact, in the first decade of the new century, Spain became a leading issuer of asset-backed securities in Europe, second only to the United Kingdom. Chart 3 depicts the growth in volume of securities on the AIAF since the start of monetary union.

In February 2001 the SENAF *(Sistema Electrónico de Negociación de Activos Financieros)* was authorized as an electronic trading platform specializing, from the outset, in Spanish book-entry public debt.

The derivatives markets have evolved very differently from the corporate bond markets. The futures and options market for fixed income (MEFF RF) developed quite well up to the introduction of the euro, but the German bund then became the benchmark for euro-denominated public debt and trading in futures and options on Spanish public debt gradually diminished, before eventually disappearing altogether.

The equity derivatives market (MEFF RV) has proved more dynamic, although it too has had to face constant competition from other European markets where similar derivatives on indices are traded. Nevertheless, this market is currently the third most active in Europe in derivatives on shares, although the first two markets represent more than four times the volume of contracts traded on the MEFF RV.

There have also been attempts in Spain to organize official derivatives markets in commodities. In 1995 a derivatives market in citrus fruit was created which operated for scarcely two years. More recently, in 2003, an olive-oil futures market (MFAO) was established that is currently at the consolidation stage, and 2011 should see the launch of a new electricity derivatives market.

A key feature shared by all the secondary markets operating in Spain in the 1980s and 1990s was that their members and shareholders all belonged to the same financial

---

[8] For more details, see Chapter 6.

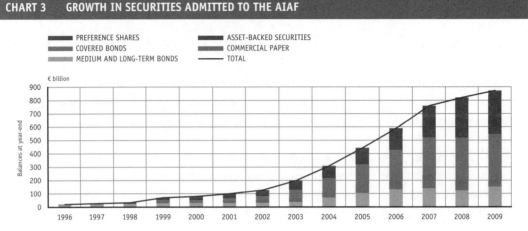

CHART 3   GROWTH IN SECURITIES ADMITTED TO THE AIAF

SOURCE: AIAF.

groups. This prompted an integration process that culminated, in December 2001, in the creation of a holding company that grouped together all its members' shares in MEFF, AIAF and SENAF and that would subsequently be included in the future BME (Bolsas y Mercados Españoles).

The BME group was established in February 2002, made up of Spain's four stock exchanges, the MEFF-AIAF-SENAF holding company and the Securities Clearing and Settlement Service (SCLV). Two years later Iberclear was created, as the result of the merger of the SCLV with the settlement and registration services for public and private debt securities managed by the Banco de España, thus bringing the entire post-trade processing of Spanish cash securities under one roof (the BME group). The Banco de España exchanged its shares in Iberclear for shares in BME, to become one of its main shareholders, a situation that continues to this day.

2.2.3   Profile of listed companies

The Securities Market Law represented considerable modernization of the Spanish markets, strengthening the Spanish business sector's capacity to raise funds.

The largest companies with the broadest shareholding base traded on the continuous market; these companies, which never numbered more than 150, were the core of the Spanish stock exchanges' market capitalization. As from 1998, the number of companies admitted to listing but not trading on the continuous market swelled (see Chart 4), reaching almost 3,200 in 2005, as a result of the influx of open-end funds (SICAVs). However in that year the tax rules were changed, with companies no longer needing to be officially listed to benefit from favorable tax treatment, and most of these funds – whose contribution to Spanish market capitalization was never significant – opted to delist.

CHART 4   LISTED COMPANIES

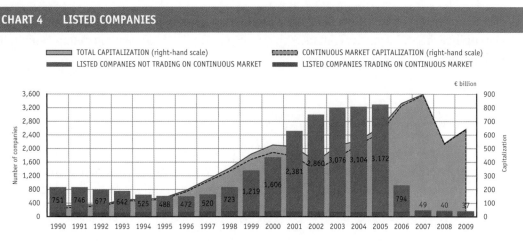

SOURCE: Compiled by the CNMV from data furnished by the Spanish stock exchanges.

The change in this rule led to the creation of an alternative trading forum for companies that found the requirements (especially the transparency requirements) of listing on an official market too demanding. This was the origin of Spain's alternative investment market, the MAB *(Mercado Alternativo Bursátil),* which operates with less strict conditions on admission and permanence and lower charges than the stock exchanges. Most investment firms that left the official market after 2006 found refuge in the MAB's open-end fund division; as in other jurisdictions,[9] there is also a division (still at the consolidation stage) for small and medium-sized enterprises in expansion.

2.2.4   Creation of an investment services industry

The intermediation model underwent rapid transformation. By the end of the 1990s there were 122 authorized securities brokers and dealers, a figure which remained quite stable up to the transposition into Spanish law of Council Directive 93/22/EEC on investment services, which allowed credit institutions to become stock-exchange members.

The effective opening-up of the activity of securities dealers and brokers – which came to be called investment services firms (ISFs) – led to a gradual decline in their numbers. Nevertheless, the ISFs linked to credit institutions did not disappear, as the growing technological complexity of electronic market transactions meant that many credit institutions chose to keep their stock market trading activities separate from their banking infrastructure, and in fact ISFs controlled by credit institutions continue to lead the stock-market trading business.

---

[9]   The most well-known are the Alternative Investment Market (AIM) managed by the LSE group, and the Alternext alternative markets of the NYSE Euronext group. Both AIM and Alternext served as benchmarks for creation of the MAB, which is part of and managed by the BME group.

The Securities Market Law also opened up the market to non-resident participants, which rapidly achieved significant market shares, especially in settlement, operating essentially through branches of foreign investment banks.

2.2.5 Consolidation of the role of supervisor

The CNMV first assumed powers over all matters relating to primary markets and admission to listing in February 1989, followed in July 1989 by powers over all matters relating to secondary markets.[10] Since then, and as Table 1 shows, the number of entities supervised has risen continuously, especially in the area of collective investment and fixed-income issuers.

From the outset, the CNMV has been a member of the international organizations of securities market regulators and supervisors. In 1989 it joined the International Organization of Securities Commissions (IOSCO) and is a member of its Technical Committee, along with the authorities of the other countries with more developed markets. The CNMV also participates in all the permanent working groups, which analyze matters relating to information on issues of securities and listed companies, the operation of secondary markets, the behavior of intermediaries and collective investment schemes, and supervisory practices. Since 2000, the IOSCO has its headquarters in Madrid; as the representative of the host country, the CNMV has a permanent seat on the Executive Committee.

During the 1990s, the CNMV signed various agreements on exchange of information and mutual assistance in the investigation of stock market violations with the main supervisors worldwide, and more recently it signed up to the IOSCO's Multilateral Agreement. Following the creation of the Committee of European Securities Regulators (CESR), comprising the securities regulators of all the EU Member States, a multilateral agreement for collaboration and exchange of information was signed between its members, replacing the previous bilateral agreements.

3 The Spanish securities markets today

3.1 The regulatory framework

As in other financial areas, Spain's current securities market regulations are based on European regulations, driven by the Financial Services Action Plan launched by the European Commission in the late 1990s. This Plan gave rise to a series of directives that have been transposed into Spanish law through successive amendments to the Securities Market Law

---

[10]   See Gil (2008) for an analysis of how the activity of the CNMV has evolved.

TABLE 1   ENTITIES SUPERVISED BY THE CNMV

	1990	1995	2000	2005	2009
Investment services firms: securities dealers and brokers	124	115	105	102	100
Portfolio managers	77	68	41	17	9
Collective investment scheme managers	125	136	124	112	120
Collective investment schemes	550	1,028	4,142	5,848	5,841
Hedge funds					67
Collective investment scheme depositaries	93	158	166	135	124
Private equity managers			20	45	74
Private equity (firms and funds)	15	22	65	121	254
Stock market governing bodies and Iberclear	5	11	11	14	14
Equity issuers	585	347	253	186	170
Fixed-income issuers	223	255	282	417	674
TOTAL	**1,797**	**2,140**	**5,209**	**6,997**	**7,447**

SOURCE: CNMV.

and complementary legislation. The relevant securities market regulations[11] essentially affect the following areas:

- Disclosure regarding financial instruments and issuers.
- Admission to listing.
- Operation and obligations of trading platforms and post-trade systems.
- Mechanisms for preservation of market integrity.
- Organization, solvency and behavior of entities specializing in intermediation and provision of investment services.

3.1.1   Regulation of disclosure regarding securities and issuers

One fundamental aim of regulation is to ensure that there is detailed and reliable information available on all securities that may be exchanged between investors or traded on official secondary markets.

When securities are placed in circulation, the prospectus is the main vehicle for disclosure. By law, any admission to listing or sale of corporate bonds or equities must be accompanied by a prospectus, the only exception to this rule being public debt or unlisted

---

[11]   See Annex at the end of this chapter for details of the most significant European legislation stemming from the Financial Services Action Plan.

instruments with a minimum investment of more than €50,000.[12] A prospectus will have two main sections:

- A securities note, outlining all the characteristics of the securities.
- A registration document, recording the business position and risks of the issuer. In Spain, these documents must be verified by the CNMV, although a prospectus approved by a competent authority in another EU Member State, through the consequent single passport, will also be valid.

In the case of securities traded on the markets, correct price formation demands regular disclosure on any developments that may affect how the securities are valued by investors. These disclosure requirements may be grouped into three different categories:

- Price sensitive information on specific events concerning issuers or securities that may reasonably affect investors' decisions to keep or sell the securities and, therefore, that may affect their price.
- Significant shareholding changes affecting the distribution of capital and voting rights of qualifying shareholders of companies whose home country is Spain and shareholdings held by their managers.
- Periodic information on the financial position and organization of listed entities, i.e. quarterly management reports, semi-annual interim financial statements and annual audited financial statements and management report. In addition, Spanish legislation also requires that companies prepare an annual corporate governance report.

Under European legislation, the consolidated financial statements of companies whose shares are listed must be drawn up in accordance with the International Financial Reporting Standards (IFRS) prepared by the International Accounting Standards Board (IASB). In the EU, these standards are applied through a convalidation process which can, in no circumstances, entail modification of the standards issued by the IASB.

The CNMV is responsible for ensuring that all issuers of securities on the Spanish markets comply with these standards.

3.1.2   Admission to listing and exclusion from trading

To be admitted to listing on an official Spanish market, regardless of the economic sector to which the issuer belongs, fixed-income issues must meet the following conditions: the securities to be admitted must represent the entire issue; the nominal value must be €200,000 or over, and the issuer must have audited financial statements for at least two years.

---

[12]   In the next review of the Prospectus Directive, this limit is expected to be raised to €100,000.

In the case of equity issues, an initial share offering must be accompanied by a prospectus and the issuer must have audited financial statements for at least three years. Moreover, in accordance with European directives, the offering must represent free float on the market of at least 25%.

One noteworthy aspect of both Spanish and European legislation is the absence of specific free-float requirements for maintenance of a stock market listing. Some European stock exchanges do have regulations that include specific conditions for permanence which must be met by all companies making initial offerings; any violation of these conditions may lead to their automatic exclusion from trading. However, although in some cases market supervisors or governing bodies may press companies to delist, none may force a delisting bid.

3.1.3 Regulation of trading and post-trade infrastructures

The Markets in Financial Instruments Directive (MiFID) is the European benchmark regulation for market infrastructures. The MiFID essentially regulates trading centers and, specifically, the rules governing official secondary markets.[13] It also removes the trading monopoly that most of these markets previously enjoyed.

The official secondary markets must meet a series of specific conditions affecting their managers, shareholders, bylaws and regulations, risk-detection systems, order-handling procedures and financial capacity.

Spanish legislation implementing the MiFID introduces certain specific requirements, such as:

- Minimum financial resources and maximum debt levels for infrastructures.
- Risk limits.
- Administrative authorization for qualifying shareholdings.
- Submission of annual budgets and confidential periodic financial and business information to the supervisor.
- Scrutiny of fees and tariffs.

The MiFID also introduces and regulates two other types of trading centers in addition to the official secondary markets:

- Multilateral Trading Facilities (MTFs), defined as facilities which, in accordance with non-discretionary rules, can bring together multiple third-party buying and selling interests in marketable securities in a way that results in binding contracts. These facilities may be managed solely by investment services firms (ISFs) and credit institutions or by governing bodies of official secondary markets.

---

[13] Under the MiFID, a "stock exchange" is a "regulated market" rather than an "official market". Here we have maintained the term "official secondary market", which must be understood to refer to any MiFID regulated market.

- Systematic Internalizers (SIs), described as ISFs or credit institutions that execute client orders relating to marketable securities against their own book, on an organized, frequent and systematic basis.

With these trading centers, the MiFID aims to increase competition and thus foster lower charges, technological innovation and cost efficiency. To ensure that these measures will not signify fragmentation of liquidity, the MiFID demands that all three types of trading centers envisaged in the regulations (official secondary markets, MTFs and SIs) comply with the same pre- and post-trade disclosure transparency rules. It also establishes the best execution principle, whereby intermediaries must execute a client's order on the market that offers the best possible results.

Pre-trade disclosure under the MiFID refers to information on buying and selling prices at any one time and on the depth of trading positions at those prices. Post-trade disclosure refers to information on the volume and price of the trade and the exact time of execution.

These rules are applicable only to shares and not to fixed-income securities, although the MiFID does allow Member States to extend them voluntarily to include trades in other kinds of financial instruments within their jurisdiction. Nevertheless, even in the case of equities, there are still significant differences between organizational and operating requirements for the official secondary markets and their participants and for the MTFs and SIs.

As indicated above, the MiFID scarcely touches on the post-trade process, although it does establish certain rules in this respect. In particular, official secondary markets must allow their members to clear and settle trades at entities or systems other than those currently used by the secondary market, and they must allow intermediaries of other States to use the central counterparty, clearing and settlement systems existing in the country in which the official secondary market operates, on the same conditions as the resident market participants.

3.1.4 Market integrity

Preventing market abuse is at the heart of the first securities market regulations and of the creation of market supervisors. There are two basic facets to the regulations: rules for the identification and use of insider information; and typification and pursuit of market manipulation.

Insider information is understood to mean specific non-public information on financial instruments within the scope of the Spanish Securities Market Law, which, if disclosed, could have a significant effect on their market price.

Regarding market manipulation, the legislation establishes that all persons or entities engaged in or connected with securities-market activities shall refrain from preparing or taking any steps that may distort free market price formation. In this respect, the scope of the Spanish Securities Market Law is somewhat broader than that of European legislation. Under Spanish legislation, all trading in securities on platforms recognized in Spanish law is automatically subject to the market abuse disciplinary and sanction regime, irrespective of whether or not the securities are admitted to listing on a European official secondary market. Thus, in contrast to the position in other jurisdictions, trades on Spain's MTFs specializing in unlisted securities, such as, for example the Latibex or the MAB, are subject to the prevention of market abuse regime.

3.1.5 Regulation of provision of investment services

The area that is most intensely regulated under the MiFID is possibly that relating to the conduct of firms providing investment services (applicable both to ISFs and credit institutions) in their relations with investors.[14]

Diligence and transparency are the essential obligations for these firms towards their clients, requiring them to look after their clients' interests as they would their own. For this reason, the three essential duties established are:

- To keep clients informed.
- To keep records of transactions.
- To apply the best execution principle, i.e. execution of client orders at the best possible price, taking into account cost, speed, likelihood of execution and settlement, size, nature or any other consideration relevant to the execution of the order.

3.1.6 The new European financial-supervision framework

To date, there has been extensive progress in financial regulation in Europe, but insufficient progress in the harmonization of supervisory practices and criteria, and this despite the existence, since the mid-2000s, of sectoral committees of financial supervisors (CESR for securities, CEBS for banking and CEIOPS for insurance). The degree of coordination between these committees, the central banks and the Community authorities has also proved insufficient to prevent and correctly handle episodes of financial instability such as those experienced since 2007.

In autumn 2010, the EU agreed on a Community regulation that entails a profound review of the existing system of financial supervision in Europe. Under the new arrangements, the national authorities remain essentially responsible for supervision of specific institutions, in keeping with the existing distribution of competencies between home and host countries. However, the new system also significantly strengthens the existing mechanisms for harmonizing supervisory criteria and coordinating actions, and it establishes a forum for joint analysis of systemic risks.

---

[14] Martínez (2007) contains a detailed description.

Specifically, the three sectoral committees become authorities: the ESMA for securities markets, the EBA for banking and the EIOPA for insurance and pensions. These new authorities, like their predecessors, will issue guidelines and recommendations; however, they will also draw up technical rules implementing European legislation, which all the Member States will have to adopt following convalidation by the European Commission. In addition, they will participate in the colleges of supervisors created to monitor financial institutions with pan-European reach and will establish a resolution mechanism for disagreements between national authorities. Lastly, in exceptional circumstances,[15] they may take decisions that will be binding on national authorities or individual institutions. The securities market authority (ESMA) will also be directly responsible for authorization and supervision of credit rating agencies and will have the power to introduce, in emergencies, measures restricting market operations (such as bans on short-selling).

Each authority will have a chairperson and an executive director, both on a full-time basis. They will also each have a Board of Supervisors, which will be the principal decision-making body, comprising representatives of the competent authority in each Member State and, as observers, representatives of the European Commission, the European Systemic Risk Board (ESRB) – created by the same Regulation – and the other two European authorities.[16] In addition, the three authorities will form a Joint Committee to facilitate coordination between them.

In the case of the ESRB, its main functions will be to compile and analyze all relevant information for the identification of systemic risk and to contribute to containing such risk. It may also issue notices, whether confidential or public, in the form of warnings and recommendations, addressed to the competent national or European authorities, and it will monitor the steps taken following such notices. The Board will consist of representatives of the ECB and the European Commission, the governors of all the EU national central banks and the chairpersons of the three sectoral European authorities, together with the chairs of an Advisory Scientific Committee (ASC) and an Advisory Technical Committee (ATC), both newly created. Representatives of the national supervisory authorities and the President of the Economic and Financial Committee (EFC) will act as observers. The Board will have a chair – initially the President of the ECB – and two vicechairs, together with a 15-member Steering Committee.[17]

---

[15]   Breach of Community law, emergency situations or in the case of failure to comply with arbitration decisions in disagreements between national authorities.

[16]   The ECB will also be an observer on the EBA.

[17]   The Chair and two Vice-Chairs of the Board, the Vice-President of the ECB, four national central bank governors, the chairpersons of the ESMA, the EBA and the EIOPA, a member of the European Commission, the President of the EFC and the chairs of the ATC and the ASC.

3.2 The current market situation in a European setting

3.2.1 Market structure

As seen in Section 2, following their demutualization, the Spanish securities markets gradually became vertically integrated around the BME group.

This contrasts with the trajectory of most European infrastructures which opted for horizontal integration, in some cases including the governing bodies of non-European markets.[18] Thus, in Europe there are currently five principal stock-exchange groups, in addition to BME:

- Euronext: the Amsterdam, Brussels, Paris and Lisbon Stock Exchanges.
- OMX: the Nordic stock exchanges (Copenhagen, Stockholm, Helsinki and Iceland) and those of the three Baltic states.
- LSE: the London Stock Exchange and, since 2007, the Milan Stock Exchange of the Borsa Italiana group.
- Deutsche Börse: the Frankfurt Stock Exchange.
- SIX Swiss: the Zurich Stock Exchange.

The OMX and Euronext groups were acquired several years ago by US market groups and were renamed NASDAQ OMX and NYSE Euronext. All these groups also include derivatives and fixed-income markets.

Deutsche Börse in Germany, SIX Swiss in Switzerland, BME in Spain and the Borsa Italiana subgroup of the LSE group in Italy all control entities that manage the securities settlement and central registration systems in the geographical markets in which they operate. However, the European market leader in the post-trade business is Euroclear, which manages, through subsidiaries, the securities settlement and central registration systems of Belgium, France, the Netherlands, Ireland, the UK, Finland and Sweden.

BME currently has nine trading centers in equities, public and private-debt securities and derivatives. These include: official markets, such as the four Spanish stock exchanges (interconnected through the SIBE); the AIAF official fixed-income market; the MEFF for financial derivatives and multilateral trading facilities such as the MAB (for small and medium-sized enterprises, open-end funds and hedge funds); the Latibex, where shares in Latin American companies are traded; and the SENAF public debt trading platform.

In the post-trade field, BME includes Iberclear which, by law, handles the settlement of all equity and fixed-income trades made on the official markets and the official registration of all holders of securities admitted to listing on these markets.

All equity trades are settled bilaterally, that is, with no central counterparty, although Iberclear guarantees compliance with the principle of assured delivery. This means that if the seller

---

[18]   Baena (2007) and García-Vaquero (2007) offer a more detailed account of this process.

fails to deliver the securities in question – usually three days after the trade (T+3) – Iberclear will obtain the securities needed to allow the trade to be completed. For this purpose, Iberclear holds collateral furnished by the market participants and operates a dissuasive penalty system.

Contrary to the usual system in other countries, in Spain equity trades are not registered by means of a system based on balances. Instead, holders of securities accounts with Iberclear must keep a record of their trades (whether on own account or for clients) using registration codes (RRs) issued by the stock markets.[19] In the settlement process, the settling party must provide Iberclear with the seller's codes corresponding to the shares to be transferred to the buyer, so that it may accept the trade and make the appropriate change in ownership.

By contrast, fixed-income settlement follows the standard system based on balances. There is a central counterparty (MEFF Clear), but it records very little activity as most transactions are settled bilaterally.

Clearing, settlement and registration on the derivatives markets – the MEFF and the MFAO (the olive oil futures market) – is made through a central counterparty.

3.2.2   Market size and activity

In equities, the BME group has a mid-market ranking among the leading European groups (see Table 2). In terms of absolute capitalization, it ranks above the Italian stock market (part of the LSE group) and the Nordic exchanges (NASDAQ OMX Nordic), but below the London Stock Exchange, the NYSE-Euronext group (comprising the French, Portuguese, Belgian and Dutch exchanges) and the German and Swiss exchanges. In terms of market capitalization as a percentage of GDP, the Spanish market also ranks above its German counterpart, but below the Nordic exchanges.

TABLE 2 STOCK EXCHANGE CAPITALIZATION OF THE MAIN EUROPEAN MARKET GROUPS		
	Value at Dec-2009 (€ million)	Capitalization as % of GDP
NYSE Euronext	1,999,967	59%
London Stock Exchange	1,950,048	82%
Deutsche Börse	900,772	35%
SIX Swiss Exchange	738,707	217%
BME (a)	584,569	51%
NASDAQ OMX Nordic	569,604	60%
Borsa Italiana	457,126	27%

SOURCES: Federation of European Securities Exchanges (FESE) and BME.

a. The BME capitalization figures exclude the Latibex and MAB MTF shares and shares of foreign companies listed on BME group stock exchanges.

---

[19]   The changes to the Iberclear regulations published in July 2010 envisage the provision of settlement and registration services for off-exchange transactions.

One less satisfactory aspect of the Spanish stock market is its free float. In fact, the IBEX is the index with the highest percentage (38%) of total capitalization at companies whose free float is below 50%. Furthermore, the Spanish market is that which has seen its average free float fall most in recent years.

To date, competition between the official equity markets of the six leading European groups has been limited, with just marginal transfers of liquidity in specific securities between markets. In fact, trading in companies' shares has tended to remain concentrated on their home markets or on the markets of the countries in which they do most of their business.

By contrast, real competition has come from the Multilateral Trading Facilities (MTFs), which have taken advantage of the greater flexibility the MiFID brought to the competitive framework to achieve significant market shares within a short space of time by means of aggressive pricing policies. As Chart 5 shows, all stock exchanges saw their trading volume decline in 2008 and again in 2009, while in the same period the volume attracted by the three most active MTFs grew significantly.

Table 3 depicts the market shares at end-September 2010 of the three most active European MTFs in the trading of shares admitted to listing on the main European markets.

The London Stock Exchange (LSE), the Deutsche Börse and NYSE Euronext have seen the most competition from MTFs, closely followed by SIX Swiss and the main NASDAQ OMX Nordic exchanges. To date, the Spanish group BME has been virtually unaffected by competition from MTFs, possibly due to the singularities of the Spanish clearing and settlement system which, as will be seen later in this chapter, may have made it more difficult for Spanish shares to be traded on these platforms.

Turning to fixed income, in the past both the stock exchanges and other official secondary markets included in the large stock market groups have attracted little trading volume in public debt securities and corporate bonds. With certain exceptions, fixed-income securities have tended to trade outside the official secondary markets and platforms linked to the large market groups.

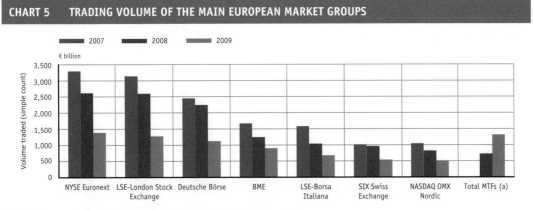

CHART 5   TRADING VOLUME OF THE MAIN EUROPEAN MARKET GROUPS

SOURCE: Own compilation, from statistical data published by the FESE.

a. The aggregate trading volume of the three leading European share trading platforms: Chi-X, BATS Europe and Turquoise.

TABLE 3   AGGREGATE MARKET SHARE OF MTFS IN SHARE TRADING

	Percentage shares of 3 MTFs (Sep-2010) (a)
LSE-London Stock Exchange *(FTSE-100)*	46%
Deutsche Börse	30%
NYSE Euronext *(main stock exchange indices, weighted)*	32%
SIX Swiss-Zurich Stock Exchange	31%
NASDAQ OMX Nordic *(main stock exchange indices, weighted)*	27%
LSE-Borsa Italiana	22%
BME	2%

SOURCE: Own compilation based on market data.

a. Data corresponding to Chi-X, BATS Europe and Turquoise. Percentage of trading of the shares admitted to listing on the markets indicated.

TABLE 4   FIXED-INCOME ACTIVITY OF THE MAIN EUROPEAN MARKET GROUPS

	Number of trades		Total volume traded (€ million)	
	2009	Change 09/08	2009	Change 09/08
CORPORATE BONDS				
BME (AIAF market + stock market fixed income)	924,410	14%	3,764,000	52%
NASDAQ OMX Nordic	170,086	35%	1,092,606	-1%
NYSE Euronext	734,773	9%	46,603	39%
LSE-London	22,611	140%	25,018	51%
SIX Swiss	106,688	29%	21,386	11%
Deutsche Börse	566,600	-1%	13,900	-6%
Borsa Italiana	467,055	14%	6,981	35%
PUBLIC DEBT				
LSE-London	318,540	15%	4,964,991	14%
NASDAQ OMX Nordic	18,458	-26%	621,704	-31%
LSE-Borsa Italiana	2,727,949	10%	211,496	27%
BME (SENAF MTF)	6,348	59%	136,301	83%
Deutsche Börse	149,434	-32%	72,113	-24%
SIX Swiss	40,165	-28%	36,004	-30%
NYSE Euronext	—		—	
INTERNATIONAL PRODUCTS				
SIX Swiss	448,353	7%	56,135	-1%
Deutsche Börse	754,727	10%	19,696	29%
LSE-London	11,051	180%	17,765	41%
LSE-Borsa Italiana	443,539	98%	12,178	113%
NASDAQ OMX Nordic	10,833	12%	1,488	-2%
BME	—		—	
NYSE Euronext	—		—	

SOURCE: FESE.

As Table 4 shows, the BME group is the European leader in corporate bond trading through the AIAF fixed-income market, followed, at a considerable distance, by the NASDAQ OMX.

In all the other groups, corporate bond trading is virtually irrelevant. The LSE group is the clear market leader in public debt, following its purchase of Borsa Italiana and consequent indirect acquisition of the MTS fixed-income markets and platforms that essentially trade EU Member States' public debt.

Cross-border competition between trading infrastructures has been much more intense in derivatives than on the stock markets. It is relatively simple to organize markets for equity, share and interest-rate derivatives, irrespective of where the underlying instruments are issued or traded, and this, together with the significant economies of scale, has favored the gradual concentration of these activities at international trading centers. As a result, two large derivatives markets have emerged in Europe: EUREX in Germany which is managed by the Deutsche Börse group (although SIX Swiss is also part of the group); and Euronext. Liffe which is headquartered in the UK and belongs to the NYSE Euronext group.

The Spanish derivatives market – the MEFF RV – ranks fourth (see Table 5), at a considerable distance from the two market leaders and also behind the Nordic group.

In post-trade, the most important infrastructures are the central securities depositories (CSDs) and the central counterparties (CCPs).

In Europe, CSDs are either subsidiaries of any of the four leading European market groups (Deutsche Börse, LSE-Borsa Italiana, SIX Swiss and BME) or they belong to Euroclear. Table 6 shows the activity of the main groups that handle settlement and registration.

TABLE 5   DERIVATIVES ACTIVITY OF THE MAIN EUROPEAN MARKET GROUPS

	Share derivatives		Index derivatives		Interest rate derivatives	
	2009	Change 09/08	2009	Change 09/08	2009	Change 09/08
EUREX	421,324,400	-12%	797,500,064	-22%	465,683,344	-29%
NYSE-Euronext.Liffe	351,915,312	14%	156,255,392	-10%	492,914,928	-11%
NASDAQ OMX Nordic	35,489,341	-39%	47,847,894	-19%	21,262,213	-21%
BME-MEFF RV	80,114,688	24%	12,942,541	-31%	—	—
LSE: EDX and IDEM	32,919,433	35%	9,658,100	-16%	—	—

SOURCE: Activity data from statistics published by the FESE.

TABLE 6   ACTIVITY OF THE MAIN EUROPEAN CENTRAL SECURITIES DEPOSITORIES (a)

	Settlement		Registration	
	Number of trades		Volume registered (€ million)	
	2009	Change 09/08	2009	Change 09/08
Euroclear	179,600,000	14%	20,200,000	12%
Deutsche Börse-Clearstream	102,000,000	-11%	10,346,000	-3%
LSE-Borsa Italiana-Monte Titoli	51,900,000	20%	2,800,000	4%
BME Iberclear	34,822,132	-14%	1,997,000	14%
SIX Swiss-SIX SIS	28,842,000	-16%	1,927,743	17%

SOURCE: Company financial statements and management reports.

a. Basis of the calculation: December 2009 for Euroclear and BME; annual average for others.

Clearing of derivatives trades is generally performed by the markets themselves; in contrast, clearing of cash market trades typically corresponds to the CCPs. Their role is essentially to interpose themselves between buyers and sellers and to determine, by position netting, the net (buying or selling) position per intermediary and the settlement value. At present, most CCPs have close ties to specific trading centers: for example, NYSE Euronext and LCH Clearnet, Deutsche Börse and Eurex Clearing, and the main MTFs and the two new European CCPs (EMCF and EuroCCP).

The Spanish stock market is an exception in this case, as it has no central counterparty. This is the result, as mentioned earlier, of the singular system of mitigation of counterparty risk in Spain, whereby the CSD (Iberclear) guarantees compliance with the principle of assured delivery.

3.2.3 Market participants

All entities wishing to participate directly on the Spanish markets, in trading and in post-trade (clearing, settlement and registration), must be registered as investment services firms (ISFs) or credit institutions.

As Chart 6 shows, the market shares of the different market participants vary enormously by activity. Thus, ISFs overall have the highest market share in trading, while branches of foreign credit institutions are the clear market leaders in settlement and resident credit institutions in registration.

Another significant industry characteristic is the high level of concentration: the top five participants in each activity account for 42% (trading), 67% (settlement) and 65% (registration) of the respective totals.

All resident credit institutions and most branches that are active in cash equity markets are present on the corporate bond markets. By contrast, ISFs have a limited presence (ten participants) in this area. This is because credit institutions that have ISFs tend to act directly as members of fixed-income market infrastructures for trading, settlement and registration. Moreover, resident credit institutions that do not operate in the equity market systems are present in corporate bonds, meaning that the fixed-income market is dominated by credit institutions.

In the case of derivatives, foreign ISFs and foreign credit institutions and their branches account for most of the volume traded (65% in 2009), reflecting the high degree of openness to competition both on the European and the Spanish derivatives markets.

4 Challenges facing the Spanish markets

The previous sections have described the context in which the Spanish markets currently operate. The medium-term outlook largely depends on two key factors: changes in the regulatory

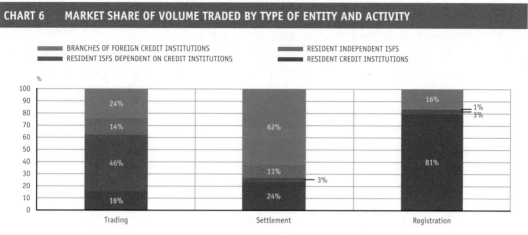

CHART 6   MARKET SHARE OF VOLUME TRADED BY TYPE OF ENTITY AND ACTIVITY

SOURCE: Own compilation.

framework, which will foreseeably become more demanding, to enhance the transparency of issuers and products, bring about improvements in market operations and place stricter rules on unregulated trading platforms; and the Spanish markets' capacity to fully adapt to the competitive environment that has built up in Europe and internationally in recent years.

4.1   Regulatory challenges

The regulatory framework described in section 3.1 largely corresponds to the principle of "better regulation" that has gradually gained ground in Europe since the end of the last century and essentially comprises three basic principles:

- Fostering competition between intermediaries and trading and settlement centers throughout Europe.
- Subjecting proposals for rules of conduct for market participants to detection of evident market failures and, in many cases, to demanding cost-benefit analysis.
- Strengthening, in exchange, the protection mechanisms for retail investors.

The financial crisis, which revealed significant shortcomings and loopholes, has brought into question the solidity of the conceptual system used to analyse securities-market regulations.

The first – and perhaps the most important – regulatory area that needs to be strengthened is transparency in all areas of financial activity. One singular aspect of the crisis that unfolded in 2007 was the breakdown in confidence, which drove credit risk spreads to unprecedented levels in recent times and paralyzed issuance and trading on many wholesale markets (such as the interbank or structured-product markets) and in other private debt securities.

One of the key points that triggered this crisis of confidence was the lack of sufficient reliable information on fundamental aspects of transactions:

- The economic and financial position of the issuers and other parties seeking funds.
- The nature of the financial products offered and, specifically, the inherent risk.
- The supply and demand conditions on the capital markets.

Post-trade is a second area in which regulatory failings have been particularly evident. As indicated previously in this chapter, to date the European regulator has paid little attention to clearing, settlement and registration, focusing instead on issuance and trading. However, the crisis has showed that the absence of reliable multilateral mechanisms for clearing bilateral trades has exacerbated counterparty risk and thus posed a threat to financial stability.

A third area in which regulations have proved insufficient is that relating to ensuring correct price formation. Specifically, it is now clear that the rules for prevention of market abuse need to be strengthened and market operations reviewed, in particular the limits on short-selling and the effectiveness of the circuit breakers used to contain volatility.

The following subsections identify and analyze a number of specific regulatory proposals in the areas indicated.

4.1.1 Issuer transparency

Issuers of securities are required to submit a wealth of information to the market (prospectus, periodic and price sensitive information, qualifying holdings, etc.), but it was possibly the information on financial statements that proved the most deficient during the crisis.

Given that the EU's current accounting regulations for all issuers of securities coincide with the International Financial Reporting Standards (IFRS), the pertinent regulatory reforms lie not with the European authorities but with the International Accounting Standards Board (IASB).

The crisis revealed certain failings in financial reporting standards: first, the lack of transparency surrounding financial corporations' exposure to the liquidity problems of vehicles promoted by them; second, the complexity and imperfections of the asset valuation standards, which possibly distorted the representation of economic reality at some entities; and third, the inappropriate treatment of impairment of loans and other assets.

Regarding the treatment of vehicles linked to firms, there has been clear progress. In particular, the IASB has amended the compulsory disclosure requirements to include exposure to vehicles related to the reporting entity, even if consolidation requirements are not met.

Definition of the valuation standards for financial assets and liabilities on financial institutions' balance sheets proves much more complex.[20] During the crisis, numerous analysts

---

[20] CESR (2009b) contains an analysis of this question. See also IASB (2009a).

and even public authorities from various countries asked the IASB to significantly narrow the scope of application of fair value, considering that this had contributed to amplifying the reach of the financial crisis.

The empirical and conceptual significance of this argument may certainly be disputed.[21] The IASB has considerably improved the valuation standards (IASB, 2009a and 2009b), specifically confining the use of fair value to equity instruments that include implicit derivatives, or fixed-income instruments that are not managed (as is normally the case with loans) on the basis of the instruments' cash flows.

Lastly, the IASB has recognized that the present standard used to reflect impairment of assets measured at cost (such as loans), based on the concept of incurred loss, was too inflexible. Accordingly, it is now considering (IASB, 2009c) replacing it with a new method that reflects the expected impairment over the residual life of the instrument. This approach is largely based on the dynamic provisioning that the Banco de España has been successfully using for the last ten years in the framework of its prudential policy.

4.1.2 Product transparency

The crisis also revealed the excesses of financial innovation, especially the opportunities for regulatory arbitrage that led the banks to create a multitude of structured products, some of which were highly complex.

These products, and especially commercial loan securitizations, effectively transferred credit risk from the originators to a wide range of investors, including other credit institutions. This meant that institutions had more funds available for lending and resulted, in some cases, in fewer incentives for appropriate credit quality assessment of borrowers.

The inherent complexity of these products, together with deficiencies in the rating agencies' credit assessment procedures, allowed them to fall into the hands of agents who lacked the capacity to estimate the risk assumed (which proved to be higher than indicated by their ratings) and to bear the impact of that risk when it materialized.[22]

Accordingly, steps have had to be taken on three fronts:

- First, restoring incentives to ensure that originator banks correctly assess the credit risk that is subsequently transferred via securitization.
- Second, strengthening the regulation of the credit rating agencies, to eliminate distortions that may affect the quality of their work.

---

[21] See Martínez and Restoy (2009), Restoy (2008a and 2008b) and Manso and Rodríguez (2008) for an analysis of this debate.

[22] See CESR (2008), Restoy (2008c) and IOSCO (2008) for an analysis of the role the credit rating agencies played in the financial crisis and the regulatory response.

- Third, enhancing transparency throughout the securitization process, including information on any change in the credit quality of the securitized assets, and promoting the simplification and standardization of these products.[23]

Regarding the incentives for originator banks, the European regulators have agreed, within the framework of amendments to the Capital Requirements Directive of 16 September 2009 (CRDII), to introduce rules that oblige investing entities to ensure that in any asset-backed securities they hold, the originators retain at least a 5% economic interest. This measure will clearly raise the incentives for originators to study loan applications diligently. How it will affect the securitization market, considering that it represents a kind of de facto tax on securitization, remains to be seen. This regulation coincides with other restrictive measures, such as the increase envisaged in regulatory capital consumption associated with investment in these instruments, their consideration as illiquid instruments for calculation of the Basel III liquidity requirements, and tightening of the conditions under which asset-backed securities may be eligible as collateral in Eurosystem operations.

In the case of the credit rating agencies, in September 2009 the European Union adopted Regulation (EC) No 1060/2009 of the European Parliament and of the Council, which establishes different requirements for agencies whose ratings are used for regulatory purposes. The European Securities and Markets Authority (ESMA) will shortly become directly responsible for authorizing rating agencies in Europe and for ensuring that these rules are met.

On the question of transparency of securitized assets, initiatives are under way in the industry[24] to develop standards on different aspects of the securitization process (credit enhancement, due diligence, disclosure requirements on securitized loans, etc.). Moreover, the ECB plans to promote the design of a standardized procedure for compilation and submission of information on securitizations in the euro area.

These initiatives are essential to restore the confidence in these instruments that is needed in order for securitization market issues and activity to be resumed. However, it is doubtful this is possible without regulatory back-up. Probably the best way to guarantee the transparency needed is to introduce disclosure requirements for asset-backed securitization vehicles. This is precisely the approach taken in Spain by the CNMV, which has established a specific accounting plan and public disclosure requirements for securitization vehicles.[25]

---

[23]   CNMV (2010) contains a description of the main initiatives in this field.

[24]   These industry initiatives notably include the proposals drawn up by the Global Joint Initiative (2008) and the Residential Securitization Transparency and Reporting (RESTART) project of the United States' American Securitization Forum (ASF). Also, see IOSCO (2009 and 2010) for its principles on transparency for securitization issues.

[25]   See Manso et al (2009) for a description of these requirements.

4.1.3   Market transparency

One of the likely causes of the malfunctioning of some securities markets during the crisis (particularly corporate bonds and credit derivatives) was the lack of sufficient public information on the transaction terms on these markets.

The consequence of the flexible approach of the current regulations is that a large proportion of securities trading activity in Europe remains hidden. This is particularly true of the corporate bond market. As indicated in section 3.1, trading in these securities is not generally subject to transparency rules, although the markets do publish some pre- and post-trade information for some (roughly half) of these securities traded on organized markets. Moreover, in the case of equities, where trading is subject to transparency rules, a significant proportion[26] of this trading is made off-exchange or in dark pools and thus escapes these rules. Transparency is even less evident in the world of derivatives, given the absence, as in the case of fixed income, of regulatory requirements in this respect and the predominance of over-the-counter (OTC) trading which accounts for some 90% of the total.

This situation is far from satisfactory. Transparency favors competition between platforms and intermediaries and cuts transaction costs. It also reduces adverse selection and helps facilitate the price search and formation process. At the same time, it allows investors to monitor managers' activity.[27]

Accordingly, European regulations in this area should be reviewed. Specifically, changes should be made to the MiFID in at least two fundamental aspects: post-trade transparency requirements should be extended to include fixed-income securities and derivatives;[28] and pre-trade transparency in the equity markets should be applied to all systematic order-matching systems (such as crossing networks), which may entail redefining the types of trading platforms regulated by the MiFID. In addition, there should be fewer exceptions to these requirements, to limit the volume of trading, for example, in dark pools, which makes no contribution to effective price formation. The review of this Directive, due to start in 2011, presents a good opportunity for such changes to be made.[29]

4.1.4   Reform of the OTC markets

The extent of the financial crisis that unfolded in 2007 was due, in part, to the shortcomings identified in the systems for clearing and settlement of certain instruments.[30] For

---

[26]   Up to one third of trading of blue chips, according to ESME (European Securities Markets Expert Group) estimates.

[27]   See Restoy and Rodriguez (2010) for a more detailed discussion of the effects of transparency on securities markets.

[28]   See the CESR proposal (2009a) and Losada (2010).

[29]   See CFA Institute (2009).

[30]   Arce et al (2010) contains an in-depth analysis of these market failings.

example, credit default swaps (CDSs), which are basically used by investors to hedge corporate bond or sovereign debt credit risk.

In order for this market to operate correctly, investors purchasing protection must be effectively protected against the credit risk of the underlying asset. In other words, the counterparty risk must be sufficiently limited.

The most effective way of limiting the counterparty risk is by establishing multilateral position netting systems (or central counterparties).[31] Projects are currently under way for the creation of central counterparties for derivatives, along with regulatory initiatives to make their use compulsory and rules on their operation and supervision.[32]

These markets would also benefit from enhanced transparency, through the creation of trade repositories, to provide information on transaction terms, and analysis – such as that currently ongoing by the Financial Stability Board (FSB) – of cases in which certain types of derivatives trades should be made through organized markets.

4.1.5   Reform of the post-trade systems

The debate on the need to strengthen the (currently under-developed) European post-trade regulations has recently intensified.

The regulatory efforts required are in two areas. First, in the legal area, developing principles to permit harmonization of the conditions of recognition of ownership of securities, and establishing uniform requirements on the organization and conduct of all entities – central securities depositories, custodian banks, etc. – holding client securities accounts.

The second area that calls for regulatory effort is clearing and settlement. At present, these services are provided by a multitude of entities, such as national (Iberclear) or international (Euroclear or Clearstream) central securities depositories, custodian banks or central counter-parties, all subject to different regulatory requirements according to their jurisdiction and to whether or not they have a banking license. The CESR-ESCB standards for clearing and set-tlement systems are the only element of convergence in this field, but they are very limited in scope: their requirements are very broadly defined; they do not cover custodian banks; and they are not binding on national regulatory and supervisory authorities.[33]

This substantial lack of regulatory uniformity within the EU means that these post-trade service providers are not competing on a level playing field, distorting the cross-border competition framework promoted by the MiFID and other EU initiatives.[34] Moreover, the lack of a common regulatory framework encourages a regulatory race to the bottom; this

---

[31]   See Cecchetti et al (2009), González Pueyo (2009) and Duffie et al (2010).

[32]   Two notable examples are the upcoming EU regulation (EMIR) and the Dodd-Frank Law in the United States.

[33]   Lastra (2007) describes this matter in detail.

[34]   See Oxera (2009) and The Giovannini Group (2001 and 2003).

could adversely affect average safety standards, heightening the systemic risk inherent in clearing and settlement.

Accordingly, steps should be taken to establish European regulations on clearing and settlement systems for all types of instruments (cash securities and derivatives) and on the providers of these services in the European Union.[35]

4.1.6 Operational reform

One point that became clear during the crisis was that, in certain cases, operational failings could help generate excess volatility in listed securities, unwarranted in terms of their fundamentals.[36]

Most securities markets worldwide operate with circuit breakers that activate halts in ordinary trading when prices move significantly above or below predefined thresholds. In the EU, these systems have generally operated satisfactorily. However, considering the growth in multilateral trading facilities (MTFs), it would seem logical to consider placing uniform circuit breakers on all markets. This may require regulatory action that can only be introduced effectively at EU level.[37]

More complex is the question of whether or not short-selling should be restricted on certain markets. Such restrictions may be justified in specific cases or circumstances; for example, a ban on naked short-selling (ie. when shares are sold by persons who at the time of the sale neither own nor have borrowed such shares) will reduce the likelihood of problems in the settlement process – delivery of shares against payment – that normally takes place several days after the trade. These problems may be a source of distortion for securities markets.

Nevertheless, before any steps are taken in this respect, prior consideration should be given to the possible adverse effects they may have on efficient market operations. For example, strict limits on short-selling may reduce market liquidity and make it more difficult to hedge long positions. Moreover, as these are asymmetrical measures, they tend to delay price moves downwards, but not upwards, thus hindering early correction of stock-market bubbles and encouraging stock-price volatility.[38]

A final point to consider is that the cost-benefit balance of certain restrictive measures may differ, according to the type of market used for their implementation analysis. For example, the cost of placing restrictions on short-selling in terms of liquidity may be

---

[35]   The European Commission is currently studying three items of legislation in this field: one on securities holding; a second on netting of OTC derivatives (EMIR); and a third, still at the early stages, on other post-trade infrastructures.

[36]   This was precisely the case of the "flash crash" on the US securities markets on 6 May 2010. During that session, the major US stock indices registered falls verging on 10%; there followed a partial recovery, but for several minutes some 200 stocks lost virtually all their value.

[37]   See Fidessa (2010).

[38]   Buenaventura (2008) contains a more in-depth review of this question.

particularly significant on bilateral markets – such as public debt markets – where trades are made through intermediaries that take buying and selling positions almost simultaneously.

In any case, the disparate regulations currently applicable in the EU should be harmonized, along the lines of the European Commission's recent legislative proposal,[39] which has three key elements:

- Adoption of a common disclosure regime for short positions in securities listed in the EU.[40]
- Establishment of procedures to strengthen settlement discipline in all markets.
- Grant of emergency powers to the European Securities and Markets Authority (ESMA) to introduce additional restrictions in all jurisdictions.

4.2 Operational challenges

4.2.1 Issuance

As seen in Section 2 of this chapter, the European financial industry has undergone extensive regulatory reform in recent years; this has significantly increased the openness of the national markets and intensified competition between intermediaries and trading centers. In light of the globalization of ownership and business activity overall, some forecasters predicted that one of the effects of this regulatory reform would be the disappearance of national niches of activity, with issuance, trading and post-trade activities becoming centralized around just one or a few financial centers.

Time has proved otherwise. In issuance, the national markets have not, in general, suffered major losses. Companies have continued to register issues in their home jurisdictions, with no major changes in market size or in the number of operations recorded.

In Spain, this is clearly linked to the fact that, despite the decline in the home bias of investment portfolios, most listed companies continue to have a national shareholder base. Moreover, international integration has consisted mainly in acquisitions of foreign firms, and even in the case of large Spanish companies that have been acquired by foreign groups or have been involved in cross-border mergers, the parent companies have preferred not to delist their Spanish subsidiaries.

Relocation of securities issues has been slightly more notable in fixed income, as some Spanish issuers have repeatedly looked to the international markets to attract large institutional investors. Nevertheless, the volume of fixed-income issues registered in Spain represents the bulk of the financing obtained through this channel by the Spanish corporate

---

[39]   See also CESR (2010).
[40]   See CESR (2010).

sector and, as shown in Table 4 of Section 3 above, the AIAF fixed-income market is still one of the largest in Europe.

In the foreseeable future it is unlikely these trends will alter dramatically. However, as the shareholder bases of Spanish companies become potentially more international, Spain needs to remain an attractive market for these issues, entailing rigorous compliance with the regulations that ensure ease of access to national markets for foreign investors and intermediaries.

One area where improvements are called for if the Spanish stock market is to remain attractive is the free float of listed companies. As seen in section 3, free float has declined significantly in recent years, partly as a result of mergers and absorptions involving various Spanish companies. Low free float makes it difficult for pricing to function correctly, which may reduce demand for securities. At present, and in contrast to the regulations on admission to listing on official markets, the regulations on securities remaining listed essentially correspond to the markets themselves.[41] Accordingly, it would make sense for Spanish market managers to introduce stricter rules on minimum free float for companies listed on official markets. Companies that failed to meet these new rules would be excluded from trading on official markets, but could possibly be listed on "unofficial" ones, such as, for example, the alternative investment market (MAB).

Lastly, the foreseeable tightening of capital regulations may dent the potential growth of credit supply,[42] encouraging companies to seek direct market financing. Hence the importance of national markets being in a position to accommodate newcomers, irrespective of size.[43] Specifically, means should be sought to reduce the cost of access to the MAB and to attract the interest of investors and analysts. One foreseeable measure to raise the profile of the alternative investment market could be to create pan-European trading platforms for securities issued on the different "unofficial" national markets.

4.2.2   Trading

As seen in earlier sections of this chapter, trades in securities admitted to listing on regulated or official markets need not necessarily be made on the markets themselves; in fact, fixed-income and derivatives market trades have tended to be made through bilateral transactions off the markets' own trading platforms. This pattern is unlikely to change dramatically, although the regulatory reforms envisaged should encourage greater uniformity of financial products, making it easier for them to be traded on multilateral facilities.

In the case of equities, since the MiFID came into force, the regulated European markets have gradually lost trading volume to the MTFs and OTC discretionary order-matching systems such as the crossing networks.

---

[41]   See López-Blanco (2008).

[42]   For more details on the changes in capital regulations, see Chapter 11.

[43]   Restoy (2010) has a more detailed analysis of this question.

To a certain extent, this shift in volume from stock exchanges to alternative trading platforms is a consequence of the regulatory failings that allow these infrastructures to operate with less demanding requirements in terms of organization, price and transparency. If the regulatory review envisaged corrects some of these failings, MTFs and crossing networks may see some decline in the rate of growth of their business.

It seems clear, however, that there is still growth potential for trading of Spanish stocks on multilateral facilities. To date, these platforms have drawn considerably less business away from the stock market in Spain than in other European markets. This may be due in part to the singular features of the Spanish settlement and registration system, which until very recently made it difficult to record changes in ownership resulting from off-exchange trades. However, given that the new Iberclear regulations – approved in July 2010 – eliminate these difficulties, the MTFs may foreseeably become more important competitors for the Spanish regulated market.

4.2.3   Post-trade processing

Clearing, settlement and registration is possibly the area of market activity where the most profound changes are foreseeable both in Spain and across Europe.

In recent years, the main barriers to integration of European financial markets have been found in this industry segment, where a high level of divergence remains in terms of the legal status of the different infrastructures, fee schedules, tax treatment and ownership recognition.

As indicated in Section 4.1 above, to date the regulatory response to these problems, identified in the Giovannini Report almost a decade ago,[44] has been rather lukewarm. This has delayed the harmonization of post-trade systems, the interconnection or consolidation of the existing infrastructures and, despite the MiFID provisions, the creation of a genuine competitive framework.

Nevertheless, in recent years some progress has been made on the construction of cross-border post-trade infrastructures. The most important of these is the TARGET2 Securities system (T2S), managed by the Eurosystem, which will integrate the handling of participants' cash and securities accounts in a single system. It will, however, maintain the role currently played by the central securities depositories – such as Iberclear in Spain – as regards registration in each national jurisdiction.[45]

The fact that post-trade processes for instruments of all kinds are converging towards a relatively well-defined basic model is assisting this progress. Broadly speaking, this model has four essential features:

-   Trades become firm upon settlement, ie. several days post-trade.
-   Trades that are not completed may be canceled.

---

[44]   See "The Giovannini Group" (2001 and 2003).
[45]   For a more detailed description, see Núñez and Jiménez (2007).

- Counterparty risk is reduced by means of central counterparties (CCPs) interposed between buyers and sellers.
- Registration of ownership is by a system based on balances.

In Spain, as discussed in Section 3.2.1 above, fixed-income and derivatives post-trade systems are essentially in line with the European model, but this is not the case in equities where the model is very different,[46] based on the following four singular features:

- Trades become firm upon execution.
- Iberclear assures delivery of securities.
- There is no central counterparty.
- Registration is based on a system of registration codes (RRs) that link purchases of securities in one person's account to sales of securities in another's.

This system has worked satisfactorily for more than 20 years. It has provided buyers and sellers with a high degree of reassurance regarding the successful completion of their trades and, via the RR system, it has provided the supervisor with an effective mechanism for monitoring of market trades and investigation of possible unlawful practices.

However, the system must evolve towards a model comparable with that in use in the rest of Europe. Efficient practices will have to be adopted to control counterparty risk (such as the creation of a central counterparty), relieving the settlement system of the need to guarantee completion of every trade. Moreover, bringing the Spanish system more in line with the European model would facilitate the integration of Spanish equity trade settlement into cross-border projects such as the T2S.

Since February 2010, the CNMV, in collaboration with the Banco de España and the industry, has been developing an ambitious reform project for Spain's clearing, settlement and registration system that will entail major changes in Spanish law and in the operations of entities active on the Spanish market. The aim is not only to introduce a model that is more compatible with that existing in most other European countries, but also to adopt procedures that will ensure that the legal and operational certainty provided by the present system is at least maintained if not enhanced.

In principle, the changes proposed should not have a significant impact on custody services. Nevertheless, the disappearance of the registration codes (RRs) will mean that formal recognition of ownership will be defined by the balances on client securities accounts held at Iberclear participants. Accordingly, more demanding requirements should be placed on these participants and a harmonized registration procedure should be adopted to facilitate periodic control both by Iberclear and the CNMV. This could prompt some decline in the number of participants actively engaged in custody services.

---

[46] See CNMV and Banco de España (2009) for a detailed description of the singularities of the Spanish model.

Clearly, the settlement business would also be affected, as trades would be cleared through a central counterparty, thus significantly reducing the number of trades to be settled. However, the reform introduces the role of trade clearing and central counterparty management, to date nonexistent on the Spanish equity market, thus opening up new business opportunities.

This new environment will mean that Spanish infrastructures will have to adjust their fee schedules and offer value-added services, either individually or through integration in pan-European initiatives. In this respect, greater market openness and competition is not only a challenge insofar as maintenance of Spanish market share is concerned, but also an opportunity to offer settlement services from Spain for trades in securities issued in other European countries.

5 Final comments

This chapter has reviewed the development and present situation of the Spanish securities markets and the outlook for the future, describing how the industry has successfully faced the main challenges posed, especially following the demutualization of the markets in the late 20th Century when the industry underwent rapid modernization and the volume of issuance, trading and post-trade activity rose, in keeping with the specific weight of the Spanish economy.

The regulatory framework was quick to adapt to these industry developments. Initially, Spanish legislation covered for the absence of sufficiently ambitious European legislation. Subsequently, European Directives were diligently transposed into Spanish law, generally taking advantage of any room for maneuver available to introduce stricter rules of conduct for market players than were required by the European provisions.

As analyzed in detail in this chapter, it is probable (and desirable) that the lessons drawn from the financial crisis will prompt major changes in securities market regulations. Thus, the rules on market transparency and organization will foreseeably soon be strengthened, to place stricter limits on the scope of activity of off-exchange trading and settlement systems. It is also likely that disclosure rules for issuers will be tightened, that incentives to create over-complex products will be reduced, that information available to the supervisor on OTC transactions will be enhanced, and that market mechanisms to prevent excess share price volatility and reduce trade settlement problems to a minimum will be improved and made more uniform. Lastly, it also seems likely that the new European financial-supervision framework will provide an effective boost to harmonization of supervisory rules and practices.

The greater rigor of prudential supervision following adoption of Basel III – the new capital accord – could reduce banks' capacity to provide companies with financing. In this context, a demand will foreseeably arise for the markets to raise their capacity to handle financial flows, especially in countries, such as Spain, with a high level of bank patronage.

The Spanish industry looks well prepared to assume the challenges identified. As a result of the demanding requirements of the national regulatory and supervisory framework and the industry dynamics, market discipline in Spain is currently higher than in other European markets. This is reflected in such aspects as the relatively low volume of OTC share trading, the virtual absence of complex structured product issues, and the existence of particularly strict controls on financial disclosures, of effective mechanisms to control financial stability and market integrity, and of a rigorous settlement-control system.

Nevertheless, further efforts are required if the Spanish industry is to fully adapt to the new competitive and regulatory environment. As explained in this chapter, the Spanish markets should generally continue to accommodate Spanish corporate bond and especially equity issues, provided that international investors are guaranteed smooth access. However, to raise the volume of securities issues, additional measures may be required in areas such as market-entry costs for small and medium-sized enterprises and the development of pan-European initiatives to raise investors' potential critical mass.

At the same time, official markets will have to face growing competition from multilateral trading facilities (MTFs), while the regulatory changes planned both in Spain and Europe in clearing and settlement systems will lead to competition between infrastructures in an industry segment where it has hitherto been virtually non-existent. These changes will also affect how the business is distributed between the different market participants, whose numbers will probably decline as a result.

All the above will require considerable management effort at the different infrastructures and entities to ensure that they remain competitive, along with far-reaching strategic decisions unprecedented to date.

Annex: Relevant Legislation

Directives relevant to the securities markets	Transposition to Spanish law
Financial instruments and intermediaries and investment services	
Directive 2004/39/EC on markets in financial instruments.	Law 47/2007 amending the Securities Market Law.
Commission Regulation (EC) No 1287/2006.	Directly applicable.
Securities issues and public offerings	
Directive 2003/71/EC on the prospectus to be published when securities are offered to the public or admitted to trading.	Royal Decree Law 5/2005, of 11 March 2005, amending the Securities Market Law.
Commission Regulation (EC) No 809/2004.	Directly applicable.
Takeover bids	
Directive 2004/25/EC on takeover bids.	Law 6/2007 reforming the Securities Market Law.
Market abuse	
Directive 2003/6/EC on insider dealing and market manipulation (market abuse).	Securities Market Law, following the reform introduced by Law 44/2002. Law 12/2006, amending the Securities Market Law. Royal Decree 1333/2005, implementing the Securities Market Law in relation to market abuse.
Directive 2003/124/EC on the definition and public disclosure of inside information and the definition of market manipulation.	Royal Decree 1333/2005.
Directive 2004/72/EC implementing Directive 2003/6/EC as regards accepted market practices, the definition of inside information in relation to derivatives on commodities, the drawing up of lists of insiders, the notification of managers' transactions and the notification of suspicious transactions.	Royal Decree 1333/2005. Law 12/2006, amending the Securities Market Law.
Transparency	
Directive 2004/109/EC on harmonization of transparency requirements in relation to information about issuers whose securities are admitted to trading on a regulated market.	Law 6/2007 reforming the Securities Market Law.
Investment services firms (ISFs)	
Directive 2006/73/EC implementing Directive 2004/39/EC as regards organizational requirements and operating conditions for investment firms.	Law 47/2007 amending the Securities Market Law.
Directive 2006/49/EC on the capital adequacy of investment firms and credit institutions.	Law 47/2007 amending the Securities Market Law.
Commission Regulation (EC) No 1287/2006 implementing Directive 2004/39/EC as regards record-keeping obligations for investment firms, transaction reporting, market transparency, admission of financial instruments to trading, and defined terms for the purposes of that Directive.	Directly applicable.

Directives relevant to the securities markets	Transposition to Spanish law
Collective investment schemes	
Directive 2009/65/EC on undertakings for collective investment in transferable securities (UCITS).	To be transposed by 30 June 2011.
Directive 2001/108/EC and Directive 2001/107/EC, amending Council Directive 85/611/EEC on the coordination of laws, regulations and administrative provisions relating to undertakings for collective investment in transferable securities (UCITS).	Law 35/2003 on Collective Investment Schemes.
International accounting standards	
Regulation (EC) No 1606/2002 on the application of international accounting standards.	Directly applicable.

References

ARCE, O., J. GONZÁLEZ-PUEYO and L. SANJUÁN (2010). *The credit default swap market: Areas of vulnerability and regulatory responses.* CNMV, Working Paper no. 42.

BAENA, N. (2007). "The consolidation of international stock exchanges", *CNMV Bulletin,* Quarter III.

BUENAVENTURA, R. (2008). "Short selling", *CNMV Bulletin,* Quarter IV.

CECCHETTI, S., J. GYNTELBERG and M. HOLLANDERS (2009). "Central Counterparties for Over-the-Counter Derivatives", *BIS Quarterly Review,* September.

CESR (2008). *The Role of Credit Rating Agencies in Structured Finance,* http://www.cesr-eu.org.

— (2009a). *Transparency of Corporate Bond, Structured Finance Product and Credit Derivatives Markets,* http://www.cesr-eu.org.

— (2009b). *Application of Disclosure Requirements Related to Financial Instruments in the 2008 Financial Statements,* http://www.cesr-eu.org.

— (2010). Model for a Pan-European Short Selling Disclosure Regime, http://www.cesr-eu.org.

CFA INSTITUTE (2009). *The Impact of Fragmentation Under the Markets in Financial Instruments Directive,* http://www.cfainstitute.org.

CNMV and BANCO DE ESPAÑA (joint report, 2007). *Los sistemas de compensación, liquidación y registro de valores en Europa. Situación actual, proyectos en curso y recomendaciones,* http://www.cnmv.es.

CNMV (2010). "Securities markets and their agents: situation and outlook", *CNMV Bulletin,* Quarter III, http://www.cnmv.es.

DUFFIE, D., A. LI and T. LUBKE (2010). *Policy Perspectives on OTC Derivative Markets Infrastructure,* Federal Reserve Bank of New York Staff Reports.

FESE (2009). *European Equity Market Report,* FESE Statistics & Market Research, http://www.fese.be.

FIDESSA (2010). *Intelligent Liquidity Access. A New Frontier for Electronic Trading in Europe. An Industry Briefing Prepared for Fidessa by A-Team Group,* http://www.fidessa.org.

GARCÍA-VAQUERO, V. (2007). "El proceso de integración de los mercados de valores", *Boletín económico,* Banco de España, October.

GIL, G. (2008). "Perspectives on the Securities Markets: Supervision and Regulation" CNMV 20th Anniversary Commemorative Book.

GONZÁLEZ PUEYO, F. J. (2009). *Organización de los mercados de derivados y las cámaras de contrapartida central,* CNMV, Working Paper n°. 35.

IASB (2009a). *Draft Guidance on Fair Value Measurement,* http://www.ifrs.org.

— (2009b). IFRS 9: *Financial Instruments (replacement of IAS 39),* http://www.ifrs.org.

— (2009c). *Financial Instruments: Amortised Cost and Impairment,* http://www.ifrs.org.

IOSCO (2008). *Code of Conduct Fundamentals for Credit Rating Agencies,* http://www.iosco.org.

— (2009). *Transparency of Structured Finance Products,* http://www.iosco.org.

— (2010). *Disclosure Principles for Public Offerings and Listing of Asset-Backed Securities,* http://www.iosco.org.

LASTRA, I. DE LA (2007). "European initiatives in clearing and settlement" *CNMV Bulletin,* Quarter IV.

LÓPEZ BLANCO, E. (2008). *Listing requirements in the regulated markets for equity,* CNMV, Working Paper no. 30.

LOSADA, R. (2010). *On the role of transparency in the ABS secondary market,* CNMV, Working Paper no. 38.

MANSO, E. and V. RODRÍGUEZ (2008). "The financial crisis and fair value: the debate on its impact and evaluation of the measures adopted", *CNMV Bulletin,* Quarter IV.

MANSO, E., B. DE ANTA and J. DOMÍNGUEZ (2009). "New aspects of the accounting standards of securitization funds", *CNMV Bulletin,* Quarter II.

MARTÍNEZ, E. (2007). "Financial analysis and rules of conduct: the regulatory path up to the MiFID", *CNMV Bulletin,* Quarter III.

MARTÍNEZ, M. and V. RODRÍGUEZ (2009). "The new structure of European financial supervision", *CNMV Bulletin,* Quarter IV.

MARTÍNEZ, M. and F. RESTOY (2009). "Las implicaciones regulatorias de la crisis financiera", *Papeles de Economía Española,* 122, pp. 38-46.

NÚÑEZ, S. and M. JIMÉNEZ (2007). "Target 2-Securities", *CNMV Bulletin,* Quarter IV.

OXERA CONSULTING (2009). *Monitoring Prices, Costs and Volumes of Trading and Post-trading Services. Report Prepared for European*

Commission DG Internal Markets and Services, http://www.oxera.com.

RESTOY, F. (2008a). "Lecciones para la regulación y supervisión financiera", in *La crisis financiera: su impacto y la respuesta de las autoridades,* at the Escuela de Finanzas Aplicadas (AFI), 12 May.

— (2008b). *The sub-prime crisis: some lessons for financial supervisors,* CNMV, Working Paper no. 31.

— (2008c). "La crisis financiera y los supervisores de valores", *Economistas,* no. extra 119, pp. 127-132.

— (2010). "Los mercados de valores en el nuevo entorno regulatorio", forthcoming in *Economistas.*

RESTOY, F. and V. RODRÍGUEZ (2010). "Transparency in securities markets", *Moneda y Crédito,* 230, pp. 249-269.

STULZ, R. M. (2010). "Credit Default Swaps and the Credit Crisis", *Journal of Economic Perspectives.*

THE DE LAROSIÈRE GROUP (2009). *High-Level Group on Financial Supervision in the EU. Chaired by Jacques de Larosière,* Report, http://ec.europa.eu.

THE GIOVANNINI GROUP (2001). *Cross-border Clearing and Settlement Arrangements in the European Union. Commission of the European Communities,* http://ec.europa.eu.

— (2003). *Second report on the EU Clearing and Settlement Arrangements, Commission of the European Communities,* http://ec.europa.eu.

9. Integration, competition and stability of the financial system

Jesús Saurina [1]
Banco de España

1 Introduction

This chapter sets out to analyze the relationships between integration, competition and financial stability in the Spanish banking sector since 1975. Rather than seek to provide concrete answers, the aim is to explore and open up a debate on a recent period of Spanish economic history full of profound changes affecting a sector which is crucial to economic development.

As explained in detail in Chapter 7, credit institutions used to be subject to rigid structural regulation. Historically, bankers have not been free to make their own decisions about prices (interest rates and fees for providing banking services), quantities (amounts

---

[1] The opinions expressed herein are solely the author's and do not necessarily represent those of the Banco de España. This paper would not have been possible without the close collaboration of José Cebrián, Alfredo Martín-Oliver and Gerard Arqué in the collection, processing and analysis of the information. I am also indebted to Alfredo Martín-Oliver for his invaluable assistance with the econometric analysis and his comments on earlier drafts of this paper. I would also like to thank José Luis Malo de Molina and Pablo Martín Aceña, the book's editors, for their suggestions and detailed comments. Finally, I would like to thank Gonzalo Gil and Jorge Pérez for their comments on this paper and, especially, Miguel Pellicer, Daniel Pérez and Vicente Salas for their careful and detailed reading of earlier versions of the text. Their comments, although not always taken into account, contributed to substantially improving the work. Any errors which remained are exclusively my responsibility.

of credit to grant, sectors to finance, businesses in which to invest) or productive capacity (numbers of branches and their geographical location). These decisions were all in the hands of the banking regulator, which back in 1975 was already the Banco de España. Moreover, there was also a strong segmentation of business between the commercial banks (mainly dedicated to corporate finance) and the savings banks (whose business was confined to their province or region of origin and focused on attracting retail depositors' savings and providing loans to households). These two groups of institutions coexisted with specialist public-sector banks which targeted specific sectors (such as farming, industry, exports, local government, and mortgage lending) and attracted very little by way of retail deposits. There was also a multitude of credit unions, (credit cooperatives) mostly operating in rural areas. Among the commercial banks there was also a degree of specialization, with a group of institutions commonly referred to as industrial banks focusing on lending for medium-to-long-term business projects.

Therefore, at the beginning of the last quarter of the 20th century, the Spanish banking system was characterized by a high degree of regulatory pressure, the almost total absence of competition between the different groups of institutions, and very little competition between the institutions within each of these groups. The banking market was fragmented into different groups of institutions and geographical areas, and there was no inter-bank market connecting lending and borrowing institutions. This resulted in a highly inefficient transfer of funds from savers to investors, with very high margins, due to negligible returns on savings (except when remunerated in ways that escaped the regulator's control), and expensive bank financing for businesses and households. These high returns were the guarantee of stability for individual institutions and the system as a whole, except in the case of institutions with serious management deficiencies.

The efficiency costs of a poorly integrated and uncompetitive banking system led to a progressive reduction of regulatory pressure so as to allow financial institutions' managers to make decisions about lending and borrowing rates, the fees to charge for the services they provided, what to do with deposits taken from the public, and where to open branches. Structural regulation was gradually replaced by prudential regulation, where the emphasis came to be placed on asset quality (and its correct valuation for the purposes of bad debt provisioning) and the existence of sufficient capital and reserves to cope with the unexpected losses that inevitably arise in the banking business. This prudential approach was the logical response to the effect of increased competition and integration on institutions' margins and yields resulting from deregulation and, therefore, on their incentives to assume greater levels of risk. This deregulation was accompanied by a sharp increase in the presence of banking in the Spanish economy, tighter integration and stronger competition between banks. This brought efficiency improvements, but also a greater need to manage risk profiles and capital and reserves properly to avoid difficulties during recessions, when risk materializes in the form of losses.

The rest of this chapter is organized as follows: Section 2 reviews a broad set of indicators of integration, competition and financial stability over the period as a whole.

Section 3 presents some of the empirical relationships between these indicators in an attempt to:

- Elucidate the relationships between structure, conduct and performance.
- Identify the source of the possible excess profits obtained by banks, separating efficiency and market power.
- Explore the possible relationship between competition and financial stability.

The last section presents some final thoughts by way of a conclusion.

2 Indicators of integration, competition and financial stability

Using a broad and diverse set of indicators, this section describes the process of banking integration and how the solvency of the Spanish banking system and the intensity of competition have evolved.

2.1 Indicators of banking integration

Given the length of the period covered and the intensity of the changes taking place in the structure of the banking sector, this section considers banking integration to mean the process by which businesses and households have a larger number of deposit-taking institutions available to them and with which they interact to obtain banking products and services, whether or not these institutions are located in the province in which these businesses and households reside. Therefore, the analysis of the banking-integration process encompasses both the general increase in bank use in Spanish society and the process of expansion undergone by numerous deposit-taking institutions outside their home markets or regions, thus giving rise to a national banking market.

Bank use has risen significantly in Spain since 1975. Credit to the resident private sector by Spanish deposit-taking institutions[2] as a share of GDP went from 63.1% in 1975, to 169% in 2008. In qualitative terms the assessment is similar, whether based on banking indicators such as bank deposits, the sum of loans plus deposits, or total assets (Chart 1). Together with the financing obtained by Spanish financial institutions abroad, attracting

---

[2] For reasons of space this chapter focuses on deposit-taking institutions, i.e. institutions which take deposits from the public. The credit system also includes other groups of financial institutions whose business focuses on granting specialist credit to particular business segments, without taking deposits directly from the public. These include institutions specializing in finance for vehicle purchases or in leasing and factoring operations. In many cases, these credit institutions are linked to banking groups. In any event, although there is a total of 66 institutions of this type, their market share in terms of total assets at the end of 2009 was just 1.6% (2.5% in terms of credit to the resident private sector). Organized financial markets are not studied here either, as they are the subject of Chapter 8 of this book. For an excellent analysis of the latter, see Pellicer (1992).

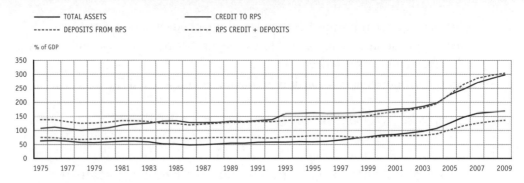

CHART 1   SPANISH DEPOSIT-TAKING INSTITUTIONS' CREDIT TO THE RESIDENT PRIVATE SECTOR (RPS), DEPOSITS FROM RPS AND TOTAL ASSETS RELATIVE TO GDP. (a)

SOURCE: Banco de España.

a. Business in Spain. Individual data.

household savings in the form of bank deposits has enabled sustained growth in the flow of credit to the private sector with which to finance the purchase of homes or consumer durables by households, business investment, and lending to government. Chart 1 also shows how Spain's membership of Economic and Monetary Union (EMU) in 1999 led to a rate of growth in credit to the resident private sector that was substantially higher than that of the sector's deposits. This was a structural change that reflects the process of bank integration in Europe, but which has recently been showing its limitations and risks.[3]

The strong presence of deposit-taking institutions throughout Spain has resulted in a high level of financial integration, with hardly any households or businesses not having access to banking services (i.e. not using a current account or savings account, fixed-term deposits, direct debits for bill payments, loans or credit, debit or credit cards, bank transfers or direct debit payments, to mention just some of the basic services that these institutions provide). The figures speak for themselves: in late 2009 deposit-taking institutions had granted more than 29.9 million loans, provided more than 27.3 million current accounts and just over 54 million savings accounts, held almost 19,000,000 fixed-term deposits, and had issued more than 78 million credit and debit cards.

The physical presence of banks in Spain has contributed to the process of financial integration among both businesses and households. Whereas in 1975 there was one bank branch for every 2,500 inhabitants, in 2009 there was one branch for every 1,000 people and for every 76 companies (Chart 2). This expansion in the number of bank branches has been partly shaped by regulatory changes. As of 1974 commercial banks were allowed to open branches nationwide, resulting in their doubling the number of branches in just two years, which demonstrates the degree of regulatory pressure that existed prior to that date. In late 1988, the prohibition on savings banks opening branches outside their home

---

[3]   For more details, see Chapter 6 of this book.

region was also lifted (this region was normally the Autonomous Community in which the savings bank had its registered office).

The entry of foreign banks in Spain as of 1978 marked the end of the Spanish banking market's long period of isolation and led to the appearance of new products that were quickly adopted by Spanish banks. It also acted as a stimulus for improvements in management, although the impact in terms of total market share was small, given the regulatory constraints that foreign institutions faced. Thus, foreign banks opened only a very limited number of branches (first three, then ten, with the restrictions finally being lifted in 1993), except in cases where they took over a crisis-stricken institution. These constraints to a large extent shaped the type of business these institutions conducted, at least until well into the 1980s. The operational limitations on foreign banks led them to specialize in the wholesale business, where they played a key role in the development of the inter-bank market, and therefore, substantially contributed to the integration of the Spanish banking market.[4]

Chart 2 shows how the number of branches of deposit-taking institutions tripled over the period 1975-2009 (quadrupling in the case of the savings banks), although the rate at which new branches were opened varied over time. As noted, deregulation and the general process of regional banks' geographical expansion, mainly in the last decade of the period, explains the steady increase in the Spanish banking sector's productive capacity (measured in terms of numbers of branches). Nevertheless, at the end of the period studied, this trend was reversed, and this looks likely to be sustained over the coming years due to the Spanish banking system's need to reduce excess capacity. Apart from the expansion of the branch network, the average size of branches (considering all types of deposit-taking institutions) has also varied substantially, ranging from about ten employees per branch at the start of the period to just over five today.

CHART 2   NUMBER OF BRANCHES

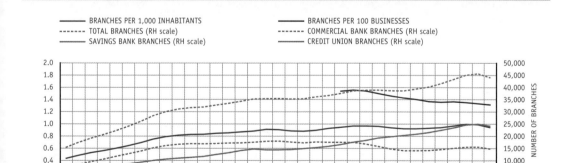

SOURCE: Banco de España.

---

[4] For more details on the presence of foreign banks in Spain and their impact, see Chapter 10 of this book.

Another factor that has made a decisive contribution to the integration of the Spanish banking system has been the fact that since 1977 commercial banks, savings banks and credit unions have been legally permitted to operate in the same business segments, and they have done so in practice since the 1980s. Thus, the banks, which had traditionally specialized in corporate lending, gradually entered the consumer-finance business, and started to provide mortgage loans for home purchases. For their part, the savings banks, previously virtually excluded from corporate finance, entered the market in the late 1980s. This led to the savings banks' market share progressively increasing (Chart 3), to the detriment of the banks.

Given the savings banks' rising penetration of the retail segment and their wider geographical coverage, their expansion has contributed to increasing the level of bank use and financial integration in Spain. The geographical expansion of the savings banks has been a gradual process. They started by extending to all the provinces of their Autonomous Community, then spreading beyond their home region to nearby Autonomous Communities. In the case of some institutions, this process ended with them having a nationwide presence. Chart 4 shows this expansion, which was particularly significant in the case of savings banks, and to a lesser extent, for credit unions and the subsidiaries of foreign banks.

The disappearance of the public-sector banks eliminated a player that had at times distorted the competitive playing field and held back the integration of the credit market. The process which first began with the consolidation of the public-sector banks and was followed by their privatization, culminated in a system in which the Spanish State has no ownership or management stake in any deposit-taking institutions. Only the Instituto de Crédito Oficial (Official Credit Institute, ICO) survives as a credit institution through which the government implements its lending policy.

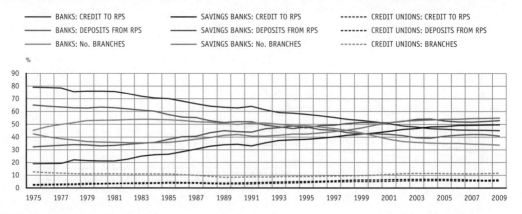

CHART 3   MARKET SHARE OF BANKS, SAVINGS BANKS AND CREDIT UNIONS IN LENDING TO RESIDENT PRIVATE SECTOR (RPS), DEPOSITS FROM RPS AND BRANCHES (a)

——— BANKS: CREDIT TO RPS   ——— SAVINGS BANKS: CREDIT TO RPS   ------- CREDIT UNIONS: CREDIT TO RPS
——— BANKS: DEPOSITS FROM RPS   ——— SAVINGS BANKS: DEPOSITS FROM RPS   ------- CREDIT UNIONS: DEPOSITS FROM RPS
——— BANKS: No. BRANCHES   ——— SAVINGS BANKS: No. BRANCHES   ------- CREDIT UNIONS: BRANCHES

SOURCE: Banco de España.

a. Business in Spain. Individual data.

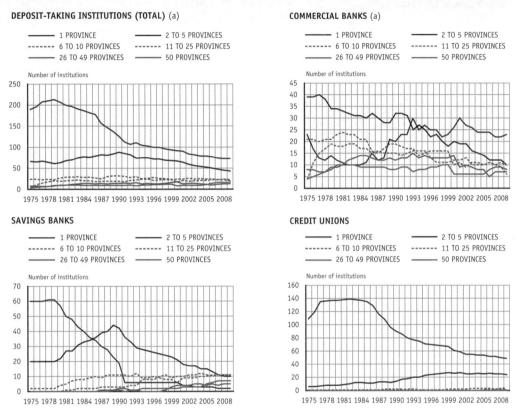

CHART 4   NUMBER OF PROVINCES IN WHICH DEPOSIT-TAKING INSTITUTIONS OPERATE.
           NUMBER OF INSTITUTIONS

SOURCE: Banco de España.

a. Excluding branches of foreign banks.

When analyzing banking integration, the wide variation in population densities between Spain's provinces, and the differences in the density of firms (the basic customers of the Spanish banking system), need to be taken into account. Thus, it can happen that institutions only expand in densely populated provinces in which there are numerous businesses, while reducing their presence, and therefore the level of banking integration, in less populated provinces. Chart 5 shows how bank use in terms of the number of branches per capita (Chart 5A) and per square kilometer (Chart 5B) increased both in less populated provinces and in those with a larger population, although, of course, the density differs substantially depending on the size of the banking markets.

A complementary way of measuring banking market integration is by means of an analysis of price dispersion between institutions.[5] However, information is only available on the interest rate offered by each institution in the case of new asset and liability operations

---

5   For a more detailed analysis see Martín-Oliver, Salas and Saurina (2008).

CAHRT 5   NUMBER OF BRANCHES IN THE FIVE MOST AND LEAST POPULATED PROVINCES IN 2008

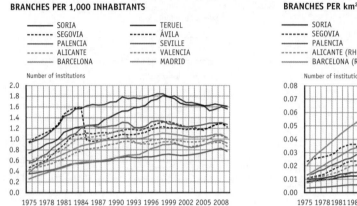

BRANCHES PER 1,000 INHABITANTS

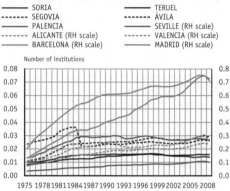

BRANCHES PER km²

SOURCE: Banco de España.

(marginal rates) since 1988. Analysis of the standard deviation of these rates shows, in general, a convergence in the marginal rates on loans (to businesses and households) and fixed-term deposits, which would suggest increased integration. Moreover, the average return on assets and average cost of liabilities have similar profiles over the period, and a stable or growing trend in the first part of the sample (up to 1988), corroborating the conclusion obtained from the marginal rates.

Nevertheless, in a period in which, for reasons unrelated to competition and integration, average interest rates have varied considerably, it is not clear that standard deviation is the best indicator of market integration. When corrected for the average (Chart 6), the coefficient of variation of marginal rates generally shows an upward trend, except in the most recent period, where the oscillations from one year to the next are considerable (the same applies to the average lending and borrowing rates), in particular in 2009, a year with very low interest rates.

CHART 6   COEFFICIENTS OF VARIATION. BANKS AND SAVINGS BANKS

SOURCE: Banco de España.

The foregoing highlights the difficulty of measuring the integration of the banking market by looking at prices. Product differentiation, through which institutions seek to maintain their excess profits, or differences in business types or bank customers' risk profiles, may explain the price dispersion observed without this implying a lesser degree of integration. Therefore, dispersion analysis, even when correcting for the average, must be interpreted with caution, unless it is possible to study a relatively uniform product. In this regard, the small, but non-zero dispersion in the home-loans market, a market in which competition has been strong over the last 10 years and products relatively uniform, highlights that, in the retail banking market, integration cannot be measured solely by price dispersion or that, alternatively, a highly integrated banking market does not translate into zero price dispersion.[6]

2.2   Indicators of banking competition

This section starts with an analysis of market-structure indicators, which yield information about the conditions under which firms make decisions. It then reviews performance indicators, which are the outcome of market structure and the behavior of market participants.

2.2.1   Market structure indicators

A first indicator of the degree of competition in a market is the number of participants.[7] The number of deposit-taking institutions at the beginning of the period was just over 300 and it rose to a maximum of 365 in 1985 (Chart 7). From that point on, until well into the current decade, the number of institutions declined gradually. This decrease was due both to the difficulties experienced by commercial banks and credit unions in the late 1970s and early 1980s, and the gradual process of bank consolidation, particularly among the savings banks, once the opening of branches was fully liberalized (between 1989 and 1991 there were 10 savings-bank mergers, resulting in 25 institutions disappearing). There was also consolidation among credit unions in the second half of the 1980s and to a lesser extent in the late 1990s.

The number of commercial banks continued to increase over the period, despite their also being affected by mergers (in particular the big four, which in 1999 and 2000 produced the two big banks present in the Spanish financial system today, Santander and BBVA,

---

[6]   This idea does not appear to be very widespread [ECB (2009) and EC Commission (2007)].

[7]   Note that the analysis of market concentration in this sector is basically at national level, in line with the idea that during that period studied there has been an integration of different local banking markets. A detailed analysis of each local market is beyond the scope of this study.

CHART 7   NUMBER OF REGISTERED DEPOSIT-TAKING INSTITUTIONS AND THEIR TYPES

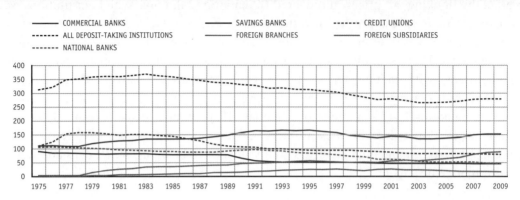

SOURCE: Banco de España.

which also have a significant presence abroad), thanks to the entry of numerous branches and subsidiaries of foreign banks.[8] However, a few of the foreign banks that entered the market at the start of the period examined ended up withdrawing from it or concentrating their business solely in the wholesale market, in view of their inability (initially as a result of legal constraints) to achieve satisfactory scale in the retail business. What at the beginning of the period seemed like a great business opportunity for large European banks, and some American and Japanese ones, ended up becoming a difficult playing field on account of the ability of national banks to react and adapt, coupled with their strong presence throughout the country with a dense network of branches, which has emerged as a crucial strategic factor.[9] The relationship-banking model developed by Spanish banks and their proximity to customers is one of their greatest strengths.[10]

The degree of concentration observed in a market offers an approximation to the competitive pressure in that market. Greater concentration not only offers opportunities for firms to coordinate their price decisions, but there is also a direct relationship between an industry's concentration and average margins even when such coordination does not take place. Chart 8 shows the year-on-year variation in the market share of the top five institutions (C5), which is one of the most widely used indicators of banking concentration. It can be observed that the Spanish banking system first underwent a relatively strong reduction in concentration up until the late 1980s (in particular, measured in terms of credit and deposit shares) and then gradually increased its level of concentration, although the market share of

---

[8]   The process of opening up to the outside world and the internationalization of the Spanish financial system is examined in Chapter 10 of this book. A complementary perspective can be found in Pérez, Salas and Saurina (2005).

[9]   Fuentelsaz and Salas (1994) highlight the fundamental importance of branches in the management of the banking business.

[10]   An analysis of the spread of relationship banking in Spain can be found in Jiménez, Saurina and Townsend (2007).

CHART 8   MARKET SHARE IN TERMS OF LOANS AND DEPOSITS FROM RESIDENT PRIVATE SECTOR
             AND BRANCHES OF TOP FIVE DEPOSIT-TAKING INSTITUTIONS IN EACH YEAR (a)

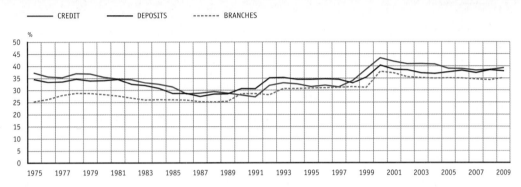

——— CREDIT   ——— DEPOSITS   ------- BRANCHES

SOURCE: Banco de España.

a. Business in Spain. Individual data.

other institutions remains over 60%. The concentration indicator increased significantly in 1999 and 2000, which is when the two major Spanish banking groups were created.

Another measure of the degree of market concentration can be obtained using the Herfindahl-Hirschman index (HHI), which is calculated as the sum of the squares of the market share of each market participant. This indicator is equal to unity (or 10,000 points) when the whole market is in the hands of a single entity, and tends to zero if market share is distributed relatively evenly among a large group of entities.[11] The picture that emerges from in Chart 9 is very similar to that obtained with the C5 indicator: a decrease

CHART 9   HERFINDAHL-HIRSCHMAN INDEX (HHI) IN TERMS OF RESIDENT PRIVATE SECTOR CREDIT
             AND DEPOSITS FOR ALL AND BRANCHES DEPOSIT-TAKING INSTITUTIONS (a)

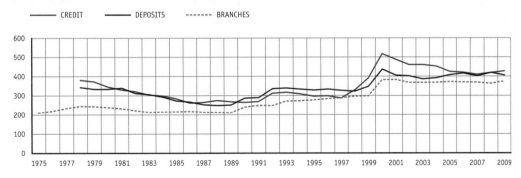

——— CREDIT   ——— DEPOSITS   ------- BRANCHES

SOURCE: Banco de España.

a. Business in Spain. Individual data.

[11]   The inverse of HHI gives a measure of the number of equivalent entities in the market; i.e. the number of identical entities with a market share that would produce the same value of the index.

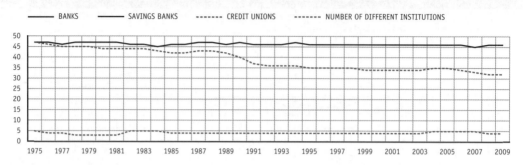

CHART 10   INSTITUTIONS WITH MOST BRANCHES IN A PROVINCE, BY INSTITUTION TYPE (a)

SOURCE: Banco de España.

a. Type of institution with biggest market share in a province. Number of different institutions that are leaders in each province and year.

in concentration at the start of the period with a gradual increase since the late 1980s, and a jump in 1999-2000, without reaching particularly high levels.[12]

The Spanish banking system had a number of specific features in the period studied: the existence of universal banks at national, regional and local level; savings banks which, initially only operated at provincial or regional level, but by the end of the period had gained national or super regional reach; and credit unions which were almost always local in scope. The existence of distinct local markets therefore makes it worth analyzing them separately. Chart 10 shows how the savings banks have a strong presence in the market in their home province, and that – with one or two notable exceptions – they lack the national presence of the major commercial banks. In fact, throughout the period examined, the savings banks, and in some cases the credit unions, are the institutions with the greatest productive capacity in each provincial market. Additionally, the number of different leading institutions in each province is relatively high although it has declined steadily. This suggests that these institutions still have a strong presence in their home region, despite the strong geographical expansion they have undergone.[13] Moreover, the savings banks have also maintained their leadership in terms of credit and deposits. Thus, at the end of the period examined, the commercial banks were the top lenders in just four provinces (one of them being Madrid) and in deposits in just one (again Madrid).

---

[12]   In some European countries the HHI is over 1,800 points, the figure which in the United States has traditionally been taken as the threshold triggering anti-trust actions. In Spain this indicator is around a quarter of this threshold. The case of C5 is similar, where some countries exceed 80% in 2008 (ECB (2009)).

[13]   A description of the different expansion strategies of Spanish deposit-taking institutions can be found in Delgado, Saurina and Townsend (2008).

2.2.2   Performance indicators

Other indirect indicators of the degree of competition in a banking market include the various margins and returns the institutions obtain. These can be expressed in terms of their returns on assets (ROA) and on equity (ROE).

Net interest margin, net income (gross margin) and, to a lesser extent, operating margin (which is no longer reported) as a proportion of each institution's total assets, have evolved similarly over the period examined (Chart 11): starting at levels that were already high, they rose further until the end of the 1970s, leveling off in the 1980s and early 1990s, and have been descending slowly but steadily since. This decline is most pronounced in the case of net interest margin (from 3.8% in 1988 to 1.4% in 2009) and less so (due to the effects of fees and earnings from financial transactions) in the case of ordinary income (from 4.4% to 2.1% over the same period). However it has been particularly noticeable in the case of operating income (from 2.5% to 1.2%), due to the sustained decline in operating expenses over the whole period, which is evidence of increased efficiency. In fact, the efficiency ratio (Chart 11B) improved by nearly 25 percentage points over the period from 1975 to 2009.

The relative decline in margins was a product of the general fall in interest rates, first as inflation was brought under control, and then during the preparations for, and subsequent membership of, EMU. Membership of the euro area has been a significant factor in the evolution of the Spanish banking market over the last decade, with implications in terms of both access to credit and debt levels of firms and households. At the same time, the way relative margins have varied suggests increased competition, both between types of institution and within each group. It also reveals how institutions have responded to these competitive pressures by diversifying their range of financial products and services and through greater cost efficiency.

| CHART 11 | MARGINS, COST AND EFFICIENCY DEPOSIT-TAKING INSTITUTIONS (a) |

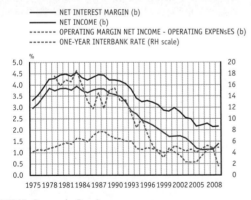

SOURCE: Banco de España.

a. Business in Spain. Individual data.
b. Percentage of total assets.

CHART 12   SPANISH DEPOSIT-TAKING INSTITUTIONS' RETURN ON ASSETS (ROA) AND RETURN ON EQUITY (ROE) (a)

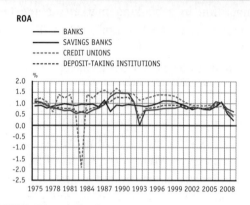

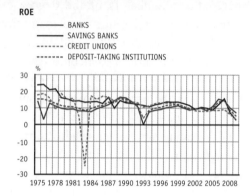

SOURCE: Banco de España.

a. Business in Spain. Individual data.

Chart 12 shows how the profitability of Spanish deposit-taking institutions[14] has been powerfully influenced by the economic cycle and particularly affected by episodes of crisis and/or bank restructuring (investment banks, and some commercial banks and rural savings banks in the early 1980s, Banesto in 1993, the savings banks today)

From the start of the period up until 1993, both ROA and ROE fell as a result of rising default rates and the corresponding write-downs of doubtful assets (Chart 13). As the Spanish economy recovered and some of the commercial banks and credit unions digested their problems, profitability again grew, reaching new highs in the late 1980s. The 1993 recession again triggered a sharp rise in doubtful assets and the provisions for them, putting downward pressure on profitability. During the second half of the 1990s, and much of the first decade of the new millennium, all three groups of institutions have obtained high

CHART 13   DEFAULT RATE ON CREDIT TO RESIDENT PRIVATE SECTOR (RPS) AND ASSET IMPAIRMENT LOSSES (a) (b). **DEPOSIT-TAKING INSTITUTIONS.**

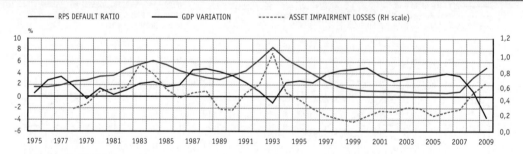

SOURCE: Banco de España.

a. Asset impairment losses. GDP variation in real terms.
b. Business in Spain. Individual data.

---

[14]   A rigorous and original analysis of the profitability of Spanish banks can be found in Martínez Méndez (1991)

levels of ROE (10.9% on average over the period 1995-2007), compared to average ten-year government bond yields of 5.5%, implying a risk premium of between four and five percentage points. This seems to indicate the existence of a certain level of excess profits on capital invested in the banking sector. At the end of the period, the marked slowdown in economic growth and, in 2009, the worst recession to affect the Spanish economy for more than 60 years, has had a negative impact on the profitability of Spanish banks due to rising defaults and write-downs, despite having a less pro-cyclical bad-debt provision system.[15] It is conceivable that in the coming years the profitability of Spanish deposit-taking institutions will be shaped by the process of digesting their exposure to the construction and property-development sector, which has been hit particularly hard by the crisis.[16]

Another indicator used as a measure of the existence of excess profits, based on market values (and thus only applicable to listed companies) is Tobin's q, which is defined as the ratio between the market value of the entity (sum of the market value of its equity and debt) divided by the cost of replacing its assets. A value above unity indicates the existence of excess profit, which may derive from the entity's market power or scarce bank-specific factors of production (such as talent, ability to manage resources, effective risk control and risk anticipation, etc.).[17] An approximate measure which may be interpreted in a similar way, but which requires less information and fewer assumptions to calculate, is the ratio of the bank's market value to book value. A value of this ratio above unity would indicate that the entity is able to generate shareholder value exceeding that of the equity invested in it. [18]

Chart 14 shows market-to-book ratio listed Spanish banks' during the period examined. The high returns obtained by Spanish banks during the period of strict regulation and strong economic growth can be observed. The economic slowdown, the ensuing crisis affecting some of the listed banks (institutions commonly referred to as industrial banks in particular, but also some commercial banks) together with the start of a process of deregulation that inevitably stimulated competition between institutions, led to a rapid contraction in excess profits, to the point that profits turned negative in the early 1980s. This was most likely a result of the doubts about the banking system's ability to recover from the economic and financial crisis in a political context that considerably exacerbated

---

[15] This provision system was calibrated with the 1993 recession, which at the time was the worst that the Spanish economy had experienced in three decades. A detailed analysis can be found in Poveda (2000), or in Saurina (2009a), explaining the changes necessary to adapt it to the new International Financial Reporting Standards (IFRS) in force since 2005. Saurina (2009b) shows the impact of this provision system on the period as a whole (from mid-2000 to the present).

[16] At the consolidated level the evolution of ROA and ROE is relatively similar up until the end of the period analyzed when the positive effects of the international diversification of business and the contributions from investments in corporate shareholdings, both financial and non-financial, are being seen. Thus, these differences have been around three percentage points over the last 10 years, although there are differences between each of the groups of institutions.

[17] See Lindenberg and Ross (1981) or Smirlock, Gilligan and Marshall (1984) for a detailed explanation of Tobin's q as an indicator of excess profits or Saurina (1992) for the case of banks.

[18] Note that equity is not adjusted for inflation, which can lead to an overestimate of Tobin's q on some measures. This adjustment, however, is not without its difficulties.

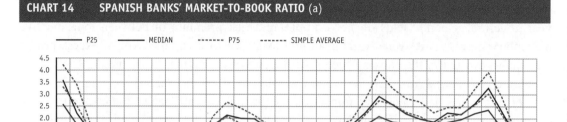

CHART 14   SPANISH BANKS' MARKET-TO-BOOK RATIO (a)

SOURCES: Banco de España, Boletín de cotizaciones de la Bolsa de Madrid, and Datastream.

a. All listed banks in each year.

investor uncertainty. As the banking and economic crises were brought under control, the market-to-book ratio again rose significantly. This probably reflected an expanding banking market divided among a smaller number of institutions in the context of a structural deregulation process that was still underway.

As of the time full competition on interest rates and, particularly, competition for cheap retail liabilities was allowed, by law in 1987, and beginning in practice in the third quarter 1989, when Santander launched a large-scale advertising campaign for its high-interest current account and other institutions gradually reacted, and the savings banks were allowed to expand throughout the country, excess profits were progressively eroded until they almost disappeared during the 1993 recession.

The gradual recovery of credit and economic growth as of the mid-1990s, and the growth in business from corporate activity, in the context of a general downward trend in interest rates, again improved the banks' prospects for obtaining excess profits. For some institutions, this coincided with the possibility of expanding outside Spain, which allowed them to export banking and management technology to markets with high growth potential, and diversify their risk. The faster pace of geographical expansion by the savings banks, which led to increased competitive pressure, and the slowing of economic growth around 2002, moderated the banking sector's excess profits, although they recovered when strong economic growth returned, driven by an unprecedented expansion of the property market and the impact this had on banks' balance sheets. The advent of the international financial crisis and subsequent recession, largely linked to the property-market crisis, significantly altered investors' expectations concerning the listed Spanish banks.

2.3 Financial-stability indicators

The stability of a financial system depends, among other things on the risk exposures of its constituent institutions, the capital and reserves these have available to cope with losses arising when these risks materialize, as well as the likelihood of contagion between institutions, which is in turn partly dependent on the level of banking integration reached. As the recent international financial crisis has shown, it is not easy to measure a bank's risk exposure, whether using market indicators or the institutions' own measures. Therefore, the discussion that follows will focus on *ex post* risk indicators, an approach which is consistent with the aim of analyzing the evolution of the banking system since 1975.

Commonly used *ex post* risk indicators include the number of bankruptcies and/or liquidations of institutions. However, this is only partial information about the extent of difficulties that the financial system has faced because, in many cases, the authorities look for solutions that avoid institutions' bankruptcy and subsequent winding up, given the systemic nature of certain institutions and the negative externalities that the failure of a deposit-taking institution can have for the national economy. Thus, the authorities aim to minimize the cost of the bankruptcy to taxpayers and the economy as a whole. It is therefore possible that intervention by the deposit-guarantee fund might be envisaged to temporarily prop up a struggling institution until a buyer can be found for part of its assets or another institution is willing to acquire it and take over its assets and liabilities. Sometimes, given the scale of the problems, the solution is for the government to take control, partially or totally, of the failing institution. Subsequently, the institution requiring public rescue may be restructured and sold.

Chart 15 shows the variation in the number of institutions which have suffered stability problems during period, requiring the intervention of the deposit-guarantee fund[19] or the

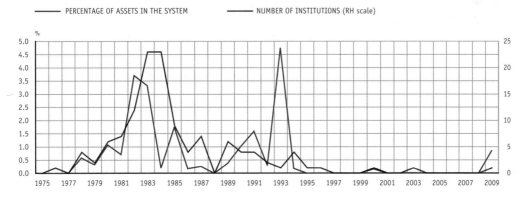

CHART 15   NUMBER OF INSTITUTIONS IN DIFFICULTIES AND THEIR RELATIVE SIZE AND SHARE OF TOTAL ASSETS (a)

SOURCES: Banco de España and 2008 Annual reports of the Deposit Guarantee Funds for the Banks, Savings Banks and Credit Unions.

a. Bankruptcy, liquidation, nationalization, aid from the Deposit Guarantee Fund and intervention of the Banco de España.

---

[19]   In Spain, unlike most other countries, the deposit-guarantee fund not only has the task of refunding deposits in the event of an institution's bankruptcy but is also authorized, when certain conditions are met, to take over and manage troubled institutions (selling off assets, restructuring, reorganizing, etc.).

direct involvement of the State (total or partial nationalization) or the Banco de España to replace the institution's managers. It also shows those that have gone bankrupt and been liquidated.[20]

The chart shows how a considerable number of institutions were affected in the late 1970s and the first half of the 1980s. This was at the time of the banking crisis, which particularly affected banks created during the first phase of financial liberalization in the 1960s, along with a significant number of rural and other savings banks that found themselves in difficulties. The economic crisis was partly due to changes in relative prices of imports (including oil, in particular), which put the productive model that had been developed in Spain during the 1960s under pressure. In part it was also linked to the increased uncertainty surrounding corporate investments in a climate of political and social change, although how the institutions concerned were managed was also a factor in this banking crisis. The cross-sectional analysis highlights that prudent lending policy, embracing everything from acceptance of risk based on selection of borrowers, their continuous monitoring, attention to excessive risk concentrations (whether individual or sector-wide), careful consideration of collateral (which can mitigate default, but is not a substitute for payment), together with liquidity and the structure of the balance sheet, has been key to explaining each institution's ability to withstand an economic crisis like that which buffeted numerous productive sectors throughout Spain during the period.[21]

Although other institutions have been taken under the authorities' control and wound up since, the number has been much smaller. However, in terms of the volume of assets affected, in addition to the banking crisis at the start of the period (which affected institutions representing slightly over 10% of total deposit-taking institutions' assets) 1993, with the rescue of Banesto (which accounted for slightly less than 5%), was another time in which excessive risks that had been taken during the preceding expansionary phase came to the fore, resulting in a crisis. Unlike the previous decade, the regulatory arsenal available to respond to distressed institutions with a view to minimizing negative externalities and the cost for taxpayers, was much greater. The Law on Discipline and Intervention in Credit Institutions was passed in 1988 and, to a large extent, incorporated the lessons that regulators, supervisors and the tax authorities had drawn from the previous crisis.

At the end of the period examined here, another bank restructuring process was underway, supported by the deposit-guarantee fund, and in particular, by the Fund for Orderly Restructuring of the Banking Sector (FROB).[22] This body was created in mid-2009 to enable the restructuring of the savings banks and was endowed with considerable resources to give it the room for maneuver necessary. Those institutions requiring

---

[20]   Chart 15 is a lower limit for the number of troubled institutions. It does not include, for example, those institutions in difficulties which were absorbed by others without the participation of the deposit guarantee fund and without their being liquidated.

[21]   Cuervo (1988) and Juan (1993) explain in detail the causes and solutions of that banking crisis.

[22]   A brief description of the FROB can be found in Box 2.1 of the Banco de España's *Informe de Estabilidad Financiera* (Financial Stability Report) for November 2009 and in Chapter 7 of this book.

recapitalization can draw upon the FROB provided they scale back their productive capacity and pay an adequate return on the capital they are provided.

The process of restructuring and elimination of excess capacity will, to a large extent, be carried out through institutional protection systems (SIP), in which a group of institutions undertake to consolidate their resources and earnings and, additionally, to create a central institution that is to ensure the solvency and liquidity of the member institutions. This core institution will have sole responsibility for the management of the group, and will be authorized to issue shares to strengthen its capital base.[23] The FROB has been backed up by a recent change in the Savings Banks Law which allows savings banks to access markets providing high quality equity (in the form of shares).

Given the scale of the restructuring process underway, it will inevitably have substantial impacts on the integration of the Spanish banking system, as it is understood in this chapter, and in the medium term, on the level of competition in the system and its stability.[24] In any event, once again, the economic crisis, linked to the limitations of the productive model that developed over the last decade, with its strong reliance on the real-estate sector, reveals errors in the way certain institutions have taken on credit risk and managed it.

Another indicator of the solvency problems in the banking sector is how problem assets which constitute an *ex post* indicator of credit risk have evolved. Chart 13 has already clearly shown that there is a high degree of (negative) correlation between doubtful assets and the different phases of the economic cycle: the recessions in 1993 and 2009 led to higher default rates, as happened during the difficulties of the early 1980s. Significantly, there is a wide variation between different institutions in terms of default rates (Chart 16) and, in particular, during recessions, as is evidenced by the inter-quartile range, which reveals the importance of risk management throughout the credit cycle in order to assess an institution's medium and long-term stability. Obviously, institutions that had put more emphasis on gaining market share during the expansionary phase of the cycle than on developing a solid business over the medium-term ended up suffering the consequences of change in economic cycle to a much greater extent.[25]

Credit risk is the most important factor that deposit-taking institutions face. Lending to the construction and property-development sector has historically shown itself to be a business segment associated with considerable credit risk, by contrast with the case of home loans. Therefore, the composition of the loan portfolio and the evolution of the real-estate sector are two factors that need to be taken into account when assessing the stability of the Spanish banking system. In the Spanish economy's last (long) expansionary phase,

---

[23] For more details of the SIPs, see Box 3.1 of Financial Stability Report, March 2010.

[24] In July 2010 the results of the stress tests performed at European level (under the coordination of the CEBS) were published. These highlighted, firstly, the existence of difficulties at a number of Spanish institutions (four) and, secondly, the high degree of resilience of the remainder of the institutions in what was an extremely demanding exercise for Spain given the extreme hypotheses used.

[25] Jiménez and Saurina (2006) find the very robust evidence for the time lag in the relationship between rapid credit growth and (future) default. Moreover, they observe that loans granted when credit grows quickly have a greater likelihood of future default than those granted during recessions. Collateral requirements also tend to be relaxed during expansionary phrases.

CHART 16   DEFAULT RATE AND ITS DISPERSION (a)

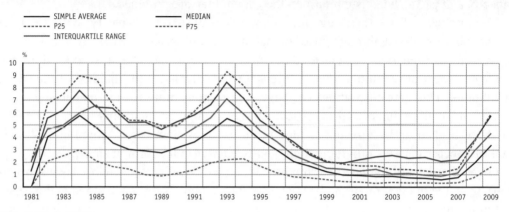

SOURCE: Banco de España.

a. All deposit-taking institutions. Business in Spain. Individual data.

the relative weight of credit linked to the real-estate sector grew substantially and recent data reveal the disparity in terms of credit risk between exposure to property developers and households buying homes (Chart 17). The variation in the default rate in the wider property sector over these years will, to a large extent, determine the ability of deposit-taking institutions to weather the crisis, individually or collectively, and the ultimate scale of the restructuring of the Spanish banking system.

CHART 17   RATE OF VARIATION OF CREDIT TO CONSTRUCTION FIRMS AND PROPERTY DEVELOPERS AND FOR HOME PURCHASES CREDIT INSTITUTIONS (a)

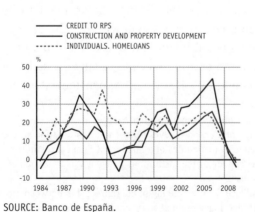

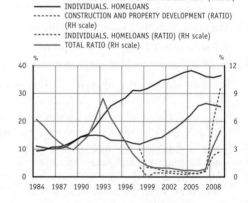

SOURCE: Banco de España.

a. Business in Spain. Individual data.

As discussed, banks have their capital and reserves (in the form of capital contributed by their owners or earnings retained to tackle unexpected losses and guarantee the institution's business continuity) as a backstop against the unexpected materialization of risks (in the form of default or asset impairment). Therefore, capital and reserves are also an indicator of financial stability. In this regard, it can be observed in Chart 18 that the value of deposit-taking institutions' market-to-book ratio has varied between 6% and 10% over the period examined.[26]

In general, this ratio increased, albeit with fluctuations, up until the early 1990s and has since been on a downward trend, with a few exceptions (for example, the last two years). However, there are significant differences between each of the groups of institutions. Thus, credit unions, given their difficulties accessing capital markets, have a higher ratio of capital to assets than other institutions. Savings banks, meanwhile, also increased their capital in the late 1970s and again in the early 1990s, given that they also have difficulty accessing the capital markets. On average, for the period as a whole, the ratio of capital plus reserves to total assets was around 7.7%, the inverse of which indicates a leverage ratio of around 13, which is well below that of banking systems in other developed countries.[27]

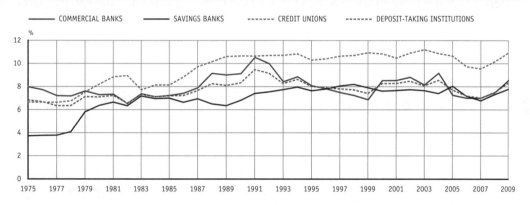

CHART 18   RATIO OF CAPITAL AND RESERVES TO TOTAL ASSETS (BOOK VALUE OF EQUITY) (a) (b)

SOURCE: Banco de España.

a. All deposit-taking institutions and by groups. Individual data.
b. Percentage of total assets.

[26] The data in Chart 18 are based on information from individual balance sheets. If this analysis were to be carried out at the consolidated level, the ratio would be slightly lower for the period where this distinction is relevant. If assets are weighted for their level of risk, consolidated solvency ratios would be substantially higher than those obtained with individual information. Given that the aim of this chapter is to analyze the Spanish banking market over an extended period of time, it seems more interesting to have a long uniform series like that shown in Chart 18.

[27] As already noted, as well as capital, since mid-2000 the Banco de España has required anti-cyclical provisions to bolster the stability of the financial system in a context of strong credit growth and highly pro-cyclical accounting standards.

Obviously, not all assets have the same level of risk. Therefore, regulatory solvency ratios are currently calculated in proportion to the risk of the asset: the greater the risk, the more capital institutions are required to hold. This is not only true in the current regulatory framework (Basel II), but in somewhat cruder form, it was also present in Basel I. In Spain, this requirement existed even earlier, given that since 1985 capital requirements have differed depending on the bank asset class in question (property, shares, loans, and also taking into account whether or not collateral had been posted, and its type).[28] Therefore, from the point of view of financial stability it is worth examining how the composition of Spanish deposit-taking institutions' assets has changed over time.

Chart 19 clearly shows how lending to businesses and households lost ground relative to government debt as the State increased public spending beyond its income (to expand the provision of public services, build infrastructure or tackle the economic crisis). Institutions therefore purchased government securities issued to cover the mismatch between revenues and expenditures, partly because they were obliged to do so by the mandatory public debt investment ratios that had been set. The chart also shows the development of the inter-bank market and the need to implement monetary policy through high minimum-reserve requirements. In the second half of the 1980s, and in particular during the post-1993 recovery, there was a significant change in the structure of deposit-taking institutions' assets, with lending to businesses and households gaining in importance relative to public debt and the inter-bank market. Obviously, institutions' risk profiles have evolved in parallel, with risk being lower, in principle, the greater the share of public debt and inter-bank assets, and rising as lending, particularly to construction

CHART 19   ASSET STRUCTURE OF SPANISH DEPOSIT-TAKING INSTITUTIONS IN PERCENTAGE TERMS (a)

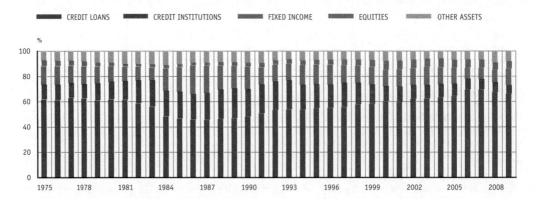

SOURCE: Banco de España.

a. Business in Spain. Individual data.

---

[28] There was also a general ratio, which is unweighted, which limited banks' leverage. A good analysis of the prudential standards is given in Trujillo, Cuervo and Vargas (1990).

firms and property developers, together with consumer lending, underwent an expansion on a scale unprecedented in recent times, as already noted. Significant differences existed between groups of institutions as regards the composition of their assets, with lending to the resident private sector having greatest weight among credit unions, followed by the savings banks, and finally, by commercial banks.[29]

Finally, it may be interesting to assess institutions' creditworthiness using a market indicator. In a way consistent with the analysis of Tobin's q, the ratio of the market value of capital and reserves to total assets can be taken (calculated as the value of capital and reserves plus liabilities). Obviously, this ratio will fluctuate much more than the book ratio and can only be calculated for listed institutions (Chart 20). The trend observed earlier in the case of the book ratio can be seen to be maintained, in general, although it is more pronounced and much more volatile. It should be noted that whereas both ratios come very close together in times of crisis, during expansionary phases, which predominate during this period, the market's assessment of creditworthiness consistently exceeds the accounting measure as it includes the capitalization of extraordinary income Beyond this ratio, it is not possible to construct any other indicators based on market information because there is no information about CDS (credit default swap) spreads for most of the institutions examined. In any case, CDSs have only existed since fairly recently. The same is true of the price of certain traded instruments, supposing that these prices (subordinated debt and preferred stock, for example) to some extent reflect the institutions' risk of bankruptcy.

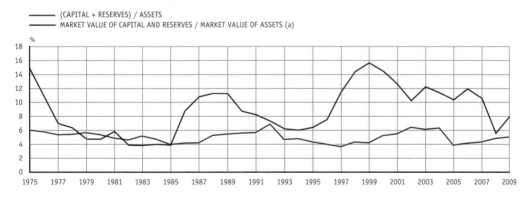

CHART 20   RATIO OF CAPITAL AND RESERVES TO ASSETS AT BOOK VALUE AND MARKET VALUE (a)

——— (CAPITAL + RESERVES) / ASSETS
——— MARKET VALUE OF CAPITAL AND RESERVES / MARKET VALUE OF ASSETS (a)

SOURCES: Banco de España, Boletín de cotizaciones de la Bolsa de Madrid, and Datastream.

a. Using the market value of capital and reserves and the book value of liabilities as an approximation. All listed bank in each year.

---

[29] These differences can also be seen in the taking of deposits from the resident private sector as a proportion of total assets.

3 Empirical analysis of the relationship between integration, competition and financial stability

The aim of this section is to explore some of the complex questions that these last 35 years of financial development have brought to light in Spain. These are issues that are pertinent to the formulation of regulatory policies for the banking industry. The intention is not to develop a new method of analysis, or even to present new findings, but simply to apply relatively simple[30] existing approaches over a long period of time in which there were many changes and significant events, with a view to stimulating a debate about their interpretation.

3.1 Market power or efficiency?

The first question that we will try to explore here is whether the high returns, albeit with the ups and downs and trend changes mentioned above, that Spanish deposit-taking institutions have obtained have been the result of market power or, on the other hand, a result of their highly efficient management of productive resources (labor, branches, technology, advertising, etc.) to produce the loans, deposits and the other banking services that they offer. These two alternative hypotheses, which need not be mutually exclusive, interpret the banking structure and its impact on institutions earnings in different ways.

On the one hand, the structure-conduct-performance paradigm's traditional interpretation is that greater concentration in the banking market translates into greater capacity for collusion and, therefore, a more oligopolistic market, which explains the level of (excess) profits obtained. On the other hand, the efficiency hypothesis interprets the greater concentration observed in the market as a response to certain institutions' more efficient use of particular factors of production (such as entrepreneurial talent, organizational management ability) or their being the first to exploit business opportunities or detect latent risks and avoid them. This greater efficiency enables them to gradually increase their market share over time at the expense of less efficient competitors.

The classic comparison of these two hypotheses to explain business earnings can be done by estimating the following relationship, as suggested by Smirlock, Gilligan and Marshall (1984):

$$R_{it} = \alpha + \beta MS_{it} + \gamma CR_t + Z_{it} + \varepsilon_{it} \qquad [1]$$

In this formula R_{it} is a measure of bank i's earnings in year t, MS_{it} is bank i's market share on that date, CR_t is an index or measure of the degree of concentration of the banking

---

[30] More precise alternative methods exist with which to estimate the degree of competition in a banking market, but it is not clear that they can be applied in this case given the detailed information they require.

market in year t, and Z_{it} is a control-variable vector: bank size measured as the logarithm of total assets on each date, variation in stock market index, to control for investors overall expectations, and variation in terms of real GDP. Finally, ε_{it} is the error term.

As a measure of the income obtained by bank i in year t, Tobin's q is used, approximated, as described earlier, by the ratio of the market value to the book value of the institution's capital and reserves. Table 1 shows the results of estimating equation [1] for all listed banks in the period 1975-2009. This is a panel with a total of 816 observations (bank-year), which includes both commercial and so-called industrial banks, for those times when this distinction existed.

The first column of Table 1 shows the results of the estimate using C5 as the market concentration index, i.e. the market share held by the top five institutions nationwide.[31]

The variable used is the number of branches. In a retail banking market, such as the Spanish market over the whole period analyzed, branches are used for lending, deposit taking and providing banking services. The market share (at national level) of each institution (MS_{it}) has been measured in a consistent way in terms of bank branches. It can be seen that both the market share parameter and the concentration indicator are positive and significant, which is evidence supporting both the hypothesis of efficiency and the structure-conduct-performance paradigm.

Part of the excess profits earned by the banks during the period would be the result of their efficient management of the resources necessary for banking intermediation. In line

TABLE 1

	Branches				Assets		Credit		Deposits	
	Coeff	t-ratio	Coeff	t-ratio	Coeff	t-ratio	Coeff	t-ratio	Coeff	t-ratio
Constant	1.017**	2.120	2.427***	5.080	0.802*	1.800	0.858*	1.900	1.608***	3.480
MS	7.052***	2.910	9.552***	3.840	4.351***	2.680	5.001***	2.760	4.721***	2.640
C5	0.087***	8.300			0.077***	10.790	0.074***	8.530	0.045***	8.180
HHI			70.415***	10.390						
Log Asset	-0.173***	-4.640	-0.224***	-5.650	-0.178***	-4.730	-0.177***	-4.450	-0.158***	-4.140
Stkmt.Ind.Var	0.368***	4.120	0.381***	4.300	0.564***	6.280	0.367***	3.940	0.409***	4.380
CR.GDP	18.835***	10.620	18.248	10.850	19.998***	11.900	17.447***	10.630	18.593***	10.700
R² (%)	15.84		19.41		23.20		16.99		15.90	
N. obs.	816		816		816		816		816	

Note:
OLS estimate of equation (1) for listed banks in the period 1975-2009, including both commercial and investment banks. The headings *Branches, Assets, Credit, Deposits* refer to regressions using these variables in the construction of the market share and concentration measures. The dependent variable is Tobin's q, approximated here by the ratio of market value to book value of the institution's capital and reserves. *C5* denotes the market share of the top five institutions at national level; *MS* is the market share of each institution; *HHI* is the Herfindahl-Hirschman index, *log Asset* is the log of the institution's total assets; *Stkmt.Ind.Var* is the variation in the stock-market index and *CR.GDP* is the variation in real GDP.
(*) Significance level of 10%.(**) Significance level of 5%.(***) Significance level of 1%.

---

[31] Although the Spanish banking market has been fragmented into provincial and even local markets, the majority of listed institutions operated at national level over most of the period analyzed, therefore making this the most significant market for them.

with the efficiency hypothesis, this could explain how more efficient institutions have gradually gained market share over time, thereby increasing the level of concentration in the Spanish banking market. However, there is also empirical evidence to support proponents of the structure-conduct-performance paradigm, where excess profits come from the position that institutions' market concentration gives them. In any event, the negative sign and significant magnitude of the variable *log Asset* suggests that it is not necessarily the largest institutions which have obtained the biggest excess profits. The signs of the other two control variables are as expected: the greater the stock market and economic activity, the greater the value of the market-to-book ratio.

The second column of coefficients in Table 1 again shows the results of estimating relationship [1], in this case using the Herfindahl-Hirschman index (HHI) as the indicator of concentration instead of C5. Again this is calculated from the number of branches at national level. As can be seen, the qualitative results are the same as in column 1: the excess profits obtained by Spanish banks are the results of greater efficiency and a certain degree of market power, which does not necessarily imply collusion between institutions. Finally, the columns for coefficients 3, 4 and 5 of Table 1 show the results of using different output measures as an approximation to the banking market: total assets, credit and deposits, respectively. Once again, the results are very similar to those already described.

3.2   Origin of the excess profits

If we accept the interpretation of Tobin's q as a measure of the excess profits obtained by an institution, it is worth asking about the origin of these profits. Whether these profits are due to market power or better utilization of factors of production, they may have their origins in the deposits market, and/or the credit market, and/or the provision of other banking services. These profits may be the direct result of greater efficiency in the use of factors of production or the fact that institutions are taking advantage of their size as a strategic variable, given the high cost of the bankruptcy of a large institution for the financial system and the national economy. It is very likely that the regulatory environment (the degree of regulatory pressure) also partly explains these profits, as regulations restricting competition (in terms of interest rates, quantities and productive capacity) create favorable conditions for excess profits to be obtained. By contrast, deregulation and liberalization, by allowing greater competition between institutions, erode these excess profits.

The traditional way (Keeley, 1990) of answering these questions is by estimating the following relationship:

$$Q_{it} = \alpha + \beta CRE_{it} + \gamma DEP_{it} + \delta COM_{it} + \theta EFI_{it} + Z_{it} + \varepsilon_{it} \qquad [2]$$

In this formula CRE_{it}, DEP_{it}, COM_{it} and EFI_{it} are variables which reflect the importance of credit, deposits and other banking services (transfers, payments, sale of other financial products, advisory services, etc), respectively, and the degree of efficiency with which institutions operate. Finally, Z_{it} is a control variable vector which includes the size of each institution on each date and the variation of the stock market index and real GDP.[32]

The first column of Table 2 shows the results of estimating relationship [2] for the period 1975-2009. Both the credit market (for which the ratio of credit to total assets is used as a proxy here) and sight deposits (for which the ratio of current account plus saving account to total assets used as the proxy) make a significant contribution to explaining the

TABLE 2

	Coeff	t-ratio	Coeff	t-ratio	Coeff	t-ratio	Coeff	t-ratio	Coeff	t-ratio
Constant	1.199**	2.350	1.562***	2.990	1.536***	2.880	3.371***	6.990	3.907***	7.660
CRE+DEP			0.726***	4.590						
CRE	1.106***	3.970			0.828***	2.700	-0.079	-0.230	-0.237	-0.720
DEP1	1.972***	4.980					1.632***	5.440	1.669***	5.610
DEP2					1.958***	6.230				
COM	1.389***	3.550	1.143***	2.890	2.038***	4.660	-0.193	-0.230	-0.653	-0.960
EFI	-0.462*	-1.890	-0.350	-1.650	-0.731***	-2.890	-0.327	-1.410	-0.329	-1.470
Log Asset	-0.065**	-2.580	-0.074**	-2.780	-0.089***	-3.310	-0.087***	-4.240	-0.094***	-4.690
Stkmt.Ind.Var	0.317***	3.110	0.238**	2.430	0.312***	3.070	0.748***	7.370	0.853***	8.310
CR.GDP	15.350***	8.610	14.989***	8.550	14.457***	8.020				
ID 1977							-1.191***	6.770	-1.170***	-6.700
ID 1978							-0.735***	-6.930	-0.775***	-7.360
ID 1981							0.114*	1.710	0.147**	2.100
ID 1984							-0.063	-0.630		
ID 1985							0.131	1.460		
ID 1987							1.006***	7.820	0.877***	10.540
ID 1989							-0.195	-1.450		
ID 1990							-0.272***	-2.670		
ID 1993							0.196**	2.340	-0.011***	-0.140
ID 1999							0.949***	2.990	0.831***	6.090
ID 2000							-0.224	-0.730		
R² (%)	20.38		14.52		22.16		45.73		44.88	
N. obs.	814		814		814		814		814	

Notes: The first three columns show the estimate of OLS in equation (2) and the last two columns that of equation (3), for the listed banks over the period 1975-2009. Both commercial and investment banks are included. The dependent variable is Tobin's q, approximated here by the ratio of market value to book value of the institution's capital and reserves. *CRE+DEP* is the sum of credit and deposits divided by total assets, *CRE* is credit divided by total assets; *DEP1* and *DEP2* are the ratios of sight deposits to total assets and deposits, respectively; *COM* is the ratio of the institution's fee earnings to its net income; *EFI* is the ratio of operating expenses to net income; *log Asset* is the logarithm of the institution's total assets; *Stkmt.Ind.Var.is* the variation in the stock market index and *CR.GDP* denotes the variation in real GDP. Finally, ID "X" is a binary variable which takes the value 1 if the year is X or later and 0 otherwise.
(*) Significance level of 10%.(**) Significance level of 5%.(***) Significance level of1%.

---

[32] A similar approach for the US case can be seen in Furlong and Kwan (2006) and an application to the Spanish banking system can be seen in Salas and Saurina (2003), although it covers a different period and takes a different sample of institutions from that analyzed here.

excess profits obtained by Spanish institutions during the period. The provision of other services (approximated by fees and commissions obtained by each institution as a share of its net income) also seems to be a source of profits, whereas a traditional measure of efficiency, namely the ratio of operating expenses to net income, is also significant. In this latter case, the negative sign indicates that a decrease in the efficiency ratio (which implies greater efficiency because operating expenses account for a smaller percentage of net income) leads to an increase in Tobin's q. The three control variables have the signs seen in the estimate of relationship (1), a result that confirms the existence of an inverse relationship between size per se and excess profits. If, instead of taking credit and deposits separately, credit and deposits for the resident private sector are considered together (second column of coefficients in Table 2), the results barely change, making this an even clearer and stronger measure of the efficiency of banking services. If the ratio of sight deposits to total deposits from the resident private sector is taken (third coefficients column in Table 2), the results are also unchanged. Indeed, they are even clearer and stronger than in the case of the measurement of efficiency and of banking services.

Sweeping deregulation and the changes in banks' behavior that came with it may have had a direct impact on the extraordinary profits institutions' obtained. In general, the regulatory measures – such as interest-rate liberalization, free opening of bank branches, the equalizing of conditions between different types of institutions or the market entry of foreign banks – can be expected to tend to increase competition, thereby eroding the incumbent banks' excess profits. By contrast, the raising of mandatory investment coefficients, or banks' decisions to embark on greater concentration in the system, may have a positive effect on these profits. Therefore, as Keeley (1990) or Salas and Saurina (2003), show, it may make sense to include a regulatory change vector in relationship (2), so as to try to measure directly the impact that changes in the regulatory environment might have on the variable used to estimate Tobin's q. Thus, the new relationship would be:

$$Q_{it} = \alpha + \beta CRE_{it} + \gamma DEP_{it} + \delta COM_{it} + \theta EFI_{it} + REG_t + Z_{it} + \varepsilon_{it} \qquad [3]$$

Here, *REG* is a dichotomous-variable vector which enables the main regulatory changes in the period analyzed to be incorporated. Most of these regulatory changes were successive stages in the process of financial liberalization, such that the most appropriate way to represent them is by means of a dichotomous step variable, with a value of zero up until the moment of the change and a value of one afterwards. For example, the change in the regulations on the entry of foreign banks promulgated in 1978 is represented as a zero prior to that date and a one after it. Specifically, for the period 1975-2009 11 regulatory and behavioral changes have been considered (Box 1).

1977: Continuation of the process of interest-rate liberalization begun in 1969 and reiterated in 1974; there was also a reduction in mandatory investment coefficients and, finally savings banks were allowed to conduct a broader range of business. These three measures tended towards an erosion of banks' excess profits, so a negative sign may be expected for the parameter associated with this dichotomous variable.

1978: Authorization given to foreign banks to enter the market, albeit with numerous restrictions on their freedom to open branches (negative sign expected).

1981: Further liberalization of interest rates and fees, although the mandatory investment coefficient was raised (sign ambiguous).

1984: Increase in reserve requirements and mandatory investments in government bonds (sign ambiguous, because the resources freely available for lending are diminished, which can be interpreted as a tax on banks).[1]

1985: New capital adequacy regulations passed, requiring capital based on asset risk, together with greater operational alignment between the banks and savings banks (sign is negative or ambiguous).

1987: Full liberalization of interest rates and fees, and reduction of the mandatory investment coefficient (sign negative).

1989: Entry into force of the freedom for savings banks to open branches throughout the country; timetable announced for the elimination of mandatory investment coefficients, and first war for cheap bank liabilities begins (launch of interest-bearing current accounts paying significantly higher rates than before), and an intensive advertising campaign was run (negative sign).

1990: Reduction of reserve requirements and strong consolidation among savings banks, a process which would continue into the following year (the expected sign should be negative given the savings banks' increased capacity to compete with the banks. However, the sign could be ambiguous if the effect of market concentration on the general level of competition is significant and if, additionally, the reduction in the reserve requirement is considered to be a reduction in the pressure on institutions' earnings).

---

[1]   For an analysis of mandatory coefficients as a tax, see Repullo (1990).

1993: Entry into force of Basel I and the Banesto crisis (sign ambiguous).

1999: Membership of the euro and merger of two of the biggest Spanish banks. On the one hand, this significantly increased market concentration, and on the other, it created opportunities for increased efficiency through the streamlining of costs by the new banking group (positive sign).

2000: Second major bank merger (positive sign).

The fourth column of coefficients in Table 2 shows the results of estimate [3].[33] This confirms that sight deposits were the biggest source of excess profits during the period analyzed, as the effect of credit disappears, along with that of fees and efficiency ratios. As regards the regulatory change or behavior variables, the liberalization of interest rates, the alignment of business possibilities in 1977, and the authorization of the entry of foreign banks in 1978, have the signs expected a priori, as do the increase in the competitive potential of the savings banks in 1990 and change in market concentration in 1999. The signs of the variables for 1987 and 1990 are harder to explain though.[34] The variable corresponding to regulatory and behavior changes in 1989 has the expected sign, although the value is not significant.

In short, using a standard methodology to analyze the determinants of excess profits in the banking sector, we obtain the result that these are largely drawn from the deposit market. This is perhaps not surprising in a banking system such as that in Spain, where institutions have dense networks of branches bringing banking services close to retail private and business customers. Nevertheless, it cannot be ruled out that these profits also come from the credit market and from the provision of banking services, as well as from the efficiency with which institutions combine their productive factors.[35] In any event, these results should be interpreted with caution in view of their exploratory nature. Above all, the aim here is to stimulate a debate on the possible existence of excess profits, their origin and measurement, and the impact of regulation on them over a relatively long period which has been marked by profound changes.

---

[33]   In order to obtain a clearer picture of the effect on the temporal dichotomous variables, the GDP variation is eliminated in this regression.

[34]   A positive sign in 1993 may be interpreted as the effect of a reduction in competition due to the Banesto crisis, as it was an institution which over the years prior to its bankruptcy had pursued an extremely aggressive policy of increasing market share. Nevertheless, the magnitude of the parameter does not seem to be proportional to the relative size of Banesto in the Spanish banking system. Therefore, a substantial part of the explanation must be related to changes in the capital regulations, given their existence in Spain from 1985. This may be interpreted as these requirements being made less demanding (leverage ratios or general coefficients disappear and there is a substantial drop in the consumption of capital by the property portfolio and industrial shareholdings), enabling capital to be freed up to increase exposure or profitability per unit invested in the business.

[35]   With fixed effects per bank, the efficiency variable (EFI) is always negative and significant.

3.3   Is there a trade-off between banking competition and financial stability?

Increased competition in a banking system tends to erode excess profits, which reduces the value of the banking franchise for institutions' shareholders and managers. Theoretically, faced with this loss of value, institutions may react by increasing their risks, in order to recover past levels of profitability, or by decreasing bankruptcy protection, as the present value of the bank has diminished. There is extensive literature on this topic, relating competition and financial stability, on both the theoretical and empirical levels.[36] The traditional way (Keeley, 1990) of contrasting whether or not this relationship exists is by means of the following empirical model:

$$RISK_{it} = \alpha + \beta Q_{it} + Z_{it} + \varepsilon_{it} \qquad [4]$$

Here, $RISK_{it}$ is a measure of the degree of financial fragility or risk to which the institution is exposed. In this case the institution's default ratio is used (doubtful assets divided by total loans), together with two measures of leverage, one based on book value and the other on market value: the ratio of capital plus reserves to total assets on the one hand and the ratio of the market value of the institution's equity capital to the market value of its assets (approximately equal to that in section 2.3) on the other. The parameter Q is expected to be negative and significant in the case of the default ratio (the higher the excess profits, the lower the tendency to take risks) and positive for the other two variables (the greater the value of the banking franchise, the greater the interest in protecting it by increasing equity capital and/or reducing the level of leverage).

The variation of real GDP, the inter-bank interest rate (when the dependent variable is the default ratio or the inverse of the book-value leverage ratio) or the variation of the stock market (when the dependent variable is the inverse of the leverage, measured at market value) have been taken as the control variables in this case, and a number of step type dichotomous variables are used to factor in the changes in accounting standards (toughening of the rules on insolvency provisions in 1988, adaptation to IFRS in 2005) and capital and reserves (replacement of the guarantee coefficients by risk-weighted capital requirements in 1985, adoption of Basel I in 1993, entry into force of counter-cyclical provisions in 2000).

Table 3 shows the results of estimate [4] over the period 1981-2009, using the default rate for the *RISK* variable and the two leverage measures (inverse) for the period as a whole. A negative coefficient with a significance of 1% is obtained for the ratio Q in relation to the default rate (first column), which supports the existence of an empirical relationship in the Spanish case between excess profits and institutions' risk exposures.[37]

---

[36]   This is the literature on bank franchise value, in particular: Suárez (1994), Demsetz, Saidenberg and Strahan (1996), Hellmann, Murdock and Stiglitz (2000), Matutes and Vives (2000) and Martínez-Miera and Repullo (2009).

[37]   The same result is obtained using the variable Q with two and three time lags.

TABLE 3

| | Default ratio | | (capital + reserves) /assets | | Market value / Assets at market value | | | | | |
			V. Inst Q_{t-2} and Q_{t-3}		V. Inst Q^{t-2} and Q_{t-3}		V.Inst ROA_{t-2} and ROA_{t-3}		V.Inst ROA_{t-2} and ROA_{t-3}	
	Coeff.	t-ratio	Coeff.	t-ratio	Coeff.	t-ratio	Coeff.	t-ratio	Coeff.	t-ratio
Constant	0.058	1.260	-0.012	-0.150	0.105***	3.870	-0.040	-0.520	0.022	0.410
Q	-0.008***	-3.330	0.110*	1.910	0.041***	4.790	0.137***	3.370	0.100***	3.300
Log Asset	0.001	-0.510	0.000	-0.070	-0.006***	-3.370	-0.002	-0.520	-0.004	-1.570
Stkmt.Ind.Var					0.009	0.980	-0.033***	-1.680	-0.017	-1.090
CR.GDP	-0.195*	-1.880	-1.986*	-1.880						
Interbank	0.001	1.280								
ID 1985			0.005	0.430	0.032***	4.960	-0.024	-0.940	-0.001	-0.080
ID 1988	0.005	0.770								
ID 1993			-0.044	-1.370	0.024***	3.470	-0.003	-0.200	0.008	0.640
ID 2000			-0.043*	-1.800	-0.005	-0.610	-0.054**	-2.160	-0.035*	-1.920
ID 2005	-0.008**	-2.500								
R^2 (%)	6.70		13.03		50,19		9.87		13.24	
N. obs.	592		689		652		689		689	

Note: The *Default ratio, (Capital+Reserves)/Assets and Market value/Market value of assets* variables refer to estimates of equation [4] considering these to be dependent variables. OLS has been estimated in the first case and instrumental variables used in the other two; the instruments are specified in the heading of each estimate (Tobin's q, ROA and ROE with two and three time lags). The sample period is 1975 to 2009 except in the case where the dependent variable is the default ratio, where it is restricted to 1981-2009. The dependent variable *Market value/assets at market value* is calculated as the ratio of the market value of the equity capital to the sum of the market value of the equity capital and the book value of liabilities. The variable Q refers to the ratio of the market value to the book value of the equity capital; *log Asset* is the logarithm of the institution's total assets; *Stkmkt.Ind.Var* is the variation in the stock-market index and *CR.GDP* is the variation in real GDP; *Interbank* is the twelve-month inter-bank interest rate. Finally, ID"X" is a binary variable which takes the value 1 if the year is X or later and 0 otherwise.
(*) Significance level of 10%. (**) Significance level of 5%. (***) Significance level of 1%.

The value of the banking franchise seems to exert a moderating effect on the banks' incentives to expose themselves to credit risk.

The second column of coefficients in Table 3 shows the results of the estimate using instrumental variables for the determinants of the inverse of the book-value leverage ratio. For instrumental variables, Tobin's q has been used with various time lags.[38] A positive and significant value (to a significance level of 10%) for the excess profits variable shows the incentive existing for banks to protect their franchise against unexpected shocks, in particular when these profits are high. This regression also shows the pro-cyclical nature of equity capital and banks' capital ratios[39]: they decrease as GDP increases; i.e., in

---

[38]   Obviously, the estimate by ordinary least squares (OLS) is not satisfactory given the highly negative correlation that exists by definition between the dependent variable and Tobin's q.

[39]   The discussion of the pro-cyclical nature of capital requirements has become more intense with Basel II. A detailed analysis of this issue for the Spanish case can be found in Repullo, Saurina and Trucharte (2009), for credit to businesses, and Saurina and Trucharte (2007), for mortgage lending.

expansionary credit phases capital and reserves, whether as determined by Basel I (or equivalent) or without a risk weighting (guarantee coefficients prior to 1985),[40] are eroded.

The most appropriate way of comparing the relationship between profit and risk is probably to use market measures of the latter. However, this has not been possible until very recently and only in a very limited way (measurements using CDS are very recent, with scant coverage of Spanish institutions and a liquidity level that is very difficult to evaluate, therefore limiting the scope for the interpretation of these data as a measure of institutions' risk). In any event, the use of stock-market information on listed banks can help mitigate this lack of information. These columns of coefficients 3, 4 and 5 in Table 3 show a positive and highly significant value for Tobin's q, both when the variable is implemented with its own lags and when using ROE or ROA, respectively, corroborating the previous results.

4 Concluding remarks

For the Spanish banking system the last 35 years has been a period of major changes and transformations, with strong market integration of the system, and a substantial increase in the levels of competition. This was accompanied by efficiency gains, product and process innovation, the development and application of new technologies for the production of banking services, increasingly openness to the exterior, the assimilation of foreign banks, and international expansion. This intense development of the banking business has gone hand in hand with significant changes in the regulatory framework, such that direct regulatory pressure on prices, quantities and productive capacity have gradually given way to a regulatory framework in which institutions are free to compete, but are subject to certain minimum regulations and prudential supervision.

Cutting across this, the period analyzed highlights that there is no one single approach to the banking business. Other institutions coexist alongside major internationally active banks that have national, regional or even local scope, with different business strategies and banking specializations that, overall, have contributed to greater bank use and financial integration in Spain, facilitating the efficient allocation of financial resources, risk transfer and, in short contributing appropriately to financing investment and economic growth. The strong development of the banking sector has been accompanied by increased competition between institutions, benefiting borrowers and depositors and consequently raising the efficiency of financial intermediation. Nevertheless, this increasing competition has not been linear, as is demonstrated by the indicators and analysis in this chapter.

---

[40] The estimate by means of fixed effects corroborates the conclusions obtained, both for the default ratio and for the book solvency ratio. In this latter case, a level of significance of 5% for Tobin's q can be observed, on the one hand, and that the substantial change in the solvency requirements introduced in 1985 translated into an effective increase in solvency ratios (unweighted) Spanish institutions, on the other, highlighting the impact of the new prudential regulations that gradually replaced structural ones. The subsequent changes in the capital and provision standards had no significant effect on this variable.

Longitudinally, the period analyzed shows several episodes of strong credit expansion, growth in bank profits, increasing productive capacity, progressive relaxation of the requirements for the granting of loans, and the correction of undigested credit excesses during recessions when differences in risk profiles during the expansionary phase materialize in the form of earnings and default rates that vary substantially from one institution to another. Thus, the banking crisis of the late 1970s and early 1980s was the response to the expansionary credit cycle of the preceding decade, combined with the idiosyncrasies that are almost always present in institutions that have been taken under the control of the authorities, liquidated or taken over by other more solvent and prudent institutions. The particular difficulties faced by some institutions and, to a lesser extent, the banking system as a whole, as a result of the 1993 recession were the product of excess lending and mismanagement during the late 1980s and early 1990s. Similarly, the restructuring process currently underway in the savings bank sector is the necessary response to the negative effects of a long phase of credit expansion, with a growing concentration of exposures to real estate and increasingly lax lending standards in the years leading up to the outbreak of the international financial crisis in 2007 followed by the subsequent severe recession in the Spanish economy.

This dialectic between the transversal and longitudinal dimensions is what has moved the Spanish financial system forward in cycles, with its alternation of boom and bust. In order for this progress to be more orderly and measured, with fewer upsets (i.e. fewer institutions affected by crisis) and with less exuberance (and excessive credit expansion, excessive concentration and ultimately, unsustainable credit growth) it may be helpful to understand the limits of the process of financial integration, namely that perfect competition is synonymous with financial instability (with high costs for the economy and social welfare) and that the banking system, in view of its systemic importance and externalities (both positive and negative) for the rest of the economy, must be regulated. This regulation should not be implemented in the form of restrictions on prices, quantities and productive capacity (which primarily generate inefficiency and excess profits) but through prudential standards that are rigorously designed and applied by banking supervisors, while paying attention to the financial position of each institution and the interactions between institutions and the business and financial cycle. In short, a model of financial regulation with two interrelated dimensions: microprudential and macroprudential.

References

BANCO DE ESPAÑA (2009). *Informe de Estabilidad Financiera,* November.

COMMISSION OF THE EUROPEAN COMMUNITIES (2007). *European Financial Integration Report.*

CUERVO, A. (1988). *La crisis bancaria en España, 1977-1985,* Ariel.

DELGADO, J., J. SAURINA and R. TOWNSEND (2008). "Estrategias de expansión de las entidades de depósito españolas: una primera aproximación descriptiva", *Estabilidad Financiera,* 15, Banco de España, pp. 99-117.

DEMSETZ, R. S., M. R. SAIDENBERG and P. E. STRAHAN (1996). "Banks with something to lose: The disciplinary role of franchise value", *FRBNY Economic Policy Review,* October, pp. 1-14.

EUROPEAN CENTRAL BANK (2009). *Financial integration in Europe,* April.

FUENTELSAZ, L., and V. SALAS (1994). *Spatial Competition in Retail Banking: Theory and Empirical Evidence from Spain and other European Countries,* Fundación BBVA.

FURLONG, F. T., and S. KWAN (2006). *Sources of Bank Charter Value, mimeo,* San Francisco Federal Reserve.

HELLMANN, T. F., K. C. MURDOCK and J. E. STIGLITZ (2000). "Liberalization, moral hazard in banking, and prudential regulation: Are capital requirements enough?", *American Economic Review,* 90, 1, March, pp. 147-165.

JIMÉNEZ, G., and J. SAURINA (2006). "Credit risk, credit cycles and prudential regulation", *International Journal of Central Banking,* 2, 2, June, pp. 65-98.

JIMÉNEZ, G., J. SAURINA and R. TOWNSEND (2007). "El número de relaciones bancarias de empresas e individuos en España: 1984-2006", *Estabilidad Financiera,* 13, Banco de España, pp. 53-72.

JUAN, A. DE (1993). "Dealing with problem banks: the case of Spain", in H. J. Blommestein and J. R. Lange (eds.), *Transformation of the banking system: portfolio restructuring, privatization and the payment system,* OECD Publications Service, París.

KEELEY, M. C. (1990). "Deposit insurance, risk and market power in banking", *American Economic Review,* 80, pp. 1183-1200.

LINDENBERG, E., and S. ROSS (1981). "Tobin's q Ratio and Industrial Organization", *Journal of Business,* 54, pp. 1-32.

MARTÍN-OLIVER, A., V. SALAS and J. SAURINA (2008). "Search Cost and Price Dispersion in Vertically Related Markets: The case of Bank Loans and Deposits", *Review of Industrial Organization,* 33, pp. 297-323.

MARTÍNEZ MÉNDEZ, P. (1991). *Los Beneficios de la Banca: 1970-1989,* Banco de España.

MARTÍNEZ-MIERA, D., and R. REPULLO (2009). "Does competition reduce the risk of bank failure?", de próxima publicación en *Review of Financial Studies.*

MATUTES, C., and X. VIVES (2000). "Imperfect competition, risk taking, and regulation in banking", *European Economic Review,* 44, pp. 1-34.

PELLICER, M. (1992). "Los mercados financieros organizados en España", *Estudios Económicos,* 50, Banco de España.

PEREZ, D., V. SALAS and J. SAURINA (2005). "Banking integration in Europe", *Moneda y Crédito,* 220, pp. 105-154.

POVEDA, R. (2000). "La reforma del sistema de provisiones de insolvencia", *Boletín Económico,* 1, Banco de España, pp. 79-91.

REPULLO, R. (1990). "The Reform of Reserve Requirements in Spain: A Technical Note", *Economic Bulletin,* Banco de España, June, pp. 85-94.

REPULLO, R., J. SAURINA and C. TRUCHARTE (2009). "Mitigating the Procyclicality of Basel II", in M. Dewatripont, X. Freixas and R. Portes (eds.), *Macroeconomic Stability and Financial Regulation: Key Issues for the G20,* CEPR.

SALAS, V., and J. SAURINA (2003). "Deregulation, market power and risk behavior in Spanish banks", *European Economic Review,* 47, pp. 1061-1075.

SAURINA, J. (2009a). *Dynamic Provisioning The Experience of Spain, The World Bank Group,* July, n.º 7.

— (2009b). "Loan loss provisions in Spain. A working macroprudential tool", *Estabilidad Financiera,* 17, Banco de España, pp. 9-26.

SAURINA, J., and C. TRUCHARTE (2007). "An assessment of Basel II Procyclicality in Mortgage Portfolios", *Journal of Financial Services Research,* 32, December, pp. 81-101.

SAURINA, J. (1992). Capítulo III of book: *Valoración económica del beneficio y el capital,* Colección Estudios, n.º 11, FEDEA, 1994, edited by Gonzalo Mato and Vicente Salas.

SUÁREZ, F. J. (1994). *Closure rules, market power and risk-taking in a dynamic model of bank be-*

havior, Discussion Paper 196, LSE, Financial Markets Group.

SMIRLOCK, M. T. GILLIGAN and W. MARSHALL (1984). "Tobin's q and the Structure-Performance Relationship", *American Economic Review,* 74(5), diciembre, pp. 1051-1060.

TRUJILLO, J. A., C. CUERVO and F. VARGAS (1990). *El sistema financiero español,* 3rd edition, Ariel.

10. The Internationalization of the Spanish financial system

Ángel Berges, Emilio Ontiveros and Francisco J. Valero
Universidad Autónoma de Madrid

1 Introduction

This chapter looks at how the Spanish financial system has opened up to the outside world in recent years. To that end, it examines the two main components of the system, namely the banking system and the stock market, and it looks at this process in both possible directions.

The international integration of Spain's financial system is hard to disentangle from that of its broader economy,[1] and this process of opening up to the outside world has been an important feature of the evolution of the country's financial system in recent years; indeed it has been one of the factors driving it.

Apart from the historical considerations, the global integration of financial systems – and Spain's is no exception – has gained special significance in the wake of the financial crisis that broke in the summer of 2007. This renewed emphasis is largely due to the fact that global integration has contributed to the rapid and intense propagation of a financial crisis that, although taking place at the heart of the global financial system, was initially a national crisis centering on local instruments of dubious credit quality, namely so-called subprime mortgages.

The intensity and speed with which the crisis spread cannot be separated from excessive

---

[1] For more, see Chapter 6 of this book.

exposure to financial risks, often of an international nature. Nor can it be separated from an inadequate and deficient control over these risks by the institutions taking them, and by the supervisory authorities overseeing those institutions.

In the Spanish case, the "international dimension" of the crisis was amplified by institutions' dependence on international wholesale markets, a dependence which had grown over the course of the preceding decade. The fact that these markets seized up entirely at certain times, and have operated erratically since the onset of the crisis, made Spain's banking system extremely vulnerable as it found itself having to meet substantial external debt repayments in a context in which it was extremely difficult to roll them over.

Beyond the specific features of the Spanish case, the speed and intensity with which the crisis spread has led to doubts about the current internationalization of the world's financial systems and its outlook. This has resulted in a sort of "homecoming" in parallel with a "back to basics" or return to "boring banking," which can be seen in certain banking institutions.

The bodies that have concerned themselves with this type of analysis include the Committee on the Global Financial System (CGFS),[2] which brings together 23 central banks from various countries around the world,[3] including the Banco de España. This committee has issued three landmark reports (CGSF 2010a, b and c), of which the third is most relevant here. This last report identifies the factors driving the global integration of the banking system and extrapolate from current trends to explore how the process may develop in the future.

This chapter, in common with the other chapters of this book, covers a fairly extensive historical period, running from a relatively remote past down to the present, and also projects forward into the future, although at this point in time any conjectures are highly speculative given the profound changes that the crisis has wrought, some of the effects of which have yet to fully manifest themselves.

This chapter's treatment of the banking system and stock market aims to sketch out an analysis of the way in which these two basic forms of financial intermediation behave in the international context, where they should be viewed as mutually complementary (see CGSF, 2010c). This will be seen in the chapter as a whole, and is the case in the Spanish financial system, where banking and the stock market have developed in parallel, although the development of the latter has been much stronger.

---

[2]   This Committee was set up in 1971 under the name of the Euro-currency Standing Committee with the aim of monitoring international banking markets. However, its focus of attention shifted over time to address broader issues, such that in 1999 its was given its present name and devoted itself to identifying and assessing possible sources of tension in global financial markets, promoting an understanding of their structural factors, and stimulating improvements in their functioning and stability.

[3]   Together with the Bank for International Settlements (BIS) which provides the Committee's secretariat.

2   The modes of internationalization of the Spanish financial system

The basic function of any financial system is to enable funds to circulate through a series of institutions and markets, so that they flow from those economic agents that have money available to other agents that need it. If the financial system did not exist, or if it operated inefficiently, requirements for funds existing in the economy would be left unmet, despite there being persons or institutions willing to lend or invest.

This central role performed by financial systems justifies the considerable attention paid to them following the outbreak of the financial crisis in the summer of 2007, and the public financial support given by the countries affected.

In relation to this basic function, it could be said that a financial system will be more internationalized, from the point of view of its external activity, the greater the weight the following factors have:

1. Funds raised abroad as a share of the system's total funding, or
2. Assets placed in other countries as a share of the total financial investments within the system.

Those are, therefore, the two dimensions of internalization: borrowing and investment. These two aspects do not always move in parallel. Indeed, as we shall see, in the case of Spanish financial system, significant imbalances built up between them over the decade prior to the crisis that began in 2007.

In any case, moving beyond the focus on foreign borrowing and investment to take a broader view, a financial system's internationalization may be defined (as shown in Figure 1) in various ways:

1. In terms of *activity:*

    a) *Foreign,* i.e. business with the rest of the world, with transactions expressed in:
        –   The national currency (currently euros), or
        –   Foreign currency
    b) In *foreign currency,* which may be:
        –   Abroad (the same as second item above)
        –   Domestic: where the counterparties are economic agents that are also resident in Spain.

2. In terms of *presence,* where this refers both to foreign entities operating in Spain and Spanish entities operating abroad. This presence can be in either of the following basic modes:

FIGURE 1   MODES OF BANKING INTERNATIONALIZATION

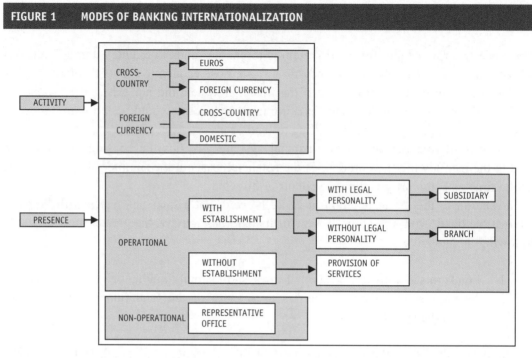

SOURCE: Valero (1994).

a) *Operational presence,* in which financial transactions may be generated in each of the modes in Figure 1, this presence may take the form of an establishment in the target country, such that this presence may have its own legal identity, as in the case of (subsidiaries), or not, as in the case of (branches). Alternatively, the presence may not involve a permanent establishment, but rather use of the freedom to provide cross-border services.

b) *Non-operational presence: representative office,* in which financial transactions are not carried out directly, but may be promoted by this office.

Internationalization based on the presence of financial entities abroad is of particular interest because, it is the most visible form of international presence. Moreover, it generates international business, particularly in those spheres where the physical proximity to customers has a value that is difficult to substitute for, such as in the case of retail banking. However, this does not prevent a large share of a financial entity's foreign business being carried out through its country of origin, and consequently, not requiring it to have a presence abroad.

In any event, as the CGFS points out (2010c, Table 1), financial internationalization has tended to become much more complex than allowed by this simple classification in terms of where business is conducted and whether or not it relies on a physical presence. This table illustrates a series of combinations of international financial transactions, highlighting their growing complexity in terms of the number of transactions and countries involved in certain transactions. The types of situations that may arise could include the following:

1. The source of funds is located in country A.
2. The entity or financial market through which the funds are intermediated is located in country B.
3. The recipient of the funds is in country C.
4. And the intermediary brokering the transaction might be a subsidiary of the entity in country B, but resident in country D, in which case the funds would not pass through country B at all, even though they form part of the international activity of the institution headquartered there.

Obviously, the situation becomes more complex the larger the number of banking institutions and countries in the chain between the source of the funds and their final destination. It is in the context of this complexity that the spread of the crisis throughout the international financial system referred to in the introduction to this chapter must be viewed.

2.1 Advantages and disadvantages of internationalization

The internationalization of the financial system presents both opportunities and risks.[4] The main advantage of international integration is improved access to new sources of funding or investment destinations, which may allow:

1. Raising larger volumes of funds and/or doing so under more favorable conditions in terms of cost, terms or risk. And in the case of risk, enabling better diversification.
2. A wider range of investment alternatives and investments than available domestically, and/or under more favorable conditions in terms of returns, terms, risk or diversification.

In short, a financial system's internationalization implies greater efficiency, and therefore a better allocation of resources by economic agents in terms of both their borrowings and investments.

In parallel, the internationalization of the financial system also brings risks. In particular, in terms of its greater external dependence. This can lead to a number of vulnerabilities:

1. Funds raised in other countries will be provided according to the goals pursued by the parties supplying them. These need not necessarily be aligned with the goals of the destination country:

---

[4] Other authors who have recently analyzed and assessed the internationalization of financial systems, particularly banking systems, include Classens (2006), Goldberg (2009), McCauley, McGuire and von Peter (2010), and Papaioannou (2009).

a) If the funds exceed the country's real needs this may lead to excess supply, with the risk of feeding bubbles in the prices of financial and other assets.

b) If foreign investors lose confidence in the country they may all rush for the exit, with depressive effects on the country's economy and financial markets.

2. Funds placed in other countries expose investors in the originating country to risks that differ from those they face in domestic markets. For example, if these countries use a different currency, they will be exposed to currency risk, which may be realized if any of the currencies is devalued, and thus the equivalent in the national currency of origin is reduced in value.

As noted previously, internationalization of the financial system is closely related to internationalization of the wider economy, although the pattern of development is not always the same, as we shall see in the Spanish case.

The increasing internationalization that has been seen in various countries' economies and financial systems in recent years has bound them all closer together. This can have negative repercussions for them in terms of risk transmission. As noted in the introduction, this is what has been happening since the crisis broke in August 2007, aided and abetted by the problems intrinsic to each country, such as an overdependence on the property sector, in Spain and other countries.

2.2 The internationalization of the Spanish economy and financial system

Spain's economy has become increasingly international, in a process closely linked to the three main stages of its integration in the European Union, namely accession (1986), the single market (1993), and Monetary Union (1999).

Chart 1 shows how financial internationalization, in the sense of foreign business, has grown over time in terms of the relative weight of the sector's overseas assets and liabilities in its aggregate financial assets and liabilities.

The relative net financial position, defined as the difference between the two weights, has always been negative for Spain (its external financial liabilities always exceeding its corresponding assets) but to make the chart more compact it is shown on the positive side.

The time horizon considered begins in 1980, the year in which the series of Financial Accounts of the Spanish Economy (CFEE) produced by the Banco de España begins. Analysis of the chart highlights the following points:

1. Throughout the period Spain has been financially dependent on the exterior as it has required more resources to finance its growth than have been available domestically. What is more, this dependence has risen significantly over time.

CHART 1   DEGREE OF FINANCIAL INTERNATIONALIZATION OF THE SPANISH ECONOMY

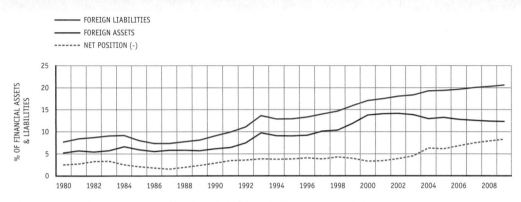

SOURCE: The authors, based on *Cuentas Financieras de la Economía Española*. Banco de España.

2. This greater dependence is reflected in a growing weight of foreign liabilities within the Spanish economy's total borrowings. This weight, which rose from 7.6% to 20.6% over the period as a whole, only fell in four years: the three-year period 1985-87, which is the period in which Spain joined the European Community, and was marked by efforts to avoid the economy overheating as a result of membership; and again 1994, when there was a European bond market crisis, which hit Spain particularly hard.

3. The persistence of a net indebtedness position relies on the sustained confidence of foreign investors in the Spanish economy.

4. Over the course of the period the financial internationalization of the Spanish economy also increased on the asset side, although to a lesser extent, and in a way that was less consistent over time. This should come as no surprise: if the economy's needs force it to turn increasingly to external sources of finance, financial investments outside the country always have the alternative of investing in the country, and vice versa.

5. The internationalization of Spain's financial investments has been declining since 2003. There was an isolated spike in 2005, primarily as a consequence of the greater demand for resources driven by the growth of the economy, and by the property boom in particular, but the downward trend resumed with the onset of the financial crisis.

6. As a result, the relative net external financial position of the Spanish economy (measured as the difference between its foreign assets and liabilities) was negative throughout the period considered and increased over the period from 2.4% at the start to 8.2% at the end.

It seems reasonable to suppose that the internationalization of an economy and its financial system follow similar patterns over time, but this is not necessarily the case, as can be seen in Chart 2, which shows the internationalization of the Spanish financial

CHART 2   COMPARATIVE DEGREE OF FINANCIAL INTERNATIONALIZATION OF THE SPANISH
            FINANCIAL SYSTEM

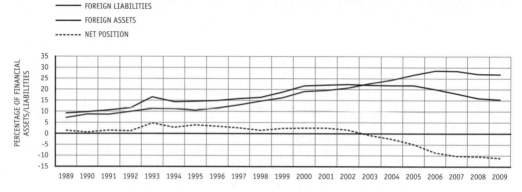

SOURCE: The authors, based on *Cuentas Financieras de la Economía Española*. Banco de España.

system. The axes of this chart are equivalent to those of the preceding one, except that the net relative position is here defined with respect to the semi-sum of the Spanish financial system's financial assets and liabilities. Moreover, given that the net external position in these cases is alternately positive and negative over time, it is not possible to make this chart as compact as the preceding one.

If we draw the lines of the relative internationalization of the Spanish economy and its financial system on Chart 3 we can observe that the latter is always above the former on the asset side, with a difference of several percentage points (p.p.).

By contrast, on the liabilities side, up to and including 1997 the internationalization of the broader Spanish economy was stronger than that of its financial system, although the difference was relatively small. Indeed, nothing prevents certain economic agents, such as

CHART 3   COMPARATIVE DEGREE OF INTERNATIONALIZATION OF THE SPANISH BANKING SYSTEM
            AND ECONOMY

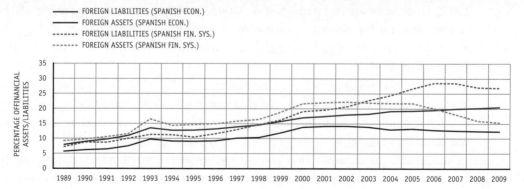

SOURCE: The authors, based on *Cuentas Financieras de la Economía Española*. Banco de España.

government bodies or large corporations, from borrowing directly from abroad, whereas Spanish financial institutions would have had to assume significant exchange rate risk if they borrowed in currencies stronger than the peseta.

The situation changed drastically with the introduction of the euro. Foreign borrowing by Spanish economy's rising net borrowing, driven by strong economic growth and the property boom that followed the introduction of the new currency, was increasingly met by Spanish financial institutions, which borrowed ever larger amounts from abroad.[5] A significant share of this external borrowing by financial institutions took the form of the issuance of mortgage-backed securities (via mortgage securitization or covered bonds), which allowed mortgages in Spain for the construction and purchase of homes to be funded.

This same pattern explains why the financial system's net external financial position has become increasingly negative since 2003, exceeding the 10% threshold in the final years of the period. As a consequence they have greatly increased their external dependence, which has been highlighted by their difficulties rolling over their debt on maturity, particularly at times of market turbulence, such as that following in the wake of the Greek and Irish crises, which affected the markets' confidence in the Spanish economy as a whole.

The following sections of this chapter will look at the internationalization of the Spanish banking industry, by far the most important part of the country's financial system, from both directions. This will be followed by a discussion of the internationalization of the Spanish stock market.

3 The presence of foreign banks in Spain

The presence of foreign banks in Spain was for a long time the most evident symbol of the internationalization of the Spanish financial system. There were two main reasons for this:

1. For many years Spain closed its doors to new foreign banks. The reasons for this included defending the *status quo* in a banking system that was highly protected from competition. It was not until 1978 that the first general regulation would be passed permitting the presence of new foreign banks in Spain.
2. Despite a penetration which, in terms of market share, was certainly small, foreign banks made a significant contribution to the development of the financial and banking systems in Spain, fostering markets such as the inter-bank market, and introducing new products, such as variable-rate loans and high-interest accounts. All these innovations laid the foundations for today's financial system that remains to this day.

---

[5] For more details, see Chapter 6 of this book.

The combination of these two factors suggests that Spanish banks, while partially protected against foreign banks for a time, learned from them how to cope in a highly competitive market, in which it is essential to have an innovative range of products and services. As a result, they have been able to defend their share of the market on their own merits.[6]

The recent history of foreign banks in Spain goes back to the period of the First World War, a conflict in which Spain remained neutral, thus favoring its economic and financial relations with other countries. The two oldest foreign branches still operating in Spain, although not necessarily under the same name throughout the period, were established in the country during the period 1916-1919.[7]

Before the Civil War there had been four foreign bank branches: two French, one British and one American. After the war, their number remained at four, although the US bank was replaced by an Italian one in 1941. From that date on, there were no new banking institutions legally classed as foreign in Spain until 1978. The development of foreign banks in Spain from this point up until 1990 is described in Álvarez and Iglesias-Sarria (1992).

Prior to 1978 there were two different channels by which foreign banks could enter the Spanish market. These were a clear expression of the reservations about this topic at the time:

1. So-called "special-status banks" under the additional provision of Decree 2248/1974, 9 August 1974, amending the regulation creating new private-sector banks, a provision which allowed foreign individuals to own a shareholding of up to 15% of their capital.

    The additional provision of this Decree authorized the Ministry of Finance, in cases of national interest, to submit applications to establish partly foreign-owned "special-status banks" to the government for approval.

    Taking advantage of this option, two Hispano-Arab banks were set up, one in 1975 and another in 1979, of which only the former remains in the Spanish market today. The participation of Arab countries and the timing of the Decree, coming shortly after the first oil shock in the 1970s, help explain the motivation behind the establishment of these banks, namely the financing of business with countries that had found themselves substantially wealthier as a result of the sudden rise in the price of oil.

---

[6]   For more details, see Chapter 9 of this book.
[7]   For more details, see Chapter 4 of this book.

2. The regulations on foreign investments in Spain (Decree 3021/1974, 31 October 1974) giving the force of law to the consolidated text of the legislative provisions on foreign investments in Spain, provided that banks in which there were foreign investments would be regulated by specific provisions.

This latter legislation allowed certain foreign banks to acquire crisis-stricken Spanish banks, thereby gaining a foothold in the Spanish market, without being officially considered foreign. This also gave them a reasonably-sized network of branches through which they could offer retail banking services; something which was prohibited for a time to the foreign banks that entered Spain after 1978. This does not mean that all these banks with a network of branches were necessarily successful in the Spanish market. Some of them ended up exiting the market or limiting themselves to the wholesale business.

Table 1 outlines the three main stages of the modern regulations governing foreign banks' access to the Spanish market. The table focuses on the legislation, as this defines the main conditions and limits to access the market:

1. Royal Decree 1388/1978 of 23 June 1978, regulating the presence of foreign banks in Spain.
2. Royal Decree 1144/1988, 30 September 1988, on the creation of private-sector banks and establishments of foreign credit institutions in Spain.
3. Royal Decree 1245/1995, 14 July 1995, on the creation of banks, cross-border activity and other points regarding the legal framework governing credit institutions.

Foreign banks were subject to significant restrictions, both in terms of licensing and minimum capital requirements. There were also limits on their operational possibilities once they had entered the Spanish market. The table does not, however, list all the restrictions under the regulations in effect at all times, but only those with greatest impact on the type of business these banks could do. Their ability to attract retail deposits was subject to strict legal constraints, not just due to express limits on deposit taking, but also the restrictions on their opening branches.

The restrictions set on foreign banks encouraged them to focus on wholesale customers. They also had a greater propensity to borrow from other institutions, thus stimulating the development of the Spanish interbank market.

Spain's membership of the EU and the subsequent implementation of the single European market ultimately led to the elimination of virtually all the existing restrictions on foreign banks, particularly in the case of banks from other EU countries. However, although it represents a barrier to entry, the increase in the minimum capital level required to operate in Spain (see Table 1) cannot be considered a discriminatory condition as long as it also applied to Spanish banks. This has served as a mechanism strengthening the Spanish banking system front to financial crises.

| TABLE 1 | REGULATION OF FOREIGN BANKS IN SPAIN. HISTORICAL OVERVIEW (1978-1995) |

Mode of Presence		Authorization			Minimum Capital (millions of pesetas)			Other requirements (a)		
		R. D. 1388/ 1978	R. D. 1144/ 1988	R. D. 1245/ 1995	R. D. 1388/ 1978	R. D. 1144/ 1988	R. D. 1245/ 1995	R. D. 1388/ 1978	R. D. 1144/ 1988	R. D. 1245/ 1995
Subsidiary		Council of Ministers	Finance Minister (b)	Finance Minister	Capital 750 (c), Issue premium 750(c)	Capital 1,500	Capital 3,000	Retail finance ≤ 40% (d) Offices ≤ 3	Retail finance ≤ 50% (e), Offices ≤ 3 (f)	If of non-EU origin (g): reciprocity and possible guarantee requirement
Branch	EU (h)	Council of Ministers	Finance Ministry	No / Finance Ministry	Capital 750 (c)	Capital 1,500	No / Capital 3,000	Retail lending ≤ 40% (d), Offices ≤ 3	Retail finance ≤ 50% (e), Offices ≤ 3 (f)	No / Reciprocity
	Non-EU									
Representative office		Finance Ministry	Finance Ministry	Banco de España	Not applicable			Cannot perform transactions or provide banking services		
Provision of services		Unregulated		Prior notification of Banco de España (i)	Not applicable			Unregulated		If of non-EU origin, guarantee of fulfillment of standards of general interest

SOURCE: The authors.

a. The restriction on retail deposit-taking refers to: borrowing on the domestic market, excluding the inter-bank market ≤ x% (investments in securities and lending to Spanish institutions + assets covering the cash ratio)

b. RD 184/1987: as of 1 Jan 1993, if origin is EU, "economic needs of the market" criteria cannot be applied.

c. 2,000 from RD 677/1983 to R. D. 184/1987.

d. Legislative RD1298/1986: 50% as of Jan 1988.

e. Legislative RD 1298/1986: 60% as of 1 Jan 1989; 70% as of 1 Jan 1990; 80% as of 1 Jan 1991; 90% 1 Jan 1992: free as of 1 Jan 1993.

f. Legislative RD1298/1986: 4 as of 1 Jan 1990; 6 as of 1 Jan 1991; 8 as of 1 Jan 1992: free as of 1-1-1993.

g. Also in RD 1144/1988.

h. Applicable to all the countries of the European Economic Area.

i. If the origin is the EU, by the supervisory authority; if not, by the institution itself.

Currently for an institution with operational capacity in another EU country, the best way of accessing the Spanish market is by setting up a branch.[8] This is basically for the following reasons:

1. It is not subject to minimum capital requirements.
2. It does not require any authorization from the banking authorities in the destination country, in this case Spain.

---

[8]   The choice between the two basic modes of operation whereby a banking institution can establish an international presence, namely through a subsidiary or a branch, is an interesting topic in this field, on which we recommend that interested readers consult Cerutti, Dell'Ariccia and Martínez (2007). The choice does not depend solely on the wishes of the banking institution, as it may be determined by the regulations and the supervisory authorities in both the countries of origin and destination. See also the following note.

3.   It is supervised by the Member State of origin.[9]

The basic legislation defining the single banking market was the Second Directive 89/646/EEC, 15 December 1989. It assumed the coordination of laws, regulations and administrative provisions relating to the taking up and pursuit of the business of credit institutions, the content of which is currently subsumed by Directive 2006/48/EC, 14 June 2006, relating to the taking up and pursuit of the business of credit institutions. Since the time this legislation came into effect, branches have been the main mechanism on which the single banking market has rested.

As a consequence, foreign branches in Spain currently comprise the biggest group of deposit-taking institutions, having overtaken credit unions in 2008.[10]

The increase in the number of foreign branches is even more striking bearing in mind the significant number exiting the Spanish market, particularly those based outside the EU. As Maravall, Glavan and Afi (2009) note (pp. 45-48), between 1986 and 2007 no less than 30 foreign branches closed in Spain, 15 of which belonged to banks headquartered outside the EU. Indeed, in 2009 only eight branches of institutions based outside the EU were present in Spain.

Banks from just two countries accounted for the bulk of closures of branches of non-EU banks in Spain. These were Japan, with seven institutions closing branches, and the United

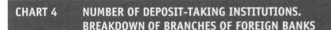

**CHART 4   NUMBER OF DEPOSIT-TAKING INSTITUTIONS.
BREAKDOWN OF BRANCHES OF FOREIGN BANKS**

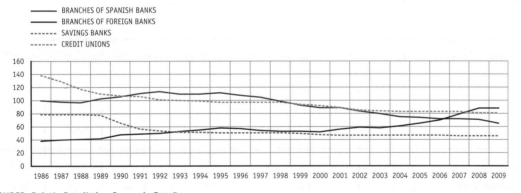

——— BRANCHES OF SPANISH BANKS
——— BRANCHES OF FOREIGN BANKS
-------- SAVINGS BANKS
-------- CREDIT UNIONS

SOURCE: *Boletín Estadístico.* Banco de España.

---

[9]   The current crisis, and in particular the collapse of the Icelandic banks, has highlighted the fact that this situation entails a degree of risk for the destination country of these branches, as it is not possible to control the possible risks that may emerge from them, except as regards their liquidity and application of monetary policy.

[10]   Nevertheless, when comparing this group of branches with Spanish deposit-taking institutions, it should be borne in mind that it is larger than it should be to act properly as a reference for them. The reason being, as their official name suggests, they are branches of foreign credit institutions, some of which might not be comparable with Spanish deposit-taking institutions, but closer in nature to other types of institution, such as credit finance institutions, etc.

States with five. In both cases, these were countries whose banking systems were undergoing significant changes at the time, particularly in the case of Japan, with a spate of takeovers and mergers among the main banks, and others, rethinking their international expansion strategies. Thus, arguably, these departures had more to do with events in the banks' countries of origin than in the Spanish market.

The evolving situation of foreign branches in Spain pictures a highly dynamic sector. It was, nevertheless, unable to translate this dynamism into significant market share.

Something similar seems to be true of subsidiaries of foreign banks, the number of which has declined significantly in recent years. According to Álvarez Canal (1998), on 31 December 1996 (i.e. the end of the first full year after the legislation regulating the presence of foreign banks in Spain came into effect) there were 25 foreign bank subsidiaries, whereas at the end of 2009 there were just 17. Underlying this decline was the significant number of banks exiting the market, although a number of other banks also entered.

Table 2 offers an overall picture of foreign banks within the Spanish banking system as a whole, as reflected by the market shares of the headline basic banking business, lending and deposit items. Obviously, given the wholesale orientation of their business, their share of customer deposits is particularly small, although it is more significant in the case of non-residents, whereas lending activities are more important, in particular in the case of loans to government.

Market share of foreign banks on 31 December 2009 was, in general, smaller than that registered at the end of 1996. It remains striking that data show a retreat by foreign banks in Spain when the single market came into effect, that is to say, after 1993-94, precisely the time when foreign banks had greater freedom to operate in Spain.

TABLE 2   MARKET SHARE OF GROUPS OF DEPOSIT-TAKING INSTITUTIONS IN SPAIN (%)

| | Spanish banks | FOREIGN BANKS | | | | TOTAL Banks | Savings banks | Credit Unions | TOTAL banking system |
| | | TOTAL | Subsi-diaries | Branches | | | | | |
				European Union	Non - European Union				
TOTAL ASSETS/ LIABILITIES	44.5	10.2	3.0	6.9	0.2	54.7	41.5	3.9	100.0
Customer credit	39.5	7.7	3.6	3.9	0.2	47.2	47.7	5.0	100.0
Government	51.0	13.2	11.6	1.5	0.0	64.1	34.0	1.8	100.0
Resident private sector	37.4	7.4	3.3	3.9	0.2	44.8	49.8	5.4	100.0
Non-residents	68.5	8.2	3.4	4.5	0.4	76.7	22.9	0.4	100.0
Customer deposits	38.7	4.6	2.5	2.0	0.0	43.3	50.8	6.0	100.0
Government	39.4	3.9	1.1	2.8	0.0	43.3	53.4	3.4	100.0
Resident private sector	34.9	4.5	2.6	1.8	0.0	39.4	54.1	6.6	100.0
Non-residents	81.4	7.0	3.1	3.8	0.1	88.4	11.0	0.4	100.0

SOURCE: Banco de España. Memoria de la supervisión bancaria 2009.

Table 3 summarizes the presence of foreign banks in Spain in each of the three modes of operation outlined above. While providing a useful overview, it should be borne in mind that the various different forms of operation cannot be aggregated horizontally as each of them has different implications for banking business. Moreover, to some extent they cannot be aggregated vertically either, given the range of activities performed under a similar model.[11, 12]

TABLE 3   PRESENCE OF FOREIGN BANKING INSTITUTIONS IN SPAIN

	Subsidiaries	Branches	Representative offices	Free provision of services
Germany	1	13	7	60
Austria			2	33
Belgium	1	3	1	10
Cyprus				4
Denmark		1	1	11
Estonia				1
Finland				7
France	4	21	3	75
Greece				1
Hungary				7
Ireland		3		38
Italy	1	3		19
Luxembourg		6	5	49
Malta				5
Netherlands		7	2	30
Poland				2
Portugal	2	10	2	16
United Kingdom	3	12	6	108
Sweden		2		9
EU TOTAL	12	81	29	485
Iceland				1
Liechtenstein				3
Norway				3
EEA TOTAL	12	81	29	492
Monaco				1
Switzerland	1	1	5	2
TOTAL EUROPE	13	82	34	495
TOTAL NON EEA	5	8	26	3
Canada			1	
United States	2	4	3	
Japan		1	1	
TOTAL OTHER COUNTRIES	2	5	5	

---

[11]   The presence under the freedom to provide services, i.e. without establishment, is subject to the same reservations as expressed in the previous note. For example, various "electronic money" institutions are present in this form, which are not at all comparable with Spanish deposit institutions and subsequently ceased to be considered credit institutions.

[12]   A quantification of this activity is only available in the case of subsidiaries and branches. At this same time, this type of table tends to underestimate the set of countries that may be present in the other's financial system. The reason being that it only covers the direct presence, when what may happen is that a country is in another through an institution in a third country, a fact that occurs fairly frequently in the EU with institutions originating outside the EU, but located in one of its Member States.

TABLE 3	PRESENCE OF FOREIGN BANKING INSTITUTIONS IN SPAIN (cont.)

	Subsidiaries	Branches	Representative offices	Free provision of services
Argentina		1	3	
Bolivia			1	
Brazil		1		
Colombia			1	
Cuba			1	
Ecuador			3	
Guatemala			1	
Mexico			1	
Venezuela			1	
TOTAL LATIN AMERICA		2	12	
Libya	1			
Mali			1	
Morocco	1		3	
TOTAL AFRICA	2		4	
OVERALL TOTAL	17	89	55	495

SOURCE: Official records of the Banco de España and own data (subsidiaries).

NOTE: One of the representative offices in Luxembourg belongs to an institution in receivership.

The most important feature of the table is that it clearly shows how the internationalization of banking tends to be very closely related overall economic integration, which in Spain's case means Europe, and in particular, the EU. This relationship is obviously two-way, as is supported by the CGFS's analysis (2010c).[13]

Indeed, 76.5% of subsidiaries, 92.1% of branches and 61.8% of offices representing foreign banks in Spain belong to banks from other European countries. Limiting ourselves to the EU, the percentages would be somewhat smaller, but not hugely so: 70.6%, 91% and 52.7%, respectively.

4   The international expansion of Spanish banks and savings banks

Although the presence of foreign banks in Spain is today entirely consolidated, and they have a stable, albeit small, market share, the direction taken by the process of internationalization of the Spanish banking system has in recent years moved in entirely the opposite direction, with Spanish deposit-taking institutions becoming increasingly international.

---

[13]   In any event, as other authors, such as Schoenmaker and Van Laecke (2007), Herrero and Navia (2003), and Herrero and Martínez Peria (2007), have pointed out, the conditions in both the origin and destination countries cannot be ignored.

This is specially the case of Spain's two largest banking groups.

The factors driving the growing presence of Spanish deposit-taking entities abroad include:

1. Expansion into other less competitive markets when the level of competition in the domestic market is particularly high and it has become progressively harder to gain market share or obtain acceptable levels of profitability.

2. The opportunity to break into markets where, due to their lower level of development compared with Spain's, stronger growth potential may be anticipated.

3. The possibility of exporting know-how developed in the Spanish market to foreign markets so as to maximize its returns.

4. The opportunity to acquire underperforming or crisis-stricken institutions at attractive prices.

The first of these causes explains why it has been mainly the large Spanish banks that have internationalized. The pressure from the savings banks, which have been gaining market share in the domestic market almost continuously in recent years, on both the deposit and lending sides, has been very intense. This has been particularly so considering that the large banks are the outcome of successive mergers between medium-sized and large banks, which have consequently closed or sold part of their branch network in order to avoid overlaps and gain in efficiency, with the consequent shrinkage of their commercial structure.

Other reasons explain why the expansion of Spain's major banks initially focused on Latin America (see Sierra Fernández, 2007), growth potential, cultural and linguistic proximity making it easier to transmit the banks' know-how.

It is true that these countries have historically been somewhat unstable from the financial point of view, with the consequent increased risk to Spanish banks' investments in them. However, banking and finance business consists precisely of taking on sufficiently profitable and controlled risks. What is more, the growth prospects in these countries are currently much stronger than those in more developed ones.

Moreover, their international diversification strategy has allowed Spain's biggest banks to reduce their relative exposure to the Spanish property market, while also avoiding exposure to toxic assets suffered by other major international banks, thus enabling them to face the crisis with better financial strength.

Additionally, the crisis has made it possible to acquire banks in other countries at attractive prices. This explains, for example, how Spain's biggest banking group acquired two credit institutions in the United Kingdom in 2008, a market in which it had already gained a significant foothold by buying one of its main banks four years earlier. These are not the only acquisitions the group has made as a result of the financial crisis, but certainly the most significant.

The factors listed are additional to the classic reason for banks' expanding abroad, which is to follow their customers (see Berges, Ontiveros and Valero (1990), Chapter 1, pp. 21-42). This is a process whereby financial institutions expand internationally because their business customers do, and they want to continue serving them in their target markets. In this sense, it is useful to recall that:

- Internationalization of banks in Spain has coincided in time with a similar process by non-financial corporations, particularly larger ones.
- Banks tend to have higher levels of penetrations among firms – especially larges ones – that saving banks also helps to explain this circumstance.

The ways in which Spanish credit institutions are present in international markets are the same as those we have already looked at in the case of foreign banks operating in Spain.

In a country where internal expansion, that is to say through the network of offices, has not been free until relatively recently, it is logical to suppose that international expansion would not have been either. Indeed, as Table 4 shows, Royal Decree 1370/1985, which declared the definitive freedom to open new branches in Spain (although not for savings banks, which would have to wait for Royal Decree 1582/1988, 29 December 1988), lays down that: "the establishment of offices abroad, whether for operations or representation, shall require in each case the authorization of the Banco de España, which shall grant or decline such authorization at its discretion."

This regime changed with Spain's membership of the European Community and the subsequent development of the Single European market, which led to Royal Decree 1245/1995, also summarized in Table 4.

Table 5 summarizes the international presence of Spanish banks and savings banks in various forms and countries.

A number of conclusions can be drawn from this table, in particular:

1. A quite diverse geopraphical presence, with a total of 52 countries and territories. However, they are concentrated in Europe (20 countries) and Latin America

TABLE 4   REGULATION OF THE INTERNATIONAL EXPANSION OF SPANISH CREDIT INSTITUTIONS (1985-1995)

Mode of presence		Authorization	
		R. D. 1370/1985	R. D. 1245/1995
Subsidiary	EU (a)	Banco de España	Destination State
	non-EU		Banco de España
Branch	EU (a)	Banco de España	Banco de España (b)
	non-EU		Banco de España
Representative office		Banco de España	Prior notification to the Banco de España
Provision of services		Unregulated	Prior notification to the Banco de España

SOURCE: The authors.

a. Applicable to all countries of the European Economic Area.
b. May only be refused on the grounds of: inadequate administrative structures, financial situation, unauthorised activities.

TABLE 5   PRESENCE OF SPANISH BANKS AND SAVINGS BANKS ABROAD 31 DEC 2009

	Subsidiaries			Branches	Representative offices
	Deposit-taking institutions	Other credit institutions	TOTAL		
Germany	1	1	2	3	8
Austria		2	2	1	
Belgium	1		1	3	2
Czech Republic		2	2		
Finland	1		1		
France	1	1	2	12	6
Hungary		1	1		
Ireland	1	1	2	2	
Italy	2	5	7	3	3
Luxembourg		1	1		
Netherlands	1		1		1
Poland	1		1	1	2
Portugal	6	4	10	34	1
United Kingdom	5	6	11	8	9
Rumania				1	
EU TOTAL	20	24	44	68	32
Norway	1		1		
EEA TOTAL	21	24	45	68	32
Andorra	1		1		
Monaco	1		1		
Russia	1		1		1
Switzerland	2		2	1	11
TOTAL EUROPE	26	24	50	69	44
TOTAL NON-EEA	50	24	74	19	76
Australia					2
United States	10	8	18	10	1
TOTAL FOR OTHER DEVELOPED COUNTRIES	10	8	18	10	3

(14 countries), the latter standing out in the case of subsidiaries that are deposit-taking institutions and representation offices, with 38% and 35.2% of the total, respectively.

Europe, and in particular the EU, stands out in terms of numbers of branches (79.3% of the total), which is consistent with the earlier discussion of the European single market, as does the absence of branches in Latin America, and subsidiaries that are other credit institutions (50% of the total).

The United States is a country that plays a key role, as it is the destination of between 11.5% (branches) and 16.7% (other credit institutions) of the international presence of Spain's institutions.

The presence in Asia only takes the form of branches (4.6% of the total) and representative offices (17.6%), with China being by far the main country in both cases.

TABLE 5   PRESENCE OF SPANISH BANKS AND SAVINGS BANKS ABROAD 31 DEC 2009 (cont.)

	Subsidiaries				
	Deposit-taking institutions	Other credit institutions	TOTAL	Branches	Representative offices
Argentina	3	1	4		5
Brazil	3	4	7		5
Chile	2	5	7		3
Colombia	2	1	3		
Cuba					4
Dominican Rep.					4
Guatemala					1
Mexico	3	2	5		9
Panama	2		2		1
Paraguay	2		2		
Peru	2		2		
Puerto Rico	5	2	7		
Uruguay	2		2		
Venezuela	1		1		6
TOTAL LATIN AMERICA	**27**	**15**	**42**	**0**	**38**
China				3	10
South Korea					2
United Arab Emirates					1
India					2
Japan				1	1
Taiwan					1
Turkey					2
TOTAL ASIA	**0**	**0**	**0**	**4**	**19**
Angola	1		1		
Algeria					1
Morocco				2	2
TOTAL AFRICA	**1**	**0**	**1**	**2**	**3**
Dutch Antilles	1		1		
Bahamas	4		4		
Cayman Is.	1		1	1	
Isle of Man		1	1		
Jersey	1		1		
Singapore				1	1
TOTAL OFFSHORE	**7**	**1**	**8**	**2**	**1**
TOTAL GENERAL	**71**	**48**	**119**	**87**	**108**
Two largest Banking groups	61	45	106	25	21
Savings bank groups	4	2	6	51	57

SOURCES: Banco de España. *Memoria de la supervisión bancaria* 2009 and AEB (2009) and CECA yearbooks (2009).

NOTE: Foreign institutions in Spain and those belonging to another Spanish group are not considered here.

In the case of so-called offshore centers, the only way in which Spanish banks have a significant presence is through deposit-taking subsidiaries, which account for almost 10% of the total.

2. The two main Spanish banking groups account for almost 90% of all foreign bank subsidiaries. They also account for 28.7% of branches and 19.4% of representative offices.[14]

Setting up a subsidiary is a more complex way, as it requires capital and submission to the jurisdiction of the destination country, with the consequent requirement to satisfy the applicable regulatory and supervisory standards. This implies a set of investments and expenses, only available to larger entities.

3. Spanish savings banks barely have any foreign subsidiaries (around 4.2 to 5.6% of the total), concentrated in the hands of just four financial groups. However, their branches and representative offices are significant, as this is where they are the majority sector, with 58.6% and 52.8% of the total, respectively.

These latter, which encompass a total of 19 countries, are explained by the more nascent nature of their international presence, as the characteristics of a representative office make it the favored means of access to a market that was previously largely or entirely unknown.

By contrast, the preponderance of foreign branches of savings banks, present in just 10 countries, is largely explained by just one of them: Portugal, accounting for 33 savings bank branches. This is a figure which is totally unparalleled in any of the other countries listed in the table in any of the modes of foreign presence abroad; Portugal's immediate proximity to Spain is no doubt the reason for this exceptional situation.

Other countries in which Spanish savings banks have a significant presence are France (6), and the United States (5), such that, together with Portugal, they account for 86.3% of this form of presence for the sector as a whole. There is no doubt that Spanish savings banks have considerable scope to internationalize their business, but to do so they would need to have sufficient financial strength and to develop an active and profitable strategy in this direction.

The aggregate activity of this overseas presence among Spanish credit institutions can be followed annually in the Banco de España's *Memoria de la supervisión bancaria* (Report on Banking Supervision), the first edition of which refers to 2001. Table 6 was constructed using the data from the first and last editions of this report, going back to 1999, the first year for which the necessary information is available.

---

[14] The preponderance of the two largest Spanish banking groups in terms of the number of subsidiary credit institutions and the number of countries in which they are present through them is a clear indication of the fact that both groups have today come to configure themselves as highly diversified geographical entities. The recent history of this process of internationalization and its outcome can be seen in Martín Aceña (2007), particularly in Chapter 7, pp. 240-337, and in González, Anes and Mendoza (2007), in particular in vol. II, Chapters X to XI, pp. 7-131. This can also be consulted in *Universia Business Review* (2008).

This year is obviously significant as it marks the launch of the euro, which helps explain the considerable shift in focus from Latin America to the EU which is observed. However, it is also the year in which the largest Spanish banking groups took on their current form as the main players in the international expansion of the Spanish banking system, as we have seen.

The foreign business of Spanish credit institutions grew at a year-on-year rate of 17% during the period considered, compared with balance sheet growth of 14.5%, which explains why their weight in the consolidated balance sheet grew by 4.2 percentage points (p.p.) over the period. This was not only due to their stepping up their international business, but also to a fall in the rate of growth of national business as a consequence of the financial crisis that began in the summer of 2007.

TABLE 6   LOCAL ACTIVITY ABROAD OF SPANISH CREDIT INSTITUTIONS (1999-2009)

	Amount (millions of euros)	% of total balance sheet	Geographical distribution (%)		
			European Union	Latin America	Other foreign
2009					
Foreign balance sheet	872,297	23.32			
Financial assets	741,714	19.83	49.55	33.39	17.06
Financial liabilities	705,696	18.87	48.03	28.74	23.24
Funds managed	155,363	4.15	14.38	83.40	2.22
Consolidated balance sheet Spanish credit institutions	3,740,696				
1999					
Foreign balance sheet	211,500	19.11			
Financial assets	138,371	12.50	22.57	58.91	18.52
Financial liabilities	125,656	11.35	16.30	58.45	25.25
Funds managed	24,668	2.23	12.16	85.98	1.86
Consolidated balance sheet Spanish credit institutions	1.106.725				
2009-1999	Overall increase (%)	Overall variations (percentage points)			
Foreign balance-sheet	312.43	4.21			
Financial assets	436.03	7.33	26.98	-25.52	-1.46
Financial liabilities	461.61	7.51	31.73	-29.71	-2.02
Funds managed	529.82	1.92	2.22	-2.57	0.36
Consolidated balance sheet Spanish credit institutions	238.00				

SOURCES: Banco de España. *Memoria de la supervisión bancaria* 2009.

NOTE: funds managed are compared with the balance-sheet total for comparative purposes.

Financial intermediation activity grew faster, at a rate of over 20% a year on average, and by 7 p.p. within the consolidated balance sheet total. By contrast, the funds managed, which grew at a similar or slightly faster rate, progressed by slightly less than 2 p.p., mainly because of their much smaller magnitude. In any event, this is an activity which clearly predominates in Latin America, which confirms the transfer of know-how to other countries referred to above.

The main conclusion to be drawn from the table is the significant increase in the relative weight registered in foreign intermediation business by Spanish credit institutions in the EU, at around 30 p.p. By contrast, the gain in the funds managed is very moderate, and is more pronounced vis-à-vis non-EU countries.

The elimination of exchange risk in transactions with other euro-zone countries that the single currency brought with it, together with the implementation and development of the common monetary policy, which stimulated cross-border inter-bank transactions, explain this substantial rise in the "Europeanization" of the Spanish banking system's foreign activity. This effect has been confirmed for the euro area as a whole by Kalemli-Ozcan, S.; Papaioannou, E.; Peydró, J. (2009).

In any case, the relative intensity of foreign business by Spanish credit institutions has placed them on the line of the general trend among European banks, as analyzed by De Haan, Oosterloo and Schoenmaker (2009), who position them as the most internationalized among the largest world banks.

If the major Spanish banks maintain, or even improve, their position, and if the savings banks, which will be fewer in number but of larger average size,[15] regain their interest in expanding their business abroad, once the crisis has been overcome, we can expect an increase in both the banks' and savings banks' foreign business in the future.

5 The international activity of Spanish deposit-taking institutions

As already noted, activity and presence do not always run parallel in international banking, but can sometimes be mutually supporting. In fact, foreign entities are the counterparts for a significant share of the total balance sheet of Spanish deposit-taking institutions, on both the assets and liabilities sides.

Starting with assets, for each group of deposit-taking institutions, Chart 5 shows the degree of openness to the exterior, i.e. the relative weight of the assets involving counterparties from the rest of the world.

The degree of internationalization of Spanish banks far exceeds that of the savings banks and credit unions, and the gap has grown even wider in recent years. This should come as no surprise given their difference in business focus, which in the case of the

---

[15]   The process of the restructuring of Spanish savings banks is described in Banco de España (2011) and in Chapter 11 of this book.

savings banks and credit unions is much more inward-looking. In the context of the financial crisis that began in mid-2007, this situation enabled the banks, particularly the two largest ones, to take advantage of their business' diversification to enable them to weather the crisis better.

As previously noted, the implementation in Spain in February 1992 of a framework allowing total freedom of movement of capital in and out of the country, imposed by the single European market, was an important milestone in the international expansion of the Spanish banking system. It helps explain why the weight of foreign assets on banks' balance sheets grew by 4.6 p.p. in 1992, despite the fact that in the summer of that year the European monetary system was hit by a severe crisis, leading to the devaluation of a number of currencies, including the peseta, an event which would be repeated four more times before the currency came to be replaced by the euro.

In 1993 Spanish banks reached a degree of internationalization of their assets of 21.2%, and this level has not since dropped below 15%. Indeed, in 2005, it reached an historic maximum of 21.9%. However, the years 1996 to 1999 marked a period of retrenchment following a phase of continuous expansion, once the two largest banking groups, which had formed in 1999, opted for a clear strategy of international expansion.

The level of internationalization of the savings banks' assets remained in the range of 0.5% (1985) to 9.5% (2000), but the most significant feature was that it has been falling from this peak almost continuously, by almost 3 p.p. in 2008, as a direct result of the financial crisis. At the end of this period the level was close to 4.5% of the total, a figure which was nevertheless significant in view of its starting point.

The savings banks had previously followed a path parallel to that of the banks, although at much lower levels. However, they diverged upwards in 1997; a sign of the interest some institutions had in gaining ground internationally (see Berges, Ontiveros and Valero, 1999). This interest tailed off as domestic business gained strength, fostered by strong economic

CHART 5   OPENING UP OF SPANISH DEPOSIT-TAKING INSTITUTIONS TO THE EXTERIOR - ASSETS (Percentage of total assets)

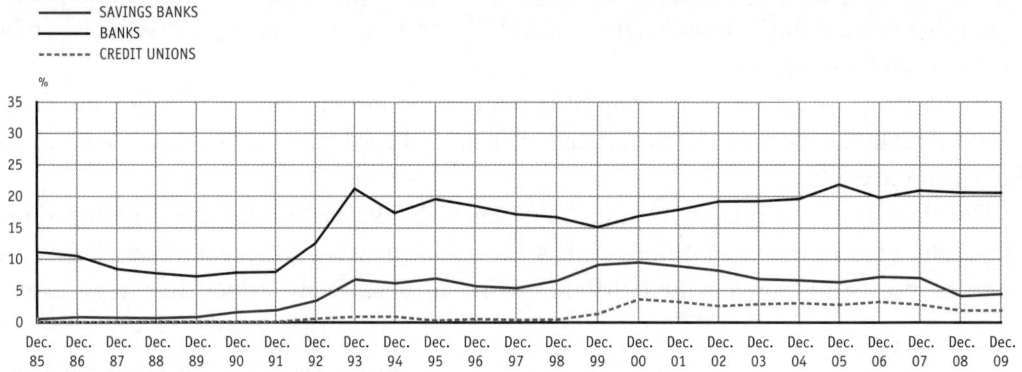

SOURCE: Boletín Estadístico de Banco de España

growth and the property boom, a strategy which ultimately has turned against them, in the light of the financial crisis and the impact it has had on the savings banks.

Credit unions, with a level of internationalization of their assets between 0% (1987) and 3.6% (2000), have followed a path parallel to that of the savings banks, ending the period with a figure of 1.8%.

The differing strengths of their international activity, and also the different size of each, explains the strong bias towards the banks in the market share of Spanish deposit-taking institutions in this field, as shown in Chart 6. There is no other major area of banking business where the predominance of these institutions in Spain is so clear. Moreover, it has increased in recent years, rising to 85.1% at the end of the period, from a minimum of 72.1% in 2000.

Despite this, the savings banks have taken a significant share in this area, accounting for 14.4% at the end of the period, down from a maximum of 27.4% in 1999, but well up from their starting point of 2.1%. Credit unions, on the other hand, have never risen above 1%, which is why they are not shown on Chart 6, as they would be barely visible.

Charts 7 and 8 are similar to the previous ones but show the liabilities side. The borrowing needs of the Spanish economy explain why, in general, the weight of the foreign sector in the liabilities of Spanish deposit-taking institutions has increased over time, particularly in the case of the banks.

In the case of savings banks, foreign liabilities have been falling continuously since 2004, after rising to a maximum of 11.8% the previous year, driven by the strength of domestic business, and then falling as a result of the financial crisis. As a result, the savings banks ended the period with a figure of 4.1%.

The banks more than doubled the share of foreign liabilities on their balance sheets, which rose from 11.1% at the start of the period to 26.1% at the end, reaching a peak of

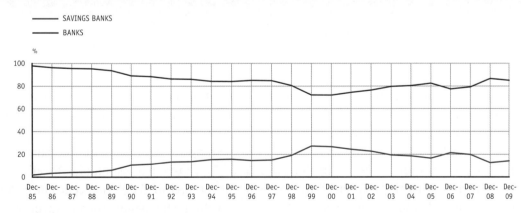

CHART 6   SHARE OF FOREIGN ASSETS IN SPANISH FINANCIAL INSTITUTIONS' TOTAL ASSETS (PERCENTAGE OF TOTAL FOR DEPOSIT-TAKING INSTITUTIONS) (PERCENTAGE OF TOTAL ASSETS)

SOURCE: *Boletín Estadístico de Banco de España.*

NOTE: The figure for credit unions is negligible.

CHART 7   OPENING UP OF SPANISH DEPOSIT-TAKING INSTITUTIONS TO THE EXTERIOR - LIABILITIES
          (percentage of total liabilities)

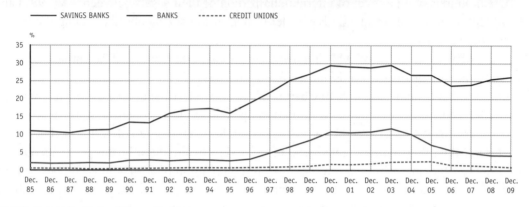

SOURCE: *Boletín Estadístico de Banco de España.*

CHART 8   BANKS' AND SAVINGS BANKS' FOREIGN LIABILITIES AS A PERCENTAGE OF THE TOTAL
          (percentages / total deposit-taking institutions)

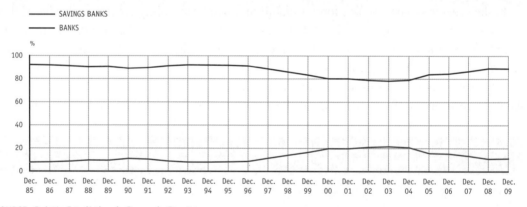

SOURCE: *Boletín Estadístico de Banco de España.*

NOTE: The figures for credit unions are insignificant.

29.5% in 2003. Around the time of the introduction of the euro (1996-2000), doubts about Spain's eventual membership of monetary union were overcome and the two major banking groups that dominate the landscape today were formed.

By contrast, from 2004 through to 2006, when the property boom took off in Spain, there was a significant drop in the internationalization of deposit-taking institutions' liabilities, a trend which was partially reversed by the banks at the end of the period, but not by the savings banks. These declines had a lot to do with the phenomenon already mentioned: increasing borrowing abroad by Spanish deposit-taking institutions by means of issuing securities backed by loans, all to finance the property boom. In some cases, these loans were not taken off the institutions' balance sheet (covered bonds) whereas in others they were (securitization).

The degree of internationalization of the liabilities of credit unions was much smaller than that of the banks and savings banks. This fact, together with their lesser importance among deposit-taking institutions as a whole, explains why they are not shown on Chart 8.

Charts 6 and 8 are similar in that, although initially, the savings banks progressively gained market share from the banks, particularly over the period 1995-2003, until they reached a 21.4% share of the foreign liabilities held by Spanish deposit-taking institutions. Since that time the gap has widened in favor of the banks. The savings banks ended the period with a share of 10.9%, 3.3. p.p. higher than their share at the start of the period.

From here it follows that savings banks have room to further internationalization particularly if they emerge strengthened from the restructuring process currently underway. The reason is that they have registered significantly higher levels than in the immediate past and, at the same time, some of these entities may opt for increased international activity in order diversify more effectively. One of the lessons of the crisis for the Spanish banks is precisely that international diversification may help maintain a better commercial and financial position, provided that the risks are duly controlled and backed with a sufficient volume of equity.

6 The internationalization of the Spanish securities market

The analysis of the internationalization of the Spanish stock market depends greatly on which of its basic functions in the economy we consider:

1. Supplying finance through the securities markets to the economic agents requiring it, (the intermediation function characteristic of the primary or issue market).
2. Regular provision of liquidity, and price determination so as to take up or unwind securities positions, with the attendant setting of market prices, a function characteristic of the secondary or trading market.

This chapter, for consistency with previous sections, will focus on the first of these perspectives, considering the Spanish economy as a whole and using the same source as before, namely the *Cuentas Financieras de la Economía Española* or CFEE.

As noted in other studies (Ontiveros and Valero, 2003 and 2004), the stock market has contributed to the transformations of the Spanish economy over the last 30 years. A first approach to its internationalization involves an analysis of the role played by what *foreign-owned securities;* securities issued by Spanish economic agents and bought by foreign agents, and securities issued in other countries that have been bought by Spanish economic agents; which we could call *foreign-issued securities.*

From this perspective, Chart 9 shows how securities as a share of GDP grew almost 23-fold between 1980 and 2009, while the weight of foreign-issued securities as a share of GDP was multiplied by a factor of 21.3 over the same period. Additionally, foreign-owned securities have always exceeded foreign-issued securities, and the gap between them has grown over time, which is a clear reflection of the fact that Spain has always been, and continues to be, dependent on outside finance.

In order to obtain a baseline for the first two trends, the CFEE's data confirms the weight of the stock market relative to the Spanish economy. This rose from 45% of GDP in 1980 to 283.2% of GDP in 2009, implying that it grew in value by a factor of 6.3 over the period. This rate is significantly slower than that of growth in foreign shares (both foreign owned and issued).

Such an increase in the financial depth of foreign securities is not unique to Spain, but should be seen within a general worldwide trend towards greater financial depth, as analyzed by Beck and Demirgüç-Kunt (2009).

As indicated in the chart above, analysis does not include holdings in investment funds (mutual funds or unit trusts), since their inclusion would lead to double accounting as their assets are also securities. The significance of these shareholdings has varied greatly over the period, from almost nothing in 1980 (0.1%) to 16.6% of GDP in 2009, and to a maximum of 37.2% of GDP in 1998.

Consistent with Spain's growing dependence on external finance the weight of foreign securities in the Spanish economy grew almost uninterrupted over the period, dropping only three times:

- 1994, 5.2 p.p., as a result of the European public-debt market crisis;
- 2002, 0.8 p.p., due to the crisis following the bursting of the dot-com bubble;
- 2008, 14.6 p.p., due to the current financial crisis.

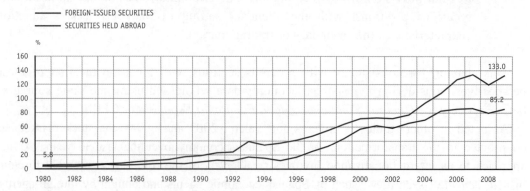

CHART 9   FOREIGN SECURITIES IN THE SPANISH ECONOMY (AS PERCENTAGE OF GDP) (a)

SOURCE: The authors, based on *Cuentas Financieras de la Economía Española*. Banco de España.

a. Excluding mutual fund investments.

The first significant increase (15.1 p.p.) took place between 1992 and 1993, as a result of the free movement of capital that was established in Spain as of the 1st February of the first of these two years, and which remains in force today. This ended 13 straight years of growth for this indicator, which advanced by 33.7 p.p. thanks to the progressive liberalization of the Spanish economy to external capital flows.

The following period of consecutive increases corresponds to the process of convergence between Spain and its EU partners, in the run-up to the euro launch on 1 January 1999. This slowed somewhat in 2002, under the influence of the dot-com crash, and represented progress of 38.8 p.p. in the importance of foreign securities in the Spanish economy for seven years.

However, a shorter, but more intense, period of sustained growth took place between 2003 and 2007, when it grew by as much as 62.4 p.p., in a period clearly dominated by the strength of the Spanish economy and, more specifically, by the real-estate boom. This growth came to a halt when the financial crisis showed its full severity in mid-2008. The following year, the greater public-debt placement abroad, made necessary by the government's increasing financial needs, made up for part of this fall.

The importance of foreign securities for the Spanish economy has evolved in a less sustained fashion than in the direction just looked at.

In any case, the internationalization of securities in both directions clearly ran parallel to one another, as the chart shows:

1. The first significant increase (5.3 p.p.) in the weight of securities held abroad took place between 1992 and 1993, as a result of the liberalization of exchange rate controls in Spain already alluded to.
2. The first period of sustained growth of this indicator took place between 1996 and 2001, increasing by a total of 49.6 p.p. There is no doubt that the reduction in the exchange-rate risk and the lower interest rate that came with the adoption of the euro stimulated foreign investment at this time to an extent that has not been seen since.
3. The last period of sustained growth in the significance of foreign securities took place between 2003 and 2007, with progress of slightly more than 28 p.p., once again coming to a halt with the emergence of a financial crisis.

This parallelism is entirely logical if we bear in mind the fact that, in a highly interconnected world such as today's, both modes of foreign securities are influenced by variables and circumstances at global, or at least international level, rather than nationally. At the same time, they are an indicator that both types of securities are looking for the destinations that are most attractive to investors, in terms of risks and returns, although in some cases investors' decisions may be influenced by strategic objectives, such as in the case of economic agents seeking to break into new markets or to diversify their economic activity.

6.1 The internationalization of fixed income and variable income

The data in CFEE not only allow an analysis of the role of foreign securities in the Spanish economy, but also the degree of internationalization of each of the groups of instruments considered in them in each of the two possible directions. In this section we will focus our attention on the two classic financing instruments: variable income (equities or shares) and fixed income, considering the Spanish economy as a whole in each case.

We will define the degree of internationalization for a given group of instruments, in each of the possible directions, as follows:

$$\frac{\text{Foreign-issue/owned securities}}{\text{Securities in the Spanish economy}}$$

That is to say, the denominator is the same in both directions, regardless of the fact that it is different for each group of securities. By relating foreign securities investments to the economy as a whole in this way, we are following a similar path to that taken previously in the case of deposit-taking institutions, when we related their foreign assets or liabilities to their total balance sheet.

Due to data limitations, the time horizon referred to here is different from that in the previous chart. In the case of fixed income it starts in 1987, which is the year in which the book-entry public debt market started in Spain, and the moment when the main fixed-income security issued in Spain began to attract the interest of foreign investors. For shares it begins in 1994, which is the year in which the CFEE started offering differentiated data on shares listed on organized markets in Spain and abroad.

In this context, the aim of this section is to offer a general analysis of the trends observed in the internationalization of securities in Spain in recent years.

Charts 10 and 11 show the internationalization of fixed-income securities in Spain, the former from the point of view of securities held by non-residents and the latter looking in the opposite direction. In the first case, a distinction is drawn between long- and short-term securities, but in the second, only long-term securities are shown, as the investment in short-term foreign securities by Spanish investors is insignificant.

Chart 10 clearly shows that fixed-income securities in Spain have become increasingly attractive to non-resident investors over the period, with a peak in 2006, both for long-term securities (51%) and fixed-income as a whole (48.5%). Since then this presence has lost momentum somewhat, as a result of the financial crisis, but remains high. By contrast, short-term fixed income securities have jumped strongly since 2006 (almost 31 p.p.) ending the period at a historic maximum, above the corresponding percentage for long-term fixed income.

Such a strong growth in the short-term fixed income securities is also related to the financial crisis, and in particular to the Treasury's borrowing strategy since the crisis began. Specifically, it incorporated a strong short-term bias (Treasury bills

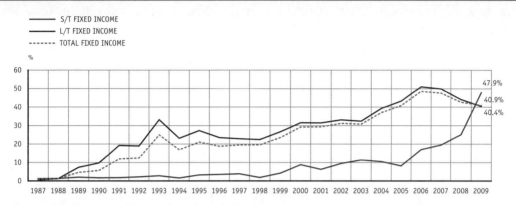

CHART 10   INTERNATIONALIZATION OF FIXED-INCOME SECURITIES IN SPAIN: FOREIGN-ISSUED SECURITIES (percentage of total securities in each group)

SOURCE: The authors, based on *Cuentas Financieras de la Economía Española*. Banco de España.

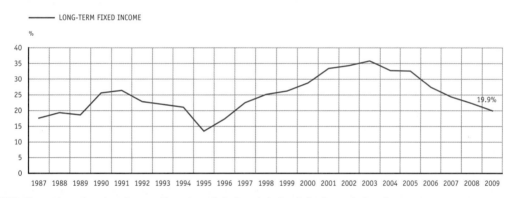

CHART 11   INTERNATIONALIZATION OF FIXED-INCOME SECURITIES IN SPAIN: SECURITIES HELD ABROAD (percentage of total)

SOURCE: The authors, based on *Cuentas Financieras de la Economía Española*. Banco de España.

or *letras del Tesoro*) in its issues, so as to gain a cost advantage on a steep interest rate curve.

Chart 11 clearly shows how internationalization of Spanish fixed-income securities abroad has declined substantially in recent years. This has been particularly so since 2003, when it reached its maximum for the period of 35.8%. This was preceded by a rise from a minimum of 13.5% in 1995. The greater borrowing requirements of the Spanish economy, in conjunction with the current financial crisis, have reduced the incentives to invest in foreign fixed-income securities. By contrast, the run up to the euro and the disappearance of exchange rate risk with respect to the other currencies replaced by the euro encouraged these investments, particularly in those cases where the goal was greater diversification and/or access to more liquid debt markets.

Charts 12 and 13 show the equivalent data for variable-income securities in Spain, the first from the perspective of investments by non-residents and the second from the opposite viewpoint. What stands out in the first of these two charts is how the internationalization of listed shares, which peaked at 43% in 2008, has remained relatively stable over the period, dropping to a minimum of 28.4% in 2000. Moreover, this level of internationalization has stayed at levels above that of unlisted shares, a fact which is explained by the greater ease with which investments can be acquired or unwound in the case of listed shares.

By contrast, the internationalization of unlisted shares has followed a basically downward path over the period, starting at its peak, dropping to a minimum of 7.5% in 2007, and recovering somewhat to end at 11.5%.

CHART 12   INTERNATIONALIZATION OF SHARES IN SPAIN: FOREIGN-ISSUED SECURITIES
(percentage of total securities in each group)

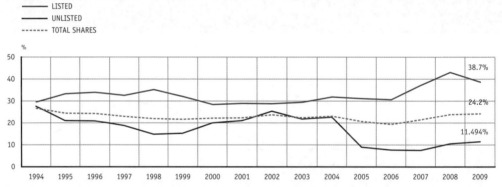

SOURCE: The authors, based on *Cuentas Financieras de la Economía Española.* Banco de España.

CHART 13   INTERNATIONALIZATION OF SHARES IN SPAIN: FOREIGN SECURITIES
(percentage of total securities in each group)

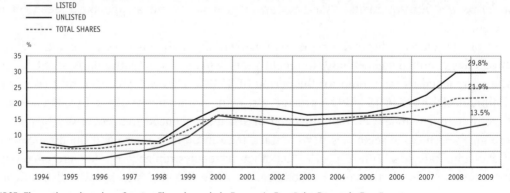

SOURCE: The authors, based on *Cuentas Financieras de la Economía Española.* Banco de España.

Although, for the economy as a whole, unlisted shares exceed listed ones by a wide margin, the opposite is true in the case of foreign investments. Therefore, the internationalization of Spanish shares as a whole is more stable than that of listed shares. Their maximum level was registered at the start of the period (26.7%) and their minimum in 2006 (19.3%).

The weight of foreign shares in the hands of residents as a proportion of the total has increased over the period as a whole in all the cases considered, such that its maximum level tends to be towards the end, except in the case of listed shares, which reached its peak in 2000 at 16.3%.

In this case, internationalization is much more intense in the case of non-listed shares, particularly in the final years of the period, which suggests that these shares in the hands of resident economic agents correspond, above all, to direct investments and, therefore, highlight the growing foreign presence of certain Spanish companies, both in financial and non-financial sectors.

7 Concluding remarks

Spain's progressive integration with the world economy, and specially with Europe, explains its growing financial internationalization over the last 30 years, which has translated into strong external dependence, as a result of its need to finance unbalanced growth, and a significant gap between domestic saving and investment needs.

Internationalization of the Spanish financial system has followed a similar path to that of the economy as a whole but it has become stronger since the introduction of the euro. The lower interest rates associated with the single currency, and the greater availability of funds in European financial markets, have undoubtedly acted as catalysts of the process of internationalization.

This process has entailed the financial system's increasing dependence on foreign finance, both as regards borrowing requirements and the greater or lesser confidence that the investors supplying these funds have in Spain, which imposes an important element of discipline on the Spanish economy and its most significant structural imbalances.

This discipline has made itself felt in the financial crisis that began in mid-2007, and subsequently with the Greek and Irish debt crisis, and the subsequent questioning of the sustainability of the euro area. As a result, the Spanish government was forced to adopt important measures to tackle Spain's economic imbalances.[16]

Key to the internationalization of the Spanish financial system has been the strong presence of foreign banks in the system; they have played an important role, more in qualitative terms than quantitative ones, given the relatively small market shares they hold. In particular, these foreign banks contributed significantly to the development of the financial

---

[16] For more details, see Chapter 6 of this book.

system, and stimulated a strengthening of the main national institutions, thereby bolstering the competitiveness of the system.

There is currently a strong, and geographically very diverse, presence of Spanish banks, abroad. This was initially focused on Latin America in the 1990s, then shifted towards Europe; it only recently gained a foothold in the United States, and is beginning to make inroads into emerging countries, such as China, which look set to have greater economic and financial weight in the near future.

The international presence of Spanish credit institutions is very much concentrated on the bigger banks, which have been pursuing an active strategy in this direction for many years. This does not prevent there being room, for example, for savings banks to progressively increase their presence, once the restructuring of the sector produces a small number of institutions, but more solid and with greater capacity to take on the risks inherent to international business. The experience of Spain's two largest banks demonstrates the benefits of pursuing a strategy of international diversification.

As a result of this international expansion, Spanish deposit-taking institutions, particularly the banks, currently perform a significant share of their business in Spain with foreign counterparties. This is a trend which has increased over time, largely as restrictions to free capital movements came down in 1992. This has strengthened the links in both directions between the banking systems in Spain and in other countries.

Over the period examined, the weight of foreign securities has grown much more rapidly than the value of securities in Spain. This has a lot to do with the full liberalization of exchange-rate controls and the subsequent shifts in the sources and destinations of investment flows. This implies Spain's growing involvement in international financial circuits strengthens the discipline that foreign investors can exercise on the Spanish economy.

In the other direction, the weight of foreign variable-income securities held by Spanish residents has also increased markedly, reflecting both the growing internationalization of Spanish firms, and the greater outward focus of financial investments in Spain, as investors look for better risk diversification. By contrast, the equivalent values for fixed income have rapidly lost ground in recent years, both before and after the financial crisis. This implies a greater preference for domestic securities among Spanish investors, who do not seem to value diversification in this case as highly as in that of variable income, among other reasons, because of the lower returns to be obtained.

References

ÁLVAREZ CANAL, P. (1998). *Evolución de la banca extranjera en el período 1992-1996,* Documentos de Trabajo, n°. 9802, Banco de España.

ÁLVAREZ, P., and E. IGLESIAS-SARRIA (1992). "La banca extranjera en España en el período 1978-1990", Estudios Económicos, 47, Banco de España.

ASOCIACIÓN ESPAÑOLA DE BANCA (AEB) (2010). *Anuario estadístico de la banca en España, 2009,* Madrid.

BANCO DE ESPAÑA (2010a). *Report on Banking Supervision,* 2009, Madrid.

— (2011). *Evolución y reforma de las cajas de ahorros,* 21 February, Madrid.

BECK, T., and A. DEMIRGÜÇ-KUNT (2009). *Financial Institutions and Markets Across Countries and Over Time - Data and Analysis,* World Bank Policy Research Working Papers, 4943, May.

BERGES, A., E. ONTIVEROS and F. J. VALERO, (1990). *Internacionalización de la banca. El caso español,* Espasa Calpe, Madrid.

— (1998). "Internacionalización de las cajas de ahorros españolas", *Papeles de Economía Española,* 74 and 75, número monográfico "Cajas de Ahorros: Realidad financiera e imagen social", pp. 55-81.

CERUTTI, E., G. DELL'ARICCIA and M. MARTÍNEZ (2007). "How Banks Go Abroad: Branches or Subsidiaries?", *Journal of Banking and Finance, 31,* pp. 1669-1692.

CLAESSENS, S. (2006). *Competitive Implications of Cross-border Banking, World Bank Policy Research Papers,* n°. 3854.

COMMITTEE ON THE GLOBAL FINANCIAL SYSTEM (CGFS) (2010a). "The Functioning and Resilience of Cross-border Funding Markets", *BIS, CGFS Publications,* 37, March.

— (2010b). "Funding Patterns and Liquidity Management of Internationally Active Banks", *BIS, CGFS Publications,* 39, May.

— (2010c). "Long-term Issues in International Banking", *BIS, CGFS Publications,* 41, July.

CONFEDERACIÓN ESPAÑOLA DE CAJAS DE AHORROS (CECA) (2010). *Anuario estadístico de las cajas de ahorros,* 2009, Madrid.

DE HAAN, J., S. OOSTERLOO and D. SCHOENMAKER (2009). *European Financial Markets and Institutions,* Cambridge University Press.

GONZÁLEZ, M. J., R. ANES and I. MENDOZA (2007). *Ciento cincuenta años, ciento cincuenta bancos,* Vol. I and II, BBVA, Madrid.

HERRERO, A., and M. MARTÍNEZ PERIA (2007). "The Mix of International Banks' Foreign Claims: Determinants and Implications", *Journal of Banking and Finance,* 31, 6, pp. 1613-1631.

HERRERO, A., and D. NAVIA (2003). *Determinants and Impact of Financial Sector FDI to Emerging Economies: a Home Country's Perspective, Occasional Paper,* n°. 0308, Banco de España, Madrid.

KALEMLI-OZCAN, S., E. PAPAIOANNOU and J. PEYDRÓ (2009). What lies beneath the euro's effect on financial integration? *Currency risk, legal harmonization, or trade?* CEPR Discussion Papers, n°. 7314.

MARAVALL, F., S. GLAVAN and ANALISTAS FINANCIEROS INTERNACIONALES (AFI) (2009). *Eficiencia y concentración del sistema bancario español,* FUNCAS, Estudios de la Fundación, Serie Análisis, July.

MARTÍN-ACEÑA, P. (2007). 1857-2007l. *Banco Santander. 150 años de historia,* Grupo Santander, Madrid.

MCCAULEY, R., P. MCGUIRE and G. VON PETER (2010). "The Architecture of Global Banking: From International to Multinational?", *BIS Quarterly Review,* March, pp. 25-37.

ONTIVEROS, E., and F. J. VALERO (2003). "El sistema financiero español desde la Constitución. Homologación internacional. Vertebración territorial", *Economía Industrial,* 349-350, pp. 111-126.

— (2004). "La transformación de los mercados de valores", *Papeles de Economía Española,* 100, pp. 246-265.

PAPAIOANNOU, E. (2009). "What Drives International Bank Flows? Politics, Institutions and Other Determinants", *Journal of Development Economics,* 88, 2, pp. 269-81.

SCHOENMAKER, D., and C. VAN LAECKE (2007). "Determinants of International Banking: Evidence From the World's Largest Banks", *Working Paper,* SSRN no. 965826.

SIERRA, M. P. (2007). "Estrategias de internacionalización de la gran banca española", *Pecnia,* 5, pp. 229-272.

UNIVERSIA BUSINESS REVIEW (2008). *Especial 150 Aniversario Banco Santander,* Primer trimestre.

VALERO, F. J. (1994). "La internacionalización de la empresa bancaria española" *Economistas,* 62, pp. 38-46.

11. The Spanish financial industry at the start of 21st century: Current situation and future challenges

Xavier Vives [1]
IESE Business School

1   Introduction

The early years of the 21st century have been a turbulent time in the financial world. The turmoil unleashed by the bursting of the United States housing bubble and the sub-prime mortgage crisis was undoubtedly the severest financial crisis since the 1930's. The scale of the crisis has highlighted weaknesses in the financial system and its regulation and represents a watershed affecting both banking business models and the regulation of the system.

This chapter focuses on the banking sector, which forms the central plank of the Spanish financial system. It examines the sector's situation before and after the crisis, and the challenges that lie ahead. The Spanish banking industry is in the midst of a process of transformation, driven by sweeping deregulation, which started relatively early and has stimulated significant international expansion. The current crisis will change the underlying trends in the sector in a reformed regulatory framework. The impact of regulatory reform, and how financial institutions respond to it, will shape the sector's future landscape.

The Spanish banking sector went into the crisis with high levels of solvency and strong profits following a period of rapid expansion, partly associated with growth in the property

---

[1]   I am grateful to Karla Perca, Jorge Paz and Miguel de Quinto from the IESE Centro Sector Público-Sector Privado for their excellent assistance with the research.

sector. As a result of its heavy reliance on external funding, which was cut short by the crisis, the Spanish banking industry has suffered its effects, despite its not being directly involved in the "originate-to-distribute" model and its associated toxic products. It is currently undergoing a process of restructuring in line with international trends, but with the specific features that will be examined in this chapter. The challenges it is facing, in both the short and long-term, are considerable.

Section 2 reviews the general trends in the sector at international level and the process of regulatory reform. Section 3 describes the situation of the Spanish banking sector before and after the crisis, and examines its strengths and weaknesses. Section 4 looks at the governance of the savings banks, given their importance in the Spanish financial system, and the process of reform in which they are involved. Finally, Section 5 considers the main challenges the sector faces and its future prospects in the wake of the financial crisis.

2   International trends in the financial sector and the impact of the crisis

This section briefly reviews the major trends shaping the banking sector at the international level prior to the outbreak of the financial crisis in 2007-8, the impact of the crisis, and the process of regulatory reform and other changes currently underway in the sector.[2]

2.1   The major trends prior to the crisis

The banking sector is undergoing a process of transformation associated with technological change (driven by information technology), globalization and market integration. To this process a shift from rigid regulation of the sector towards a more flexible approach has been added and this allows and encourages competition between financial institutions. The sector has gone from being a tightly regulated system with infrequent crises, between the 1940's and 1970's, to a liberalized sector suffering major crises, culminating in the crisis of 2007-8, which has come at a high cost for both the Treasury and the wider economy. The changes in the sector have resulted in the traditional business of holding deposits and granting loans losing weight in favor of providing services to investors and businesses. This has been accompanied by a restructuring of the industry, which has consequently undergone significant consolidation.

The Spanish financial and banking sector is caught up in international developments and has experienced a profound transformation, taking it from being a highly regulated and controlled sector to a liberalized one. Chapter 7 of this book discusses the major mile-

---

[2]   See Vives (2011) for an account of trends in banking, the role of competition and its interaction with regulation and the stability of the system, and the implications in the context of the crisis, and the EEAG (2010) for an analysis of the factors leading up to the crisis.

stones in this process. These include freedom for the banks to open offices since 1974; freedom of entry for foreign banks (with certain restrictions) as of 1978; freedom over asset types in 1981; elimination of investment ratios; total liberalization of liability types in 1987; the freedom for savings banks to open offices outside their Autonomous Community (region) in 1989; and a drastic reduction in minimum reserve requirements. The European single banking license made it easier for European competitors to establish themselves in the country. This process introduced the potential for a significant increase in competition, by removing the restrictions on rivalry between institutions, allowing banks and savings banks to operate on a similar footing, and facilitating market entry.[3]

This liberalization process was accompanied – and stimulated – by advances in information technology and transaction processing (ATMs, telephone and electronic banking), together with developments in hedging techniques (for example, with innovations such as the use of derivatives and securitization). These developments raised productivity and produced economies of scale in domestic business while creating the need for highly qualified specialist human capital. The liberalization of international capital movements was a fundamental part of the process.

The outcome of the liberalization process has been an increase in competition both from within and outside the banking industry, with banks facing direct competition from financial markets, and the advance of disintermediation and financial innovation. At the same time there has been rapid expansion of financial markets and intermediation, and a transformation of the banking business to put greater emphasis on the provision of services. This has been accompanied by an increased concentration in the industry.

2.1.1   Disintermediation

The proportion of bank assets relative to those of non-bank financial intermediaries has fallen in the developed economies (in the Unites States, up until 2000), (see Chart 1A). Developments in the United States contrast with those in Spain, where the decline of the banks has been much more moderate, and insurance companies and pension funds hold much smaller market shares, and these have recently even shrunk somewhat (Chart 1B). In the euro area (Chart 1C) banks account for a smaller percentage of assets than in Spain, and the decline has been less pronounced. The market share accounted for by insurance and pension funds is greater, however.

An intensive process of *financial disintermediation* is underway in the United States, Europe and Spain. The importance of market-related financial assets is growing in relation to bank assets, although in Spain bank assets are holding their ground better (deposits lost share up until 2006, but lending gained share, see Chart 2).

---

[3]   See Caminal, Gual and Vives (1990).

CHART 1A   DISTRIBUTION OF FINANCIAL ASSETS IN THE US HELD BY MAIN TYPES OF FINANCIAL INTERMEDIARIES

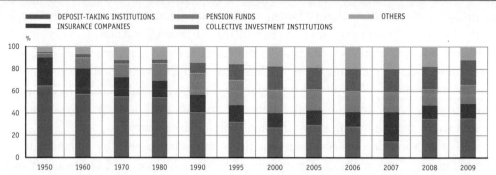

SOURCE: Barth et al. (1997), completed with data from Flow of Fund Accounts, Board of Governors of the Federal Reserve System. (a)

a. The "others" category includes: Closed-end funds and Exchange-traded funds, ABS issuers, Finance companies, Mortgage companies, REITs, Brokers and dealers and Bank personal trusts and estates. Deposit-taking institutions includes: Commercial banks, Savings institutions and Credit unions.

CHART 1B   DISTRIBUTION OF FINANCIAL ASSETS BY TYPE OF INTERMEDIARY (SPAIN, INCLUDING BANCO DE ESPAÑA). UNCONSOLIDATED EARNINGS

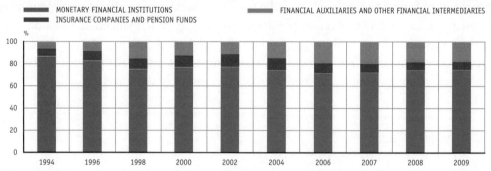

SOURCE: Eurostat.

CHART 1C   DISTRIBUTION OF FINANCIAL ASSETS BY TYPE OF FINANCIAL INTERMEDIARY (EURO AREA, INCLUDING CENTRAL BANKS) (a). UNCONSOLIDATED EARNINGS

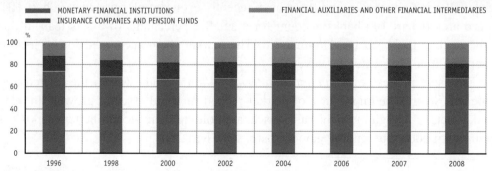

SOURCE: Eurostat.

a. Excluding Luxembourg, Ireland (1996–2000), Cyprus (2008) and Malta (2008).

CHART 2   PERCENTAGE OF FINANCIAL ASSETS HELD IN FORM OF EACH TYPE OF INSTRUMENT
IN SPAIN

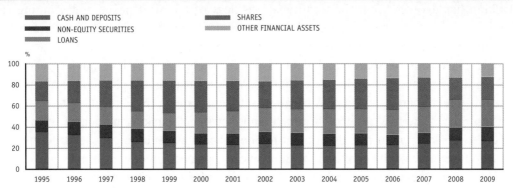

SOURCE: Eurostat.

2.1.2   Expansion of financial intermediation

The liberalization process has also led to significant *expansion of financial intermediation,* with a sharp increase in intermediaries' financial assets as a percentage of GDP (in the United States the figure was 98% in 1952, rising to a peak of 306% in 2007, with commercial banks' assets ranging from 51% to 84% of GDP over the same period). In the euro zone, the percentage of financial assets held by intermediaries was 277.5% in 1995 and 506.7% in 2008; for Spain the figures were 218% in 1995 and 429.7% in 2008 (see Chart 3).

This effective expansion of the financial market has meant that even the banks have grown in real terms, despite the advance of disintermediation.

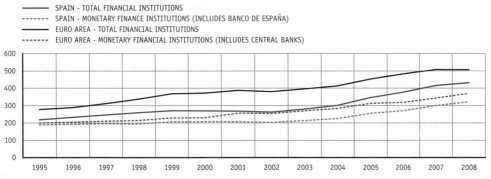

CHART 3   FINANCIAL ASSETS (% GDP). SPAIN AND EURO AREA (a).
UNCONSOLIDATED EARNINGS

SOURCE: Eurostat.

a. The euro-area data are a simple average of the ratios of financial assets to GDP in each country. The euro-area series excludes Luxembourg, Ireland (1995–2000), Cyprus (2008) and Malta (2008).

2.1.3   Transformation of the banking business

Banking has evolved from the traditional business of taking deposits and granting (and monitoring) loans, to the provision of investor services (managing investment funds/assets, consulting and insurance) and business services (consulting, insurance, mergers and acquisitions, placement of shares and debt issuance, securitization, risk management), and making investments with their own resources. Within financial conglomerates it is possible to identify retail banks, investment banks, asset management, investments with own funds, and insurance. The now reviled "originate and distribute" banking model, in which banks sought to off-load credit risk by originating mortgage loans and quickly securitizing them, is a good example of the evolution of the banking business. Interest revenues gave way to fee income and there was a switch from investing in infrastructure at branches to investing in communications networks, information technology and skilled human capital. This process has also taken place to some extent at Spanish banks, although they did not adopt the "originate and distribute" model. After the crisis, interest revenues have regained importance (at least as a result of central banks' low interest rate policies) and the weight of banking assets is tending to rise. This return to traditional banking has also been observed in the United States, where recently the volume of commercial bank assets grew faster, in real terms, than the total held by financial intermediaries.

2.1.4   Consolidation and increased concentration

Restructuring is taking the form of consolidation, with similar reductions in the number of banks between 1997 and 2007 in both the United States and in Europe (down 22% in the United States and 29% in the EU-15). In Europe, domestic mergers have predominated, although more recently there have been some cross-border mergers in Europe and interstate mergers in the United States. One consequence is that, despite an increase in concentration nationally in the United States over the last 20 years, concentration at local level shows, if anything, a downward trend (Berger, Demsetz and Strahan (1999), Table 7 in White (2009)).

In Europe, the prevalence of domestic mergers has tended to increase local concentration (for example, in 19 of the 27 EU markets the CR5 concentration ratio for assets was over 50% in 2007). In the EU-15 the CR5 ratio for assets increased from 37.6% in 2001 to 44.3% (weighted average) in 2009. Spain is close to the EU-15 weighted average, which is higher than the level in the United States (Chart 4).

The effects of liberalization in Spain did not take long to emerge, with a significant increase in competition between institutions.[4] The sector has undergone a restructuring process that

---

[4]   For example, with successive "wars" in the sector: the "super accounts" battle in 1989, mutual funds from 1991, mortgages from 1993, etc. See, for example, Vives (1990) for a brief analysis of the new competitive context introduced by the 'super accounts'.

CHART 4   CR-5 RATIO FOR SPAIN AND EU-15. SHARE OF DEPOSITS HELD BY THE TOP FIVE INSTITUTIONS AS A PERCENTAGE OF TOTAL ASSETS

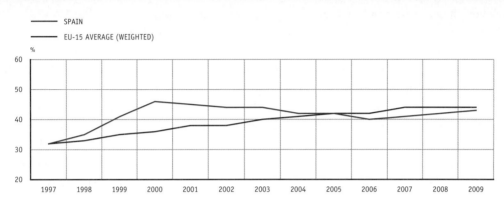

SOURCE: European Central Bank.

led to the emergence of two major banks (Santander and BBVA), and there has also been a significant number of mergers involving small- and medium-sized banks. In this competitive scenario, the savings banks have competed effectively with the commercial banks, gaining market share, as discussed below, in both in credit and deposit markets, with the exception of mortgage lending. Foreign banks, however, have not made significant inroads into the Spanish market. Also, financial institutions, particularly banks, have managed to lead and manage a large share of the disintermediation process.

In summary, liberalization has been associated with an increase in the level of competition faced by financial intermediaries. At the same time, banking has been transformed into the provision of services, and restructuring has tended to increase aggregate concentration (although the consequences of this may have been different in local retail markets in the United States and in Europe). The crisis marks a return to traditional banking (with an increase in the weight of credit institutions in intermediated financial assets, particularly in the United States but also in euro area and Spain) and is tending to accentuate the trend towards consolidation, although it remains to be seen whether this is a lasting or temporary reaction.

2.2   The crisis and regulatory reform

The process of liberalization in the banking industry has been accompanied by prudential requirements allowing the banks to use their own internal models to evaluate and control risk, accompanied by information disclosure requirements on financial institutions in order to increase transparency and promote market discipline. The Basel II framework takes a flexible view of the minimum capital requirements, supervisory review, and market discipline which form its pillars. This framework aimed to make capital requirements more sensitive to risk. Supervisors were supposed to evaluate how well banks were adjusting their capital to the risks they were incurring, and banks were expected to disclose information about their capital structure, accounting practices, risk exposures and capital adequacy. However, the crisis has put this regulatory scheme in question.[5]

The financial crisis marks a change in the trends in the banking sector in terms of regulatory requirements, business models, and the role of innovation and internationalization. The banks' solvency and liquidity requirements will increase significantly under the new Basel rules (known as "Basel III"). The aims of the regulations are for institutions to be able to survive unexpected losses and to curb the potential for contagion between institutions. There will be an increase in the quantity (stricter solvency ratios) and quality of institutions' capital (fewer hybrid instruments such as preference shares or subordinate debt in relation to core capital, comprising ordinary shares and reserves, net of goodwill). Countercyclical provisions are envisaged, as are requirements to adjust liquidity and to moderate maturity transformation by the industry.

In the Basel committee's new proposals, the existing minimum requirements for risk weighted asset capital ratios of 2% for Core Tier 1 (common stock and retained earnings, net of goodwill), 4% for Tier 1 (including non-accumulative perpetual preference shares), and 8% for total regulatory capital (including perpetual preference shares and hybrid debt/equity instruments, subordinate debt and general provisions) will rise. This will be progressive in the case of the first two, rising to values of 4.5% and 6% by 2015.[6] The proposal includes a capital conservation buffer that will increase to 2.5%, and total requirements for Core Tier 1, Tier 1 and total regulatory capital that will reach 7%, 8.5% and 10.5%, respectively, by the end of 2018.[7] Depending on circumstances in each country, a countercyclical buffer of up to an additional 2.5% of ordinary capital will also be activated in order to control the systemic risk associated with periods of excessive aggregate credit growth. The risk weighting of assets is also undergoing a limited review.

To mitigate the vulnerability of wholesale funding that became apparent during the crisis, a Liquidity Coverage Ratio (LCR), which is a measure of short-term liquidity, is being introduced, to cover 30 days' cash withdrawals with liquid assets, along with a longer term, Net Stable Funding Ratio (NSFR) to encourage long-term funding and mitigate maturity transformation (i.e. to avoid long-term assets being financed from short-term borrowing).[8] The NSFR is intended to provide for a one-year buffer with which to tackle an institution's profitability or solvency problems.

The new Basel III proposals also include a leverage ratio intended to provide a simple, transparent, and non-risk-based indicator as an additional measure to supplement the Basel

---

[5]   For an analysis of the financial crisis and its impact on regulation, see Vives (2010).

[6]   See BIS (2010a) and the July and September 2010 annexes.

[7]   As losses reduce this buffer, restrictions on the distribution of profits will be increased, so as to give priority to strengthening the capital base over payment of dividends and discretional bonuses.

[8]   The liquidity coverage ratio will have a transitional "observation" period that will start in 2011 and end in 2015 with the introduction of the minimum requirements. The net stable funding ratio will be monitored as of 2012 and will not come into effect until 2018 and may yet undergo certain modifications. For more details, see BIS (2010b).

II risk-weighted ratio. This indicator, which will apply worldwide, will require banks to hold Tier 1 capital equal to 3% of (non-risk-weighted) total assets.[9]

These requirements represent an increase in costs and potential reduction in levels of credit. The high returns of the past will not be repeated and a lower-risk, lower-profit sector is taking shape. Also, if the original ideas are maintained, the proposed changes in the calculation of core capital will penalize banks with minority interests and shareholdings, as well as those with insurance business. Indeed, minority interests are not consolidated in core capital (tier 1),[10] although they are computed as risk-weighted assets (the reason being that minority interests can cover a related subsidiary's risk but not the group's risk, so as to avoid possible regulatory arbitrage); significant holdings (over 10%) in non-consolidated financial institutions (banks, insurance companies, and other financial institutions) can also be included in the core capital calculation up to a limit of 10% of ordinary shares (to prevent problems spreading between group subsidiaries).

Assessing the impact of the Basel reform on economic growth is complex. In the long term, it should enhance growth by helping make financial crises less likely and less severe and therefore reducing the GDP losses they cause. At the same time it may raise the cost of financial intermediation by increasing the margins needed to recoup the additional costs of the increased capital and liquidity requirements. However, it should be borne in mind that the increased capital requirements make banking safer and should therefore reduce the cost of capital. The Bank for International Settlements (BIS) has run a simulation of the Basel reform and concluded that its impacts are positive over a wide range of higher capital requirements than at present (up to approximately twice the current requirements).[11] However, the cost of the transition to the new system also needs to be considered.[12]

Although the details (which will be crucial) have yet to be defined, the Basel III proposals for capital tend to penalize banking joint ventures, therefore limiting their potential benefits in terms of market entry, exchange of know-how and good practice, and they may lead to reduced diversification both geographically and into other business segments such as insurance. The proposals regarding liquidity will have implications for the banks' maturity-transformation function, given that they aim to limit maturity transformation and so may penalize retail banking (deposit financing being considered relatively unstable).

A more complex issue is the likely influence at the interface between intermediation and the market. The envisaged liquidity requirements on the asset side will make loans less attractive while making bonds more so, particularly government bonds, and on the liability side, deposits will take precedence over wholesale funds.

Regulatory reform can have a major impact on the internationalization of the banking sector. Indeed, the tendency to isolate institutions' problems in the country in which they

---

[9]   Banks will be obliged to publish this ratio as of 2015 and to comply with the 3% requirement as of 2018.

[10]   Certain minority interests in foreign bank subsidiaries may be booked as core capital so as to back specific losses at these subsidiaries.

[11]   BIS (2010c) and BIS (2010d).

[12]   BIS (2010e).

arise may lead to supranational conglomerates forming, comprising subsidiaries which are capitalized, regulated and supervised independently. For example, in the EU this would mean replacing branches by national subsidiaries. This could put a damper on the integration of the European financial market. In the EU, and in the euro area in particular, mechanisms are needed for resolving crises arising at pan-European institutions that establish *ex ante* how restructuring is to be financed. Such mechanisms need to be accompanied by a harmonized deposit insurance at European level to avoid problems such as those clearly highlighted by the bankruptcy of Fortis. This is an issue that is on the agenda for discussion at EU level. Also, the treatment given to minority shareholdings in the capital requirements will have significant repercussions for financial institutions' international expansion.

Regulation now faces the challenge of how to make the financial system more resilient and stable without stifling development and innovation. The financial sector faces the challenge of restoring trust and rebuilding its reputation, and of adapting to a stricter new regulatory environment, resulting from the view that the sector has enjoyed high returns as a result of excessive risk-taking. The consequences of these regulatory changes will be crucial to the definition of business models and internationalization strategies.

3   Situation of the Spanish banking sector

This section will first describe the state of play before the crisis erupted in 2007, then analyze the impact of that crisis, and finally assess the sector's strengths and weaknesses.[13]

3.1   The banking sector on the eve of the crisis

Prior to the outbreak of the crisis, the Spanish banking industry was characterized by: (i) strong growth in credit focused particularly on the property market; (ii) the centrality of the banking system in the economy, despite the development of the financial markets; (iii) funding from deposits and wholesale markets; (iv) increased concentration, with growth in the number of offices and a high branch network density; (v) considerable market power, although on a downward trend; (vi) high returns, solvency at EU-15 levels, and low default rates; (vii) and, rapid international expansion.[14]

---

[13]   The data in this section are from: Banco Central Europeo (2010), Banco de España (2010), BIS (2010f), Escrivá (2009), Eurostat, International Monetary Fund (2009, 2010), Maudos and Fernández de Guevara (2008) and Roldán (2010).

[14]   For more details, see Chapter 9 of this book.

3.1.1   Expansion, specialization and the central position of the Spanish banking sector

The Spanish banking sector expanded rapidly in parallel with the Spanish economy's period of strong growth that began in 1997. Indeed, bank assets grew by a factor of 3.5 from 1997 to 2007 (against a factor of 2.14 for the euro area as a whole), growing at rates above GDP during the period.

Lending to the (non-bank) private sector grew five-fold in Spain between 1997 and 2007 (compared to a factor of 2.15 in the euro area) reaching 169.1% of GDP (113.6% of GDP in the euro area) (see Chart 5).

The increase in mortgage lending has been spectacular (an annual average of over 19% between 2002 and 2007, compared with 9% in the euro area). Moreover, home loans accounted 22% of the growth in the sector's balance sheet in Spain and 12% growth in the euro area. Spanish banks are highly *specialized in the mortgage market* (for example, in 2004 mortgage loans represented 55% of banks income from households, compared with 33% in the EU-25). Even so, the ratio of mortgage debt to GDP in Spain is in line with the EU-25 average.

The result has been that, as a share of GDP, bank assets grew by 1.7 points between 1997 and 2007 (by 1.4 in the euro area), but left Spain still well below the euro area average in 2007 (see Chart 6). Nevertheless, the weight of the financial sector in the economy remains below the European average (in 2007 financial intermediation accounted for 5.3% of GVA and just under 2.0% of employment in Spain, whereas in the EU-15 these percentages were 5.6% and 2.9% respectively), but it has a productivity (in terms of GVA per employee) that is high compared to EU-15 (financial-sector productivity in Spain compared to the total economy in 2007 was 270% and that of the EU-15 was 181.5%)

The banking system retains a *central position* in Spain, despite the progressive development of the financial markets. For example, in 2007 bank lending to the private (non-bank)

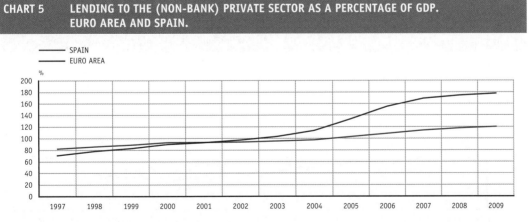

CHART 5   LENDING TO THE (NON-BANK) PRIVATE SECTOR AS A PERCENTAGE OF GDP. EURO AREA AND SPAIN.

SOURCES: European Central Bank and Eurostat.

a. i.e., except monetary financial institutions, resident in the euro area

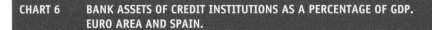

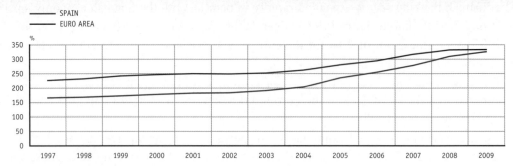

CHART 6   BANK ASSETS OF CREDIT INSTITUTIONS AS A PERCENTAGE OF GDP.
           EURO AREA AND SPAIN.

SOURCES: European Central Bank and Eurostat.

sector[15] was equivalent to 169% of GDP, while market capitalization was equivalent to 117%. The banks are increasingly significant as sources of credit for businesses. Additionally, a large share of market-related activity, such as investment funds and pension funds, is managed by the banking sector.

3.1.2   Deposit funding and reliance on foreign funding sources

The sector's expansion has been largely funded from deposits. Non-interbank deposits in 2007 represented 48.7% of the sector's balance sheet compared with 30% for the euro area. Even so, deposits (from the private sector, excluding central government and monetary fi-

---

[15]   ECB data (as in Chart 5).

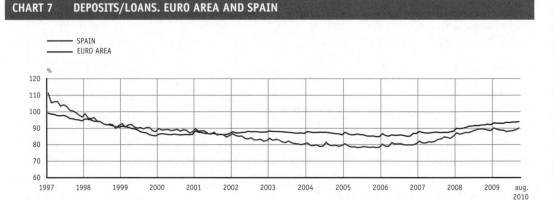

CHART 7   DEPOSITS/LOANS. EURO AREA AND SPAIN

SOURCE: European Central Bank.

nancial institutions) dropped from 111% of lending to the private sector (excluding banking and finance) in 1997, to 82% in 2007, while in the euro area, this percentage went from 99% to 88%. (See Chart 7). The industry has needed to increase the amount of funding it obtains from wholesale markets (interbank, bond issues, and securitization) as deposits grew by 14% a year (average) between 1997 and 2007, while loans to the private sector (non-bank) grew by an average of 17.5%.

Spain's securitized assets rose from 3% of GDP in 2000 to 33% of GDP in 2007, of which the percentage of securitized assets held on the banking sector's balance sheet reached 50% in 2007, with rates of foreign investment of over 60%. Savings banks have been the biggest issuers of covered bonds.

3.1.3   Market structure, consolidation and extension of the network

The European banking industry underwent consolidation between 1997 and 2007, with the number of institutions contracting by almost 29% in the euro area (14.2% in Spain). This process was accompanied by an increase in concentration: CR5 in terms of assets rose 9 points to 41% in 2007 in Spain, but remained below the 44.2% euro-area average (weighted average, see Chart 4). The Herfindahl index of asset concentration rose by more than 61% over the period, but remained low in the European context (459 in Spain compared with 655 in the euro area in 2007). During that period there were a few mergers between savings banks and three acquisitions of banks by savings banks.

In late 2007 there were 151 commercial banks accounting for 54.8% of total credit institutions' assets (with savings banks and credit unions). The 46 savings banks had a market share of 40%. The remainder were credit unions and specialist credit institutions. Over the period 1997-2000 the savings banks clearly won market share from the domestic banks (see Chart 8).

CHART 8   MARKET SHARE OF CREDIT INSTITUTIONS IN SPAIN

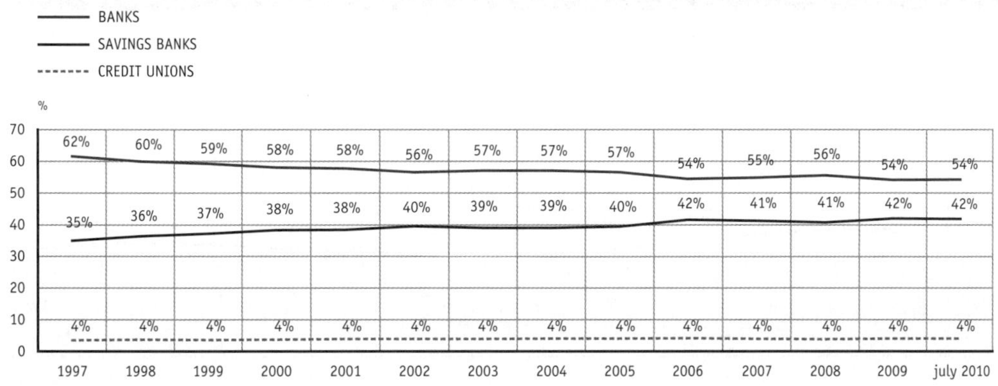

SOURCE: Banco de España.

In the EU (excluding Spain), the network of bank branches has shrunk since 1997 while in Spain it has expanded (by 19.6% up until 2007), yielding a high network density (with the smallest number of inhabitants per branch in the euro area and relatively few inhabitants per ATM). For example, whereas the population per bank branch increased in the EU from 2,482 in 1997 to 2,720 in 2007, in Spain it dropped to below 1,000 (from 1039 in 1997 to 977.5 in 2007). Spanish bank branches are small compared to those in the EU, both in terms of employees and assets managed (they are smallest in the euro area on both measures). Part of the explanation for this high network density is Spain's low population density and the relative specialization in retail banking. Another noteworthy feature is that the penetration of ATMs and point-of-sale terminals is very much higher in Spain than in its European neighbors. However, by contrast, the penetration of Internet banking is weaker (in 2007, 16% of the population aged over 16 used online banking, whereas in the EU-25 the share was 27%), although it is growing rapidly. The explanation lies in the relatively low penetration of broadband in Spain, in conjunction with the population's lower relative educational attainment.

Contrary to the trend in the EU-15, where the number of banking employees has declined, in Spain it has risen. The growth in the number of offices and in employment is mainly due to the expansion of the savings banks (between 2000 and 2007 the banks slimmed their networks down slightly, whereas the savings banks expanded theirs by 26.6%; in terms of employment, between 2000 and 2007 the savings banks increased their workforce by 30% whereas the banks reduced theirs by 4%. See Chart 9).

3.1.4 Level of competition

The indicators of the degree of competition (Lerner index, Panzar-Rosse H-statistic) suggest that the Spanish banking industry's market power is above the European average although

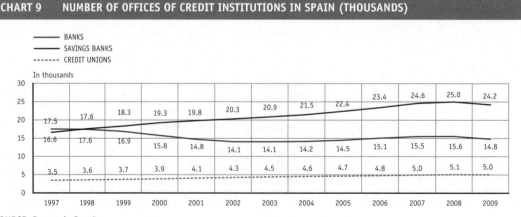

CHART 9   NUMBER OF OFFICES OF CREDIT INSTITUTIONS IN SPAIN (THOUSANDS)

SOURCE: Banco de España.

the difference has tended to narrow.[16] Between 1997 and 2005, the trend in both Spain and Europe as a whole was towards increased market power.[17] There are wide variations between segments, however, because whereas margins on sight deposit and consumer loans are higher than the European average, those on business loans, mortgages and term deposits are lower. During the period prior to the crisis, there was a marked fall in the margins on assets products. In any case, the savings banks have made a big contribution to competition in the market.[18]

3.1.5   Earnings and solvency

The earnings of the Spanish banking sector compare favorably with those of other European banks, despite their lower leverage. Spanish banks' return on assets (ROA) and return on equity (ROE) were 1.4 times higher than the euro area average in 2007.

The Spanish banks have higher margins (both financial and ordinary) but these have declined faster than in the EU. Both in Spain and in Europe as a whole, banks have increased fee income and revenues from financial transactions, which rose to almost 50% of earnings in 2006. At the same time Spanish banks have slightly higher average costs than in Europe (their costs were more than 10% higher than the average for the EU-15 in 2006, for example), despite cost-containment efforts, especially by the banks. From 1997 to 2007, the Spanish banks improved their ratio of operating expenses to gross income by about 30% and reduced average costs by 63%, while ordinary income fell by 27%. For the EU-15, the figures were 10%, 30% and 16%, respectively.[19] The ratio of operating expenses to gross income was 33% below the European average in 2007.

Before the crisis, the banking system looked well capitalized; it had a total solvency ratio slightly below the EU-15 average (10.7% in Spain compared with 11.6% on average in the EU-15 in 2007, although this ratio does not fully include the general provisions the Banco de España requires Spanish banks to set aside in times of surplus). The downward trend in the solvency ratio in both the EU and Spain should also be noted. The level of provisions to cover defaults (doubtful loans) is high (214.6% in December 2007 according to the IMF, compared with 83.5% in the EU-15, excluding Denmark, Finland, Luxembourg, the Netherlands and the UK, or 86.1% in the euro area, excluding Luxembourg, the Netherlands and Finland) due to the increase in reserves during the period of rapid credit growth. The default rate is low, at 0.9% of total doubtful loans in December 2007, compared with 1.7% in the EU-15 in 2007 (excluding the Netherlands).

---

[16]   See Maudos and Fernández de Guevara (2008).

[17]   According to the Panzar-Rosse H-statistic, the Spanish banking industry's market power declined after the mid-1980's when liberalization measures were imposed, reaching a minimum in the final five years of the century, and then subsequently rising. See Gutiérrez de Rozas (2007).

[18]   For more details of the degree of competition in the Spanish banking system, see Chapter 9 of this book.

[19]   See Maudos and Fernández de Guevara (2008).

3.1.6   Internationalization

Spanish banks have internationalized more rapidly than the European banking industry as a whole, although the weight of foreign business on their balance sheet is substantially lower than the euro-area average (in 2007, it was 14.16% on the asset side, as an investment destination, compared to a figure of 33.3% for the euro area; and on the liabilities side, as a source of funding, it was 15.01% compared to 22.3%). The EU-15 is both the main source of external funding (almost 90%, mainly from Germany, France, the Netherlands and the United Kingdom) and the main destination for Spanish foreign investments (59.4% of Spanish banking assets invested abroad in 2006 were invested in the EU-15). These foreign investments are largely the result of the major Spanish banks' international expansion since the mid-1990s, first in Latin America, and then in the United States and Europe (in the UK in particular). Early internationalization of the Spanish banking system was uneven, with the two biggest banks being highly internationalized (with foreign assets accounting for approximately half of their revenues in 2008). There has been a small, but significant, international presence among medium-sized banks, but relatively few savings banks (with one or two recent exceptions) have any presence abroad. The presence of large Spanish institutions in Asia is small, despite the incipient investments being made. Moreover, the penetration of foreign banks in Spain is also low: in 2007 the share of total assets belonging to branches and subsidiaries of foreign banks in Spain was 11.6%, compared to a euro-area average of 20%.[20]

3.2   The impact of the financial crisis

The impact of the financial crisis which broke in August 2007 has made itself felt in the sector. When the wholesale markets dried up, Spanish banks had to compete to attract more deposits (primarily from mutual funds), pay more for liquidity, turn to the ECB for financing (with a doubling of their recourse to the ECB compared to pre-crisis levels) in line with other European banking systems, and draw upon the government's liquidity programs (the *Fondo de Adquisición de Activos Financieros* or FAAF, a financial asset purchase fund, and guaranteed issues). Deposit rates rose relative to ECB rates, and in general they did so more in the case of the savings banks than the banks. The disparities between institutions in terms of their remuneration of liquidity and recourse to the ECB increased as the crisis progressed. Securitization of real-estate assets continued, but primarily so that the securities produced could be submitted to the ECB as collateral for finance operations.

Credit growth slowed significantly, with a slight contraction in credit in 2009 (an increase in credit institutions' lending to the resident private and non-bank sectors of 6.2% between December 2007 and December 2008 followed by a drop of 2% between December 2008

---

[20]   For more details of the level of competition in the Spanish banking system, see Chapter 10 of this book.

and December 2009) due to supply and demand factors (as a result of more stringent loan approval criteria). It should be noted, however, that credit in 2009 fell by 2%, less than nominal GDP, which contracted by more than 3% (see Chart 10A). Growth in lending for home purchases also fell markedly, with zero growth in 2009 (see Chart 10B).

The surge in credit growth in relation to the euro area, and the contraction caused by the crisis, can be seen in Chart 11.

The banking sector was not materially affected in a direct way by the toxic products in the United States sub-prime mortgages market and their consequences. The crisis in Spain initially involved a combination of disruption to the liquidity of wholesale and interbank markets – a factor contributing to precipitating the property-market adjustment – which forced widespread deleveraging, with tensions rising later as a result of the devaluation of assets and a poorer outlook for economic growth. The result was a *significant increase in*

CHART 10A   ANNUAL GROWTH IN LENDING TO THE PRIVATE SECTOR (NON-BANK AND RESIDENT) BY CREDIT INSTITUTIONS IN SPAIN (a)

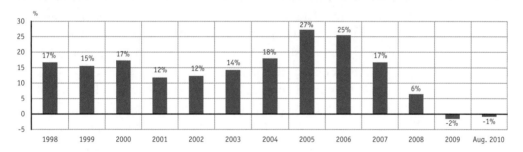

SOURCE: Banco de España.

a. Excludes general government and non-resident credit institutions. For 2010, the figure is the rate from August 2009 to August 2010.

CHART 10B   ANNUAL GROWTH OF LENDING TO HOUSEHOLDS FOR HOME PURCHASES IN SPAIN (a)

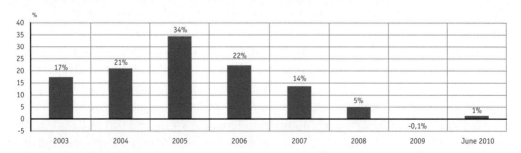

SOURCE: Banco de España.

a. For 2010, the figure is the rate from June 2009 to June 2010.

CHART 11   LENDING TO THE (NON-BANK) PRIVATE SECTOR, ANNUAL VARIATION IN OUTSTANDING
            BALANCE: SPAIN AND EURO AREA (EXCLUDING SPAIN)

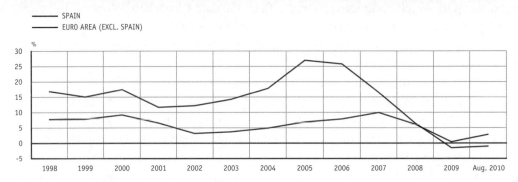

SOURCE: European Central Bank.

defaults and the banks taking real estate directly onto their balance sheets. Default rates rose from less than 1% in 2007 to around 5.5% in July 2010, with a much more pronounced rate of defaults among businesses than families (defaults by businesses in the second quarter of 2010 rose to almost 7% whereas the rate among households stayed at less than 3.5%). Both banks and savings banks experienced similar default rates. The annual growth of bad loans fell between January 2009 (when it reached a peak of about 300%) and August 2010 (14%).

In general, default rates in the construction and property sector were highest, in comparison with other sectors, and they increased markedly (with the percentage of doubtful loans rising from 0.3% in 2007 to almost 11% in June 2010). This hit the savings banks harder than the banks, given their greater exposure to the sector (in comparative terms, the banks have been worse affected by defaults on consumer credit, with a default rate of 9.2%, whereas the default rate for the savings banks in the case of consumer credit is 3.8%). The percentage of doubtful loans in the construction and property development sector (over 10%) contrasts with that on home loans (2.5%, see Chart 12). Among the reasons for this is the strong preference for homeownership in Spain, together with the personal guarantees needed in order to take out a mortgage (in contrast to the situation in the United States, for example).

In December 2009, the exposure to the construction and property development sector accounted for 25% of total lending to households and businesses and 12% of the consolidated balance sheet of deposit-taking institutions. The default rate on this lending was 9.6%, although it varied widely from one institution to another, in terms of their exposure to the sector, as well as their default rates. Thus, exposure to the construction and property-development sector by deposit-taking institutions varied from 6% to 50%, and default rates varied between 2.3% and 28%. Potentially problematic exposures need to be understood in conjunction with the information on the foreclosure of property assets and substandard loans. Estimates up until June 2010 would put the percentage of potentially troubled assets at over 40% of total credit investments in construction and property-development companies

CHART 12   PERCENTAGE OF DOUBTFUL LOANS AS A SHARE OF THE TOTAL IN EACH SECTOR

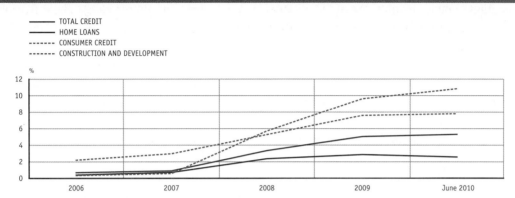

———— TOTAL CREDIT
———— HOME LOANS
------- CONSUMER CREDIT
------- CONSTRUCTION AND DEVELOPMENT

SOURCE: Banco de España.

TABLE 1   DEFAULT RATES: DOUBTFUL LOANS AS A PERCENTAGE OF TOTAL LENDING
(BY CREDIT INSTITUTIONS) TO THE PRIVATE SECTOR (RESIDENT AND NON-BANK)

	% 1993	% 2009
Default rate	8.9	5
GDP growth	-1.2	-3.6
Unemployment	22	18.8
Government deficit	6.7	11.1

SOURCES: Banco de España and Instituto Nacional de Estadística.

and with coverage (including general provisions for business in Spain) of a third of the value of these assets.

Generally speaking, the increase in default rates has *varied widely* between institutions, with a marked increase in the standard deviation of the default rate since the start of the crisis. It cannot be ruled out that the banks' default rate will rise further than those of the savings banks given their greater exposure to personal and commercial credit, which is backed with relatively little collateral.

It is interesting to compare the present case with the 1993 recession, when default rates rose further, probably as a result of higher interest rates. This suggests that the current situation may be vulnerable to a rise in interest rates (see Table 1).

The provision-coverage ratio has fallen to below 60% (December 2009) and general provisions have been largely used up. In 2009, 67% of the sector's operating margin had to be devoted to provisions, in contrast with the final phase of the expansion in 2006, when just 20% had to be.[21] The heterogeneity of institutions translates into a dispersion of capital

---

[21]   Banco de España, Financial Stability Report (March 2010).

ratios and the rate at which general provisions are exhausted (as of December 2008 from a maximum among institutions of 8% of assets to a minimum of almost zero). The differences are also reflected in an increase in the dispersion between institutions and debt ratings and CDS levels.

Institutions with higher default rates, which have relied more heavily on the ECB or the government's liquidity programs, and consequently have lower credit ratings, have had to offer higher interest rates on deposits.[22] This phenomenon has arisen in other crises, such as the S&L crisis in the United States, and indicates that institutions in difficulties and with greater borrowing needs are willing to take on more risk and take advantage of the umbrella offered by the financial system's stability and insurance mechanisms. In this regard, competition may be excessive and could undermine financial stability.[23]

The market trajectory of the large banks (measured in terms of share prices) has remained on the same upward path as their European counterparts (focusing on retail banking, such as Unicredito, ING or BNP Paribas). Before the Greek debt crisis in January 2010, CDS levels were similar and have since risen. In fact, up until 2009 the Spanish banking system demonstrated greater earnings stability than systems in other European countries, with limited losses from financial-asset impairment and with no need for injections of public capital.

According to the ECB, Spanish banks continued to have the second-highest rate of return on assets (ROA) in the euro area in 2008 (0.68% compared with a euro-area average of 0.13%) and the third-highest in 2009 (0.6% compared to the 0% average for the euro area). Moreover, the rates of return on equity (ROE) in 2008 and 2009 were the second-highest, at over 12% and 9% respectively, compared to a euro-area average of -0.5% and -1.6%.

3.3   Strengths and weaknesses

The Spanish banking and finance sector grew strongly during the period of growth that began in 1996 and was further stimulated by the adoption of the euro in 1999. This led to an increase in the weight of banking in the Spanish economy and growth in credit as a percentage of GDP, both of which reached levels above the European averages. The euro offered the prospect of a permanent reduction in borrowing costs for the economy and a revaluation of assets such as building land, which, in conjunction with the ECB's policy of low interest rates, drove growth in real-estate asset prices and investments in homes, accompanied by a significant expansion of credit. This growth was underpinned by certain factors which represent strengths and others which represent weaknesses.

The first strength is the banking system's traditional retail orientation, with a strong basis of deposits and traditional lending (mortgages, consumer and business loans), free from

---

[22]   With data from the beginning of 2009 and interest rates on a 9-month deposit (see BBVA).
[23]   See Matutes and Vives (2000) and Vives (2011) for an analysis of this phenomenon.

exposure to complex off-balance sheet structures (conduits/SIV), which were responsible for the financial crisis unleashed in the United States by sub-prime mortgages.

The second strength is the high apparent level of efficiency, which has enabled cost-containment and growth of the banking business with smaller relative growth in the numbers of branches and size of the workforce (particularly in the case of the banks). Both the average size of bank branches and productivity rates have increased. These have risen at rates exceeding the European average (EU-15 or euro area) due to the use of information technology, and higher levels of human capital and total factor productivity.[24] Operating expenses relative to net income went from 64% in 1997 to 45% in 2007, whereas in the euro area they went from 66% to 56%. It should be noted, however, that variations in margins take into account both efficiency factors and market power.

The third is a high yield (above the European average in terms of both ROE and ROA) based on efficiency, rapid growth and market power, which, although possibly in relative decline, enabled higher margins.[25] In the period immediately following Spain's joining the euro (1997 to 2003), there was a convergence with Europe in terms of levels of competition, with a fall in the Lerner index for deposits relative to the pre-euro period 1988 to 1996 (and a rise in the index in the case of credit).[26]

The result was a level of solvency that exceeded the minimum requirements, but which has suffered as a result of the long expansion phase. Up until 2008, it was accompanied by low levels of default and high levels of provisions, thanks in part to the general provisioning system implemented by the Banco de España. Solvency ratios improved as of 2007.

Finally, it is worth mentioning that the internationalization of certain institutions followed a process which went from Latin America to Europe and the United States, and is now beginning in Asia. International expansion was made possible by the early liberalization of the Spanish financial sector, which increased levels of competition and forced banking institutions to restructure and make improvements in efficiency.

The process of growth and the financial crisis that broke in 2007 have revealed significant weaknesses.

First of all, the *high degree of exposure to real estate* (construction and property development, in particular). Thus, in late 2007 lending to the construction industry and real-estate developers represented around 26% of lending to the private sector (an increase of 14 points relative to 1997). This percentage was higher in the case of the savings banks than in that of the banks (almost 29% compared to 25% in the case of the banks). This exposure left certain institutions' bottom line vulnerable. As Chart 12 shows, the significant increase in defaults in the construction and property-development sector is the most problematic. Moreover, whereas in the euro area home loans in 2007 accounted for less than 12% of the credit institutions'

---

[24]   There is also evidence of the impact of membership of the euro in terms of operating cost reductions on both the deposits and lending sides (Martín-Oliver (2010)).

[25]   See Maudos and Fernández de Guevara (2008).

[26]   See Martín-Oliver (2010).

aggregate balance sheet, in Spain the figure was almost 21%. In 2009, real-estate related lending, whether to the construction industry or for home purchases, accounted for almost 60% of all lending, and as in 2007, this was equivalent to over 100% of GDP. The exposure of the savings banks was greater than that of the banks (69% of total credit to the private sector was provided by 53% of the banks in 2009) although the banks have reoriented their activity more towards the property sector in relative terms, due to the initial position of the savings banks in the mortgage market. It is also worth noting that the vast majority of mortgage lending is variable rate, therefore the banking sector does not bear the interest rate risk but does bear the credit risk, which is sensitive to interest rate rises. Overall increases in defaults rose strongly in Spain and in 2008 reaching a level of 3.4%, which far exceeds the EU-15 percentage of 2.5% (excluding the Netherlands, Denmark and Luxembourg).

The second weakness is the *high degree of dependence on external financing* and, in general, on market sources that are more expensive than deposits. Indeed, credit has grown faster than deposits and the sector has had to finance itself from the interbank market or through bond issues and securitizations. The weight of deposits has risen since 2007, due to the efforts institutions have made to attract deposits in response to their problems accessing international financing (in 2009 they reached 90% of loans, a percentage which is still below the 93% euro area average).

Securitizations in Spain left the risk on the originating institutions' balance sheet as they took the form of covered bonds (backed by the issuer's entire mortgage loan portfolio) or used simple securitized mortgage bond structures (backed only with the asset securitization fund) in which originators retain the first losses. Moreover, due to mortgage market regulations in Spain, originators continue to play the role of credit managers with responsibility for monitoring and supervision. The result is that banks have used securitization as a funding mechanism (or even simply as a means of producing collateral for discounting with the ECB) rather than to transfer risk. This has meant that the Spanish banking sector has directly assumed the property sector's risk. At the same time, the financial crisis has highlighted the liquidity risk inherent in these sources of funding.

The third weakness is the presence of significant *excess capacity* following the phase of rapid expansion. The branch network is now oversized because the levels of credit growth associated with the property sector will not return, and because there is likely to be a downsizing of the sector due to the increased capital and liquidity requirements (under Basel III) and in response to the financial crisis.[27] The excess capacity uncovered by the crisis is most evident in the case of the savings banks, which had significantly expanded their branch networks. Whereas the banks' branch network shrank by 15% between 1997 and 2009, that of the savings banks grew by 45%.

The process of restructuring this excess capacity has begun. Between late 2008 and December 2009, the banks and saving banks closed approximately 800 branches each.

---

[27]   For example, Spain has the lowest number of inhabitants per bank office in the EU-15: 989 in 2008 compared with a euro-area average of 1,730, for example.

Interestingly, this excess capacity also extends to electronic banking. Indeed, the penetration rate of Internet banking, the number of ATM transactions and the number of transactions per POS terminal are all very low compared to the European average is (the latter two are around half the European average).

Finally, we should mention two factors whose implications are somewhat harder to elucidate. The first is the increased market power of Spanish banks. This enables them to enjoy higher profit margins, but at the same time one might question the sustainability of this differential over European banks when the penetration of electronic banking and the population's financial literacy have both increased. In short, the market power of the banks in Spain is a strength that that is declining as a result of the maturing of the market, excess capacity and the sector's limited growth prospects.

The second factor is that the internationalization of the two big Spanish banks has led to a significant concentration of risk in emerging countries (particularly Brazil and Mexico), although this has been offset more recently by expansion in Europe and United States. Spanish banks' foreign operations represented 23.5% of total consolidated assets in June 2009. As a percentage of GDP, the Spanish banking system's exposure to emerging countries in terms of financial assets as a fraction of GDP (December 2009) is approximately 28% (mainly in Latin America). This is higher than the exposure of the United Kingdom (20.6%), the Netherlands (21.2%) and Switzerland (19.5%) but lower than that of Austria (32.7%). Internationalization brings diversification to Spanish banks, an obvious strength in the current financial crisis, but entails a significant exposure to Latin America, which is a potential weakness given its relatively high volatility. It is therefore important that the diversification of the major Spanish banks be balanced between developed and emerging countries and be spread across geographical regions.

4   The savings banks and corporate governance

Overall, during the current financial and economic turmoil, the Spanish savings banks have revealed themselves to be weaker than the banks. For example, during the period, two savings banks have had to be taken over by the authorities, and excess capacity and exposure to the property market have been more pronounced in this part of the financial system. This has led to the need to embark on a process of restructuring. The fact that these institutions have performed worse than the banks during this period can be linked, in part, to their peculiar legal status. The structure of the savings banks as non-profit social undertakings (entities with the legal status of a foundation) is complex and results in a model lacking explicit owners and including stakeholders with a multiplicity of objectives. The mission of the savings banks, the outcome of a historical evolution from institutions (*montes de piedad,* mutualism) which sought to generate trust among small savers, has focused on providing financial services under conditions of economic efficiency while addressing financial exclusion, conducting community welfare activities, and pursuing the economic development of the regions in which they operate. A connection can be drawn between each of the savings banks' goals and the relevant stakeholder group. Thus, the founding organizations aim to promote thrift, to prevent financial exclusion and provide social and community services; depositors want to invest with confidence, obtain good service and, in the early days of the savings banks, to be able to avoid usury and obtain loans at reasonable interest rates; local authorities aim to use them to promote regional development; and the employees' main concerns are their pay and working conditions. Naturally, the public authorities are also interested in promoting thrift among the working class and avoiding financial exclusion (universal access to financial services, in the modern version), in the stability and soundness of the financial system, and in investor protection (the role of the regulator), as well as in defending competition in the sector (perhaps a modern version of the fight against usury). However, it is not clear that the protection of the interests of depositors/customers and employees is not already guaranteed by the savings banks' financial and supervision contracts (the banking supervisor acts as the representative of the interests of the financial institutions' customers) on the one hand, and by employment contracts and the relevant supervisory bodies (the Labor Authority) and legal bodies on the other.

This focus on multiple stakeholders potentially weakens the savings banks' corporate governance system. Firstly, the lack of a clear mission gives greater freedom to managers to put their own interests ahead of profitability criteria. Secondly, the stakeholders' multiple divergent interests can be an obstacle to decision-making. Thirdly, there is an increased likelihood of political interference, leading to decisions being motivated by factors other than business logic, and greater regulatory risk and management instability arising from political changes. Conflicts of interest may also arise when the authorities in the Autonomous Community are represented on the governing body of the savings bank, particularly if the regional authority also has responsibility for the savings bank's supervision.

The agency problem, arising between the theoretical "owners" of a savings bank and its managers is therefore more acute than in the case of a commercial bank (organized as a corporation), whose shareholders have incentives to control the managers. In Spain, the likelihood of a change of managers at a bank has been found to increase when its earnings (return on assets) deteriorate, whereas this relationship does not hold in the case of savings banks.[28] Additionally, if the shareholders do not control the managers properly, such that they fail to optimize the value of the company, they may be ousted by a hostile takeover bid, leading to a change of management, although this mechanism is weaker in the banking sector due to regulatory intervention (making it less common in Spain than in the United States). Finally, shareholders typically demand dividend payments. This reduces the available cash flow for managers and therefore reduces their scope for dissipating the business's earnings on unproductive expenditure.

The problem of managers' autonomy is not unique to the savings banks; it may also arise in the case of banks when ownership is dispersed. This excess of autonomy clearly

---

[28] See Crespí, García-Cestona and Salas (2004), using data from 1986 to 2000.

emerges when the managers can change the "rules of the game" or the institutions' bylaws when it suits them.[29] Managers can also protect themselves from corporate market control by means of anti-takeover measures, such as voting restrictions, non-voting shares, restrictions on board membership or presidency of the bank, or "supermajority" requirements for certain decisions such as mergers (in 2000 two-thirds of listed banks in Spain still had such mechanisms in place). There is also the problem that bank shareholders will tend to urge the managers to take on more risk than is socially appropriate (from the point of view of depositors and taxpayers). This is due to financial institutions' having limited liability, together with the explicit and implicit insurance mechanisms (whether deposit insurance or financial aid in the case of bankruptcy). In this case, the alignment of the interests of the shareholders and managers leads to high levels of risk when regulation is inadequate. There is recent evidence that this happened during the run-up to the crisis.[30]

In principle, the savings banks should align their management better with the preferences of depositors in relation to risk, given that the conflict of interest between depositors and shareholders should not arise in the case of the savings banks. The limited liability of a bank's shareholders may lead the banks and managers to take on more risk than the depositors might care for. In principle, therefore, one would expect the managers of savings banks to be more conservative than those of banks.[31] However, a savings bank may have incentives to pursue excessive growth and may be subject to political interference, meaning that the savings banks do not necessarily enjoy lower interest-rate and credit risk. Their overexposure to real estate makes them vulnerable to a crisis in this sector, and rapid expansion of their branch network tends to increase the proportion of problem loans.[32] Moreover, their possession of a portfolio of investee companies has important effects on the risk of the group (given that, in principle, industrial shareholdings are more sensitive to the economic cycle, whereas services may provide more stability).

The governance structure of the savings banks translates into potential differentials with the banks in terms of costs, risks, and proximity to their geographical region. Thus the savings banks have tended to reduce costs more moderately than have the banks (although part of their higher costs may arise from their greater specialization in retail banking); although in principle they should have tended to better align their management with depositors' risk preferences (they have concentrated very much on the real-estate sector). They have also provided a local customer service which can offer advantages in lending to families and

---

[29] Hellwig (2000) has described, for example, the case of successive changes in shareholders' rights (registered stock, 5% cap on voting rights even when the shareholder group owns more than 5% of the shares, etc.) at the bank UBS in order for managers to maintain control.

[30] See Vives (2010).

[31] Hermalin and Wallace (1994) have studied the S&L crisis in the United States and shown that listed S&Ls are more efficient and less likely to go bankrupt than mutual S&Ls in the same lines of business. However, if the data are not controlled for business lines, the result would be the opposite. The reason for this is that listed S&Ls choose higher risk business lines than mutual S&Ls.

[32] See Salas and Saurina (2002).

small businesses by being able to use non-verifiable ("soft") information in their decisions, and not merely basing themselves on the quantitative and verifiable ("hard") information on which standard procedures are based.

In response to these challenges, the international trend has been to seek explicit owners for institutions of this kind. Thus, in the United States, the savings and loans virtually disappeared in the wake of the major crisis in the 1980s. In Italy they have become corporations, and their social work has been transferred to independent foundations. In France they have become credit unions. In Germany it has been necessary to explicitly recognize public ownership rather than give a public guarantee. In the United Kingdom many building societies have chosen to demutualise, and in Norway, in order to bolster their capitalization, the savings banks can issue primary capital certificates, which are listed on the stock market, have voting rights and open up a route for their voluntary conversion into a corporation.[33]

Although the Spanish savings banks' model looks almost unique in the world, up until the current crisis the savings banks had achieved very satisfactory results: they have wrested market share from the banks, maintained high levels of profitability, and undertaken significant amounts of community work. In fact, the savings banks, which are non-profit institutions, have managed to obtain better returns than the banks, whose goal is to maximize profits. The explanation for this paradox lies in a combination of factors:

- When competing, the goal of savings bank's managers to maximize volume can turn out to be a strategic advantage. This is because it leads to more aggressive competition between the savings banks in terms of opening branches.[34] Furthermore, this growth target imposes discipline, as it requires resources, and savings banks cannot rely on capital increases to fund their growth.
- The inefficiencies intrinsic to the savings bank's governance system are limited by market discipline, competition from other savings banks and from commercial banks, and the possibility of mergers with other savings banks if they underperform.[35] There is evidence in Spain that the possibility of mergers does in fact impose discipline on the managers of savings banks.[36]
- The savings bank brand builds trust and is associated with community work. In modern terms, a savings bank is an enterprise with "social responsibility" built into its charter. Customers appreciate this and therefore savings banks are differentiated in a way that gives them significant market power. This phenomenon is also linked to the fact that the savings banks target a less financially literate clientele and concentrate on geographical regions in which there is less competition.

---

[33] The conversion of the biggest savings bank in to a listed corporation, merging with banking and financial corporations from outside the savings banks sector, points in the direction of the sector's new perspectives.

[34] See Purroy and Salas (2000).

[35] See Allen and Gale (2000) and Vives (2000).

[36] See Crespí et al. (2004).

– Finally, the savings banks' success is due in large part to the fact that their traditional business, retail banking, has developed enormously, a situation the savings banks have taken advantage of by making strategic investments. These savings banks have exploited the gaps left by the major banks as a result of mergers and their expansion in Latin America.

The general good performance of the savings banks until the current economic and financial crisis suggests that changes were not on the cards. The crisis has transformed the scene, however, bringing three fundamental weaknesses to the fore in a scenario characterized by excess capacity and the need for quality equity. First, up until the reform in July 2010, the status of the savings banks did not, in effect, allow for certain types of restructuring, for example, that a savings bank in one Autonomous Community acquire a savings bank in another (although, what it can do, just like a bank, is acquire the branch network of the savings bank in question and integrate it with its own). In principle, this restriction could represent an obstacle to an efficient restructuring of the financial sector. Secondly, shareholdings without voting rights have not satisfied capital needs. *Cuotas participativas,* or non-voting equity instruments, can provide resources to shore up the institution's solvency and enable it to grow, and can introduce market discipline by requiring the savings banks to give a minimum return (especially if these equity instruments are publicly traded). At the same time this raises the question of whether the introduction of non-voting equity instruments is not simply adding another stakeholder to the long list of groups that already exists – each with their own goals – to the joint control of the savings banks and thus increasing the likelihood of internal conflicts. Thirdly, political interference in the governance of the savings banks has frequently occurred in many Autonomous Communities (although not all) and the professionalism of their governing bodies has, at times, been called into question.

The crisis has highlighted the need to strengthen the savings banks' governance, by re-inforcing internal and external control mechanisms and shielding them from political interference. It has also demonstrated the need to equip them with mechanisms with which to increase their capital. Any reform to the status of the savings banks should begin by asking what the mission of these institutions is. Once this has been established, the next step is to determine the most appropriate structure with which to achieve it. The purpose of a savings bank is to perform community welfare work focused on a particular geographical area. From this perspective, the "principal" of the banking business must be this community welfare work (its representatives), which must continue to be provided through an entity in the form of a foundation. The "principal" should have as its objective the goal of maximizing the financial returns from the banking business in order to generate the greatest possible resources to devote to community welfare work and establish a code of ethics in the banking business which, without jeopardizing profitability or solvency, makes this activity compatible with its ultimate goals. The reform must allow the savings banks to keep their independence and institutional diversity, provide choices, and encourage the desired transformation by the more dynamic savings banks, allowing them the possibility of maintaining their traditional structure provided there is a strengthening of good governance and the ability to increase their capital. From this point on, the most appropriate institutional form must be left to the process of evolution in a competitive environment. An essential corollary to this is therefore ensuring that the market remains competitive and that the savings banks are overseen professionally and competently in all areas.[37]

The savings-bank reform passed in July 2010 points in this direction by recognizing the social role of the savings banks, while introducing mechanisms to facilitate their access to capital markets, to professionalize their management and allow them to operate through banking institutions.[38]

In terms of corporate governance, the reform recognizes the representation of the Autonomous Communities in their governing bodies, and sets a limit of 40% on the voting rights held by government entities and public bodies. This limit was 50% in the previous legislation.[39] Moreover, elected political representatives and senior government officials will not be eligible for membership of the governing body of a savings bank. The reform also reinforces the requirements for professionalism and experience as prerequisites for membership of the governing bodies.[40] Mergers between savings banks may only be refused by regional governments with a resolution stating the reasons and taking into account objective requirements envisaged in Autonomous Community legislation. It also establishes that any changes to the legal nature of the savings banks must be approved by a two-thirds majority. Moreover, in order to enhance transparency, all savings banks must submit an annual corporate governance report.

The change is also aimed at making equity instruments more attractive to investors. To this end, when targeted at the general public, they must be traded on secondary markets and shareholders may potentially be given voting rights in proportion to their equity interest. Limits on the size of the stake belonging to an individual holder are also eliminated (the limit under the previous law was 5% of the total equity units issued) as are those on their remuneration. However, the limit on the issuance of equity instruments at 50% of equity remains in force. These changes seek to strengthen the savings banks' standards of solvency, and their liquidity and leverage ratios, in order to adapt them to the future requirements of Basel III.

The reform also envisages new organizational models. The savings banks may choose to exercise their financial activity directly, indirectly through a bank, or become a foundation and transfer their financial business to a bank. The organizational options open to the savings banks under the new rules are:

---

[37]   The IMF recommends that the savings banks' legal structure be adapted to the new context in order to reduce political influence, enhance their ability to increase their capital, and offer the savings banks the opportunity to transform themselves into corporations, or even require them to do so, in the case of those of greatest systemic importance.

[38]   Royal Decree-Law 11/2010, 9 July 2010 on governing bodies and other aspects of the savings banks' legal framework.

[39]   The presence of a representative of the Autonomous Community on the audit board has also been eliminated.

[40]   The Law establishes that the general manager and at least half of the members of the Board of Directors must have accredited knowledge and experience relevant to their responsibilities.

1. Keeping their status as savings banks and incorporating the new regime of equity instruments (with or without voting rights) and adapting to the new corporate governance standards.
2. Transferring some or all of their financial business (that of various savings banks) to a bank through the institutional protection system *(sistema institucional de protección,* SIP).[41]
3. Transferring their financial business to a bank and retaining their status as a savings bank (the community welfare activities and portfolio of shares remaining with the savings bank) provided that control of the bank is maintained.
4. Converting into a special foundation, keeping their community welfare activity as the core activity of the foundation and transferring their financial business to a bank (in exchange for a shareholding).

In scenarios (2), (3) and (4), the bank is directly exposed to market discipline, which obliges it to be managed professionally, but means it can increase its capital. The restructuring of the sector is encouraged by the fact that there are no obstacles to mergers and acquisitions between banking institutions. Capital increases in scenarios (2) and (3) may be limited by the idiosyncrasies of the savings bank's governance model.[42] In scenario (1) it may be expected that capital increases will require that shareholders be given voting rights, and will put the stability of the system of savings-bank equity instruments to the test (Norway's experience may be useful in this regard).

5   Challenges and outlook

The Spanish banking sector is facing the current crisis with a legacy of efficiency, profitability and solvency that has enabled it to weather the first phase of the turmoil well. However, structural weaknesses exist that could undermine banks' performance and their ability to contribute to the optimal functioning of the economy in the second phase, as the problems arising from adjustments in the property market and the economic recession are digested.

Section 2 has discussed how the problems that emerged with the crisis will mark a watershed in the banking sector's regulation and business model. The originate-and-distribute

---

[41]   It is stipulated that the central institution in the SIP must be at least 50% owned by the savings banks and be incorporated as a corporation. If this shareholding drops below 50%, the member savings banks will be obliged to convert into special foundations and assign their banking business to the SIP's central institution. The individual institutions under the SIP retain their legal identity, governing bodies and community welfare activities, and operate as mutual support mechanisms providing each other with liquidity and solvency, consolidating their earnings and balance sheet (sharing policies on risk, treasury, internal control, credit rating and solvency and liquidity ratios under certain conditions for a minimum period of 10 years).

[42]   In cases (2) and (3) the savings bank would have to appoint representatives on the Board of Directors of the bank, "to this end, assessing the representation of the different groups on its Board."

model, which is at the heart of the crisis, is not the model applied by banks in Spain in view of their retail focus and the fact that risk largely remains on institutions' balance sheets. Therefore, the business model will be less affected than elsewhere. Even so, the outcome of the crisis will be a transformed banking system. This section gives an overview of the specificities of the sector in Spain, and the challenges it faces, and concludes with the lessons that can be drawn from the crisis, and the future outlook of the sector.

5.1   Specificities of the Spanish banking sector

The Spanish banking sector fits into the international context with certain specificities.

First of all, it *operates in a macroeconomic environment suffering from low growth prospects and sovereign risk issues,* due to rising government deficits, and *potential instability in the euro area,* which raises financial institutions' borrowing costs. The problems of the deficit and debt in the countries on the periphery of the euro area are a breeding ground for possible speculative attacks on sovereign debt. These problems may originate in either the public or private sector (when the public sector underwrites or assumes private-sector debt). The failure of an initial-aid plan for Greece led the EU to establish a financial-stabilization fund, and for the ECB to buy government bonds in order to curb speculative attacks. The tensions to which Spanish public debt is subject are strongly reflected in the situation of the banking sector.

Secondly, the *delayed emergence of losses.* This is a result of the cushion provided by general provisions, non-exposure to toxic derivatives (unlike United States banks), together with the resistance of property prices to decline. The potential insolvency problems among certain entities in the Spanish banking system have emerged with a time lag as the crisis has unfolded and largely depend on developments in the economy. Uncertainty about the magnitude of the necessary adjustment has hovered over the sector, although this largely dissipated with the publication of the results, at individual level, of the stress tests performed in July 2010. The heterogeneity of default rates and differences in credit worthiness among institutions stand out in particular.

In terms of public support in Spain, there has been a limited program of debt guarantees and quality asset purchases, together with the extension of deposit insurance coverage. So far two savings banks have needed to be rescued (Caja Castilla la Mancha – CCM – and Cajasur) and several savings banks have merged with support from the Fund for Orderly Restructuring of the Banking Sector (FROB). Total public capital injections represent[43] approximately 1.4% of GDP. Financial support for banks across Europe has had an impact on institutions competing in the international market, given that other institutions have received aid that has lowered their cost of capital. In fact, the very perception that a bank is too big to fail lowers its cost of capital. Spain's two biggest banks drew upon the capital

---

[43]   Including preference shares and asset protection schemes.

markets in 2008 and 2009 without public support, although confidence in European markets limited access to capital markets in 2010. Confidence began to return, however, following the publication of the banking stress tests.

Thirdly, excess capacity arising from rapid credit growth during the recent expansion phase, focusing especially on the financing of real-estate assets. This overcapacity is also distributed unevenly between institutions, with some of the savings banks in the lead. The adjustment will therefore affect different institutions to a varying extent. This excess capacity is tied to the extraordinary growth of real-estate lending financed with money from abroad.

5.2 The challenges

Against the backdrop of the specificities described above, the Spanish banking sector faces a number of interrelated challenges.

The first major challenge in the short to medium term is that of *restoring the health of the sector's balance sheet.* In July 2010 the EU decided to publish the results of the stress tests conducted on a total of 91 banks (representing 65% of the banking industry's total assets). In the case of Spain, eight listed banks and all the savings banks (45 institutions in all or 19 groups, given that in the case of the savings banks undergoing consolidation, the group level was considered) were tested, although the minimum commitment at European level was to subject 50% of each country's banking system to evaluation. Moreover, Spain presented more information (and in additional formats) than was required by the European Community.

Transparency is obviously essential in a context in which international capital markets doubt the creditworthiness of certain institutions; without it, troubled institutions could all too easily contaminate healthy ones or the system as a whole. At the same time, greater transparency accelerates the process of restoring balance sheets to health and restructuring the institutions concerned.[44]

According to the results of the stress tests, the Spanish banking system has sufficient resources to absorb the impact of the theoretical impairment considered. The adverse macroeconomic scenario in Spain envisages a key relative decline of 2.6% of GDP in 2010 and 2011.[45] In this somewhat unlikely scenario (according to the IMF forecasts -0.3% in 2010 and +0.7% in 2011) all the institutions, except for four groups of savings banks, exceeded 6% of Tier 1 capital, the target ratio set by the Committee of European Banking Supervisors (CEPS)[46] and three groups would not have passed the test without the financial

---

[44] In May 2010 the IMF recommended that transparency be increased, with a diagnosis of the situation bank by bank.

[45] A drop of 28% in house prices from their peak is assumed, a 50% drop in the value of homes under construction and a 61% drop in the value of land.

aid previously granted to them by the FROB. Following additional recapitalization (either through the market or the FROB), by December 2011 the Spanish banking system overall will have a Tier 1 ratio of 8.3%.[47] It should be noted that the requirement for 6% of Tier 1 capital is 50% higher than the required legal limit, but less than the 8.4% that will ultimately be required by the Basel III process. At the same time, the stress tests did not take possible liquidity problems into account.

In the adverse scenario, asset impairments to a value of 7.3% of these sectors' aggregate assets (and 9.5% of the savings banks aggregate assets) were calculated.[48] The provisions accumulated by Spanish banking institutions enable them to absorb 34% of this impairment (29% in the case of the savings banks) and, by generating income, they would be able to absorb a further 48% (the savings banks could absorb an additional 23%).

The stress tests have made it possible to identify the most vulnerable institutions in the financial system; these now have the option of recapitalization from the markets or the FROB.

Given the turmoil in the euro area (based on the information from the stress tests), Spanish banks' exposure to sovereign debt in certain countries on the periphery of the EU, in particular Italy and Portugal, apart from Spain, should also be noted.

The second major challenge, deriving from the previous one, is the sector's *restructuring* to reduce excess capacity and ensure adequate capitalization. The first element to consider is the heterogeneity of institutions. On average, the banks have better profitability and efficiency and lower exposure to the property sector, and the savings banks have similar default rates due to lower levels of default on consumer credit. Even so, the range of variation in parameters such as ROA, and operating costs/gross margin, foreclosure and capitalization, are higher among the banks than the savings banks.[49] Excess network capacity and employment is particularly evident among the savings banks and the FROB is intended in part to eliminate this and provide quality equity capital to those institutions that need it.

---

[46]   The four savings banks that did not achieve 6% Tier 1 capital must increase their equity capital by €1.835 billion (taking into account the funding already provided by the FROB and the Deposit Guarantee Fund, support funds comes to a total of €16.193 billion). Cajasur did not pass the test either, but does not require a capital increase as it is being taken over by BBK.

[47]   At European level, seven out of a total of 91 institutions evaluated did not pass the tests. Of these, five are Spanish (including Cajasur), one is German and another is Greek. Germany tested 14 institutions and Greece six.

[48]   The potential impairment of €207,403 million represents 11.3% of private sector lending (non-bank and resident) in March 2010, with realized losses of 2.7% of lending. The impairment originates primarily in the loan portfolio (84% of gross impairment). Of this impairment, €76,012 million corresponds to the property-developers portfolio (in the case of the savings banks it corresponds to 63% of impairment on the lending portfolio). Total accumulated provisions as at December 2009 came to €69,918 million, such that net impairment is €137,555 million (€75,711 million in the case of the savings banks). If we also take into account institutions ordinary earnings and capital gains, and finally the tax effect, the net impairment of the system is €28,075 million (in the savings banks, in particular, the net impairment comes to €38,686 million due to their lesser capacity to generate earnings with which to absorb impairment).

[49]   Carbó and Maudos (2010).

The FROB is managed by the Banco de España and has potential financing of €99 billion available. It is intended to contribute to the restructuring (to reduce excess capacity) and capitalization of the Spanish banking system and the winding up of institutions with solvency problems (supplementing deposit guarantee funds). The rescue of non-viable institutions is envisaged (to date, only Cajasur has been given aid from the FROB, CCM having received aid from the savings banks' Deposit Guarantee Fund) and for the FROB to take control over them. It also facilitates the integration of viable institutions to bolster their capital with preferred stock, paid at 7.75% (with a staggered annual increase) for a term of five years, conditional on their restructuring.[50] Integration may be through the institutional protection system (SIP), which is structured through a bank in which all the institutions participate (promoting integration between savings banks in different Autonomous Communities) or through one of the institutions. Reform of savings bank legislation in July 2010 modified the FROB so that, exceptionally, it can support the recapitalization of credit institutions which are basically sound but which the Banco de España considers need to shore up their equity.

The 45 existing savings banks have been reduced to 18 groups through a process of consolidation (involving 94% of the sector's assets). Eight of these have received assistance from the FROB and five others have not, currently leaving five independent savings banks (see Table 2). Five of these mergers have taken place through the SIP. The average size of the savings banks in asset terms has more than doubled[51] and significant reductions in the number of branches and employees are foreseen (between 10% and 30%).

The process of restructuring the savings banks will have impacts in at least four areas: efficiency, diversification, ability to access capital markets, and market power. Various issues therefore arise. The first is the difficulty of getting the process started (accelerated when Cajasur was taken into the control of the authorities, and by the initial deadline of 30 June 2010 for FROB aid for voluntary restructuring processes, subsequently extended to 31 December). The second is how well suited this process of mergers is to solving the problems of solvency and efficiency. The question is whether the merged savings banks will be more efficient and be able to find the synergies they need. More specifically, there is the question of how many of the ongoing mergers respond to complementarities and achievable synergies. It needs to be borne in mind that the evidence on economies of scale in the banking industry is far from conclusive and many studies suggest that they are soon exhausted. Mergers between savings banks in the same Autonomous Community potentially offer a better likelihood of removing excess capacity by eliminating overlaps in networks, but mergers between savings banks in different regions would foster diversification. Market power, which depends on the concentration of local markets in retail segments, will increase yet further in the case of mergers between savings banks in the same region. In terms of solvency, it should be

---

[50] The deadline for voluntary restructuring with FROB aid was initially set as June 2010, but following approval from the European Commission this was extended to December 2010.

[51] The average size (assets) will go from €28.504 million to €71.260 million following the restructuring.

	FROB	Without FROB
SIP	Base: Caja de Ahorros del Mediterráneo (CAM) - Cajastur - Caja Extremadura - Caja Cantabria - Caja Castilla La Mancha Júpiter: Caja Madrid - Bancaja - la Insular de Canarias - Caixa Laietana - Caja de Ávila - Caja Segovia - Caja Rioja Mare Nostrum: Caja Murcia - Caja Granada - Caixa Penedès - Sa Nostra	Banca Cívica: Caja Canarias - Caja Burgos - Caja Navarra Caja3: Caja Badajoz - Caja Círculo de Burgos - Caja Inmaculada de Aragón
Non-SIP	CatalunyaCaixa: Caixa Catalunya - Caixa Tarragona - Caixa Manresa Unnim: Caixa Sabadell - Caixa Terrassa - Caixa Manlleu Espiga: Caja Duero - Caja España Breogán: Caixa Galicia - Caixanova BBK - Cajasur	Unicaja - Caja Jaén Cajasol - Caja Guadalajara La Caixa - Caixa Girona

TABLE 2   RESTRUCTURING OF THE SAVINGS BANKS. GROUPS FORMED AS AT SEPTEMBER 2010

NOTE: No integration process in the case of Ibercaja, Caja Ontinyent, Pollença, Kutxa and Caja Vital.

noted that mergers between troubled institutions do not produce a stronger institution, per se, although larger institutions may find it easier to access capital markets. The third issue is the effectiveness and stability of virtual mergers through the SIPs. Indeed, for the SIP to work, and provide a guarantee of solvency and liquidity, there must be a common policy, which entails a de facto integration by the institutions. It will also be necessary to see how their *cuotas participativas* or equity instruments evolve, for instance how well they are accepted by the market. The success of the capital increases by the savings banks' holding banks has also yet to be seen, given their institutional particularity.

It may be surmised that the wave of mergers taking place in the first semester of 2010 is only a first step in the sector's restructuring process. It is also possible that some medium-sized banks with significant exposure to the Spanish market will follow the path of restructuring and consolidation to adapt their capacity to the new environment and compete more effectively in the international market.[52]

The third major challenge is the *contribution of the banking sector to the deleveraging and financing* of the economy. Achieving this goal may require changes to their *business model*.

The level of debt among Spanish households is well above the euro-area average (86% of GDP in Spain compared with 69% in the euro area (excluding Italy) in 2009).[53] Holding

---

[52] So far there has been a merger between Banco Sabadell and Banco Guipuzcoano.

[53] Eurostat data.

interest rates low in the short term, however, would help contain the financial burden. At the same time, the high percentage of households owning their own homes (83% in Spain compared with an EU-15 average of 67% in 2007) gives stability to efforts to pay mortgages. Nevertheless, the prospect of high unemployment sustained over many years may complicate the situation, given the close correlation between default rates and unemployment rate. Business borrowing is also higher than the euro-area average (140% of GDP in Spain compared to 103% in the euro area in 2009). This is due to lending to the construction industry and the real-estate sector (for example, 46% of business lending in 2009 was to construction firms and property developers). The question is how real-estate companies are going to pay their debts in a context of recession and stagnation in the sector. Generally speaking, a portfolio of variable interest rate bank loans is extremely vulnerable to increases in market interest rates.

Shoring up the balance sheet in the banking sector is essential if it is to play a positive role in the post-crisis recovery. The industry needs to address the issue of deleveraging sectors with an excessive debt burden (particularly the real-estate sector) and redirecting lending to other more productive sectors of the economy and, in particular, emerging sectors and segments.[54] It is worth noting that the balance sheet of credit institutions in Spain grew by 1% in 2009, during the crisis, whereas it decreased by more than 2% in the euro area. This is despite the decrease in lending to the private sector (resident and non-bank), where there have been negative growth rates in all segments except services (0.4% increase) and housing (0.86% increase). Early recognition of the real-estate sector's losses, accompanied by the necessary restructuring, would potentially free up resources and (depending on the economic recovery) so enable credit to be channeled to other sectors.

In a context of economic recession, it is difficult to distinguish between supply and demand factors in the drying-up of credit. The recession reduces solvent demand. Credit supply by banks may be curtailed by their balance sheet difficulties and their need for liquidity to refinance their own debt on maturity. In surveys conducted by the ECB,[55] companies in Spain reported a tightening of the conditions on which credit could be obtained (rationing and more stringent terms) and worse future expectations of access to credit than elsewhere in the euro area. Moreover the banks acknowledged that they had tightened the conditions under which they granted credit. At the same time, the percentage of small and medium-sized companies which reported that their earnings had worsened in relation to the previous semester was 60% compared with a euro-area average of 34%. It is therefore plausible that both supply and demand factors were at work in the reduction in credit levels.

In the short term there is the question of how the banking industry will contribute to the necessary financing of productive sectors in a context in which balance sheet problems

---

[54]   Caballero, Hoshi and Kashyap (2008) offer evidence of how in Japan financing insolvent firms and sectors was harmful to solvent ones and to the economy as a whole.

[55]   Second semester 2009.

persist and capital requirements are tightened. In the medium term, the reduction in excess capacity must be accompanied by a significant relative decrease in lending to construction companies and property developers, accompanied by a shift towards corporate finance, and in particular towards riskier and more innovative business projects. Projects of this kind tend to suffer funding constraints as a result of information asymmetry issues, high levels of uncertainty, and imperfections in capital markets. This shift would represent a culture shift in the sector, particularly but not exclusively for the savings banks, given that the human capital necessary to monitor innovative projects cannot be improvised. Tensions may therefore arise in risk management as business activities extend beyond the functions of traditional banking.

In any case, capital markets for private debt and venture capital need to develop further in Spain (and in Europe as a whole) in order to provide the necessary credit to businesses and to foster innovative projects (and to do so transparently). Importantly, in a functional venture capital market, projects are monitored by their financiers much more closely than is the case with traditional projects, and this implies a degree of loss of control for the entrepreneur.[56]

Additionally, the resizing of the sector, due to a combination of the end of the property boom and stricter regulation, raises the issue of a possible expansion of business outside the financial sector to take advantage of a larger customer base, the distribution network of products and services involving bank branches and the considerable capacity to manage information and data with the IT systems available. Banks could follow the same path as other companies (in distribution or equipment, such as in the automotive industry) which have achieved significant market shares in consumer credit. It needs to be borne in mind here, however, that the advantages of exploiting potential synergies in the banking network by offering non-financial products have to be weighed up against the advantages of focusing on the financial business, in view of its idiosyncrasies, such as the fundamental role of trust. A failure in a non-financial business line could tarnish confidence in the institution as a whole.

The new conditions under which the banking business will develop are likely to include greater pressure on margins due to a combination of increased use of electronic banking, enhanced transparency requirements to meet regulatory demands, and the closer integration of European financial markets. These factors will increase the pressure to achieve efficiency improvements.

The fourth major challenge is to *rethink the balance sheet structure* in a context of increased capital and liquidity requirements, and where the Spanish economy's need for external finance will remain high. Even in a context of a recovery in the interbank market and in the secondary market for asset-backed securities, the relative shares of the different sources of financing need to be reconsidered, so as to place less reliance on wholesale funding.

In the short-to-medium term, liquidity management will be a key issue in a context in which the impact of rising risk premiums and downgrades by the ratings agencies of the credit rating on Spanish public debt are passed on to bank-debt. In effect, the financing

---

[56]   See Aoki (2000).

situation of Spanish public debt is affected by how the sovereign-debt crisis develops and the prospect of a possible rise in interest rates when the European economy recovers adds further uncertainty. On top of this comes the phasing out of the ECB's extraordinary liquidity measures and the government guarantees for bank-debt issues. Liquidity tensions, exacerbated by the instability in the euro area since the outbreak of the Greek debt crisis, are manifesting themselves in the battle for deposits between institutions that began in 2009 and 2010, offering depositors rates well above the interbank rate.

The regulatory changes will have a big influence on the structure of institutions' liabilities. In 2008, Spanish banks' total solvency ratio was 11.3%, below the EU-15 average of 12.1% (in the United States it was 12.7%).[57] It should be noted, however, that Spanish banks have not had large-scale public capital injections. Solvency ratios have improved since 2007, approaching a total solvency ratio of 12% in mid-2010. The impact of more stringent capital requirements, in terms of both quantity and quality, may be very significant for commercial banks in Spain, given the importance of hybrid capital such as preference shares and, even more so, in the case of the savings banks which have intrinsic problems raising capital (other than by retaining earnings) unless they take advantage of the options offered by the reforms.

Given the gradual transition envisaged in the Basel III reform process, due to be rolled out between now and 2019, the Spanish banking industry is likely to be able to adapt its levels of capital and liquidity by a combination of changes in balance-sheet structure, accumulation of reserves, and capital increases. Changes in balance-sheet structure may include divestments of real estate and of financial and industrial holdings, sale and lease back of branch networks, the return of investment and pension funds on to the balance sheet, and changes in the maturity structure of credit and deposits to reduce maturity transformation (so as to obviate the maturity mismatch). The sector's heterogeneity also means that some institutions will need to make much bigger changes to their balance sheet than others owing to their lack of access to capital markets or because they wish to avoiding diluting their capital. In any case, better capitalized institutions with greater access to international markets may increase their market share at the expense of others.

Apart from the effects on capital and credit, together with the redefining of the boundary between markets and intermediation, the new regulation may have a major impact on financial institution's holdings in industrial and insurance companies, particularly in the case of the savings banks, and on their international business in the case of organizations basing their financial expansion on minority shareholdings.

5.3   Lessons of the crisis and outlook

The outcome of the crisis and regulatory reform will be a profound transformation of the Spanish banking industry in a context of slower growth and lower profits, accompanied

---

[57]   ECB and IMF data.

even by a decline in some segments of financial business, which will result in the more robust institutions growing stronger at the expense of the weaker ones. The savings banks, and to a lesser extent, medium-sized banks, will be the leading players in this transformation.

The lessons of the crisis for regulators are the fragility of wholesale funding, the need to pay attention to a concentration of risk in a single sector (in this case the real-estate sector) and the importance of acting quickly and effectively as soon as institutions face solvency problems. Once a crisis has erupted, regulators must be particularly vigilant to ensure that banks recognize their losses and that balance sheet reorganization is not postponed. This has been a recurrent problem in financial crises, and one which causes them to last longer and raises their cost (Japan is a case in point).[58] Consequently there is a need to promote transparency, raise capital requirements and impose liquidity requirements. The Banco de España has been a pioneer in requiring dynamic provisioning to cushion the pro-cyclical impact of capital requirements, and has required the consolidation of off-balance-sheet financial structures that implied additional risks for banks. It has also made the accounting rules on the provisioning of foreclosed assets more stringent. In the context of the crisis and the restructuring process, regulators must also pay attention to excessive competition, from the point of view of deposit insurance, and ensure that restructuring aid does not affect the sector's stability. The current crisis has highlighted two further issues: the importance of the ability to expand Tier 1 capital if necessary (and this applies in particular to the savings banks), and the importance of geographical and sector diversification.

The evolution of the European regulatory architecture depends on the reform of the governance mechanisms to stabilize the euro area (including stability funds and sovereign-debt restructuring processes). Progress towards resolving the issue of regulatory fragmentation in the EU will come from the micro- and macro-prudential committees that are being set up, although the problems of bailing out pan-European institutions continue to exist and discussion of a Europe-wide deposit insurance fund (at least for these institutions) is on the agenda. Other factors are the regulation of hedge funds and venture capital, compensation policies, and managing the conflicts of interest that arise. In the EU context, the system in Spain is in the vanguard, with the Banco de España as the accounts regulator, a deposit guarantee fund and dynamic provisioning.

The general lessons for the sector are similar to those for regulators as regards wholesale funding, risk concentration, transparency and diversification. Of course, from the industry's standpoint this is compounded by the uncertainty created by the new regulations, in particular the new liquidity requirements, given their novelty, as well as the window for implementation. Indeed, the pace of implementation, or the point in the economic cycle at which it takes place, are crucial variables in any assessment of the impact on the sector and the economy as a whole. Moreover, the industry needs to think about how to establish mechanisms to restore trust and deal with reputational risk.

The diversity of banks also implies different challenges and strategies for the future.

---

[58]   See Hoshi and Kayshap (2000).

The two big banks need to step up their international expansion and diversification process, based on the model of traditional banking that they dominate and which, in the wake of the crisis, has once again been placed at the heart of the business. The medium-sized banks should continue to pursue their growth and consolidation to achieve the necessary economies of scale and adequate diversification. The savings banks are caught up in a sweeping process of restructuring from which groups with sufficient size and diversification should emerge. These should be more professional, have depoliticized governing bodies, and be able to expand their capital (with the corresponding voting rights or through banking institutions) when necessary. The new savings banks should also be able to embark on a process of international diversification based on their retail specialization (and with possible alliances), but before they can do so they must overcome significant management capacity limitations. The reform can and must be made compatible with keeping their community welfare work a priority, and without severing their ties to their home region. The sector's restructuring, which still has some way to go, may be completed with more consolidation between savings banks or the participation of banks and partial sales of branch networks. This process could also enable the entry of a foreign bank through the acquisition of a branch network or through a direct investment in an institution needing to increase its capital.

The diversity of possible institutional models in the reform process means that it will be for the market to decide which are stable and which will ultimately prevail. In the case of those savings banks that retain the traditional model and wish to increase their capital, shareholders must be given a place on their governing bodies. Both these institutions and those that conduct their financial business through a bank that retains the savings bank "brand", but has access to capital markets, may find themselves limited by the peculiarity of the model. Those savings banks that are organized within an SIP need to make progress towards integration to ensure stability. Finally, those savings banks that choose to conduct their social work through a foundation in which they invest but which they do not necessarily control, the investee bank retains the savings bank "brand" in its community-welfare activities but in the financial business it becomes blurred.

Finally, a pending issue for the Spanish financial system is to improve the performance of mutual and pension funds, which are subject to high fees but give poor results in relation to the performance of the market. Increasing transparency for investors, and competition between institutions, would give the sector a major boost and help restore investor confidence, which has been badly damaged by the financial crisis. It should be noted that the weight of the investment fund industry in Spain is much less than that in countries such as France or Germany, for example.[59] An additional benefit would be the development of corporate bond markets, which will be necessary to provide funding to companies in a context in which banks will tend to restrict credit. The development of pension funds could also provide capital to finance stable holdings in industrial and service corporations that are

---

[59]   17.5% of GDP in Spain compared with over 50% in Germany or close to 80% in France (in 2009).

currently partly owned by the savings banks and which, in the new environment of capital requirements and demands for returns for the entry of private capital, perhaps ought to, at least, partly divest them.

In summary, the challenges facing the Spanish banking industry in the wake of the 2007-2008 crisis are formidable: a long-term transformation in the very structure of banking and its regulation, potential turbulence in the euro area in the short term, and the associated strains on liquidity. The response by both the private and public sector must be commensurate with these challenges.

References

ALLEN, F., and D. GALE (2000). "Corporate Governance and Competition", in X. Vives (Ed.), *Corporate Governance; Theoretical and Empirical Perspectives,* University Press, Cambridge.

AOKI, M. (2000). "Information and Governance in the Silicon Valley Model", in X. Vives (Ed.), *Corporate Governance: Theoretical and Empirical Perspectives,* pp. 169-195, University Press, Cambridge.

BANCO DE ESPAÑA (2010). "Financial Stability Report", March.

BANK FOR INTERNATIONAL SETTLEMENTS (BIS) (2010a). Basel III: *A Global Regulatory Framework for More Resilient Banks and Banking Systems.*

— (2010b). Basel III: *International Framework for Liquidity Risk Measurement,Standards and Monitoring.*

— (2010c). *An Assessment of the Long-term Economic Impact of Stronger Capital Requirements.*

— (2010d). Final Report: *Assessing the Macroeconomic Impact of the Transition to Stronger Capital and Liquidity Requirements.*

— (2010e). *Results of the Comprehensive Quantitative Impact Study.*

— (2010f). *Consolidated Banking Statistics.*

BARTH, J. R., D. E. NOLLE and T. N. RICE (1997). *Commercial Banking Structure, Regulation, and Performance: an International Comparison,* Economic Working Paper, 97-6, Office of the Comptroller of the Currency, Washington, D.C.

BERGER, A., R. DEMSETZ and P. STRAHAN (1999). "The Consolidation of the Financial Services Industry: Causes, Consequences, and Implications for the Future", *Journal of Banking & Finance,* 23, 2-4, pp. 135-194.

CABALLERO, R., T. HOSHI and A. KASHYAP (2008). "Zombie Lending and Depressed Restruc-

turing in Japan", *American Economic Review,* 98, pp. 5, 1943-1977.

CAMINAL, R., J. GUAL and X. VIVES (1990). "Competition in Spanish Banking", in J. Dermine (Ed.), *European Banking in the 1990's,* Basil Blackwell.

CARBÓ, S., and J. MAUDOS (2010). *Diez interrogantes del sector bancario español.* Cuadernos de Información Económica, 215, pp. 89-105

CRESPÍ, R., M. A. GARCÍA-CESTONA and V. SALAS (2004). "Governance Mechanisms in Spanish Banks. Does Ownership Matter?", *Journal of Banking and Finance,* 28, 10, pp. 2311-2330.

EEAG (2010). *The EEAG Report on the European Economy 2010,* with G. Corsetti, M. P. Devereux, L. Guiso, J. Hassler, G. Saint-Paul, H. W. Sinn, J. E. Sturm and X. Vives, CesIFO.

ESCRIVÁ, J. L. (2009). *El futuro del sistema financiero español. La profundidad de la crisis y su repercusión en el sector financiero y otros sectores de la economía,* presentation available at: http://serviciodeestudios.bbva.com/KETD/fbin/mul t/090618_el-futuro delsistema financiero espanol_tcm346-196767.pdf?ts=2362010.

EUROPEAN CENTRAL BANK (2010). *Structural Indicators for the EU Banking Sector, EU Banking Sector Stability.*

GUTIÉRREZ DE ROZAS, L. (2007). *Testing for Competition in the Spanish Banking Industry: The Panzar-Rosse Approach Revisited,* Working Paper no. 0726, Banco de España.

HELLWIG, M. (2000). "On the Economics and Politics of Corporate Finance and Corporate Control", in X. Vives (Ed.), *Corporate Governance: Theoretical and Empirical Perspectives,* Cambridge University Press.

HERMALIN, B., and N. WALLACE (1994). "The Determinants of Efficiency and Solvency in Savings and Loans", *Rand Journal of Economics,* 25, 3, pp. 361-381.

HOSHI, T., and A. KASHYAP (2000). "The Japanese Banking Crisis: Where Did it Come From and How Will it End?", NBER Chapters, in NBER *Macroeconomics annual 1999,* 14, pp. 129-201.

INTERNATIONAL MONETARY FUND (2009). *Spain: Selected Issues,* IMF Country Report no. 09/129.

— (2010). *Global Financial Stability Report.*

MARTÍN-OLIVER, A. (2010). *From Proximity to Distant Banking: Spanish Banks in the EMU,* Working Paper no. 1008, Banco de España.

MATUTES, C., and X. VIVES (2000), "Imperfect Competition, Risk Taking and Regulation in Banking", *European Economic Review,* 44, 1, pp. 1-34.

MAUDOS, J., and J. FERNÁNDEZ DE GUEVARA (2008). *El sector bancario español en el contexto internacional. Evolución reciente y retos futuros,* Fundación BBVA.

PURROY, P., and V. SALAS (2000). "Strategic Competition in Retail Banking Under Expense Preference Behavior", *Journal of Banking and Finance,* 24, 5, pp. 809-824.

ROLDÁN, J. M. (2010). *The Spanish Banking Sector: Outlook and Perspectives,* presentation available at http://www.bde.es/prensa/intervenpub/diregen/regula/regula280510e.pdf.

SALAS, V., and J. SAURINA (2002). "Credit Risk in Two Institutional Regimes: Spanish Commercial and Savings Banks", *Journal of Financial Services Research,* 22, 3, pp. 203-224.

VIVES, X. (1990). "La nueva competencia", *Papeles de Economía Española,* 44, pp. 20-25.

— (2000). "Corporate Governance: Does it Matter?", in X. Vives (Ed.), *Corporate Governance; Theoretical and Empirical Perspectives,* Cambridge University Press.

— (2011). *Competition and Stability in Banking,* in *Monetary Policy under Financial Turbulence,* Proceedings of the Annual Conference of the Central Bank of Chile, Bank of Chile.

— (2010). "La crisis financiera y la regulación", in *La crisis de 2008,* colección Mediterráneo Económico, pp. 77-92.

WHITE, L. (2009). *Financial Regulation and the Current Crisis: A Guide for the Antitrust Community,* mimeo.

Index